CW00969760

THE PILLAR NEW TESTAMENT COMMENTARY

General Editor
D. A. CARSON

The Letters to the
COLOSSIANS
and to
PHILEMON

DOUGLAS J. MOO

WILLIAM B. EERDMANS PUBLISHING COMPANY
GRAND RAPIDS, MICHIGAN / CAMBRIDGE, U.K.

APOLLOS
NOTTINGHAM, ENGLAND

First published 2008
in the United States of America by
Wm. B. Eerdmans Publishing Co.
2140 Oak Industrial Drive N.E., Grand Rapids, Michigan 49505 /
P.O. Box 163, Cambridge CB3 9PU U.K.
www.eerdmans.com

and in the United Kingdom by
APOLLOS
Norton Street, Nottingham,
England NG7 3HR

Printed and bound in Great Britain by the MPG Books Group

13 12 11   7 6 5 4 3 2

Library of Congress Cataloging-in-Publication Data

Moo, Douglas J.
The letters to the Colossians and to Philemon / Douglas J. Moo.
p.   cm.   — (Pillar New Testament commentary)
Includes bibliographical references and indexes.
ISBN 978-0-8028-3727-1 (cloth: alk. paper)
1. Bible. N.T. Colossians — Commentaries.
2. Bible. N.T. Philemon — Commentaries.   I. Title.

BS2715.53.M66   2008
227'.7077 — dc22

2008011989

British Library Cataloguing in Publication Data

A catalogue record for this book is available from the British Library.
Apollos ISBN 978-1-84474-341-4

Contents

CONTENTS

THE LETTER TO PHILEMON

Editor's Preface

Commentaries have specific aims, and this series is no exception. Designed for serious pastors and teachers of the Bible, the Pillar commentaries seek above all to make clear the text of Scripture as we have it. The scholars writing these volumes interact with the most important informed contemporary debate, but avoid getting mired in undue technical detail. Their ideal is a blend of rigorous exegesis and exposition, with an eye alert both to biblical theology and the contemporary relevance of the Bible, without confusing the commentary and the sermon.

The rationale for this approach is that the vision of "objective scholarship" (a vain chimera) may actually be profane. God stands over against us; we do not stand in judgment of him. When God speaks to us through his Word, those who profess to know him must respond in an appropriate way, and that is certainly different from a stance in which the scholar projects an image of autonomous distance. Yet this is no surreptitious appeal for uncontrolled subjectivity. The writers of this series aim for an evenhanded openness to the text that is the best kind of "objectivity" of all.

If the text is God's Word, it is appropriate that we respond with reverence, a certain fear, a holy joy, a questing obedience. These values should be reflected in the way Christians write. With these values in place, the Pillar commentaries will be warmly welcomed not only by pastors, teachers, and students, but by general readers as well.

*   *   *

For many years Doug Moo and I served on the same faculty. His move from Trinity to Wheaton, however much a gain for the latter, was a personal loss. Mercifully, we have continued to collaborate on various projects, and he is surely among the two of three scholars with whom I am most happy to work in close association. Readers of this series will already be familiar with his Pillar commentary on James — and that after writing, for another series, what is still the best English-language commentary on Romans.

Colossians and Philemon speak powerfully to many issues in the twenty-first century. What has consumed a great deal of energy in contemporary scholarship on these epistles, however, has often been the construction of plausible "backgrounds" that then determine (I almost said "domesticate") the interpretation of the documents. These backgrounds are now so plentiful and so diverse that the corresponding interpretations are equally plentiful. One of the many strengths that Dr. Moo brings to this commentary is an ability to evaluate the relative merits of diverse appeals, and even to point out what one cannot know when the evidence is not all that secure — and then to work carefully through the text in an exegetical and theological manner to make clear what the text itself does say. All of this is couched in lucid prose with transparent hints as to the bearing of the biblical texts on today's church. Anyone who reads through this commentary will emerge with a stronger grasp of what is disclosed in these two letters. I shall not be surprised if it becomes a "standard" among pastors for many years to come. And once again I am deeply indebted to a friend.

D. A. CARSON

Author's Preface

Writing this commentary felt like coming home. The first book I studied in Greek was Colossians, in a class in New Testament Exegesis at Trinity Evangelical Divinity School in 1972. The notes from that class are the bottom layer (deeply buried now, alas) of this commentary. I have also had the opportunity to teach Colossians in academic settings and to teach it and preach it in several churches. All these experiences, and the things that I learned from those who studied with me, have fed my interpretation of this great letter. Philemon I have studied and taught less. But I do remember a series of three sermons on the book that I preached at a summer conference in the 1980s, and I surprised myself by basically confirming many of the points that I made about this book at that time.

I want to express appreciation to research assistants (and colleagues) Matt Harmon, Elisee Ouoba, and Laurie Norris for help with bibliography and proofreading. My wife, Jenny, read the entire MS in its last stages and offered invaluable suggestions about content (perhaps I should have listed her as coauthor!). I am also grateful to my former colleague Don Carson for allowing me to contribute this volume to the Pillar series. I dedicate this book to Murray J. Harris. He was my professor for that 1972 Colossians class, and his teaching in that class, elaborated and put into written form in his very useful exegetical commentary, has been foundational to my own thinking about Colossians. But he has taught me even more by his example as a scholar and a Christian gentleman. I am grateful to have studied under him and to have served with him.

DOUGLAS J. MOO

Abbreviations

AB	Anchor Bible
ABD	*Anchor Bible Dictionary*
ABR	*Australian Biblical Review*
ACCS	Ancient Christian Commentary on Scripture
AnBib	Analecta Biblica
ANF	*Ante-Nicene Fathers*
ANRW	*Aufstieg und Niedergang der römischen Welt*
ANTC	Abingdon New Testament Commentaries
ASNU	Acta seminarii neotestamentici upsalienses
ATANT	Abhandlungen zur Theologie des Alten und Neuen Testaments
ATD	Das Alte Testament Deutsch
AUSS	*Andrews University Seminary Studies*
BBR	*Bulletin for Biblical Research*
BDAG	W. Bauer, W. F. Arndt, F. W. Gingrich, and F. W. Danker, *Greek-English Lexicon of the New Testament* (2d ed.)
BDB	F. Brown, S. R. Driver, and C. A. Briggs, *The New Brown-Drivers-Briggs-Gesenius Hebrew-English Lexicon*
BDF	F. Blass, A. Debrunner, and R. W. Funk, *A Greek Grammar of the New Testament and Other Early Christian Literature*
BDR	F. Blass, A. Debrunner, and F. Rehkopf, *Grammatik des neutestamentlichen Griechisch*
BETL	Bibliotheca ephemeridum theologicarum lovaniensium
BevT	Beiträge zur evangelischen Theologie
BFCT	Beiträge zur Förderung christlicher Theologie
BHT	Beiträge zur historischen Theologie
Bib	*Biblica*

ABBREVIATIONS

BibLeb	*Bibel und Leben*
BN	*Biblische Notizen*
BNTC	Black's New Testament Commentaries
BR	*Biblical Research*
BSac	*Bibliotheca Sacra*
BT	*The Bible Translator*
BTB	*Biblical Theology Bulletin*
BWANT	Beiträge zur Wissenschaft vom Alten und Neuen Testament
BZ	*Biblische Zeitschrift*
BZNW	Beihefte zur Zeitschrift für die neutestamentliche Wissenschaft
CBC	Cambridge Bible Commentary
CBQ	*Catholic Biblical Quarterly*
CC	Continental Commentaries
CGTC	Cambridge Greek Testament Commentary
CNT	Commentaire du Nouveau Testament
ConBNT	Coniectanea biblica: New Testament Series
CTJ	*Calvin Theological Journal*
CTQ	*Concordia Theological Quarterly*
CurTM	*Currents in Theology and Mission*
CTM	*Concordia Theological Monthly*
DPL	G. F. Hawthorne, R. P. Martin, and D. G. Reid (eds.), *Dictionary of Paul and His Letters*
ÉBib	Études bibliques
EDNT	H. Balz and G. Schneider (eds.), *Exegetical Dictionary of the New Testament*
EKKNT	Evangelisch-katholischer Kommentar zum Neuen Testament
ESV	English Standard Version
ETL	*Ephemerides theologicae lovanienses*
ETR	*Etudes théologiques et religieuses*
EvQ	*Evangelical Quarterly*
EvT	*Evangelische Theologie*
ExAud	*Ex Auditu*
ExpTim	*Expository Times*
FB	Forschung zur Bibel
FRLANT	Forschung zur Religion und Literatur des Alten und Neuen Testaments
GNS	Good News Studies
HBT	*Horizons in Biblical Theology*
HCSB	Holman Christian Standard Bible
HKNT	Handkommentar zum Neuen Testament
HTKNT	Herders theologischer Kommentar zum Neuen Testament
HNT	Handbuch zum Neuen Testament

HNTC	Harper's New Testament Commentaries
HTR	*Harvard Theological Review*
HUT	Hermeneutische Untersuchungen zur Theologie
IBC	Interpretation: A Bible Commentary for Teaching and Preaching
ICC	International Critical Commentary
Int	*Interpretation*
ITQ	*Irish Theological Quarterly*
IVPNTC	InterVarsity Press New Testament Commentary
JAAR	*Journal of the American Academy of Religion*
JBL	*Journal of Biblical Literature*
JETS	*Journal of the Evangelical Theological Society*
JSNT	*Journal for the Study of the New Testament*
JSNTSup	Journal for the Study of the New Testament: Supplement Series
JTS	*Journal of Theological Studies*
JTSA	*Journal of Theology for Southern Africa*
KD	*Kerygma und Dogma*
KEK	Kritisch-exegetischer Kommentar über das Neue Testament (Meyer-Kommentar)
KJV	King James Version
LASBF	*Liber annuus Studii biblici franciscani*
LCL	Loeb Classical Library
LD	Lectio divina
LN	J. P. Louw and E. Nida, *Greek-English Lexicon of the New Testament: Based on Semantic Domains*
LSJ	Liddell-Scott-Jones, *Greek English Lexicon*
LTQ	*Lutheran Theological Quarterly*
LXX	Septuagint
MBS	Message of Biblical Spirituality
MM	J. H. Moulton and G. Milligan, *The Vocabulary of the Greek New Testament*
MT	Massoretic Text
NA^{27}	E. Nestle and K. Aland (eds.), *Novum Testamentum Graece* (27th ed.)
NAB	New American Bible
NAC	New American Commentary
NASB	New American Standard Bible (rev. ed.)
NCBC	New Century Bible Commentary
NEB	New English Bible
Neot	*Neotestamentica*
NewDocs	*New Documents Illustrating Early Christianity*

ABBREVIATIONS

NET	New English Translation
NIB	*New Interpreters' Bible*
NIBCNT	New International Biblical Commentary on the New Testament
NICNT	New International Commentary on the New Testament
NIDNTT	C. Brown (ed.), *The New International Dictionary of New Testament Theology*
NIGTC	New International Greek Testament Commentary
NIV	New International Version
NIVAC	New International Version Application Commentary
NJB	New Jerusalem Bible
NKJV	New King James Version
NLT	New Living Translation
NovT	*Novum Testamentum*
NovTSup	Supplements to Novum Testamentum
NPNF	*Nicene and Post-Nicene Fathers*
NRSV	New Revised Standard Version
NRTh	*La nouvelle revue théologique*
NSBT	New Studies in Biblical Theology
NTAbh	Neutestamentliche Abhandlungen
NTD	Das Neue Testament Deutsch
NTS	*New Testament Studies*
NTTS	New Testament Tools and Studies
ÖTK	Ökumenischer Taschenbuch-Kommentar
PG	Patrologia graeca
PNTC	Pelican New Testament Commentaries
RB	*Revue biblique*
REB	Revised English Bible
ResQ	*Restoration Quarterly*
RevExp	*Review and Expositor*
RevScRel	*Revue des sciences religieuses*
RHPR	*Revue d'histoire et de philosophie religieuses*
RNT	Regensburger Neues Testament
RRef	*La revue reformée*
RSV	Revised Standard Version
RTR	*Reformed Theological Review*
SANT	Studien zum Alten und Neuen Testaments
SBB	Stuttgarter biblische Beiträge
SBL	Society of Biblical Literature
SBLDS	Society of Biblical Literature Dissertation Series
SBLMS	Society of Biblical Literature Monograph Series
SBLSP	*Society of Biblical Literature Seminar Papers*

SBM	Stuttgarter biblische Monographien
SBT	*Studies in Biblical Theology*
SEÅ	*Svensk exegetisk årsbok*
SJLA	*Studies in Judaism of Late Antiquity*
SJT	*Scottish Journal of Theology*
SNT	Studien zum Neuen Testament
SNTSMS	Society for New Testament Studies Monograph Series
SNTSU	Studien zum Neuen Testament und seiner Umwelt
SP	Sacra Pagina
ST	*Studia theologica*
Str-B	H. L. Strack and P. Billerbeck, *Kommentar zum Neuen Testament aus Talmud und Midrasch*
SUNT	Studien zur Umwelt des Neuen Testaments
SVTQ	*St. Vladimir's Theological Quarterly*
SwJT	*Southwestern Journal of Theology*
TDNT	G. Kittel and G. Friedrich (eds.), *Theological Dictionary of the New Testament*
TEV	Today's English Version
TBei	*Theologische Beiträge*
Them	*Themelios*
THKNT	Theologischer Handkommentar zum Neuen Testament
TJ	*Trinity Journal*
TLG	*Thesaurus linguae graecae*
TNIV	Today's New International Version
TNTC	Tyndale New Testament Commentaries
TTE	*The Theological Educator*
TU	Texte und Untersuchungen
TynBul	*Tyndale Bulletin*
TZ	*Theologische Zeitschrift*
UBS	United Bible Societies Greek New Testament (4th ed.)
UNT	Untersuchungen zum Neuen Testament
VE	*Vox evangelica*
WBC	Word Biblical Commentary
WD	*Wort und Dienst*
WMANT	Wissenschaftliche Monographien zum Alten und Neuen Testament
WTJ	*Westminster Theological Journal*
WUNT	Wissenschaftliche Untersuchungen zum Neuen Testament
ZB	Zürcher Bibel
ZBK	Zürcher Bibelkommentare
ZNW	*Zeitschrift für die neutestamentliche Wissenschaft*
ZTK	*Zeitschrift für Theologie und Kirche*

Texts and Translations

The commentary is based on the Today's New International Version (TNIV). The text of this version is quoted at the beginning of every commentary section, with paragraphing and spacing kept intact. All quotations from the English Bible are also from the TNIV, unless otherwise indicated.

Quotations from the Greek New Testament are from *Novum Testamentum Graece* (Nestle and Aland, 27th ed.) and from the Hebrew/ Aramaic Old Testament from *Biblica Hebraica Stuttgartensia*. Translations of the Apocrypha are from the NRSV; of the Pseudepigrapha from *The Old Testament Pseudepigrapha* (2 vols.; ed. J. H. Charlesworth; New York: Doubleday, 1983, 1985); and of the Dead Sea Scrolls from *The Dead Sea Scrolls Study Edition* (2 vols.; ed. F. G. Martínez and E. J. C. Tigchelaar; Leiden: Brill, 1997).

The Letter
to the
COLOSSIANS

Select Bibliography

Commentaries on Colossians

The commentaries listed here are referred to in the commentary with the last name of the commentary author only.

Abbott, T. K. *A Critical and Exegetical Commentary on the Epistles to the Ephesians and to the Colossians*. ICC. Edinburgh: T&T Clark, 1897.

Aletti, Jean-Noël. *Epître aux Colossiens*. Ébib. Paris: Gabalda, 1993.

Barth, Markus, and Helmut Blanke. *Colossians: A New Translation with Introduction and Commentary*. AB 34B. New York: Doubleday, 1994.

Bengel, Johann Albrecht. *Gnomon Novi Testamenti*. Reprint, Edinburgh: T&T Clark, 1857.

Bieder, Walter. *Der Kolosserbrief*. Prophetei. Zurich: Zwingli, 1943.

Bruce, F. F. *The Epistles to the Colossians, to Philemon, and to the Ephesians*. NICNT. Grand Rapids: Eerdmans, 1984.

Calvin, John. *The Epistles of Paul the Apostle to the Galatians, Ephesians, Philippians and Colossians*. Grand Rapids: Eerdmans, 1965.

Dibelius, Martin. *An die Kolosser, Epheser, an Philemon*. 3d ed. rev. H. Greeven. HNT 12. Tübingen: Mohr Siebeck, 1953.

Dunn, James D. G. *The Epistles to the Colossians and to Philemon*. NIGTC. Grand Rapids: Eerdmans, 1996.

Eadie, John. *Commentary on the Epistle of Paul to the Colossians*. N.p.: Richard Griffin, 1856. Reprint, Grand Rapids: Zondervan, 1957.

Ernst, J. *Die Briefe an die Philipper, an Philemon, an die Kolosser, an die Epheser*. RNT. Regensburg: Pustet, 1974.

Furter, Daniel. *Les Épîtres de Paul aux Colossiens et à Philémon*. Commentaire

Évangélique de la Bible 8. Vaux-sur-Seine: Faculté libre de théologie évangélique, 1988.

Garland, David E. *Colossians and Philemon.* NIVAC. Grand Rapids: Zondervan, 1998.

Gnilka, Joachim. *Der Kolosserbrief.* HTKNT 10.1. Freiburg: Herder, 1980.

Gorday, Peter, ed. *Colossians, 1-2 Thessalonians, 1-2 Timothy, Titus, Philemon.* ACCS. Downers Grove, Ill.: InterVarsity, 2000.

Harris, Murray J. *Colossians and Philemon.* Exegetical Guide to the Greek New Testament. Grand Rapids: Eerdmans, 1991.

Hay, David M. *Colossians.* ANTC. Nashville: Abingdon, 2000.

Houlden, J. L. *Paul's Letters from Prison.* PNTC. London: SCM, 1977.

Hübner, Hans. *An Philemon, an die Kolosser, an die Epheser.* Tübingen: Mohr Siebeck, 1997.

Huby, Joseph. *Les Épîtres de la captivité: Colossiens, Philémon, Ephésiens, Philippiens, aux Colossiens.* Verbum Salutis. Paris: Beauchesne, 1947.

Hugedé, N. *Commentaire de l'Épître aux Colossiens.* Genève: Labor et Fides, 1988.

Lightfoot, J. B. *Saint Paul's Epistles to the Colossians and to Philemon.* London: Macmillan, 1897. Reprint, Grand Rapids: Zondervan, 1971.

Lincoln, Andrew T. "The Letter to the Colossians." In *The New Interpreter's Bible.* Nashville: Abingdon, 2000.

Lindemann, Andreas. *Der Kolosserbrief.* ZBK 10. Zürich: Theologischer Verlag, 1983.

Lohmeyer, Ernst. *Die Briefe an die Philipper, an die Kolosser und an Philemon.* KEK 9. Göttingen: Vandenhoeck & Ruprecht, 1964.

Lohse, Eduard. *Colossians and Philemon.* Hermeneia. Philadelphia: Fortress, 1971.

Lucas, R. C. *The Message of Colossians and Philemon: Fullness and Freedom.* The Bible Speaks Today. Downers Grove, Ill.: Inter-Varsity, 1980.

Luz, Ulrich. "Der Brief an die Kolosser." In *Die Briefe an die Galater, Epheser und Kolosser,* by Jürgen Becker and Ulrich Luz. NTD 8.1. Göttingen: Vandenhoeck & Ruprecht, 1998.

MacDonald, Margaret Y. *Colossians and Ephesians.* SP 17. Collegeville, Minn.: Liturgical Press, 2000.

Martin, Ernest D. *Colossians, Philemon.* Believers Church Bible Commentary. Scottdale, Pa.: Herald Press, 1993.

Martin, Ralph P. *Colossians and Philemon.* NCBC. Grand Rapids: Eerdmans, 1973.

―――. *Ephesians, Colossians, and Philemon.* IBC. Atlanta: John Knox, 1991.

Masson, Charles. *L'Épître de Saint Paul aux Colossiens.* CNT 10. Neuchâtel: Delachaux, 1950.

Melick, Richard R., Jr. *Philippians, Colossians, Philemon.* NAC 32. Nashville: Broadman, 1991, 2000.

Meyer, H. A. W. *Kritisch-exegetisches Handbuch über die Briefe an die Philipper, Kolosser und an Philemon.* KEK 9. Göttingen: Vandenhoeck & Ruprecht, 1859.

Moule, C. F. D. *The Epistles of Paul the Apostle to the Colossians and to Philemon.* CGTC. Cambridge: Cambridge University Press, 1968.

O'Brien, Peter T. *Colossians, Philemon.* WBC 44. Waco, Tex.: Word, 1982.

Pokorný, Petr. *Colossians: A Commentary.* Peabody, Mass.: Hendrickson, 1991.

Schweizer, Eduard. *The Letter to the Colossians: A Commentary.* Minneapolis: Augsburg, 1982.

Thompson, Marianne Meye. *Colossians and Philemon.* The Two Horizons New Testament Commentary. Grand Rapids: Eerdmans, 2005.

Wall, Robert W. *Colossians and Philemon.* IVPNTC. Downers Grove, Ill.: InterVarsity, 1993.

Wilson, R. McL. *A Critical and Exegetical Commentary on Colossians and Philemon.* ICC. Edinburgh: T&T Clark, 2005.

Wolter, Michael. *Der Brief an die Kolosser. Der Brief an Philemon.* ÖTK 12. Gütersloh: Gerd Mohn, 1993.

Wright, N. T. *The Epistles of Paul to the Colossians and to Philemon.* TNTC. Leicester, U.K.: Inter-Varsity, 1986.

Other Works on Colossians

Aasgaard, R. *"My Beloved Brothers and Sisters!" Christian Siblingship in Paul.* JSNTSup 265. Edinburgh: T&T Clark, 2004.

Aland, K. "The Problem of Anonymity and Pseudonymity in Christian Literature of the First Two Centuries." *JTS* 12 (1961), 39-49.

Aletti, J.-N. *Colossiens 1,15-20: Genre et exégèse du texte: fonction de la thématique sapientielle.* AnBib 91. Rome: Pontifical Biblical Institute, 1981.

———. "Colossiens: un tournant dans da christologie Néotestamentaire: problèmes et propositions." *LASBF* 49 (1999), 211-36.

———. "Créés dans le Christ, Col. 1,15-20." *Christus* 23 (1976), 343-56.

Allen, W. "The English for *Agôna* at Colossians 2:1." *Reformation Biblical Studies Bulletin* 1 (1990), 10-12.

Allmen, D. von. "Réconciliation du monde et christologie cosmique de 2 Cor. 5:14-21 à Col. 1:15-23." *RHPR* 48 (1968), 32-45.

Anderson, C. P. "Who Wrote the Epistle from Laodicea?" *JBL* 85 (1966), 436-40.

Anwander, A. "Zu Kol 2:9." *BZ* (1965), 278-80.

Argall, R. A. "The Source of a Religious Error in Colossae." *CTJ* 22 (1987), 6-20.

Argyle, A. W. "Colossians 1:15." *ExpTim* 66 (1955), 318-19.

———. *"Prōtotokos Pasēs Ktiseōs* (Colossians 1:15)." *ExpTim* 66 (1954), 61-62.

Arnold, C. E. *The Colossian Syncretism: The Interface between Christianity and Folk Belief in Colossae.* WUNT 77. Tübingen: Mohr Siebeck, 1995.

———. "Jesus Christ: 'Head' of the Church (Colossians and Ephesians)." Pages 346-66 in *Jesus of Nazareth, Lord and Christ: Essays on the Historical Jesus and New Testament Christology.* Edited by J. B. Green and M. Turner. Grand Rapids: Eerdmans, 1994.

———. *Powers of Darkness: Principalities and Powers in Paul's Letters.* Downers Grove, Ill.: InterVarsity, 1992.

Attridge, H. W. "On Becoming an Angel: Rival Baptismal Theologies at Colossae." Pages 481-98 in *Religious Propaganda and Missionary Competition in the New Testament World.* Edited by L. Bormann, K. Del Tredici, and A. Standhartinger. Leiden and New York: Brill, 1994.

Balch, D. L. "Household Codes." Pages 25-50 in *Greco-Roman Literature and the New Testament: Selected Forms and Genres.* Edited by D. E. Aune. Atlanta: Scholars Press, 1988.

———. *Let Wives Be Submissive: The Domestic Code in I Peter.* SBLMS 26. Chico, Calif.: Scholars, 1981.

Balchin, J. F. "Colossians 1:15-20: An Early Christian Hymn? The Arguments from Style." *VE* 15 (1985), 65-94.

Bammel, E. "Versuch Col 1:15-20." *ZNW* 52 (1961), 88-95.

Bandstra, A. J. "Did the Colossian Errorists Need a Mediator?" Pages 329-43 in *New Dimensions in New Testament Study.* Edited by R. N. Longenecker and M. C. Tenney. Grand Rapids: Zondervan, 1974.

———. *"Plērōma* as *Pneuma* in Colossians." Pages 96-102 in *Ad Interim: Festschrift für R. Schippers.* Kampen, Netherlands: J. H. Kok, 1975.

Barbour, R. S. "Salvation and Cosmology: The Setting of the Epistle to the Colossians." *SJT* 20 (1967), 257-71.

Barclay, J. M. G. *Colossians and Philemon.* New Testament Guides. Sheffield: Sheffield Academic Press, 1997.

———. "Ordinary but Different: Colossians and Hidden Moral Identity." *ABR* 49 (2001), 34-52.

Barclay, W. *The All-Sufficient Christ: Studies in Paul's Letter to the Colossians.* Edinburgh: Saint Andrew, 1978.

Barth, M. "Christ and All Things." Pages 160-72 in *Paul and Paulinism: Essays in Honour of C. K. Barrett.* Edited by M. D. Hooker and S. G. Wilson. London: SPCK, 1982.

Bauckham, R. "Colossians 1:24 Again: The Apocalyptic Motif." *EvQ* 47 (1975), 168-70.

————. "Where Is Wisdom to Be Found? Colossians 1.15-20 (2)." Pages 129-38 in *Reading Texts, Seeking Wisdom: Scripture and Theology*. Edited by D. F. Ford and G. Stanton. Grand Rapids: Eerdmans, 2003.

Baugh, S. M. "The Poetic Form of Col 1:15-20." *WTJ* 47 (1985), 227-44.

Beasley-Murray, G. R. "Second Chapter of Colossians." *RevExp* 70 (1973), 469-79.

Beasley-Murray, P. "Colossians 1:15-20: An Early Christian Hymn Celebrating the Lordship of Christ." Pages 169-83 in *Pauline Studies*. Edited by D. A. Hagner and M. J. Harris. Grand Rapids: Eerdmans, 1980.

Beetham, C. "Echoes of Scripture in the Letter to the Colossians." Ph.D. diss., Wheaton College, 2005.

Behr, J. "Colossians 1:13-20: A Chiastic Reading." *SVTQ* 40 (1996), 247-64.

Bellai, Z. "Traces of the Ancient Church's Liturgy of Baptism in the New Testament (Col. 1:15-20)." *Theologiai Szemle* 28 (1986), 6-9.

Benoit, P. "Colossians 2:2-3." Pages 41-51 in *The New Testament Age: Essays in Honor of Bo Reicke*. Vol. 1. Edited by W. C. Weinrich. Macon, Ga.: Mercer University Press, 1984.

————. "L'hymne christologique de Col I,15-20: jugement critique sur l'état des recherches." Pages 226-63 in *Christianity, Judaism, and Other Greco-Roman Cults: Studies for Morton Smith at Sixty*. Edited by J. Neusner. Leiden and New York: Brill, 1975.

————. "Pauline Angelology and Demonology: Reflections on Designations of Heavenly Powers and on the Origin of Angelic Evil according to Paul." *Religious Studies Bulletin* 3 (1983), 1-18.

————. "The 'Plērōma' in the Epistles to the Colossians and the Ephesians." *SEÅ* 49 (1984), 136-58.

————. "Rapports littéraires entre les Épîtres aux Colossiens et aux Éphésiens." Pages 11-22 in *Neutestamentliche Aufsätze: Festschrift für Prof. Josef Schmid zum 70. Geburtstag*. Edited by J. Blinzler, O. Kuss, and F. Mussner. Regensburg: Friedrich Pustet, 1963.

————. "Ἅγιοι en Colossiens 1.12: hommes ou anges?" Pages 83-101 in *Paul and Paulinism: Essays in Honour of C. K. Barrett*. Edited by M. D. Hooker and S. G. Wilson. London: SPCK, 1982.

Berkhof, H. "The Holy Spirit and the World: Some Reflections on Paul's Letter to the Colossians." *JTSA* 29 (1979), 56-61.

Best, E. "Who Used Whom? The Relationship of Ephesians and Colossians." *NTS* 43 (1997), 72-96.

Betz, H. D. "Paul's 'Second Presence' in Colossians." Pages 507-18 in *Texts and Contexts: Biblical Texts in Their Textual and Situational Contexts*. Edited by T. Fornberg and D. Hellholm. Oslo: Scandinavian University Press, 1995.

Beuttler, U. "Christus, das Heil der Natur." *Glaube und Denken* 12 (1999), 81-88.

Bevere, A. R. *Sharing in the Inheritance: Identity and the Moral Life in Colossians.* JSNTSup 226. Sheffield: Sheffield Academic Press, 2003.

Blanchette, O. A. "Does the Cheirographon of Col 2:14 Represent Christ Himself?" *CBQ* 23 (1961), 306-12.

Bock, D. L. "'The New Man' as Community in Colossians and Ephesians." Pages 157-67 in *Integrity of Heart, Skillfulness of Hands: Biblical and Leadership Studies in Honor of Donald K. Campbell.* Edited by C. Dyer and R. B. Zuck. Grand Rapids: Baker, 1994.

Bockmuehl, M. "A Note on the Text of Colossians 4:3." *JTS* 39 (1988), 489-94.

Bornkamm, G. "Die Hoffnung im Kolosserbrief: Zugleich ein Beitrag zur Frage der Echtheit des Briefes." Pages 56-64 in *Studien zum Neuen Testament und zur Patristik: Erich Klostermann zum 90 Geburtstag dargebracht.* TU 77. Edited by O. Eissfeldt. Berlin: Akademie Verlag, 1961.

———. "The Heresy of Colossians." Pages 123-45 in *Conflict at Colossae: A Problem in the Interpretation of Early Christianity Illustrated by Selected Modern Studies.* Edited by F. O. Francis and W. A. Meeks. Missoula, Mont.: Scholars Press, 1973.

Botha, J. "A Stylistic Analysis of the Christ Hymn (Col 1:15-20)." Pages 238-51 in *A South African Perspective on the New Testament: Essays by South African New Testament Scholars Presented to Bruce Manning Metzger during His Visit in South Africa in 1985.* Edited by J. H. Petzer and P. J. Hartin. Leiden and New York: Brill, 1997.

Bouttier, M. "Complexio Oppositorum: sur les formules de I Cor 12:13; Gal 3:26-8; Col 3:10, 11." *NTS* 23 (1976), 1-19.

———. "Petite suite Paulinienne." *ETR* 60 (1985), 265-72.

Bowen, C. R. "The Original Form of Paul's Letter to the Colossians." *JBL* 43 (1924), 177-206.

Bowers, W. P. "A Note on Colossians 1:27a." Pages 110-14 in *Current Issues in Biblical and Patristic Interpretation.* Edited by G. F. Hawthorne. Grand Rapids: Eerdmans, 1975.

Bradley, J. "The Religious Life-Setting of the Epistle to the Colossians." *SBT* 2 (1972), 17-36.

Bratcher, R. G., and E. A. Nida. *A Translator's Handbook on Paul's Letters to the Colossians and to Philemon.* Stuttgart: United Bible Societies, 1977.

Bruce, F. F. "Colossian Problems, Pt. 1: Jews and Christians in the Lycus Valley." *BSac* 141 (1984), 3-15.

———. "Colossian Problems, Pt. 2: The 'Christ Hymn' of Colossians 1:15-20." *BSac* 141 (1984), 99-111.

———. "Colossian Problems, Pt. 3: The Colossian Heresy." *BSac* 141 (1984), 195-208.

OTHER WORKS ON COLOSSIANS

———. "Colossian Problems, Pt. 4: Christ as Conqueror and Reconciler."
BSac 141 (1984), 291-302.

Bujard, W. *Stilanalytische Untersuchungen zum Kolosserbrief als Beitrag zur
Methodik von Sprachvergleichen.* SUNT 11. Göttingen: Vandenhoeck &
Ruprecht, 1973.

Buls, H. H. "Luther's Translation of Colossians 2:12." *CTQ* 45 (1981), 13-16.

Burger, C. *Schöpfung und Versöhnung: Studien zum Liturgischen Gut im Kolosser-
und Epheserbrief.* WMANT 46. Neukirchener: Neukirchener Verlag,
1975.

Cahill, M. "The Neglected Parallelism in Colossians 1:24-25." *ETL* 68 (1992),
142-47.

Callow, J. *A Semantic and Structural Analysis of Colossians.* 2d ed. Dallas: SIL International, 2002.

Campbell, D. A. "The Scythian Perspective in Col 3:11: A Response to Troy
Martin." *NovT* 39 (1997), 81-84.

———. "Unravelling Colossians 3.11b." *NTS* 42 (1996), 120-32.

Cannon, G. E. *The Use of Traditional Material in Colossians.* Macon, Ga.: Mercer
University Press, 1983.

Carlos Reyes, L. "The Structure and Rhetoric of Colossians 1:15-20." *Filologia
Neotestamentaria* 12 (1999), 139-54.

Carr, W. "Two Notes on Colossians." *JTS* 24 (1973), 492-500.

Carrez, M. "Souffrance et gloire dans les épîtres Pauliniennes (contribution à
l'exégèse de Col 1:24-27)." *RHPR* 31 (1951), 343-53.

Cerfaux, L. "En faveur de l'authenticité des épîtres de la captivité: et
l'influence des 'mystères' sur les épîtres de S. Paul." Pages 265-85 in
*Recueil Lucien Cerfaux. études d'exégèse et d'histoire religieuse de Monsei-
gneur Cerfaux.* Gembloux: J. Duculot, 1962.

Chadwick, H. "'All Things to All Men.'" *NTS* 1 (1955), 261-75.

Chester, A. "Jewish Messianic Expectations and Mediatorial Figures and
Pauline Christology." Pages 17-89 in *Paulus und das Antike Judentum:
Tübingen-Durham Symposium im Gedenken an den 50. Todestag Adolf
Schlatters (19 Mai 1938).* Edited by M. Hengel and U. Heckel. Tübingen:
Mohr Siebeck, 1991.

Christopher, G. T. "A Discourse Analysis of Colossians 2:16–3:17." *Grace
Theological Journal* 11 (1990), 205-20.

Cleveland, R. E. "Colossians: Polemic or Paraenesis?" Ph.D. diss., Fordham
University, 2000.

Cole, H. R. "The Christian and Time-Keeping in Colossians 2:16 and
Galatians 4:10." *AUSS* 39 (2001), 273-82.

Collins, R. F. *Letters That Paul Did Not Write: The Epistle to the Hebrews and the
Pauline Pseudepigrapha.* GNS 28. Wilmington, Del.: Michael Glazier,
1988.

9

Constantelos, D. J. "Religious Cultural Diversity and Christian Unity in the Church of Colossae: An Exegesis of Colossians 2:16 to 3:4." Pages 53-61 in *Agape and Diakonia: Essays in Memory of Bishop Gerasimos of Abydos.* Edited by G. Papadopoulos and P. A. Chamberas. Brookline: Holy Cross Orthodox Press, 1998.

Cope, L. "On Rethinking the Philemon-Colossians Connection." *BR* 30 (1985), 45-50.

Coutts, J. "Relationship of Ephesians and Colossians." *NTS* 4 (1958), 201-7.

Craddock, F. B. "'All Things in Him' — A Critical Note on Col 1:15-20." *NTS* 12 (1965), 78-80.

Cranfield, C. E. B. "Dying with Christ and Being Raised with Christ." *Metanoia* 2 (1992), 99-102.

Crouch, J. E. *The Origin and Intention of the Colossian Haustafel.* FRLANT 109. Göttingen: Vandenhoeck & Ruprecht, 1972.

Dahl, N. A. "Adresse und Proömium des Epheserbriefes." *TZ* 7 (1951), 241-64.

DeMaris, R. E. *The Colossian Controversy: Wisdom in Dispute at Colossae.* JSNTSup 96. Sheffield: JSOT Press, 1994.

Donelson, L. R. *Pseudepigraphy and Ethical Argument in the Pastoral Epistles.* HUT 22. Tübingen: Mohr Siebeck, 1986.

Drake, A. E. "The Riddle of Colossians: Quaerendo Invenietis." *NTS* 41 (1995), 123-44.

Dübbers, M. *Christologie und Existenz im Kolosserbrief: Exegetische und Semantische Untersuchungen zur Intention des Kolosserfriefes.* WUNT 191. Tübingen: Mohr Siebeck, 2005.

Dunn, J. D. G. "Anti-Semitism in the Deutero-Pauline Literature." Pages 151-65 in *Anti-Semitism and Early Christianity: Issues of Polemic and Faith.* Edited by C. A. Evans and D. A. Hagner. Minneapolis: Fortress, 1993.

———. "The 'Body' in Colossians." Pages 163-81 in *To Tell the Mystery.* Edited by T. E. Schmidt and M. Silva. Sheffield: JSOT Press, 1994.

———. "The Colossian Philosophy: A Confident Jewish Apologia." *Bib* 76 (1995), 153-81.

———. "Deutero-Pauline Letters." Pages 130-44 in *Early Christian Thought in Its Jewish Context.* Edited by O. L. Yarbrough. New York and Cambridge: Cambridge University Press, 1996.

Dupont, J. *Gnosis: la connaissance religieuse dans les épîtres de Saint Paul.* Paris: Gabalda, 1949.

Efird, J. M. *Christ, the Church, and the End: Studies in Colossians and Ephesians.* Valley Forge, Pa.: Judson, 1980.

Egan, R. B. "Lexical Evidence on Two Pauline Passages." *NovT* 19 (1977), 34-62.

Eitrem, S. "*Embateuō*: note sur Col 2:18." *ST* 2 (1949), 90-94.

Eller, V. *Christian Anarchy: Jesus' Primacy over the Powers*. Grand Rapids: Eerdmans, 1987.

Ellingworth, P. "Colossians I.15-20 and Its Context." *ExpTim* 73 (1962), 252-53.

Ellis, E. E. "Colossians 1:12-20: Christus Creator, Christus Salvator." Pages 415-28 in *Interpreting the New Testament Text: Introduction to the Art and Science of Exegesis*. Edited by D. L. Bock and B. M. Fanning. Wheaton, Ill.: Crossway, 2006.

———. "Pseudonymity and Canonicity of New Testament Documents." Pages 212-24 in *Worship, Theology and Ministry in the Early Church: Essays in Honor of Ralph P. Martin*. Edited by M. J. Wilkins and T. Paige. Sheffield: Sheffield Academic Press, 1992.

Evans, C. A. "The Colossian Mystics." *Bib* 63 (1982), 188-205.

———. "The Meaning of *Plērōma* in Nag Hammadi." *Bib* 65 (1984), 259-65.

Ferguson, E. "Spiritual Circumcision in Early Christianity." *SJT* 41 (1988), 485-97.

Feuillet, A. "La creation de l'univers dans le Christ d'après l'épitre aux Colossiens (1:16a)." *NTS* 12 (1965), 1-9.

Flemington, W. F. "On the Interpretation of Colossians 1:24." Pages 84-90 in *Suffering and Martyrdom in the New Testament*. Edited by H. Merklein. London: Cambridge University Press, 1981.

Foerster, W. "Die Irrlehrer des Kolosserbriefes." Pages 71-80 in *Studia biblica et semitica: Theodoro Christiano Vriezen qui munere professoris theologiae per xxv annos functus est, ab amicis, collegis, discipulis dedicata*. Wageningen, Netherlands: Veenman, 1966.

Fossum, J. "Colossians 1:15-18a in the Light of Jewish Mysticism and Gnosticism." *NTS* 35 (1989), 183-201.

———. "The Image of the Invisible God: Colossians 1.15-18a in the Light of Jewish Mysticism and Gnosticism." Pages 13-39 in *The Image of the Invisible God: Essays on the Influence of Jewish Mysticism on Early Christology*. Göttingen: Vandenhoeck, 1995.

Fowl, S. E. *The Story of Christ in the Ethics of Paul: An Analysis of the Function of the Hymnic Material in the Pauline Corpus*. JSNTSup 36. Sheffield: JSOT Press, 1990.

Fox-Genovese, E., and E. D. Genovese. "The Divine Sanction of Social Order: Religious Foundations of the Southern Slaveholders' World View." *JAAR* 55 (1987), 211-33.

Francis, F. O. "The Background of *Embateuein* in Legal Papyri and Oracle Inscriptions." Pages 197-206 in *Conflict in Colossae: A Problem in the Interpretation of Early Christianity Illustrated by Selected Modern Studies*. Edited by F. O. Francis and W. A. Meeks. Missoula, Mont.: Scholars Press, 1973.

———. "Christological Argument of Colossians." Pages 192-208 in *God's*

Christ and His People. Edited by J. Jervell and W. A. Meeks. Oslo: Universitetsforlaget, 1977.

————. "Humility and Angelic Worship in Col 2:18." Pages 163-95 in *Conflict in Colossae: A Problem in the Interpretation of Early Christianity Illustrated by Selected Modern Studies.* Edited by F. O. Francis and W. A. Meeks. Missoula, Mont.: Scholars Press, 1973.

————. "Humility and Angelic Worship in Col 2:18." *ST* 16 (1962), 109-34.

————. "Visionary Discipline and Scriptural Tradition at Colossae." *LTQ* 2 (1967), 71-81.

Francis, F. O., and W. A. Meeks. *Conflict at Colossae: A Problem in the Interpretation of Early Christianity Illustrated by Selected Modern Studies.* Sources for Biblical Study 4. Missoula, Mont.: Scholars Press, 1973.

Fuchs, E. "Das Neue Testament und das hermeneutische Problem." *ZTK* 58 (1961), 198-226.

Gardner, P. D. "'Circumcised in Baptism — Raised through Faith': A Note on Col 2:11-12." *WTJ* 45 (1983), 172-77.

Gewiess, J. "Die apologetische Methode des Apostels Paulus im Kampf gegen die Irrlehre in Kolossä." *BibLeb* 3 (1962), 258-70.

Gielen, M. "Zur Interpretation der Paulinischen Formel *Hē Kat' Oikon Ekklēsia.*" *ZNW* 77 (1986), 109-25.

Giem, P. "*Sabbatōn* in Col 2:16." *AUSS* 19 (1981), 195-210.

Giles, K. "The Biblical Argument for Slavery: Can the Bible Mislead? A Case Study in Hermeneutics." *EvQ* 66 (1994), 3-17.

Glasson, T. F. "Col. 1,18.15 and Sir 24." *NovT* 11 (1969), 154-56.

————. "Colossians 1:18, 15 and Sirach 24." *JBL* 86 (1967), 214-16.

Gnilka, J. "Das Paulusbild im Kolosser- und Epheserbrief." Pages 179-93 in *Kontinuität und Einheit: Festschrift für Franz Mussner.* Edited by P.-G. Müller and W. Stenger. Freiburg: Herder, 1981.

Goulder, M. D. "Colossians and Barbelo." *NTS* 41 (1995), 601-19.

————. "Vision and Knowledge." *JSNT* 56 (1994), 53-71.

Grässer, E. "Kol 3,1-4 als Beispiel einer Interpretation Secundum Homines Recipientes." *ZTK* 64 (1967), 139-68.

Grudem, W. "Does *Kephale* ('Head') Mean 'Source' or 'Authority Over' in Greek Literature: A Survey of 2,336 Examples." *TJ* 6 (1985), 38-59.

Gunton, C. "Atonement and the Project of Creation: An Interpretation of Colossians 1:15-23." *Dialog* 35 (1996), 35-41.

————. "Christus Victor Revisited: A Study in Metaphor and the Transformation of Meaning." *JTS* 36 (1985), 129-45.

Halter, H. "Kol 1,12-14: Errettet aus dem Machtbereich der Finsternis, Erlöst im Lichreich des Sohnes." *Freiburger Theologische Studien* 106 (1977), 183-90.

————. "Kol 2,6-23: Begraben und Auferweckt mit Christus, Befreit von

Sündentod und kosmichen Mächten." *Freiburger Theologische Studien* 106 (1977), 190-204.

———. "Kol 3,1-4: Gestorben und erweckt mit Christus: Suchet, was 'oben' ist." *Freiburger Theologische Studien* 106 (1977), 204-9.

———. "Kol 3,5-17: Der alte Mensch ist abgetan, ain neuer ist geworden." *Freiburger Theologische Studien* 106 (1977), 209-25.

Hanson, S. *The Unity of the Church in the New Testament: Colossians and Ephesians.* ASNU 14. Uppsala: Almqvist & Wiksell, 1946.

Hanssler, B. "Zu Satzkonstruktion und Aussage in Kol 2,23." Pages 143-48 in *Wort Gottes in der Zeit.* Edited by H. Feld and J. Nolte. Düsseldorf: Patmos, 1973.

Harrington, D. J. "Christians and Jews in Colossians." Pages 153-61 in *Diaspora Jews and Judaism.* Edited by J. A. Overman and R. S. MacLennan. Atlanta: Scholars Press, 1992.

Harrisville, R. A. "God's Mercy — Tested, Promised, Done (An Exposition of Genesis 18:20-32; Luke 11:1-13; Colossians 2:6-15)." *Int* 31 (1977), 165-78.

———. "The New Testament Witness to the Cosmic Christ." Pages 39-63 in *Gospel and Human Destiny.* Edited by V. Vajta. Minneapolis: Augsburg, 1971.

Hartman, L. "Code and Context: A Few Reflections on the Parenesis of Col 3:6–4:1." Pages 237-47 in *Tradition and Interpretation in the New Testament.* Edited by G. F. Hawthorne. Grand Rapids: Eerdmans, 1987.

———. "Doing Things with the Words of Colossians." Pages 195-210 in *Text-Centered New Testament Studies: Text-Theoretical Essays on Early Jewish and Early Christian Literature.* Tübingen: Mohr Siebeck, 1997.

———. "Humble and Confident: On the So-Called Philosophers in Colossae." Pages 25-39 in *Mighty Minorities.* Oslo: Scandinavian University Press, 1995.

———. "Some Unorthodox Thoughts on The 'Household-Code Form.'" Pages 219-32 in *Social World of Formative Christianity and Judaism.* Edited by J. Neusner. Philadelphia: Fortress, 1988.

———. "Universal Reconciliation (Col 1,20)." *SNTSU* 10 (1985), 109-21.

Harvey, A. E. "The Use of Mystery Language in the Bible." *JTS* 31 (1980), 320-36.

Hatina, T. R. "The Perfect Tense-Form in Colossians: Verbal Aspect, Temporality and the Challenge of Translation." Pages 224-52 in *Translating the Bible: Problems and Prospects.* Edited by S. E. Porter and R. S. Hess. Sheffield: Sheffield Academic, 1999.

Haulotte, E. "Formation du corpus du Nouveau Testament: recherche d'un "module" génératif intratextuel." Pages 255-439 in *Le canon des Écri-*

tures: études historiques, exegetiques, et systematiques. Edited by J.-N. Aletti and C. Theobald. LD 140. Paris: Cerf, 1990.

Hayes, H. D. "Colossians 2:6-19." *Int* 49 (1995), 285-88.

Helyer, L. R. "Arius Revisited: The Firstborn over All Creation (Col 1:15)." *JETS* 31 (1988), 59-67.

————. "Colossians 1:15-20: Pre-Pauline or Pauline?" *JETS* 26 (1983), 167-79.

————. "Cosmic Christology and Col 1:15-20." *JETS* 37 (1994), 235-46.

————. "Recent Research on Col 1:15-20 (1980-1990)." *Grace Theological Journal* 12 (1991), 51-67.

Hendricks, W. L. "All in All: Theological Themes in Colossians." *SwJT* 16 (1973), 23-35.

Hengel, M. "Das Christuslied im Frühesten Gottesdienst." Pages 357-404 in *Weisheit Gottes — Weisheit der Welt.* Edited by W. Baier. St. Ottilien: EOS, 1987.

————. "Hymnus und Christologie." Pages 3-23 in *Wort in der Zeit: Neutestamentliche Studien. Festgabe für Karl Heinrich Rengstorf zum 75. Geburtstag.* Edited by W. Haubeck and M. Bachmann. Leiden and New York: Brill, 1980.

Hinson, E. G. "Christian Household in Colossians 3:18–4:1." *RevExp* 70 (1973), 495-506.

Hockel, A. *Christus der Erstgeborene: Zur Geschichte der Exegese von Kol 1,15.* Düsseldorf: Patmos, 1965.

Hofius, O. "'Erstgeborener vor aller Schöpfung' — 'Erstgeborener aus den Toten': Erwägungen zu Struktur und Aussage des Christushymnus Kol 1,15-20." Pages 185-203 in *Auferstehung-Resurrection: The Fourth Durham-Tübingen Research Symposium.* Edited by F. Avemarie and H. Lichtenberger. Tübingen: Mohr Siebeck, 2001.

Hollenbach, B. "Col 2:23: Which Things Lead to the Fulfilment of the Flesh." *NTS* 25 (1979), 254-61.

Hölscher, A. "Christus als Bild Gottes: Zum Hymnus des Kolosserbriefes." Pages 114-33 in *Religiöse Sprache und ihre Bilder: Von der Bibel bis zur modernen Lyrik.* Edited by A. Hölscher and R. Kampling. Berlin: Morus, 1998.

Hooker, M. D. "Were There False Teachers in Colossae?" Pages 315-31 in *Christ and Spirit in the New Testament: Studies in Honour of Charles Francis Digby Moule.* Edited by B. Lindars and S. S. Smalley. Cambridge: Cambridge University Press, 1973.

————. "Where Is Wisdom to Be Found? Colossians 1.15-20 (1)." Pages 116-28 in *Reading Texts, Seeking Wisdom: Scripture and Theology.* Edited by D. F. Ford and G. Stanton. Grand Rapids: Eerdmans, 2003.

Howington, N. P. "Liberating Christ (Colossians 3:1-11)." *RevExp* 55 (1958), 196-202.

Hunt, J. P. T. "Colossians 2:11-12, the Circumcision/Baptism Analogy, and Infant Baptism." *TynBul* 41 (1990), 227-44.

Hurtado, L. W. *Lord Jesus Christ: Devotion to Jesus in Earliest Christianity.* Grand Rapids: Eerdmans, 2003.

———. *One God, One Lord: Early Christian Devotion to Jesus and Ancient Jewish Monotheism.* Philadelphia: Fortress, 1988.

Johnston, G. "'Kingdom of God' Sayings in Paul's Letters." Pages 143-56 in *From Jesus to Paul: Studies in Honour of Francis Wright Beare.* Edited by P. Richardson and J. C. Hurd. Waterloo: Wilfrid Laurier University Press, 1984.

Jones, P. "L'évangile pour l'âge du verseau: Colossiens 1:15-20." *RRef* 50 (1999), 13-23.

Karris, R. J. *A Symphony of New Testament Hymns.* Collegeville, Minn.: Liturgical, 1996.

Kasali, M. D. "The Concept of Hope in Paul: Studies in Selected Passages." Ph.D. diss., Trinity Evangelical Divinity School, 1994.

Kiley, M. C. *Colossians as Pseudepigraphy.* The Biblical Seminar. Sheffield: JSOT Press, 1986.

Knight, G. W. "Husbands and Wives as Analogues of Christ and the Church: Ephesians 5:21-33 and Colossians 3:18-19." Pages 165-78 in *Recovering Biblical Manhood and Womanhood: A Response to Evangelical Feminism.* Edited by J. Piper and W. Grudem. Wheaton: Crossway, 1991.

Knowles, M. P. "'Christ in You, the Hope of Glory': Discipleship in Colossians." Pages 180-202 in *Patterns of Discipleship in the New Testament.* Edited by R. N. Longenecker. Grand Rapids: Eerdmans, 1996.

Kremer, J. "Was an den Bedrängnissen des Christus Mangelt: Versucht einer Bibeltheologischen Neuinterpretation von Kol 1,24." *Bib* 82 (2001), 130-46.

Ladd, G. E. "Paul's Friends in Colossians 4:7-16." *RevExp* 70 (1973), 507-14.

Lähnemann, J. *Der Kolosserbrief: Komposition, Situation und Argumentation.* SNT 3. Gütersloh: Mohn, 1971.

Lamarche, P. "Structure de l'épître aux Colossiens." *Bib* 56 (1975), 453-63.

Lamp, J. S. "Wisdom in Col 1:15-20: Contribution and Significance." *JETS* 41 (1998), 45-53.

Lampe, G. W. H. "New Testament Doctrine of *Ktisis.*" *SJT* 17 (1964), 449-62.

Lane, W. L. "Creed and Theology: Reflections on Colossians." *JETS* 21 (1978), 213-20.

Langkammer, H. "Die Einwohnung der 'Absoluten Seinsfülle' in Christus Bemerkungen zu Kol 1,19." *BZ* 12 (1968), 258-63.

———. "Jesus in der Sprache der Neutestamentlichen Christuslieder." Pages 467-86 in *Vom Urchristentum zu Jesus: Für Joachim Gnilka.* Edited by H. Frankemölle and K. Kertelge. Freiburg: Herder, 1989.

────. "Zum Ursprung der kosmologischen Christologie im NT." *BN* 16 (1982), 30-38.

Leaney, R. "Colossians 2:21-23 (the Use of *Pros*)." *ExpTim* 64 (1952), 92.

Legaré, C. "La dimension pathémique dans l'épître aux Colossiens." Pages 215-27 in *Temps de la lecture: exègése biblique et semiotique: recueil d'hommages pour Jean Delorme*. Edited by L. Panier. LD 155. Paris: Cerf, 1993.

Leppä, O. *The Making of Colossians: A Study on the Formation and Purpose of a Deutero-Pauline Letter*. Publications of the Finnish Exegetical Society 86. Göttingen: Vandenhoeck & Ruprecht, 2003.

Levison, J. R. "2 Apoc Bar 48:42–52:7 and the Apocalyptic Dimension of Colossians 3:1-6." *JBL* 108 (1989), 93-108.

Lewis, E. "Paul and the Perverters of Christianity: Revelation through the Epistle to the Colossians." *Int* 2 (1948), 143-57.

Lightfoot, J. B. "The Colossian Heresy." Pages 13-59 in *Conflict in Colossae: A Problem in the Interpretation of Early Christianity Illustrated by Selected Modern Studies*. Edited by F. O. Francis and W. A. Meeks. Missoula, Mont.: Scholars Press, 1973.

Lillie, W. "The Pauline House-Tables." *ExpTim* 86 (1975), 179-83.

Lincoln, A. T. "The Household Code and Wisdom Mode of Colossians." *JSNT* 74 (1999), 93-112.

────. "Liberation from the Powers: Supernatural Spirits or Societal Structures?" Pages 335-54 in *The Bible in Human Society: Essays in Honor of John Rogerson*. Edited by M. D. Carroll, D. J. A. Clines, and P. R. Davies. Sheffield: Sheffield Academic Press, 1995.

Lincoln, A. T., and A. J. M. Wedderburn. *The Theology of the Later Pauline Epistles*. Cambridge: Cambridge University Press, 1993.

Lindemann, A. "Die Gemeinde von 'Kolossä', Erwägungen zum 'Sitz in Leben' eines pseudopaulinischen Briefs." *WD* 16 (1981), 111-34.

Lohse, E. "Christologie und Ethik im Kolosserbrief." *BZNW* 30 (1964), 156-68.

────. "Christusherrschaft und Kirche im Kolosserbrief." *NTS* 11 (1965), 203-16.

────. "Die Mitarbeiter des Apostels Paulus im Kolosserbrief." Pages 189-94 in *Verborum Veritas: Festschrift für Gustav Stählin zum 70. Geburtstag*. Wuppertal: Theologischer Verlag Rolf Brockhaus, 1970.

────. "Ein Hymnisches Bekenntnis in Kol 2,13-15." Pages 427-35 in *Mélanges bibliques en hommage au R. P. Béda Rigaux*. Gembloux: Duculot, 1970.

Lona, H. E. *Die Eschatologie im Kolosser- und Epheserbrief*. FB 48. Würzburg: Echter, 1984.

Longenecker, R. N. *Patterns of Discipleship in the New Testament*. McMaster New Testament Studies. Grand Rapids: Eerdmans, 1996.

Louw, J. P. "Reading a Text as Discourse." Pages 17-30 in *Linguistics and New Testament Interpretation*. Edited by D. A. Black. Nashville: Broadman, 1992.

Löwe, H. "Bekenntnis, Apostelamt und Kirche im Kolosserbrief." Pages 299-314 in *Kirche: Festschrift für Günther Bornkamm*. Edited by D. Lührmann and G. Strecker. Tübingen: Mohr Siebeck, 1980.

Lyonnet, S. "L'épître aux Colossiens (Col 2:18) et les mystères d'apollon clarien." *Bib* 43 (1962), 417-35.

――――. "Paul's Adversaries in Colossae." Pages 147-61 in *Conflict in Colossae: A Problem in the Interpretation of Early Christianity Illustrated by Selected Modern Studies*. Edited by F. O. Francis and W. A. Meeks. Missoula, Mont.: Scholars Press, 1973.

MacDonald, M. Y. "Citizens of Heaven and Earth: Asceticism and Social Integration in Colossians and Ephesians." Pages 269-98 in *Asceticism and the New Testament*. Edited by L. E. Vaage. New York: Routledge, 1999.

Manns, F. "Col 1:15-20: Midrash chrétien de Gen 1:1." *RevScRel* 53 (1979), 100-110.

Marshall, I. H. "Mutual Love and Submission in Marriage." Pages 186-204 in *Discovering Biblical Equality: Complementarity without Hierarchy*. Edited by R. W. Pierce and R. M. Groothuis. Downers Grove, Ill.: InterVarsity, 2004.

Martin, R. P. "An Early Christian Hymn (Col. 1:15-20)." *EvQ* 36 (1964), 195-205.

――――. "Reconciliation and Forgiveness in Colossians." Pages 104-24 in *Reconciliation and Hope: New Testament Essays on Atonement and Eschatology*. Edited by R. Banks. Grand Rapids: Eerdmans, 1974.

Martin, T. "But Let Everyone Discern the Body of Christ (Colossians 2:17)." *JBL* 114 (1995), 249-55.

――――. *By Philosophy and Empty Deceit: Colossians as Response to a Cynic Critique*. JSNTSup 118. Sheffield: Sheffield Academic Press, 1996.

――――. "Pagan and Judeo-Christian Time-Keeping Schemes in Gal 4.10 and Col 2.16." *NTS* 42 (1996), 105-19.

――――. "The Scythian Perspective in Col 3:11." *NovT* 37 (1995), 249-61.

――――. "Scythian Perspective or Elusive Chiasm? A Reply to Douglas A. Campbell." *NovT* 41 (1999), 1256-64.

McCarthy, J. "Le Christ cosmique el l'âge de l'écologie: une lecture de Col. 1,15-20." *NRTh* 116 (1994), 27-47.

McCown, W. "The Hymnic Structure of Colossians 1:15-20." *EvQ* 51 (1979), 156-62.

Meecham, H. G. "Colossians 1:15." *ExpTim* 66 (1955), 124-25.

Meeks, W. A. "The 'Haustafeln' and American Slavery: A Hermeneutical Challenge." Pages 232-53 in *Theology and Ethics in Paul and His Inter-*

preters. Edited by E. H. Lovering and J. L. Sumney. Nashville: Abingdon, 1996.

———. "In One Body: The Unity of Humankind in Colossians and Ephesians." Pages 209-21 in *God's Christ and His People.* Edited by J. Jervell and W. A. Meeks. Oslo: Universitetsforlaget, 1977.

———. "'To Walk Worthily of the Lord': Moral Formation in the Pauline School Exemplified by the Letter to Colossians." Pages 37-58 in *Hermes and Athena: Biblical Exegesis and Philosophical Theology.* Edited by E. Stump and T. P. Flint. Notre Dame: University of Notre Dame Press, 1993.

Merk, O. "Erwägungen zu Kol 2,6f." Pages 407-16 in *Vom Urchristentum zu Jesus: Für Joachim Gnilka.* Edited by H. Frankemölle and K. Kertelge. Freiburg: Herder, 1989.

Merklein, H. "Eph 4:1-5,20 als Rezeption von Kol 3:1-17: Zugleich ein Beitrag zur Problematik des Epheserbriefes." Pages 194-210 in *Kontinuität und Einheit: Festschrift für Franz Mussner.* Edited by P.-G. Müller and W. Stenger. Freiburg: Herder, 1981.

———. "Im Spannungsfeld von Protologie und Eschatologie: Zur kurzen Geschichte der aktiven Beteiligung von Frauen in paulinischen Gemeinden." Pages 231-59 in *Eschatologie und Schöpfung: Festschrift für Erich Gräßer zum siebzigsten Geburtstag.* Edited by M. Evang, H. Merklein, and M. Wolter. New York: de Gruyter, 1997.

———. "Paulinische Theologie in der Rezeption des Kolosser und Epheserbriefes." Pages 25-69 in *Paulus in den neutestamentlichen Spätschriften.* Edited by K. Kertelge. Freiburg: Herder, 1981.

Moir, I. A. "Some Thoughts on Col. 2,17-18." *TZ* 35 (1979), 363.

Motyer, S. "The Relationship between Paul's Gospel of 'All One in Christ Jesus' (Galatians 3:28) and The 'Household Codes.'" *VE* 19 (1989), 33-48.

Moule, C. F. D. "New Life in Colossians 3:1-17." *RevExp* 70 (1973), 481-93.

Müller, K. "Die Haustafel des Kolosserbriefes und das antike Frauenthema: Eine kritische Rückschau auf alte Ergebnisse." Pages 263-319 in *Die Frau im Urchristentum: Quaestiones Disputatae.* Edited by G. Dautzenberg, H. Merklein, and K. Müller. Freiburg: Herder, 1983.

Mullins, T. Y. "The Thanksgivings of Philemon and Colossians." *NTS* 30 (1984), 288-93.

Münderlein, G. "Die Erwählung durch das *Plērōma* — Kol 1:19." *NTS* 8 (1962), 264-76.

Munro, W. "Col 3:18–4:1 and Eph 5:21–6:9: Evidences of a Late Literary Stratum?" *NTS* 18 (1972), 434-47.

Murphy-O'Connor, J. "Tradition and Redaction in Col 1:15-20." *RB* 102 (1995), 231-41.

Murray, J. *Principles of Conduct: Aspects of Biblical Ethics*. Grand Rapids: Eerdmans, 1957.

Mussner, F. "Das Reich Christi: Bemerkungen zur Eschatologie des *Corpus Paulinum.*" Pages 141-55 in *Im Gespräch mit dem Dreieinen Gott: Elemente einer trinitarischen Theologie: Festschrift zum 65. Geburtstag von Wilhelm Breuning*. Edited by M. Bohnke and H. Heinz. Düsseldorf: Patmos, 1985.

Nash, H. S. "*Theiotēs — Theotēs*, Rom. i.20; Col. ii.9." *JBL* 18 (1899), 1-34.

Nash, R. S. "Heuristic Haustafeln: Domestic Codes as Entrance to the Social World of Early Christianity: The Case of Colossians." Pages 25-50 in *Religious Writings and Religious Systems*. Edited by J. Neusner. Atlanta: Scholars Press, 1989.

Nauck, W. "Salt as a Metaphor in Instructions for Discipleship." *ST* 6 (1952), 165-78.

O'Brien, P. T. "The Church as a Heavenly and Eschatological Entity." Pages 88-119 in *The Church in the Bible and the World*. Edited by D. A. Carson. Exeter: Paternoster, 1987.

———. "Col 1:20 and the Reconciliation of All Things." *RTR* 33 (1974), 45-53.

———. "Principalities and Powers: Opponents of the Church." *Evangelical Review of Theology* 16 (1992), 353-84.

O'Donnell, M. B. *Corpus Linguistics and the Greek of the New Testament*. New Testament Monographs 6. Sheffield: Sheffield University Press, 2005.

Oke, C. C. "A Hebraistic Construction in Colossians I.19-22." *ExpTim* 63 (1952), 155-56.

Olbricht, T. H. "Colossians and Gnostic Theology." *ResQ* 14 (1971), 65-79.

———. "The *Stoicheia* and the Rhetoric of Colossians: Then and Now." Pages 308-28 in *Rhetoric, Scripture and Theology: Essays from the 1994 Pretoria Conference*. Edited by S. E. Porter. Sheffield: Sheffield Academic Press, 1996.

Ollrog, W.-H. *Paulus und seiner Mitarbeiter: Untersuchungen zu Theorie und Praxis der paulinischen Mission*. WMANT 50. Neukirchen-Vluyn: Neukirchener, 1979.

O'Neill, J. C. "The Source of the Christology in Colossians." *NTS* 26 (1979), 87-100.

Overfield, P. D. "*Plērōma*: A Study in Content and Context." *NTS* 25 (1978), 384-96.

Percy, E. *Die Probleme der Kolosser- und Epheserbriefe*. Lund: Gleerup, 1946.

———. "Zu den Problemen des Kolosser- und Epheserbriefes." *ZNW* 43 (1951), 178-94.

Perriman, A. C. "The Pattern of Christ's Sufferings: Colossians 1:24 and Philippians 3:10-11." *TynBul* 42 (1991), 62-79.

Peterson, J. "'The Circumcision of the Christ': The Significance of Baptism in Colossians and the Churches of the Restoration." *ResQ* 43 (2001), 65-77.

Piper, O. A. "Savior's Eternal Work: An Exegesis of Colossians 1:9-29." *Int* 3 (1949), 286-98.

Pöhlmann, W. "Die hymnischen All-Prädikationen in Kol 1:15-20." *ZNW* 64 (1973), 53-74.

Polhill, J. B. "Relationship between Ephesians and Colossians." *RevExp* 70 (1973), 439-50.

Pollard, T. E. "Colossians 1:12-20, a Reconsideration." *NTS* 27 (1981), 572-75.

Porter, S. E. "P Oxy 744.4 and Colossians 3:9." *Bib* 73 (1992), 565-67.

Porter, S. E., and K. D. Clarke. "Canonical-Critical Perspective and the Relationship of Colossians and Ephesians." *Bib* 78 (1997), 57-86.

Reicke, B. I. "Historical Setting of Colossians." *RevExp* 70 (1973), 429-38.

———. "Zum sprachlichen Verständnis von Kol 2:23." *ST* 6 (1952), 39-53.

Reumann, J. H. P. "The Scope of Christ's Lordship." Pages 63-118 in *Christ and Humanity: A Workshop in Christian Social Ethics*. Edited by I. Asheim. Philadelphia: Fortress, 1970.

———. "Colossians 1:24 ('What Is Lacking in the Afflictions of Christ'), History of Exegesis and Ecumenical Advance." *CurTM* 17 (1990), 454-61.

———. "Jewish Mystical Experience in the Early Christian Era as Background to Understanding Colossians." *Neot* 32 (1998), 161-89.

Robinson, D. W. B. "Who Were 'the Saints?" *RTR* 22 (1963), 45-53.

Robinson, J. M. "A Formal Analysis of Colossians 1:15-20." *JBL* 76 (1957), 270-87.

Rollins, W. G. "Christological *Tendenz* in Colossians 1:15-20: A *Theologia Crucis*." Pages 123-38 in *Christological Perspectives: Essays in Honor of Harvey K. McArthur*. Edited by R. F. Berkey and S. A. Edwards. New York: Pilgrim Press, 1982.

Roose, H. "Die Hierarchisierung der Leib-Metapher im Kolosser- und Epheserbrief als 'Paulinisierung': Ein Beitrag zur Rezeption paulinischer Tradition in pseudo-paulinischen Briefen." *NovT* 47 (2005), 117-41.

Ross, A. "The Epistle to the Colossians and Its Message for Today." *EvQ* 30 (1958), 43-48.

Rowland, C. "Apocalyptic Visions and the Exaltation of Christ in the Letter to the Colossians." *JSNT* 19 (1983), 73-83.

Royalty, R. M. "Dwelling on Visions: On the Nature of the So-Called 'Colossians Heresy.'" *Bib* 83 (2002), 329-57.

Rusam, D. "Neue Belege zu den *stoicheia tou kosmou* (Gal 4,3.9, Kol 2,8.20)." *ZNW* 83 (1992), 119-25.

Sanders, E. P. "Literary Dependence in Colossians." *JBL* 85 (1966), 28-45.

Sappington, T. J. *Revelation and Redemption at Colossae.* JSNTSup 53. Sheffield: JSOT Press, 1991.

Scharlemann, M. H. "The Scope of the Redemptive Task (Colossians 1:15-20)." *CTM* 36 (1965), 291-300.

Schenk, W. "Christus, das Geheimnis der Welt, als dogmatisches und ethisches Grundprinzip des Kolosserbriefes." *EvT* 43 (1983), 138-55.

Schenke, H. M. "Der widerstreit gnostischer und kirchlicher Christologie im Spiegel des Kolosserbriefes." *ZTK* 61 (1964), 391-403.

Schottroff, L. "Ist Allein in Christus Heil? Das Bekenntnis zu Christus und die Erlösung (Kol 1,15-20)." Pages 79-89 in *Antijudaismus im Neuen Testament? Grundlagen für die Arbeit mit biblischen Texten.* Edited by D. Henze. Gütersloh: Kaiser, 1997.

Schweizer, E. "Altes und neues zu den 'Elementen der Welt' in Kol 2,20; Gal 4,3-9." Pages 111-18 in *Wissenschaft und Kirche.* Edited by K. Aland. Bielefeld: Luther-Verlag, 1989.

———. "Askese nach Kol 1,24 oder 2,20f." Pages 340-48 in *Neues Testament und Ethik.* Edited by H. Merklein. Freiburg: Herder, 1989.

———. "Christ in the Letter to the Colossians." *RevExp* 70 (1973), 451-67.

———. "Christus und Geist im Kolosserbrief." Pages 297-313 in *Christ and Spirit in the New Testament.* Edited by B. Lindars. Cambridge: Cambridge University Press, 1973.

———. "Church as the Missionary Body of Christ." *NTS* 8 (1961), 1-11.

———. "Colossians 1:15-20." *RevExp* 87 (1990), 97-104.

———. "Die 'Elemente der Welt' in Gal 4,3 9; Kol 2,8 20." Pages 245-59 in *Verborum Veritas: Festschrift für Gustav Stählin zum 70. Geburtstag.* Edited by K. Haacker and O. Böcher. Wuppertal: Brockhaus, 1970.

———. "Slaves of the Elements and Worshipers of Angels: Gal 4:3, 9 and Col 2:8, 18, 20." *JBL* 107 (1988), 455-68.

———. "Traditional Ethical Patterns in the Pauline and Post-Pauline Letters and Their Development." Pages 195-209 in *Text and Interpretation: Studies in the New Testament Presented to Matthew Black.* Edited by E. Best and R. Wilson. New York and Cambridge: Cambridge University Press, 1979.

———. "Versöhnung des Alls." Pages 487-501 in *Jesus Christus in Historie und Theologie: Festschrift für Hans Conzelmann zum 60. Geburtstag.* Edited by G. Strecker. Tübingen: Mohr Siebeck, 1975.

———. "Zur neueren Forschung am Kolosserbrief (seit 1970)." Pages 163-91 in *Theologische Berichte V.* Edited by J. Pfammatter and F. Furger. Zurich: Benziger, 1976.

Shogren, G. S. "Presently Entering the Kingdom of Christ: The Background and Purpose of Col 1:12-14." *JETS* 31 (1988), 173-80.

Sittler, J. "Called to Unity." *CurTM* 16 (1989), 5-13.

Sloyan, G. S. "Jewish Ritual of the 1st Century C.E. and Christian Sacramental Behavior." *BTB* 15 (1985), 98-103.

Smith, I. K. *Heavenly Perspective: A Study of the Apostle Paul's Response to a Jewish Mystical Movement at Colossae.* Library of New Testament Studies 346. Edinburgh: T&T Clark, 2006.

Söding, T. "Die Welt als Schöpfung in Christus: Der Beitrag des Kolosserbriefes zum interreligiösen Dialog." *Religionspädagogische Beiträge* 31 (1993), 20-37.

Stagg, F. "The Gospel, Haustafel, and Women: Mark 1:1; Colossians 3:18–4:1." *Faith and Mission* 2 (1985), 59-63.

Standhartinger, A. "Colossians and the Pauline School." *NTS* 50 (2004), 572-93.

———. *Studien zur Entstehungsgeschichte und Intention des Kolosserbriefs.* NovTSup 94. Leiden and New York: Brill, 1999.

Standhartinger, A., and B. McNeil. "The Origin and Intention of the Household Code in the Letter to the Colossians." *JSNT* 79 (2000), 117-30.

Stegemann, E. "Alt und neu bei Paulus und in den Deuteropaulinen (Kol-Eph)." *EvT* 37 (1977), 508-36.

Stettler, C. *Der Kolosserhymnus: Untersuchungen zu Form, Traditionsgeschichtlichem Hintergrund und Aussage von Kol 1,15-20.* WUNT 131. Tübingen: Mohr Siebeck, 2000.

Stettler, H. "An Interpretation of Colossians 1:24 in the Framework of Paul's Mission Theology." Pages 185-208 in *The Mission of the Early Church to Jews and Gentiles.* Edited by J. Ådna and H. Kvalbein. WUNT 127. Tübingen: Mohr Siebeck, 2000.

Stockhausen, C. L. *Letters in the Pauline Tradition: Ephesians, Colossians, 1 Timothy, 2 Timothy and Titus.* MBS 13. Wilmington: Michael Glazier, 1989.

Strecker, G. "Die neutestamentlichen Haustafeln (Kol 3,18–4,1 und Eph 5,22–6,9)." Pages 349-75 in *Neues Testament und Ethik.* Edited by H. Merklein. Freiburg: Herder, 1989.

Stuhlmacher, P. "Christliche Verantwortung bei Paulus und seinen Schülern." *EvT* 28 (1968), 165-86.

———. "Predigt im ökumenischen Wortgottesdienst." Pages 156-61 in *Heute von Gott reden.* Edited by M. Hengel and R. Reinhardt. Munich: Kaiser, 1977.

———. "Überlegungen zur Menschlichkeit des Menschen nach dem Neuen Testament." Pages 71-93 in *Gesellschaft ohne Humanität: Zur Frage nach der Menschlichkeit in der Gesellschaft.* Edited by K. Röhring and H. Schulze. Göttingen: Vandenhoeck and Ruprecht, 1971.

Sumney, J. L. "Those Who 'Pass Judgment': The Identity of the Opponents in Colossians." *Bib* 74 (1993), 366-88.

Swart, G. J. "Eschatological Vision or Exhortation to Visible Christian Conduct? Notes on the Interpretation of Colossians 3:4." *Neot* 33 (1999), 169-77.

Thompson, G. H. P. "Ephesians 3:13 and 2 Timothy 2:10 in the Light of Colossians 1:24." *ExpTim* 71 (1960), 187-89.

Thornton, T. G. C. "Jewish New Moon Festivals, Galatians 4:3-11 and Colossians 2:16." *JTS* 40 (1989), 97-100.

Thraede, K. "Zum historischen Hintergrund der 'Haustafeln' des NT." Pages 359-68 in *Pietas*. Edited by E. Dassmann. Münster: Aschendorff, 1980.

Tise, L. E. *Proslavery: A History of the Defense of Slavery in America, 1701-1840.* Athens, Ga.: University of Georgia Press, 1987.

Trudinger, L. P. "Further Brief Note on Colossians 1:24." *EvQ* 45 (1973), 36-38.

Van Broeckhoven, H. "The Social Profiles in the Colossian Debate." *JSNT* 66 (1997), 73-90.

Vawter, B. "Colossians Hymn and the Principle of Redaction." *CBQ* 33 (1971), 62-81.

Walsh, B. J. "Late/Post Modernity and Idolatry: A Contextual Reading of Colossians 2:8–3:4." *ExAud* 15 (1999), 1-17.

Walsh, B. J., and S. C. Keesmaat. *Colossians Remixed: Subverting the Empire.* Downers Grove, Ill.: InterVarsity, 2004.

Walter, N. "Die 'Handschrift in Satzungen' Kol 2:14." *ZNW* 70 (1979), 115-18.

———. "Geschichte und Mythos in der urchristlichen Präexistenzchristologie." Pages 224-34 in *Mythos und Rationalität*. Edited by H. H. Schmid. Gütersloh: Gütersloher Verlaghaus Mohn, 1988.

Weiss, H. F. "Gnostische Motive und antignostische Polemik im Kolosser- und im Epheserbrief." Pages 311-24 in *Gnosis und Neues Testament: Studien aus Religionswisschaft und Theologie*. Edited by K.-W. Tröger. Gütersloh: Gütersloher Verlaghaus Mohn, 1973.

Wengst, K. *Christologische Formeln und Lieder des Urchristentums.* SUNT 7. Gütersloh: Gütersloher, 1972.

———. "'Einander durch Demut für Vorzüglicher zu halten': Zum Begriff 'Demut' bei Paulus und in paulinischer Tradition." Pages 428-39 in *Studien zum Text und zur Ethik des Neuen Testaments: Festschrift zum 80. Geburtstag von H. Greeven*. Edited by W. Schrage. Berlin: Walter de Gruyter, 1986.

———. "Versöhnung und Befreiung: Ein Aspekt des Themas 'Schuld und Vergebung' im Lichte des Kolosserbriefes." *EvT* 36 (1976), 14-26.

Wenham, J. W. "The Identification of Luke." *EvQ* 63 (1991), 3-44.

Wessels, G. F. "The Eschatology of Colossians and Ephesians." *Neot* 21 (1987), 183-202.

Westermann, W. L. *The Slave Systems of Greek and Roman Antiquity.* Philadelphia: The American Philosophical Society, 1955.

Wiedemann, T. *Greek and Roman Slavery.* Baltimore: Johns Hopkins University Press, 1981.

Wilson, W. T. *The Hope of Glory: Education and Exhortation in the Epistle to the Colossians.* NovTSup 88. Leiden and New York: Brill, 1997.

———. "The 'Practical' Achievement of Colossians: A Theological Assessment." *HBT* 20 (1998), 49-74.

Wink, W. *Cracking the Gnostic Code: The Powers in Gnosticism.* Atlanta: Scholars, 1993.

———. "The 'Elements of the Universe' in Biblical and Scientific Perspective." *Zygon* 13 (1978), 225-48.

———. *Engaging the Powers: Discernment and Resistance in a World of Domination.* Minneapolis: Fortress, 1992.

———. "The Hymn of the Cosmic Christ." Pages 235-45 in *The Conversation Continues: Studies in Paul and John in Honor of J. Louis Martyn.* Edited by R. T. Fortna and B. R. Gaventa. Nashville: Abingdon, 1990.

———. *Naming the Powers: The Language of Power in the New Testament.* Philadelphia: Fortress, 1984.

Wood, K. H. "The 'Sabbath Days' of Colossians 2:16, 17." Pages 338-42 in *The Sabbath in Scripture and History.* Edited by K. A. Strand and D. A. Augsburger. Washington, D.C.: Review and Herald, 1982.

Wright, N. T. "Adam in Pauline Christology." *SBLSP* 22 (1983), 359-89.

———. "Poetry and Theology in Colossians 1:15-20." *NTS* 36 (1990), 444-68.

Yamauchi, E. M. "Qumran and Colosse." *BSac* 121 (1964), 141-52.

Yates, R. "The Christian Way of Life: The Paraenetic Material in Colossians 3:1–4:6." *EvQ* 63 (1991), 241-51.

———. "Colossians 2:14: Metaphor of Forgiveness." *Bib* 71 (1990), 248-59.

———. "Colossians 2:15: Christ Triumphant." *NTS* 37 (1991), 573-91.

———. "Colossians and Gnosis." *JSNT* 27 (1986), 49-68.

———. "From Christology to Soteriology." *ExpTim* 107 (1996), 268-70.

———. "Note on Colossians 1:24." *EvQ* 42 (1970), 88-92.

———. "A Reappraisal of Colossians." *ITQ* 58 (1992), 95-117.

———. "'The Worship of Angels' (Col 2:18)." *ExpTim* 97 (1985), 12-15.

Yinger, K. "Translating *Katabrabeuetō* ['Disqualify,' NRSV] in Colossians 2.18." *BT* 54 (2003), 138-45.

Zeilinger, F. *Der Erstgeborene der Schöpfung: Untersuchungen zur Formalstruktur und Theologie des Kolosserbriefes.* Vienna: Herder, 1974.

Zimmerman, R. "Lügen für die Wahrheit? Das Phänomen urchristlicher Pseudepigraphie am Beispiel des Kolosserbriefs." Pages 257-72 in *Lügen und Betrügen: Das Falsche in der Geschichte von der Antike bis zur Moderne.* Edited by O. Hochadel and U. Kocher. Köln: Böhlau, 2000.

Introduction to Colossians

Paul's letter to the Colossians has had an impact on Christian theology and practice out of proportion to its size. Christian thinkers since the patristic period have turned to its teaching about Jesus' role in creation and his preeminence over the church to formulate their Christology. Paul's warnings about people who insist on following certain kinds of rules as basic to spiritual growth have been cited by theologians and laypeople alike to hold up the principle of Christian liberty. And the paraenetic section of the letter, though brief, is typified by a collection of broad ethical principles that have provided significant guidance for believers seeking to translate their commitment to the Lord Jesus into practice. In the pages that follow, we will try to describe as accurately as we can just what this small but powerful letter has to say on these issues, as well as the many others touched on in the letter. Our concern will be to discern what this portion of God's Word has to say to Christians today.

But this goal can be attained only as we carefully and patiently describe what this letter would have meant in its first-century context. As a letter, Colossians is an "occasional" document whose meaning and significance are closely related to (even if they are not finally limited to) its circumstances. Our first task, then, will be to describe these circumstances as the necessary context within which the meaning of the text can be uncovered. Determining these circumstances is, however, particularly complicated in the case of Colossians. For the place of the letter in early Christianity is a matter of considerable dispute. Many scholars are convinced that the letter was written not by Paul but by a follower of his after his death. If this were the case, it would skew our conclusions about the meaning of both a number of specific texts as well as about the overall theological significance of the letter. A second particularly complicating matter in "locating" Colossians accurately is the nature of the false teaching to which Paul is responding. We will deal with both these key issues, as well as several others less debated and less significant in the following sections. Six questions will structure our discussion: To whom was the letter written? Who wrote it? When and where was it written? Why was it written? What is the letter about? And how is it organized?

I. TO WHOM WAS THE LETTER WRITTEN? COLOSSAE AND THE COLOSSIANS

In his classic commentary on the letter, J. B. Lightfoot claimed that "Colossae was the least important church to which any epistle of St. Paul was addressed."[1] Colossae had not always been so insignificant a city. Located in the Lycus River valley of west-central Asia Minor, Colossae was apparently the most important city in its vicinity in the fourth and third centuries before Christ. It was known as being the center of a thriving textile industry, to the point that a certain kind of high-quality dark red wool was known as "Colossian wool." Its prominence was due especially to its location at the crossroads of two well-traveled highways: one that ran east and west, connecting the coastal cities of Ephesus (120 miles to the west) and Sardis with the interior east; and another running north and south. When, however, the latter road was moved west to pass through Laodicea, Colossae began to decline. In Paul's day it was not as large or important as the neighboring cities of Laodicea (twelve miles to the west) or Hierapolis (fifteen miles northwest). Both these communities also had Christian churches (see Col. 2:1), and Paul wrote a (now lost) letter to the Laodiceans (see Col. 4:16). An earthquake devastated the area sometime in the early 60s.[2] We know that Laodicea was quickly rebuilt (as Tacitus suggests; and see Rev. 3:14-22, probably written in the 90s) and that Colossae eventually was rebuilt also, though we do not know how quickly. The city has been in ruins (which have never been excavated) for centuries.

Geographically, Colossae belonged to the region of Phrygia and in Paul's day was part of the Roman province of Asia. Its location on an im-

---

1. Lightfoot, 16.

2. The Roman historian Tacitus refers to an earthquake that destroyed Laodicea in A.D. 60-61 (*Annals* 14.27), while the Christian historian Eusebius mentions an earthquake that devastated Laodicea, Hierapolis, and Colossae in A.D. 64 or so (*Chronicle* 1.21-22). They are probably referring to the same event. Lightfoot was open to the possibility that Eusebius's date might be correct (38-40), but we cannot know for sure.

portant highway at a time of considerable mobility and the mixing of different ethnic groups that typified the Roman Empire meant that the population of Colossae was very diverse. A majority were undoubtedly Gentile, but we have good reason to think there was also a substantial number of Jews. According to the Jewish historian Josephus, the Seleucid ruler Antiochus III ("the Great") had settled two thousand Jewish families in the general area in 213 B.C. (*Antiquities* 12.3.4). And the Roman man of letters Cicero, in the first century B.C., refers to the Roman seizure of a significant amount of money contributed by Jews in the area to support the Jerusalem Temple (the "temple tax"; see Cicero's letter *Pro Flacco* 28). The diversity of population and exposure to the latest ideas via travelers on its major highway meant that Colossae was a place where many different religious and philosophical viewpoints thrived and probably mixed together. This diversity helps explain the apparently syncretistic religious movement that was affecting the Colossian Christians and that gave rise to the letter. At the same time, as we will see below, this diversity makes it notoriously difficult to pin down the exact contours of this movement.

As far as we know, Paul had never visited Colossae, and he certainly was not the founder of the Christian community there (see Col. 2:1). This honor goes to Epaphras, whom Paul warmly commends in the letter (1:7-8; 4:12-13). It is likely that Epaphras was a convert of Paul's from the time of his almost three-year ministry in Ephesus on the third missionary journey (Acts 19). As a major commercial center, Ephesus was a place that people from all over the province would visit, and it was in this way that, through Paul's ministry in Ephesus, "all the Jews and Greeks who lived in the province of Asia heard the word of the Lord" (Acts 19:10). Epaphras, we may surmise, was one of those who heard the word of the Lord from Paul and believed. He was himself from Colossae ("one of you" [4:12]), and so we can imagine him preaching the good news there and establishing a Christian church in the town. He had traveled to where Paul was in prison "for the sake of the gospel," and had, apparently, even joined Paul in his imprisonment (in Phlm. 23 Paul calls him a "fellow prisoner"). He was not able, then, to travel back to Colossae with the letter that Paul writes, so Paul commissions Tychicus to do this job instead (Col. 4:7-8). Epaphras's reason for making this trip to visit Paul was almost certainly that he wanted to enlist the apostle's help in dealing with a dangerous yet slippery variation on the Christian gospel that had arisen in the community. Paul writes to a community, then, that he has "grandfathered" through his "son," Epaphras.

The letter suggests that most of the Christians in Colossae were Gentiles. Paul describes the conversion of the Colossian Christians in terms that, while perhaps not altogether impossible to apply to Jews, more naturally describe those who were at one time "separate from Christ, excluded from citizenship in Israel and foreigners to the covenants of the promise, without hope and without God in the world" (Eph. 2:12). See especially Colossians 1:12 — "[the Father] has qualified you to share in the inheritance of his people in the kingdom of light" — and Colossians 1:21 — "Once you were alienated from God and were enemies in your minds because of your evil behavior." Paul's mention of the fact that it was "among the Gentiles" that God had chosen to make known his mystery (1:27) points in the same direction. The sins that characterized these believers before they came to Christ — "sexual immorality, impurity, lust, evil desires and greed, which is idolatry" (3:5) — are also more typically Gentile than Jewish. In addition to these positive indications, there are also two arguments from silence that cohere with (though certainly do not prove) a mainly Gentile audience: the lack of any explicit Old Testament quotations; and the lack of any explicit reference to the law.[3]

II. WHO WROTE THE LETTER? AUTHORSHIP

Colossians, of course, claims to have been written by the apostle Paul (1:1), and this claim is fleshed out with considerable personal and circumstantial detail. The author speaks at length of his special ministry as a "servant" of the gospel (1:23), a representative of Christ in his suffering (1:24), and a steward of the "mystery" revealed in the last days (1:25-26). He requests prayer that he might be able to continue, even in prison, to proclaim Christ boldly (4:3-4). Timothy is his "brother" (1:1), he names six other men, with some degree of circumstantial detail, as his ministry associates (4:7-15), and he urges one man to "complete" his work (4:17). He mentions that he "contends" for Christians in both Colossae and the neighboring Laodicea, even though he has never met them personally (2:1). He is sending a letter to Laodicea that he wants the Colossians to read after they have, in turn, shared their letter with the Laodiceans (4:16). And he concludes the letter by saying "I, Paul, write this greeting in my own hand" (4:18).

We list these details so that we might have a full picture of the matter before us. The letter's claim to be written by Paul is no casual matter. It is a claim that is built into the warp and woof of the letter, elaborated

3. Most commentators make these points; for a brief statement, see Moule, 29.

with detail after detail. Any ultimately convincing alternative to Pauline authorship will have to deal adequately with this rather extensive series of details. As John Barclay notes, "If Colossians is by a later Paulinist, it is unparalleled in its sophisticated adaptation of incidental details to camouflage its inauthenticity."[4] It will not be enough, then, simply to cite other pseudepigraphical writings from antiquity to show that Colossians might also be pseudepigraphical. We need evidence on two key points: (1) that people in the ancient world wrote *letters* in other people's names; and (2) that they wrote letters with the kind of corroborating detail that we have in Colossians. Further, if Colossians is to retain its status as a canonical document with moral authority, we will want to find evidence (3) that such letters were not regarded as deceptive frauds but were recognized and accepted as belonging to a well-used literary genre.

As this introduction to the matter reveals, the belief that Colossians is a pseudepigraphical work, a letter written by a follower of Paul's in his name after his death, is widely held in the scholarly community. Raymond Brown estimates that 60 percent of current scholars think that Paul did not write Colossians.[5] Yet this view of the authorship of the letter is relatively recent. No early Christian doubted Paul's authorship, and the letter to the Colossians was received into the developing Christian canon

4. John M. G. Barclay, *Colossians and Philemon* (New Testament Guides; Sheffield: Sheffield Academic Press, 1997), 24.

5. R. E. Brown, *An Introduction to the New Testament* (New York: Doubleday, 1997), 610. Among recent interpreters who contest Pauline authorship are Mark Kiley, *Colossians as Pseudepigraphy* (The Biblical Seminar; Sheffield: JSOT Press, 1986); Wolter, 27-33; Gnilka, 19-26; Ernst, 141-52; Pokorný, 3-10; Luz, 184-90; Lincoln, 577-83; MacDonald, 6-9; Wilson, 9-35; Outi Leppä, *The Making of Colossians: A Study on the Formation and Purpose of a Deutero-Pauline Letter* (Publications of the Finnish Exegetical Society 86; Göttingen: Vandenhoeck & Ruprecht, 2003); Walter Bujard, *Stilanalytische Untersuchungen zum Kolosserbrief als Beitrag zur Methodik von Sprachvergleichen* (SUNT 11; Göttingen: Vandenhoeck & Ruprecht, 1973); Wolfgang Schenk, "Der Kolosserbrief in der neueren Forschung (1945-1985)," *ANRW* 2.25.4, 3327-49; Raymond F. Collins, *Letters that Paul Did Not Write: The Epistle to the Hebrews and the Pauline Pseudepigrapha* (GNS 28; Wilmington, Del.: Michael Glazier, 1988), 171-208. Those who think Paul did write the letter include Ernst Percy, *Die Probleme der Kolosser- und Epheserbriefe* (Lund: Gleerup, 1946), 16-136; Werner Georg Kümmel, *Introduction to the New Testament* (rev. ed.; London: SCM, 1975), 340-46; Donald Guthrie, *New Testament Introduction* (4th ed.; Downers Grove, Ill.: InterVarsity, 1990), 572-77; Aletti, 277-80 (slight preference); Bruce, 28-33; Moule, 13-14; Wright, 31-34; O'Brien, xli-xlix; Harris, 3-4; Barth/Blanke, 114-26. Uncertain about authorship are Paul J. Achtemeier, Joel B. Green, and Marianne Meye Thompson, *Introducing the New Testament: Its Literature and Theology* (Grand Rapids: Eerdmans, 2001), 418-20; Hay, 21-24. Still others associate the letter with Paul but as written under his supervision or auspices: Luke Timothy Johnson, *The Writings of the New Testament: An Interpretation* (rev. ed.; Minneapolis: Fortress, 1999), 393-95; Dunn, 38-39.

of Scripture with no apparent controversy.[6] "[T]here is no shred of evidence that the Pauline authorship of the whole or any part of this epistle was ever disputed until the nineteenth century."[7] It was at this time that the rise of historical criticism led to challenges of many traditionally accepted views of Scripture.[8] The famous and influential German critic F. C. Baur rejected Pauline authorship, and the matter has been a topic of scholarly debate ever since, with, as we have noted, a majority of contemporary scholars deciding against authenticity.

Why do so many think that Paul could not have written the letter? Basically, these scholars are convinced that the Greek of the letter and/or the theology of the letter are different enough from those of the authentic letters of Paul so as to make it impossible for Paul to have written it himself. We will deal first with the issue of the Greek and then with theology.

Debates about the authorship of disputed New Testament books invariably involve discussion of the Greek in which they were written. The issue is a simple one: could the person who wrote the Greek in book x (and/or y, z, etc.) also have written the Greek in the book over which there is debate? In this case, we might ask: could the person who wrote Romans, 1 and 2 Corinthians, Galatians, Philippians, 1 Thessalonians, and Philemon (the seven-book "critical canon" of Paul as determined by current scholarship) also have written Colossians? A number of scholars answer "no." They note, first, that Colossians uses a number of words that are not found in any of these other letters: 87, to be exact. Yet Philippians, generally agreed to be Pauline, uses 79 words not found in the other six letters. Furthermore, vocabulary is very much dependent on the subject matter. The author of Colossians is dealing with issues, raised by a certain form of false teaching, that are not present in the other letters. Of course the vocabulary will be different! And, in fact, most contemporary critics admit that the argument from vocabulary is not very convincing.

But more significant, many of these critics assert, is style, which does not change as much as vocabulary. And the style of Colossians shows some significant variations from that of the other letters of Paul. For instance, the author of Colossians loves to string together genitives in a way that we do not find as consistently elsewhere in Paul. See, for instance, "the word of the truth of the gospel" (1:5); "all riches of the full-

---

6. Abbott provides a useful summary (l-li). Justin, in the second century, appears to refer to the letter (*Dialogue with Trypho* 85.2; 138:2), and it is explicitly cited by Irenaeus (*Against Heresies* 3.14.1), as well as by Clement, Tertullian, and Origen. Abbott summarizes: "The external evidence for the genuineness is in no wise defective" (li).

7. Guthrie, *New Testament Introduction*, 576.

8. According to Collins (*Letters*, 171-72), Edward Evanson in 1805 raised the first questions; but it was E. T. Mayerhoff in 1838 who first offered a substantial argument.

ness of understanding" (2:2); "the participation of the inheritance of the saints" (1:12); "the kingdom of the Son of his love" (1:13); "the riches of the glory of this mystery" (1:27); "knowledge of the mystery of God, of Christ" (both in 2:2); "the faith of the working of God" (2:12; all my own translations). Other peculiarities of a similar nature are noted, all of them together making for long, complex sentences in a kind of "liturgical-hymnic" style that is distinct from the more argumentative style of the authentic Paulines.[9] Of course, this claim is very generalized, for there are, in fact, many passages in Colossians that do not fit this description. Still, there is some substance to the observation: the letter does, in many paragraphs, exhibit a style that is a bit different from that found in most other Pauline letters. The question, however, is whether this style is one that would have been impossible for Paul to write in. While certain features of a person's style tend to be stable, other features will vary, depending on the audience being addressed and the issues being dealt with. Moreover, as we argue below, Colossians was probably written in A.D. 60-61, three to ten years after most of Paul's critically accepted letters (Philemon is, of course, an exception; and Philippians may be). What kind of style might Paul have developed over time?

And there is a further factor that complicates any argument from the Greek of the letter. It is generally agreed that Paul used an amanuensis (or scribe) to write his letters, and Paul's "signature" in 4:18 suggests that this may have been the case in Colossians: after the work of his amanuensis, Paul writes a final greeting in his own hand. We also know that writers would sometimes give their amanuenses a certain amount of compositional freedom. Could Timothy (1:1) have served as Paul's amanuensis in the case of Colossians? Of course, we cannot know. But it is at least possible that Timothy, or some unknown amanuensis, is responsible for some of the word choices and style of the letter. The amanuensis variable, along with the natural variability in word choice and style that pertains to any author, means that the Greek of Colossians offers little basis for judgments about ·authorship.[10] This is now generally admitted by scholars of various persuasions,[11] and the focus has thereby shifted to other arguments.

9. See esp. Lohse, 88-89; Bujard, *Stilanalytische Untersuchungen*.

10. After a careful analysis, Percy (*Die Probleme der Kolosser- und Epheserbriefe*, 16-66) concludes that the Greek of Colossians speaks more for than against authenticity. He thinks Colossians shows a gradual development of Pauline style. Bujard, on the other hand, is equally convinced that the Greek could not be Paul's (*Stilanalytische Untersuchungen*).

11. E.g., Lohse: "on the basis of the observations made about the language and style of the letter, no final decision can yet be reached on the question of Pauline or non-Pauline authorship of the letter" (91).

Scholars on both sides of the debate on authorship, then, generally agree that the critical evidence in deciding the issue is the theology of the letter. Everyone agrees that some of the letter's theological perspectives are an advance on what we find in the authentic letters of Paul. The question of authorship, then, basically gets down to this: could Paul have developed his theology in the ways we find in Colossians within his lifetime, or not? The answer is finely balanced. Scholars on both sides of the question admit that Colossians stands in a kind of transitional zone: either very late in Paul's theological development or very early in the "deutero-Pauline" movement. With a certain qualification, the former alternative, we think, best explains the letter.

Four theological issues are consistently mentioned in terms of the Pauline character of Colossians: the teaching of the letter on authority, on Christ, on the church, and on eschatology.[12]

The stance toward authority in the letter is said to fit with the early stages of what scholars have dubbed "early Catholicism." "Early Catholicism" is the name that has been given to an alleged later development in the history of the early church characterized by waning of belief in an imminent return of Christ and consequent emphasis on the authority of tradition and accommodation with the world. Colossians, it is argued, betrays this perspective not only in its eschatology (see below) but also in its emphasis on tradition and in its characterization of Paul as an apostle with universal authority. The language of "receive" in 2:6 suggests a concern with the preservation of tradition, and this is reinforced by the concern that the Colossians maintain "the faith" that they have been given (1:23; 2:7).[13] Paul is presented as the "universal apostle" (1:23, 24), whose authority is transferred, by all the laudatory statements about him, to Epaphras (1:7-8; 4:12-13). The author thereby seeks to attach Paul's authority to the generation of teachers that have arisen after Paul's death.[14]

However, in addition to larger questions about the whole "early

---

12. Good overviews of these arguments are found in Lohse, 177-83; Angela Standhartinger, "Colossians and the Pauline School," *NTS* 50 (2004), 572-93; Johannes Lähnemann, *Der Kolosserbrief: Komposition, Situation und Argumentation* (SNT 3; Gütersloh: Mohn, 1971).

13. See, e.g., Angela Standhartinger, *Studien zur Enstehungsgeschichte und Intention des Kolosserbriefs* (NovTSup 94; Leiden: Brill, 1999).

14. See, e.g., MacDonald, 185-88; Willi Marxsen, *Introduction to the New Testament* (Philadelphia: Fortress, 1968), 177-86. Somewhat related is the contention that the author portrays Paul as a "heroic figure" of the past. Reference is made, e.g., to 1:24, with its unusual reference to the vicarious sufferings of Paul (see esp. Hans Dieter Betz, "Paul's 'Second Presence' in Colossians," in *Texts and Contexts: Biblical Texts in Their Textual and Situational Contexts* [ed. Tord Fornberg and David Hellholm; Oslo: Scandinavian University Press, 1995], 507-18).

Catholic" concept, there are also problems with this way of reading the letter. The commendation of Epaphras, while clear and strong, does not go beyond what Paul himself says elsewhere about ministry associates (e.g., Phil. 2:25-29). Moreover, this commendation of Epaphras makes perfect sense in a letter devoted to a defense of the truthfulness of the message that the community received through that same person. It is not Epaphras that Paul is so concerned to elevate but the message of the gospel that Epaphras brought to them. And the same point applies, of course, to the respect accorded to tradition in the letter in general. Paul himself refers to the importance of respecting tradition that has been "handed down" (1 Cor. 15:1-3). Is it not entirely natural to think he would make this point very strongly to a church tempted by another form of teaching, another "tradition" (2:8; cf. 2:22)? Moreover, the claim that the letter elevates Paul to a role that he did not claim in his lifetime is simply wrong (cf. Rom. 1:5-6; 15:14-33). There is nothing in Colossians, then, about authority that can even be called an advance on what we find in the teaching of the seven critically accepted letters.[15]

The christological teaching of Colossians, on the other hand, certainly does move beyond what we find in the other Pauline letters. In none of the other letters is the cosmic significance of Christ so clearly or consistently portrayed. He is the "image of the invisible God" (1:15), the one through whom God created all things (1:16), and the one through whom he has reconciled all things (1:20). He is the head of every spiritual power (2:10; cf. 2:15; 1:16, 20). "All the fullness" — the fullness of God himself — has come to dwell in him (1:19; 2:9). Moreover, it has been argued that some of these conceptions reflect late-first-century ideas, such as the language of "fullness," which is often ascribed to gnostic influence. To begin again, however, with this last point, the argument for thinking that fullness language is a reflection of gnostic ideas is now, rightly, rejected. To be sure, the universal supremacy of Christ is not so clearly taught in any other letter of Paul. But we find texts that clearly anticipate this direction of thought, such as 1 Corinthians 8:6 — "yet for us there is but one God, the Father, from whom all things came and for whom we live; and there is but one Lord, Jesus Christ, through whom all things came and through whom we live" — or, still more clearly, Philippians 2:5-11. Again, we have to ask: could Paul, as a response to the apparent denigration of Christ and cosmic speculations of the false teachers in Colossae, have developed the cosmic Christology of Colossians? Is it easier to attribute this teaching to an anonymous and unknown follower of

15. So also, e.g., George E. Cannon, *The Use of Traditional Materials in Colossians* (Macon, Ga.: Mercer University Press, 1983).

Paul's shortly after his death or to Paul himself, an acknowledged theological genius?

Another theological development in Colossians is the conception of the universal church as the "body of Christ" (1:18, 24; 2:19; cf. 2:17). In the seven-letter critical Pauline "canon," "church" *(ekklēsia)* refers to local gatherings of believers, and this local *ekklēsia* is sometimes compared to a body, or the body of Christ (e.g., 1 Corinthians). But in Colossians (and Ephesians), the "church" becomes a universal phenomenon and is identified with Christ's body (1:18, 24). Here again, it is alleged, we have a development that goes beyond Paul's teaching. Particularly would this be the case if the conception depends — as is often alleged — on Stoic or gnostic ideas that are foreign to Paul's basic way of thinking.[16] There is no need, however, to explain the identification of the church with Christ's body by recourse to such backgrounds. The concept of Christ as an "inclusive figure," an idea rooted solidly in Old Testament and Jewish perspectives, provides a much more likely and quite adequate explanation for the development of this conception in Colossians and Ephesians. And calling the church the "body of Christ" is not that great an advance on the idea of individual Christians as making up the "body of Christ" that we find in 1 Corinthians (see esp. 10:16: "And is not the bread that we break a participation in the body of Christ?"; 12:27: "Now you are the body of Christ").

The theological teaching of Colossians that is usually said to offer the clearest contrast with the genuine Pauline letters is its eschatology. Paul's eschatology is characterized by a temporal dualism, in which what God has "already" done in Christ is balanced and kept in tension with what has "not yet" happened. Yet Colossians replaces the temporal scheme of "already" and "not yet" with the spatial scheme of "below" and "above" (3:1-4) and teaches a "realized" eschatology that ignores the Pauline temporal tension. The resurrection of believers is no longer a future, bodily experience, but a past, spiritual one: we "have been raised with Christ" (2:12; 3:1; cf. 2:13). The defeat of the spiritual powers is no longer to take place in the future (e.g., 1 Cor. 15:24) but has already taken place (1:20; 2:10, 15). Missing from Colossians are also any explicit references to the return of Christ or to the coming judgment.[17] Yet, to begin our response, both of these latter are clearly presupposed in Colossians. Christ's return is alluded to in 3:4, where Paul says that Christians will

16. E.g., Hanna Roose, "Die Hierarchisierung der Leib-Metapher im Kolosser- und Epheserbrief als 'Paulinisierung': Ein Beitrag zur Rezeption paulinischer Tradition in Pseudo-Paulinischen Briefen," *NovT* 47 (2005), 117-41.

17. For a summary of these criticisms, see esp. Günther Bornkamm, "Die Hoffnung im Kolosserbrief: Zugleich ein Beitrag zur Frage der Echtheit des Briefes," in *Studien zum Neuen Testament und zur Patristik* (Berlin: Akademie Verlag, 1961), 56-64.

"appear with him in glory." And the coming judgment is clearly used as a warning to encourage holy living in 3:6: "because of these [sins], the wrath of God is coming." It is simply not true, then, that spatial categories have squeezed out temporal ones in the eschatology of Colossians. Of course, Colossians does not refer to future eschatology to the degree that many of Paul's other letters do. But such arguments from silence are very precarious, since they appear to assume that Paul must explicitly include the same theological themes (and apparently in the same proportion!) in every one of his letters. But the circumstantial nature of his correspondence makes this *a priori* unlikely, and a glance at the accepted letters of Paul confirms the point. There is, for instance, very little future eschatology in Romans, a much longer letter than Colossians.

The more significant issue, then, is not whether Colossians is silent about theological points found elsewhere in Paul but whether Colossians contradicts Paul. This is often said to be the case with respect to the present resurrection of believers. But two points need to be made in response. First, it should be noted that this teaching does not necessarily contradict the conception of a future bodily resurrection (although, admittedly, Colossians makes no reference to it). And, second, the idea of a present resurrection of believers with Christ is clearly hinted at (and some would say, explicitly taught) in Romans 6. In v. 13, Paul claims that Christians have "been brought from death to life," and he has explicitly referred to resurrection earlier in the chapter (vv. 4, 5, 8). Moreover, the logic of v. 4b — "in order that, just as Christ was raised from the dead through the glory of the Father, we too may live a new life" — implies a present identification with Christ's resurrection. And some think Paul explicitly takes this step in vv. 5 and 8. This is, perhaps, unlikely. But the basic point still stands: the logic of Romans 6 presumes something pretty close to what Colossians 3:1 explicitly affirms. As Johnson puts it, "The language is slightly different, but the thought is virtually identical to that found in Rom. 6:1-14."[18] The eschatology of Colossians is strongly tilted toward the "already" side of the typical Pauline eschatological tension. But this is not unexpected in a letter that must make the case for the sufficiency of Christ's work for spiritual victory and fulfillment in the present.

If differences with Paul's theology are discerned in these areas, other significant Pauline theological conceptions are notable for their absence in Colossians.[19] Missing are typical Pauline words and concepts such as "sin" (in the singular), "justify," and "to believe." Granted the legalistic tendencies of the false teachers, the lack of any reference to "law"

18. Johnson, *Writings*, 394. See also our comments on 3:1-4.
19. See the succinct overview in Luz, 186-87.

is surprising. Particularly striking is the failure to develop a theology of grace (it is mentioned only in the formulas in 1:2 and 4:18; 1:6; and perhaps 4:6) or to refer to the Spirit in connection with Christian obedience (the Spirit is mentioned only in 1:8, 9; 3:16). The failure to develop these points is, to be sure, somewhat surprising. On the other hand, we cannot expect a letter as brief as Colossians to develop every point of Paul's theology. The argument from silence with respect to theological themes works only if the omission involves a theological concept that Paul simply could not have left out in anything he wrote. Colossians does not omit references to the Spirit or to God's grace (as we have seen above): does the failure to develop them any further stand as a decisive argument against Paul's authorship? We think not.

We are not at all convinced, then, that Colossians stands in theological contrast with the other Pauline letters in the four areas usually mentioned.[20] Our own evaluation is that the failure of Colossians to develop certain ideas in the way that we might expect from Paul's other letters is the more serious theological argument against Pauline authorship. Yet neither do we think these omissions are sufficient to overturn the very strong indications that the letter was, in fact, written by Paul.

And, of course, if Ephesians is brought into the picture, the distance between the theology of Colossians and Paul is virtually eliminated. For, as we have noted in our comments above, Colossians and Ephesians share many of the emphases that have led scholars to dismiss Colossians as Pauline. Indeed, so similar are the letters, in theology, general content, and even (at a number of places) in exact wording, that scholars are united in thinking that these two letters have a very close relationship. The virtual "consensus of critical scholarship" is that Ephesians depends on Colossians, and most who hold this view also think that Ephesians is pseudepigraphical.[21] We have therefore left Ephesians out of consideration in our evaluation of Colossians above. But we think that a good case can be made for the Pauline authorship of Ephesians.[22] And, in any case, we are not as convinced as many that Ephesians clearly borrows from Colossians. The relationship between the two, as Ernest Best has shown, is such that simple literary dependence one way or the other does not of-

---

20. See also the conclusions of Percy, *Die Probleme der Kolosser- und Epheserbriefe*, 67-136.

21. For a recent full statement of the position, see Andrew T. Lincoln, *Ephesians* (WBC 42; Dallas: Word, 1990), xlvii-lxxiii. John Coutts ("Relationship of Ephesians and Colossians," *NTS* 4 [1958], 201-7), however, argues that Colossians is later than Ephesians; and Peter T. O'Brien (*The Letter to the Ephesians* [Pillar; Grand Rapids: Eerdmans, 1999], 8-21) is uncertain about the direction of dependence.

22. See esp. O'Brien, *Ephesians*, 4-47.

fer the best explanation. The random nature of the similarities suggests, he thinks, that the author of one of the letters had the words of the other in mind as he wrote. Such a relationship is compatible with pseudepigraphical authorship of both letters (and Best leans this way himself). But this kind of relationship also fits extremely well with the hypothesis that Paul has written both letters at about the same time.[23]

We must now evaluate more broadly the pseudepigraphical hypothesis, especially in light of the letter's claim to authorship and the many details pertaining to Paul personally that we surveyed at the beginning of this section. As we noted there, any alternative theory of the authorship of Colossians must provide a satisfactory explanation for this claim and for these details. Those who think that Colossians was written by someone other than Paul offer two explanations. Some think that these details were added to create the impression that Paul was, indeed, the author: the real author was trying to deceive his audience about the origin of the letter. But the majority of interpreters think that these details are features of an ancient literary style that the author has adopted. This author is not being deceptive, since he is writing within the conventions of a known and recognized style that would have been recognized by the readers of the letter. The author would be claiming simply to be writing within the authoritative tradition initiated by Paul — and his readers would have understood his claim in just this way. R. E. Brown, a good representative of a middle-of-the-road critical viewpoint, summarizes this general approach very clearly:

> One of the Pauline "school" of disciples took it upon himself to write a letter in Paul's name because he wanted it to be received authoritatively as what Paul would say to the situation addressed. Such a situation makes sense if one supposes that Paul was dead and the disciple considered himself an authoritative interpreter of the apostle whose thought he endorsed. Attribution of the letter to Paul in those circumstances would not be using a false name or making a false claim that Paul wrote the letter. It would be treating Paul as the author in the sense of the authority behind a letter that was intended as an extension of his thought — an assumption of the great apostle's mantle to continue his work.[24]

<hr/>

23. Ernest Best, "Who Used Whom? The Relationship of Ephesians and Colossians," NTS 43 (1997), 72-96; see also Barth/Blanke, 72-114.
24. Brown, Introduction, 586; the fullest statement of this hypothesis is David G. Meade, Pseudonymity and Canon (WUNT 39; Tübingen: Mohr Siebeck, 1986). See also Collins, Letters, 254-58; James D. G. Dunn, "Pseudepigraphy," in Dictionary of the Later New Testament and Its Developments (ed. Ralph P. Martin and Peter H. Davids; Downers Grove, Ill.: InterVarsity, 1997), 984; Lincoln, 577-83.

However, despite the frequency with which this claim about an innocent, "transparent" literary device of pseudonymity is made in the literature, it stands on very shaky foundations. For the argument to stand, one would have to find a substantial body of literature sharing the basic generic features of Colossians that (1) was written in someone else's name; and (2) was both recognized as pseudepigraphical and still accepted as authoritative. Parallels to pseudepigraphical letters such as Colossians from both the Jewish and the Greek world are known, and some of them are at least arguably in the same generic class as Colossians.[25] So we may accept, at least for the sake of argument, that the first condition is met. But how about the second? If the literary device were so widespread, we would have expected early church fathers to recognize it and identify the letter accordingly. But we do not have a single shred of evidence that any of them did so. The comment of Serapion, Bishop of Antioch (c. 200), seems to represent the universal viewpoint of the early church on the issue of pseudepigraphy: "We receive both Peter and the other apostles as Christ; but as experienced men we reject the writings falsely inscribed with their names, since we know that we did not receive such from our fathers" (Eusebius, *Ecclesiastical History* 6.12.1-6). The notion of an innocent, "transparent" literary device of epistolary pseudepigraphy, in other words, appears to be largely a modern scholarly invention, designed to reconcile a "false" claim of authorship in a letter with the acceptance of that letter as an authoritative and canonical witness to the truth of Christ.[26]

The options before us, then, appear to be only two: (1) Paul wrote Colossians; or (2) someone else wrote Colossians in a way that sought to convince people that Paul really had written it.[27] Despite his apparent de-

25. See, e.g., Standhartinger, *Studien*, 29-59. From the Jewish world, the *Epistle of Jeremiah* and *The Letter of Aristeas* are usually cited. But even a superficial reading of these books reveals how different they are from Colossians. In the Greco-Roman world, the pseudonymous letters that were produced by the Pythagorean, Cynic, and neo-Platonist "schools" are mentioned (e.g., Lewis R. Donelson, *Pseudepigraphy and Ethical Argument in the Pastoral Epistles* [HUT 22; Tübingen: Mohr Siebeck, 1986], 7-66; Lincoln, 582).

26. See esp. Donelson, *Pseudepigraphy*; E. Earle Ellis, "Pseudonymity and Canonicity of New Testament Documents," in *Worship, Theology and Ministry in the Early Church: Essays in Honor of Ralph P. Martin* (ed. Michael J. Wilkins and Terrence Paige; JSNTSup 87; Sheffield: Sheffield Academic Press, 1992), 212-24; Terry Lee Wilder, *Pseudonymity, the New Testament and Deception: An Inquiry into Intention and Reception* (Lanham, Md.: University Press of America, 2004); Lee Martin MacDonald and Stanley E. Porter, *Early Christianity and Its Sacred Literature* (Peabody, Mass.: Hendrickson, 2000), 388-93; D. A. Carson and Douglas J. Moo, *An Introduction to the New Testament* (2d ed.; Grand Rapids: Zondervan, 2005), 337-50.

27. Among those who recognize that a false claim to authorship is deceptive, see esp. Donelson, *Pseudepigraphy*; and also Wayne A. Meeks, "'To Walk Worthily of the

fense of the "transparent literary device" view (see the quotation above), Brown indicates the realities very nicely:

> Yet how could a writer of that school address Col to the Lycus River valley Christians who possessed the letter sent to Philemon twenty-five years previously? Presumably it would have mattered to them if they knew that Col, despite surface appearances, was not actually written by Paul who had died long before. If therefore the writer desired to gloss over the pseudonymous character of the letter, he might have presented Col as stemming from long ago, namely, at the same time as Phlm, but only recently recovered. In the course of addressing the area around Colossae, now in ruins from an earthquake — an area to a house-church of which Paul once wrote Phlm — the writer in the Pauline school of the 80s would be wrapping himself in the apostle's mantle by borrowing from Phlm the dramatis personae who constituted Paul's connection to the Lycus Valley. A syncretistic false teaching now threatened the next generation of Christians there, and the writer's intention would have been to remind them of what Pauline missionaries had told them about Christ and to develop that christology to refute the new error.[28]

Donelson recognizes the dilemma and puts it clearly: "The embarrassment of pseudepigraphy strikes at the heart of scriptural authority. The vehemence of conservative scholars who resist the whole notion of pseudepigrapha in the canon is well-founded, for to admit it would be to admit that the canon is not what they want it to be."[29] Some who choose

---

Lord': Moral Formation in the Pauline School Exemplified by the Letter to Colossians," in *Hermes and Athena* (ed. Eleonore Stump and Thomas P. Flint; Notre Dame: University of Notre Dame Press, 1993), 37-58.

28. Brown, *Introduction*, 616. Brown appears to be attempting to offer an explanation of a specific problem in accepting Colossians as a pseudepigraphical letter: why would a later Paulinist have chosen the city of Colossians as the destination? As Reicke remarks, "No forger would have been interested in producing a quasi-Pauline letter to Colossae in a period when no city or at least no church of importance existed there" (Bo Reicke, *Re-examining Paul's Letters: The History of the Pauline Correspondence* [Harrisburg, Pa., and Philadelphia: Trinity Press International, 2001], 77) (the city, it will be remembered, was destroyed by an earthquake in A.D. 60-61). Lincoln tries to turn this problem into a virtue for the pseudepigraphical hypothesis: a later Paulinist would have chosen Colossae as the address precisely because it would have been known that no church existed there at the time (580). But how does this square with the elaborate attempts to create an impression of a specific situation with the greetings, etc.?

29. Donelson, *Pseudepigraphy*, 201. Contra, e.g., Wall, who claims that scholars make a "fundamental mistake in equating a book's *authority* with the question of its *authorship*" (15). Deceptive authorship, bordering on fraud, must inevitably raise questions about authority.

the second option nevertheless argue that Colossians should be retained as a valuable New Testament document. For a book's canonical status does not rest on human authorship but on divine authentication, as confirmed by the early Christians. Their decision stands, even if they mistakenly accepted the letter on the assumption that it was written by Paul — much as we keep Hebrews in the canon even though it was not written by Paul (although arguably, it made it into the canon because people thought that Paul had written it). However, it is one thing to accept a book as canonical that makes no claim about authorship, even if early Christians made certain assumptions along these lines (e.g., the Gospels, Acts, Hebrews). It is quite another to retain as a canonical witness a book whose author is guilty of deceptive claims.

Of course, what we have said in the preceding paragraph is no argument against the pseudepigraphical nature of Colossians. But it does make clear just what the stakes are. More importantly, for our present purposes, it suggests that the overt claims about authorship in the letter, along with the corroborating personal details, must be given great weight in evaluating the issue of authorship. One must take seriously the significant internal conflict between a high moral tone, an emphasis on the importance of truthfulness (e.g., 1:5, 6), and a prohibition of lying (3:9), on the one hand, and an intent to deceive about authorship, on the other. Are the two compatible? Of course they are, as many convincing frauds in history make clear. But the degree of hypocrisy involved makes it difficult to give the writer any credibility at all.

As we have made clear, we are not convinced that we are faced with so unpalatable an option. For we are not convinced that the arguments against the Pauline authorship of Colossians are finally very convincing. As an authentic letter of Paul (and so recognized by the earliest Christians), Colossians richly deserves its place in the Christian canon. Of course, the likely involvement of an amanuensis means that we have to define carefully what we mean by "Pauline authorship." Johnson, for instance, argues that Paul "authored" Colossians but did not necessarily "write" it: "Paul, as head of a missionary school, commissioned and supervised the production of the letter."[30] However, in addition to the issue of the "school" hypothesis (for which there is little evidence), this way of putting the matter distances Paul too far from the writing of Colossians: there are simply too many specific personal claims woven throughout the letter.[31] The same objection applies to the hypothesis of Schweizer and

---

30. Johnson, *Writings*, 271-73, 395.

31. See also Wilson's remarks (31) on the danger of using the amanuensis hypothesis to "have our cake and eat it too": to claim a letter is genuinely Pauline while attribut-

Dunn that Timothy wrote under loose supervision from Paul.[32] Timothy may well have had significant involvement in the writing of the letter (as 1:1 may imply), perhaps acting as amanuensis and therefore possibly having some influence on its wording. But Paul must be seen as the real author.

III. WHEN WAS THE LETTER WRITTEN? DATE AND PLACE OF WRITING

If Colossians is pseudepigraphical, then it could have been written at almost any time. Some scholars even think it could have been written within Paul's lifetime, his imprisonment making it impossible for him to write directly.[33] But most advocates of the pseudepigraphical origins of the letter date it around 80 — not too far removed from Paul's own theology and before Ephesians.[34] However, if, as we have argued, Paul did in fact write Colossians, we must turn to evidence from his life and letters to situate it. The book of Acts says nothing explicit about this matter; in fact, it never even mentions the city of Colossae. The only real evidence we have in trying to locate Colossians within Paul's ministry comes from the letter itself. And the key issue from the letter is the fact that Paul was a prisoner when we wrote it (4:3, 18). The question of "when?" then, can be answered only by answering the question "where?"

Unfortunately, answering this question about the "provenance" (place of writing) is not easy. The book of Acts refers explicitly to three imprisonments of Paul: overnight in Philippi (16:19-34); for two years in Caesarea (23:23–26:32; cf. 24:27); and for two years in Rome (28:11-31; cf. v. 30). But Paul's claim that he had "been in prisons" very frequently (2 Cor. 11:23) implies that he was imprisoned more often than on these three occasions. So it is possible that Colossians was written during an imprisonment that Luke does not include in his narrative. Many scholars point to Paul's three-year stay in Ephesus as the time of one of those additional imprisonments. The New Testament itself may imply such an imprisonment, and early Christian tradition supports the possibil-

---

ing all its linguistic oddities to the amanuensis. He rightly argues that the amanuensis hypothesis, if taken too far, is hardly distinguishable in practice from pseudepigraphy.

32. Schweizer, 15-24; Dunn, 38-39; see also Allan R. Bevere, *Sharing in the Inheritance: Identity and the Moral Life in Colossians* (JSNTSup 226; Sheffield: Sheffield Academic Press, 2003), 54-59; Hay, 21-24 (possibly).

33. Luz, 189-90; MacDonald, 10, entertains this hypothesis.

34. E.g., Brown, *Introduction*, 615-16; Lohse, 182-83.

ity.[35] Since the overnight stay in Philippi is obviously excluded from consideration, we have, therefore, three viable candidates for the location from which Paul wrote Colossians: Ephesus (c. A.D. 52-55), Caesarea (c. A.D. 57-59), or Rome (c. A.D. 60-62).

In evaluating these options, we have to take into consideration not only the evidence of Colossians but also of Ephesians and Philemon. For, while Paul wrote four other letters while he was in bondage — Ephesians, Philemon, Philippians, and 2 Timothy — only Ephesians and Philemon are closely related to Colossians. There are four reasons to think that these three letters were written at the same time and, therefore, of course, from the same place of imprisonment. First, they are all addressed to Christians living in the same general area. Ephesus is only 120 miles from Colossae, while Philemon lives in Colossae (cf. 4:9, which refers to Philemon's slave, Onesimus, as "one of you"). Second, both Colossians and Ephesians were entrusted to the same messenger, Tychicus, for delivery (4:7-8; Eph. 6:21-22). Third, the lists of companions from whom Paul sends greetings in Colossians and Philemon are almost identical:

Colossians 4:10-14	Philemon 23-24
Aristarchus	Epaphras
Mark	Mark
Jesus who is called Justus	
Epaphras	Aristarchus
Luke	Demas
Demas	Luke[36]

And, fourth, there is considerable overlap between Ephesians and Colossians, in both shared vocabulary and in theological themes (for more detail on this relationship, see above). From which of Paul's imprisonments, then, were these three letters written?

The traditional answer to this question has been "Rome," and it is the answer that most scholars who defend the Pauline authorship of Colossians continue to advocate.[37] But advocates of Ephesus have been

35. See esp. G. S. Duncan, *St. Paul's Ephesian Ministry* (London: Hodder and Stoughton, 1929).

36. For the unlikely hypothesis that Philemon also refers to "Jesus who is called Justus," see the notes on Phlm. 23.

37. Most of the early commentators place these letters in Rome. The "Marcionite Prologue" identifies Ephesus as the place where Colossians was written; but this same document places Philemon in Rome. Modern defenders of the Roman provenance include: Bruce, 193-96; Moule, 21-25; O'Brien, xlix-liii; Barth/Blanke, *Philemon*, 121-26; Harris, 4; Garland, 307-8; Guthrie, *Introduction*, 577-80; Carson/Moo, *Introduction*, 521-22.

growing in number.[38] Caesarea, on the other hand, has never been a very popular option, and it has few recent defenders.[39] We think this lack of recent defenders is both telling and appropriate, and we will accordingly concentrate on the two main options of Rome and Ephesus in our discussion.

Which provenance provides the best "fit" with evidence from the book of Acts? Luke, of course, says nothing anywhere about Paul's letter-writing, so we have no explicit information on this matter. But comparisons can be made between the situations that the letters assume and Acts. First, it might be immediately objected that it is quite unlikely that Paul would have to "send" Tychicus with a letter to Ephesus (Eph. 6:22) when he is imprisoned there. The many scholars who think that Ephesians was written after Paul's death by one of his followers would, of course, dismiss this objection. But even if we attribute Ephesians to Paul (as we do), the objection is not decisive. For Ephesians might be a circular letter that Paul sent to churches in the area of Ephesus, along with Ephesus itself. Second, all three letters assume that Paul has the freedom to interact with a wide variety of people. He requests prayer that he might be able boldly to proclaim the gospel (Eph. 6:19-20; Col. 4:3-4), and he is able to receive visitors (Col. 4:7-14; Phlm. 23-24). This degree of relative freedom was certainly true of Paul's Roman imprisonment: "For two whole years Paul stayed there in his own rented house and welcomed all who came to see him. He proclaimed the kingdom of God and taught about the Lord Jesus Christ — with all boldness and without hindrance!" (Acts 28:30-31). Whether this measure of freedom was also true of his Ephesian imprisonment, of course, we have no way of knowing.

A third point of comparison between the letters and Acts involves the companions that Paul mentions. As we have seen above, Colossians and Philemon mention six individuals who are with Paul. Of these six, two — Epaphras and Jesus called Justus — are not mentioned elsewhere in the New Testament and so, of course, provide no basis for comparison. Another, Demas, is not mentioned in Acts but is referred to in 2 Timothy 4:10 as a minister associated with Paul who has "deserted" him. Aristarchus is mentioned three times in the book of Acts. According to 19:29, he was seized by the mob in Ephesus; in 20:4 he is listed as one of Paul's

38. E.g., J. F. Collange, *L'Épître de Saint Paul à Philemon* (CNT; Geneva: Labor et Fides, 1987), 21-23; Lohse, 188; Schweizer, 24-26; J. Fitzmyer, *The Letter to Philemon: A New Translation with Introduction and Commentary* (AB 34C; New York: Doubleday, 2000), 9-11; P. Stuhlmacher, *Der Brief an Philemon* (4th ed.; EKKNT 18; Neukirchen/Vluyn: Neukirchener, 2004), 21; Wright, 34-37; Jerome Murphy-O'Connor, *Paul: A Critical Life* (Oxford: Clarendon, 1996), 175.

39. See, however, Reicke, *Re-examining Paul's Letters*, 73-76.

companions on his journey with the "collection" to Jerusalem; and in 27:2 he is listed as a shipmate of Paul's on his voyage to Rome. Mark is almost certainly the same as the "John Mark" who appears several times in the book of Acts and also in 1 Peter 5:13. The early Jerusalem church met in his mother's house for a time (12:12), and he was enlisted by Paul and Barnabas to assist them in the ministry in Antioch (11:27-30). They then took him with them on the first missionary journey, but his failure to stick with the journey led to a split between Paul and Barnabas (15:37-39). Luke, finally, is mentioned only one other time in the New Testament (2 Tim. 4:11), but he is indirectly mentioned often in Acts, since, as its author, he includes himself by using first-person plural verbs. These "we" passages make clear that Luke was a frequent companion of Paul, participating with him in ministry in Madeconia (Acts 16:8-17), on his trip back to Palestine after the third missionary journey (Acts 20:5-15; 21:1-18), and on the "shipwreck" voyage to Rome (Acts 27:1–28:16). Taken together, these references to companions favor a Roman provenance. To be sure, Aristarchus may have been imprisoned in Ephesus (Acts 19:29), although the text suggests a brief detention by the mob rather than arrest and imprisonment. But Acts 27:2 indicates that he accompanied Paul to Rome, and it is natural to think that he may have stayed on there with him (perhaps as a "volunteer" prisoner; cf. Col. 4:10). Mark, as Paul's commendation of him in Colossians shows, was eventually reconciled with Paul, and how soon this reconciliation took place is impossible to say. He could, therefore, have ministered with Paul in Ephesus. On the other hand, 1 Peter 5:13 furnishes pretty strong evidence that Mark was in Rome in the early 60s.[40] Finally, if we go by the "we passages" in Acts, Luke was with Paul in Rome, but not in Ephesus.

A second set of issues to consider are the various journeys that are assumed or referred to in the letters. There are four: Epaphras's trip to Paul (Col. 1:7-8); Onesimus's trip to Paul (Phlm. 8-12); the trip of Tychicus and Onesimus to Ephesus and Colossae (Eph. 6:22; Col. 4:7-8; Phlm. 12); and the projected trip of Paul to Colossae (cf. Phlm. 22, where he asks Philemon to prepare a guest room for him). The sheer number of these trips is easier to envisage the closer Paul is to these places, and this is naturally an argument in favor of Ephesus. And this argument can be strengthened by considering two further aspects of these trips. As we will see, the reason why Onesimus ended up with Paul is unclear. If he was a runaway slave, a "fugitive," it is hard to see that either Ephesus or Rome is favored. Ephesus is, of course, closer; but, for a runaway trying to es-

---

40. Most scholars think that 1 Peter was written in the early 60s from Rome, taking "she who is in Babylon" (1 Pet. 5:13) as a cryptic reference to the church in Rome.

cape his master, the distance of Rome might also have been attractive.[41]
Paul's impending visit to Colossae, on the other hand, is usually thought
to favor an Ephesian provenance. According to Romans 15:14-33, Paul
planned to visit Rome on his way to new ministry horizons in Spain. If
written from Rome, then, Philemon would assume a change in plans. Yet
such a change of plans is not to be ruled out. For, first, Paul ended up in
Rome in circumstances he did not envisage when writing Romans (after a
two-year imprisonment in Caesarea and an indefinite time of imprisonment in Rome). Furthermore, if we consider the Pastoral Epistles as genuinely Pauline letters, such a change of plans is virtually certain. For they
were almost certainly written after Paul's "first" Roman imprisonment,
yet they assume a significant time of Pauline ministry back in the Eastern
Mediterranean. While, then, the evidence from the travels is not as decisive a consideration as some scholars suggest, it nevertheless does support an Ephesian provenance.

A third issue to consider in locating these letters is the nature of the
false teaching that lies behind them (Colossians explicitly; Ephesians perhaps implicitly). Scholars in the past tended to associate this false teaching with some form of (incipient) Gnosticism. And, since full-blown
Gnosticism was a late (second century) development, the later one could
date the letters, the better sense they made. Those who did not simply relegate them to the postapostolic era (partly for this reason), then, tended
to favor Rome over Ephesus. But this argument holds little weight, and
for two reasons. First, the supposition that Gnosticism, in any form, was
involved in the false teaching is far from certain. Second, even if some
form of incipient Gnosticism is assumed in the letters, the difference of a
few years will hardly be significant.

A fourth issue is related to this third one. Whatever the false teaching, Paul responds with arguments about the cosmic significance of
Christ and the conception of the church as the body of Christ that are generally thought to be something of an "advance" of the theology we find
in other Pauline letters. Again, so "advanced" is this teaching that many
are convinced that it must come from a follower of Paul after his death.
But if it is the true voice of Paul himself (as we think it is), then, again, the
later we date the letters the better; and Rome would again be favored.
This argument has some force, but it is certainly not decisive. Tracking
the trajectory of "development" in the theology of someone like Paul,
who wrote occasional letters over at least fifteen years, is precarious in-

41. S. Llewelyn cites evidence from ancient sources indicating that some runaway
slaves tended to stay in their own countries while others sought refuge in distant large
cities (*NewDocs* 8:45).

deed. So-called "advanced" theological ideas may be the result not of Paul's own more mature theology but of reflection on a new set of issues. How early could Paul have developed the Christology and ecclesiology taught in Ephesians and Colossians? Could not the pressure of new forms of false teaching have led him to do so in the middle 50s? It is certainly possible.

A fifth, and final, issue to consider comes not from the New Testament but from secular history. As we noted above, a Roman historian indicates that an earthquake devastated the area of Colossae in A.D. 60-61 — just about the time when, on the hypothesis of a Roman provenance, Paul would be writing Colossians and Philemon. The significance of this consideration depends on the precise timing of two events, neither of which, unfortunately, can be timed very closely at all: the earthquake and Paul's imprisonment in Rome. If the earthquake took place early in 60 and Paul did not arrive in Rome until early 60, Epaphras may not have had time to leave Colossae before the city was ruined. On the other hand, if the earthquake took place later in 60 or 61, then Epaphras could easily have left before it and found Paul in Rome sometime in 60. In any case, the imprecision in dating means that this consideration should not be given a very important role in our decision.

A fair evaluation of the evidence we have set forth makes clear that certainty, or even, perhaps, strong probability about the provenance of these letters is impossible. Considerations based on Philemon alone favor Ephesus; and most scholars who think that Ephesians and Colossians are post-Pauline naturally locate Philemon in Ephesus. However, if we accept all three letters as Pauline (as we do), and all the evidence above is taken into consideration, there is a slight preference, we think, for Rome as the place of writing. One can, on the assumption that Paul is writing from Rome in A.D. 60-61, explain the circumstances presupposed in Philemon. A Roman provenance fits well the circumstances of Paul's imprisonment, and it provides the best fit with what we know about the movements of Paul's associates in the rest of the New Testament.

IV. WHY WAS COLOSSIANS WRITTEN? THE FALSE TEACHING

The letter makes no explicit claim about its purpose. But the warnings about not being "deceived by fine-sounding arguments" (2:4) and about those who would take others "captive through hollow and deceptive philosophy" (2:8), who are "judging" others (2:16) and "disqualifying" them

(2:18), make clear that one of its purposes is to encourage the Colossians to resist some kind of erroneous teaching. And, since "the best defense is a good offense," Paul urges, as the most effective antidote to this teaching, that the Colossians maintain their disciplined and firm faith (2:5) and hold on tightly to the good teaching that they have received (2:7-8). Scattered allusions to the power and importance of the gospel truth they have received (1:5-8, 23, 29; 2:2; 3:1-2, 16) suggest that much of the rest of the letter is also oriented to this concern. The purpose of the letter, then, is to provide the resources that the Colossian Christians need to fend off some kind of false teaching to which they are exposed. Epaphras, we may assume, has journeyed all the way to Rome just to present his mentor, the apostle Paul, with the problem and to enlist his help in responding to it.

We have used the phrase "false teaching," but some justification of this language is necessary. In several other letters, Paul deals with false teachers, and he usually refers to them quite specifically and criticizes them overtly (see, e.g., Gal. 1:8; 4:17; 5:12; 6:12-13; 2 Cor. 11:4-5, 13-15, 20-23; 12:11; Phil. 3:2, 18-19; 1 Tim. 1:3-7; 4:1-3; 6:3-5). In comparison with these explicit and sometimes quite blunt descriptions of false teachers, the language of Colossians is quite restrained.[42] Paul never refers to a particular false teacher, or false teachers, warning instead quite generally about "no one" (*mēdeis*, 2:4, 18) or "anyone" (*tis*, 2:8, 16). Nor does he describe very clearly just what the false teaching is — as the bewildering variety of scholarly reconstructions (see below) bears witness to. It is no wonder, then, that Morna Hooker has questioned whether there was any particular "false teaching" being propagated at Colossae.[43] She argues that Paul is not attacking a particular teaching. He is simply issuing warnings about tendencies within the environment of the church that are potentially damaging to the Colossians' faith. Hooker makes some good points. The letter gives no indication that the Colossians were facing teachers who had come to them from outside their community. Indeed, by warning about people "who have lost connection with the head [Christ]" (2:19), Paul implies that the threat arose from among fellow Christians.[44] But it is hard finally to avoid the impression that the threat was a definite one and that it involved a single, relatively coherent, teaching: what Paul labels in 2:8 a "philosophy." The connections among the several warnings in chapter 2 are pretty tight, suggesting that a single

42. E.g., Dunn, 25.
43. Morna D. Hooker, "Were There False Teachers in Colossae?" in *Christ and Spirit in the New Testament: Studies in Honour of Charles Francis Digby Moule* (ed. Barnabas Lindars and Stephen S. Smalley; Cambridge: Cambridge University Press, 1973), 315-31.
44. Contra, e.g., Wolter, 162-63. Whether these Christians were part of the same community addressed by Paul is more difficult to know.

"movement" is in view throughout. However, Hooker's protest may be justified to the extent that the false teachers were perhaps seeking to win people over less by overt proselytizing than by an attitude of smug and prideful superiority. To be sure, some English versions refer to these people as "insisting on" certain practices (2:18), but the verb should probably be translated "delight in." Paul's warnings about being "taken captive" (2:8) or "judged" (2:16) or "disqualified" (2:18) suggest that the people within this movement were advocating an alternative teaching that exerted an attraction on the other Christians. Paul criticizes the false teachers for their arrogance (2:18), and numerous examples from every age of the church enable us to construct a profile of people who claim to have the "inside track" on spiritual truth and disdain as "unenlightened" those who do not follow their program.

Paul's language and manner of dealing with the problem suggest, then, that certain Christians in Colossae had adopted and were advocating an approach to Christianity that stood in contrast to the teaching that the Colossians had received from Epaphras and that Paul judged ultimately to be not only deficient but ultimately dangerous to one's spiritual health (see 2:19). Some therefore call the movement a "heresy."[45] Others, fearing that talk of heresy goes too far or that it presumes an "orthodoxy" that might not have existed in Paul's day, prefer the term Paul himself uses, "philosophy."[46] But the time-honored phrase "false teaching" is also appropriate and, we think, finally the best option. Advocates of the movement were certainly "teaching" their philosophy, even if they were not actively proselytizing, and the teaching is certainly "false," since it has the potential to move people away from "the hope held out in the gospel" (1:23) and from Christ, the source of all spiritual power (2:19).[47]

Our interpretation of Colossians would be more exact if we could identify this false teaching. Letter writers in the New Testament are engaged in a long-distance conversation. In the text of Scripture we possess one side of that conversation. Thus in Colossians we hear Paul's response

45. E.g., Lightfoot, 73-113.
46. E.g., Dunn, 24-35; Wright, passim.
47. Dunn protests that calling the movement a "false teaching" ignores the many points of agreement between the "teachers" and the gospel as Paul understands it (35; see also 25). But, of course, all "false teaching" is similar to true teaching in varying degrees. To label something "false teaching" does not imply that every part of the teaching is false but that it contains one or more errors at critical points, rendering the whole dangerously misleading. The "agitators" in Galatia agreed with Paul on a great deal, but Paul can nevertheless claim that their overall teaching is "another gospel" (Gal. 1:6-7). Dunn's view, as he makes clear on p. 25, assumes a fairly expansive view of the parameters of Christian "orthodoxy" in the early decades.

to the issues at Colossae as communicated to him by Epaphras. But we do not have direct access to the other side of the conversation. In this case the crucial conversation partner is not the Colossians themselves but the false teachers. Paul and the false teachers are indirectly engaged in a sort of debate that the Colossians are listening in to. What exactly the false teachers were saying can be determined only by analyzing the nature of Paul's response to them against the background of what we know generally about the first-century world of Colossae. But this process is a very inexact and uncertain one. Paul naturally presupposes that the Colossians know what the false teachers were saying, and so he only alludes to their teaching in making his own points. And these allusions involve some of the most debated exegetical points in the letter. Moreover, it is sometimes difficult to know when Paul is describing what the false teachers were saying and when he is characterizing their teaching in his own terms. And, finally, we do not know nearly as much as we would like about the Colossians' own "world." What we do know about it suggests that it was very complex, with many religious, philosophical, and cultural movements jostling for attention.

All of this makes it extraordinarily difficult to pin down the exact contours of the false teaching that Paul opposes in Colossians and explains why scholars come to so many different conclusions about it. Indeed, we are not convinced that the letter provides enough information for us to be even reasonably sure about the identification of the false teaching. As Lincoln puts its, "Although the prescription for cure comes across reasonably clearly to the present-day reader of Colossians, the ailment defies a really detailed diagnosis on his part."[48] Such an uncertain conclusion is disappointing in some respects but is, in another respect, hermeneutically fruitful. For it means that we can apply Paul's teaching in the letter to a wide variety of historical and contemporary movements that share the general contours of the false teaching. Our inability to pin down the false teaching does not mean that we cannot describe some of its basic tenets. In what follows, then, we will first gather some of the evidence from the letter itself, and then evaluate various options in light of this evidence before drawing some tentative conclusions.

One of the difficulties we face in reconstructing the false teaching is deciding what evidence in Colossians should "count." We have seen that the letter as a whole is concerned with the false teaching. But, of course, this does not mean that every verse or every point that Paul makes directly takes up the language or ideas of the false teachers. In his concern

---

48. Lincoln, 561. Barclay expresses a similar uncertainty about the false teaching (*Colossians and Philemon*, 52-54).

to present the truth of the gospel as an antidote to the false teaching, Paul will naturally rehearse many gospel truths that do not necessarily run directly counter to the false teaching.[49] In surveying the evidence from Colossians, then, we will move from the direct to the less direct, suggesting at each point something of the range of opinion.[50] (Readers should refer to the commentary for more detailed discussion of the relevant verses.)

The clearest statements about the false teaching come in 2:8-23, where Paul is directly concerned with warning the Colossians about this teaching (vv. 8, 16, 18). Methodologically, then, it is appropriate to begin here, and to begin with direct statements about the false teaching before moving on to indirect ones. We list these direct statements, with comment where necessary. (See the comments on specific verses for elaboration.)

1. The false teaching is a "hollow and deceptive philosophy" (v. 8). The word "philosophy" was applied to a wide range of belief systems in the ancient world, so it tells us little about the origin or nature of the teaching. It does suggest, however, that the teaching involved a somewhat coherent system.

2. The false teaching "depends on human tradition" (v. 8; cf. also v. 22). The similarity of this wording with Jesus' denunciation of scribal "tradition" in the Gospels (e.g., Mark 7) has suggested to some that the false teaching was Jewish in nature. But the language is too general to justify such an inference.

3. The false teaching "depends on . . . the elemental spiritual forces of this world" (v. 8). Nothing certain can be determined from this phrase. For (1) the referent of the key Greek word in this phrase — stoicheia — is very uncertain (spiritual beings? elementary teachings? physical components?); and (2) it is unclear whether the word was being used by the false teachers themselves to describe their teaching or whether Paul has chosen to apply it to their teaching.

4. The false teaching does not "depend on . . . Christ" (v. 8).

5. The false teachers were advocating the observance of certain food restrictions and of certain Jewish "holy days" (v. 16).

6. The false teachers practiced ascetic disciplines (v. 18; cf. also v. 23).

---

49. The process of reconstructing the background of a letter from its incidental references has been dubbed "mirror reading," and the challenges facing this procedure have frequently been noted.

50. See also, for this method, Barclay, Colossians and Philemon, 48-52; Robert E. Cleveland, "Colossians: Polemic or Paraenesis?" (Ph.D. diss., Fordham University, 2000); Richard E. DeMaris, The Colossian Controversy: Wisdom in Dispute at Colossae (JSNTSup 96; Sheffield: JSOT Press, 1994), 43.

While there is some discussion about the meaning of "humility" *(tapeinophrosynē)*, most agree that the word refers to ascetic practices such as fasting.

7. The false teachers focused attention on angels (v. 18). The phrase "worship of angels" is one of the most debated in the letter and, at the same time, a critical "hinge point" in larger reconstructions of the Colossian false teaching. It may refer to some kind of worship, or veneration, offered to angels by humans; or to the participation of humans in the worship performed by angels. Also important, and debated, is the relationship between this reference to "angels" and the references to the "powers and authorities" elsewhere in the letter (1:16, 20; 2:10, 15).[51]

8. The false teachers made a great deal about visions they had seen (v. 18). There is considerable controversy over the exact meaning of the phrase translated in the TNIV "go into great detail about what they have seen." But there is general agreement that "what they have seen" refers to visionary experiences.

9. The false teachers are proud: "their unspiritual minds puff them up with idle notions" (v. 18).

10. The false teachers are losing connection with "the head" of the body, Christ (v. 19). Paul here repeats and elaborates the "not according to Christ" of v. 8, using wording that suggests the false teachers were at least claiming to be Christians.

11. The false teachers were propagating various rules — which Paul regards as "worldly" — as an important means of spiritual growth (vv. 20-23).

These points are relatively clear, and most scholars agree that they are appropriately used to reconstruct the false teaching. Several other details in this section and from the letter as a whole are also sometimes thought to reflect the false teaching, but they are less clear and there is no agreement about their relevance.

1. The false teachers were using the language of "fullness" (cf. 1:19; 2:9, 10). Some interpreters think that this language suggests a gnostic or Stoic element in the false teaching. We think this is unlikely. But we do feel that Paul's use of this language suggests that the false teachers were claiming to offer a "fullness" of spiritual experience that could not be found through Christ alone.[52]

2. The false teachers were advocating circumcision (v. 11; cf. v. 13;

---

51. Schenk perceptively notes that a key question in evaluating the Colossian false teaching is whether the false teachers feared the angels or venerated them ("Kolosserbrief," 3350) — or, we might add, both.

52. See, e.g., Lähnemann, *Der Kolosserbrief*, 103-4.

3:11). It is possible that Paul refers to circumcision because the false teachers were advocating circumcision or at least were Jewish. But circumcision is mentioned so casually (in a metaphor in 2:11 [cf. v. 13] and in a traditional formula in 3:11) that it is also possible that Paul has introduced the language without regard to the false teaching.

3. The false teachers denigrated Christ. The assumption, widespread in the literature, that the false teachers were directly questioning the supremacy or sufficiency of Christ, especially in comparison with other spiritual beings, is based on what Paul says positively about Christ. In 2:8-23 alone he asserts that Christ is the one in whom "all the fullness of the Deity lives" (v. 9); that Christ is "the head of every power and authority" (v. 10) and that "in Christ" (or "through the cross") God has triumphed over these spiritual beings (v. 15); that believers "in Christ" are brought to "fullness" (v. 10) and "with him" experience new life (vv. 12-13); that the "reality" is found in Christ (v. 17); that Christ, as "head" of the body, empowers its growth (v. 19); and that "with Christ" believers have "died . . . to the elemental spiritual forces" (v. 20). And, of course, when we expand our horizons to include the rest of the letter we find considerable reinforcement for this last point.

Of course, Christ is the central theme of all of Paul's letters, and much of the language about Christ can be found in these other letters as well. But the density of references to Christ, the critical contribution of some of these references (e.g., 2:6), and some unusual christological expressions cause Colossians to stand out in this regard in comparison with the other letters of Paul. It should also be noted that, while possessing great value for the construction of a theoretical Christology, the Christology of Colossians has a very practical concern: to demonstrate the sufficiency of Christ for the believer's every spiritual need. It is just in these terms that Paul "applies" his christological teaching in the key polemical passage, 2:6-23. Christ, and Christ alone, as "head" of the body, empowers Christian living (v. 19). Believers have been bought to fullness in him, as they die and are raised with him to new life (vv. 11-13, 20). Believers thus need to continue to orient themselves to the all-encompassing Lord (v. 6).

There can, then, be no doubt about Paul's intention to make the centrality and supremacy of Christ, especially with respect to other spiritual beings, a central plank in his response to the false teachers. The question, however, is whether this emphasis is a direct or indirect response to the false teachers. In other words, is Paul's christological focus directed against people who were explicitly questioning the supremacy and sufficiency of Christ? Or is he highlighting these christological points because he wants believers to recognize that Christ meets their every spiritual need and that they therefore have no need to succumb to the alternative spiritual program being propagated by the false teachers? We cannot decide definitively between these scenarios, but we do think the second is a serious possibility.[53]

With these points about the false teaching from the letter before us, we are now in a position to analyze some of the main options. We begin with three preliminary points. First, while "Gnosticism" has frequently been invoked to explain the false teaching, it is unlikely to be very helpful.[54] As is now commonly recognized, "Gnosticism," as a coherent system, arose only in the second century. Various teachings that later became part of this system certainly existed in Paul's day, and so some interpreters will speak of "incipient Gnosticism" as a factor in the false teaching. But even this more modest suggestion is probably not appropriate, since there is nothing in Colossians to suggest a coalescence of typically gnostic elements. Any allegedly gnostic elements that are hinted at seem to involve ideas that were more generally part of the first-century intellectual environment. Second, the false teaching has a Jewish component. Despite some attempts to explain the text in other ways, Colossians 2:16-17 makes this clear. The threefold "religious festival, New Moon celebration, or Sabbath" (heortē, neomēnia, sabbatōn) is a common Old Testament way of summarizing Jewish "holy days." And the "shadow"/"reality" language of v. 17 also points to a contrast between Old Testament and New. Third, at the risk of complicating the matter, we have to recognize that the false teaching may be composed of a mixture of elements, drawn from various religious, philosophical, and cultural contexts, and that we may not be able to affix a simple label to it. Colossae, as we have seen, was a cosmopolitan city, with a significant Jewish population, open to all manner of influences from almost any part of the Roman Empire and even beyond.

With these preliminary observations before us, it will be useful to

53. See also, e.g., Hooker, "False Teachers in Colossae," 322-26; Walter T. Wilson, *The Hope of Glory: Education and Exhortation in the Epistle to the Colossians* (NovTSup 88; Leiden: Brill, 1997), 145-46.

54. Contra, e.g., Lightfoot, 73-113; Günther Bornkamm, "The Heresy of Colossians," in *Conflict at Colossae: A Problem in the Interpretation of Early Christianity Illustrated by Selected Modern Studies* (rev. ed.; ed. and trans. Fred O. Francis and Wayne A. Meeks; Sources for Biblical Study 4; Missoula, Mont.: Scholars, 1973), 123-45; Harold W. Attridge, "On Becoming an Angel: Rival Baptismal Theologies at Colossae," in *Religious Propaganda and Missionary Competition in the New Testament World* (ed. Lukas Bormann, Kelly Del Tredici, and Angela Standhartinger; Leiden: Brill, 1994), 481-98; Lohmeyer, 3-8; Pokorný, 117-20; Lohse, 129 ("pre-gnostic"). See also Dibelius, who thinks the language of 2:18 reflects the technical terminology of the gnostic-oriented mystery religions (Martin Dibelius, "The Isis Initiation in Apuleius and Related Initiatory Rites," in *Conflict at Colossae*, 61-121).

describe and briefly analyze the three specific proposals that meet the qualifications we have set out above and that at the same time have commanded some significant support in the literature.[55]

1. Jewish mysticism. This is the proposal that has probably had the greatest support over the course of the last half-century.[56] It is rooted in a particular interpretation of the phrase "worship of angels" in 2:18. This phrase has usually been taken to mean "worship offered to angels by human beings." But in the Greek the phrase is ambiguous; it could also refer to "worship engaged in by angels" (i.e., *tōn angelōn* might be a "subjective" genitive rather than an "objective" genitive). At first blush, this interpretation of the phrase might not seem to make much sense. But, read against the background of Jewish apocalyptic, it is argued, it makes very good sense. For in these books, the seer would often experience visions in which he or she was invited to participate in heaven with the angels in the worship of God. And evidence that Paul might have had just this in view comes from the two references that surround this phrase: "false humility" and "go into detail about what they have seen." The former phrase translates a single Greek word, *tapeinophrosynē*, "humility," and it was sometimes used to refer to fasting and other ascetic practices. The apocalyptic visionaries would often seek to induce visions by fasting. The second phrase, as we noted above, is translated in several different ways, but some reference to visionary experience seems to be intended. Putting these elements together yields, then, a coherent picture: the false teachers engage in ascetic practices such as fasting to prepare them to receive visions, visions in which they participate with angels in the worship of God. Since the mystical experience grows out of Judaism, a predilection to observe Jewish rituals would not be unexpected. And Paul's emphasis on the sufficiency of Christ would be a natural response: believers have no need of "adding" mystical experiences as a way of relat-

---

55. For good surveys of the many more options, see esp. Bevere, *Sharing in the Inheritance*, 13-46; Aletti, 14-28; DeMaris, *The Colossian Controversy*, 18-40; Barclay, *Colossians and Philemon*, 40-48.

56. It was first clearly proposed by Fred O. Francis in 1962: "Humility and Angel Worship in Col. 2:18," *ST* 16 (1962), 109-34 (the article has been republished with a series of other essays on the Colossian false teaching in *Conflict at Colossae*, 163-95). Ian K. Smith provides perhaps the fullest analysis of Colossians along these lines: *Heavenly Perspective: A Study of the Apostle Paul's Response to a Jewish Mystical Movement at Colossae* (Library of New Testament Studies 346; Edinburgh: T&T Clark, 2006). See also O'Brien, xxxvii-xxxviii; William L. Lane, "Creed and Theology: Reflections on Colossians," *JETS* 21 (1978), 216-18; Craig A. Evans, "The Colossian Mystics," *Bib* 63 (1982), 195-201; Thomas J. Sappington, *Revelation and Redemption at Colossae* (JSNTSup 53; Sheffield: JSOT Press, 1991); Bruce, 22-26; Wilson, *The Hope of Glory*, 34-38 (he thinks it may foreshadow the specific teaching of a second-century Jewish prophet named Elchasai).

ing to God. This view is able to account for all the elements we have identified as probable references to the false teaching and, moreover, can account satisfactorily for Paul's teaching in the rest of the letter.[57]

It has, however, several weaknesses. First, the interpretation of "worship of angels" that it assumes is not altogether persuasive (see our notes on 2:18). Second, it does not provide an obvious explanation of why Paul would be so intent on demonstrating Christ's superiority to spiritual beings elsewhere in the letter (1:16, 20; 2:10, 15). To be sure, advocates of the "Jewish mysticism" view often argue that the "angels" in 2:18 are not the same as the "powers and authorities" of these other verses. But it might make more sense to tie all these texts together, yielding a consistent picture in the letter of spiritual beings. Third, this view may not provide an adequate explanation of the emphasis on "rules." These rules appear to have greater significance than as a preparation to receive visions. Colossians 2:20-23 suggests that the false teachers are making adherence to these rules a central plank in their platform. We therefore are not convinced that "Jewish mysticism" is the best single option for describing the false teaching. This does not mean, however, that Jewish mysticism may not have played some role in the false teaching.

2. Quite similar to the first view, but without quite so much of an emphasis on mysticism, is the view of James Dunn. Dunn argues that the "philosophy" was nothing more than Judaism, as it was being taught and practiced in the local synagogues. There is no need, contra so many interpreters, to appeal to some kind of syncretistic mix of religious and/or philosophical traditions. The data of the text can all be adequately explained against a background of standard Jewish teaching. Dunn points to several parallels with Galatians, where all agree that the false teaching was Jewish in nature: a concern with circumcision (see Col. 2:11, 13; 3:11); a polemic against the "elements of the world" (2:8, 20; cf. Gal. 4:3, 9, the only other place this language occurs in Paul); the observance of Jewish food laws and holy days (2:16; cf. 2:11-14; Gal. 4:10); a concern with "purity" issues (2:20-23; cf. Gal. 2:11-14); and a concern with angels, in connection with the law (2:14-15; cf. Gal. 3:19). In addition, Dunn finds allusions to Old Testament language that suggest that Paul in Colossians is claiming that Christians are the legitimate heirs of the Old Testament promises (e.g., 1:12-14; 3:12).[58] Dunn makes some good points, and he has certainly underscored the need to see a significant Jewish element in the

57. See esp. Smith, *Heavenly Perspective*.

58. James D. G. Dunn, "The Colossian Philosophy: A Confident Jewish Apologia," *Bib* 76 (1995), 153-81; see also Dunn, 23-35; Wright, 24-27; Schenk, "Kolosserbrief," 3351-54; Bevere, *Sharing in the Inheritance*, 59-147.

Colossian "philosophy." We have no significant quarrel with the positive evidence he adduces.[59]

Our criticism is, rather, whether "standard Judaism" adequately explains all the data about the false teaching and Paul's response to it. Dunn acknowledges that Paul's response in Colossians is far more restrained than in Galatians, but explains this by suggesting that the "philosophy" was not "a sustained attempt to undermine or further convert the Colossians, but a synagogue apologetic promoting itself as a credible philosophy."[60] But does this description account adequately for Paul's concern that the Colossians might be "taken captive" by this philosophy (2:8)? Such language suggests that the false teachers were more active in promoting their view than Dunn has allowed. And if this is true, and if Judaism were the "philosophy" involved, we would have expected a stronger polemic, more along the lines that we find in Galatians. Another problem with Dunn's view is that he thinks the philosophy is an attractive rival "worldview" within the Colossian community rather than a teaching being propagated from within the Colossian church. As we noted above, however, Colossians 2:19 appears to support the latter. Dunn responds that there may have been fluidity between the church and the synagogue in Colossae so that the person Paul has in view in 2:19 might have been on the boundary between the two.[61] Of course, we must be careful not to read into first-century Colossae the kind of clear distinction between Christianity and Judaism that we find in the second century. But Dunn tends, in contrast, to blur the line between the two in the first century in a way that does not adequately explain the rather clear distinction that Paul regularly makes in his letters.

What is particularly troublesome for Dunn's view, however, is the silence of Colossians on three key elements of Judaism (in virtually any form): the Old Testament, circumcision, and the law. Colossians has no quotations from the Old Testament. While allusions to the Old Testament are certainly present,[62] we would have expected a more overt appeal to the Old Testament if the rival claims of Jews and Christians were being debated in Colossae.[63] Circumcision is, of course, mentioned in Colossians (2:11; cf. 2:13; 3:11), and Dunn and a number of other interpreters argue that these allusions reveal that circumcision was an issue in

---

59. DeMaris, however, argues that the strict rigor of the false teachers' ascetic disciplines (2:21-23) goes beyond a Jewish viewpoint (*Colossian Controversy*, 56-58).

60. Dunn, 35.

61. Dunn, 185.

62. See esp. Christopher Beetham, "Echoes of Scripture in the Letter to the Colossians" (Ph.D. diss., Wheaton College, 2005).

63. Hay, 33; Lincoln, 567-68.

the false teaching. But these references are very incidental. One simply uses circumcision as a metaphor (2:11, 13), and the other involves a quotation from a standard formula (3:11). It is very surprising that Paul does not say something more about circumcision if the "philosophy" was a form of standard Judaism. The third surprising omission is the law, which is never mentioned in Colossians (except perhaps allusively in 2:14). This omission is especially striking since Ephesians, which is so similar to Colossians and probably written at the same time, does refer to the law, and in a text that develops an extensive and pointed defense of the inclusion of the Gentiles in the new covenant community (2:11-22). We would have expected this kind of polemic in Colossians if the "philosophy" were fundamentally Jewish. For, on Dunn's view, what the advocates of the "philosophy" were teaching was that Judaism provided the resources necessary to deal with the threat to human beings from sin and spiritual beings. Judaism insists that adherence to the covenant of God with the patriarchs and obedience to the law is where such refuge is to be found. Yet Paul simply does not bring up these issues in Colossians. Again, we hasten to say that the issues we have raised do not demand that Dunn's view be rejected — especially since some of the criticisms involve arguments from silence. Still, we believe the objections are sufficient to make it doubtful that we can describe the false teaching simply as "basic Judaism."

3. The majority of scholars, confronted with the wealth of data about the false teaching, have argued that it is syncretistic, a mix of two or more religious and/or philosophical traditions.[64] While a quite astonishing variety of specific "mixes" has been proposed, the best argued and most persuasive has been presented by Clinton Arnold in a major monograph on the Colossian false teaching. Arnold argues, "The Colossian 'philosophy' . . . represents a combination of Phrygian folk belief, local folk Judaism, and Christianity. The local folk belief has some distinctive Phrygian qualities, but it also has much in common with what we could also describe as magic or ritual power."[65] Arnold bases his understanding of the false teaching on a thorough study of local (Phrygian) attitudes and practices. He thinks there is good evidence for a widespread

64. E.g., Gnosticism and Jewish Essenism (Lightfoot, 73-113); Iranian myth, Phrygian religion, Hellenistic Judaism, mystery religions (Lähnemann, *Der Kolosserbrief*); Judaism and "middle Platonism" (DeMaris, *Colossian Controversy*); Pythagoreanism and Judaism (Schweizer, 125-33); "Judaized Hellenism" (J. Bradley, "The Religious Life-Setting of the Epistle to the Colossians," *SBT* 2 [1972], 17-36). See also Moule, 29-34.

65. Clinton Arnold, *The Colossian Syncretism: The Interface between Christianity and Folk Belief in Colossae* (WUNT 77; Tübingen: Mohr Siebeck, 1995; repr., Grand Rapids: Baker, 1996), 243.

57

"apotropaic" appeal to spiritual beings: that is, the appeal to angels, accompanied with various practices, to ward off evil. He therefore holds that the controverted phrase in 2:18 is Paul's own way of describing this invocation of angels, as a kind of "veneration" of angels (he insists that the genitive *angelōn* must be objective). The people combined this "veneration of angels" with ascetic practices and rituals drawn both from paganism and Judaism, thereby creating a local syncretistic belief system that was being picked up and propagated by some Christians in Colossae.

Arnold's view has the virtue of being based on solid research about the specific situation of Colossae (rather than on vague generalities about broad movements). It accounts for the evidence of the letter tolerably well. To be sure, some object to his (and many others') characterization of the false teaching as syncretistic, arguing that this approach is simply an easy way out of the problems the letter poses. Rather than working hard to fit the disparate evidence of the letter into a single coherent belief system, one simply attributes the bits and pieces to whatever belief system they might fit and labels the whole "syncretism." One thus creates, it is alleged, an unlikely mishmash of beliefs and practices. To the extent that syncretistic descriptions are based on superficial exegesis or offer an unlikely combination of elements, this objection has merit. On the other hand, syncretistic proposals such as Arnold's arguably reflect the realities of life, in which most people do not hold a "pure" form of any religion or philosophy, but a set of beliefs drawn from an often bewildering variety of sources. People in Colossae, a cosmopolitan city exposed to a wide variety of religions and philosophies, were likely quite susceptible to these kinds of mixtures. It is this possibility that bedevils any attempt to come up with a "neat" identification of the false teaching. Even Dunn's view must confront the question about the particular kind of Judaism taught and practiced in the Colossian synagogues. Was it not likely somewhat influenced by the surrounding culture and by other movements?[66]

All in all, then, we think that Arnold's reconstruction offers the single best explanation of the false teaching that Paul opposes in Colossians.[67] Still, his view is not without its problems. Much of Arnold's evidence for "folk belief" in Colossae comes from later (second- and third-century)

---

66. See esp. Bevere, *Sharing in the Inheritance*, who argues for an "assimilated" Judaism, a Judaism affected by its environment. Historians have disputed the evidence about how "syncretistic" Phrygian Judaism might have been. Some think it was quite syncretic (e.g., Bruce, 12-13), but others doubt it (Paul Trebilco, *Jewish Communities in Asia Minor* [SNTSMS 69; Cambridge: University Press, 1991], 127-44 [although he confines himself in this chapter to a study of certain divine titles]); Dunn, 31.

67. See also Lincoln, 560-68.

sources. His reconstruction tends to make angel veneration the center of the movement, whereas Paul's polemic suggests that a preoccupation with rules was the more fundamental practical problem. Paul also implies that the main deficiency that the false teachers found in Christ was his inability to provide ultimate spiritual "fulfillment" rather than his inadequacy in warding off evil. And, like every other specific proposal, Arnold's view depends on a particular interpretation of some very finely balanced exegetical issues (e.g., the meaning of "worship of angels" in 2:18).

Scholars are notoriously prone to advance sweeping theses on the basis of sometimes quite flimsy and debatable evidence. Sometimes we simply have to admit that we cannot know enough to be sure. This would seem to be one of those instances. We conclude, then, that we must be content with the kind of generalized description of the false teaching that we have given in the eleven points above. The false teachers were probably people from within the Colossian Christian community who were bragging about their ability to find ultimate spiritual "fulfillment" via their own program of visions and asceticism. This program was drawn partly from Judaism, particularly in its focus on rules about eating and observing certain days. They were preoccupied with spiritual beings, probably because they viewed them as powerful figures capable of having a significant influence on their lives. Here we must take note of a fundamental feature of first-century Hellenistic culture that would inform this kind of concern with spiritual beings: *Weltangst*, anxiety about the world and one's place in it. Wilson puts it well:

> It seemed that the universe, in all its vastness and intricacy, was beyond human comprehension or control, being governed instead by a host of wrathful gods and indifferent supernatural powers. Human beings could do little more than struggle against the relentless tide of "Fate." For them, personal and material insecurity, not to mention moral and spiritual indeterminacy, characterize the human condition, which often amounts to little more than a fruitless search for meaning that ends with death and oblivion. . . .
>
> Often abetting this "common core" was the belief that the very fabric of the universe suffered from some sort of irreparable rift. The two fundamental realms of reality that make up the universe, the celestial and the terrestrial, are set in opposition to one another on account of some cosmic crisis, variously described. . . .
>
> In response to this unsettled state of affairs, mortals sought some understanding of and access to the supernatural powers that controlled their lives, often via intermediary or daemonic beings or through mystical experiences. This would involve discovering some sort of effectual means for appeasing, worshipping, or manipulating these powers in

order to obtain a degree of protection or in order to escape the corrupted, terrestrial world, either in this life or the next.[68]

The false teachers were appealing to spiritual beings, visions, and rules to find security in this very uncertain universe. In doing so, they were questioning the sufficiency of Christ. They may have done so directly, but it is more likely that their questions about Christ were implicit in their approach and that it is Paul who draws out the implications of this "philosophy" for Christology. The false teachers were so preoccupied with their own program for spiritual fullness that they were separating themselves from the only true source of spiritual power: the Lord Jesus Christ, the one in whom God in all his fullness is to be found and the one through whom God has accomplished the reconciliation of the world. Here is the essence of the false teaching: it is "not according to Christ" (2:8). And, at the risk of generalizing unduly, we might suggest that here as well is the point of contact for the application of the message of Colossians to a wide variety of historical and contemporary teachings. Any teaching that questions the sufficiency of Christ — not only for "initial" salvation but also for spiritual growth and ultimate salvation from judgment — falls under the massive christological critique of Colossians.

V. WHAT IS COLOSSIANS TEACHING? THE THEOLOGY OF THE LETTER

The New Testament, claims C. F. D. Moule, "debates from a single platform, but from different corners of it; and so far as it does lean over towards any extremes, it is because the writers, at those points, recognize particularly clearly what are the positions that are being occupied by error and recoil violently from them."[69] What Moule says of the New Testament in general certainly applies to Paul in particular. In none of Paul's letters can we find his "theology," considered in the abstract. What we find, instead, is contextualized theology, particular points and emphases from the "platform" of his theological convictions that he uses in debating with his opponents and correcting his flock. So in Colossians. The theology that comes to expression in this letter is intended to convince the Colossian Christians not to succumb to the false teaching that has

---

68. Wilson, *The Hope of Glory*, 3-4.

69. C. F. D. Moule, *The Birth of the New Testament* (3d ed.; San Francisco: Harper & Row, 1982), 220-21.

arisen in their midst. The letter's theological emphases are therefore largely polemical thrusts against a particular form of erroneous teaching. We have described the general contours of this false teaching in the last section. Here we provide a brief overview of the main points that Paul makes in responding to it.[70]

A. Christ

"[T]he key religious theme throughout Colossians is the centrality and supremacy of Jesus."[71] The most famous christological passage is the "hymn" of 1:15-20, where Paul (whether he is the original author of the hymn or not) asserts Christ's centrality in both creation and new creation. Using language and concepts from both the creation account and from Old Testament and Jewish teaching about wisdom and "word" *(logos)*, Paul begins generally by announcing Christ's unique relationship to God — Christ is his "image" — and Christ's supremacy over creation — Christ is the "firstborn" over creation (v. 15).[72] These two christological themes dominate the letter. Indeed, the heart of Paul's argument is found just here, in the juxtaposition of these two themes. Because Christ stands in a unique relationship to God, he, and only he, is able to bring all things in creation back under God's sovereignty and thereby provide believers with the resources that they need to live and flourish in a world dominated by hostile powers. Christ's relationship to God is emphasized again within the hymn, with v. 19 claiming that "all [God's] fullness" dwells in Christ. Paul reiterates this same point in 2:9. And in both these texts, Paul immediately relates this claim about God's unique and full presence in Christ to his significance for the world — "reconciling all things" to God (1:20) — and for believers — we are "full" in Christ (2:10). These connections reveal as clearly as any text in the New Testament the intimate relationship between theology and practice, between ontology and ethics. Only if Christ is who Paul claims he is can he provide the "fullness" that the false teachers are claiming to offer in their alternative construal of religious experience.

While the hymn of 1:15-20 is the christological high point of the letter, it would be a mistake to ignore the degree to which Colossians is suf-

---

70. A particular good survey of Colossians' theology, with stimulating reflection on its significance, is found in Thompson, 111-91.

71. Larry Hurtado, *Lord Jesus Christ: Devotion to Jesus in Earliest Christianity* (Grand Rapids: Eerdmans, 2003), 505.

72. For the concept of supremacy in the word "firstborn" (πρωτότοκος), see the notes on 1:15.

INTRODUCTION TO COLOSSIANS

fused with Christology. Indeed, the two themes we have identified above are present throughout the letter. First, we take note of the constant reiteration of the unique relationship between Christ and God. God is "the Father of our Lord Jesus Christ" (1:3); Jesus is "the Son he loves" (1:13). The "word of God" (1:25) is also "the word of Christ" (3:16; my trans.). The "mystery of God" is "Christ" (2:2). It was God's working that raised Jesus from the dead (2:13). It is by holding on to Christ, the "head," that God provides growth to the body (2:19). Christ is now seated at "the right hand of God" (3:1), and believers' lives are now "hidden with Christ in God" (3:3). All that believers do and say should be done "in the name of the Lord Jesus, giving thanks to God the Father through him" (3:17). Paul asks prayer that God might "open a door" so that he can proclaim "the mystery of Christ" (4:3). The "kingdom of God" (4:11) can also be called "the kingdom of the Son he loves" (1:13). The cumulative effect of these references, when set beside the explicit assertions in 1:15, 1:19, and 2:9, is to suggest that Christ is divine: he is himself God. Colossians is therefore a prime witness to the "christological monotheism" that characterizes early Christianity.[73]

The theme of Christ's sufficiency for Christian spiritual experience is also woven throughout the fabric of the letter. The Colossians' faith is in Christ (1:4; 2:4); Epaphras is a "faithful minister of Christ" (1:7; see 4:12); the kingdom in which believers find rescue from darkness belongs to "the Son he loves" (1:13); it is "Christ's physical body" that has reconciled the Colossians to God, and it is before him that the Colossians will be presented holy (1:22); Paul's ministry is bound up with and empowered by Christ (1:24, 28, 29); the "mystery" that God has disclosed to his saints in the last days is "Christ in you" (1:27) or, simply, "Christ" (2:2; cf. 4:3); Christ is the one in whom are hidden "all the treasures of wisdom and knowledge" (2:3); the "tradition" the Colossians received can be summed up as "Christ Jesus as Lord" (2:6); believers have been "raised with Christ," they are now "hidden with Christ," and they will appear "with him" in glory (3:1-4); "Christ is all, and is in all" in the new creation (3:11); it is Christ's peace that should rule in our hearts (3:15) and his message that should dwell among us (3:16); everything the believer does should be done "in the name of the Lord Jesus" (3:17); household relationships are governed by the Lord (3:18, 20, 22-24; 4:1); and the ministry of Paul's associates is bound up with the Lord (4:7, 17). Of course, much

73. See esp. on this theme Richard Bauckham, *God Crucified: Monotheism and Christology in the New Testament* (Grand Rapids: Eerdmans, 1999), 25-42; Hurtado, *Lord Jesus Christ*, 29-53; N. T. Wright, *The Climax of the Covenant: Christ and the Law in Pauline Theology* (Minneapolis: Fortress, 1993), 56-136.

of this language is paralleled in Paul's other letters and, indeed, in the New Testament generally. But some of the expressions in the letter are unique — the syntactical formulation "Christ Jesus as Lord" in 2:6; "the peace of Christ" in 3:15 — and their concentration is impressive.

We have noted above, in discussing the false teaching, that Paul uses his teaching about Christ in Colossians especially to make the point that Christians find all that they need in him. Virtually every "theoretical" statement about Christ in the Christ "hymn" is picked up and applied to this concern later on in the letter. Indulging in a bit of "mirror-reading," we may deduce from this that the false teachers were not so much contesting traditional Christian teaching about Christ as they were implicitly questioning Christ's adequacy to supply all their spiritual needs. In any case, the Christology of Colossians is eminently practical, providing the basis on which Paul can claim that genuine spiritual experience can be found only in Christ.[74]

B. Cosmology and the Powers

Christology is the theological heart of Colossians, and, like the spokes of a wheel, all the other themes of the letter radiate from it. The Christ hymn, as we have noted, emphasizes Christ's role in relationship to the entire created world. He is "firstborn" over creation (v. 15), and this prominence is seen in the fact that he is the instrument, goal, and sustaining power of the universe (vv. 16-17). Christ holds the same central position in the new creation, as it is through his death that all things are "reconciled" to God (v. 20). Colossians, in relation to the other letters of Paul, "paints the christological picture more boldly on a cosmological canvas."[75] God's determination to create a people "for his name" is a central theme of the Bible. But God has not abandoned the world even as he calls out and forms his people from the world. The story of the Bible is not just about "salvation history" but about history more broadly conceived. The Christology of Colossians is a strong reminder of the significance of the cosmos in God's continuing work. The cosmological Christology of Colossians is, of course, a reaction to the false teachers, who were apparently suggesting that Christ was not sufficient to protect believers from all the "powers" rampant in the world.

---

74. See Michael Dübbers, *Christologie und Existenz im Kolosserbrief: Exegetische und Semantische Untersuchungen zur Intention des Kolosserbriefes* (WUNT 191; Tübingen: Mohr Siebeck, 2005), 176-77.

75. Thompson, 143; cf. also Lähnemann, *Der Kolosserbrief*, 152.

In our day, interpreters from a wide variety of perspectives have turned to the cosmic Christology of Colossians as a theological resource to address the church's role in the world. Two examples will suffice. Several theologians have suggested that Colossians' image of the "cosmic Christ" may serve as a means to think about the unity of all religions: Christ, in some fashion, penetrates and is present in every faith.[76] "All things" are reconciled to God in Christ. But this perspective, quite congenial in our age of tolerance and inclusiveness, misses the point of the "cosmic Christology" of Colossians. Colossians 1:20 teaches that God in Christ has provided the means to bring all the universe back under his sovereign control — not that everything in the universe is brought into salvific relationship to God (see the notes on this verse). This positive relationship to God in Christ, Colossians makes clear, is available only in the church, the universal gathering of all who acknowledge Christ as Lord.[77] A more appropriate application of the cosmology of Colossians is found among a number of Christian environmentalists. The "all things" of Colossians 1:20 includes the world of nature, and this text therefore taps into the strong Old Testament teaching about God's creation of and continuing concern for the created world.[78]

In both parts of the hymn that stresses Christ's role with respect to the cosmos, a particular focus on spiritual beings is present. The "all things" created in Christ include "things in heaven and on earth, visible and invisible, whether thrones or powers or rulers or authorities" (v. 16); the "all things" reconciled to God through Christ's death include "things on earth" and "things in heaven." This same concern with spiritual beings surfaces elsewhere in the letter: Christ is "the head over every power and authority" (2:10), and God in Christ (or through the cross) has "disarmed the powers and authorities" (2:15). Some think that all the references in Colossians have in view "good" angels. But this view is hard to reconcile with both 1:20 — why would good angels need to be reconciled? — and, still more, with 2:15 — why would God have to "lead" good angels in "triumphant procession"? More likely, then, 1:16 and 2:10 refer to all spiritual beings, whereas 1:20 and 2:15 focus implicitly on evil spiritual beings.[79] As we have noted above, this quite ex-

76. See, e.g., the 1961 WCC address of Joseph Sittler, "Called to Unity," published in *CurTM* 16 (1989), 5-13; and Matthew Fox, *The Coming of the Cosmic Christ: The Healing of Mother Earth and the Birth of a Global Renaissance* (San Francisco: Harper & Row, 1988).

77. Robert S. Barbour, "Salvation and Cosmology: The Setting of the Epistle to the Colossians," *SJT* 20 (1967), 257-71.

78. See Douglas J. Moo, "Nature in the New Creation: New Testament Eschatology and the Environment," *JETS* 49 (2006), 469-74.

79. See Wesley Carr, *Angels and Principalities: The Background, Meaning and Develop-*

traordinary emphasis on spiritual beings can make sense only if the false teachers were questioning the sufficiency of Christ to deal with the threat these powers posed to human beings. In responding to this false teaching, Paul contributes significantly to our appreciation of God's sovereignty in Christ over every spiritual being. Through Christ's death God has provided for their ultimate subjection; even now, they are defeated powers, unable to hold sway over believers, who belong to their sovereign, the Lord Jesus.

In many parts of the world, belief in spiritual beings remains strong, and their power to determine human affairs is both recognized and feared. Appropriating the teaching of Colossians about God's victory over the spiritual powers is especially important in such contexts. In many other parts of the world, however, belief in spiritual beings has waned or disappeared. How is Paul's teaching to be appropriated in this context? One possibility is to "demythologize" the language of the "powers" by "updating" the worldview of Paul, with its belief in spiritual beings, to fit with our own worldview, where the "powers" are now seen to be the institutions and "invisible forces" of our cultures.[80] Liberation theologians have used the language of the "powers" in this way to rail against exploitative governments or oppressive economic systems. Social critics have used the language to condemn the technological society. However, such a process of outright "demythologizing" is to be rejected as an unjustified imposition of our worldview on that of the Bible. Our task is, rather, to take seriously the explicit teaching of the Scriptures about the reality of spiritual beings and adjust our worldview accordingly.

Does this mean, then, that it is illegitimate to apply the language about spiritual beings in Colossians to these other "powers"? Perhaps.[81] However, since Paul himself probably held the view, widespread in his day, that these spiritual beings stood behind the various structures and institutions of the world and held sway over humans through them, we may be justified in making the hermeneutical move to apply the lan-

ment of the Pauline Phrase hai archai kai hai exousiai (SNTSMS 42; Cambridge: Cambridge University Press, 1981), 47-85.

80. See esp. the wide-ranging three-volume work of Walter Wink: *Naming the Powers: The Language of Power in the New Testament* (Philadelphia: Fortress, 1984); idem, *Unmasking the Powers: The Invisible Forces That Determine Human Existence* (Minneapolis: Fortress, 1986); idem, *Engaging the Powers: Discernment and Resistance in a World of Domination* (Minneapolis: Fortress, 1992); and, for a particular application of this hermeneutical strategy, see Brian J. Walsh and Sylvia C. Keesmaat, *Colossians Remixed: Subverting the Empire* (Downers Grove, Ill.: InterVarsity, 2004).

81. See esp. Clinton E. Arnold, *Ephesians: Power and Magic* (SNTSMS 63; Cambridge: Cambridge University Press, 1989), 48-51; idem, *Powers of Darkness: Principalities and Powers in Paul's Letters* (Downers Grove, Ill.: InterVarsity, 1992).

guage in Colossians at these points to various entities in our day.[82] Nevertheless, identifying which "structures" have been so taken over by evil spiritual beings as to render them evil themselves is a precarious undertaking. It is far too easy for Christians of various theological and political persuasions simply to label any structure they don't like as one of the "powers" and relegate it to Satan's control.

C. The Church

As we have seen, the Christ "hymn" falls into two basic sections, one celebrating the supremacy of Christ in creation and the other the supremacy of Christ in the new creation. As we argue in our notes on 1:18, we think that the conclusion of this verse, "so that in everything he might have the supremacy," refers to Christ's "inaugurated" rule: already raised and installed as Lord of all at God's right hand, Christ must nevertheless still manifest that rule in the world. And the assertions about Christ's supremacy in the church at the beginning of the verse suggest that it is through the church that Christ's supremacy is now revealed and advanced in the world. The connection between supremacy in creation and the church as the place where that supremacy comes to expression is typical of the letter as whole. Colossians, David Hay argues, uses a "totalizing rhetoric" that affirms "both the universality of Christ's lordship and the particularity of the Christian community as that portion of humanity that confesses his secret supremacy."[83] The distinctive concept of the "universal church" that emerges in Colossians may then be a product of Paul's universal Christology. As there is a single "creation" over which Christ rules, so there must be a single, all-inclusive "new creation," a "church" *(ekklēsia)* where — and only where — Christ can be known, worshipped, and proclaimed. The development from the typical conception of the "church" as a local (physical) assembly of believers in Paul's earlier letters (and cf. Col. 4:15, 16) into the "church" as a universal spiritual entity (Col. 1:18, 24) is a natural one in light of this universalism.[84]

Paul expresses this universal conception of the church in the meta-

82. Andrew T. Lincoln, "Liberation from the Powers: Supernatural Spirits or Societal Structures?" in *The Bible in Human Society: Essays in Honor of John Rogerson* (ed. M. Daniel Carroll, David J. A. Clines, and Philip R. Davies; JSOTSup 200; Sheffield: Sheffield Academic Press, 1995), 335-54.

83. Hay, 35.

84. P. T. O'Brien, on the other hand, thinks that the development toward a universal "church" took place via the conception of the heavenly "assembly" of believers (*DPL*, 125-26).

phor of the "body of Christ" (1:18, 24; cf. 2:19). Paul calls local churches a "body" in his earlier letters, but the universal application here in Colossians (and Ephesians) is clearly anticipated in these letters as well (e.g., 1 Cor. 12:13). How Paul arrived at the notion of the church as Christ's body is debated. But almost surely involved was the idea of Christ as a "corporate person," one who, like Adam in the old creation, represents the totality of God's new creation. New in Colossians, however, is the further step of identifying Christ as the "head" of the body (1:18; 2:19). This identification, if pressed in any literal sense, is illogical: Christ cannot be both the body and its head (distinguished from the body) at the same time. Of course, no such logical consistency is demanded in the world of metaphors, which often overlap in just these ways. Theologically, what is important is to identify what Paul intends to convey with the metaphor. The Greek word for "head" *(kephalē)* generally implies authority of some kind, and this is part of what Paul intends: Christ is the ruler of the church. But, as 2:19 strongly suggests, Christ's "headship" also involves sustenance. Just as the ancients thought of the head, physiologically, as the directing source of the body's movements, so Christ, affirms Paul, is the directing source of the body of his people. Only by staying connected to this "head," therefore, can Christians grow.

D. The Gospel

The false teachers, as we have seen, were making some kind of claim about "visions" that they had seen (2:18). We have also seen that it is very difficult to know just what was involved in these visions, but that it is possible that the false teachers were making a claim to have received new revelations, needed to supplement the original gospel. Certainly Paul's emphasis on the significance and power of the gospel in Colossians would make sense if this were the case. But even if the false teachers were not making this kind of claim, what Paul says in the letter about the source and finality of God's revelation in Christ would be apropos. For the false teachers were apparently suggesting that Christians needed to go "beyond" the gospel that Epaphras had taught the Colossians in order to experience spiritual "fullness." And so it is often the case with false teachers, who err not always in subtracting from the gospel but in seeking to add to it. The gospel can be perverted through addition just as easily as through subtraction.

    While no section of the letter is devoted to this topic, Paul weaves language about the power of the gospel into the fabric of the letter. We are using the word "gospel" as a catchall for the various terms that Paul uses in the letter to describe the message about Christ. This emphasis frames the first major section of the letter (1:3-23). From Epaphras, the Colossians have heard the "truth," "the gospel," and learned from it about the secure hope they have (1:5-8). This gospel itself, Paul emphasizes, is powerful and productive: it has led to growth among the Colossians as well as in the rest of the world (1:6). After reminding the Colossians of what God has done for them through his supreme and pre-eminent Son, Paul then concludes the section on a similar note, reminding them that they will be able to appear faultless before God only if they "do not move from the hope held out in the gospel" (1:23).

The next section (1:24–2:5) also makes significant claims about the finality of God's revelation in Christ. Paul's task is to present to the Colossians "the word of God in its fullness" (1:25), the word that unveils the mystery of Christ himself dwelling among the Gentiles. It is by understanding this mystery, the mystery that is bound up with Christ himself, that the Colossians will be able to understand the world and God's ways in it, for "all the treasures of wisdom and knowledge" are found in Christ (2:3). The key transitional verses in the letter, 2:6-7, carry on this theme. By using the language of "receive" (v. 6), Paul evokes the concept of a tradition that the Colossians have received, an idea that is probably reinforced with "the faith" in v. 7. Fundamental to the direct polemic about the false teachers in 2:8-23, then, is the contrast between "human tradition" (2:8, 22) and that divine tradition, the gospel, which manifests the "reality" of new covenant truth (cf. 2:17).

In the paraenetic section of the letter (3:1–4:6), Paul urges the community to dwell on the "message" about Christ in its communal activities (3:16). It is this same message that Paul is determined, with the aid of the Colossians' prayers, to continue to proclaim (4:3-4). The flip side of this emphasis on the power of God's word is the importance that Paul accords to the Colossians' learning and knowing this word. As the Colossians have "truly understood" God's grace through Epaphras (1:7), so he prays that they might be filled "with the knowledge of his will through all the wisdom and understanding that the Spirit gives" (1:9), "growing in the knowledge of God" (1:10). We easily read over these many assertions about the gospel without giving them the attention they deserve. Yet when considered in their totality, and in light of the false teaching, the power and finality of God's word in Christ emerges as a key theme of the letter.

E. Eschatology

We noted above that many scholars are convinced that Paul could not have written Colossians because of its eschatology. The "authentic" Paul maintains a tension between "realized" and future eschatology, between what God has "already" done in Christ and what God has "not yet" done. Colossians, it is argued, reduces or eliminates that tension by concentrating so much on the "already."[85] We have "already" been brought into God's kingdom (1:13); the gospel has "already" been proclaimed to "every creature under heaven" (1:23); we have "already" been made alive with Christ (2:13) and been raised with him into heaven (3:1); and God has "already" disarmed the powers and authorities (2:15).[86]

Yet, as we argued above, there is a clear "not yet" side to the eschatology of Colossians as well. Yes, we have been "raised with Christ," but we have "not yet" appeared with him in glory (3:4). "Not yet" have the Colossians been "presented" before God in the judgment (1:22; cf. 1:28). The concept of hope, which bookends the first major section of the letter (1:3-23), is a particularly clear example of the typical Pauline already/not yet eschatological tension. Hope, by its very definition, is forward-looking, yet it is already "stored up for you in heaven" (v. 5). And it is this hope, "held out in the gospel," that the Colossian Christians must hang onto by continuing in their faith (v. 23). While it is true, then, that Colossians focuses on realized eschatology, future eschatology is not abandoned. The Pauline eschatological tension is maintained. At the same time, since the false teachers are questioning the adequacy of God's present provision in Christ for spiritual fullness, Paul quite naturally moves to that side of the platform to make his points.[87]

F. The Christian Life

Few texts in the New Testament make the case so clearly that Christian living must be rooted in Christ. He is the "head" who supplies power to the whole body (2:19). It is by our existence "in him," the "new self," or "new man," that renewal in the image of God takes place (3:10). He is the repository of all wisdom (2:3), the "reality" or "substance" of new cove-

85. E.g., Horacio E. Lona, *Die Eschatologie im Kolosser- und Epheserbrief* (FB 48; Würzburg: Echter, 1984).

86. See the section on authorship in the Introduction and comments on 3:1-4 for a defense of the compatibility of this teaching with Paul's major epistles.

87. See, e.g., A. T. Lincoln, *Paradise Now and Not Yet: Studies in the Role of the Heavenly Dimension in Paul's Thought with Special Reference to His Eschatology* (SNTSMS 43; Cambridge: Cambridge University Press, 1981), 131-34; Sappington, *Revelation*, 225-28; Franz-Josef Steinmetz, *Protologische Heils-Zuversicht: Die Strukturen des soteriologischen und christologischen Denkens im Kolosser- und Epheserbrief* (Frankfurter Theologische Studien 2; Frankfurt: Josef Knecht, 1969); Barth/Blanke, 458-61.

nant truth (2:17). Our very mind-set must be governed by "the things above," where Christ is and with whom we have been raised to new life (3:1-2).

One important implication of this focus on Christ is a negative one: a "rules-oriented" lifestyle is not the means to true spiritual growth. It is this point that Paul singles out in his references to the false teachers, who were apparently promising ultimate spiritual power through adherence to their rules (2:16, 20-23). Paul is clear about the poverty of these rules to deliver on what they promise: they have the "appearance of wisdom," "but lack any value in restraining sensual indulgence" (2:23).

Of course, Paul does not mean by this polemic to dismiss the value of all "rules" from the conduct of the Christian life. He certainly elsewhere upholds the continuing importance of God's "commandments" for Christian living (e.g., 1 Cor. 7:19). And, if not exactly rules, the exhortations of 3:5-4:1 reveal that Paul is not at all shy about urging believers to behave in certain ways. The problem with the rules of the false teachers, however, is that they stemmed from human tradition rather than from Christ (2:8). We may, then, formulate a theology of rules from Colossians 2 along these lines: Rules must never take the place of Christ as the source of spiritual nourishment and growth; and any rules that we propose to follow must be clearly rooted in and lead back to Christ. These principles will not, of course, solve all our debates about rules: for example, does Colossians 2:16 imply that Sabbath observance is optional for Christians? or does it teach only that Sabbath observance not rooted in Christ is wrong? But Colossians 2 does strongly remind us of where the true and only source of our spiritual growth is to be found and stands therefore as a stark warning about the perennial tendency toward legalism within the Christian church.

On a more positive note, Colossians 3:1-4:1 provides a succinct but beautifully rich overview of the life God calls us to in Christ. The opening paragraph roots this new life firmly in the Christology of the earlier part of the letter: because we have been raised with Christ (see 2:12), who is seated at right hand of the Father, we are to set our hearts and minds on "the things above" (3:1-2). The false teachers were perhaps bragging about their visions of heaven (see 2:18); here Paul affirms that there is nothing wrong with a heavenly perspective, as long as it is christologically focused. In fact, the foundation and essence of Christian living is the application to all our daily experience of a heavenly mind-set. In 3:5-9a, Paul contrasts this heavenly mind-set with the old life that we have left behind.

Paul then touches on another key principial foundation for the Christian life in 3:9-11, where he contrasts the "old self" with the "new."

This contrast is rooted in Paul's salvation-historical contrast between Adam (*the* "old man") and Christ (*the* "new man"). Because believers are "in Christ," the new man, they themselves become the new man, a corporate entity that God is in the process of renewing so that it more and more resembles Christ himself. The imagery of vv. 10-11 shows that the Christian life is a corporate life, a life lived out with others who also belong to Christ. Paul focuses on this corporate dimension of the Christian life in 3:12-17.

Sitting somewhat unexpectedly in a context that focuses so much on the transformation of life in Christ is 3:18–4:1, a passage that calls believers to rather ordinary and commonly accepted roles in their households. Indeed, considerable controversy surrounds this passage and the other "household codes" that we find in the New Testament. Surely their call to maintain "the status quo" in relationships of subordination — wives to husbands, children to parents, slaves to masters — stands in at least tension with, if not outright contradiction to, the principle of all believers being "one" in Christ (Gal. 3:28)? So, it is sometimes argued, we should, in effect, ignore these passages as traditional and culturally conditioned expressions of what was expedient for that time and place. However, it is preferable rather to think about these passages as important correctives to an overly "enthusiastic" appropriation of the "all one in Christ" principle. These passages warn us that our common life in Christ does not erase the responsibilities we have toward one another within the family and society. They are rather set on a new footing and given a new motivation: reference to "the Lord" permeates this passage. To be sure, this passage must not be seen as an endorsement of all these relationships: marriage and childbearing are God's good gifts; slavery is a perversion of his will for human relationships. But Paul's point, rooted in the "not yet" of eschatological realization, is that believers, while they must think in "heavenly" ways, still find themselves living on earth and obliged in all kinds of ways to relationships that are earthly in nature.

Commentary on Colossians

I. THE LETTER OPENING: "JUST AS YOU RECEIVED CHRIST JESUS AS LORD . . ." (1:1–2:5)

Letters from the world of Paul's day exhibit certain standard features. At its most basic, the "epistolary form" consists of an opening, a body, and a closing. Since they are regular components of letter openings, the prescript (1:1-2) and thanksgiving (1:3-12) must at least be included in this opening section. But 1:13-20 are firmly attached to vv. 3-12 through a series of relative clauses that describe the work (vv. 13-14) and person (vv. 15-20) of Christ. Paul's description of the Colossians' transfer from alienation to reconciliation (1:21-23) might appear to begin a new section, but this paragraph is tied to the immediately preceding verses via the topic of reconciliation (v. 20) and to the thanksgiving section by several key words and ideas (see below for details). Many commentators posit a rather significant break after v. 23.[1] But Paul's rehearsal of his own ministry (1:24–2:5) elaborates themes that have been important throughout chapter 1: the universally available power of the gospel to transform those who respond to its message and the full knowledge of God that the gospel, and the Son it proclaims, is uniquely able to provide. We therefore suggest, following Wright, that 1:1–2:5 is a discrete section of the letter, in which Paul greatly expands his typical thanksgiving by reflecting on the ultimate cause of that thanksgiving: the power and sufficiency of the Word of the gospel.[2] This letter opening sets the stage for Paul's warnings

---

1. E.g., Dunn, 53; Wolter, 49; Luz, 193; Lohse, 13; Lincoln, 554.
2. Wright, 48; see also R. E. DeMaris, *The Colossian Controversy* (Sheffield: JSOT Press, 1994), 41-42; J. Lähnemann, *Der Kolosserbrief* (Gütersloh: Mohn, 1971), 60; Franz

about the false teaching in 2:8-23. He wants the Colossians to understand that their adherence to the gospel of God's Son provides for all the spiritual blessing and power that they will ever need. They have "received Christ Jesus as Lord"; what they need to do simply is to "continue to live your lives in him" (2:6).

A. Prescript (1:1-2)

> ¹*Paul, an apostle of Christ Jesus by the will of God, and Timothy our brother,*
> ²*To God's holy people in Colossae, the faithful brothers and sisters in Christ: Grace and peace to you from God our Father.*

Letter openings typically begin with an identification of the sender and of the recipients, along with a greeting. This basic pattern, A to B, "Greetings,"[3] is found in all thirteen of his letters, but Paul always expands on it, adding various qualifying words and phrases. By doing so, he often furnishes some clues about the main concerns and emphases of the letter to follow. In Colossians, however, the additions are minor and conventional, providing very little basis for speculation about what is to come.

1 As in all his letters, Paul begins by identifying himself as the writer of the letter. The name *Paul (Paulos)* was probably the name by which the Jew Saul was known among Greek- (and Latin-) speakers.[4] Paul quickly establishes his right to address the Colossian Christians by claiming to be *an apostle* (as he does in all his letters except Philippians, 1 and 2 Thessalonians, and Philemon). The word *apostolos* has a range of meaning in Paul's letters, sometimes designating simply a "messenger" (e.g., Phil. 2:25; 2 Cor. 8:23) and at other times an "accredited missionary" (e.g., 1 Cor. 9:5-6; 15:7; Gal. 2:9; Acts 14:4, 14).[5] But in his letter openings, Paul clearly intends the word to have its full "official" sense: a person

---

Zeilinger, *Der Erstgeborene der Schöpfung: Untersuchungen zur Formalstruktur und Theologie des Kolosserbriefes* (Vienna: Herder, 1974), 34-49.

3. Examples of this simple epistolary formula are found in Acts 15:23; 23:26; Jas. 1:1.

4. The name "Paul" (Παῦλος) is almost certainly his *cognomen*, the Hellenized form of his Hebrew name Saul (e.g., F. F. Bruce, *Paul: Apostle of the Heart Set Free* [Grand Rapids: Eerdmans, 1977], 39).

5. On this latter category, see esp. E. E. Ellis, "Paul and His Co-Workers," in *DPL*, 186. See also R. Schnackenburg, "Apostles before and during Paul's Time," in *Apostolic History and the Gospel: Biblical and Historical Essays Presented to F. F. Bruce on His 60th Birthday* (ed. W. Ward Gasque and Ralph P. Martin; Grand Rapids: Eerdmans, 1970), 287-303.

called by Christ himself to represent Christ and proclaim Christ and thereby serve as the "foundation" of the new people of God (Eph. 2:20). Though Paul did not found the church at Colossae and had never visited it (2:1, 5), he is, nevertheless, through his convert Epaphras (1:7), the "apostle" of the church in that city.[6]

Christ Jesus may be added to *apostle* to indicate that it was Christ who called Paul (*Christou Iēsou* as a subjective genitive; see Gal. 1:1 for the idea) but more likely simply indicates that Paul's apostleship is bound up with Christ Jesus in a way that cannot be precisely defined (genitive of relationship).[7] *Christ* is used so often in Paul that many scholars think it has lost its titular significance and become not much more than a proper name.[8] However, it must be questioned whether a Jew like Paul, converted to a new movement whose distinguishing claim was that God's promised Messiah was none other than Jesus of Nazareth, crucified by the Romans, could ever have fully discarded the rich associations of the word.[9] While the title is not common in either the Old Testament or in Judaism, it was used by early Christians to identify Jesus of Nazareth as the man in whom the entire line of promise about a great Davidic king to come had reached its fulfillment. The almost formulaic language of these letter openings renders it unlikely that Paul has thought too much about his choice of words here. But we may still insist that his use of *Christ* would remind the Gentile Christians in Colossae of the Old Testament roots of their faith.[10]

As Acts 9 so vividly reveals, Paul's apostleship was not a matter of choice on his part but on God's part: it was *by the will of God*. In a context where Paul must establish his credentials against contrary claims, this assertion carries a polemical thrust; see Galatians 1:1 for a particularly clear example. But there is no evidence that Paul's claim to authority was being contested at Colossae. Probably, then, as with the same expression in 1 Cor. 1:1, 2 Cor. 1:1, Eph. 1:1, and 2 Tim. 1:1 (and note "by the command of God our Savior and of Christ Jesus our hope" in 1 Tim. 1:1), *by the will of God* carries no polemical overtones here.[11]

While we regularly identify Colossians as a letter of Paul, the pre-

---

6. O'Brien, 2.

7. See BDF §162.

8. E.g., Lohse, 6.

9. Douglas J. Moo, "The Christology of the Early Pauline Epistles," in *Contours of Christology in the New Testament* (ed. Richard N. Longenecker; Grand Rapids: Eerdmans, 2005), 186-87; Ben Witherington III, "Christ" and "Christology," in *DPL*, 98; Barth/Blanke, 137.

10. Dunn, 46.

11. Lightfoot, 131.

script in fact identifies two authors: Paul and *Timothy our brother*. Timothy, enlisted among Paul's co-workers at the beginning of the second missionary journey (Acts 16:1-3), became the most important of Paul's ministry associates. *Brother*, therefore, is probably intended to suggest Timothy's close association with Paul in ministry.[12] What role does Timothy play in the composition of this letter? Schweizer and Dunn, among others, suggest that Timothy may have been the actual writer of the letter, with Paul perhaps reading and "signing off" on what Timothy had written.[13] But this may give Timothy more credit than he deserves. First-person plural verbs occur only in 1:1-9, 1:28, and 4:3, and some of these may be "editorial plurals," intending to refer to Paul alone. Particularly difficult for any joint authorship theory are the many personal references that could apply to Paul only (1:23-27, 29; 2:1-5; 4:3-4, 7-15, 18). And Paul refers to Timothy in the openings of other letters that are patently Paul's own composition (2 Cor. 1:1; 1 Thess. 1:1; 2 Thess. 1:1; Phil. 1:1; Phlm. 1). To be sure, Timothy's inclusion in the prescripts of these other letters can readily be explained in terms of his involvement with those churches.[14] No such ministry with the Colossians can be documented (Timothy is not mentioned elsewhere in either Colossians or Philemon). But we know that Timothy was with Paul for at least some of the apostle's three-year Ephesian ministry (Acts 19:22), so it is entirely possible that Timothy could have come to know Epaphras and perhaps other Colossian Christians during that time.

2 Paul describes his addressees as *brothers and sisters*, the inclusive rendering of the TNIV appropriately bringing out the intended breadth of the Greek *adelphoi* (traditionally, "brothers"). This word was apparently widely used in the ancient world within various associations to stress the intimacy of relationship within these associations; members called one another *adelphos* as a way of indicating that the association was a "second home."[15] Because this language is so common in the New Tes-

---

12. O'Brien, 3.

13. Schweizer, 29-30, 23-34; Dunn, 47, 38-39. Harris, 8, speculates that Timothy may have been the amanuensis.

14. Timothy was involved in the initial establishment of the church in Corinth (Acts 18:5; cf. 2 Cor. 1:19) and was Paul's trusted emissary in his dealings with that church (1 Cor. 4:17; 16:10; cf. Acts 19:22). Timothy played a similar role in Thessalonica (1 Thess. 3:2, 6; cf. Acts 17:14, 15) and Philippi (Timothy was probably left behind in Philippi when Paul and Silas moved on to Thessalonica — cf. Acts 17:4 with 17:14, 15; cf. also Phil. 2:19, 22).

15. See esp. Philip A. Harland, "Familial Dimensions of Group Identity: 'Brothers' (ΑΔΕΛΦΟΙ) in Associations of the Greek East," *JBL* 124 (2005): 491-513; and see also Reidar Aasgard, *"My Beloved Brothers and Sisters!" Christian Siblingship in Paul* (JSNTSup 265; London: T&T Clark, 2004). It is very unlikely that ἀδελφοί is restricted to Paul's co-workers (who would have been responsible for reading the letter to the congregation)

tament, we can easily overlook its significance. It reminds us that we are members of the same family and that we should adopt the attitudes and actions necessary to maintain our familial unity.[16]

These fellow members of the new family of God are located, from an earthly perspective, *in Colossae*. Colossae had been the chief city of the Lycus valley for at least five centuries before Christ but was losing ground to Laodicea (cf. 2:1; 4:13, 15, 16), eleven miles away, during the first centuries B.C. and A.D. Located on a major trade route about 120 miles east of Ephesus, Colossae was a cosmopolitan city, exposed to diverse cultural and religious movements — including Judaism, which had a significant presence in the city.[17] These influences doubtless help explain the tendencies toward apparent theological syncretism that Paul seeks to correct in this letter.

But more important than their physical location is their spiritual "location": they are *in Christ*. This little phrase is one of Paul's favorites. It occurs thirty-three times in his letters (but only once else in Colossians, 1:28), and the fuller "in Christ Jesus [our Lord]" (see v. 4) occurs forty-eight times. To be "in Christ" is to belong to him as the originator and ruler of the new age of redemption that his death and resurrection inaugurated (in contrast to being "in Adam"; see 1 Cor. 15:22; 2 Cor. 5:14-17; Rom. 5:12-21). Paul uses the phrase in a rich variety of ways that cannot be precisely outlined.[18] Indeed, to seek a definite list of meanings would be to miss the inclusive sense that Paul usually seems to have in mind. "In Christ" is Paul's way of saying that believers are now "located" in a new "place" — the kingdom of God's Son (v. 13) — that carries with it a total reorientation of one's existence.[19]

(contra E. Earle Ellis, "Colossians 1:12-20: Christus Creator, Christus Salvator," in *Interpreting the New Testament Text: Introduction to the Art and Science of Exegesis* [ed. Darrell L. Bock and Buist M. Fanning; Wheaton, Ill.: Crossway, 2006], 415).

16. See esp. David G. Horrell, *Solidarity and Difference: A Contemporary Reading of Paul's Ethics* (London: T&T Clark, 2005), 110-15.

17. On Colossae, see, e.g., *ABD* 1.1089-90.

18. BDF claim that Paul's ἐν Χριστῷ "utterly defies definite interpretation" (§219 [4]); see also Wallace, *Greek Grammar*, 375.

19. Paul's "in Christ" is probably rooted in his conception of salvation history, with Adam as the representative head of the old realm and Christ as the head of the new. As all people are found, because of sin, "in Adam," so by God's grace they may be transferred into the new realm over which Christ reigns and so be found "in Christ" (see esp. 1 Cor. 15:22; 2 Cor. 5:14-17; Rom. 5:12-21; and on the general "in Christ" idea, H. N. Ridderbos, *Paul: An Outline of His Theology* [Grand Rapids: Eerdmans, 1974], 57-62; for a history of interpretation, see esp. M. Bouttier, *En Christ: Étude d'exégèse et de théologie pauliniennes* [Paris: Presses Universitaires de France, 1962]; F. Neugebauer, *In Christus (EN ΧΡΙΣΤΩΙ): Eine Untersuchung zum paulinischen Glaubensverständnis* [Göttingen: Vandenhoeck & Ruprecht, 1961], 18-33).

Paul also characterizes his readers as *holy* and *faithful;* but the meaning of these words and their relationship to the other elements in the address are not clear. Both words can be taken as adjectives modifying *brothers and sisters;* for example, NIV: "To the holy and faithful brothers in Christ at Colossae."[20] But most English versions, as does the TNIV, take the adjective *hagiois* as a substantive: "holy people," or "saints." This rendering is a bit more likely than the other because it follows the typical pattern of Paul's opening addresses.[21] The term *hagios* taps into an important Old Testament tradition, according to which Israel was called out from among the nations to be God's own people (see esp. Exod. 19:6; Dan. 7:18, 22, 25, 27). Some of the modern translations seek to capture this nuance by translating *God's holy people* (TNIV; NLT) instead of the traditional "saints." As Moule remarks, "'Saint' is, to modern ears, misleading, for the Hebrew and Greek words are concerned less with any excellence of character (however much that may be implied as a *result*) than with the commitments and loyalties of the Church to the God who had made her his own."[22] While calling his readers "holy" is typical for Paul, addressing them as "faithful" is not. Only in the address of Colossians does Paul use this word *(pistos),* which might be translated either "believing" (see REB: "our fellow-believers in Christ")[23] or "faithful" (so most other modern English versions).[24] The former translation suggests that Paul is simply characterizing the Colossians as believers in Christ (as opposed to unbelievers). "Faithful," on the other hand, could be a generic description of Christian experience (people who are dedicated to God) but could also, in a polemical sense, single out the Colossians as faithful believers in contrast to other Christians who are not.[25] Since characterizing the Colossians as "believing" would add little to the idea of *brothers*

---

20. See, e.g., Moule, 45; Luz, 192; Barth/Blanke, 139. Advocates of this arrangement point to the single article, τοῖς, that would suggest that the words ἁγίοις ("holy") and πιστοῖς ("faithful") are to be taken closely together.

21. Paul uses ἅγιος to characterize his readers in Rom. 1:7; 1 Cor. 1:2; 2 Cor. 1:1; Eph. 1:1; and Phil. 1:1. The word is clearly substantive in the latter three; and almost certainly so in the former two as well (where the sequence κλητοῖς ἁγίοις probably means "called to be holy people"). See, e.g., Lightfoot, 132; Harris, 9; O'Brien, 3.

22. Moule, 45. See also O. Procksch, *TDNT* 1.107. Dunn characteristically stresses the connection thus established between the Colossians and Israel (48).

23. O'Brien, 3-4.

24. So most commentators. Paul uses πιστός with these two basic meanings about equally: "believing" is the main idea in 2 Cor. 6:15; Gal. 3:9; 1 Tim. 4:3, 10, 12; 5:16; 6:2 [twice]; Titus 1:6); "faithful" in 1 Cor. 4:2, 17; 7:25; Eph. 6:21; Col. 1:7; 4:7, 9; 1 Tim. 1:12; 3:11; 2 Tim. 2:2 (some, to be sure, are difficult to put neatly into one category or the other).

25. Lightfoot, 132: "he means the true and stedfast [sic] members of the brotherhood. In this way he obliquely hints at the defection." See also Thompson, 14.

and sisters in Christ, the translation "faithful" is more likely. Paul chooses this unusual word to remind his readers of their need to continue to maintain allegiance to the gospel tradition that they have been taught (1:5-7; 2:6).

As is his custom, Paul modifies the usual ancient epistolary "greetings" *(chairein)* by substituting the similar-sounding "grace" *(charis)* and by adding "peace." Grace is a key theological concept for Paul. It expresses a fundamental characteristic of God's new covenant people: that their status is ultimately dependent on God's own unmerited intervention on their behalf (see esp. Rom. 5:2). Paul does not refer to grace very often in Colossians (clearly again in 1:6; 4:18; possibly in 3:16 and 4:6). But his frequent reference to "giving thanks" is an oblique and practical reminder of this basic theological theme. "Peace" has more traditional roots, reflecting the Old Testament prophetic hope for an era of *shalom,* when God's people would be delivered from their enemies and enjoy both physical and spiritual well-being. In every one of his other letters, Paul expresses his wish that his readers might enjoy "grace" and "peace" from God the Father and from Jesus Christ.[26] To be sure, a significant number of manuscripts here add "and from our Lord Jesus Christ" at the end of the verse,[27] but this addition is rightly suspect since it could so easily have been added in imitation of Paul's other salutations. In light of the christological focus of Colossians, the omission of Christ here is a bit unexpected. Perhaps, however, Paul is preparing us for the unusual language of v. 3, in which he calls God *the Father of our Lord Jesus Christ.*[28]

B. The Powerful Gospel of God's Son (1:3-23)

Strongly suggesting that these verses constitute a single major argument is the similarity between its beginning and its ending. Paul begins by thanking God for the Colossians' faith in Christ and love for all God's people, and claims that these are rooted in the hope stored up for them in heaven and about which they have heard in "the true word of the gospel" (1:4-5). He ends by warning the Colossians that their expectation of being presented before God "without blemish" in the judgment depends on their holding firmly to their faith and not moving from "the hope held out in the gospel" (1:23). This passage, then, is about the power of the

26. A partial exception to this rule is 1 Thess. 1:1, where neither God the Father nor Jesus Christ is mentioned; but both are mentioned in the previous clause.

27. See KJV and NKJV.

28. See Gordon D. Fee, *Pauline Christology: An Exegetical-Theological Study* (Peabody, Mass.: Hendrickson, 2007), 292-93.

gospel, the gospel that has at its heart (vv. 15-20) the Son of God, supreme in creation and the church.

1. The Evidence of the Gospel's Power among the Colossians (Thanksgiving and Prayer) (1:3-14)

[3]*We always thank God, the Father of our Lord Jesus Christ, when we pray for you, [4]because we have heard of your faith in Christ Jesus and of the love you have for all his people — [5]the faith and love that spring from the hope stored up for you in heaven and about which you have already heard in the true word of the gospel [6]that has come to you. In the same way, it is bearing fruit and growing throughout the whole world — just as it has been doing among you since the day you heard it and truly understood God's grace. [7]You learned it from Epaphras, our dear fellow servant, who is a faithful minister of Christ on our behalf, [8]and who also told us of your love in the Spirit.*

[9]*For this reason, since the day we heard about you, we have not stopped praying for you. We continually ask God to fill you with the knowledge of his will through all the wisdom and understanding that the Spirit gives, [10]so that you may live a life worthy of the Lord and please him in every way: bearing fruit in every good work, growing in the knowledge of God, [11]being strengthened with all power according to his glorious might so that you may have great endurance and patience, [12]and giving joyful thanks to the Father, who has qualified you to share in the inheritance of his people in the kingdom of light. [13]For he has rescued us from the dominion of darkness and brought us into the kingdom of the Son he loves, [14]in whom we have redemption, the forgiveness of sins.*

Paul usually gives thanks to God for his readers and God's work among them in the opening of his letters (only in Galatians and Titus is such a thanksgiving lacking). O'Brien isolates two basic types of Pauline thanksgivings, a simpler one that contains an expression of thanks followed by a reason for the thanks and a more complex type.[1] The thanksgiving in Colossians is of the latter kind. It may be outlined as follows, with the numbered elements reflecting the standard seven features of Paul's complex thanksgiving.[2]

---

1. Peter T. O'Brien, *Introductory Thanksgivings in the Letters of Paul* (NovTSup 49; Leiden: Brill, 1977), 6-15.
2. See O'Brien, 8-9. Some commentators include all of vv. 3-23 in the "thanksgiving" section (e.g., Lincoln, 589).

1. *we . . . thank* (v. 3) (the expression of thanks)
   2. *God, the Father of our Lord Jesus Christ* (v. 3) (the one to whom thanks are offered)
   3. *always . . . when we pray* (v. 3) (a verbal clause expressing the frequency of the thanks)
   4. *for you* (v. 3) (a phrase identifying the object of the thanks)
   5. *praying* (v. 3) (a temporal participle)
   6. *because we have heard* (v. 4) (a participle expressing the basis for the thanks)
      about your faith . . . love . . . hope (vv. 4b-5a) (what Paul has heard that motivates his giving thanks)
         which you . . . heard in the . . . gospel (v. 5b) (the source of the Colossians' faith, hope, and love)
            that has come to you. . . .
               bearing fruit and growing throughout the whole world . . .
               since the day you heard it . . . from Epaphras (vv. 6-8)
   we have not stopped praying for you (v. 9a)
   7. *to fill you with the knowledge of his will* (v. 9b) (purpose of the thanksgiving [usually with *hina*])
      so that you may live a life worthy of the Lord (v. 10a)
      bearing fruit in every good work, *growing* (v. 10b)
      being strengthened (v. 11a)
      giving joyful thanks to the Father (v. 12a)
      who has qualified you . . . (v. 12b)
      he has rescued us . . . into the kingdom of the Son he loves (v. 13),
         in whom we have redemption (v. 14)

This elaborate thanksgiving section is framed by the verb "give thanks" *(eucharisteō)* in vv. 3 *(thank)* and 12 *(giving . . . thanks)*. As the outline reveals, Paul considerably elaborates even this "complex" thanksgiving form. Particularly striking are (1) the digression about the Colossians' reception of the gospel and its parallel in the wider world (vv. 6-8); (2) Paul's concern about the Colossians' "knowledge" (v. 6: *heard . . . and truly understood*; v. 7: *learned*; v. 9: *knowledge of his will through all wisdom and understanding*; v. 10: *growing in the knowledge of God*); and (3) the concluding section about the Father's redeeming work in the Son (vv. 12-14). Indeed, so unusual is this final section that a number of interpreters think that it should be separated from the thanksgiving section. Some feel that "giving thanks" in v. 12 marks the conclusion of the thanksgiving, with the description of God's work through his Son (v. 13) introducing a new section.[3] The most popular alternative, however, is that the reference to thanksgiving in v. 12 — perhaps construed as an imperative: "give thanks" — introduces a new section, with vv. 12-14, then, functioning, with vv. 21-23, as a frame around the hymn to Christ in vv. 15-20.[4] But, while there is something to this suggestion, we should probably keep vv. 12-14 with vv. 3-11 (see below on v. 12). All three of the additions we have identified serve Paul's overall purpose in the letter. The false teaching will hold no attraction for the Colossians if they truly come to know and understand that they have already received the "true word of God" and that they have been transferred by God's own power into the new realm of God's own Son.

3 The first-person plural form of the verb *thank* again raises the question of authorship. Since Timothy is specifically included in the pre-script (v. 1), it is natural to think that the thanksgiving comes from both Paul and Timothy. To be sure, as we noted in our comments on v. 1, Paul clearly emerges as the basic writer of this letter; and some therefore argue that the first-person plural verbal form includes Paul alone.[5] But the proximity of the thanksgiving to v. 1 makes it more likely that, though written by Paul specifically, the thanksgiving, along with the reiterated prayer expression in v. 9, is intended to include Timothy.[6] Paul is the author, but he includes Timothy here as a courtesy to his fellow worker.

Paul's thanks for the Colossians are expressed to *God, the Father of our Lord Jesus Christ.*[7] This mode of address is unusual. Paul usually expresses his thanks to both God and Jesus Christ, and he normally portrays God as the Father of believers rather than as the Father of Jesus Christ. Probably not too much should be made of this, since Paul's letters reveal considerable variety in the juxtaposition of God, Father, and

---

3. E.g., John Callow, *A Semantic and Structural Analysis of Colossians* (2d ed.; Dallas: SIL International, 2002), 13-14.

4. See, e.g., Michael Dübbers, *Christologie und Existenz im Kolosserbrief: Exegetische und semantische Untersuchungen zur Intention des Kolosserbriefes* (WUNT 2.191; Tübingen: Mohr Siebeck, 2005), 130-32, who (rightly) notes the importance of "thanksgiving" language in Colossians; also Hübner, 51; R. Martin, 53; Ellis, "Colossians 1:12-20," in *Interpreting the New Testament* (Wheaton, Ill.: Crossway, 2006), 418-19.

5. E.g., Lohse, 14, who cites Rom. 1:5 and 1 Thess. 3:1.

6. E.g., O'Brien, 9; Bruce, 41; Wilson, 81. Lohse's parallel texts (see previous note) are not all that germane. Romans includes Paul alone in the prescript, while 1 Thess. 3:1 is far removed from the plurality of authors identified in 1:1.

7. We are assuming that the text printed in NA[27] and translated in most modern English versions is correct. A number of manuscripts insert a καί ("and") between *God* and *Father* (hence NKJV: "We give thanks to the God and Father of our Lord Jesus Christ"), but this reading is almost surely an assimilation to Paul's usual way of speaking (see, e.g., Lightfoot, 133).

Christ.[8] Nevertheless, the fact that Paul focuses (unusually) on the Father alone also in his grace and peace wish (v. 2) suggests that his mode of address is deliberate. Perhaps, in a letter that elevates Christ, Paul wants at the outset to anchor the person of Christ firmly to God the Father.[9] As supreme as Christ is in the work of both creation and redemption, his identity and his work cannot be understood apart from his relationship to God his Father. Indeed, Paul will suggest in a variety of ways in this letter that Christ is himself in some sense God.[10] As a kind of *inclusio* in this section, Paul sounds a similar note in vv. 12-14, attributing the work of rescue and redemption to the Father, who works in and through the Son.

Most English versions, like the TNIV, attach the adverb *always* to the main verb, *thank* (see also NIV; ESV; NAB; RSV; NRSV; NLT; TEV) rather than to the subordinate verb *praying* (though see KJV; NKJV; NASB; NJB). This is probably correct, since it reflects the usual pattern in Paul's thanksgivings,[11] but it makes little difference to the meaning. The TNIV, along with most of the English versions, gives the Greek participle *proseuchomenoi* a temporal sense: *when we pray for you*. This makes explicit what is in any case clear enough in Paul's other expressions of "continual" thanksgiving for his readers: Paul prays frequently and regularly for his readers and always gives thanks for them when he does so. This dedication to prayer is especially remarkable when it involves Christians whom Paul has neither evangelized nor, apparently, even visited.

8. The closest parallels, using, however, the language of "blessing" (εὐλογητός) rather than thanksgiving, are 2 Cor. 1:3 and Eph. 1:3: "Blessed be the God and Father of our Lord Jesus Christ." Paul calls God the Father of Jesus elsewhere in Rom. 15:6; 2 Cor. 11:31; and see also Eph. 1:17: "God of our Lord Jesus Christ, the glorious Father." Paul's other formulations are: "God our Father and the Lord Jesus Christ" (Rom. 1:7; 1 Cor. 1:3; 2 Cor. 1:2; Gal. 1:3; Eph. 1:2; Phil. 1:2; 2 Thess. 1:1; Phlm. 3); "God the Father and [Christ]" (Gal. 1:1; Eph. 6:23; 1 Thess. 1:1; 2 Thess. 1:2; 1 Tim. 1:2; 2 Tim. 1:2; Titus 1:4); "one God, the Father . . . and the Lord . . ." (1 Cor. 8:6); "one God and Father of all" (Eph. 4:6); "our Lord Jesus Christ . . . and God our Father" (2 Thess. 2:16); "our God and Father and our Lord Jesus" (1 Thess. 3:11).

9. Wright, similarly, suggests that the language is an important reminder of the new Christian understanding of God (50). Dunn, 55-56, suggests that Paul wants to make clear that his strong christological affirmations in no manner attack traditional Jewish monotheism.

10. See the section on the Christology of Colossians in the Introduction, 61-63.

11. Lightfoot, 133; Moule, 49; Harris, 15; for the contrary view, Wright, 50. Other thanksgivings that use πάντοτε (as does Col. 1:3) where it clearly modifies εὐχαριστέω are 1 Cor. 1:4; 1 Thess. 1:2; 2 Thess. 1:3; with a different construction, see also Eph. 1:16. Philemon 4 is ambiguous, but Phil. 1:3-4 and 2 Tim. 1:3, though using a different construction, attach πάντοτε to the "pray" rather than to "give thanks." Though it is not an opening thanksgiving, Eph. 5:20, "always giving thanks" (εὐχαριστοῦντες πάντοτε), is also significant. Paul exhibits no clear pattern in his sequencing of πάντοτε and the verb it modifies.

4 Although expressed in Greek as a simple participle, the "hearing" of v. 4 is rightly taken by all the English translations in a causal sense: *because we have heard*. Verses 4-5 explain why Paul gives thanks for the Colossians: they are exhibiting the three cardinal Christian virtues of faith, love, and hope. Faith, as the fundamental means by which God's grace in Christ is appropriated, is naturally put first. The English phrase *faith in Christ Jesus* most naturally suggests that Christ Jesus is the object of the Colossians' faith. It is objected to this interpretation, however, that the Greek (the noun *pistis*," faith," followed by the preposition *en*) means not that Christ Jesus was the object of the Colossians' faith but that he was "the sphere in which 'faith' lives and acts."[12] There is some point to this objection. Yet it can be argued that Paul uses this same phrase, and ones similar to it, to indicate the general idea of a "faith that has Jesus Christ as its ultimate reference point."[13]

Since, for Paul, genuine Christian faith is ever active in works of love (Gal. 5:6), it is quite natural that Paul should next mention the love that the Colossian Christians are showing *for all his people*. His (e.g., Christ's) *people* translates Greek *hagioi*, traditionally rendered "saints" (and so many other English versions). However, as we noted in commenting on v. 2, the biblical-theological focus of this word is on the fact of

---

12. Quoting O'Brien, 11; see also, e.g., Lightfoot, 133; Bruce, 41; Harris, 16; Lohse, 16; Hübner, 45; Lincoln, 590. The grammatical basis for this view is the contention that Paul rarely, if ever, confuses the prepositions εἰς and ἐν (e.g., Zerwick, *Biblical Greek*, §35; Turner, *Syntax*, 254-57). Therefore, had he wanted to indicate Christ as the object of faith, he would have used εἰς (see Col. 2:5) or perhaps πρός (1 Thess. 1:8; Phlm. 5).

13. The occurrences are all debated, but the following verses probably use ἐν with Christ to denote this idea: Eph. 1:15; 1 Tim. 3:13; 2 Tim. 3:15. Some think that Gal. 3:26 should also be included in this list; see NIV: "You are all sons of God through faith in Christ Jesus." But most commentators probably rightly think that "in Christ Jesus" is an independent adverbial clause; as in TNIV: "in Christ Jesus you are all children of God through faith." While not exactly comparable, 1 Tim. 1:14 and 2 Tim. 1:13 are also probably relevant: "faith and love in Christ Jesus." If "in his blood" in Rom. 3:25 goes with "faith," we would have another parallel construction; but "in his blood" probably modifies "sacrifice of atonement." Note also 1 Cor. 2:5: "faith . . . not *in* (ἐν) human wisdom but *in* (ἐν) God's power." Also relevant might be Paul's use of the dative case after the verb πιστεύω, since the pure dative and ἐν + dative overlap considerably in NT Greek (Gal. 3:6; 2 Thess. 2:12; 2 Tim. 1:12; Titus 3:8). Part of the problem in this debate is the language of Christ as the "object" of faith. Paul never uses Christ, or God, as the "object" of the verb πιστεύω (i.e., as an accusative after the verb), but other, more indirect constructions (dative case [Rom. 4:3; Gal. 3:6; 2 Tim. 1:12]; εἰς [Rom. 10:14; Gal. 2:16]; ἐπί [Rom. 4:5, 24; 9:33; 10:11; 1 Tim. 1:16]; genitive case [Rom. 10:14]). These constructions are probably roughly equivalent to πίστις ἐν Χριστῷ Ἰησοῦ here. Dunn, noting that the clearest evidence for ἐν having an objective sense after "faith" comes in letters whose Pauline authorship is disputed, finds the locution here to be an indication that Paul did not write it. But the evidence on this point is both too sparse and too debated for any such conclusion.

belonging to God's people and not on any inherent moral qualities (as the English word "saint" is liable to mean). In speaking of *all his people*, Paul of course means those fellow Christians with whom the Colossians have relationships: members of churches in the Lycus valley and other Christians who might be traveling through the city. The focus is not extensive — every single Christian everywhere — but intensive — every Christian that comes across their path.

5   The TNIV (and NIV before it) specify that it is *the faith and love* of v. 4 that rest on the hope of v. 5: *the faith and love that spring from the hope.* . . . This is an interpretation of the Greek, since v. 5 begins generally with the prepositional phrase "because of the hope," with no specific connection to anything before it (see, e.g., ESV). Some commentators therefore think that the phrase modifies the main verb of the previous sentence, "give thanks" — "we give thanks because of the hope"[14] — or "love" only — "your love is rooted in your hope" — or has only a general relationship to vv. 3-4.[15] But most commentators follow the TNIV interpretation, and this is the most likely way to connect v. 5 with what comes before it (see also NET; NLT; REB; TEV).[16] While Paul often juxtaposes faith, love, and hope, only here does he make hope the basis for love and faith (although Titus 1:1-2 probably presents the "hope for eternal life" as the basis for "faith" and "knowledge"). Paul often uses "hope" to refer to the attitude of hope (e.g., Rom. 4:18; 5:5; 2 Cor. 3:12). Here, however, it pretty clearly denotes that which Christians hope for: "the totality of blessing that awaits the Christian in the life to come"[17] (as also in, e.g., Titus 1:2, where the hope consists in eternal life, and 1 Pet. 1:4, where it is virtually identified with the "inheritance"). Faced with teaching that led them to wonder whether Christ could supply all their spiritual needs, the Colossians need to be reminded that their present experience of faith and love rests on the solid foundation of what God has committed to do for them in the future.

Paul accentuates this point by asserting that this hope is *stored up for you in heaven*. While not yet something the Colossians have experienced, their ultimate salvation already exists, "reserved"[18] for them in heaven, the spiritual realm in which God "dwells."[19] Note the close parallel in

14. Abbott, 196; Masson, 91.
15. Lohse, 17.
16. E.g., Lightfoot, 134; Moule, 49; Harris, 17; Pokorný, 40; Wolter, 52.
17. BDAG, s.v. ἀπόκειμαι. See also Harris, 17, along with most commentaries.
18. The verb is ἀπόκειμαι, used, e.g., of a coin "put away" for safekeeping (Luke 19:20); see also 2 Tim. 4:8, with reference to the "crown of righteousness"; Heb. 9:27.
19. E.g., *heaven*. The Greek word is plural (οὐρανοῖς), as in 1:16 and 1:20, although it is singular in 1:23 and 4:1 (following the general Pauline pattern, with eleven singular and ten plural). Paul usually uses the plural form in a singular sense (following Heb.

1 Peter 1:4-5, which speaks of an inheritance "kept in heaven for you" and a salvation "ready to be revealed in the last time." Some critics suggest that the "spatial" conception that occurs here is somewhat removed from Paul's typical temporal focus.[20] But, in fact, Paul's eschatology, rooted in Jewish apocalyptic conceptions, combines the spatial and the temporal: that which will be "revealed" even now exists in the transcendent realm of God's person and purposes. Colossians combines the spatial and the temporal in just this way: Christians are even now "hidden with Christ," who is at the right hand of the Father (spatial), and when he appears, they will appear with him (temporal) (Col. 3:1-4).

Introducing a theme that will be important in the letter, Paul now reminds the Colossians that they first heard about the hope stored up in heaven for them through the *true word of the gospel*. Even as "thanksgiving" frames vv. 3-14, so this focus on the hope that the proclamation of the gospel has brought to the Colossians frames the larger section vv. 3-23 (see v. 23: *the hope held out in the gospel*; v. 23: *the gospel that you heard*). TNIV's *have already heard* translates a verb that could also be rendered "hear before" (e.g., ESV), leading to the question, "before what?" Moule thinks that Paul might be reminding his readers that they heard the gospel before the false teaching came along,[21] but it is more likely that he means simply that the Colossians have heard the gospel before he writes this letter to them.[22] Nevertheless, as Schweizer suggests, comparing 1 John 1:1; 2:17, 24; 3:11 (also written to counter false teachers), Paul may also want to stress the foundational nature of the gospel message.[23]

Paul uses three words to describe this message — "word," "truth," and "gospel" — and their relationship to each other is uncertain (they are linked in the Greek via the genitive case). The TNIV translation, *the true word of the gospel*, takes "truth" as an adjectival modifier of "word" (attributive genitive), and probably intends "gospel" to be taken in apposition to this phrase: "the true word that is the gospel."[24] Another option is to connect "truth" to "gospel" in a similar manner; see REB's "the message of the true gospel."[25] But, considering the importance of the concept

---

שָׁמַיִם [cf. BDF §141(1)]). No difference in meaning between the singular form and the plural can be detected in Paul (cf. 2 Cor. 5:1 and 5:2; Eph. 6:9; and Col. 4:1) (contra Dunn, who suggests that the plural here might reflect Jewish notions of tiers in heaven [59-60]).

20. E.g., Lohse, 17-18; Lindemann, 18; Wolter, 52-53.
21. Moule, 50.
22. BDAG.
23. Schweizer, 34-35.
24. So also, e.g., Moule, 50; Harris, 18; Turner, *Syntax*, 213.
25. The REB, presumably, takes ἀληθείας as an attributed genitive (to use Wallace's category; *Greek Grammar*, 89-91). Dunn compares Gal. 2:5 and 14, "the truth of the gos-

"truth" in both the Old Testament and the New Testament, it might be better to give independent significance to the word: "the message that is (or contains, or reveals) the truth, the message, that is, of the gospel" (cf. esp. Eph. 1:13; cf. also 2 Cor. 6:7; 2 Tim. 2:15).[26] In the Old Testament, "truth" often involves the ideas of reliability and authenticity, and this meaning carries over to the New Testament. A "word of truth," then, is a word, or message, that can be relied upon. See, for example, Ps. 119:43, where the psalmist pleads with God to retain his "word of truth" in a context in which he reaffirms hope in God's judgments.[27] The gospel, then, Paul implies, is to be contrasted with the false teaching, which cannot offer a reliable basis for hope.

6   Paul now elaborates on the Colossians' experience of the gospel, reflecting further on the circumstances in which they first heard it (vv. 7-8) and on the power to transform people that it has revealed not only among the Colossians but also in "the whole world" (v. 6). This last point is the center of vv. 3-8.[28]

The Greek syntax of v. 6 is awkward, but it seems that Paul wants to make two basic comparisons between the Colossians' experience and the experience of Christians elsewhere in the Mediterranean basin: (1) the gospel has come to the Colossians[29] just as it has to other people; and (2) the gospel is transforming people and communities in Colossae just as it has in other parts of the world.[30] Faced with false teachers who appar-

---

pel," arguing that Paul may intend here in Colossians, as he does in Galatians, a contrast with a narrowly exclusive, Jewish gospel (61). But the connection is tenuous.

26. On this interpretation, ἀληθείας would be an epexegetic, or perhaps objective, genitive; εὐαγγελίου would be epexegetic in relationship to λόγῳ (less probably, epexegetic in relationship to truth [mentioned by Turner, Syntax, 213]).

27. See O'Brien, 12.

28. As Lamarche points out, vv. 3-8 display a concentric structure, with reports about the Colossians' love (and faith) as the outer "ring" (vv. 4, 8), references to their hearing the gospel forming the next ring (vv. 5b, 6b), and the power of the gospel to stimulate growth at the core of the paragraph (v. 6a) (Paul Lamarche, "Structure de l'épître aux Colossiens," Bib 56 [1975], 453-54).

29. That has come to you; Gk. τοῦ παρόντος εἰς ὑμᾶς. The combination of the verb πάρειμι plus the preposition εἰς signifies movement (εἰς) followed by rest (πάρειμι), "arrival at" (see BDAG; Josephus, Antiquities 1.285, 337): "[the gospel] did not come and go away, but . . . remained and was there" (Chrysostom, "Homilies on Colossians" [NPNF 13.259, quoted from ACCS 9.3]) (O'Brien, 12-13).

30. The syntactical awkwardness is created by the two occurrences of καθώς, "just as," in the verse. Paul probably intended initially to compare simply the arrival of the gospel in Colossae with its propagation in "all the world": "the gospel has come to you, just as it has to the rest of the world" (the first καθώς). But he then decided to speak not simply of the gospel's arrival but of its power (ἐστὶν καρποφορούμενον καὶ αὐξανόμενον — a compound periphrastic present). The second καθώς is therefore introduced to make this

ently encouraged Christians to look beyond the gospel for ultimate spiritual fulfillment, Paul stresses the inherent power of the gospel itself.

The language *bearing fruit and growing* is reminiscent of the Genesis creation story, where God commands human beings to "be fruitful and increase in number" (Gen. 1:28; see also 1:22). After the Flood the mandate is reiterated (Gen. 8:17; 9:1, 7), and the same language is later used in God's promises to Abraham and the patriarchs that he would "increase" their number and "multiply" their seed (e.g., Gen. 17:20; 28:3; 35:11). The nation Israel attains this blessing in Egypt (Gen. 48:4; Exod. 1:7) but then, of course, suffers judgment and dispersal. So the formula appears again in God's promises to regather his people after the exile (Jer. 3:16; 23:3). Paul may, then, be deliberately echoing a biblical-theological motif according to which God's original mandate to humans finds preliminary fulfillment in the nation Israel but ultimate fulfillment in the worldwide transformation of people into the image of God by means of their incorporation into Christ, *the* "image of God." Colossians 3:10 echoes the same idea, referring to the "new self" (the new people of God in Christ) as "renewed in knowledge in the image of its Creator" (see also v. 10 and cf. 1:15).[31] To be sure, the verb "bear fruit" does not occur in the Old Testament formula, but Paul may have substituted this verb (and placed it first) because it conveys better than "multiply" the results of the gospel in the lives of believers.[32]

Paul's claim that the gospel is exerting this power *throughout the*

---

comparison: "the gospel is bearing fruit and growing in all the world, just as it is also among you." See, essentially, Lightfoot, 135, for this interpretation, followed by most commentaries. Romans 3:8 and 1 Thess. 4:1 furnish partial analogies to this double καθώς construction.

31. See esp. C. Beetham, "Echoes of Scripture in the Letter to the Colossians" (Ph.D. diss., Wheaton, 2005), 51-74; G. K. Beale, *The Temple and the Church's Mission: A Biblical Theology of the Dwelling Place of God* (NSBT 17; Downers Grove, Ill.: InterVarsity, 2004), 263-67; Wright, 53-54. While the allusion to this OT motif is probable, it must be noted that the linguistic match is not exact. In the LXX of Gen. 1:28, the verbs αὐξάνω and πληθύνω are combined; and this same formula occurs also in Gen. 1:22; 8:17; 9:1, 7; 17:20; 28:3; 35:11; 47:27; 48:4; Exod. 1:7; Jer. 3:16; 22:3. Paul, on the other hand, uses the combination αὐξάνω and καρποφορέω (the latter verb occurs only in Hab. 3:17; Odes Sol. 4:17; Wis. 10:7 in the LXX, all with a literal reference; nor does the LXX elsewhere ever translate the Hebrew verb rendered by καρποφορέω in Hab. 3:17 [פָּרָה] with πληθύνω). For these reasons, Ernst (158), e.g., doubts that an allusion to Gen. 1 is present.

32. It is also possible that Paul's wording is influenced by the teaching of Jesus: the verb καρποφορέω is not common in the NT (eight occurrences), and four of these references occur in the gospel accounts of the Parable of the Sower (Matt. 13:23; Mark 4:20, 28; Luke 8:15; cf. Bruce, 42; O'Brien, 23). The verb is in the middle voice here in v. 6 but is in the active voice in the parallel formula in v. 10. Some scholars think that the middle may suggest the "intrinsic potency of the gospel" (Harris, 19; Lightfoot, 135), but others doubt that any difference in meaning can be detected (e.g., Turner, *Syntax*, 55; Moule, 50; Lohse, 20).

whole world points to a theme that is important in the opening part of the letter: the universality of the gospel. Especially striking, and closest in both form and meaning to this text, is Colossians 1:23, where Paul claims that the gospel "has been proclaimed to *every* creature [or "in the whole creation"; see the notes on the verse] under heaven" (see also the celebration of Christ's universal rule in vv. 15-20, and Paul's desire to "present *everyone* fully mature in Christ" [1:28]). It is possible that Paul uses "world" to mean his own "world" of the Roman Empire,[33] but the expression (especially in light of v. 23) is more likely to be simply a "rhetorical exaggeration."[34] The point is that the gospel is exerting its power widely, in many different places, and, by doing so, attests to its validity. The widespread experience of the gospel is testimony to its truthfulness over against the claims of the false teachers, who are propagating a local heresy.[35]

Another tactic Paul uses to counter the false teaching is to highlight the reality of the Colossian Christians' past experience with the gospel. Not only has it exerted transforming power among them,[36] but it has been doing so *since the day you heard it and truly understood God's grace*. The Colossians have true and reliable knowledge about God and his purpose for them and for the world in Christ. Paul's summary of this gospel message with the word *grace* reveals just how central this concept is to Paul's understanding of the gospel (see also Rom. 5:2). Paul again emphasizes the "truth" of this gospel of grace (cf. v. 5), and again it is not entirely clear how we should attach the word to the larger clause. The TNIV interprets the relevant phrase (Gk. *en alētheia*) in an adverbial sense (*truly*; cf. also NRSV), and this seems to be the most likely option here. Paul wants to remind them that they have *truly* — really, authentically, reliably — come to understand the gospel of grace. It is worth noting that Paul in this verse seeks to ground the Colossians spiritually by appealing both to the truth of the gospel and to its life-changing power. The gospel is authenticated not by its truth only nor by its power in people's lives only but by both working in tandem.

7-8 Paul turns from message to messenger.[37] Not only is the gos-

---

33. E.g., Schweizer, 35.

34. BDAG; similar expressions with similar intention are found in Rom. 1:8; 10:18; 1 Pet. 5:9.

35. Lightfoot, 134-35; Abbott, 197.

36. The Greek is ἐν ὑμῖν, which could mean "in each one of you," but almost certainly here means "among you" (as almost all the translations interpret it).

37. The Greek text connects v. 7 with the preceding via yet another καθώς ("just as"; see ESV; NASB). The word probably serves very generally to connect the commendation of Epaphras with the discussion of the gospel's arrival and power in Colossae. Nothing is lost by its omission in translation.

pel they have heard an authentic and life-transforming reality, but it has also been brought to them by one who is a *dear fellow servant* and a *faithful minister of Christ on our behalf*. Epaphras is mentioned only in Colossians and in Philemon (v. 23) in the New Testament.[38] Little is known about him, though we can infer that he was a native of Colossae and that he was perhaps converted by Paul himself during the apostle's ministry in Ephesus. The mention of a co-worker at this point in a Pauline epistle is unusual, and the strength of Paul's endorsement of him is also striking (note also 4:12-13). Perhaps Epaphras's reliability and commitment to the Colossians was being questioned by them and/or challenged by the false teachers.[39] On the other hand, the peculiar circumstances of Paul's letter to the Colossians may better explain this emphasis: writing to Christians he has never visited demands that Paul go out of his way to accredit his representative among them.[40] Paul speaks to the Colossians of Epaphras's relationship to himself, and of his role as emissary from Colossae to himself.

Calling Epaphras a *fellow servant* in relationship to himself highlights Epaphras's significance in Paul's eyes: he applies *fellow servant* (Gk. *syndoulos*) to a co-worker only once else (Tychicus in 4:7 of this letter), and he rarely uses even the simple "slave" (Gk. *doulos*) to refer to co-workers (again in 4:12 with reference to Epaphras; cf. also 2 Cor. 4:5; Phil. 1:1). Paul uses "slave" language to connote the Christian's total dependence upon and dedication to the Lord Jesus.[41] Epaphras exhibits such dedication and is, moreover, *dear* (or *beloved*; Gk. *agapētos*) to Paul also.

Shifting language, Paul calls Epaphras a *faithful minister of Christ* in relationship to the Colossians. *Minister* translates the Greek *diakonos*,

---

38. While the name Epaphras originated as a shortened form of Epaphroditus (BDF §125[1]), "Epaphras" became an independent name in its own right. It is therefore very unlikely that the Colossian Epaphras is the same as the emissary to Philippi, Epaphroditus (Phil. 2:25; 4:18) (*NewDocs* 4.22-23; Harris, 21).

39. See esp. Wall, 42-43, who goes so far as to claim that "I am convinced that Epaphras's relationship with the Colossian church is a key to unlocking the reason Paul wrote Colossians" (p. 43). Wall finds vv. 7-8 to be the center of a chiastic structure and thus the most important element in these verses. Such a conclusion only raises questions about too strict an insistence on chiastic structures and where the emphatic element within such a structure must occur. Commentators who question the Pauline authorship of Colossians sometimes suggest that a stress on Paul's emissaries is a natural result of the need to accredit these workers in a post-Pauline environment (e.g., MacDonald, 42-45). But (1) Paul emphasizes ministry associates in the acknowledged "authentic" Paulines (see esp. Phil. 2:19-24); and (2) there is good reason for Paul's concern about Epaphras here (see above).

40. See O'Brien, 15.

41. See esp. Murray J. Harris, *Slave of Christ: A New Testament Metaphor for Total Devotion to Christ* (NSBT 8; Downers Grove, Ill.: InterVarsity, 1999).

"servant" (NASB; NLT; NJB). While the New Testament in general makes clear that all Christians are "servants" or "ministers" in the service of God to one another (e.g., 1 Pet. 4:10-11), Paul confines the language of "servant" to specific forms of ministry — thus "minister" is probably a good rendering.[42] All these "ministers" belong to and are ultimately in the service of God, or Christ, as the *of Christ* in our text makes clear. But on whose behalf is Epaphras's ministry carried out? A textual variant makes the answer to this question difficult, a problem to which recent translations bear witness: TNIV, *on our behalf* (also NIV; RSV; NASB; NET; NJB; REB); ESV, "on your behalf" (also NRSV; NLT; HCSB; NAB). Accepting the latter would mean that Paul is simply highlighting Epaphras's faithful ministry to the Colossians; accepting the former would suggest that Paul adds the nuance that this ministry (implicitly to the Colossians) is ultimately on Paul's own behalf. Since Paul is clearly at pains in this context to stress Epaphras's reliability as a conduit for Paul's gospel, we think the TNIV rendering is probably slightly preferable.[43] Epaphras, both when he originally brought the gospel to Colossae and now as he seeks to counteract the influence of the false teachers, is acting on Paul's own behalf. This clause would then reinforce the first clause in the verse, a relationship neatly conveyed in the NET Bible: "You learned the gospel from Epaphras, our dear fellow slave — a faithful minister of Christ on our behalf. . . ."

If v. 7 is primarily about Epaphras's faithfulness as a minister to the Colossians on behalf of Paul, v. 8 is about his reliability as a messenger to Paul on behalf of the Colossians. For Epaphras has communicated to Paul that the Colossians are continuing to manifest a key quality of Christian existence: love (cf. v. 4).[44] In adding that this love is *in the Spirit*, Paul

42. He uses διάκονος to refer to Christ (Rom. 15:8; Gal. 2:17), to himself (Col. 1:23, 25; Eph. 3:7), to himself and (implicitly) others of his stature (1 Cor. 3:5; 2 Cor. 3:6; 6:4; 11:23), to Tychicus (Eph. 6:21; Col. 4:7), to Timothy (1 Tim. 4:6), to "deacons" in the churches (Rom. 16:1 [probably]; Phil. 1:1; 1 Tim. 3:8, 12), and to government officials (Rom. 13:4). On the technical sense of διάκονος in Paul, see E. E. Ellis, "Paul and His Co-Workers," *NTS* 17 (1970-71), 441-43.

43. The variation in the Greek involves one vowel only — ὑμῶν ("your") vs. ἡμῶν ("our") — and is, accordingly, one of the most common textual variations in the NT. External evidence in favor of each reading is pretty evenly divided, with perhaps the combination of the proto-Alexandrian tradition (א and B) and the western (D) giving a slight advantage to ἡμῶν (e.g., Lightfoot, 136; Abbott, 200; Harris, 22; and most commentaries). "Our" is probably also the more difficult reading, since mention of ministry would naturally suggest a direct reference to the ones on behalf of whom the ministry is carried out. The NA and UBS committees, on the other hand, favor ὑμῶν because it has broader external support and may have been changed under the influence of ἡμῶν earlier in the verse and ἡμῖν in v. 8 (Metzger, *Textual Commentary*, 552-53; Bruce, 40).

44. In light of the context, Paul could mean that Epaphras's love is directed toward

91

probably intends to suggest that it is the Holy Spirit who stimulates this love; see NLT: "the great love for others that the Holy Spirit has given you."[45]

9 As we noted above, Paul regularly moves from thanksgiving to petition in these opening sections of his letters. Thus, after giving thanks for the Colossians' reaction to the proclamation of the gospel in their midst (vv. 3-8), Paul now prays that they might continue on the course they have begun. In the Greek text, vv. 9-14 is a single complex sentence that may usefully be broken down into three main parts. There is (1) Paul's assertion of regular prayer on behalf of the Colossians along with the basic content of that prayer: knowledge of God's will and the manifestation of that knowledge in a lifestyle pleasing to God (vv. 9-10a); (2) a further description of what this lifestyle looks like, employing (in the Greek) four participles: "bearing fruit," "growing," "being empowered," and "giving thanks" (vv. 10b-12a); and (3) a rehearsal of the deliverance from sin provided to the readers by God the Father through the Son (vv. 12b-14). A noteworthy feature of this prayer are the number of parallels with the thanksgiving section:

"since the day you heard"	v. 6	"since the day we heard"	v. 9
"thank"	v. 3	"giving . . . thanks"	v. 12
"always"	v. 3	"not stopped"	v. 9
"when we pray for you"	v. 3	"praying for you"[46]	v. 9
"understood"	v. 6	"knowledge"[47]	v. 9, v. 10
"bearing fruit and growing"	v. 6	"bearing fruit . . . growing"	v. 10

The parallels are numerous enough to suggest that Paul is deliberately echoing the language of the thanksgiving in his petition. The effect is to subtly remind the Colossians again that they must continue on the course they have already begun.

Paul's petition for the Colossians proceeds directly from his thanksgiving for them, as the connecting phrase *for this reason* makes

---

himself (Gordon D. Fee, *God's Empowering Presence: The Holy Spirit in the Letters of Paul* [Peabody: Hendrickson, 1994], 639). But, in light of v. 4, he probably means that Epaphras loves other Christians in general.

45. The ἐν ("in") is, in this case, instrumental; Harris, 23, cites Rom. 15:30, where the genitive τοῦ πνεύματος is almost certainly subjective: "love stimulated by the Spirit" (cf. also Fee, *God's Empowering Presence*, 639). All English versions capitalize *Spirit*, reflecting the majority view among commentators, that the reference is to the Holy Spirit (though cf. Moule, 52, for a contrary view).

46. The Greek is slightly different, with the preposition περί in v. 3 and ὑπέρ in v. 9.

47. The Greek root is the same: ἐπιγινώσκω in v. 6; ἐπίγνωσις in v. 9.

clear.[48] Especially in the face of the threat posed by the false teachers, the Colossians' good start and genuine progress should lead not to complacency but to renewed effort.[49] Yet it is not simply the threat of false teaching that stimulates Paul's prayer for them, for he has been regularly praying for the Colossians ever since he first heard about their conversion through the ministry of Epaphras. Paul uses two verbs to indicate his prayer: "praying" (proseuchomenoi) and "asking" (aitoumenoi). (For stylistic reasons — to break up an otherwise intolerably long sentence — the TNIV has put the verbs in separate sentences.) They form a hendiadys, with "asking" perhaps added to enforce the idea of petition in the otherwise general "praying."[50]

What[51] Paul prays for is that the Colossians "might be filled with the knowledge of his [God's] will." The verb (plērōthēte) is a "divine passive," with God as the implied agent: "filled by God." Several English translations, including the TNIV, express this idea by explicitly adding a reference to God and turning the verb into an active: we continually ask God to fill you (cf. also NIV; NLT; NET; REB). The language of "fulfill" or "fullness" occurs at some crucial junctures in Colossians (1:19; 2:9-10), leading some interpreters to suggest that the language may have played a role in the false teaching. We think this is probably the case, although it must be noted that Paul does use this verb in similar contexts elsewhere (Rom. 15:13; Eph. 3:19; Phil. 2:2; 4:19; 2 Thess. 1:11; 2 Tim. 1:4). Paul has given thanks that the Colossians have truly understood (epegnōte) God's grace; now he correspondingly prays that they may be filled with the knowledge (epignōsin) of his will. What Paul has in mind is not some particular or special direction for one's life (as we often use the phrase "God's will"), but a deep and abiding understanding of the revelation of Christ and all that he means for the universe (vv. 15-20) and for the Colossians (vv. 21-23).[52]

48. The τοῦτο in the phrase διὰ τοῦτο thus almost certainly refers to the whole of vv. 3-8 (Harris, 29).
49. See David Pao, Thanksgiving: An Investigation of a Pauline Theme (NSBT 13; Downers Grove, Ill.: InterVarsity, 2002), 107.
50. See also the only other place in the NT where both verbs are used together, Mark 11:24, where most English translations treat the construction as a hendiadys: "ask in prayer" (e.g., ESV; TNIV; NAB). While αἰτέω is quite common in the Gospels as a way of indicating prayer, this usage is rare in Paul (only here and in Eph. 3:13, 20). The middle form of αἰτούμενοι is probably not to be distinguished from the active in meaning (BDAG; see also Jas. 4:2-3, where little difference between active and middle can be discerned).
51. The Greek conjunction ἵνα that Paul here uses to introduce the prayer generally indicates the content of the prayer rather than the purpose of the prayer (BDAG; they point out that the ἵνα clause functions in a way similar to an infinitive construction).
52. Paul's use of the compound ἐπίγνωσις in preference to the simple noun γνῶσις is taken by some commentators as connoting a special sense of "knowledge": either, e.g., a

Paul makes clear just what kind of *knowledge* he is talking about by adding the phrase *through all the wisdom and understanding that the Spirit gives*. Indeed, the TNIV's *through* suggests that the phrase describes the means by which God will fill the Colossians with knowledge of his will. But it is better to view the phrase as qualifying *knowledge* by indicating two other qualities that are to accompany it.[53] *Wisdom (sophia)* and *understanding (synesis)* are two of the three chief "intellectual" virtues, according to Aristotle (the third is *phronēsis*, "prudence"; cf. *Nicomachean Ethics* 1.13); and they are frequently paired in the Greek Old Testament and in Judaism. Some sense of the meaning of the pairing arises from the contexts in which it is used. These virtues are essential to the godly leader (e.g., Moses [Exod. 31:3; 35:31]; Solomon [1 Chron. 22:12; 2 Chron. 1:10, 11, 12]; the "shoot from the stump of Jesse" [Isa. 11:2]) and are given to those who fear the Lord (Prov. 1:7; 2:2, 3, 6; 9:10; 24:3; Job 12:13; 28:20).[54] The combination thus suggests the ability to discern the truth and to make good decisions based on that truth. Of course, as the Old Testament contexts make clear, this truth comes only from God, a claim that Paul elaborates in a christological way in 2:3: in Christ (and in Christ alone) are hidden *all the treasures of wisdom and knowledge*. As the TNIV interprets it, the adjective "spiritual" *(pneumatikos)* is getting at this same point: the Spirit is the source of the wisdom and understanding that the Colossians require as they negotiate their way through the maze of first-century worldview options.[55]

10 Spirit-given insight into the will of God, as important as it is, is not an end in itself. Echoing a consistent biblical theme, Paul indicates that the Colossians' mental and attitudinal realignment is to produce behavioral transformation. The verb at the beginning of v. 10, an infinitive

---

more thorough knowledge (Lightfoot, 138) or the direction of the knowledge (MacDonald, 47). But no consistent difference in meaning between γνῶσις and ἐπίγνωσις (or between γινώσκω and ἐπιγινώσκω) can be discovered in Paul; and so we should probably not attach any special nuance to the word here.

53. TNIV's *through* translates ἐν, which can be rendered several ways in English. In preference to the instrumental interpretation (for which see, e.g., Harris, 30; MacDonald, 47), we prefer an associative rendering ("with"; cf. Wright, 58).

54. Dunn again finds in the phrase a polemic against a torah-based false teaching, since Deut. 4:6 specifies that God's decrees and laws produce σοφία and σύνεσις (70).

55. The translation "spiritual" found in many English versions is accurate enough, but leaves open a myriad of possible interpretations, especially in a culture like ours where "spiritual" can mean so many different things. As Fee emphasizes, however, Paul's view of what is "spiritual" is overwhelmingly determined by his experience of the Holy Spirit; and the TNIV rendering *that the Spirit gives* highlights this idea (*God's Empowering Presence*, 641-43). As O'Brien puts it, *wisdom and understanding* "comes through the insight God's Spirit imparts" (22; cf. also Dunn, 71). Πνευματικός, as also the adjective πάσῃ that precedes the phrase, modifies both nouns (e.g., Abbott, 202; Lohse, 27).

in Greek (*peripatēsai*, "to walk"), might indicate either result — "with the result that you will walk" — or purpose — "with the purpose that you might walk."[56] The difference between these two ideas in the context of a prayer is slight, but perhaps purpose, with its implied exhortation, fits better. Paul's use of the verb meaning "walk" (see also 2:6; 3:7; 4:5) picks up a common Jewish and biblical idiom, according to which a person's lifestyle is pictured as a road that one travels along. Frequently, especially in Wisdom literature, two paths or ways are contrasted as a way of confronting the righteous with the decisive choice that they must make; and the command to "walk" (Heb. *hlk*) is naturally used in these contexts.[57] Representative is Proverbs 2:12-20:

> Wisdom will save you from the ways of wicked men, from men whose words are perverse, who have left the straight paths to walk in dark ways, who delight in doing wrong and rejoice in the perverseness of evil, whose paths are crooked and who are devious in their ways. Wisdom will save you also from the adulterous woman, from the wayward woman with her seductive words, who has left the partner of her youth and ignored the covenant she made before God. Surely her house leads down to death and her paths to the spirits of the dead. None who go to her return or attain the paths of life. Thus you will walk in the ways of the just and keep to the paths of the righteous.

Some English versions choose to retain the idiom and its associated ideas (e.g., ESV; NASB; HCSB), while most (losing the metaphor but gaining clarity for many English readers) interpret the metaphor, often with the language of "live" (NIV; TNIV; NRSV; NLT; NET; NJB; REB).

Paul describes the nature of this new "walk": it is to be *worthy of the Lord* and to *please him in every way*. The decision of the TNIV to view these two constructions as parallel descriptions of "live" (followed also by NIV; NLT; NET; REB) is one possible way to construe the Greek syntax.[58] But it is also possible that the second phrase elaborates the first phrase (cf. ESV: "to walk in a manner worthy of the Lord, fully pleasing to him") or that it indicates the purpose or result of the first phrase (cf. NAB: "to

56. Result: Harris, 31; Lightfoot, 139; Dunn, 71; purpose: Lohse, 27; O'Brien, 22; Gnilka, 41.

57. As Lohse (27) especially emphasizes, this imagery is common in the Dead Sea Scrolls (e.g., 1QS 3:17-26; 5:8-11). The imagery is so widespread, however — as are the other parallels between Colossians and the DSS that Lohse notes here — that conclusions about any special dependence on Qumran ideas are speculative.

58. The second phrase, *please him in every way*, is preceded by the preposition εἰς, which these versions are apparently assuming is to be connected to the main verb, περιπατῆσαι.

live in a manner worthy of the Lord, so as to be fully pleasing").[59] Paul elsewhere urges believers to live "worthily" of the gospel (Phil. 1:27), their calling (Eph. 4:1), and God (1 Thess. 2:12). Here it is *the Lord* who sets the standard of our "worthy walk." The immediate context (see esp. 1:3; 2:6), as well as the syntax of this particular construction,[60] suggests that the *Lord* is Jesus Christ — yet another example of the very high Christology that typifies this letter. The Greeks often used the language of "pleasing" with a negative nuance, signifying an obsequious attitude of currying favor. But it was also frequently used in a positive way, and this usage, of course, determines the meaning of the language here. "Pleasing" God is not a common Old Testament expression, but is found more often in Judaism and in the New Testament (in Paul; cf. Rom. 8:8; 1 Cor. 7:32; 1 Thess. 2:4; 4:1).[61] The Greek text has nothing that explicitly corresponds to the *him* found in most English translations, and a few commentators have thought that Paul might be referring to actions that please both the Lord and other people.[62] But the context strongly suggests a limitation to behavior that is pleasing to the Lord.

The end of v. 10 provides a further description of the life that is worthy of the Lord and that pleases him in every way: *bearing fruit in every good work, growing in the knowledge of God.*[63] The two participles are bound closely together (connected with *kai*, "and") and probably are intended to be read together. Paul echoes the language of v. 6: the Colossians are to continue to do what the gospel is already accomplishing among them.[64] As we noted in our comments on v. 6, *bearing fruit* and *growing* is language rooted in the creation story, carrying the implication, perhaps, that God is seeking through response to the gospel to confirm his original purpose in creation and establish human beings in his own image. In v. 6,

59. In this case, εἰς will depend on the phrase ἀξίως τοῦ κυρίου ("worthy of the Lord").

60. When Paul uses an article before κύριος ("Lord"), as he does here, he usually refers to Christ (e.g., Harris, 31).

61. In the Old Testament, the expression (with the verb ἀρέσκω) occurs only in Num. 23:27; Ps. 68:32; Prov. 24:18; Isa. 59:15; Mal. 3:4. Philo uses the language quite frequently.

62. E.g., Barth/Blanke, 178.

63. The participles Paul uses here — καρποφορούμενοι and αὐξανόμενοι — are in the nominative case. Since participles dependent on an infinitive — περιπατῆσαι at the beginning of the verse — should technically be accusative, it is possible that the participles should be construed as dependent on πληρωθῆτε ("that you might be filled") in v. 9. But it is perhaps more likely that they are loosely attached to περιπατῆσαι (see Lohse, 28).

64. In v. 6, Paul used the middle participle καρποφορούμενον. His shift to the active form here (καρποφοροῦντες) is probably not indicative of any change in meaning (see O'Brien, 23).

the focus was on the extension of the gospel to many people; here, however, it is the intensive growth within each believer that is the focus.[65] The clause has a chiastic structure in Greek, with the two participles in the "center" surrounded by qualifying phrases. "Bearing fruit" is to manifest itself in "every kind of" (the force probably of *panti*;[66] cf. NJB; REB) good work. And *growing* happens in some relationship to the "knowledge of God" (the preposition translated *in* by TNIV is *en*). The relationship could be one of sphere, paraphrased nicely in the NLT: "you will learn to know God better and better."[67] Or the *en* could have instrumental force: growing takes place by means of our knowledge of God.[68] The importance of a clear understanding of God and his purposes in this opening section (see vv. 6, 9) points to the former as the better option.

11 Paul continues the syntax that ended v. 10 by adding another participle to his list: a life worthy of the Lord and that pleases him (v. 10a) will consist in (1) bearing fruit and growing (v. 10b); and (2) *being strengthened*. As O'Brien notes, this clause indicates "how the conduct, worthy of the Lord, was to be achieved."[69] Living a life worthy of the Lord is a high and difficult calling. In typical New Testament fashion, Paul reminds us that God gives what he demands. And the form of the participle (the present tense) suggests that God's provision of strength is continuously available to his people. References to the Spirit are surprisingly sparse in Colossians (only 1:8; but *pneumatikos* in 1:9 and 3:16 probably also alludes to the Spirit). But Paul's broader teaching certainly justifies our thinking that this divine enablement comes through the indwelling Holy Spirit.

Verse 11 describes the extent and purpose of God's empowerment of the believer. First, the *strengthening* comes *with all power*. The word "all" (Gk. *pas*) has a variety of nuances. Here it signifies a "marker of the highest degree": "complete," "unlimited" power.[70] The word *power* is closely related to the word "strengthen" (*dynamis* and *dynamoō*, respectively): we might paraphrase "strengthened by God with the greatest strength imaginable."

Paul further emphasizes the extent of God's empowering, as well as making explicit its source, with the next description: *according to his glorious might*. *Might* translates a word that is typically associated with

65. See Harris, 32, for this distinction.
66. See BDAG, Def. 5 for πᾶς.
67. See Harris, 32; Wright, 58.
68. Lightfoot, 139; Abbott, 203; Lohse, 29. In either case, the genitive τοῦ θεοῦ ("of God") is objective: it is God who is the "object" of our knowing (see Wallace, *Greek Syntax*, 119).
69. O'Brien, 24.
70. The relevant definition in BDAG.

God in the New Testament; in fact, half of its occurrences are in doxologies (1 Tim. 6:16; 1 Pet. 4:11; 5:11; Jude 25; Rev. 1:6; 5:13; see also Luke 1:51; Acts 19:20; Eph. 1:19; 6:10; Heb. 2:14). As so often in Colossians, the closest parallel is in Ephesians: "I pray that the eyes of your heart may be enlightened in order that you may know the hope to which he has called you, the riches of his glorious inheritance in his people, and his incomparably great power for us who believe. That power is the same as the mighty **strength** he exerted when he raised Christ from the dead and seated him at his right hand in the heavenly realms" (1:18-20). The translations are almost unanimous in using the adjective "glorious" to qualify this divine might, echoing the opinion of most commentators that *doxēs* should be construed as a qualitative genitive.[71] But one might wonder if this interpretation gives appropriate value to the very significant word "glory." This word occurs frequently in Scripture as a very basic characterization of God, signifying his "weighty," overwhelming presence. The English "glorious" is too easily cast loose from this God-focused meaning (as when we speak of a "glorious sunset"). It might, then, be preferable to take the genitive as possessive: the strength that God supplies his people is in accordance with (and is the expression of) his own intrinsic glory.[72]

Paul, second, says that the purpose of God's strengthening is that the Colossians *may have great endurance and patience. Great* translates *pas,* the third time we have encountered this word in a verse and a half: *every* good work (v. 10b); *all* power (v. 11a); *great* endurance and patience (*pas* probably modifies both nouns). As in v. 11a, the word probably connotes degree: "the very greatest possible endurance and patience." Paul's decision to use two words naturally leads us to ask about a possible distinction in their meanings. Some commentators think that the former (Gk. *hypomonē*) connotes the ability to "bear up" (corresponding to the etymology of the Greek word) under difficult circumstances, while the latter *(makrothymia)* suggests long-suffering toward people. As Wright puts it: "[Endurance] is what faith, hope and love bring to an apparently impossible situation, [patience] what they show to an apparently impossible

71. E.g., Bruce, 47; Dunn, 73. Many commentators, indeed, appear to assume that the meaning is so obvious as not to require comment.

72. Paul uses the genitive δόξης as a qualifier of a noun or pronoun twenty other times. In Eph. 1:17, a qualitative interpretation might be preferable ("the glorious Father"). But in all the other verses, "glory" is best seen as an important entity in its own right; see, e.g., Col. 1:27b: "the hope *of glory*"; and the formula "the praise *of his glory*" (Eph. 1:6, 12, 14). See also Rom. 5:2; 8:21; 9:23; 1 Cor. 2:8; 2 Cor. 4:4, 6, 17; Eph. 1:18; 3:16; Phil. 3:21; Col. 1:27a; 2 Thess. 2:14; 1 Tim. 1:11; Titus 2:13. See, on Col. 1:11, Moule, 54; Masson, 95; Wilson, 111.

person."[73] Contemporary linguistics properly encourages wariness about these kinds of distinctions — especially when they are so homiletically attractive! But, without insisting that this difference between the two is always to be assumed, the usage of the relevant words in the New Testament does suggest that a general distinction of this sort may be justified.[74]

12 Paul adds a final participle to the sequence describing the life worthy of the Lord that he began in v. 10b: "giving thanks." This verb reminds us of the leading verb in v. 3 and, when combined with reference to the *Father* (a title absent in vv. 4-11),[75] there is good reason to think that Paul is signaling that he is now rounding off the thanksgiving/prayer section of the letter. Indeed, as we noted above (see the introduction to vv. 3-14), many scholars think that these same parallels suggest that a new section of the letter begins here, with the participle *eucharistountes* being interpreted as imperatival: "Give thanks to the Father. . . ." And there is a shift in focus, as Paul turns from praying for the Colossians to rehearsing what God has done for them. Accenting this switch is the move from the second person — "you" — to the first person — "us" — in v. 13. A few interpreters even suggest that in vv. 12-14 Paul reproduces a confession of the early church as a kind of "introit" to the Christ hymn that follows.[76] However, independent imperatival participles are very rare in the New Testament, and so it is more natural to connect this participle with what precedes. On this reading, which we prefer, *giving . . . thanks* describes a fourth element of the fruitful Christian life. The TNIV follows this interpretation, translating the beginning of v. 12 as the continuation of the sentence that began in v. 9b: *and giving joyful thanks*.

The TNIV's *joyful* translates a prepositional phrase (*meta charas*;

73. Wright, 60; see also Lohse, 30-31; similar are Lightfoot, 140; Barth/Blanke, 182-83.

74. "Endurance" (ὑπομονή) does not occur elsewhere in Colossians; the one other occurrence of μακροθυμία (3:12) denotes an attitude that enables believers to "bear with each other" (3:13). The two words (and their cognate verbs) occur in fairly close proximity in the NT elsewhere in Rom. 2:4-7; 1 Cor. 13:4-7; 2 Cor. 6:4-6; 2 Tim. 3:10; Jas. 5:7-11.

75. A few MSS have "God" (θεῷ) in place of "Father" (πατρί), while still others compromise with both "God" and "Father." But the support for "Father" is both early and diverse.

76. See, e.g., Ernst, 163-64; Lohse, 33; Schweizer, 40; Furter, 92; George E. Cannon, *The Use of Traditional Materials in Colossians* (Macon, Ga.: Mercer University Press, 1983), 12-14; J. Lähnemann, *Der Kolosserbrief* (Gütersloh: Mohn, 1971), 34-35. Evidence, however, for a clear-cut tradition is in this case wanting. Paul may be citing some traditional language (see, e.g., Wolter, 57-58; Pokorný, 51; Gnilka, 45; O'Brien, 25; T. J. Sappington, *Revelation and Redemption at Colossae* [Sheffield: JSOT Press, 1991], 193-97), but he is almost certainly the one who composed these verses.

"with joy"). Some commentators[77] and versions (e.g., RSV; ESV) hold that this prepositional phrase (which precedes the participle) goes with the end of v. 11 rather than with v. 12. On this reading, it is the Colossians' endurance and patience that would be accompanied by joy. But Paul has modified each of the other participles in this series with a prepositional phrase, so it is likely that he is doing the same here: "bearing fruit in every good work"; "growing in the knowledge of God"; "being strengthened with power"; "giving thanks with joy."[78] This same pattern argues that the participle is modal and, and along with the other participles in vv. 10b-11, modifies "so that you may live" in v. 10a.[79] It might seem a bit surprising that Paul would include thanksgiving in a short list of activities that comprise the life that is "worthy of the Lord" (v. 10). But the giving of thanks plays a prominent role in Colossians (see, in addition to v. 3, 2:7; 3:17; 4:2) — perhaps, among other reasons, because it signals the reality of their spiritual experience in Christ.[80] For the giving of thanks implies that what has been received has not been earned but is a gift. Thanksgiving is therefore the flip side of a key Pauline theological claim: that Christians are saved by and live in grace.[81] The reminder of this fundamental gospel truth would be especially important in a context where false teachers were insisting on a program of rules for true spiritual fulfillment (cf. 2:16-23).

Paul has steadily been moving away from the starting point of the long sentence that began in v. 9. His prayer that the Colossians might grow to know God better led naturally into the purpose of that knowledge: leading a life pleasing to God. The nature of that life has occupied Paul in vv. 10b-12a. In vv. 12b-14 Paul takes a step back, reminding the Colossians of the foundation for their new life in the redemptive work of the Father through the Son. Transfer from one power into that of another marks this section and suggests that Paul may be elaborating v. 11a: *being strengthened with all power according to his glorious might.* God's power has, first, *qualified you*[82] *to share in the inheritance of his peo-*

77. Lightfoot, 140; Moule, 55; Barth/Blanke, 183.

78. This option is supported by most of the commentaries; see, e.g., Harris, 33; O'Brien, 25; Abbott, 205; Lohse, 33.

79. Aletti, 76-77, responding to those who see the participle as imperatival. He also appeals to the pattern of modal participles in 2:6-7; 3:9-10, 12-13; 16; 4:3, 5. Whether one can speak of a "pattern" is questionable, but the sequence in 2:6-7 does have some parallels with this text.

80. Masson, 95.

81. Lincoln, 576.

82. The better manuscripts here read ὑμᾶς, "you," and this reading is properly accepted by most of the commentators and English translations. The alternative, ἡμᾶς, "us," is, however, adopted by the NASB. The variant has little bearing on the sense of the passage.

ple in the kingdom of light (v. 12b). The transitive use of the verb "qualify" in English (found in most of the translations) is awkward but mirrors an equally unusual construction in Greek (the verb *hikanoō* + *eis*).[83] Paul's intended meaning, however, is clear enough: God the Father has himself provided what sinners need to be considered worthy to join the people of God.

Paul's description of the new spiritual status for which believers are qualified is rather elaborate: literally, "for a share of the inheritance of the holy ones in the light." Paul uses two words that overlap in meaning: *meris* and *klēros*, which both mean "share" or "portion." The two occur together in rough parallelism several times in the LXX and once in the New Testament (Acts 8:21); see, for instance, Deuteronomy 10:9: "That is why the Levites have no share *(meris)* or inheritance *(klēros)* among their fellow Israelites; the LORD is their inheritance, as the LORD your God told them." This verse reflects the most common use of the words in the Old Testament, where they are often applied to the territories allotted to Israel's tribes in the land of Israel. The translation "inheritance," found in most of the English versions, is a natural extension of meaning: that which is "allotted" is an inheritance.[84] In a move typical of the New Testament "christifying" of the Old Testament "land" theme,[85] Paul applies this language to the spiritual privilege enjoyed by God's new covenant people — including, in a particularly significant salvation-historical development, the Gentiles, such as the Colossians (see esp. the significant development of this theme in Eph. 2:11-22; note also Acts 20:32). This *inheritance* belongs to "the holy ones" *(tōn hagiōn)*, which some take to be a reference to the angels.[86] The LXX uses *hagios* to refer to angels (e.g., Deut. 33:3; Ps. 89:6), and especially persuasive to some scholars is the parallel

---

83. The verb appears only once elsewhere in the NT: 2 Cor. 3:6, where Paul claims that God has "made us competent (ἱκάνωσεν ἡμᾶς) as ministers of a new covenant." The verb appears fifteen times in the LXX, but usually in the passive, in the sense "it is enough."

84. It is instructive in this regard that the LXX often translates the Hebrew word behind κλῆρος in Deut. 10:9 and other passages (חֵלֶק) with the usual word for "inheritance" in Greek: κληρονομία.

85. See esp. W. D. Davies, *The Gospel and the Land: Early Christianity and Jewish Territorial Doctrine* (Berkeley: University of California Press, 1974).

86. E.g., Wolter, 65; Lohse, 36; R. P. Martin, 54; Pokorný, 52; MacDonald, 50; Gnilka, 47; A. T. Lincoln, *Paradise Now and Not Yet* (Cambridge and New York: Cambridge University Press, 2004), 119-20 (probable). Pierre Benoit ("Ἅγιοι en Colossiens 1.12: hommes ou anges?" in *Paul and Paulinism: Essays in Honour of C. K. Barrett* [ed. M. D. Hooker and S. G. Wilson; London: SPCK, 1982], 83-101), Sappington (*Revelation*, 199-200), and Wilson (113-14) think the reference is to both angels and fellow religionists (as, they allege, at Qumran).

between Colossians 1:12 and 1QS 11:7-8: "To those whom God has selected he has given them an everlasting possession; and he has given
them an inheritance in the lot of the holy ones." Against this is the pre-
dominant New Testament usage, where "the holy ones" almost always
refers to Christians (as it does consistently in Colossians; see 1:2, 4, 26;
also 1:22; 3:12).[87] Note also some roughly parallel wording from Ephesians: "the riches of his glorious inheritance in his people ["the holy
ones"]" (Eph. 1:18); "fellow citizens with God's people ["the holy ones"]"
(2:19). This New Testament evidence makes it likely that "holy ones" refers to the people of God (see TNIV). God has made it possible for the
Gentiles to have a share in the inheritance "that belongs to God's people"
or "that is destined for God's people."[88]

At the end of this description of the new covenant inheritance,
Paul adds the prepositional phrase "in the light" (en tō phōti). The obvious contrast with "dominion of darkness" in v. 13 suggests that "light"
is here shorthand for the "realm" or "kingdom" of light (cf. REB;
TNIV).[89] But to what are we to attach the phrase? Is Paul suggesting
that it is the inheritance that exists in this realm of light?[90] Or is it "the
holy ones" who exist in this realm of light (cf. NLT: "God's holy people,
who live in the light")? Or, as most commentators think, does "in the
light" modify the entire preceding sequence: "the share of the inheritance that belongs to his people is in the realm of light"? A decision is
difficult, but perhaps a reference to "inheritance" provides the most
natural connection.

13 As the TNIV's "for" suggests (for which there is nothing explicit in the Greek), v. 13 elaborates v. 12b. God the Father's bestowal of
the inheritance on his new covenant people takes the form of a rescue
and transfer operation. The rescue and transfer (TNIV, "brought") may
be sequential — first he "rescued," then he "transferred," or "brought"
— but it may be better to take them as concurrent: a "rescue by transfer-

---

87. "Holy ones" (τῶν ἁγίων) refers clearly to angels in Jude 14, which, however, is a
quotation from 1 En. 1:9. Most commentators also think the "holy ones" who accompany
Jesus at his return in 1 Thess. 3:13 are angels (cf. Zech. 14:5; and Gene Green, The Letters to
the Thessalonians [Pillar; Grand Rapids: Eerdmans, 2002], 181). Four passages use ἅγιος to
modify ἄγγελος (Mark 8:38; Luke 9:26; Acts 10:22; Rev. 14:10). In these verses, however, it
may be significant that ἅγιος by itself is apparently felt to be insufficient to mark the reference to angels.

88. The former translation implies a possessive genitive; the latter an objective
genitive (for which see Dübbers, Christologie und Existenz, 136). On this general interpretation, see, e.g., O'Brien, 26; Dunn, 76-77; Schweizer, 51. For ἅγιοι as a reference to God's
people, see the note on 1:2.

89. See Harris, 35.

90. Harris, 35; Abbott, 207; Bruce, 50.

ence."[91] Most interpreters think that Paul alludes here to the rescue of God's people from Egypt.[92] And there is some reason to see a connection. Note especially the programmatic text of Exodus 6:6-8:

"Therefore, say to the Israelites: 'I am the LORD, and I will bring you out from under the yoke of the Egyptians. I will free (LXX, *rhyomai*) you from being slaves to them, and I will redeem *(lytroō)* you with an outstretched arm and with mighty acts of judgment. I will take you as my own people, and I will be your God. Then you will know that I am the LORD your God, who brought you out from under the yoke of the Egyptians. And I will bring you to the land I swore with uplifted hand to give to Abraham, to Isaac and to Jacob. I will give it to you as a possession *(klēros)*. I am the LORD.'"

The parallels between this text and Colossians 1:12-14 are obvious: in both, God "rescues" *(rhyomai; cf. v. 13)* and "redeems" *(lytroō; cf. "redemption" in v. 14)* people, taking them out of a situation of bondage and bringing them into an "inheritance" *(klēros; cf. v. 12)*.[93] Nevertheless, some interpreters have overemphasized the degree to which Paul's language in this and other passages echoes the exodus.[94] In fact, one could make an equally strong or even stronger case for an allusion to the deliverance Israel experienced when God brought his people back from exile. Psalm 107 celebrates this "redemption" *(lytroō* occurs twice in v. 2; cf. *apolytrōsis* in v. 14), using the language of "rescue" *(rhyomai; vv. 6, 20)* and speaking of the way the Lord brought the exiles "out of darkness and the deepest gloom" (v. 14). Isaiah, who had so much influence on Paul, often depicts the deliverance from exile as a "redemption," and uses "darkness" to describe the exilic condition and "light" the new state into which the Lord brings his people (e.g., 42:7, 16; 49:9). Of course, these options are not mutually exclusive, since the exodus experience becomes paradigmatic for Israel's rescue from exile — a "new Exodus." But it is the latter — which of course itself becomes paradigmatic in turn for God's ultimate "rescue" of his people — that Paul may be highlighting here. The

---

91. Harris, 36.

92. See esp. Wright, 62.

93. For this parallel, see esp. Fee, *Pauline Christology,* 297.

94. The verb "rescue" (ῥύομαι) refers to the exodus only four times (Exod. 5:23; 6:6; 14:30; Ps. 22:4) in over 200 occurrences in biblical Greek; the verb "brought" (μεθίστημι) never refers to the exodus. To be sure, the language of "redemption" (esp. the verb λυτρόω; cf. ἀπολύτρωσιν in v. 14) is more often applied to the exodus; note esp. Exod. 6:6, where ῥύομαι and λυτρόω occur together. But λυτρόω, out of almost 100 occurrences in the LXX, refers to the exodus only 18 times, while the verb ἀπολυτρόω (only two times in the LXX) and the noun ἀπολύτρωσις (only once in the LXX) never do.

true and ultimate rescue from exile comes not in (physical) return to the land but in (spiritual) redemption from sin through Christ.[95] It is also intriguing to speculate on the degree to which Paul's own experience of "deliverance," when the Lord appeared to him on the Damascus Road, may have influenced his wording here. Note the similarities between Acts 26:12-18 and Colossians 1:12-14:

> "On one of these journeys I was going to Damascus with the authority and commission of the chief priests. About noon, King Agrippa, as I was on the road, I saw a light from heaven, brighter than the sun, blazing around me and my companions. We all fell to the ground, and I heard a voice saying to me in Aramaic, 'Saul, Saul, why do you persecute me? It is hard for you to kick against the goads.'
>
> "Then I asked, 'Who are you, Lord?'
>
> "'I am Jesus, whom you are persecuting,' the Lord replied. 'Now get up and stand on your feet. I have appeared to you to appoint you as a servant and as a witness of what you have seen and will see of me. I will rescue you from your own people and from the Gentiles. I am sending you to them to open their eyes and turn them from darkness to light, and from the power of Satan to God, so that they may receive forgiveness of sins and a place among those who are sanctified by faith in me.'"[96]

As Israel during her exile lived in darkness, so the Colossians have lived in *the dominion of darkness*. "Darkness" (genitive *skotous*) might be another way of describing the *dominion* (epexegetic genitive),[97] but is more likely characterizing that dominion (descriptive genitive).[98] People who have not been rescued by God in Christ live in a power structure that is characterized by the forces of chaos, evil, and judgment. As we suggested above, God has accomplished this rescue by transferring us from this dominion of darkness into *the kingdom of the Son he loves*. In comparison with the extensive use of the language in the Gospels, "kingdom" language is relatively rare in Paul (only thirteen times). Many scholars

95. N. T. Wright has especially emphasized this "ultimate return from exile" motif in the NT (e.g., *The New Testament and the People of God* [Minneapolis: Fortress, 1992], 268-71, passim). We think he has exaggerated its importance, but it clearly does play a role in the NT conception of God's deliverance of his people in Christ.

96. Reference should also be made to the Jewish tradition of using the transference from darkness to light to depict conversion (e.g., *Joseph and Aseneth*) and the extensive use of the "darkness"/"light" contrast in the Dead Sea Scrolls (e.g., 1QS 3:13–4:1).

97. Wallace, *Greek Grammar*, 100.

98. Harris, 36. There is insufficient evidence to suggest that Paul sees a personal reference here (e.g., NLT: "rescued us from the one who rules in the kingdom of darkness").

emphasize the futuristic nature of the kingdom in Paul, and they therefore think that the focus here on the kingdom as a present reality is yet another sign that Paul did not write the letter.[99] In fact, however, the use of kingdom language in the critically accepted seven Pauline letters is by no means standard: while four are pretty clearly future-oriented (1 Cor. 6:9, 10; 15:50; Gal. 5:21), three are present-oriented (Rom. 14:17; 1 Cor. 4:20, 15:24; 1 Thess. 2:12 is unclear).[100] It can hardly be argued that the kingdom language of Colossians (see also 4:11) is any departure from the "authentic" Paul.

Jesus habitually spoke of the "kingdom of God" (or "of heaven" as a periphrasis for God). Another indication of Paul's high Christology, then, is his reference to this kingdom as *the kingdom of the Son he loves* (see also 1 Cor. 15:24; 2 Tim. 4:1). *Son he loves* translates a Greek genitive construction that would be literally rendered "the Son of the love of his." The TNIV, with most commentaries, takes *agapēs* ("of love") as a descriptive genitive and *autou* as possessive: "the Son characterized by the love that belongs to God."[101] The closest parallel to this language in Scripture comes in God's commendation of Christ at his baptism: "This is my beloved Son" (ESV; *ho huios mou ho agapētos*) — language that alludes to the presentation of the (messianic) king in Psalm 2:2. Paul may also be alluding to another key Old Testament messianic prophecy, 2 Samuel 7:12-16, which uses the title "Son" and stresses God's eternal love for him:

> "When your days are over and you rest with your ancestors, I will raise up your offspring to succeed you, who will come from your own body, and I will establish his kingdom. He is the one who will build a house for my Name, and I will establish the throne of his kingdom forever. I will be his father, and he will be my son. When he does wrong, I will punish him with a rod wielded by human beings, with floggings inflicted by human hands. But my love will never be taken away from him, as I took it away from Saul, whom I removed from before you. Your house and your kingdom will endure forever before me; your throne will be established forever."

99. E.g., Lohse, who claims that "whenever Paul mentions the 'rule of God' (βασιλεία τοῦ θεοῦ) in his letters, the futuristic meaning of the concept is presupposed . . ." (pp. 37-38).

100. Despite the claim of some (e.g., O'Brien, 28), it does not seem possible to distinguish temporal references on the basis of whether God or Christ occurs with the word.

101. The construction υἱός plus descriptive genitive may reflect Semitic syntax (Moule, *Idiom Book*, 175; Turner, *Syntax*, 214). It is also possible that, for the same reason, αὐτοῦ should be connected with υἱός (Turner; Zerwick, *Biblical Greek*, §42).

When taken in conjunction with explicit mention of the kingdom in this context, it seems clear that Paul is drawing our attention to Jesus' messianic and kingly status.[102]

14 Paul concludes his brief rehearsal of God's work of deliverance by shifting the focus to general Christian experience ("we" as opposed to the "you" of vv. 3-13) and to the present (present focused verb in v. 14 vs. the aorists of vv. 12-13). *Redemption* taps into a key New Testament image of the effects of Jesus' death on those who belong to him. The language would have brought to mind in the first century the transaction by which a slave paid a price to secure his or her release from slavery. Christ came to "redeem" *(lytroō, apolytroō)* sinners from their slavery to sin by offering his own life as a "ransom" *(lytron)* (see esp. Mark 10:45 par. Matt. 20:28; Rom. 3:24).[103] But, as we noted in our comments on v. 13, the language may also allude to Israel's experience of the exodus — though the case is not as strong as is sometimes suggested.

The appositive description of this redemption — *the forgiveness of sins* — again raises questions about the author of this letter. Paul uses forgiveness language to depict the work of Christ for us only six times: five of them occur in Colossians or Ephesians (Col. 1:14; 2:13; 3:13; Eph. 1:7; 4:32), and the one other comes in an Old Testament quotation (Rom. 4:7). The motif is then alleged to indicate that Paul is not himself the author of Colossians or of Ephesians.[104] Our response to this objection will hinge on a cluster of other considerations, including our understanding of the nature of the claim made in the openings of both letters, the overall "fit" between the language and ideas of these letters in comparison with the other letters of Paul, and — not least — the degree to which we must give an author such as Paul the latitude to bring in new ideas for particular purposes on particular occasions. On the basis of these points, and others, we are strongly disposed to think that Paul was indeed the writer of this letter (see the Introduction, 28-41, for discussion). While it is quite speculative, then, we might wonder if the false

102. See esp. Wright, 62-63; Fee, *Pauline Christology*, 295-98; Beetham, "Echoes of Scripture," 121-43.

103. Scholars sometimes think that the idea of a "price paid" for release has been lost via the use of this language in the LXX (see esp. David Hill, *Greek Words with Hebrew Meanings: Studies in the Semantics of Soteriological Terms* [SNTSMS 5; Cambridge: Cambridge University Press, 1967], 58-80). But the case for finding a reference to "ransoming" specifically in the NT is a strong one, classically argued by Leon Morris, *The Apostolic Preaching of the Cross* [Grand Rapids: Eerdmans, 1955], 9-26). Note esp. 1 Pet. 1:18: "For you know that it was not with perishable things such as silver or gold that you were redeemed from the empty way of life handed down to you from your forefathers"; and also 1 Cor. 6:20: "You were bought at a price."

104. See, e.g., Dunn, 81.

teachers in Asia Minor were making some kind of claim about their spiritual experiences that led Paul to bring up this concept in these letters. It is possible, for instance, that they were questioning the adequacy of Christ to take care of their sin problem (see also 2:14-15). Further, Paul may have introduced the language in this context because of its association with a cluster of ideas that were communicated to him in the commission the resurrected Christ gave to him on the Damascus Road (note the way the quotation from Acts 26:12-18, cited above, ends). In any case, the idea of forgiveness is, of course, very common in first-century Judaism and elsewhere in the New Testament, so reference to the idea here is certainly fitting.[105]

2. The Heart of the Gospel: The Supremacy of Christ in Creation and Redemption (1:15-20)

[15]The Son is the image of the invisible God, the firstborn over all creation. [16]For in him all things were created: things in heaven and on earth, visible and invisible, whether thrones or powers or rulers or authorities; all things have been created through him and for him. [17]He is before all things, and in him all things hold together. [18]And he is the head of the body, the church; he is the beginning and the firstborn from among the dead, so that in everything he might have the supremacy. [19]For God was pleased to have all his fullness dwell in him, [20]and through him to reconcile to himself all things, whether things on earth or things in heaven, by making peace through his blood, shed on the cross.

This passage, the most famous in the letter, is one of the christological high points of the New Testament and provides a critical basis for the teaching of the letter. As Thompson has put it, "One of the distinctive contributions — if not the distinctive contribution — of Colossians is its comprehensive vision of reality with the focal point of christology."[106] The passage stands out from its surrounding context. The reader of the Greek text senses the shift instinctively, but the shift can also be documented with some data. Comparison can be made with vv. 3-8 and 9-14, both of which are about the same length as vv. 15-20, and with vv. 21-23, which is about two-thirds the length of vv. 15-20. Typical of Paul's normal style are rather long, complex sentences, in which the key structural

---

105. See esp. Paul's proclamation in Acts 13:38.
106. Thompson, 155; cf. also J.-N. Aletti, "Colossiens: un tournant dans la christologie néotestamentaire: problèmes et propositions," *LASBF* 49 (1999), 211-36; J. M. G. Barclay, *Colossians and Philemon* (Sheffield: Sheffield Academic Press, 1997), 77-92.

component is the adverbial participle. Six occur in vv. 3-8; six in vv. 9-14; four in vv. 21-23; but only one in vv. 15-20. The flip side of this statistic is the much greater occurrence of main clause indicative verbs in vv. 15-20: seven, in comparison with two in vv. 3-8, one in vv. 9-14, and two in vv. 21-23. The context surrounding vv. 15-20 also contains features, natural to a letter, that focus on the readers: pronouns that refer to the reader and/or the writer (nine in vv. 3-8; four in vv. 9-14; two in vv. 21-23) and first- or second-person verbs (six in vv. 3-8; four in vv. 9-14; three in vv. 21-23). Neither feature appears at all in vv. 15-20. These features combine to set vv. 15-20 apart from their context. In these verses Paul strings together brief assertions about Christ, while in vv. 3-14 and 21-23 (as in the rest of the letter), he uses complex sentences to mount arguments. To be sure, it needs also to be said that the relative pronoun opening v. 15 can be seen as integrating this passage firmly in its context: "He [the Father] has rescued us . . . and brought us into the kingdom of the Son he loves, in whom we have redemption . . . [who] is the image of the invisible God. . . ." While these connections should not be overlooked, the syntactical features we have enumerated still mark out this paragraph in its context.

The most common explanation for this syntactical distinctiveness is that Paul is here quoting traditional material, a "hymn" or confession about Christ.[107] Other evidence cited in favor of this hypothesis is (1) the relative pronoun that opens the passage (hos, for which TNIV has sup-

---

107. The traditional character of the passage was first extensively argued by E. Norden, *Agnostos Theos: Untersuchungen zur Formgeschichte religiöser Rede* (4th ed.; Darmstadt: Wissenschaftliche Buchgesellschaft, 1956), 250-54. But it should be noted that the distinctive syntactical features that we have enumerated above are less evident in vv. 19-20 than in vv. 15-18. It is possible, then, that Paul has more significantly modified this latter part of the hymn or even that Paul's "quotation" ends at v. 18. See Pierre Benoit, "L'hymne christologique de Col I, 15-20: jugement critique sur l'état des recherches," in *Christianity, Judaism and Other Greco-Roman Cults: Studies for Morton Smith at Sixty* (ed. Jacob Neusner; SJLA 12; Leiden: Brill, 1975), 237-60; Wayne G. Rollins, "Christological Tendenz in Colossians 1:15-20: A *Theologia Crucis*," in *Christological Perspectives: Essays in Honor of Harvey K. Mcarthur* (ed. Robert F. Berkey and Sarah A. Edwards; New York: Pilgrim Press, 1982), 123-38. For a thorough analysis of the passage, with consideration of various hypotheses, see esp. H. J. Gabathuler, *Jesus Christus. Haupt der Kirche — Haupt der Welt. Der Christushymnus Colosser 1,15-20 in der theologischen Forschung der letzten 130 Jahre* (ATANT 45; Zurich: Zwingli, 1965); Christoph Burger, *Schöpfung und Versöhnung: Studien zum Liturgischen Gut im Kolosser- und Epheserbrief* (WMANT 46; Neukirchen/Vluyn: Neukirchener, 1975), 3-53; Jean-Noël Aletti, *Colossiens 1,15-20: Genre et exégèse du texte: fonction de la thématique sapientielle* (AnBib 91; Rome: Pontifical Biblical Institute, 1981); and esp. Christian Stettler, *Der Kolosserhymnus: Untersuchungen zu Form, traditionsgeschichtlichen Hintergrund und Aussage von Kol 1,15-20* (WUNT 2.131; Tübingen: Mohr Siebeck, 2000).

plied the antecedent, *Son*), which is said to be typical of New Testament "hymns" (e.g., Phil. 2:6; 1 Tim. 3:16); (2) the occurrence of some words that are rare or absent in Paul's own vocabulary;[108] and (3) the repetition of some key words and phrases. Further speculation about the original hymn's content, structure, and life-setting in the church has generated a veritable academic cottage industry. And "speculation" is, all too often, the appropriate word, for many of the theories rest on pretty weak or greatly debated foundations. Where these theories affect our interpretation of the passage, we will bring them into our discussion either here or at the relevant point in the exposition.

However, a preliminary question must be raised: is it, after all, quite so clear that vv. 15-20 could not have been composed by Paul? Syntactical distinctiveness and parallelism might point to careful composition of a "hymn"-like passage, but could not Paul, either before Colossians, or as he writes the letter, have been its author? Unusual vocabulary is always a slender basis for conclusions about authorship, since authors often employ unusual vocabulary for distinctive purposes. Moreover, some of the ideas in the "hymn" — such as "image of God," Christ as "head of the body," and the language of reconciliation — are distinctively Pauline. Furthermore, the language and concepts of the passage are picked up throughout the rest of the letter, as the following chart reveals.

"in him all things were created, things in heaven and on earth, visible and invisible, whether thrones or powers or rulers or authorities; all things have been created through him and for him" (v. 16)

"He is the head over every power and authority" (2:10b)

"he is the head of the body, the church" (v. 18a)

"They have lost connection with the head" (2:19)

"God was pleased to have all his fullness dwell in him" (1:19)

"in Christ all the fullness of the Deity lives in bodily form" (2:9)

"and through him to reconcile to himself all things, whether things on earth or things in heaven, by making peace through his blood, shed on the cross" (1:20)

"having disarmed the powers and authorities, he made a public spectacle of them, triumphing over them by the cross" (2:15)

108. O'Brien, 40-41, provides a handy survey.

Paul obviously uses the language and concepts of the hymn as his christological ammunition in fighting the false teachers. This consonance between "hymn" and the rest of the letter can be explained in two ways. (1) Paul quotes a hymn that provides the theology he needs to combat the false teachers. (2) Paul composes a hymn that enunciates the theology he will use to combat the false teachers.[109] Deciding between these options is difficult. On the one hand, favoring Pauline authorship is the improbability that he would find a ready-made hymn that so nicely dovetailed with the theology he needed to bring to bear against this particular false teaching. But, on the other hand, some of the concepts of the "hymn" are not clearly (or only indirectly) taken up in the rest of the letter (e.g., "image of God"; "firstborn over creation"; "in him all things hold together"; "the beginning and the firstborn from the dead"). Moreover, we have to allow for the possibility that Paul has "redacted" an earlier hymn by adding elements particularly relevant to the false teaching (many scholars think the language about spiritual beings in vv. 16 and 20 falls into this category).[110] We slightly incline to this latter option as the most likely: Paul has quoted and redacted an earlier hymn. But there is enough uncertainty about the matter to caution us about resting exegetical arguments on assumptions about authorship or redaction. We will accordingly continue to speak of vv. 15-20 as a "hymn" (the quotation marks signaling that the passage does not quite fit the usual "hymn" genre[111]), but we will leave open the question of authorship. It is methodologically important, however, to make clear that whatever is asserted in these verses is genuinely "Pauline," whether he composed the whole passage from the ground up or whether he has taken over and modified for his own purposes a traditional text.

The traditional language that Paul uses in this passage (whether he quotes or not) is designed to establish common ground with his Colossian audience. To be sure, Paul is quite forthright about the authority of

109. Some of those who opt for or are very open to Pauline authorship are: Steven M. Baugh, "The Poetic Form of Col 1:15-20," *WTJ* 47 (1985), 228; O'Brien, 40-42; Moule, 60-62; Barth/Blanke, 234-36; N. T. Wright, *The Climax of the Covenant: Christ and the Law in Pauline Theology* (Minneapolis: Fortress, 1991), 118-19; Larry R. Helyer, "Colossians 1:15-20: Pre-Pauline or Pauline," *JETS* 26 (1983), 167-79; A. Feuillet, *Le Christ sagesse de Dieu, d'après les épîtres pauliniennes* (EBib; Paris: Gabalda, 1966), 262-69; Stettler, *Kolosserhymnus*, 299 (possible); Seyoon Kim, *The Origin of Paul's Gospel* (Grand Rapids: Eerdmans, 1981), 147; Smith, *Heavenly Perspective*, 147-52.

110. For a representative presentation, see Jerome Murphy-O'Connor, *Paul: A Critical Life* (New York: Oxford University Press, 1997), 242-46.

111. See, for this point, the analysis of Stephen E. Fowl, *The Story of Christ in the Ethics of Paul: An Analysis of the Function of the Hymnic Material in the Pauline Corpus* (JSNTSup 36; Sheffield: JSOT Press, 1990), 40-45.

his own apostolic pronouncements. But he also manifests a desire to ground his own teaching in the "received" tradition of the church (e.g., 1 Cor. 15:1-3). It would not be at all surprising if Paul decided that the christological foundation for his argument could best be established by reminding the Colossians (whom, we must remember, Paul had never met), of some traditional christological teaching.

But why bring in this high Christology here? The Christology serves the greater purpose of the letter by setting forth Christ as the exclusive instrument through whom God created the universe (vv. 15-17) and through whom he is in the process of pacifying the universe (vv. 18-20). The word *pas* (variously translated "all," "every," "each"), occurring eight times in these verses, is the thread that binds the verses together. Whatever precise form the false teaching at Colossae took, it is at least clear that it was tending to question Christ's exclusive role in providing spiritual growth and security, and, thereby, his exclusive role in the universe at large (see, e.g., 2:9-10, 19). The false teachers, it appears, argued from cosmology to spirituality: because the universe was filled with spiritual powers of various sorts, ultimate spiritual "fullness" could be achieved only by taking them all into consideration (see esp. Paul's counterargument in 2:14-15). Thus Paul in the hymn places particular emphasis on the supremacy of Christ — in both creation and redemption — over the powers (vv. 16, 20).

But the high Christology of vv. 15-20 also serves Paul's immediate argument. As Morna Hooker puts it, "These verses, then, give us christological statements which back up the reality of what Paul has said about the Colossians' redemption in verses 12-14, a theme he takes up again in verses 21-23."[112] Our "rescue" from the "dominion of darkness" (v. 13) is certain and lasting because God accomplished it through none other than the one who is Lord of the universe. Indeed, the passage uses language that associates Christ intimately with God the Father himself. As Richard Bauckham has put it, ". . . what the passage does is to include Jesus Christ in God's unique relationship to the whole of created reality and thereby to include Jesus in the unique identity of God as Jewish monotheism understood it."[113]

The background for the high Christology of this hymn (particularly vv. 15-18a) is debated. We will comment on specific words and phrases below, but it might be helpful here to note the main options. The majority of

112. M. D. Hooker, "Were There False Teachers in Colossae?" in *Christ and Spirit in the New Testament* (Cambridge: Cambridge University Press, 1973), 322.
113. Richard Bauckham, "Where Is Wisdom to Be Found? Colossians 1.15-20 (2)," in *Reading Texts, Seeking Wisdom: Scripture and Theology* (ed. David F. Ford and Graham Stanton; Grand Rapids: Eerdmans, 2003), 133.

scholars think that the figure of "wisdom" *(sophia)*, as portrayed in some Old Testament texts and especially as developed in Judaism in association with the concept of the "word" *(logos)*, is the major influence on the hymn. Based on Old Testament texts such as Proverbs 8:22-31, and seen in its most developed form in Philo, the tradition personified the concepts of wisdom and the "word" to such an extent that they could appear at times to be independent entities. But "appear" is an important word here. We should not be misled by the high degree of personification to think that any Jewish author conceived of "wisdom" or "word" as entities distinct from God: even in Philo, who goes the furthest in this direction, "wisdom" and "word" remain what Hurtado calls "personified divine attributes." Jewish authors spoke of these divine attributes as a way of explaining how a transcendent God could be active in a material and fallen world.[114] It is in this light, then, that Jewish authors portray wisdom and word as intermediaries between God and his world, especially in creation. Colossians 1:15-20 has many resemblances to this tradition. Christ is presented as God's intermediary in creation (v. 16), and he is given titles that were often connected with wisdom/word: especially "image" and "firstborn" in v. 15, and "beginning" *(archē)* in v. 18. Two texts from Philo that illustrate these parallels are *Allegorical Interpretation* 1.43 and *Special Laws* 1.81:

> "And God planted a pleasaunce in Eden toward the sun-rising, and placed there the man whom he had formed." By using many words for it Moses has already made it manifest that the sublime and heavenly wisdom is of many names; for he calls it "beginning" *(archē;* cf. v. 18), and "image" *(eikona;* cf. v. 15) and "vision of God."

> And the image *(eikōn;* cf. v. 15) of God is the Word, through whom the whole universe was framed [cf. v. 16].

This wisdom/word tradition undoubtedly provides the greatest number of parallels to the particular combination of ideas that we find in 1:15-20.[115] To be sure, some scholars have overemphasized the linguistic con-

114. See esp. Larry Hurtado, *One Lord, One God: Early Christian Devotion to Jesus and Ancient Jewish Monotheism* (Philadelphia: Fortress, 1988), 41-46; cf. also James D. G. Dunn, *Christology in the Making: A New Testament Inquiry into the Origins of the Doctrine of the Incarnation* (Philadelphia: Westminster, 1980), 172.

115. See esp. Beetham, "Echoes of Scripture," 175-77, for a summary of the parallels between the wisdom/word tradition and Col. 1:15-20; and also Jeffrey S. Lamb, "Wisdom in Col 1,15-20: Contribution and Significance," *JETS* 41 (1998), 45-53; Harald Hegermann, *Die Vorstellung vom Schöpfungsmittler im Hellenistischen Judentum and Urchristentum* (TU 82; Berlin: Academie, 1961), 67-101. On the wisdom influence, see esp. Aletti, *Colossiens 1:15-20,* 141-82, who argues that the hymn extensively employs wisdom motifs but does not identify Christ with the figure of wisdom per se and Feuillet, *Le*

nections between Colossians 1:15-20 and this tradition;[116] and, in terms of Philo's writings, the greater number of parallels are, in fact, with his teaching about the "word," not with wisdom per se.[117] Still, once we recognize the high degree of overlap between wisdom and "word" in Philo,[118] it would seem to be quite appropriate to combine these two traditions in identifying the background to Colossians 1:15-20.[119]

A second source of some of the language and activities attributed to Christ in 1:15-20 is the Genesis creation story.[120] The language of "image of God" naturally draws our attention to the foundational text of Genesis 1:26-28; and "image of God" language in both the Old Testament and Judaism was more often related to humans than to anything else. Moreover, it is possible that the language of "beginning" (archē) and also, perhaps, "firstborn" could be traced to the influence of the creation story.[121] This

---

Christ sagesse de Dieu, 170-238, who sees Prov. 8:22 to be particularly influential. Ben Witherington III, on the other hand, thinks that Wisdom of Solomon provides the key influence (*Jesus the Sage: The Pilgrimage of Wisdom* [Minneapolis: Fortress, 1994], 266-67).

116. On this in general, see esp. Fee's vigorous criticism of the wisdom hypothesis in his *Pauline Christology*, 317-25, 595-619; his overall conclusion is that ". . . Wisdom Christology is *not* found in Paul's letters and thus has no role in the reconstruction of Paul's Christology" (619). Fee appropriately criticizes a tendency toward an uncritical acceptance of, and overemphasis on, Wisdom Christology (e.g., Dunn: "By common consent, it [the language of 1:15-20] was drawn from earlier Jewish reflection on divine Wisdom" (*The Theology of Paul the Apostle* [Grand Rapids: Eerdmans, 1998], 269). But, with respect at least to Col. 1:15-20, Fee's failure to consider the larger wisdom/word tradition as found in Philo renders the strength of his conclusion questionable. For a degree of skepticism about the importance of wisdom in this text, see also Aletti, "Colossiens," 213-14; Fowl, *The Story of Christ*, 118-21.

117. Hence several scholars argue that the "word" tradition is the dominant influence on our passage (e.g., Lightfoot, 143-44; Wolter, 76; Hegermann, *Die Vorstellung vom Schöpfungsmittler*, 67-101).

118. E.g., *Allegorical Interpretation* 1.65; cf. Wisdom 9:1-2.

119. Stettler, *Kolosserhymnus*, 134-47; Gnilka, 59-60. While Dunn notes this convergence (p. 88), he effectively ignores it through most of his exposition, focusing only on wisdom.

120. Wright, 66-68; Masson, 98-99.

121. An ingenious proposal by C. F. Burney connects much of the language of Col. 1:15-20 to the word רֵאשִׁית, used with reference to wisdom in Prov. 8:22 — "The LORD brought me forth as the **first** of his works" — and in the creation story at Gen. 1:1 — "In the **beginning**, God. . . ." Since these passages use the same word, good rabbinic practice equated them, justifying the assertion that "by wisdom God created the world." Burney then traced other key words in Col. 1:15-20 back to רֵאשִׁית (e.g., "beginning," "firstborn," "head") ("Christ as the ΑΡΧΗ of Creation [Prov. viii 22, Col. i 15-18, Rev. iii.14]," *JTS* 27 [1926], 160-67; cf. also Wright, 66-68; W. D. Davies, *Paul and Rabbinic Judaism: Some Rabbinic Elements in Pauline Theology* (rev. ed.; New York: Harper & Row, 1948), 151; Martin H. Scharlemann, "The Scope of the Redemptive Task (Colossians 1:15-20)," *CTM* 36 (1965), 289-300; Stettler, *Kolosserhymnus*, 314-16; Lincoln, 604-5; Smith, *Heavenly Perspective*, 156-57.

background would also fit the scheme of "creation"/"new creation" that many think dominates the passage. And, of course, the portrayal of Christ in Adamic terms would mesh nicely with a major Pauline christological conception. Finally, though less significant than these other two, the messianic concept of the Old Testament and Judaism has also probably influenced the text at specific points.[122]

Such a combination of backgrounds should not surprise us. Early Christians naturally mined all the rich resources of the Old Testament and the Jewish world to develop and express their understanding of Christ. And, as N. T. Wright has pointed out, the general structure of the "hymn," asserting as it does that Christ is the center of God's work in both creation and redemption, echoes a widespread Old Testament/Jewish pattern.[123] This pattern is reflected, moreover, in some key New Testament christological passages: note especially the very significant 1 Corinthians 8:6: "one Lord, Jesus Christ, through whom all things came and through whom we live."[124] And this point, in turn, reminds us that this "hymn" — whether written by Paul or by someone before him — is not based simply and directly on either the Old Testament or Judaism. It reflects the reality of Christ as he was experienced in the early church.[125] Through Jesus' mighty acts, and especially in light of his resurrection and exaltation, Christians began quite early to "redefine" Jewish monotheism by including Jesus Christ in their understanding of God. This step was one for which there were no real precedents in the Jewish (or Greco-Roman) world.[126]

Finally, we must consider briefly the structure of this passage. Determining the structure is complicated by the possibility that Paul is quoting an underlying hymn. The literature is littered with reconstructions of the alleged original hymn, with the redactional elements added by Paul and perhaps others stripped away.[127] It is not out of order to indulge in

122. Hübner (53-54) argues that the Lordship of Christ portrayed in vv. 15-20 reflects the messianic ideas of vv. 13-14.

123. *Climax of the Covenant*, 107-8.

124. Fee (*Pauline Christology*, 302) also notes that two of the key terms that govern each section of the hymm — εἰκών ("image") and πρωτότοκος ("firstborn") — are also used together in Rom. 8:29.

125. See, e.g., the intriguing suggestion of Kim (*Origins of Paul's Gospel*, 193-268) that Paul's understanding of Christ as "the image of God" was a deduction from Christ's appearance to him on the Damascus Road.

126. See esp. Hurtado, *Lord Jesus Christ;* Wright, *Climax of the Covenant*, 114-18; Bauckham, *God Crucified*.

127. See the survey of possibilities in C. Burger, *Schöpfung und Versöhnung* (Neukirchen-Vluyn: Neukirchener Verlag, 1975), 3-18; Gnilka, 53-54. John F. Balchin ("Colossians 1:15-20: An Early Christian Hymn? The Arguments from Style," *VE* 15

some speculation along these lines. But we have to admit at the end of the day that we just don't know enough to establish any theory as very likely.[128]

We can more profitably concentrate on the text now before us. Most scholars identify two basic stanzas on the basis of similar language and structure: the phrase *who is* (v. 15 [TNIV, "The Son is"], v. 18); the word *firstborn* (vv. 15, 18); the phrase (in reverse sequence) *things in heaven and on earth* (vv. 16, 20); the sequence of assertion plus elaboration introduced with *for* (*hoti*; vv. 16, 19); the sequence of three prepositions: *in* (*en*; vv. 16a, 19) — *through* (*dia*; vv. 16b, 20a) — *for* (*eis*; vv. 16b, 20 ["reconcile all things 'unto' himself"]). But opinions diverge from here, with three proposals deserving mention. The first takes its key from the shift in focus from "creation" to "church" that occurs at v. 18a. The two stanzas would then comprise vv. 15-17 and vv. 18-20.[129] The second proposal focuses on the parallel language in v. 15 and v. 18b: "who is" (*hos estin*) and "firstborn" (*prōtotokos*). Verses 15-18a and vv. 18b-20 would then comprise the two stanzas.[130] A third alternative, recognizing some point in each of these considerations, posits two main stanzas (vv. 15-16, vv. 18b-20), with a transitional stanza between the two (vv. 17-18a).[131] This last suggestion seems to offer the best account

[1985], 65-94) notes that the number of competing schemes suggests that the attempt to reconstruct an "original" hymn is doomed. Most often thought to be redactional additions by Paul are "of the church" in v. 18 (adapting an alleged original "cosmological" idea of "body" to Paul's ecclesial purposes) and the phrase "blood of the cross" in v. 20 (see, e.g., Schweizer, 58-60; Lohse, 42-43; Gnilka, 57-58). Cited a bit less frequently is the enumeration of the "powers" in v. 16 (Schweizer, 60-61; Ernst, 76). Various theories about the origin of the hymn have been propounded over the years. Ernst Käsemann's suggestion that the passage grew out of a non-Christian hymn about the Gnostic redeemer ("A Primitive Christian Baptismal Liturgy," in *Essays on New Testament Themes* [London: SCM, 1964], 149-68) was popular for a time, but has now fallen out of favor (see Lohse, 45, for a brief rebuttal). Ernst Lohmeyer traced the hymn to the Day of Atonement festival (Lohmeyer, 41-47).

128. Those skeptical of discerning redactional additions are Robert J. Karris, *A Symphony of New Testament Hymns* (Collegeville, Minn.: Liturgical Press, 1996), 65-66; Stettler, *Kolosserhymnus*, 94-100; Barth/Blanke, 227-34.

129. Paul Ellingworth, "Colossians I.15-20 and Its Context," *ExpTim* 73 (1962), 252-53; Harris, 42; Dibelius/Greeven, 10; Stettler, *Kolosserhymnus*, 86-94.

130. Wolter, 72-73; Dunn, 84; Schweizer, 56-58; Lohse, 42; Ernst, 174-76; Aletti, *Colossiens 1:15-20*, 25-45; Hay, 51.

131. This is the general preference among recent interpreters. See, e.g., Luis Carlos Reyes, "The Structure and Rhetoric of Colossians 1:15-20," *Filologia neotestamentaria* 12 (1999), 140-46; Bruce, 55-56; Benoit, "L'hymne christologique," 226-32; Otfried Hofius, "'Erstgeborener vor aller Schöpfung' — 'Erstgeborener aus den Toten': Erwägungen zu Struktur und Aussage des Christushymnus Kol 1,15-20," in *Auferstehung-Resurrection* (ed. Friedrich Avemarie and Hermann Lichtenberger; Tübingen: Mohr Siebeck, 2001),

of the passage, especially when it is recognized that the interim stanza exhibits an inclusion structure of its own ("he is . . . he is"). The resulting structure is best appreciated by means of a structural layout (with key structural clues highlighted):

> ¹⁵The Son [who] **is** the image of the invisible God,
>   the <u>firstborn</u> over all creation.
>   ¹⁶FOR *in* him all things were created:
>   <u>things in heaven and on earth,</u>
>   visible and invisible,
>   whether thrones or powers
>   or rulers or authorities;
>   ALL THINGS have been created
>   *through* him
>   and *for* [*eis*] him.
> ¹⁷He *(autos)* is before all things,
> and in him all things hold together.
> ¹⁸And he *(autos)* is the head of the body, the church;
>
> he [who] **is** the beginning
> and the <u>firstborn</u> from among the dead,
>   so that in everything he might have the supremacy.
>   ¹⁹FOR God was pleased
>   to have all his fullness dwell *in* him,
>   ²⁰and *through* him to [*for; eis*] reconcile to himself
>   all things,
>   whether <u>things on earth or things in heaven,</u>
>   by making peace through his blood,
>   shed on the cross.

15 The TNIV's *The Son* represents a relative pronoun in the Greek *(hos)*, which continues the sequence of relative pronouns that begins in v. 13: "*the Father* [v. 12] **who** [TNIV *he*] brought us into the kingdom of the

190-91; Pokorný, 59; Paul Beasley-Murray, "Colossians 1:15-20: An Early Christian Hymn Celebrating the Lordship of Christ," in *Pauline Studies* (ed. D. A. Hagner and M. J. Harris; Grand Rapids: Eerdmans, 1980), 169-70; Dübbers, *Christologie und Existenz*, 86-91. Somewhat related to this three-stanza structure is the proposal of Wright, who finds four parts, chiastically arranged (vv. 15-16, v. 17, v. 18a, vv. 18b-20; cf. *Climax of the Covenant*, 101; see also Aletti, 89-92). Zeilinger also identifies four parts, two "stanzas" (15-16, 18b-20a), a "mediating strophe" (vv. 17-18a), and an "Abgesang" (v. 20b) (Franz Zeilinger, *Der Erstgeborene der Schöpfung: Untersuchungen zur Formalstruktur und Theologie des Kolosserbriefes* [Vienna: Herder, 1974], 39-43).

Son he loves, in **whom** we have redemption . . . **who** is the image. . . ." If Paul is quoting a "hymn," he has probably replaced the original noun with the relative pronoun to connect the hymn to the context.[132] The hymn opens with two parallel depictions of the Son: *image of God* and *firstborn over all creation.* "Image" (Gk. *eikōn*) is basically something that looks like, or represents, something else. Its most common reference in biblical Greek is to objects that are designed to represent other gods. "Image" is the name given to the statue that Nebuchadnezzar has erected in Daniel; and in Revelation, for instance, the word occurs ten times to refer to the "image" of the "beast" who seeks to displace God. Related to this usage is the application of the word to the stamped portrait of Caesar found on many first-century coins (e.g., Matt. 22:20 par. Mark 12:16 par. Luke 20:24). In relationship to God, as in v. 15, the most important text is, of course, the account of the creation of human beings:

> Then God said, "Let us make human beings in our image (*eikōn*), in our likeness, so that they may rule over the fish in the sea and the birds in the sky, over the livestock and all the wild animals, and over all the creatures that move along the ground." So God created human beings in his own image (*eikōn*), in the image of God he created them; male and female he created them. God blessed them and said to them, "Be fruitful and increase in number; fill the earth and subdue it. Rule over the fish in the sea and the birds in the sky and over every living creature that moves on the ground." (Gen. 1:26-28)

"Image of God" has this general sense elsewhere in the Old Testament (Gen. 5:1) and in the New Testament (1 Cor. 11:7), and, most interesting for our purposes, in Colossians 3:10, where Paul says that the "new self" is "being renewed in knowledge in the image of its Creator."[133]

Theologians have long debated just what this "image of God" in which humans were created might be. But this issue is only tangentially related to the question of what it means for Christ to be "the image of God." In both texts where Paul asserts this about Christ (here and in 2 Cor. 4:4), the focus is on Christ's revelation of God. He *is* the "image" in accordance with which human beings are formed.[134] According to both

---

132. Another possibility is that the original hymn was a "blessing" that began "blessed is the Lord **who**" (Stettler, *Kolosserhymnus,* 79-86).

133. It should be noted that Philo, who is often cited as a source for "image" = wisdom or the "word," in fact uses "image of God" language most often in reference to the creation of humans (over thirty times).

134. See, e.g., Stettler, *Kolosserhymnus,* 104-10, who rightly distinguishes between Christ, who *is* the image of God, and human beings, who are created *according to* or *in* that image.

the Old Testament and Judaism, as John puts it, "no one has ever seen God" (1:18); he is, as Paul puts it here, *invisible (aoratos).*[135] A major question, therefore, in Jewish theology at the time, with parallels in the Greco-Roman world, was this: where can God be seen? In this respect, Colossians 1:15 is similar to John's depiction of the "Word" in 1:1-18 — the Word was "with God" and "was God" (v. 1) and thus has "made him known" (v. 18) — and to Hebrews 1:3 — "the Son is the radiance of God's glory and the exact representation of his being."[136] The opening line of our hymn may, then, identify Christ as that original image in accordance with which human beings were created.[137]

However, the revelatory focus of "image of God" here might point to a different background: the wisdom/word tradition.[138] While lacking Old Testament support, the identification of wisdom or the word with the image of God is found in Jewish writings (Wis. 7:25 and esp. Philo[139]), and often in contexts that focus on the way God can now be known. This latter tradition is almost certainly influential here since, as we will see, this tradition has influenced the hymn at a number of places. But this tradition itself incorporated allusion to Genesis 1 as its starting point. Philo, for instance, regularly connects the "image" with Genesis 1, even as he identifies the image with wisdom or the word. We should probably conclude, therefore, that our hymn, similarly, alludes to both these traditions. In place of the Jewish tradition, which finds the image to be expressed in

135. There is, to be sure, a tension within the OT on this point. Several texts speak of people "seeing" God (e.g., Gen. 12:7; 18:1; 32:30; Exod. 33:11; Num. 12:8; Deut. 34:30; Isa. 6:1-5), but God warns Moses, "You cannot see my face, for no one may see me and live" (Exod. 33:20). We may ease the tension if the former texts refer to seeing some kind of image of God rather than God himself.

136. The Hebrews text suggests another tie with the wisdom tradition, since the word ἀπαύγασμα (translated "radiance") refers to wisdom in its only occurrence in the LXX (Wis. 7:6).

137. See esp. Ridderbos, *Paul,* 70-73; Masson, 98-99; Hugedé, 50-58; Beasley-Murray, "Colossians 1:15-20," 170-71; T. E. Pollard, "Colossians 1:12-20, a Reconsideration," *NTS* 27 (1981), 572-75. Dübbers (*Christologie und Existenz,* 92-95), on the other hand, thinks that the hymn identifies Christ not with Adam, created "in" the image of God, but with the original "image" according to which Adam was created (an idea that parallels Philo's interpretation of the Genesis tradition in terms of the "Word").

138. As Kim (*Origins of Paul's Gospel,* 266) notes, "Adam Christology" tends to focus on anthropology and soteriology, while "Wisdom Christology" comes to the aid of the ideas of creation and revelation.

139. "Wisdom" is related to "image of God" in *Allegorical Interpretation* 1.43; *On the Migration of Abraham* 40; *Who Is the Heir?* 112, "Word" (closely allied with wisdom in Philo) is related to "image of God" in *Allegorical Interpretation* 3.96 (?); *On the Confusion of Tongues* 97; 147; *On Dreams* 1.75; 1.239; 2.45; 3.83 (?); *On the Special Laws* 1.81, and *On Flight and Finding* 101.

wisdom or the word, the hymn claims that the original image is to be found in the person of Jesus Christ, God's Son. And this decision came via the early Christians' confrontation with the reality of the resurrected and glorified Christ, whom they recognized to be "the perfect manifestation of the invisible God."[140]

The "hymn" adds a second depiction of the Son in its opening line: *the firstborn over all creation.* Calling Christ "firstborn," especially in the common translation "firstborn *of* all creation" (e.g., ESV; NRSV; NASB), could suggest that Christ is a created being, a conclusion that the church leader Arius drew early in the fourth century. Arius's views stimulated considerable christological reflection and resulted in the Nicene Creed's affirmation that Christ was "eternally begotten of the Father, . . . begotten, not made, of one Being *(homoousios)* with the Father."[141] But what can we then say about Colossians 1:15? The TNIV, by translating the Greek genitive construction *(pasēs ktiseōs)* as "over all creation," hints at the answer. The word *prōtotokos* ("firstborn"), while often used in the literal sense of the first to come from the womb, takes on a metaphorical significance based on the ancient attribution of preeminence to the first to be born. Thus, Israel is called God's "firstborn" (Exod. 4:22), and God says of David in Psalm 89:27 that "I will appoint him to be my firstborn, the most exalted of the kings of the earth." This latter text is probably especially important for Colossians 1:15, since Psalm 89 rings with messianic allusions, and Paul has just been describing Christ in messianic/kingly terms (vv. 12-14). It may be noted in this regard that the author to the Hebrews also uses *prōtotokos* as a christological title in a messianic context (Heb. 1:6; cf. v. 5). Philo also uses *prōtotokos* and its close equivalent, *prōtogonos,* to refer to the "word,"[142] so there could also be allusion here to the wis-

---

140. Kim, *Origins of Paul's Gospel,* 259.

141. For a history of interpretation, see Alfred Hockel, *Christus der Erstgeborene: Zur Geschichte der Exegese von Kol 1,15* (Düsseldorf: Patmos, 1965).

142. πρωτότοκος: *Who Is the Heir?* 117-19; πρωτόγονος: *On Husbandry* 51; *On the Confusion of Tongues* 146-47; *On Dreams* 1.215; *On Agriculture* 51. See Lightfoot, 146; Schweizer, 68. Dunn is representative of those who suggest that the figure of "Wisdom" may be the background (see also Feuillet, *Le Christ sagesse de Dieu,* 185-94). But this is more questionable. We have no extant text that calls "wisdom" πρωτότοκος, contrary to the implication in Dunn's claim (p. 90) that "the antecedent for the use of the word πρωτότοκος . . . is most obviously wisdom" (Prov. 8:22, 25; Philo, *On Drunkenness* 30-31; *Questions and Answers on Genesis* 1, 2, 3, 4 4.97; cf. *On the Virtues* 62)." Proverbs 8:22 and 25 do, indeed, claim that "The LORD brought [wisdom] forth as the first of his works" and that "before the mountains were settled in place, before the hills, I [wisdom] was given birth," but the word πρωτότοκος is not used in the LXX. Nor does any of the Philo texts use πρωτότοκος. This is not to deny, of course, that there may be a conceptual parallel; but the lack of a linguistic connection does raise questions. See also, on the wisdom background, Schweizer, 67; Lohse, 48; Ernst, 166-67.

dom/word tradition.[143] Against this background, then, and since the "hymn" goes on to affirm Christ's mediatorial role in all of creation (v. 16) — and hence his existence before creation — it is clear that the word is used here in this sense of "supreme over."[144] The supremacy asserted in the hymn may be over "every creature,"[145] but the translation "all creation," found in the English versions, is preferable.[146] As the first predicate in v. 15 presents Christ in unique relationship to God, so the second asserts his unique relationship to creation: he is "the acting subject who extends God's activity to the creatures that follow him."[147]

16 Christ's supreme role in creation is now cited as evidence (*for; hoti*) that he is, indeed, the *firstborn over all creation*. The extent of this supremacy is emphasized by citing three specific ways in which Christ and the creation are related: *in him all things were created . . . all things have been created **through** him and **for** him*. The sequence of three prepositions is significant, as seen in the fact that the second main strophe of the hymn features the same progression (see above on structure). The translation of the first clause is uncertain, the ambiguity of the Greek preposition *en* being the issue. A number of English versions (e.g., NIV; ESV; NLT; NASB; HCSB; NET; TEV) and interpreters[148] take the word in an instrumental sense: "**by** him all things were created" (NIV). It is argued that this interpretation fits with language about God creating "through" his word or wisdom in the Old Testament and about Christ and creation used elsewhere in the New Testament (esp. John 1:3 and 1 Cor. 8:6). It is also said to be supported by the explicit language about Christ as mediator of creation later in the verse ("through" him). But the latter point actually cuts both ways. Which is more likely: that the "hymn" repeats the idea of

143. Some also see allusion to the creation of humans/Adam tradition (e.g., Ridderbos, *Paul*, 81), and others to Israel (Hay [57] cites the fragmentary first-century *Prayer of Joseph*, in which Jacob is called "the firstborn of every living thing to whom God gives life" [frag. A, 2,3]).

144. Lohse, 48-49; Wallace, *Greek Grammar*, 104 (he identifies the genitive as a "genitive of subordination"). Others suggest that the word may have the sense "prior to" (Abbott, 210-12; Schweizer, 67); while still others want to combine "supreme over" with "prior to" (Moule, 64-65; Wright, 71).

145. Abbott, 212-13; Masson, 99; Stettler, *Kolosserhymnus*, 147-48.

146. Lightfoot, 148; Furter, 100; Barth/Blanke, 197. Paul's usual usage of κτίσις favors this meaning. Some argue for the alternative on the basis of the anarthrous construction (πάσης κτίσεως), which would normally in Greek indicate "every . . ." rather than "the whole of . . ." (e.g., Stettler, *Kolosserhymnus*, 147-48). But this "rule" is frequently violated in the NT (see esp. Turner, *Syntax*, 199-200; F. C. Conybeare and St. George Stock, *A Grammar of Septuagint Greek* [Boston: Ginn and Company, 1905], 63.c), so context is the only sure guide.

147. Schweizer, 67; cf. also Masson, 98-99.

148. E.g., Lohse, 50; Stettler, *Kolosserhymnus*, 146-47.

Christ's instrumentality in creation or that the opening line makes a different point? The latter might seem at least as probable. Moreover, it may be significant that John 1:3 and 1 Corinthians 8:6 both use *dia* (as later in this verse) and not *en*. Positively, Paul uses the preposition *en* quite a lot in Colossians with Christ as its object; and most of them — perhaps even all of them — express the idea of sphere (1:4, 14, 17, 19; 2:6, 7, 9, 10, 11; 3:18, 20; 4:7, 17). We think it more likely, then, that this opening line is claiming that Christ is the one "in" whom all things were created.[149] As so often when we confront Paul's "in Christ" language, it is difficult to put into words the precise point that is being made. But perhaps our problem is that we are seeking a specificity that Paul does not intend. He wants to make the very general point that all of God's creative work took place "in terms of" or "in reference to" Christ.

The universality expressed in "all things" *(ta panta)* is a leitmotif of the "hymn," the construction here suggesting a collective sense: "the entire universe."[150] This point receives considerable emphasis by the addition of three sets of qualifiers: *things in heaven and on earth; [things] visible and invisible; thrones or powers or rulers or authorities.* These qualifiers disrupt the simple sequence of clauses about Christ and creation; and many scholars therefore suppose that some or all of these have been added to the "original" hymn.[151] The scenario is certainly possible, since we can well imagine Paul adding language to focus attention on the "powers" in light of the apparent concern about them in the Colossian situation (see 2:10, 15, 18). But, as we noted earlier, the scant and debated evidence regarding the "hymn's" authorship and history makes it necessary to exercise considerable caution about these matters.

The first set of qualifers, *things in heaven and on earth,* is clear enough. "Heaven and earth" is a common biblical merism, that is, a construction in which two elements function together to indicate a single whole: in this case, the created order, the universe (e.g., Gen. 1:1, passim).[152] It is more difficult to know what in particular is intended in the

149. As TNIV; RSV; NRSV; NJB; REB; NAB; see also O'Brien, 45; Fowl, *The Story of Christ*, 108-9. A few commentators think that both instrument and locality may be expressed (Moule, 65).

150. See Harris, 44, on the significance of the article with πάντα.

151. The most popular option holds that the last series of four spiritual beings has been added by Paul (Schweizer, 60-61; Ernst, 176; Dunn, 92-93). Contra, see Barth/Blanke, 203. Lohse (43) thinks they were added to the original hymn but before Paul. Stettler's claim that the list exemplifies standard early Christian teaching (*Kolosserhymnus*, 166-98) founders on the unusual reference to "thrones."

152. Lincoln, however, suggests that the emphasis on heaven and earth here may reflect the typical Hellenistic sense of the separation of the two realms (cf. also v. 20) (*Paradise Now and Not Yet*, 120-21).

pairing *visible and invisible.* This pair is not common,[153] so we do not have much to go on. It is easiest to assume that they restate the first pair in chiastic arrangement *(heaven = invisible; earth = visible).*[154]

The relationship between the last set of four qualifiers and the previous ones is again disputed. Some think that both earthly rulers and heavenly rulers — spiritual beings — are intended, so that the four elaborate the pair that precedes them: *[things] visible and invisible.*[155] But it is more likely that all four are describing spiritual beings, and that they are elaborating the word *invisible. Thrones,* to be sure, occurs very often throughout Scripture in its literal sense and often also in the metaphorical sense of that which the throne represents, power. But its placement here suggests that, like the other three in the series, it refers to personal beings, a usage attested outside Scripture.[156] The second term in the series, *powers,* translates a Greek word, *kyriotēs,* that occurs elsewhere in the New Testament and in Jewish writings as a reference to spiritual beings (Eph. 1:21; cf. 2 Pet. 2:10; Jude 8[157]). The last two, *rulers* and *authorities (archai and exousiai),* are better known from the Pauline letters. They occur together in six verses as references to spiritual powers (1 Cor. 15:24; Eph. 1:21; 3:10; 6:12; Col. 2:10, 15; cf. also *archē* in Rom. 8:38; in Titus 3:1 [and Luke 12:11], they refer to earthly authorities).[158]

Also disputed is whether the four titles refer to all spiritual beings (e.g., angels, both good and bad)[159] or to evil spiritual beings only.[160] It is certainly the case that 1:20 and 2:15 imply hostility toward God and/or

153. The pairing occurs nowhere else in Scripture; cf. *T. Reuben* 6:12, which speaks of "wars visible and invisible"; also Philo, *On the Creation of the World* 12.

154. O'Brien, 46.

155. Lightfoot, 152-53; Thompson, 34; Ernst Bammel, "Versuch Col 1:15-20," *ZNW* 52 (1961), 88-95. Walter Wink argues that language about the "powers" in the NT, against the worldview of that day, would naturally refer to "power" in its broadest sense *(Naming the Powers* [Philadelphia: Fortress, 1984], 39; he refers explicitly here to Col. 1:16).

156. See 2 *En.* 20:1; *Apoc. El. (H)* 1:10-11; *T. Levi* 3:8. The location of these "thrones," just below the archangels, in the latter text may suggest that the word denotes one of the highest of heavenly powers (O. Schmitz, *TDNT* 3:166-67).

157. A reference to spiritual beings in the Ephesians text is pretty clear; but the meaning in the 2 Peter and Jude passages (which are roughly parallel) is quite disputed.

158. See also *1 En.* 6:7-8 (Gk. frag.); *3 Bar.* 12:3; *T. Abraham* 13:10 (shorter res.). For these references and discussion, see Clinton Arnold, *Colossian Syncretism* (Tübingen: Mohr Siebeck, 1995), 253-55.

159. See esp. the thorough analysis of Stettler, *Kolosserhymnus,* 166-98. Wesley Carr *(Angels and Principalities* [Cambridge and New York: Cambridge University Press, 2005], 48-52) minimizes here, as elsewhere in the letter, reference to evil spiritual beings, arguing that they are neutral at worst.

160. E.g., Dunn, 92-93.

humans on the part of the powers; but the inclusive language of this verse suggests that Paul is setting up that specific point by asserting Christ's supremacy over the entire angelic realm. The existence of spiritual beings of various sorts and their critical impact on the affairs of human beings were fundamental components of the ancient worldview. This belief was apparently an important catalyst for the Colossian false teaching, and Paul's emphasis here on Christ's supremacy to these powers reminds the Colossians that they are utterly unable to rival Christ in any way. Translation of this emphasis into our culture is contested. On the one hand, the ancient worldview about the significance of spiritual beings for the affairs of this world is, in a fundamental sense at least, the biblical worldview as well. Spiritual powers, while defeated in Christ (2:15), are still active and powerful. More contested is whether we are justified in finding reference in a text such as this one to the various structures, persons, and institutions through whom evil "powers" might be working today. On this view, the language of v. 16 can be applied, as Wright puts it, to "unseen forces working in the world through pagan religion, astrology, or magic, or through the oppressive systems that enslaved or tyrannized human beings."[161]

Having asserted in the opening of the verse the general relationship of Christ to creation, the final line specifies by focusing on the beginning and end of creation. Christ stands at the beginning of creation as the one *through (dia)* whom all things were created. This concept probably again alludes to the widespread teaching about wisdom/word. Note, for example, Psalm 104:24: "In wisdom have you [the LORD] made them all"; Proverbs 3:19: "The LORD by wisdom founded the earth's foundations"; Wisdom 9:1: "O God of my ancestors and Lord of mercy, who have made all things by your word"; cf. 8:5, "wisdom, the active cause of all things"; and the Philo reference quoted above. And, while the text does not clearly assert wisdom's mediation in creation, Proverbs 8:22-31 should certainly also be cited in this regard:

"The LORD brought me forth as the first of his works, before his deeds of old; I was formed long ages ago, at the very beginning, when the world came to be. When there were no oceans, I was given birth, when there were no springs abounding with water; before the mountains

---

161. Wright, 72. See, for this general way of thinking about the "powers" in the NT, the three-volume project of Walter Wink (*Engaging the Powers, Naming the Powers, Unmasking the Powers: The Invisible Forces That Determine Human Existence*); and for a stimulating application of this idea, Brian Walsh and Sylvia Keesmaat, *Colossians Remixed* (Downers Grove, Ill.: InterVarsity, 2004). Arnold is reluctant to make this hermeneutical move (*Powers of Darkness* [Downers Grove, Ill.: InterVarsity, 1992]).

were settled in place, before the hills, I was given birth, before he made the world or its fields or any of the dust of the earth. I was there when he set the heavens in place, when he marked out the horizon on the face of the deep, when he established the clouds above and fixed securely the fountains of the deep, when he gave the sea its boundary so the waters would not overstep his command, and when he marked out the foundations of the earth. Then I was constantly at his side. I was filled with delight day after day, rejoicing always in his presence, rejoicing in his whole world and delighting in humankind."

While it is likely, then, that the assertion of Christ's relationship to creation here owes something to the wisdom/word tradition, it is important again to insist that the concept does not depend on that tradition. Still less can we interpret the text as though its assertions about Christ as mediator of creation serve only to show that Christ is the "climactic manifestation" of wisdom and imply nothing about his preexistence.[162] And the final assertion in this verse about Christ's relationship to creation, that *all things have been created*[163] . . . *for him*, goes beyond any Jewish tradition about wisdom.[164] Christ stands at the "beginning" of the universe as the one through whom it came into being, and he stands at its end as the goal of the universe. O'Brien aptly cites Ephesians 1:10, which asserts that God plans to "bring unity to all things in heaven and on earth under Christ."[165] The vision of Christ in relationship to creation is thus comprehensive, and reminds us that "For those who have been redeemed by Christ, the universe has no ultimate terrors; they know that their Redeemer is also creator, ruler, and goal of all."[166]

17 As we argued above, the two lines of this verse, along with the first line of v. 18, are best seen as a brief intermediary strophe between the two larger strophes in the "hymn." All three lines begin with *kai*, "and" (left untranslated by the TNIV in the first line), and the first and third also

162. So Dunn, 89; cf. *Christology in the Making* (Grand Rapids: Eerdmans, 1996), 190. In his *Theology*, Dunn is more nuanced, claiming that Christ's preexistence is, indeed, taught in this passage but that the preexistence involves "the divine fullness whereby God's presence fills the universe and which is now embodied (incarnate?) in Christ" (p. 277; see also p. 292). The preexistence of Christ *as a person* still appears to be denied by Dunn.

163. The verb here is in the perfect tense — ἔκτισται — in contrast to the aorist ἐκτίσθη in the opening line. The change in tense could be purely stylistic (so Turner, *Syntax*, 70), but it is perhaps more likely that it signals a greater emphasis in the last part of the verse on the enduring state of creation (Zerwick, *Biblical Greek*, §287; Harris, 45).

164. O'Brien, 47. See, however, the rabbinic saying about the Messiah: "The world was created for the sake of the Messiah" (*b. Sanhedrin* 98b).

165. O'Brien, 47.

166. Bruce, 63.

use the nominative personal pronoun *autos* ("he").[167] The opening line clearly looks back to vv. 15-16, with their focus on Christ's relationship to creation, while the last line introduces the focus on Christ's redemptive work that typifies vv. 18b-20. The center line — *and in him all things hold together* — seems to look both directions and functions not only as the center of this brief strophe but perhaps of the hymn as a whole.[168]

The claim that Christ is *before all things* is somewhat ambiguous in English and even more so in Greek, where the preposition *pro* can designate either priority in time (e.g., Eph. 1:4, "before the foundation of the world") or priority in rank (e.g., 1 Pet. 4:8, "above all"). But the latter usage is quite rare in the New Testament, while all of Paul's uses of the word have a temporal sense.[169] So this text is best taken as referring to Christ's preexistence.[170] There are again wisdom parallels for this idea; see Proverbs 8:22-31, cited above, and also, for example, Sirach 1:4, "Wisdom was created before all things." But while these texts assert that wisdom was the first thing created, the claim in our verse is bolder: Christ existed before creation itself.

The hymn thus far has focused on Christ's role at the beginning ("in him," "through him," "before all things") and at the end ("for him") of creation. Now the focus turns to the present role of Christ in creation: *in him all things hold together*. The verb here (*synestēken*, from *synistēmi*) means, in this context, "hold together," "cohere,"[171] and the use of the perfect tense suggests a stative idea: the universe owes its continuing coherence to Christ. This concept has analogies in the wisdom/word tradition,[172] which, in turn, is probably reflecting certain Platonic and Stoic emphases about the cohesion of the universe. Again, however, the idea that an aspect of God's character or immaterial concept holds the universe together is a far cry from the startling claim that a man who had recently lived and been crucified by the Romans was the one in whom all things are held together. What holds the universe together is not an idea

---

167. The nominative pronoun may be emphatic, as it often is in the NT (Greek not requiring it for sense) — cf. NRSV and NET, "he himself is before all things" (e.g., Turner, *Syntax,* 40 ["he, and no other"]; Lightfoot, 156; Harris, 46), but it is perhaps more likely that it is used for rhetorical effect.

168. E.g., Baugh, "The Poetic Form of Col 1:15-20," 237; Beasley-Murray calls it the "pivotal line" ("Colossians 1:15-20," 174).

169. Rom. 16:7; 1 Cor. 2:7; 4:5; 2 Cor. 12:2; Gal. 1:17; 2:12; 3:23; Eph. 1:4; 2 Tim. 1:9; 4:21; Titus 1:2.

170. So most commentators; Masson, 101, takes it to mean precedence in rank; others, to both time and rank (Wallace, *Greek Grammar,* 379; Dunn, 93; Wright, 73).

171. The only other NT occurrence with a similar meaning is 2 Pet. 3:5.

172. See, e.g., Sir. 43:26, "by his word all things hold together." There are many similar references in Philo.

or a virtue, but a person: the resurrected Christ. Without him, electrons would not continue to circle nuclei, gravity would cease to work, the planets would not stay in their orbits. As is true of every line in this "hymn," there is particular application to the Colossian Christians, who were perhaps being tempted to find coherence by pursuing other religious options in their context. In response, Paul wants them to understand that things make sense only when Christ is kept at the center.

18 The opening line of this verse is the most difficult to fit into the structure of the "hymn." On the one hand, the content of the line, with its shift of attention to the church, suggests that it should be seen as the beginning of a new strophe, focusing on the "new creation," just as vv. 15-17 have focused on creation as such. On the other, the form of the line suggests that it be seen as the conclusion to the first strophe. For it resembles v. 17a — "and he is" *(kai autos estin)* — while it is with the second line — "he is the beginning" *(hos estin archē)* — that we get the formal equivalent to v. 15a. Traditions-analysis posits a solution to this dilemma: the original "hymn" lacked any reference to the church, asserting simply that "he [Christ] is the head of the body," "body" *(sōma)* being used in a cosmological sense to denote the universe. Paul has added "of the church" *(tēs ekklēsias)* to suit his own argument.[173] But attempts to reconstruct an original hymn are fraught with difficulties of all sorts (see above). Moreover, it is questionable whether the term "body" could refer to the cosmos apart from an extended metaphor.[174]

We must deal with the text as it stands. And, as we suggested above, a solution that does justice to both the form and content of this line is at hand: it should be seen as the last line of an intermediate strophe. As the opening line of the strophe points back to the first strophe, so this line points forward to the strophe that follows. The "hymn" equates the "body" with the church,[175] utilizing a metaphor that is distinctive to

173. The suggestion is very widespread; see esp. Lohse, 53-54, who provides examples from ancient literature; cf. also Hanna Roose, "Die Hierarchisierung der Lieb-Metapher im Kolosser- und Epheserbrief als 'Paulinisierung': Ein Beitrag zur Rezeption paulinischer Tradition in Pseudo-Paulinischen Briefen," *NovT* 47 (2005), 117-41; Schweizer, 58-59; Ernst, 175; Gnilka, 57-58; Dunn, 94-95; Wolter, 81-82.

174. Beasley-Murray, "Colossians 1:15-20," 180-82; cf. also Stettler, *Kolosserhymnus,* 231-34; N. Kehl, *Der Christushymnus im Kolosserbrief: Eine motivegeschichtliche Untersuchung zu Kol 1,12-20* (SBM 1; Stuttgart: Katholisches, 1967), 93. In the key texts usually cited as parallels (Plato, *Timaeus* 31–32; the *Orphic Fragment* 168; Philo, *On Dreams* 1.128), "body" is usually explicitly qualified; e.g., "the body of the world" (τὸ τοῦ κόσμου σῶμα) in *Timaeus* 32c. See also Dübbers, *Christologie und Existenz,* 17-25, who notes that the literary judgment about the originality of τῆς ἐκκλησίας is too tied to a dubious historical judgment about the dominance of a "lordship" christological model in Colossians.

175. The genitive τῆς ἐκκλησίας is an obvious epexegetic genitive.

Colossians (1:24; 2:19; 3:15) and Ephesians (1:23; 4:4, 12, 16; 5:23, 30). But the metaphor is a natural extension of the simile in the earlier letters of Paul, according to which the church is compared to a body.[176] That the two are closely related is evident from the continuing use of the imagery of the physical body to denote the church and its growth (Col. 2:19; Eph. 4:16).

Scholars debate the source of this metaphor.[177] Various ancient writers from differing backgrounds used the metaphor of the body, and we cannot exclude the possibility that Paul has been influenced by one or more of them. But his distinctive understanding of Christ as a "corporate person," who, in a sense, "contains" all those who belong to him, has probably been a more immediate influence.[178] Whatever its derivation, the application of the metaphor to the church falls into line with the broad canvas on which Paul paints in both Colossians and Ephesians. The *ekklēsia* is no longer, as is typical in New Testament usage of the word elsewhere, the local "gathering" of believers (although this usage, of course, continues [4:15, 16]). It is a worldwide entity, embracing all who acknowledge Christ as Lord.[179] While many find in this development an indication of a post-Pauline author,[180] the move is, in fact, an evolutionary one, rooted perhaps in the Old Testament use of equivalent words to describe the (one) "assembly" of Israel.

But our passage takes a further step in the evolution of the metaphor. Christ is not pictured as the body per se but as the "head" *(kephalē)* of the body (cf. also 2:10, 19; Eph. 1:22; 4:15; 5:23). Again, there are paral-

---

176. A development already well under way (or even completed!) in 1 Corinthians; cf. 1 Cor. 12:27: "you are the body of Christ."

177. See the discussion in, e.g., Lohse, 54-56.

178. See esp. Ernest Best, *One Body in Christ: A Study of the Relationship of the Church to Christ in the Epistles of the Apostle Paul* (London: SPCK, 1955); Bruce, 68-69.

179. O'Brien, however, thinks that the concept of "assembling" may still be present in this universal application of ἐκκλησία: "Men and women were called into membership of this one church of Christ, the heavenly assembly, through the preaching of the gospel. They were brought into fellowship with God's Son, and to speak of their membership of this heavenly gathering assembled around Christ is another way of referring to this new relationship with him. They and other Christians were to assemble in local congregations here on earth, for this was an important way in which their fellowship with Christ was expressed. Further, as they came together with others who were in fellowship with him, so they not only met with each other — they also met with Christ himself who indwelt them corporately and individually" (60-61; cf. also idem, *DPL* 124-26); cf. also Robert Banks, *Paul's Idea of Community: The Early House Churches in Their Historical Setting* (Grand Rapids: Eerdmans, 1980), 44-47.

180. E.g., "the understanding of the church in Colossians cannot be explained as a simple evolution from earlier beginnings within Pauline theology" (Lohse, 55; cf. also Dunn, 95).

lels to this conception in the Hellenistic world, and these parallels may facilitate the language that is used here.[181] But the basic conception is again a rather straightforward elaboration of the metaphor, based on the standard Christian conception of Christ as the Lord of his people. In the ancient world, the head was conceived to be the governing member of the body, that which both controlled it and provided for its life and sustenance.[182] Christ is "the locus of the church's unity and coherence, the source of the church's sustenance and direction."[183] And this development may very well have been stimulated by the Colossian false teaching itself. Against people who were arguing that ultimate spiritual experience had to be found in places in addition to Christ, Paul holds up Christ as the one who is the true and only source of life for the body.[184] Just as Christ is preeminent in the universe, so he is preeminent within the new creation, the assembly of new covenant believers. But there is this difference: as the metaphor of body and head implies, Christ is in organic relationship to his people in a way that is not true of the creation in general.

With the second line of v. 18, we move into the second strophe (anticipated in v. 18a), which elaborates Christ's preeminence in the new creation. *He is the beginning, the firstborn from the dead* clearly echoes v. 15a, *The Son is the image of the invisible God, the firstborn over all creation.* The cor-

181. See esp. the *Orphic Fragment* 168, where Zeus is named the "head" (κεφαλή) and is described as the one in whose body all things exist. The text in Philo in which the logos is said to be the "head" of the universe (*Questions and Answers on Exodus* 2.117) is textually uncertain and may be a Christian interpolation.

182. See esp. Clinton E. Arnold, "Jesus Christ: 'Head' of the Church (Colossians and Ephesians)," in *Jesus of Nazareth, Lord and Christ: Essays on the Historical Jesus and New Testament Christology* (ed. Joel B. Green and Max Turner; Grand Rapids: Eerdmans, 1994), 350-55. See, e.g., Philo, *On Rewards and Punishments* 125: "The virtuous one, whether single man or people, will be the head [κεφαλή] of the human race and all the others will be like the parts of the body which are animated by the powers in and above the head." Dübbers argues that the elaboration of the metaphor of "head" in 2:19 is decisive in favor of the idea here not so much of Lordship but of "ground of existence" (*Christologie und Existenz*, 104-8). Influential on Pauline usage is also the LXX, where κεφαλή often translates ראש in the sense "leader," "ruler" (cf. Judg. 11:11: "So Jephthah went with the elders of Gilead, and the people made him head [ראש; κεφαλήν] and commander [ἀρχηγόν] over them." For discussion, see, e.g., S. M. Bedale, "The Meaning of κεφαλή in the Pauline Epistles," *JTS* 5 (1954): 211-15; the interchange between Wayne Grudem and Richard Cervin (Grudem, "Does κεφαλή mean 'Source' or 'Authority Over' in Greek Literature? A Survey of 2,336 Examples," *TJ* 6 [1985], 38-59; Cervin, "Does κεφαλή Mean 'Source' or "Authority Over" in Greek Literature? A Rebuttal," *TJ* 10 [1989], 85-112; Grudem, "The Meaning of κεφαλή ("Head"): A Response to Recent Studies," *TJ* 11 [1990], 3-72; and A. C. Perriman, "The Head of a Woman: The Meaning of Κεφαλή in 1 Cor. 11:3," *JTS* 45 (1994), 602-22.

183. Fowl, *The Story of Christ*, 112-13.

184. See esp. Bruce, *Paul*, 421; O'Brien, 49-50.

relation is much closer in the Greek text, which uses relative pronouns in both lines: *hos estin eikōn* . . . ; *hos estin archē*. . . . The Greek *archē* has a wide variety of meanings, but the temporal idea of "beginning" predominates, and most scholars agree that the word here has this basic sense (the translations agree).

But more than simple temporal rank is surely intended. Christ stands at the head of the new creation as the *firstborn from the dead*, the one who initiates the eschatological resurrection (see 1 Cor. 15:20).[185] "Beginning" here thus implies "founder," a meaning that *archē* appears to have in Genesis 49:3 LXX (especially interesting because *archē* occurs here with *prōtotokos* ["firstborn"]): "Reuben, you are my firstborn, my strength and the founder [*archē*] of my children" (see also Deut. 21:17).[186] Note also Revelation 3:14, where Christ is called the "beginning [*archē*] of God's creation" (ESV).[187] Some allusion to the wisdom/word tradition may again be present here. The Old Testament proclaims that wisdom was created in the "beginning" (Prov. 8:23) as the "first" of God's works (Prov. 8:22); and Philo calls wisdom "the beginning" (*Allegorical Interpretation* 1.43 [with "image"; cf. v. 15]).

In the roughly parallel v. 15, "firstborn" (*prōtotokos*), we have argued, refers to Jesus' supreme rank over all the created world. There may be some allusion to the same idea here in v. 18, but clearly the focus is now on temporal priority. But the word may have more than a simply temporal nuance. Jewish theology, following the hints of some Old Testament passages (esp. Dan. 12:1-2; Ezekiel 37), viewed the resurrection of physical bodies from the state of death as an eschatological event, signaling the coming of God in final kingdom power.[188] The resurrection of Christ initiates this end-time resurrection; his resurrection guarantees and, indeed, stimulates the resurrection of all who follow (1 Cor. 15:20; cf. Acts 26:23; Matt. 27:52-53). In this sense, he is not only the first one to experience resurrection; he is the "founder" of the new order of resurrection (see the remarks above on Gen. 49:3). He is the "firstborn (*prōtotokos*) among many brothers and sisters."

The outcome of Christ's being "beginning" and "firstborn" is that

185. Dunn, 97. A number of commentators combine this sense with the third (e.g., Wright, 74; Pokorný, 83; Beasley-Murray, "Colossians 1:15-20," 175-76).
186. See Moule, 69; O'Brien, 50; R. P. Martin, 59; MacDonald, 62.
187. The ESV is quoted because the TNIV interprets ἀρχή as "ruler." For a defense of the translation "beginning," see Greg Beale, *A Commentary on the Book of Revelation* (NIGTC; Grand Rapids: Eerdmans, 1999), 298-301.
188. On resurrection in Jewish theology, see esp. N. T. Wright, *The Resurrection of the Son of God* (vol. 3 of Christian Origins and the Question of God; Minneapolis: Fortress, 2003), 129-206.

in everything he might have the supremacy. In everything could also be translated "among all people" (if we take *pasin* as masculine rather than neuter), but the usual rendering is to be preferred in a hymn that is so deliberately cosmic in its scope. The TNIV's *he might have the supremacy*
renders a Greek periphrastic verbal[189] that can be rendered either "that
he might become supreme" or that "he might be supreme." But the difference between these two is minor; in either case, Christ's supremacy is
seen to be the result of his resurrection. This, of course, takes nothing
away from the reality of Christ's eternal sovereignty over all creation
(vv. 15-17). But it reflects the common New Testament understanding of
Christ's resurrection as having established his power over a fallen and
rebellious world in a new degree (Acts 2:36; Rom. 1:4; Phil. 2:9-11). Most
interpreters affirm or assume that this preeminence is an established
fact.

However, while it is no doubt true that Christ, through his resurrection, has been installed as lord over all, it is also true that he has yet to
manifest that Lordship over fallen and rebellious creation. We do "not
yet" see all things placed under his feet (1 Cor. 15:25-28; Heb. 2:8; cf. Phil.
2:11). We therefore suggest that the clause here is a true purpose clause,
expressing God's intention of ultimately bringing all of creation under
his rule through Christ.[190] Christ rules the church with the purpose of
bringing all things ultimately within the scope of that rule (see, perhaps,
the reference to the "reconciliation of all things" in v. 20). What is perhaps
even more significant for the situation in Colossae is the emphasis that
Christ is just as preeminent in the realm of redemption as he is in the
realm of creation. Christ's universal Lordship is not just a theoretical affirmation about the way the world is; it holds wide-ranging implications
for the way Christians are to find spiritual "fulfillment" (see esp. the application of these ideas in 2:9-23). It is this focus that the "in all things"
may emphasize.

19 The way in which the two main stanzas of our hymn mirror
each other is seen again by noting how the progression from v. 18b to v. 19
is similar to the move from v. 15 to v. 16. In both texts, strong christological claims by means of two titles — "image of God" and "firstborn
over all creation" in v. 15; "beginning" and "firstborn from the dead" in
v. 18b — are followed by an elaboration introduced with "for" *(hoti)*. But
we should note the differences as well. First, the result clause at the end
of v. 18 has no counterpart in vv. 15-16. Second, the elaboration in v. 16

189. On γένηται plus πρωτεύων as a periphrastic construction, see, e.g., BDF §354.
190. Eadie, 66. The clause, introduced with ἵνα, is often taken as indicating result
(e.g., Abbott, 218).

takes the form of grammatically simple claims about Christ's involvement in creation. In vv. 19-20, however, we find a longer, more complex sentence, with a main verb, two infinitives, and a participle: "was pleased" . . . "to dwell" . . . "to reconcile" . . . "making peace." The structure of this sentence is more typical of Paul's normal style and may signal that the "hymn" ends at v. 18 or that Paul has more radically modified a possible earlier hymn in these verses.

Before turning to the details of these verses, we must first pin down more specifically the structure of the sentence. The difficulty is created by the ambiguity of the function of the phrase "all the fullness" in the sentence. Since this phrase is neuter in Greek *(pan to plērōma)*, it could be either (1) the (nominative) subject of the verb "was pleased" or (2) the (accusative) subject of the infinitive "to dwell," in which case we have to supply "God" as the subject of "was pleased" (it is normal for verbs in Greek to have an unexpressed subject supplied from the context). Thus we could translate either (1) "all the fullness was pleased to dwell . . . and to reconcile" (cf. RSV; NRSV; ESV; NAB);[191] or (2) "God was pleased that all his fullness should dwell . . . and to reconcile" (TNIV; NIV; HCSB; NASB; NLT; NET; NJB; TEV).[192] In favor of the former rendering is: (1) the fact that we do not need to supply a subject (the alleged subject, "God," last occurs in v. 15 and then not as a subject); and (2) "fullness" is clearly the subject of the verb "dwell" in the parallel passage in 2:9. In favor of the latter rendering is: (1) the masculine form of the participle "making peace," which would normally echo the form of the subject of the main verb ("God" being masculine); (2) the awkwardness of the combination "all the fullness was pleased . . . to reconcile." However, both these latter problems are considerably alleviated if we take "all the fullness" to mean, as we probably should (see below), "God in all his fullness." In addition, as we will note below, it is very possible that Paul is alluding to Psalm 68:16, which also uses the verb "be pleased" *(eudokeō)* with the infinitive "to dwell" *(katoikein);* and the structure of option one is closest to this verse.[193] On the whole, then, taking "all the fullness" as the subject of this sentence is probably the better option. We may now turn to the details of v. 19.

The verb "was pleased" sometimes comes close to the idea of "choose" or "elect" (cf. Luke 12:32; 1 Cor. 1:21; Gal. 1:15), and this is prob-

191. Although most of the English versions favor option two, most commentators prefer this option; see esp. Moule, 70-71; O'Brien, 51.
192. See, e.g., Lightfoot, 159; Aletti, 109. A third, less likely, possibility is that "the Son" is the subject of the verb (Fee, *Pauline Christology*, 308-13). But the phrase "in him" (ἐν αὐτῷ) makes this option very difficult (O'Brien, 51).
193. This is the only other combination of these verbs in biblical Greek.

ably the case here.[194] We might paraphrase, "God in all his fullness has chosen to dwell in Christ." The absolute form of "all the fullness" (fullness of what?) has led to considerable speculation about the meaning of the phrase. For instance, since the Gnostics used "fullness" language quite a lot,[195] it has been suggested that the phrase betrays the fact that the "original" hymn was in praise of a gnostic redeemer figure. A more plausible variation of this thesis suggests that the hymn may have picked up the language from the Colossian false teachers and turned it against them. Although it is unlikely that "fullness" reflects gnosticism in any direct fashion, there is some reason to think that the word may, indeed, have a polemical thrust. This is because the word is never used absolutely elsewhere in the New Testament (at least with this sense), and all the other passages where it has a christological significance are closely related to this passage (Col. 2:9; Eph. 1:23; cf. 4:13). We might surmise, then, that the false teachers in Colossae were inviting the Christians there to experience true "fullness" by following their philosophy (2:8) and rules (cf. 2:16-23); to which Paul responds: the "fullness" that you are seeking is to be found in Christ. And the use of the word "all" *(pan)* here confirms this supposition, since it is tautologous: "fullness" itself indicates totality.[196] *"All* the fullness" reflects the exclusive emphasis that is the warp and woof of Paul's response to the Colossian false teachers: *only* in Christ can "fullness" be found. This "fullness," as Colossians 2:9 makes clear, is the "fullness of God," or "God in his fullness."

Other suggestions for the derivation of the "fullness" language here are less convincing. The Old Testament never uses "fullness" in connection with God, nor are the passages in which God is said to "fill" *(plēroō,* the verb cognate to "fullness") the earth very close to what we have here in Colossians.[197] Nor are suggested wisdom or "word" backgrounds very helpful.[198] On the other hand, the claim that all the fullness "was pleased to

---

194. BDAG suggest the definition "to consider someth. as good and therefore worthy of choice, *consent, determine, resolve."*

195. See esp. the evidence amassed in Lightfoot, 264-68.

196. O'Brien, 52; cf. also Dibelius-Greeven, 53; contra Arnold, *Colossian Syncretism,* 262-63; Pierre Benoit, "The 'Pleroma' in the Epistles to the Colossians and the Ephesians," *SEÅ* 49 (1984), 137-42.

197. See Ps. 72:19 (πληρόω); Jer. 23:24; Isa. 6:3; Ezek. 43:5; 44:4 (πλήρης). See, for these references, O'Brien, 52.

198. Contra, e.g., Dunn, 99-100 (cf. also Feuillet, *Le Christ sagesse de Dieu,* 236-38), who stresses again here the wisdom tradition — despite the fact that we have no extant example of "fullness" being attributed to wisdom and only an indirect relationship between "filling" and wisdom (in Wis. 1:6-7, which Dunn cites, while wisdom is the general topic, the specific language of "filling" is connected with the Spirit). Similarly, attempts to connect the "filling" idea with the "word" concept (e.g., Schweizer, 78) are not persua-

dwell in him" probably echoes Old Testament descriptions of God "dwelling" in the temple. See especially Psalm 68:16, which describes the temple mount: "God has been pleased to dwell in it" (my trans. from the LXX [67:17]).[199] In a typical New Testament emphasis, Christ replaces the temple as the "place" where God now dwells. It is probably fruitless to speculate about the moment when God in his fullness "took up his residence" in Christ;[200] what is important is that this is now where all that can be known and experienced of God is to be found.

20 As we have seen, the sentence begun in v. 19 continues into this verse. "God in all his fullness was pleased to dwell in Christ" *and through him to reconcile to himself all things.* The TNIV's word order in this verse reflects the Greek, with "through him" *(dia autō)* standing in the emphatic first position and echoing the similar placement of "in him" in v. 19 (TNIV in this case moves the prepositional phrase to the end). The Greek behind "to himself" is *eis auton;* and this sequence "in him" — "through him" — "for him" may echo the similar sequence of v. 16: "*in him* all things were created . . . all things have been created *through him* and *for him.*" This parallel also throws into relief a key question about the pronoun *himself.* TNIV, along with most of the English versions, uses a reflexive pronoun, interpreting the one to whom all things are reconciled as "God" (the subject of the sentence, or at least of the infinitive "to reconcile").[201] But the Greek word is a simple personal pronoun,[202] and the same pronoun refers to Christ in v. 19, later in v. 20 *(his blood),* and, indeed, throughout vv. 15-19.[203] It is quite possible, then, to interpret the

---

sive (the most relevant text is Philo, *On Dreams* 1.75, where the word is described as "the fullness of God" [using, however, πληρέστατος rather than πλήρωμα]).

199. εὐδόκησεν ὁ θεὸς κατοικεῖν ἐν αὐτῷ. See esp. Beetham, "Echoes of Scripture," 184-202; Beale, *Temple,* 267-68. Cf. also Stettler, *Kolosserhymnus,* 255-61, who thinks that the "filling" language might also pick up OT language about God filling the temple with his presence (e.g., Isa. 6:1; cf. Rev. 15:8).

200. The "Christ event as a whole" (Lohse, 58); the resurrection (Gnilka, 73; Beasley-Murray, "Colossians 1:15-20," 177-78); perhaps most likely, the incarnation (Stettler, *Kolosserhymnus,* 263-65).

201. And see, for this view, Wilson, 154.

202. To be sure, there is some doubt about this, since the reflexive pronoun in Greek could sometimes be indicated by nothing more than a rough breathing mark (αὑτόν instead of αὐτόν), and breathing marks were usually not included in the earliest MSS (cf. Moule, *Idiom Book,* 119; Turner, *Syntax,* 43). Many commentators therefore posit an original αὑτόν here because they think that God must be the object of the reconciliation (e.g., Bruce, 74; Wright, 76).

203. Yet another personal pronoun referring to Christ would be present if we include the contested words δι' αὐτοῦ — "through him" — just before the reference to "things on earth or things in heaven." These words are included in some good MSS (P⁴⁶, ℵ, A) and are thought to be original by many scholars (e.g., Lightfoot, 160; Dunn, 83;

passage to mean that "God has reconciled all things to Christ."[204] It is objected that elsewhere in the New Testament theological "reconciliation" is always directed toward God, whose wrath against sin is the background for the concept.[205] But the language is used in an unusual way in this passage in any case; and we should probably respect Paul's apparent choice of pronoun here.[206] Moreover, a christological focus here would mirror the resolutely christological focus of the "hymn" as a whole.

In speaking of the reconciliation of all things to Christ, the "hymn" presupposes that the Lordship of Christ over all things (vv. 15-18) has somehow been disrupted. Though created through him and for him, "all things" no longer bear the relationship to their creator that they were intended to have. They are therefore in need of reconciliation. But what is the nature of this reconciliation? The verb used here, *apokatallassō*, occurs only twice elsewhere in the New Testament (v. 22; Eph. 2:16); but its base form, *katallassō*, is found also in Romans 5:10 (twice); 1 Corinthians 7:11; 2 Corinthians 5:18, 19, 20; while the cognate noun occurs in Romans 5:11; 11:15; 2 Corinthians 5:18, 19.[207] In each of these verses (with the exception of 1 Cor. 7:11, where the language refers to marriage partners), "reconcile"/"reconciliation" refers to the restoration of fellowship between God and sinners. It is understandable, then, that some would argue that the reconciliation in this verse is restricted to human beings who respond to the invitation to be reconciled.[208] But the context makes this kind of limitation on the scope of reconciliation very problematic. The "all things" of v. 20 occurs five other times in the context, and in each case the referent is

---

Wright, 76; Metzger, *Textual Commentary*, 554). And see the NASB: "having made peace through the blood of His cross; through Him, I say, whether things. . . ." This reading can also be argued to be the more difficult (as the NASB rendering attests). The failure to include these words explicitly in many translations (NIV; TNIV; ESV; NET) does not mean that the translators have decided to reject these words on text-critical grounds; it might reflect simply a decision about the best way to handle these words in translation.

204. E.g., Lohse, 59; Aletti, 111; Masson, 103; Barth/Blanke, 214; Fee, *Pauline Christology*, 308-13.

205. E.g., Harris, 50.

206. Especially is this so since, as Fee points out, the usual textual variants reflecting a reflexive interpretation are absent in this verse (*Pauline Christology*, 311).

207. The compound form of the verb (which occurs only here and in v. 22 and Eph. 2:16 in the NT), which is unattested before Paul, might emphasize the idea of a restored relationship (Beasley-Murray, "Colossians 1:15-20," 178-79) or, perhaps more likely, the completeness of the restoration (Harris, 50). On the other hand, *koinē* Greek was known for its preference for compound forms, so the verb might carry no particular emphasis (Barth/Blanke, 214).

208. I. Howard Marshall, "The Meaning of 'Reconciliation,'" in *Unity and Diversity in New Testament Theology: Essays in Honor of George E. Ladd* (ed. Robert A. Guelich; Grand Rapids: Eerdmans, 1978), 126-27.

the created universe. And, of course, in this context, Paul goes on to specify that the scope of "all things" includes *things on earth or things in heaven*. The neuter form (Gk. *ta . . . ta*) and the parallelism with v. 16 make clear that all created things are included.

Since at least the time of Origen, then, some interpreters have used this verse to argue for universal salvation: in the end, God will not (and often, it is suggested, *can*not) allow anything to fall outside the scope of his saving love in Christ. Universal salvation is a doctrine very congenial to our age, and it is not therefore surprising that this verse, along with several others in Paul, is regularly cited to argue for this belief.[209] This is not the place to refute this doctrine, which, we briefly note, cannot be reconciled with clear New Testament teaching about the reality and eternality of Hell.[210] But particularly relevant to the meaning of v. 20 is Paul's teaching in 2:15 that God, "having disarmed the powers and authorities, . . . made a public spectacle of them, triumphing over them by the cross." The spiritual beings to which Paul refers explicitly in v. 20 are not saved by Christ but vanquished by him (see 2:15).[211]

Another option arises especially if we think that Paul is quoting a hymn that reflects Hellenistic (-Jewish) ideas. An apparently widespread assumption in the world of Paul's day was that the elements of the universe were in conflict with one another, owing partly to the influence of baneful spiritual powers. Verse 20 might then claim that God in Christ has brought an end to this cosmic conflict.[212] Advocates of this interpretation often think that Paul has added *through his blood, shed on the cross*[213] in order to "Christianize" the idea.[214] However, as we have noted above, the supposition that these words have been added to the hymn is fraught with difficulty. Moreover, there is little in the context of Colossians to support the idea of a conflict among created beings; the basic fault line, in

---

209. Some of the others are Rom. 5:18-19; 11:32; 1 Cor. 15:24-28.

210. See, e.g., Douglas J. Moo, "What Does Paul Teach about Hell?" in *Hell under Fire: Modern Scholarship Reinvents Eternal Punishment* (ed. Christopher W. Morgan and Robert A. Peterson; Grand Rapids: Zondervan, 2004), 92-109.

211. Stettler, *Kolosserhymnus*, 295-96.

212. See, e.g., Philo, *On the Special Laws* 2.190; and cf. Eduard Schweizer, "Versöhnung des Alls (Kol 1,20)," in *Jesus Christus in Historie und Theologie: Festschrift für Hans Conzelmann zum 60. Geburtstag* (ed. Georg Strecker; Tübingen: Mohr Siebeck, 1975), 487-501; Lars Hartman, "Universal Reconciliation (Col 1,20)," *SNTSU* 10 (1985), 109-21; Wolter, 86-88; Gnilka, 75.

213. In the Greek text, the pronoun — αὐτοῦ — follows "cross"; hence the rendering "the blood of his cross" (ESV). But Greek word order allows this pronoun to modify the "lead" noun, making the TNIV's *his blood* also an option.

214. See, e.g., A. J. M. Wedderburn (with A. T. Lincoln) in *The Theology of the Later Pauline Letters* (Cambridge: Cambridge University Press, 1993), 39-41, 66-69.

keeping with the New Testament elsewhere, runs between God and his creation.[215]

But it is also likely that the concept is both broader and more biblically oriented. Key to understanding "reconcile all things" is the elaboration of this idea in the participial clause, *by making peace through his blood, shed on the cross.* This language picks up the widespread Old Testament prediction that in the last day God would establish universal *shalōm,* "peace," or "well-being."[216] The Old Testament prophets focus, naturally enough, on the way this "peace" would bring security and blessing to Israel as the people live in the land God gave them; but they also suggest that the wider creation in general suffers from the effects of human beings' fall into sin and is in need of restoration. Paul picks up this point very clearly in Romans 8:19-22. In a manner typical of New Testament fulfillment, then, Paul proclaims that this peace has now been established in Christ. By responding to the gospel, the Colossians have experienced this reconciliation (vv. 21-22).[217] They are therefore enabled, as God's new covenant people, to live in a still dangerous and hostile world in peace. They need not fear the spiritual powers that were believed to be so determinative of one's destiny.

Colossians 1:20 teaches, then, not "cosmic salvation" or even "cosmic redemption," but "cosmic restoration" or "renewal."[218] Through the

215. See esp. Dübbers, *Christologie und Existenz,* 117-26.

216. See esp. Isa. 52:6-10; and, inter alia, Isa. 9:7; 26:3, 12; 27:5; 52:7; 55:12; 66:12; Jer. 29:11; 30:10; 33:6, 9; 46:27; Ezek. 34:29; 37:26; Mic. 5:5; Hag. 2:9; Zech. 9:10. See, e.g., Pokorný, 89; Arnold, *Colossian Syncretism,* 265-69.

217. Note the clearly "two-stage" nature of reconciliation in 2 Cor. 5:19-21: God has "reconciled the world to Christ" (v. 19); but it is by responding to the message of reconciliation that the Corinthian Christians have experienced its benefits (vv. 20-21).

218. For this view, often called "pacification," see, e.g., Bruce, 74-76; O'Brien, 52-57; Aletti, *Colossiens 1:15-20,* 112-13; Arnold, *Colossian Syncretism,* 269. Hartman suggests that Philo, who attributes to the Jewish cult the power to bring harmony in the disorder of creation (*On the Special Laws* 1.97; 2.188-89; *On the Life of Moses* 2.133-34; *On the Decalogue* 178), may furnish a partial parallel to Paul's conception ("Universal Reconciliation," 109-21). Somewhat similar is Thomas Torrance's notion of redemption as a "reordering" of the cosmos, a restoration of the God-given order present in creation (cf. *Divine and Contingent Order* [Oxford: Oxford University Press, 1981], 138). Cf. also Alister E. McGrath, *The Reenchantment of Nature: The Denial of Religion and the Ecological Crisis* (New York: Doubleday, 2002), 175-76. The implications of this reconciliation for unbelievers is not entirely clear from Scripture. As we have noted above, Scripture as a whole certainly forbids us from concluding (as much as we might in a certain sense wish to) that all unbelievers will be "saved." Nor is the idea that unbelievers will one day be annihilated a biblical concept. Perhaps, however, we might tentatively think that reconciliation will mean that unbelievers will themselves, though suffering the torments of Hell, nevertheless cease to sin and express remorse for their sin. See for this idea Henri Blocher, "Everlasting Punishment and the Problem of Evil," in *Universalism and the Doctrine of Hell* (ed.

work of Christ on the cross, God has brought his entire rebellious creation back under the rule of his sovereign power. Of course, this "peace" is not yet fully established. The "already/not yet" pattern of New Testament eschatology must be applied to Colossians 1:20. While secured in principle by Christ's crucifixion and available in preliminary form to believers, universal peace is not yet established.[219] It is because of this work of universal pacification that God will one day indeed be "all in all" (1 Cor. 15:28) and that "at the name of Jesus every knee should bow, in heaven and on earth and under the earth, and every tongue acknowledge that Jesus Christ is Lord, to the glory of God the Father" (Phil. 2:10-11). While modern theologians have therefore often greatly exaggerated the implications of v. 20 in the service of an unbiblical universalism, this passage does, indeed, assert a thoroughly biblical universalism: that God's work in Christ has in view a reclamation of the entire universe, tainted as it is by human sin (cf. Rom. 8:19-22). That fallen human beings are the prime objects of this reconciliation is clear from the New Testament generally and from the sequel to this text (vv. 21-23). But it would be a serious mistake (not always avoided) to limit this "reconciling" work to human beings. The "peace" that God seeks is a peace that not only applies to humans in their relationship to God but also to humans in their relationship with one another (hence the mandate for social justice) and to humans in their relationship with the natural world (hence the mandate for a biblically oriented environmentalism).[220]

3. The Hope Held Out in the Gospel (1:21-23)

[21]*Once you were alienated from God and were enemies in your minds because of your evil behavior.* [22]*But now he has reconciled you by Christ's physical body through death to present you holy in his sight, without blemish and free from accusation —* [23]*if you continue in your faith, established and firm, and do not move from the hope held out in the gospel. This is the gospel that you heard and that has been proclaimed to every creature under heaven, and of which I, Paul, have become a servant.*

Nigel M. de S. Cameron; Grand Rapids: Baker, 1992), 282-312; Stephen N. Williams, "The Question of Hell and Salvation: Is There a Fourth View?" *TynBul* 57 (2006), 263-83.

219. Nothing in the wording of v. 20 settles the "time" of the reconciliation (contra, e.g., Gnilka, 76, who notes that the verbs are aorist; aorist infinitives [e.g., ἀποκαταλλάξαι] and participles [e.g., εἰρηνοποιήσας] are not necessarily past-referring). The timing of these events is appropriately to be seen in light of typical NT patterns of fulfillment.

220. See D. J. Moo, "Nature in the New Creation: New Testament Eschatology and the Environment," *JETS* 49 (2006), 469-74; Wright, 79-80.

At the heart of this paragraph is a favorite literary device of Paul's: a contrast between "once" and "now." "Once" the Colossians were estranged from God because of their evil thoughts and deeds (v. 21). "But now" they are reconciled to God through Christ's death and with the hope of being presented before God as blameless (v. 22). But this hope is contingent on their continuing in the faith, as Paul adds in a concluding warning statement (v. 23). The gospel, the source of this hope, has had a powerful effect on the Colossians (1:6). But it will secure what the Colossians hope for only if they continue in their faith. This brief paragraph is marked by a shift in style. The impersonal, third-person, descriptive style of vv. 15-20 is dropped in favor of direct address in the second person: *once you. . . . he has reconciled you . . . if you continue*. The high theology of vv. 15-20 is being applied. And, of course, the focus on reconciliation in vv. 21-22 shows that it is the universal reconciling work of God in Christ (v. 20) that is being especially applied here.[221] Because God in all "his fullness" is present in Christ (v. 19), his death (v. 20) and resurrection (v. 18) have the power to initiate ("beginning," "firstborn" in v. 18) a new creation ("the body, the church," v. 18). This new creation work rests on the universal reconciling, or "peacemaking" power of the cross of Christ. It is God's intention to bring "peace" to his fallen and fractured universe, to bring all things again into subjection to his sovereignty, to bring all his enemies into subjection. This intention will be finally accomplished only when Christ returns in glory to establish the kingdom in its final form (cf. 1:22b; 3:4). But God invites human beings in the present time both to participate in this reconciliation and to become agents through whom God's work of reconciliation can begin to be carried out.[222] Because they have responded to this invitation, the Colossians have been turned from God's enemies into his "friends" and anticipate the day when they will stand before God fully transformed into his image — if, that is, they continue to maintain their commitment to the gospel (v. 23).

But the paragraph is tied not only to vv. 18-20, but to other parts of the letter, both preceding and following it. Especially important is the way that these verses pick up the theme of a "transfer" from one spiritual realm to another from vv. 12-14. The connections are well summarized by Morna Hooker: "Those who were at one time alienated (21) are those who have now been given a share in the inheritance of God's holy ones (12); those who were hostile in mind and evil deeds (21) are those who have been rescued from the power of darkness (13) and whose calling is

---

221. Indeed, Stettler (*Kolosserhymnus*, 270) suggests that the focus on reconciliation at the end of the hymn is the reason that Paul quotes it.
222. See esp. Dunn, 104.

the knowledge of God and every good deed (9-10); those who are reconciled through the death of Christ (22) are those who have been transferred into his kingdom (13); those whom he now presents as holy, blameless and irreproachable (22) are those who in him have redemption, the forgiveness of sins (14)."[223] Verse 23 also picks up some themes from earlier in the letter: the universal nature of the gospel — compare "to every creature under heaven" and "bearing fruit and growing throughout the whole world" (v. 6) — and the importance of faith and hope (cf. vv. 3-5). At the same time, v. 23 anticipates key developments in the letter, not only the focus on Paul's own ministry (1:24–2:4) but also the central rhetorical issue of the letter: the need for the Colossians to continue in their faith (cf. 2:7) in the face of the false teaching (2:6-23).[224]

21 The TNIV (cf. also NIV; HCSB) translates vv. 21-23 with two sentences, the break coming at the end of v. 21. In the Greek, however, we have one long sentence, whose main verb, a form of "reconcile," comes in v. 22a. Verse 21 identifies the people who receive this reconciling action; v. 22b tells us the purpose of the reconciliation; and v. 23 introduces the condition for the continuing efficacy of the reconciliation. The bare bones of the sentence therefore are: *you . . . he reconciled . . . to present you . . . if you continue.* By placing the object of the verb first in the sentence, Paul highlights the transition from the theological assertions of the "hymn" to its application in these verses. ESV (following RSV) brings out this emphasis nicely: "And you, who once were alienated. . . ." *Were alienated* translates a periphrastic construction that may highlight the continuing nature of the Colossians' state of separation.[225] Some interpreters think that the participle might be concessive — "although you were formerly alienated" (NASB)[226] — but this may detract from the emphatic contrast that Paul intends: "it is precisely you who were alienated whom God has reconciled."

Paul does not specify from whom the Colossians were once alienated, and the parallels in Ephesians (the only other New Testament occurrences of this verb) offer conflicting evidence. The focus in Ephesians 2:12 is on the alienation of Gentiles from Jews: they are "excluded from citizenship in Israel." In Ephesians 4:18, on the other hand, the alienation is vertical, as Paul describes the situation of the "Gentiles" (= unbelievers): "separated from the life of God." Dunn suggests that the former may be somewhat in view here, the "you" being seen as Gentiles.[227] But noth-

---

223. Hooker, "False Teachers," 321-22.
224. For these connections, see esp. Lähnemann, *Der Kolosserbrief,* 42-43; also Lamarche, "Structure," 456; Aletti, 119-22; Dunn, 105.
225. BDF §352; O'Brien, 60.
226. Harris, 57.
227. Dunn, 106; cf. also Thompson, 40.

ing in the context would prepare us for an ethnic distinction at this point; so it is almost certainly Ephesians 4:18 that furnishes the more apt parallel.[228] And this seems all the more likely when we note that both Ephesians 4:18 and Colossians 1:21 refer to the "understanding," or the "mind" *(dianoia)*, as an element in the alienation (Paul uses this word one other time, in Eph. 2:3). This word refers not simply to the "mind" as an organ of intellectual thought but to the "mind-set," or disposition of the person; cf. REB, "enemies in heart and mind" (in the LXX, *dianoia* usually translates *lēb*, "heart").[229] It is this basic mind-set of the non-Christian that is "hostile" toward God; as TNIV puts it, *enemies in your minds.*[230]

Enmity is the natural contrast to reconciliation (cf. Rom. 5:10), the condition that makes reconciliation necessary. The Scriptures present human beings in their natural state as hostile to God because of their involvement in Adam's primal sin. As Paul puts it in Romans 1:21, "their thinking became futile and their foolish hearts were darkened." Other texts teach that God, being perfectly holy and just, reacts to human sin with wrath; so the hostility works both ways (both are probably intended in Rom. 5:10). In our text, however, the context suggests that it is human enmity toward God that is in view.[231] For Paul goes on to say that our being "enemies" is *because of your evil behavior.*[232] *Because of* translates a Greek preposition that has a wide range of meaning. The TNIV has taken the word in a causal sense,[233] but this is probably not the best way to construe the relationship. Rather than our evil behavior being the reason why our minds are hostile, it is more natural to think that our evil behavior is the result of the hostility of our minds.[234]

22 Paul loves to highlight the glorious new status that believers enjoy by contrasting it with our former life of sinfulness and condemnation (see also 1:26; Rom. 3:21; 6:22; 7:6; Eph. 2:13; 5:8; 2 Tim. 1:10; Phlm. 11). So here Paul contrasts the former state of enmity with the present state of reconciliation ("once . . . but now"). As we have seen, the main verb in the long sentence that spans vv. 21-23 comes at the beginning of this verse: *he has reconciled.* All the English translations have this same ba-

228. Wright, 81.
229. BDAG.
230. The dative τῇ διανοίᾳ may be either locative or referential (Harris, 57); and the singular is probably distributive (hence TNIV, "your minds").
231. E.g., Lightfoot, 161; Moule, 72.
232. TNIV's "evil behavior" translates the Gk. τοῖς ἔργοις τοῖς πονηροῖς, "evil works."
233. Harris, 57. See also HCSB; NAB.
234. The preposition ἐν would then specify the means by which the enmity located in the disposition comes to expression (cf. the note in the NET Bible; REB; and Bruce, 76; O'Brien, 67; Wolter, 92-93).

sic wording, but an important variant in the Greek text needs to be noted, which would yield the rendering "you were reconciled." While this variant does not have as much manuscript support as the reading assumed in the English versions, it is undoubtedly the "more difficult" reading (because of the awkward syntax that would result) and so is supported by a number of scholars.[235] But this may be one of those occasions when a reading is too difficult to be accepted; the reading assumed in the English translations should probably be retained.[236] The translations also reflect the fact that the Greek does not specify the subject of the verb "reconciled." The TNIV implies that "God" is the subject by making explicit the intended antecedent of the pronoun *autou* later in the verse: *he has reconciled you by Christ's physical body* (and cf. REB). For this very reason, however, some interpreters insist that Christ must be the subject of the verb.[237] The pronoun at the end of the verse — *to present you holy in his sight* — does not help us decide, since it could refer to either God or Christ (see below). However, other considerations favor a reference to God. However we construe the debated syntax of v. 19, "God" or "God in all his fullness" is the one who reconciles *through* Christ; and this same pattern is found in all Paul's other references to reconciliation. Probably, then, God should be assumed to be the subject of *has reconciled* in v. 22.[238]

Just as the "hymn" specifies "his blood, shed on the cross" as the means by which God reconciles, so here Paul asserts that God has reconciled *by Christ's physical body through death*. TNIV's "physical body" translates a phrase, literally rendered, "the body of his flesh" (or "his body of flesh"; cf. ESV). Paul uses the word "flesh" (Gk. *sarx*) in a variety of ways, and its particular nuance in any given occurrence is very much context dependent.[239] Sometimes *sarx* has a clearly negative connotation, refer-

235. E.g., Lightfoot, 161, 251-52; Bruce, 76 (?); Dunn, 105; Fee, *Pauline Christology*, 313-16. Two of the better MSS of the Pauline letters read this variant (ἀποκατηλλάγητε): B, P46 (the latter has misspellings that reflect an original ἀποκατηλλάγητε [Metzger, *Textual Commentary*, 554-55]).

236. The sequence with the active infinitive παραστῆσαι ὑμᾶς is especially problematic; "you were reconciled in order to present you" is almost intolerable. (Lightfoot's suggestion, that the infinitive is governed by the verb εὐδόκησεν in v. 19 [161], ignores the rather clear break between vv. 20 and 21.) The infinitive would seem to demand that the subject of the main verb be God or Christ (though note Metzger's personal note in the *Textual Commentary*, 555).

237. E.g., Gnilka, 89; Bruce, 78. NLT assumes this reading: "He has brought you back as his friends. He had done this through his death on the cross in his own human body."

238. E.g., Harris, 57; Lohse, 64.

239. Anthony Thiselton, *The Two Horizons: New Testament Hermeneutics and Philosophical Description with Special Reference to Bultmann, Heidegger, Gadamer, and Wittgenstein* (Grand Rapids: Eerdmans, 1979), 408-11.

ring to the nature of life in the "old age" (this is clearly its meaning in 2:18, 23, and perhaps in 2:11, 13). In other texts, however, *sarx*, probably reflecting its Hebrew equivalent *(bśr)*, refers simply to "human mortality," to the physical nature of life here on earth (in Colossians: 1:24; 2:1, 5; 3:22; perhaps in 2:11, 13).[240] This is clearly the sense of the word in our context (hence TNIV's "physical"), but it remains to ask why Paul has introduced the word, since "body" *(sōma)* in itself would have seemed to carry this significance. The simplest explanation is that Paul wants clearly to differentiate his use of "body" here from the previous occurrence of the word, where it is a metaphor for the church (v. 18).[241] Others think that Paul might also be responding to a docetic-like tendency among the false teachers to denigrate the significance of Christ's humanity.[242] But the most likely explanation is that the qualification is added to focus attention on Christ's susceptibility to suffering — a nuance that the addition of the phrase *through death* explicates.[243]

The purpose of God's reconciling work is that believers might be presented as *holy (hagious) . . . without blemish (amōmous) and free from accusation (anenklētous).* Biblical parallels suggest that Paul refers to the last judgment, when Christians will have to stand before "God's judgment seat" (Rom. 14:10).[244] Particularly close to our passage (as so often) is a

240. James D. G. Dunn, *The Theology of Paul the Apostle* (Grand Rapids: Eerdmans, 1998), 62-70; cf. also Dunn's "Jesus — Flesh and Spirit: An Exposition of Romans I.3-4," *JTS* 24 (1973), esp. 44-51; W. D. Stacey, *The Pauline View of Man: In Relation to Its Judaic and Hellenistic Background* (London: Macmillan, 1956), 154-73; Douglas J. Moo, "'Flesh' in Romans: A Challenge for the Translator," in *The Challenge of Bible Translation: Communicating God's Word to the World* (ed. Glen S. Scorgie, Mark L. Strauss, and Steven M. Voth; Grand Rapids: Zondervan, 2003), 365-79. As Dunn points out, Colossians uses σάρξ more often in this "neutral" sense than is typical in Paul (James D. G. Dunn, "The 'Body' in Colossians," in *To Tell the Mystery* [ed. Thomas E. Schmidt and Moisés Silva; Sheffield: JSOT Press, 1994], 168-69). This need carry no implications for authorship, however — there are good circumstantial reasons for Paul to stress this point in Colossians.

241. Lightfoot, 162; Dunn, 108-9; Wolter, 93; Luz, 207; Pokorný, 92.

242. E.g., Abbott, 226; O'Brien, 68.

243. The only biblical parallel to σῶμα plus σάρκος is found in 2:11, where the meaning is debated (cf. also Sir. 23:16, which refers to a man committing adultery in "his fleshly body"). Lohse (64) perhaps aptly mentions 1QpHab 9:2, which refers to the Teacher of Righteousness suffering "vengeful acts on his body of flesh" (Heb. בגוית בשרו). The qualification "of his flesh" also makes it unlikely that "body" has any allusion to the church or to Christ as a "corporate" figure (contra, e.g., Wright, 82; Schweizer, 91-92).

244. The verb that Paul uses here — παρίστημι — is used in a variety of contexts by Paul, but refers to the "presentation" of believers in the judgment in Rom. 14:10; 2 Cor. 4:14; 11:2; Eph. 5:27; and cf. v. 28 in this chapter. Note also the significance of the combination ἅγιος and ἀμώμος (see text above). See, e.g., Sappington, *Revelation*, 188-91. Lightfoot (162-63) and MacDonald (73), on the other hand, think that Paul refers to the present standing of believers before God.

text from Ephesians: "Christ loved the church and gave himself up for her to make her holy, cleansing her by the washing with water through the word, and to present *(parastēse)* her to himself as a radiant church, without stain or wrinkle or any other blemish, but holy *(hagia)* and blameless *(amōmos)*" (Eph. 5:25b-27; cf. also Eph. 1:4). In this text the one to whom believers are presented in the judgment is Christ (as also in 2 Cor. 11:2), making it possible that here also Paul thinks of Christ as the one before whom believers will appear.[245] But it is perhaps more likely, despite this parallel, that Paul has God in mind.[246]

As we indicated above, the TNIV description of the qualities that believers should have in the judgment rests on three Greek adjectives, each of which begins with the same letter (an *alpha;* the need to represent the Greek rough breathing mark with an *h* obscures this in the transliteration *hagious*). This makes it likely that Paul has chosen these three words at least partly for literary reasons, to create an alliteration. "Holy" and "without blemish" are each used in the Old Testament to refer to sacrifices, and some interpreters think that sacrificial imagery might be found in our passage also.[247] But in the only passages in biblical Greek where they appear together as parallel adjectives, the reference is the last judgment (Eph. 1:4; 5:27). This fact, along with the distinctly legal connotation of the word *anenklētos* (brought out well in the TNIV's "free from accusation"), confirms what we suggested earlier: Paul has in view the final judgment.[248] While celebrating the new status that believers enjoy — "reconciled"; cf. also vv. 12-14 — Paul at the same time reminds us that this new status is not an end in itself but has a further goal in view: that we who are already "holy" in status should become "holy" in reality. As we have noted in commenting on Paul's emphasis on hope in 1:5, the future prospect of judgment is one that Paul holds before the Colossians in order to stimulate their continuing growth in the true gospel of God. And, while God himself supplies this growth, the growth nevertheless does not take place apart from the willingness of believers — as v. 23 forcefully indicates.

23 As we have seen, in v. 23 Paul introduces — albeit somewhat obliquely — the central concern of the letter: to encourage the Colossian Christians to resist the blandishments of the false teachers and to continue to grow in their knowledge of Christ. While it might seem at first

---

245. Aletti, 124-25.

246. The Greek behind TNIV's "in his sight" is κατενώπιον αὐτοῦ, which could also be translated "before him"; and the only other occurrences of κατενώπιον in the NT have reference to people being presented before God in judgment (Eph. 1:4 and Jude 24). See also, for the general idea, 1 Thess. 3:13; Rom. 14:10; 2 Cor. 4:14.

247. See esp. Lightfoot, 162.

248. See esp. O'Brien, 68-69.

sight, then, that the verse is a bit of an afterthought, it is, in fact, a very important indication of where the argument of the letter is going to go (see 2:6-23). The verse takes the form of a long and complex conditional clause. It is probably to be attached to the word "present" in v. 22: "God has reconciled you with the purpose of presenting you as holy before him — but you will, in fact, only be presented as holy before him if. . . ."[249] The precise nuance of the conditional construction that Paul uses here is debated. Some believe that the construction (ei ge) suggests uncertainty — "if, though I doubt it" — while others think it connotes confidence — "if, as I am sure." Pauline evidence points in both directions, Galatians 3:4 falling into the former category and 2 Corinthians 5:3 and Ephesians 3:2; 4:21 into the latter. Since most of the parallels point to the idea of confidence, and because Paul expresses confidence in the Colossians elsewhere (see esp. 2:5), it is this direction that we should probably take here.[250] Nevertheless, the condition is a real one, and it is very important not to rob the words of their intended rhetorical function. As his strong pleas in 2:16-23 make clear, Paul is genuinely concerned that the false teachers might "disqualify" the Colossian Christians (2:18). This being the case, Paul would clearly want his words here to be taken with great seriousness. He wants to confront the Colossians with the reality that their eventual salvation depends on their remaining faithful to Christ and to the true gospel. Only by continuing in their faith can they hope to find a favorable verdict from God on the day of judgment. We have in this verse, then, a real warning. This warning, along with many similar ones, presents the "human responsibility" side in the biblical portrayal of final salvation. God does, indeed, by his grace and through his Spirit, work to preserve his people so that they will be vindicated in the judgment; but, at the same time, God's people are responsible to persevere in their faith if they expect to see that vindication.

The perseverance in *faith* that Paul urges in this verse can be taken in two ways. On the one hand, Paul might be emphasizing the need to continue to believe, an interpretation that the TNIV implies by translating *your faith* (see also REB).[251] But the *your* in this translation represents

249. It is just possible, however, that the conditional clause should be attached to the main verb of the previous sentence: "he has reconciled" (Bengel, 164). The idea that one's present spiritual state is conditioned on future perseverance is not unknown in the NT (Heb. 3:6, 14).

250. M. E. Thrall, *Greek Particles in the New Testament* (Leiden: Brill, 1962), 87-88; cf. also, e.g., Judith M. Gundry-Volf, *Paul and Perseverance: Staying In and Falling Away* (WUNT 2.37; Tübingen: Mohr Siebeck, 1990), 197; Harris, 60; O'Brien, 69.

251. E.g., Lightfoot, 163. Faith has this subjective sense in 1:4; 2:5, 12. The verb πιστεύω does not occur in Colossians.

the Greek article; so we could also translate "the faith," implying that faith refers here not to the act of believing but to what is believed: Christian truth (so most of the translations).[252] "Faith" probably has this latter meaning in the roughly parallel 2:7. But 1:23, unlike 2:7, includes an explicit mention of this element of Christian truth by referring to the gospel. On the whole, then, it might be preferable to take v. 23 as referring to the need to continue in belief.

How may the Colossians continue in their faith? Positively, by being *established and firm*; negatively, by not being *moved from the hope held out in the gospel*. Both positive descriptions have their background in the world of building. The Greek verb behind *established (themelioō)* refers to "laying the foundation" of a building (cf. Matt. 7:25), and its form (a perfect tense) highlights the need for believers constantly to live in a state of "being securely founded." *Firm* is not so clearly intended to connote the idea of a building; and, in general, we must remember that even words that originally referred to a particular activity often lose that connotation as they are more widely used (e.g., they become "dead metaphors"). Nevertheless, Paul does use a cognate word *(hedraiōma)* with apparent reference to building in 1 Timothy 3:15, so perhaps we are justified in retaining the building metaphor.[253] There is also some evidence that Paul uses this language as a general way of insisting on firm continuance in the faith. For in 1 Corinthians 15:58, he uses the same combination of positive and negative imagery that we find in this verse: "stand firm *(hedraios)*. Let nothing move you *(ametakinētoi)*." Rather than using the adjective of the 1 Corinthians text, Paul here employs the cognate verb *(metakineō,* found only here in the New Testament), but the meaning is the same. This negative counterpart to "continuing in your faith" has in view the false teachers, who are trying to move the Colossians away from *the hope held out in the gospel*. The TNIV "held out in" is an apt translation of a genitive construction in Greek that is almost certainly to be taken in a "subjective" sense: the hope "stored up in heaven" for believers is produced by the gospel.[254] As he did earlier in chapter 1 (v. 5), Paul urges the Colossians to focus on the hope that comes through response to the gospel in distinction from the false hope being held out by the false teachers.

Paralleling again the earlier passage, Paul qualifies this gospel in three ways: it has been heard by the Colossians (v. 6: "since the day you heard it"); it has universal significance (v. 6: "bearing fruit and growing throughout the whole world"); and it has been proclaimed by an individ-

---

252. Cf. O'Brien, 69; Gnilka, 91.
253. O'Brien, 70.
254. E.g., Lightfoot, 163; Abbott, 227; Harris, 61.

ual servant (vv. 7-8: "you learned it from Epaphras . . . a faithful minister"). The first and third of these qualifications are clear enough in their meaning. But the second is more problematic, especially in the TNIV rendering: *proclaimed to every creature under heaven* (cf. also RSV; NRSV; NJB; NAB). For it is obvious that the gospel in Paul's day had not been proclaimed to every creature under heaven. Mitigating the difficulty somewhat is the alternative rendering "proclaimed in all creation under heaven" (ESV; cf. also NASB; HCSB; NET; REB). The qualifier "under heaven" might favor the translation "creature";[255] but Pauline usage of the word *ktisis* and the particular Greek construction that Paul uses here favor "creation."[256] What Paul is probably saying, then, is not that the gospel has been proclaimed *to* every creature but *throughout* the whole creation.[257]

But our problem, while lessened, still remains. O'Brien suggests that Paul is thinking of key "gospel centers" from which the message of Christ can spread more widely.[258] Others suggest that the reference is to God's general revelation, a revelation that, as Paul puts it, quoting Psalm 19:4 in a discussion about the gospel, "has gone out into all the earth . . . to the ends of the world" (Rom. 10:18). Yet another option is that Paul is thinking of a process that is underway. Jesus predicted that the gospel would be preached "throughout the world" (Mark 14:9; Matt. 24:14), and, as Paul and others spread the good news among the Gentiles, this worldwide proclamation is happening.[259] But the simplest solution is that Paul

255. "Under heaven" is used nowhere else in Paul, but it is standard OT language to describe something that is universal (e.g., Exod. 17:14; Deut. 29:19; Dan. 7:27; 9:12; cf. Acts 2:5; 4:12). In favor of a reference to "creature," see, e.g., Harris, 61; Lohse, 66; O'Brien, 70. Note particularly Mark 16:15 (v.l.), where Jesus commands his disciples "to preach the gospel to all creation" (κηρύξατε τὸ εὐαγγέλιον πάσῃ τῇ κτίσει — the dative here might suggest "to every creature" [articular κτίσει not necessarily being a problem for this meaning; cf. Turner, *Syntax*, 200]).

256. Of Paul's ten other uses of κτίσις, eight refer pretty clearly to "creation" (Rom. 1:20; 8:19, 20, 21, 22; 2 Cor. 5:17; Gal. 6:15; Col. 1:15); two probably mean "creature" (Rom. 1:25; 8:39). The Greek construction we refer to is the use of the preposition ἐν (translated "to" in TNIV) instead of the simple dative. No clear example of the combination κηρύσσω ("preach") plus ἐν meaning "preach to" is found in the NT. On the other hand, this combination does refer to preaching "in" a certain location (Matt. 3:1; 11:1; 24:14; 26:13; Mark 1:39; 5:20; 14:9; Acts 9:20; 2 Cor. 1:19; Gal. 2:2; 1 Tim. 3:16). The anarthrous κτίσει is no problem for this rendering, since πᾶς with anarthrous nouns often means "the whole of" in the NT (Moule, *Idiom Book*, 94-95). For the meaning "creation," see, e.g., Dunn, 111.

257. There is then no reason to limit the reference of κτίσις to humanity.

258. O'Brien, 71; cf. 13.

259. Wright, 84-85. The usual English past-time translation, "which has been proclaimed," might seem to stand in the way of this view. But there is some question whether the aorist participle here (κηρυχθέντος) has this kind of time significance. Aorist adjectival participles can sometimes be simply "definitional"; i.e., here, "the proclaimed-in-all-creation gospel."

is simply exaggerating to make his point; and there are New Testament parallels for this usage. See, for instance, Acts 2:5, which claims that Jews "from every nation under heaven" were present at Pentecost. To be sure, this exaggeration nevertheless makes an important point: the reconciliation of "all things" accomplished in the cross of Christ (v. 20) has its counterpart in the proclamation of this event in "the whole creation."[260] Paul wants the Colossians to understand the gospel is the one, universal answer to the quest for spiritual fulfillment.

Paul ends the verse with a final relative clause, inserted to prepare for the direction the letter will now take. It was on the Damascus Road that Paul was called by God to *become a servant* of the gospel. "Servant" (*diakonos*) usually is followed by a personal object, designating the one who is being served (see 1:25). Here, however, Paul designates the gospel as his object of service, probably in the sense that he owes his allegiance to it (see the parallel in Eph. 3:7; also 2 Cor. 3:6: "servants of a new covenant" [my trans.]). It is unusual for Paul to name himself in the course of one of his letters. Perhaps he does so here to distinguish himself from Timothy (1:1).

C. The Mystery of Christ in Paul's Ministry and Christian Experience (1:24–2:5)

24*Now I rejoice in what I am suffering for you, and I fill up in my flesh what is still lacking in regard to Christ's afflictions, for the sake of his body, which is the church.* 25*I have become its servant by the commission God gave me to present to you the word of God in its fullness —* 26*the mystery that has been kept hidden for ages and generations, but is now disclosed to the Lord's people.* 27*To them God has chosen to make known among the Gentiles the glorious riches of this mystery, which is Christ in you, the hope of glory.*

28*We proclaim him, admonishing and teaching everyone with all wisdom, so that we may present everyone fully mature in Christ.* 29*To this end I strenuously contend with all the energy Christ so powerfully works in me.*

2:1*I want you to know how hard I am contending for you and for those at Laodicea, and for all who have not met me personally.* 2*My goal is that they may be encouraged in heart and united in love, so that they may have the full riches of complete understanding, in order that they may know the mystery of God, namely, Christ,* 3*in whom are hidden all the treasures of*

260. Pokorný, 94; Hay, 69.

wisdom and knowledge. ⁴*I tell you this so that no one may deceive you by fine-sounding arguments.* ⁵*For though I am absent from you in body, I am present with you in spirit and delight to see how disciplined you are and how firm your faith in Christ is.*

Paul's reference to himself as a "servant" of the gospel at the end of v. 23 leads into this section, which focuses on the ministry of Paul. The personal focus of the section is seen in the dominance of the first-person singular (1:24-25, 29; 2:1, 4-5); the shift to the first-person plural in v. 28 is probably just a stylistic variation. Paul speaks generally about his ministry in 1:24-29 and then applies what he has said to the Colossians in 2:1-5. Three themes stand out. First, at the heart of the word of God that Paul proclaims is the "mystery." With an emphasis entirely typical of Colossians, Paul defines this mystery christologically: "Christ in you" (1:27); "Christ" (2:2). Second, Paul highlights the extent to which his proclamation of the gospel involves suffering (1:24) and struggle (1:29; 2:1). Both of these themes are designed to encourage the Colossian Christians to withstand the false teaching and maintain their adherence to the true gospel. Third, the christological focus of God's word and purpose provides theological motivation for "staying the course," while the example of Paul's sacrificial ministry on their behalf provides personal motivation toward the same end.

The passage exhibits a chiastic arrangement:[1]

A	"Rejoice" *(chairō)*, "flesh" *(sarx)*	1:24
B	"make known," "riches," "mystery"	1:27
C	"contend"	1:29
C'	"contending"	2:1
B'	"knowledge," "riches," "mystery"	2:2
A'	"delight" *(chairō)*, "body" *(sarx)*	2:5

Whether Paul has deliberately organized the section along these lines is difficult to say, but the list does highlight some of the key themes of the section. In addition to the mystery and Paul's suffering, which we have mentioned above, we should also note the high concentration of "knowledge" language: "make known" (v. 27); "wisdom" (v. 28); "complete understanding" (2:2); "know" (2:2); "wisdom" (2:3); "knowledge" (2:3). The concern expressed in these words is evident also in 1:9-10, as we have seen earlier. Wisdom and knowledge were very common goals in the ancient world, and it is possible that the false teachers were claiming that it

---

1. Dunn, 128; Pokorný, 108.

was through their doctrines and practices that ultimate knowledge could be attained. Paul's response is again christological: *"all* the treasures of wisdom and knowledge" are found in Christ (2:2). This last quotation picks up another key theme that is continued from 1:3-23: the universality of the gospel and the exclusiveness of Christ. Paul preaches the word "in its *fullness"* (1:25); he proclaims Christ with *"all* wisdom," seeking to present *"everyone"* mature in Christ (1:28); he strives for *"all* who have not met me personally" (2:1), hoping that they would have "the *full* riches of *complete* understanding" (2:2). Paul wanted those to whom he preached to experience the "fullness" of Christ himself.[2]

The sequence of topics here in Colossians bears a general similarity to the sequence found in Ephesians 2:11–3:13, but with some telling differences. As he does in Colossians 1:21-22, Paul celebrates reconciliation in Christ in Ephesians 2:11-18 — but with a focus on the reconciliation of Jew and Gentile. Then, as in 1:23, Paul refers to the "foundation" of the new community (Eph. 2:19-22). But what is simply affirmed in Ephesians becomes in Colossians a warning, required because of the false teaching. Paul then, as in Colossians, moves into discussion of his own ministry, with reference to his sufferings (3:1, 13), the mystery (3:3-6), and the making known of God's wisdom (3:10). Again, however, the focus on the inclusion of the Gentiles that we find in Ephesians is almost entirely missing from Colossians. These differences suggest again that Paul has contextualized some basic themes in his preaching for two different situations; and that one difference in the situations is that inclusion of Gentiles is not a significant issue in Colossae.

24 *Now* (Gk. *nyn*) normally, of course, functions as a temporal adjective, and the majority of commentators believe it has this significance here also — cf. NJB: "It makes me happy to be suffering for you now."[3] But at times the word loses most of its temporal significance and functions more as a transitional conjunction, as when, for instance, we say, "Now I would like you to understand that. . . ."[4] This function makes better sense here. Having referred to himself as a servant of the gospel, Paul "now" goes on to elaborate the nature of that ministry and particularly its significance for the Colossians. That the Colossians are in mind right from the beginning is clear from the opening statement: *I rejoice in what I am suffering for you.* Paul did not found the church at Colossae, nor has he visited the church (2:1; cf. 1:8). Yet in some manner the suffering that Paul undergoes in his gospel ministry has benefits for the

2. J. Lähnemann, *Der Kolosserbrief* (Gütersloh: Mohn, 1971), 45-46.
3. So the majority of commentators.
4. Cf. 1 Cor. 5:11; 12:20; cf. Wright, 89-90; Barth/Blanke, 253.

Colossians. Paul never explains quite how this can be, but the rest of the
verse suggests a possible answer.

Getting at this answer is not easy, however, since v. 24b is one of the
more difficult passages in the letter.[5] As we have suggested, the clause beginning with *and* likely functions to explain how it is that Paul's sufferings
are "on behalf of" (Gk. *hyper;* TNIV, "for") the Colossians.[6] The end of the
verse suggests a partial answer: Paul's sufferings as a servant of the gospel
are *for the sake of* (*hyper* again) *his body, which is the church.* The language is
reminiscent of 1:18, where "church" refers not to a local assembly of believers (as is usually the case in the New Testament) but to the "universal
church."[7] By referring to the church as Christ's body, Paul highlights the
corporate solidarity that Christ's people enjoy with him. The Colossians,
of course, are members of this worldwide assembly of believers, so they
are among the beneficiaries of Paul's sufferings. But just how does Paul's
suffering benefit the church at large? And how can Paul claim that his sufferings are *filling up . . . what is still lacking in regard to Christ's afflictions?*

As a first step toward answering these questions, we need to determine the exact meaning of the verb translated *fill up* in the TNIV. This rare
Greek verb (occurring only here in biblical Greek) is a double compound,
made up of two prepositions (*anti* and *ana*) plus the verb *plēroō* ("fill,"
"fulfill"). A simpler form of this verb, *anaplēroō,* occurs elsewhere in Paul
with the sense "fill up [completely]" (note esp. 1 Cor. 16:17 and Phil. 2:30,
where it is used with *hysterēma*).

But the problem is to determine what nuance the addition of the
preposition *anti* gives to this verbal idea. There are five main possibilities.
(1) The verb could mean "fill up in place of" — Paul suffers in place of the
church.[8] (2) It could mean "fill up on behalf of," simply emphasizing the
later preposition "on behalf of."[9] (3) It could mean "fill up in response to"
— Paul's sufferings respond to what is lacking.[10] (4) The *anti* could have a
reciprocal significance — Paul, in his turn (after Christ), suffers for the
sake of the church.[11] (5) Granted the tendency of *koinē* Greek to use com-

5. For a history of interpretation, see Jacob Kremer, "Was an den Bedrängnissen
des Christus Mangelt: Versucht einer bibeltheologischen Neuinterpretation von Kol
1,24," *Bib* 82 (2001), 130-46.

6. Harris, 65, who translates καί "in that."

7. In 1:18 Paul uses the genitive τῆς ἐκκλησίας following "body," which is to be interpreted as an epexegetic genitive. Here he uses a relative clause, ὅ ἐστιν ἡ ἐκκλησία. The
two are semantic equivalents, with the more compact genitive construction fitting the
style of the hymn.

8. E.g., Wright, 90.

9. Moule, *Idiom Book,* 71.

10. O'Brien, 80.

11. See esp. Lightfoot, 165; also BDAG.

pound verbs, it could indicate simply what its simple form means: "fill up."[12] The rarity of the verb makes a decision difficult, and we should certainly not let a decision about this verb dictate the meaning of the passage. But perhaps the third option makes most sense of the other examples of the verb and the context here. So we hesitantly adopt the sense "I am filling up in order to complete" *what is lacking in regard to Christ's afflictions.*[13]

Paul is not, of course, suggesting that the *redemptive* suffering of Christ requires any supplementation. As 1:19-20 and 2:15 in this letter make clear (quite apart from the evidence of other Pauline letters), Paul is convinced that Christ's death on the cross is completely and finally capable of taking care of the human sin problem. It is not that there is anything lacking "in" the atoning suffering of Christ but that there is something lacking "in regard to" (TNIV) the tribulations that pertain to Christ as the Messiah as he is proclaimed in the world.[14] The difference may even be suggested in the vocabulary that Paul uses, since he shifts from "sufferings" (Gk. *pathēma*) to "afflictions" (Gk. *thlipsis*), this latter word never being used in the New Testament for Christ's redemptive sufferings.

Jewish literature speaks of the "messianic woes," tribulations to be endured by God's people in the days immediately before the coming of the Messiah.[15] Jesus and New Testament authors use similar language to describe the "last days," initiated with Christ's first coming and awaiting their fulfillment with the glorious return of Christ (see esp. Matt. 24:4-14 and par.). The early Christian consciousness, surely shared by Paul, that Christ's coming had inaugurated the "last days," is an important backdrop to what Paul is saying here.[16] There are also hints that the amount

12. Barth/Blanke, 256.

13. Note that several versions (RSV; NRSV; NLT; HCSB; REB) use the verb "complete" in their translations here. The phrase "in my flesh" simply emphasizes the physical nature of the sufferings. In the Greek text, this phrase (ἐν τῇ σαρκί) follows "what is lacking in regard to Christ's afflictions," so it could modify "what is lacking" (Wolter, 102). But the English translations are surely right to attach the phrase to the verb (see C. Stettler, *Der Kolosserhymnus* [Tübingen: Mohr Siebeck, 2000], 187).

14. Lightfoot, 166, distinguishes between the "satisfactory" sufferings of Christ and his "ministerial" sufferings. The precise nuance of the two genitives in the phrase τὰ ὑστερήματα τῶν θλίψεων τοῦ Χριστοῦ is therefore very important. The first could be partitive, "the lacking parts within the tribulations" but, on the interpretation advanced above, it is better taken as genitive of reference, as in TNIV: "what is still lacking in regard to Christ's afflictions." The second genitive might be objective — "tribulations for the sake of Christ" (Abbott, 230-32; Schweizer, 102-4), but it is probably possessive, with the nuance "the tribulations that relate to Christ."

15. See esp. O'Brien, 79-80.

16. Lohse, 70, correctly notes that our passage is suffused with "apocalyptic" language (cf. esp. "mystery," "disclosed"). See also F. Zeilinger, *Der Erstgeborene der Schöpfung* (Vienna: Herder, 1974), 82-94.

and time of these tribulations have been determined by God. In the New Testament, see especially Revelation 6:9-11:

> When he opened the fifth seal, I saw under the altar the souls of those who had been slain because of the word of God and the testimony they had maintained. They called out in a loud voice, "How long, Sovereign Lord, holy and true, until you judge the inhabitants of the earth and avenge our blood?" Then each of them was given a white robe, and they were told to wait a little longer, until the full number of their fellow servants and brothers and sisters were killed just as they had been.[17]

What is lacking, then, needing to be "filled up," are the tribulations that are inevitable and necessary as God's kingdom faces the opposition of the "dominion of darkness" (cf. v. 13). As members of Christ's own body, his people participate in the sufferings of Christ himself.[18]

There is much to be said for this reading of the text, but it fails to account for the focus on Paul's special role as "servant of the body."[19] Paul's ministry has a special eschatological significance. It is telling, for instance, that, even as he identifies Christ as the "suffering servant" of Isaiah, so he also applies that servant language to himself (see esp. Acts 13:47). Two texts in 2 Corinthians help illuminate the idea that Paul expresses here in Colossians 1:24: "For just as we share abundantly in the sufferings of Christ, so also our comfort abounds through Christ. If we are distressed, it is for your comfort and salvation; if we are comforted, it is for your comfort, which produces in you patient endurance of the same sufferings we suffer" (1:5-6); "We always carry around in our body the death of Jesus, so that the life of Jesus may also be revealed in our body. For we who are alive are always being given over to death for Jesus' sake, so that his life may also be revealed in our mortal body. So then, death is at work in us, but life is at work in you" (4:10-12). Because Paul's apostolic ministry is an "extension" of Christ's work in the world, Paul identifies his own suffer-

---

17. See on this, briefly, Clinton E. Arnold, "Colossians," in *Zondervan Illustrated Bible Backgrounds Commentary* (4 vols.; Grand Rapids: Zondervan, 2002), 3.381-82. He also quotes *4 Ezra* 4:36-37: "For [God] has weighed the age in the balance, and measured the times by measure, and numbered the times by number; and he will not move or arouse them until that measure is fulfilled."

18. See, e.g., E. Percy, *Die Probleme der Kolosser- und Epheserbriefe* (Lund: Gleerup, 1946), 128-34.

19. See Masson, 110-11; Richard Bauckham, "Colossians 1:24 Again: The Apocalyptic Motif," *EvQ* 47 (1975), 168-70; Hanna Stettler, "An Interpretation of Colossians 1:24 in the Framework of Paul's Mission Theology," in *Mission of the Early Church to Jews and Gentiles* (Tübingen: Mohr Siebeck, 2000), 192-208.

ings very closely with Christ's. These sufferings have no redemptive benefit for the church, but they are the inevitable accompaniment of Paul's
"commission" to proclaim the end-time revelation of God's mystery (vv.
25-27). It is in this way that Paul's sufferings are "on behalf of" the church,
including the Colossian Christians. And, of course, as a prisoner for the
gospel, Paul is suffering for them even as he writes. As members of the fellowship of those raised with Christ and forming therefore part of Christ's
body, we also are the beneficiaries of Paul's suffering.

25 In 2:1, Paul continues the line of thought that he began in v. 24:
as a servant of the gospel, Paul "contends," even to the point of suffering,
for the church, including the Christians in Colossae and Laodicea. In vv.
25-29 Paul detours slightly from this path to talk about the purpose of his
ministry, focusing on the message he is called to proclaim (vv. 25-27) and
the purpose of that proclamation (v. 28) before transitioning back to the
theme of his apostolic "striving" (v. 29).

In v. 23, Paul claims to be serving the gospel, in v. 24 Christ's body,
the church. Elsewhere in Paul, he describes his role as "servant"/"minister" (diakonos) in terms of the message that he serves (2 Cor. 3:6; Eph. 3:7).
But nowhere else does he claim to be a "servant" of the church — especially of the "universal" church. This language has been taken by a number of scholars to indicate the work of a Pauline disciple, seeking to elevate Paul's authority to the level of the worldwide church.[20] Of course,
this view faces the rather daunting task of explaining the emphatically
personal language of the passage before us. But it also overlooks the way
in which Paul commonly stresses the universal scope of his call. For instance, Paul explains why he can claim some measure of authority over
the Christians in Rome — even though he had never visited them — by
appealing to his apostolic commission (1:5; 11:13; cf. 1:13-14; 15:16).
Something very similar may be going on in our text, since, of course, here
also Paul is addressing a church that he has neither founded nor visited.
And the universal focus of Paul's ministry matches the universal proclamation of the gospel (v. 23).

The same issue arises with respect to Paul's claim to be serving by
the commission God gave me. Commission (oikonomia) sometimes refers to an
office, as in Jesus' parable about the "shrewd manager," whose office is
called an oikonomia (Luke 16:2-4). Many interpreters accept that meaning
for this verse (cf. RSV, "divine office"),[21] and some then go on to insist
that we are facing again a post-Pauline "institutionalizing" of the minis-

20. E.g., Wolter, 102.
21. The meaning is favored by BDAG; see also Lohse, 72-73; T. J. Sappington, *Revelation and Redemption at Colossae* (Sheffield: JSOT Press, 1991), 183-85.

try of the apostle.[22] But it is doubtful whether "office" is a fair translation of the word anywhere in the New Testament. It has a more dynamic connotation, even in passages such as Luke 16:2-4: "stewardship," "custodianship," or perhaps "commissioning" (1 Cor. 9:17). Some argue that *oikonomia* here means "plan," as it probably does in Ephesians 3:9, which is somewhat parallel to this text.[23] But the Ephesians texts that are closest to our verse are 3:2 and 7: "Surely you have heard about the administration of God's grace that was given to me for you"; "I became a servant of this gospel by the gift of God's grace given me through the working of his power" (cf. vv. 23, 25, and 29). In these texts, the "administration" (Gk. *oikonomia*) in v. 2 appears to be equivalent to the "gift of God's grace" in v. 7 and refers to Paul's apostolic commission. And Paul uses similar language elsewhere to describe his apostleship (note the language of "which was given me by God" in Rom. 12:3; 15:15; 1 Cor. 3:10; Gal. 2:9).[24] These parallels suggest that *oikonomia* refers to his apostolic ministry. God chose Paul before his birth (Gal. 1:15) to become an apostle, with particular responsibility to bring the good news to the Gentiles (Acts 9:15; 22:21; 26:17-18; see v. 27). This is the "commission" of which he speaks here.

As he has done in v. 24 — *suffering for you* — Paul again gives his apostolic commission personal application to the Colossians: *to present to you the word of God in its fullness.* The TNIV rendering brings together two phrases that are distinct in the Greek text, in which Paul says of his apostolic commission that it is "directed toward you" and that it consists in "fulfilling (Gk. *plērōsai*) the word of God." The "you" may simply be a way of speaking of the Colossian Christians. But it may carry more significance than this. Paul often refers specifically to his calling to the Gentiles when he mentions his apostolic ministry. The text roughly parallel to our passage in Ephesians goes on to speak of the "mystery" and defines it with reference to Gentiles being "heirs together with Israel" (3:2-6; see v. 6). Similarly, in this passage, Paul goes on to refer to the way that God has made known "among the Gentiles the glorious riches of this mystery" (v. 27). Therefore, Paul could be thinking of the "you" here in terms of the Colossians' Gentile identity (see NLT).[25] Nevertheless, we should be cautious about thinking this is the case, since (as we noted above) Paul in general says much less explicitly about Gentile inclusion here in Colossians than he does in Ephesians. The second clause is best taken as a definition of the commission that Paul has been given.[26] The verb *plēroō*

22. E.g., Wolter, 103.
23. Esp. O'Brien, 81.
24. E.g., Dunn, 118.
25. Eadie, 93; O'Brien, 82.
26. The infinitive πληρῶσαι is epexegetical (Harris, 68).

that Paul uses means "fill." God's word is not "filled" when it is preached only, but when its preaching accomplishes the purpose God has for it: when it is heard and produces growth and fruit in the lives of those who respond (see vv. 5-6). Paul uses the same verb with reference to the gospel in a similar way in Romans 15:19.

26 A typical Pauline sentence resembles a series of Russian dolls: the main, or "outer" clause yields to a series of subordinate, or "inner" clauses. So here. The sentence that began in v. 24 continues into this verse: "I rejoice in what I am suffering . . . and I fill up in my flesh . . . for the sake of his body, . . . the church, of which I am a servant . . . by the commission . . . to fulfill the word of God, which is the mystery. . . ." As this paraphrase indicates, Paul defines the word of God in v. 25 as the *mystery (mystērion)*. This word is one of the most interesting in Paul's theological vocabulary. It is particularly prominent in Ephesians and Colossians, where half of the twenty Pauline occurrences are found (in Colossians, see also 1:27; 2:2; 4:3). In the heyday of the history-of-religions approach to Paul, his use of this word was thought to reflect the larger Greco-Roman world, particularly the "mystery religions." But it is now generally recognized that Paul borrows this word from the Old Testament and Judaism (esp. Qumran). Particularly significant are the occurrences of the word in Daniel 2 (translating Heb. *rāz*), where it refers to the "mystery" of King Nebuchadnezzar's dream — a mystery that God reveals to Daniel. Paul, similarly, uses the word characteristically to denote truth about God and his plan of salvation that had remained hidden in the past but that had now been revealed.[27] The general application of the word here to the revelation of gospel truth in general (which continues in the other Colossian occurrences) is similar to the use of the word in Romans 16:25 — where Paul claims that his gospel and preaching are "according to the revelation of the mystery hidden for long ages past" — and in Ephesians 1:9 and 6:19. However, in Ephesians 3:1-9, the passage that, as we have seen, offers the most parallels to Colossians 1:24-29, Paul applies the "mystery" specifically to the inclusion of Gentiles within the new covenant people of God (v. 6). Since Paul brings the Gentiles explicitly into the picture as he continues to speak of mystery in v. 27, he may have in view this particular aspect of the word of God (but see on this our notes on the next verse).

27. For the background of the word, see esp. R. Brown, *The Semitic Background of the Term "Mystery" in the New Testament* (Philadelphia: Fortress, 1968); on Paul's use, Markus N. A. Bockmuehl, *Revelation and Mystery in Ancient Judaism and Pauline Christianity* (WUNT 2.36; Tübingen: Mohr Siebeck, 1990); D. A. Carson, "Mystery and Fulfillment: Toward a More Comprehensive Paradigm of Paul's Understanding of the Old and the New," in *Justification and Variegated Nomism*, vol. 2: *The Paradoxes of Paul* (ed. D. A. Carson, Peter T. O'Brien, and Mark A. Seifrid; WUNT 2.181; Tübingen: Mohr Siebeck, 2004), 390-436.

Paul's assertion that the mystery has been *kept hidden* but is now *disclosed* (or "revealed")[28] has its background in apocalyptic Judaism, with its focus on "revealing" (*apokalyptō;* hence "apocalyptic") realities about God, the world, and the culmination of God's purposes in the world. Paul refers specifically to this scheme elsewhere when he speaks of the mystery (see Rom. 16:25, quoted above; 1 Cor. 2:7; Eph. 3:4-6, 9). A few commentators have argued that the particular wording of this text suggests that *ages and generations* refer to spiritual powers (cf. 1 Cor. 2:6-8; Eph. 3:10).[29] But Paul never elsewhere uses either of these words to refer to spiritual beings,[30] so the meaning will have to be temporal — as the *now* in the subsequent clause strongly suggests. The coming of Christ and the accompanying gift of the Spirit, the climactic event in salvation history, reveal to *the Lord's people* (*hagiois*, "saints"; see the note on v. 2) God's ultimate purpose and plan. Paul emphasizes the point, of course, to remind the Colossians that it is by receiving (1:5) and holding fast (1:23) to the gospel that they have access to this ultimate knowledge — not via the program of the false teachers.

27 Most of the English versions begin a new sentence in this verse, but in the Greek Paul's run-on sentence continues. This part of his sentence elucidates the mystery mentioned in v. 26. So, varying his language but not his idea, Paul says again that *God has chosen to make [it] known* to the Lord's people. What God has made known is *the glorious riches of this mystery.* This, the TNIV rendering, is one way to piece together three words whose relationship to one another is expressed very generally in Greek: the substantive "riches" followed by two words in the genitive, "glory" and "mystery." A straightforward rendering of the three in English would be "the riches of the glory of this mystery" (NASB; ESV). The TNIV, along with several other versions (e.g., HCSB; NET), takes "of the glory" (*tēs doxēs*) as a descriptive genitive; hence, "riches characterized by glory," "glorious riches."[31] Granted the sequence of words in this context, this seems to be the best option. Yet we would want to register again our

28. The verb here is φανερόω ("disclose," "make known"), but it is virtually equivalent to ἀποκαλύπτω ("reveal") in these contexts (cf. Rom. 1:17 with 3:21; Rom. 16:25 and 26). In parallel with "kept hidden" (ἀποκεκρυμμένον), a participle, we would expect φανερόω also to take the form of a participle. Instead, we find an aorist indicative, which may be used for emphasis ("this mystery, hidden for ages — it has now been disclosed!" cf. Lightfoot, 169).

29. E.g., Dibelius-Greeven, 24. The construction is ἀποκρύπτω (here as a perfect participle, "now hidden") plus ἀπό ("from"). In this combination, which is rare, the object of the preposition is usually a person from whom a secret is hidden (2 Kgs. 4:27; Ps. 118:19; Isa. 40:27; Jer. 32:17 [= LXX 39:17]; Luke 10:21; Hermas, *Similitudes* 9.11.9).

30. Despite BDAG on αἰών.

31. So also many commentators, e.g., Harris, 70; Gnilka, 102.

concern that the theologically very "weighty" word "glory" not be weakened to a mere adjective (see our comments on v. 11). If we take the word as a description of "riches," we should at the same time insist that it connotes the presence of God himself. As O'Brien puts it, "The apostle wished to emphasize that this wonderful mystery partook of the character of God himself."[32]

The TNIV construes "of this mystery" (*tou mystēriou toutou*) as an epexegetic genitive, specifying the content of the riches ("the riches that are the mystery"). This makes good sense because the word "riches" in itself lacks specific content. Paul uses a number of similar expressions, particularly in Ephesians and Colossians: "riches consisting in [God's] goodness" (Rom. 2:4); "riches consisting in [God's] glory" (Rom. 9:23); "riches consisting in generosity" (2 Cor. 8:2); "riches consisting in [God's] grace" (Eph. 1:7); "glorious riches consisting in the inheritance" (Eph. 1:18); "riches consisting in [God's] grace" (Eph. 2:7); "riches consisting in Christ" (Eph. 3:8); "riches consisting in [God's] glory" (Eph. 3:16); "riches consisting in the full measure of understanding" (Col. 2:2) (all translations mine). The word obviously underscores the value of what is indicated by the word it governs. Another word in the Greek text, not directly translated in the TNIV, may serve a similar purpose. Immediately preceding "the riches" is an interrogative particle (*ti*), which means, in a context such as this, "what sort of."[33] But the effect of adding it to the word "riches" is to heighten the value of those riches;[34] hence RSV/NRSV/ESV: "to make known how great among the Gentiles are the riches . . ." (and note the close parallels in Eph. 1:19; 3:18).

The strongly christological orientation of Colossians is seen again in Paul's definition of the mystery: *Christ in you, the hope of glory* (see also 2:2; 4:3).[35] Only in these verses in Colossians does Paul equate the mystery with Christ. To be sure, Ephesians 3:4 also refers to the "mystery of Christ," but goes on to define this mystery in terms of the inclusion of Gentiles as "heirs together with Israel" in one body. Many interpreters think that Paul is here also interpreting the mystery with particular refer-

32. O'Brien, 86.
33. BDAG.
34. Abbott, 234.
35. The definition is accomplished by means of a relative clause, introduced with ὅ, that has as its antecedent (probably) μυστηρίου. Some good manuscripts have the masculine pronoun ὅς in place of the neuter ὅ, but the reading is probably secondary, an assimilation to the case of Χριστός. A few commentators (e.g., Eadie, 97; Barth/Blanke, 265) think that the antecedent of the relative pronoun is the entire preceding idea (which is certainly grammatically possible). But the "mystery" seems to be the main idea in this clause, and it is preferable to see it as the antecedent.

157

ence to Gentile inclusion. But this view depends on how we construe two phrases in this verse: "among the Gentiles" and *en hymin*, which could be translated either "in you" or "among you." The TNIV, like most of the other versions, follows the majority of commentators in attaching the former phrase to the main verb, "make known," and translating the second phrase "in you." The result is a rather general definition of the mystery in terms of the "indwelling Christ," a mystery that has been proclaimed "among the Gentiles."[36]

But it is also possible to attach "among the Gentiles" to "this mystery" — "how great are the glorious riches of this mystery [displayed] among the Gentiles."[37] And "in you" might mean, specifically, "in each of you Gentiles" or "among you Gentiles."[38] Accepting these options gives the "mystery" more of a focus on the Gentiles: it is among *them* that its riches are displayed, and it is in (or among) *them* that Christ dwells.[39] And this definition fits well with the parallel text in Ephesians, as we have seen. Nevertheless, caution is in order. Appeal to the Ephesians parallel is a double-edged sword, for, as we have seen, it is the explicit material about the inclusion of Gentiles in Ephesians that is omitted in Colossians. Moreover, Paul has done nothing to draw attention to the ethnic status of the Colossian Christians: this is the first (and only) place in the letter where the word "Gentile" (*ethnos*; plural *ethnē*) occurs. On the whole, then, we are inclined to follow the TNIV in attaching "among the Gentiles" to the verb and in translating *en hymin* as "in you" rather than "among you."

It is, of course, true that the Colossian Christians are Gentiles, and that there might therefore be some hint of the distinctive new covenant blessing of the extension to the Gentiles of the ministry of Christ, the Jewish Messiah. And Paul's specific reference to the mystery being made known "among the Gentiles" obviously touches on this epochal salvation-history shift. But the motif is far less prominent than it is in Ephesians. Nor should we feel any compulsion to come up with a single specific referent for Paul's "mystery." He uses the term in a functional more than in a topical manner, applying it to a number of different, albeit usually related, aspects of God's climactic work in Christ.

36. The verse would have even less reference to the Gentiles if we translated ἐν τοῖς ἔθνεσιν as "among [or "to," if ἐν = εἰς] the nations."

37. The paraphrase is from Harris (71), who thinks word order favors this view.

38. For this latter rendering, adopted in NASB; NJB; NAB; NET, see esp. Lohse, 75-76, who comments: "Doubtless this does not mean the pneumatic indwelling of the Lord in the hearts of believers, but rather the Christ preached among the nations, the Lord proclaimed in the community's midst" (p. 76). See also, e.g., Moule, 85; Gnilka, 102; Pokorný, 103; Masson, 113. In favor of rendering "in [each one of] you," see esp. Dunn, 122-23.

39. See esp. Dunn, 121-22, for this line of interpretation.

Paul's focus here is on how God's new covenant people are completely identified with their representative, Christ, and how that new identity gives hope for the future. Paul often speaks of Christians as those who are "in Christ" (see 1:2), but only rarely does he reverse the imagery and refer to Christ "in" us (Rom. 8:10; 2 Cor. 13:5; Gal. 2:20; 4:19; Eph. 3:17).[40] But the point of both expressions is the same (cf., e.g., Rom. 8:1 and 10), stressing the intimate relationship between Christ and his people and the way in which, because of this relationship, Christ fully represents us. It is because of this that we can have *the hope of glory*, that is, the certainty that we will experience final glory (cf. Rom. 5:2). Paul here returns to a key theme in this opening chapter (1:5, 23) in order to remind us again that hope is tied to Christ, and to Christ alone.

28 The *him* in TNIV and other English versions translates a Greek relative pronoun, as Paul's sentence takes yet another step forward. At the beginning of this long sentence, Paul focused on his apostolic suffering (v. 24) and his commission to preach the word of God (v. 25). In vv. 26-27 he has elaborated the nature of this word that he preaches. Now he returns to where the sentence began, referring (reversing the order in vv. 24-25) to his apostolic preaching (v. 28) and his suffering (v. 29). Verse 28 elaborates what Paul means when he says at the end of v. 25 that he has been given the task "to present to you the word of God in its fullness," or "fill up the word of God." One difference between v. 28 and vv. 24-25 (and v. 29) should be noted, however: while the earlier text (and again v. 29) uses the first-person singular, we have here the first-person plural. Probably, as in vv. 3-9, Paul includes fellow workers such as Timothy (1:1) and Epaphras (1:7-8).[41] But it is not impossible that the shift is stylistic only, the so-called "editorial we," and that Paul thus continues to refer to himself alone.

The verse is remarkable for its emphasis on universality: the Greek word *pas* occurs four times: "admonishing *everyone*," "teaching *everyone* with *all* wisdom,"[42] "that we may present *everyone* fully mature in Christ." Particularly striking is the threefold "every person" (*panta anthrōpon*). This emphasis continues a theme that runs through chapter 1;

---

40. Paul can also occasionally use similar language about the Spirit "in us" or "among us" (Rom. 8:9, 11; 1 Cor. 3:16; 6:19; 2 Tim. 1:14); and with similar meaning (cf. Rom. 8:9 and 11 with Rom. 8:10).

41. So most commentators. Lohse, 76, suggests that the "we" includes Epaphras, who is included within Paul's apostolic commission by virtue of his extension of Paul's ministry in Colossae.

42. Some manuscripts (D F G 0278 33 614 629 and a few others) omit this second πάντα ἄνθρωπον; but it has probably been accidentally omitted because of the two other occurrences of the same phrase.

see v. 6, "the gospel is bearing fruit and growing throughout the whole world"; and v. 23, "the gospel . . . has been proclaimed to every creature under heaven." Paul may again direct this emphasis against the false teachers, who were perhaps advocating an elitism in which salvation was confined to certain "special" people.[43] Since Paul has not visited Colossae, and in light of the claim about universal reconciliation in v. 20, "every person" cannot be restricted to "every person in Colossae" (cf. REB). On the other hand, it cannot mean "every person in the universe" either. It is best taken in this context to mean "every person we encounter," "every person God brings into the scope of our ministry." The repetition of the phrase therefore emphasizes the full measure of gospel proclamation that Paul and his associates bring to every person they encounter. Each one is "admonished" and "taught" with the goal that each one might be presented fully mature in Christ.[44] It is possible that the language has yet a further nuance. Paul sometimes uses *pas* to mean "every kind of person" with a particular focus on the breakdown of ethnic distinctions (Jew vs. Gentile) (see, perhaps, Rom. 11:32). While this distinction does not seem to play a significant role in the Colossian situation, Paul has just mentioned the mystery and its significance for the Gentile world.[45]

"Proclaim" *(katangellō)* is a particularly Pauline word in the New Testament, referring to his preaching in most of its occurrences in Acts and used elsewhere only by Paul. This general word for the preaching of the gospel is broken down here into two of its specific components: "admonishing" (from *noutheteō*) and "teaching" (from *didaskō*). Lightfoot seems to suggest that the former may be directed to non-Christians (to stimulate repentance) and the latter to Christians (to enhance faith).[46] But the goal of the proclamation here makes it more likely that both activities are directed to Christian converts. As the English "admonish" implies, *noutheteō* focuses on the preacher's warning of Christians who might be tempted to stray (see esp. Acts 20:31; 1 Cor. 4:14; 1 Thess. 5:14; 2 Thess. 3:15; it also occurs in Rom. 15:14; Col. 3:16; 1 Thess. 5:12). "Teaching," on the other hand, is the more positive activity of communicating Christian truth. It denotes the same activity as the Colossians' "hearing" and "learning" of the gospel (1:5, 7) from the standpoint of the speaker, in this case Epaphras (cf. also 2:7). The verb and its corresponding nouns,

43. Lightfoot, 170; Lohse, 74.
44. Wright, 93.
45. Dunn, 125; Barth/Blanke, 267.
46. Lightfoot says that the two words are "complementary aspects of the preacher's duty, and are related one to the other, as μετάνοια to πίστις, 'warning to repent, instructing in the faith'" (p. 170). He refers to Acts 20:21.

"teacher" and "teaching," are often used in the New Testament to denote this authoritative communication of gospel truth (see esp. 1 Cor. 12:28-29; Eph. 4:11, 21; 1 Tim. 1:10; 5:17; 2 Tim. 1:11; 2:2; Titus 1:9). At the same time, this truth is reinforced as believers "teach" one another (Col. 3:16).

This close relationship between faithful teaching and faith-filled hearing of the gospel is reinforced with the addition of the phrase "with all wisdom," which matches what Paul has said earlier about the Colossians' understanding of God's will (1:9). As people need wisdom to know how to live out true knowledge of God, so the preacher needs wisdom to know how to teach and admonish the people. Paul will again have one eye on the situation in Colossae, where the believers need great wisdom in negotiating the competing religious teachings they are hearing. And it is perhaps significant in this regard that three of the four Pauline occurrences of the phrase "in/with all wisdom" *(en pasē sophia)* occur in Colossians (1:9, 28; 3:16; cf. also Eph. 1:8; and note also "in wisdom" [TNIV, "Be wise in the way you act"] in Col. 4:5).

Paul and his associates labor in preaching so that *we may present everyone fully mature in Christ.* As in v. 22, "present" (from *paristēmi*) probably has an eschatological focus, referring to the presentation of every believer before God at the final judgment.[47] The Greek word rendered "fully mature" in TNIV — *teleion* — is one difficult to translate into English. Most of the versions opt for some form of "mature" (RSV; NRSV; ESV; HCSB; NET; REB), but some prefer "perfect" (NIV; NJB; NAB). Neither quite captures the sense of the word. "Perfect" is too strong, "mature" too weak. Rarely does the word in the New Testament have the sense of our English "perfect," with its connotations of absoluteness (though see, perhaps, Rom. 12:2; Jas. 1:17, 25; 1 John 4:18). "Mature," on the other hand, is too relative, inviting us to think that we are *teleios* as long as we are doing a bit better than some other Christians we could name. Similar to the Hebrew *tamim* (which is translated by *teleios* five times in the LXX), *teleios* connotes the quality of being so wholehearted in one's devotion to the Lord that one can be said to be blameless in conduct (see esp. Matt. 5:48; 19:21; Eph. 4:13; Heb. 5:14; Jas. 1:4b). Schweizer puts it well: to be *teleios* is the "complete and undivided way in which a person, with all one's positive and negative attributes, is oriented toward God or toward Christ."[48] Noah was one who was "blameless" in this way (Gen. 6:9), and the people of Israel were similarly to be "blameless" before the Lord (Deut. 18:13). The Hebrew *tamim* was used especially often

47. So most commentators. See, however, Lohse, 78-79, who holds that it must refer to the current conduct of the community.
48. Schweizer, 112.

in the Dead Sea Scrolls to denote this total commitment and blameless conduct. Some commentators have speculated that *teleios* was a goal that the false teachers were promising their adherents and Paul therefore uses the word here polemically: it is through Christian proclamation that people can become *teleios*.[49] There is some precedent for a polemical use of the term in Paul (Phil. 3:15), but we do not have enough evidence to suppose this was the case in Colossae.

29 Paul ends the paragraph (and the long Greek sentence) by returning to where he began (v. 24): his apostolic labor on behalf of the Colossian Christians and others. The verb in this verse shifts back to the first-person singular, suggesting that, though Paul includes his associates in v. 28, his focus is on his own ministry throughout. *To this end* translates a Greek relative clause, which is attached to v. 28: Paul *strenuously contends* in his ministry in order to "present everyone fully mature in Christ." *Strenuously contends* translates a phrase that contains a Greek indicative verb — "labor" — and adverbial participle — "fighting, struggling."

"Labor" *(kopiaō)* is a general verb for any kind of work (e.g., Luke 5:5; 1 Cor. 4:12; Eph. 4:28; 2 Tim. 2:6), but Paul uses it most often to refer to the "work" of ministry (e.g., Rom. 16:6, 12; 1 Cor. 15:10; 16:16; Gal. 4:11; Phil. 2:16; 1 Thess. 5:12; 1 Tim. 4:10; 5:17). Similarly, the Greek verb behind "contend" *(agōnizomai)* referred originally to "competing" as an athlete and then developed into the more general sense "fight" — whether physical (e.g., 2 Macc. 8:16; John 18:36) or mental (e.g., Luke 13:24; cf. Col. 4:12 with reference to prayer). The verb here may allude to athletic competition, since Paul does use the verb in this way (1 Cor. 9:25; 2 Tim. 4:7).[50] But whether or not this is the case,[51] the sense of "contend [for the faith]," "strive," is clear enough. Lightfoot thinks that the "inward striving" of prayer is particularly in view.[52] But, while not excluding prayer, the word here, combined with "labor," more likely refers to the general work of ministry: preaching the gospel, admonishing converts, resisting false teachers.[53] Only here and in 1 Timothy 4:10 does Paul use the two verbs — "labor" and "contend" — together to denote his apostolic ministry, and it is surely no coincidence that both contexts deal with false teaching.

As he has done earlier in v. 11 with reference to the Colossians' life

49. This view is especially popular among those who think the pagan "mysteries," with their promises of "perfection," are behind the false teaching (Lightfoot, 170-71; Lohse, 78).

50. Dunn, 126.

51. Victor C. Pfitzner calls it a "pale transferred sense" (*Paul and the Agon Motif: Traditional Athletic Imagery in the Pauline Literature* [NovTSup 16; Leiden: Brill, 1967], 109).

52. Lightfoot, 170 (on 2:1 and referring to 4:12).

53. See esp. Pfitzner, *Paul and the Agon Motif*, esp. 109-12; O'Brien, 90.

of Christian obedience, Paul again stacks up words referring to power: *with all the energy Christ so powerfully works in me;* or, more literally, "according to his [Christ's] energy which is working in me in power."[54] And the ultimate aim is much the same: to balance human effort with the enabling grace of God in Christ. All Paul's work would be of little effect if it was not done through[55] the power of Christ. Paul can brag that "I worked harder than all of them" (1 Cor. 15:10), but at the same time what he accomplishes in ministry is always and only "through him who gives me strength" (Phil. 4:13). "Energy" and "works" come from the same Greek root *(energeia/energeō),* which often refers in the New Testament to the power of God (e.g., Gal. 2:8; Eph. 1:11, 19-20; 3:7, 20; Phil. 2:13; 3:21; Col. 2:12). The combination of the three words is found nowhere else in the New Testament (though cf. Eph. 1:19-20).

2:1 It is possible that chapter 2 introduces a new stage in Paul's argument,[56] but, as we have noted above, 2:1-5 is closely related to 1:24-29. Paul continues in this new paragraph to talk about his ministry. But his attention shifts a bit, from general discussion of himself and his ministry to the significance of his ministry for the Colossians and for the threat of false teaching that they are facing. Aletti discerns a chiasm in this paragraph, with vv. 1 and 5 focusing on the readers, vv. 2a and 4 on the reaction Paul hopes to stimulate from his readers, and vv. 2b and 3 on the central truth to which his readers need to respond: Christ, the mystery of God, the repository of "all the treasures of wisdom and knowledge."[57]

Though not explicitly translated in the TNIV, v. 1 begins with a conjunction, *gar,* "for." It may suggest that 2:1-5 explain why Paul has written 1:24-29,[58] but it more likely simply connects 2:1 to 1:29, as Paul illustrates and elaborates his apostolic "struggle."[59] *I want you to know* draws attention to what Paul is about to say.[60] The suffering and struggle attendant on

---

54. TNIV rightly takes ἐν δυνάμει adverbially ("powerfully"). It also assumes that the participle ἐνεργουμένην is middle rather than passive (for the latter option, see O'Brien, 91).

55. The preposition at the head of this phrase (κατά) may indicate instrument (Harris, 74).

56. See, e.g., Gnilka, 107, who notes the use of παρακαλέω in v. 2 (a word that sometimes marks the transition to a new section of exhortation in the NT letters) and the first explicit mention of false teachers in v. 4.

57. Aletti, 147-48.

58. Wright, 94.

59. Harris, 78.

60. This phrase occurs elsewhere in Paul only in 1 Cor. 11:3; but the negatively expressed "I [we] do not want you to be ignorant" (Rom. 1:13; 11:25; 1 Cor. 10:1; 12:1; 2 Cor. 1:8; 1 Thess. 4:13) functions in the same way. Both phrases are found quite commonly in ancient letters.

Paul's apostolic ministry are not only directed to people with whom he has personally worked but also to people, such as the Colossians, whom Paul has never met. The close connection between 1:29 and 2:1 is signaled especially by the language of "contending," a form of the same word occurring here in 2:1 (the noun *agōn*), which has also been used in 1:29 (the verb *agōnizomai*). As in 1:29, Paul characterizes his ministry as involving hard work, often in difficult circumstances and against dedicated opponents.

Three groups are the beneficiaries of this apostolic "contending": *you* (e.g., the Colossians), *those at Laodicea,* and *all who have not met me personally.* The last phrase translates a Greek construction that would literally be rendered "as many as have not seen my face in the flesh." "Face" in the biblical languages often expresses the idea of personal presence; hence our idiom "face-to-face" (which is employed here in several English versions: NRSV; ESV; NET; NAB).[61] The TNIV therefore accurately renders the metaphor into standard contemporary English. Laodicea was an important city, with a significant Jewish population, about twelve miles from Colossae. The church there (which is warned about spiritual lethargy in Rev. 3:14-22) was probably founded by Epaphras.[62] The Laodicean Christians are referred to again in Colossians 4:13-16, where there is also mention of Hierapolis, another city of the Lycus valley. Why Paul fails to mention Hierapolis here is not clear.[63] Some (noting the lack of reference to the church in Revelation 2–3 and the merely passing reference in Colossians 4) suggest that the gospel did not take root there as successfully as in Colossae and Laodicea.[64] However, the church in Hierapolis is certainly known to have flourished in later years.[65] Others suggest, perhaps more plausibly, that the false teaching had not infected Hierapolis to the same degree as Colossae and Laodicea, so there was less need for Paul to assert apostolic authority over the church there.[66] Nevertheless, the Christians in Hierapolis are certainly included in the last category, which includes "all" those who, like the Colossians and Laodiceans, have never met Paul.[67] Whether this group is restricted to other believers

61. E.g., Gen. 46:30: "Then Israel said to Joseph, 'Now let me die at this time, having seen your face, that you are still alive.'"
62. See F. F. Bruce, *ABD* 4.230-31.
63. Some scribes decided that they should be included: a clearly secondary textual variant adds "and those in Hierapolis."
64. Dunn, 129.
65. See Bruce, *ABD* 3.195-96.
66. Lightfoot, 170.
67. The nominative form of ὅσοι is unexpected, since it appears to depend on the preposition ὑπέρ (which takes the genitive). But the construction is, in fact, a fairly common one (see, e.g., Gal. 6:16), with ὅσοι dependent on an understood pronoun such as πόσων or τούτων or τοσούτων: "on behalf of those, as many as have not seen . . ." (Harris, 79).

in the immediate vicinity of Colossae[68] or includes in a general way Christians whom Paul has not met but for whom Paul feels some ministerial responsibility is not clear.[69]

2   Paul strives so hard for these converts with the purpose that *they may be encouraged in heart.* The word translated "encourage" in TNIV and in most English versions is *parakaleō,* a verb that occupies a wide spectrum of meaning. Paul often uses it to introduce a command, in which case it means "exhort" or "urge" (e.g., "As a prisoner for the Lord, then, I urge you to live a life worthy of the calling you have received" [Eph. 4:1]). When he uses it absolutely, as here, the verb usually has the sense of "comfort" or "encourage." O'Brien correctly argues that "comfort," supported by some interpreters, is too weak here.[70] He argues for "strengthen," but, in view of parallel texts, this may be too strong.[71] We should probably follow TNIV and most English versions and render "encourage." The Greek text has "their hearts" as the subject of the passive verb "be encouraged" (cf. NASB); the idea is captured accurately in the TNIV's *encouraged in heart.* References to the "heart" in the Bible require English speakers to "distance" themselves from their own culture. For the strong tendency in modern English is to use heart with reference to the emotions, whereas in Scripture "heart" designates the center of the personality, the source of willing and thinking in addition to feeling. Hence it is a new heart that God promises in order to transform his people's basic orientation toward himself (Ezek. 36:26). "Encouraged in heart" or "to have hearts encouraged" is therefore a way of referring to an encouragement that touches the deepest part of our being and that affects every aspect of our persons.

A second purpose of Paul's apostolic "striving" is that Christians would be *united in love.* A number of English versions, following the Greek literally, subordinate this verb to "encourage"; for example, ESV: "that their hearts may be encouraged, being knit together in love."[72] But the

68. O'Brien, 92; Harris, 79; Wilson, 183.

69. In any case, there is no warrant for finding in the phrase a universalizing emphasis stemming from an author after Paul's day (contra, e.g., Wolter, 109-10).

70. O'Brien, 93.

71. Paul uses παρακαλέω with "heart" in three other texts, all of them supporting the meaning "comfort" or "encourage" (Eph. 6:22; Col. 4:8; 2 Thess. 2:17 [O'Brien argues that this last text supports the meaning "strengthen," but it does so only if παρακαλέσαι is parallel in meaning to στηρίξαι — and this is by no means clear]).

72. Some versions, because of the aorist form of the participle, suggest that "being knit together" is the basis or presupposition for the "encouragement" (e.g., NASB; NET; NJB reflects the same idea by placing the "uniting" clause ahead of the "encouraging" clause). The masculine plural form of the participle does not agree with the subject of the sentence, "hearts" (which is feminine). The participle has been understood as imperatival (Gnilka, 110), but this is unlikely (cf. Wallace, *Greek Grammar,* 652). The simplest ex-

Greek participle frequently adds a relatively distinct verbal idea to the verb it modifies, and this seems to be a case in point. Paul hopes that his ministry will both encourage these believers he has never met and foster unity among them at the same time. The concern for unity seems a bit unexpected in this context, particularly if it is a basis for the *full riches of complete understanding*, as the TNIV suggests. It is possible, then, that this verb (a passive form of *symbibazō*), instead of being translated *united*, as in almost all the English versions, should be translated "having been taught." The verb means "teach" in Acts 19:33 and 1 Corinthians 2:16 (quoting Isa. 40:13) and in all its LXX occurrences,[73] and "being taught in love" would provide a natural basis for *full riches of complete understanding*.[74] However "being taught in love" is itself an odd combination, and Paul uses this same verb with the general sense "unite" in 2:19 with reference to the "body" of the church, "*held together* by its ligaments and sinews" (cf. Eph. 4:16). Moreover, the idea of love as a unifying force is clearly enunciated elsewhere in Colossians: "And over all these virtues put on love, which binds them all together in perfect unity" (3:14). Overall, then, the usual English translation should be preferred. "Love," then, will be either the means by which unity is achieved (as 3:14 would suggest; cf. NLT: "knit together by strong ties of love") or, more likely, the sphere in which the unity exists. It is true that Paul has not touched on unity among believers yet in the letter. Nevertheless, as we have seen, Paul associates interaction among the members of the body with spiritual growth later in the letter (2:19). So a reference to the importance of unity is certainly not out of place.

As we noted above, the TNIV suggests that the phrase *the full riches of complete understanding* is the result or purpose of both "encouraged in heart" and "united in love" (so also, it would seem, NRSV; HCBS; REB). However, in the Greek, a *kai* (often "and" in English) precedes the phrase *so that they might have the full riches of complete understanding*.[75] This raises the possibility that this clause is not dependent on the first part of the verse but parallel to it. See, for example, NLT: "For I want you to know how much I am struggling for you and for those in Laodicea. . . . I want them to be encouraged and knit together by strong ties of love. I want them to have complete confidence. . . ."[76] *Full riches of complete understand-*

---

planation is a "construction according to the sense," with the masculine participle used because Paul is thinking of the people to whom he ultimately refers (Harris, 80; Wilson, 184).

73. In Acts 9:22 and 16:10, it means "demonstrate."

74. Dibelius-Greeven, 25-26; O'Brien, 93; Zeilinger, *Der Erstgeborene der Schöpfung*, 108.

75. It is omitted in one MS (D), but the omission is secondary.

76. Harris, 78, 81.

ing translates another one of Paul's "run-on" genitive phrases that are so common in Colossians.[77] Dunn speaks somewhat disparagingly of an "awkward echo of the prayer already offered in 1:9-10, with a somewhat tautologous alliterative piling up of the thought of completeness."[78] The reference back to 1:9-10 is, indeed, quite clear,[79] as is the alliteration: *pan ploutos tēs plērophorias tēs syneseōs*. But "awkwardness" is in the eye of the beholder (or the reader), and the repetition of ideas may be emphatic rather than simply repetitious. Paul is again piling up words in order to hammer home the truth that Christ, and Christ alone, is the source of every conceivable bit of spiritual knowledge worth having.

Still, this truth leaves the structure to be sorted out. The ESV reflects the Greek structure rather closely: "all the riches of full assurance of understanding." This does not make for very comprehensible English, however, so almost all the other versions (including the usually very "literal" NASB) introduce other nuances. The two main issues to be settled are (1) the meaning of *plērophorias*; and (2) the semantic function of the two genitive expressions, *tēs plērophorias* and *tēs syneseōs*. The word *plērophoria* occurs four times in the New Testament. Once it clearly means "full assurance" (1 Thess. 1:5), but in its other three occurrences it could mean either "full assurance" or simply "fullness" (Heb. 6:11; 10:22; and here). A number of possibilities emerge from the intersection of these two issues, but two options are particularly likely. First, *plērophoria* might mean "fullness," so that it will function essentially to reiterate the completeness of the understanding that Paul is talking about (so, basically, TNIV).[80] Second, *plērophoria* might mean "full assurance," in which case it will add the idea that true understanding brings with it an assurance; see REB, "the full wealth of conviction which understanding brings."[81] A choice between these options is not easy to make, but the focus on the exclusivity of Christ might favor the former.

This exclusivity emerges explicitly at the end of v. 2, in a phrase in

---

77. See Percy, *Die Probleme der Kolosser- und Epheserbriefe*, 26-27, who notes that Ephesians and Colossians have in common a higher frequency of genitive strings than the other Pauline letters.

78. Dunn, 131.

79. See also Wolter, 111.

80. In this case, τῆς πληροφορίας is best taken as what Wallace (*Greek Grammar*, 89-91) calls an "attributed genitive": "the characterized-by-fullness understanding"; hence TNIV's "complete understanding." For this general interpretation, see Lohse, 81; Barth-Blanke, 279; Gnilka, 110.

81. In this case, τῆς πληροφορίας would be an epexegetic genitive and τῆς συνέσεως a source or subjective genitive. See Turner, *Syntax*, 211; Moule, 86; Dunn, 131. There are, of course, a number of possible variations. Note, e.g., the NET, which takes τῆς πληροφορίας as a subjective genitive: "all the riches that assurance brings."

which Paul "defines" *complete understanding:* it consists in nothing more nor less than knowing *the mystery of God, namely, Christ.* This way of relating the two "knowing" phrases — having "full riches of complete understanding" and "knowing the mystery of God" — views the latter as repeating and elaborating the former.[82] The TNIV, on the other hand, takes the second as the purpose of the former: *the full riches of complete understanding, in order that they may know . . .* (cf. also NASB).[83] A third option is to view the latter phrase as parallel to the former, both indicating the purpose of the encouragement (and unity) (v. 2a) or of Paul's contending (v. 1) (cf. RSV; NRSV; ESV; REB). We slightly prefer the first of these, since it appropriately highlights what appears to be the critical and summarizing point.

The ultimate purpose of Paul's ministry, including this very letter to the Colossians, is that believers might *know the mystery of God, namely, Christ.* The Greek text underlying the last four words in this phrase is very confused, with a tangled web of textual variants facing the interpreter. But most scholars concur that the reading assumed in the TNIV translation — and in virtually all the other English translations — is the correct one.[84] If this reading is accepted, the Greek text again confronts us with a series of three genitives. But, in this case, the significance of each one is relatively clear. The first, *tou mystēriou* — *the mystery* — indicates the object of the verbal noun "knowledge" (TNIV, *may know*). The second is possessive: the mystery "belongs to" God. It is only with the third — *Christou* — that there can be any question. A very few commentators have attached the word to the immediately preceding word, God: "the mystery of the God who belongs to Christ" (cf. "the God of our Lord Je-

82. This construal of the phrases is suggested by the lack of a conjunction introducing the final phrase; it implies that "Paul is here redefining his aim by stating it comprehensively" (Harris, 81). So most commentators; e.g., Barth/Blanke, 279; Aletti, 149; Gnilka, 110. The two phrases are both introduced with the preposition εἰς followed by a noun. This preposition frequently functions to introduce a purpose or result phrase and is often best translated into English with a corresponding result or purpose phrase plus verb. Thus, in the TNIV, εἰς πᾶν πλοῦτος becomes "so that they may have the full riches" and εἰς ἐπίγνωσιν becomes "in order that they may know." Most other English translations do something similar.

83. Lohse, 81.

84. There are no fewer than fifteen textual options. The text assumed by the English translations is τοῦ θεοῦ, Χριστοῦ, which has good external support (it is attested in two very good manuscripts — P[46] and B). But it is to be preferred especially on internal grounds, since this reading best explains all the others. See esp. Metzger, *Textual Commentary,* 555; also Lightfoot, 252-53. For a contrary view, defending the shortest reading — simply τοῦ θεοῦ — see Pierre Benoit, "Colossiens 2:2-3," in *The New Testament Age: Essays in Honor of Bo Reicke* (ed. William C. Weinrich; Macon, Ga.: Mercer University Press, 1984), 1:41-51.

sus" in Eph. 1:17; "God, the Father of our Lord Jesus Christ" in 1:3).[85] But, in light of the very clear lead given us in 1:28, where the "mystery" is defined as "Christ in you," we should construe *Christou* as an epexegetic genitive dependent on "mystery": *the mystery of God, namely, Christ;* "God's mystery, which is Christ" (ESV). Earlier in the letter, in a somewhat parallel passage, Paul made "God's will" (v. 9) or "God" (v. 10) the object of our "knowing" *(epignōsis)*. Now, in light of the high Christology of 1:15-20, Paul makes "the mystery of God" the object of that knowing and identifies that mystery with Christ.

3　This verse is the christological high point of the letter.[86] It does not match the "hymn" of 1:15-20 for exalted language in reference to Christ, but it expresses beautifully and compactly the cutting-edge christological point that is Paul's driving concern: Christ is the one in whom is to be found *all* that one needs in order to understand spiritual reality and to lead a life pleasing to God. The all-encompassing nature of the knowledge to be found in Christ is highlighted by yet another occurrence of "all" *(pas)* and by the use of the two terms "wisdom" *(sophia)* and "knowledge" *(gnōsis)*. The latter term occurs only here in Colossians, although its cognate compound form, *epignōsis*, occurs frequently (1:9, 10; 2:2; 3:10; the verb *epiginōskō* occurs in 1:6). It is unlikely that there is any difference in meaning between the two.[87] Paul probably chooses the simpler form here because of its more biblical, and especially wisdom, orientation.[88] The simple form *gnōsis* occurs almost forty times in the wisdom books of the Old Testament and the Apocrypha (Proverbs, Ecclesiastes, Wisdom, Sirach), whereas *epignōsis* occurs only once in these books. Moreover, *gnōsis* is paired with

---

85. E.g., Abbott, 239-40. A few interpreters (e.g., Hilary of Poitiers, according to Aletti, 150) have viewed Χριστοῦ as an epexegetic genitive dependent on τοῦ θεοῦ: "God, who is Christ." But this interpretation does not match the context well and creates theological problems, suggesting that God can be exhaustively defined by Christ.

86. The relative pronoun ᾧ refers to Christ, not to the mystery (contra the NJB and Abbott, 241): hence "whom" rather than "which" in the TNIV.

87. So most modern commentators, in distinction from many in the past, who often suggested that ἐπίγνωσις indicated a "larger and more thorough knowledge" (Lightfoot, 136 [on 1:9]).

88. There might also be a stylistic reason for preferring γνῶσις to ἐπίγνωσις. The latter word occurs fifteen times in Paul, and in eleven of these occurrences it is followed by a genitive object. The former, on the other hand, occurs twenty-three times in Paul and is followed by a genitive object only four times. This pattern holds for three of the four uses of ἐπίγνωσις in Colossians (3:10 is the exception). It may be, then, that Paul naturally prefers the simple noun in an absolute construction, such as we have in v. 3. (My thanks to Moisés Silva, whose comments on the related issue of the relationship between οἶδα and γινώσκω in Paul suggested such a pattern: "The Pauline Style as Lexical Choice: ΓΙΝΩΣΚΕΙΝ and Related Verbs," in *Pauline Studies* [ed. D. A. Hagner and M. J. Harris; Grand Rapids: Eerdmans, 1980], 184-207).

sophia in several texts (Rom. 11:33; Eccl. 1:17; 2:26; 9:10; cf. Eccl. 7:12; 12:9; Sir. 21:13, 18), whereas *epignōsis* is never used with *sophia*. This background quite adequately explains the presence of the word here, without recourse to a connection with an alleged "proto-gnostic" heresy in Colossae. At the same time, it is possible that Paul's concern with true understanding stands in contradistinction to the claims that the false teachers were making. "Wisdom," of course, refers to practical knowledge, the ability to understand reality from God's perspective and to act on that understanding. "Knowledge," on the other hand, has a more intellectual focus. But we should probably not make too much of the distinct ideas each term communicates. Paul connects the two words by using a single article to govern both of them, and he probably therefore wants us to focus on the entire phrase rather than on the individual words.

Labeling "wisdom and knowledge" *treasures* may also reflect Old Testament wisdom tradition. Proverbs 2:1-8, for instance, includes many of the key words that Paul uses in this and related contexts in Colossians; and "treasures" is among them (we note parallel words in the LXX):

> My son, if you accept my words and store up (*krypsēs;* "hide"; cf. v. 3) my commands within you, turning your ear to wisdom (*sophia;* cf. v. 3) and applying your heart (*kardia;* cf. v. 2) to understanding — indeed, if you call out for insight (*sophia;* cf. v. 3) and cry aloud for understanding (*synesis;* cf. v. 2), and if you look for it as for silver and search for it as for hidden treasure (*thēsauros;* cf. v. 3), then you will understand the fear of the LORD and find the knowledge (*epignōsis;* cf. v. 2) of God. For the LORD gives wisdom (*sophia;* cf. v. 2); from his mouth come knowledge (*gnōsis;* cf. v. 3) and understanding (*synesis;* cf. v. 2). He holds success in store (*thēsaurizō;* cf. v. 3) for the upright, he is a shield to those whose walk is blameless, for he guards the course of the just and protects the way of his faithful ones.[89]

Paul rarely uses the word "treasure" (*thēsauros;* only elsewhere in 2 Cor. 4:7), making it even more likely that its presence here is owing to a reminiscence of this kind of wisdom teaching (see also Wis. 7:12-14; Sir. 1:25). It serves to underscore the value of wisdom and knowledge that is found in Christ. As the quotation from Proverbs 2 shows, Paul's claim that these treasures are *hidden* in Christ might also depend on this wisdom tradition.[90] However, Lightfoot and others have argued that the

89. Cf. R. P. Martin, 76, for this parallel.
90. The word (*apokryphoi*) comes last in the Greek sentence, probably for emphasis (Wilson, 188). English versions, even when they place the word last in the sentence (HCSB; NJB) cannot capture the same sense of emphasis.

presence of hiddenness language again is a parry against a gnostic-type false teaching.[91] And still others suggest, more plausibly, that the language is rooted in Jewish apocalypticism. This background seems clearly to lie behind the "hidden"/"revealed" language of 1:26, as we have seen, so we might expect this also to be the background here, where again Paul speaks of the mystery (v. 2).[92] But it is also possible that we can read too much into the imagery. The combination of "hidden" and "treasure" is a natural one, then and now, since hiding the treasure was often the means of securing and protecting it.[93] And the use of "hidden" in this verse does not have an implicit contrast with "revealed," since Paul's point, of course, is that wisdom and knowledge are now freely available in Christ. They are "hidden" in Christ in the sense that they are "treasures" that have been deposited in him and are now stored up in him. Anyone who comes to know Christ by faith can draw from his store all the wisdom and knowledge that exists.

   4 The transition between vv. 3 and 4 is abrupt, with no particle or conjunction linking the two verses.[94] And for the first time, Paul warns explicitly about false teaching. These factors have led some interpreters to conclude that a new section of the letter begins with this verse.[95] Moule, for instance, argues that the pronoun *this (touto)* refers forward to the second part of v. 4, which he thinks might be imperatival in force: "What I mean is this: let no one lead you astray. . . ."[96] This is unlikely.[97]

91. Lightfoot, 174.

92. See esp. Andrew J. Bandstra, "Did the Colossian Errorists Need a Mediator?" in *New Dimensions in New Testament Study* (ed. Richard N. Longenecker and Merrill C. Tenney; Grand Rapids: Zondervan, 1974), 341-43. Jacques Dupont (*Gnosis: la connaissance religieuse dans les épîtres de Saint Paul* [Paris: Gabalda, 1949], 16-18) and Dunn (132) suggest that an anti-torah polemic may be intended, since Jewish tradition often celebrated the torah as the place where wisdom and knowledge could be found (e.g., Rom. 2:20; Sir. 24:23-25). But we are not persuaded in general that Colossians betrays a concern with torah in this sense. And note that in, e.g., Isa. 33:5-6, the "treasures" of "wisdom and understanding" (σοφία καὶ ἐπιστήμη) are found in the Lord himself.

93. See, e.g., O'Brien, 95; and cf. Isa. 45:3; Dan. 11:43 (Θ); 1 Macc. 1:23; Matt. 13:44; 2 Bar. 41:14; 54:13.

94. The "And" in KJV and "Now" in NKJV reflect a secondary textual variant (δέ, found in the majority text and a number of other MSS).

95. E.g., Harris, 85-86. In two of the three other occurrences of τοῦτο [δὲ] [οὖν] λέγω, the τοῦτο is prospective: Gal. 3:17; Eph. 4:17; in 1 Cor. 7:6 it is retrospective. Cf. also τοῦτο δὲ φήμι in 1 Cor. 7:29 and 15:50, where the τοῦτο is in each case prospective. None of these, however, is parallel syntactically to Col. 2:4, where a ἵνα is used in the next clause.

96. He derives the imperatival force from ἵνα ("so that"), which can, indeed, sometimes have this significance (Moule, 86; cf. idem, *Idiom Book*, 145; and Bruce, 92). On "imperatival ἵνα," see BDF §388; Turner, *Syntax*, 94-95.

97. See esp. O'Brien, 97.

And, however we translate, it is likely, following most of the commentators, that we should view vv. 4-5 more as the conclusion to the section that begins in 1:24 than as the introduction to what follows. As we noted above in the introduction to this section, v. 5, with its expression of Paul's personal concern and the language of "flesh," returns to themes found in 1:24-25, suggesting that it closes off an argument that begins there. It also has clear connections with 2:1: "those who have not seen my face in the flesh"; "absent [from you] in the flesh" (my own translations). And it is v. 6, rather than v. 4, that marks the stronger transitional moment in the letter. Of course, this does not mean that vv. 4-5 have no relation to what follows. They are clearly transitional, as Paul moves from the initial christologically oriented rehearsal of the benefits the Colossians enjoy (1:3-23) and his own particular role in mediating these benefits (1:24–2:3) to direct address of the Colossians. In view of the climactic significance of v. 3, it is probably to Christ as the one in whom is found all wisdom and knowledge that *this (touto)* specifically refers.[98] But that verse also summarizes the essential christological teaching of chapter 1. In this sense, Paul refers to all that he has written in the letter so far.

The theology, and especially the high Christology, of 1:1–2:3 has, then, a direct practical purpose: to keep believers from being deceived by[99] *fine-sounding arguments*. This phrase translates a single Greek word *(pithanologia)*, which has a neutral meaning, "plausible arguments" (ESV); "persuasive argument" (NASB). But the context here obviously requires a negative connotation, such as is reflected in the TNIV (see also RSV, "beguiling speech"; NJB and NAB, "specious arguments"; NET, "arguments that sound reasonable"). And there is some lexical basis for this nuance, since Plato associates *pithanologia* with "popular oratory" and warns about accepting conclusions on this basis rather than on the basis of a "cogent proof" *(apodeixis; Theaetetus 162E)*.[100] So for us: paying too much attention to *fine-sounding arguments* can *deceive* us about religious and spiritual truth. Paul has no doubt about the vital importance of spiritual truth, and he knows how perilously easy it is for believers to be led astray by high-flown rhetoric (or, in our day, by "multimedia presentations"). The antidote for such false teaching is the "cogent proof" of Christ's absolute supremacy and exclusivity.

5   In this verse Paul explains *(gar;* "for") why he thinks it appropri-

---

98. So, e.g., Abbott, 242; R. P. Martin, 76; O'Brien, 97 (v. 3 and indirectly vv. 1-3 also). Other interpreters think that τοῦτο refers to 1:24–2:3 (Barth/Blanke, 285; Aletti, 152), vv. 1-3 (Lightfoot, 175; Gnilka, 113), or vv. 2-3 (Dunn, 133).

99. The ἐν is clearly instrumental.

100. BDAG; Louw-Nida 33.31. The word does not occur elsewhere in biblical Greek; nor does Philo or Josephus use it.

ate for him to issue warnings, such as we have in v. 4, to the Colossian Christians. Part of the explanation has already been implicitly given in 1:24-29: Paul has been called to minister to the entire "body," the church, and especially to Gentiles. He therefore has "authority," in some sense, over the Colossians. In this verse he meets another objection: his physical absence from Colossae. What gives Paul the right, under house arrest in Rome and far removed from the Colossians, to warn and rebuke them? The answer is his presence with them "in spirit." Paul sets this in contrast to his absence from them "in the flesh (sarx)."[101] The TNIV's in body captures well the sense that the elusive word sarx has here (almost all the English translations do the same).[102] The contrast with "body" would naturally suggest that "spirit" (pneuma) refers to the human spirit. Indeed, the language is popular in our own culture as a way of indicating a nonphysical, empathetic "withness." However, as Gordon Fee has argued, it is doubtful whether Paul ever uses the language of "spirit" without some reference to the Holy Spirit. Here, then, while the immediate reference may be, indeed, to Paul's own "spirit," it is his spirit as taken up into the Holy Spirit. His "presence" with the Colossians, then, is not a simple "you will be in my thoughts and prayers," but involves a profound corporate sense of identity, based on and mediated by the Spirit of God.[103] It is on the basis of this union, effected in and by Christ and mediated by the Spirit, that Paul can address the Colossian Christians.

But the communication that takes place in "S/spirit" goes both directions. Not only does Paul, by letter, warn the Colossians; he also is "delighted to see" that they are at present doing well in the faith. The TNIV's delight to see translates two parallel Greek participles: chairōn kai blepōn, literally, "rejoicing and seeing." Some interpreters insist that the two participles, because of the kai between them, must be given independent force: "rejoicing because he sees" or "rejoicing and [then] looking" — in the sense that Paul continues to look because "he derives satis-

101. The Greek is in the form of a conditional sentence, with the protasis introduced by εἰ ("if"). A καί in the first clause lends a concessive force to it — "if, indeed, I am absent in spirit" — while the ἀλλά introducing the apodosis reinforces this idea: "yet" (RSV; NRSV; ESV; cf. BDB §471.5). The datives in the contrast "in body" (τῇ σαρκί)/"in spirit" (τῷ πνεύματι) may be "adverbial" — "absent in a fleshly way"; "present in a spirit way" (Turner, Syntax, 239) — but perhaps they are better seen as "datives of respect" — "absent with reference to the flesh"; "present with reference to the S/spirit."

102. Cf. BDAG. Wilson (189) notes the roughly parallel 1 Cor. 5:3, where σῶμα appears in place of σάρξ: "even though I am not physically present, I am with you in spirit."

103. Gordon Fee, God's Empowering Presence (Peabody, Mass.: Hendrickson, 1994), 24-26; 645-46; cf. also Dunn, 134. Contra, e.g., Lightfoot, 173; Abbott, 243, who see here a reference simply to the human spirit. Fee suggests rendering "S/spirit," but this really cannot be used in a translation!

173

faction from it."[104] But it makes better sense of the verse if the two participles function within a mutually interpreting hendiadys, such as the TNIV and all the other English versions assume.[105]

Paul's seeing is accompanied by rejoicing. And what he rejoices to see is *how disciplined you are and how firm your faith in Christ is.* The TNIV freely renders the Greek, which would be literally translated "your order and the firmness of your faith in Christ." Both "order" *(taxis)* and "firmness" *(stereōma)* are used in military contexts, and a number of interpreters think that Paul uses them in this sense.[106] Paul is like a general, inspecting his troops and rejoicing to see that they are displaying the disciplined formation *(taxis)* and strong force *(stereōma)* that they will need to fight the false teachers. Interpreting the words in this fashion makes for good preaching, but it is dubious lexicography. Both terms do, indeed, occur as technical military terms, but they also occur much more widely in the general sense simply of "order" and "firmness."[107] The Greek does not make it clear whether we should construe "your faith in Christ" with both words or only with "firmness." The English translations, explicitly or implicitly, take the latter view, as do most of the commentators.[108] If this is correct, then the genitive *tēs . . . pisteōs* could be subjective — "firmness created by faith" — or, more probably, loosely possessive — "the firmness that belongs to your faith," for example, "your strong faith" (NLT).[109] Paul's affirmation of the solid spiritual state

104. For the former, Wright, 96; for the latter (with what he insists is the more natural relationship between the participles), Lightfoot, 176; Abbott, 243; similarly, Barth/Blanke, 286-87.

105. See BDB §471.5 and most of the commentaries (e.g., Harris, 87; O'Brien, 98-99; Lohse, 83-84).

106. Lightfoot, 174; Lohmeyer, 95; R. P. Martin, 76-77. Lightfoot speculates that it was Paul's daily contact with Roman soldiers that might have stimulated the language here (174). Henry Chadwick ("'All Things to All Men,'" *NTS* 1 [1955], 272-73) suggests the terms may be derived from gnostic-oriented false teachers.

107. Lohse, 84; Wolter, 114; O'Brien, 99. Paul uses τάξις only one other time, with no clear military connotations (1 Cor. 14:40). The word also occurs in the LXX, the NT, and in Philo and Josephus numerous times with the general meaning "order," "arrangement." The word στερέωμα occurs only here in the NT and twenty-three times in the LXX, where it often refers to the "firmament" or "vault" of the sky (the sky being pictured as a beaten-out piece of metal, hence "something firm"; e.g., Gen. 1:6; cf. also the derived references to God's throne in Ezekiel [1:22, 23, 25]). The word does sometimes have a military flavor (e.g., Ezek. 13:5, 1 Macc. 9:14, and perhaps in those places where the Lord is called the believer's στερέωμα ["fortress"; cf. 17:3; 70:3]). Only in Col. 2:4 do the two words occur together.

108. An exception is apparently Dunn, 135.

109. Harris, 88. This general interpretation is confirmed by the two verses in which other words from the same root as στερέωμα are used with reference to faith: Acts 16:5 and 1 Pet. 5:9 (cf. O'Brien, 99).

of the Colossians might seem surprising in light of the urgency of his concern about false teaching in the community. Dunn suggests that Paul here expresses "more . . . of what he would hope to see were it possible."[110] But there is little reason to introduce such a hypothetical notion. Paul's commendation of the Colossians is in keeping with his other direct reference to their spiritual state (1:4-6). And the language he uses later in this chapter suggests that the false teaching is something to be resisted, not something that has already infected the church. The Colossian Christians have started well (1:7-8), and they are continuing well. It is the future for which Paul is concerned.[111] As Wink puts it, "The epistle is a vaccination against heresy, not an antibiotic for those already afflicted."[112]

II. THE LETTER BODY: ". . . CONTINUE TO LIVE YOUR LIVES IN HIM" (2:6–4:6)

While stretched considerably, in both length and complexity, beyond the normal boundaries, 1:3–2:5 nevertheless appears to function formally as the "opening" of the letter to the Colossians. The "body," the second and normally most substantive section of the ancient letter, can be identified, then, as 2:6–4:6.[1] The beginning of the section is marked by a transitional clause, *just as you received Christ Jesus as Lord,* which, particularly in its christological focus, nicely summarizes the opening part of the letter.[2] Paul has spotlighted the person of Christ, ruler of both the old creation and the new (1:15-20), substance of the "mystery," God's plan for human history (1:27; 2:2), and repository of all wisdom and knowledge (2:3). And he has reminded the Colossians that they have responded to the message about this new Lord of the universe and given themselves to his service (1:5-8, 21-23).

The focus of v. 6, however — and, in a sense, the focus of the entire letter — is the response that Paul now calls on his readers to make: *continue to live your lives in him.* As they have begun, so they must continue, looking to Christ, and Christ alone, for all their spiritual needs. This imperative at the end of v. 6 is the first in the letter, and the first of a series of commands that dominates the flow of 2:6–4:6: "See to it" (2:8); "do not let

110. Dunn, 134.
111. O'Brien, 99.
112. Wink, *Naming the Powers,* 73.
1. This division is widely acknowledged (see, e.g., Wright, 96; Dunn, 136; Wolter, 114-16; Lincoln, 555).
2. J. Lähnemann, *Der Kolosserbrief* (Gütersloh: Mohn, 1971), 49.

anyone judge you" (2:16); "Do not let anyone . . . disqualify you" (2:18); "set your hearts on things above" (3:1); "Set your minds on things above" (3:2); "Put to death" (3:5); "you must . . . rid yourselves" (3:8); "Do not lie to each other" (3:9); "clothe yourselves" (3:12); "Bear with each other" (3:13); "forgive one another" (3:13); "forgive" (3:13); "put on love" (3:14); "let the peace of Christ rule in your hearts" (3:15); "be thankful" (3:15); "Let the message of Christ dwell among you richly" (3:16); "do it all" (3:17); "Wives, submit yourselves to your own husbands" (3:18); "Husbands, love your wives" (3:19); "Children, obey your parents" (3:20); "Fathers, do not embitter your children" (3:21); "Slaves, obey your earthly masters" (3:22); "work at it with all your heart" (3:23); "Masters, provide your slaves with what is right and fair" (4:1); "Devote yourselves to prayer" (4:2); "pray for us, too" (4:3); "Be wise" (4:5); "Let your conversation be always full of grace" (4:6). This series of general commands to the Colossian Christians comes to an end in 4:6, and 4:7 marks the transition into the letter "closing," with its focus on people, plans, and logistics.

Colossians, then, provides perhaps the clearest example of the "indicative"–"imperative" sequence that is widely noted as a feature of the New Testament letters. However, we must avoid giving the impression that this scheme divides the letter into watertight compartments. Theological teaching in the indicative continues to be significant in 2:6–4:6 (see esp. 2:9-15; 3:3-4), while "quasi-commands" pop up in the opening section, with the indirect exhortations of the prayer-wish in 1:9-14, along with the warnings of 1:23 and 2:4-5. Paul could never talk about theology for long without application; nor could he speak for long about the Christian life without allusion to the theology that buttresses and gives shape to that life.

The paragraph divisions within 2:6–4:6 are, for the most part, clearly marked. Colossians 2:6-7, with its central command to "continue to live your lives in him," states the overarching point of the whole letter body. Paul then elaborates the negative side of this command in 2:8-23 by warning about the false teachers. This section breaks down into a more positive expression of the fullness of life available in Christ (2:8-15) and a more negative assessment of the false teaching. The positive side of the general exhortation in 2:6 is developed in 3:1–4:1, which can be divided into four basic parts: the call to develop a thoroughly Christian mind-set (3:1-4); a series of commands warning against (especially communal) sins (3:5-11); a series of commands to "put on" various Christian virtues (3:12-17); and a Christian "household code," summarizing the responsibilities of the various members of the Christian extended family (3:18–4:1). The letter body concludes with an outward-looking focus, as Paul requests prayer for his work of evangelism and encourages the Colossians to be active in the same ministry (4:2-6).

A. The Heart of the Matter: Remaining Centered on Christ (2:6-7)

6So then, just as you received Christ Jesus as Lord, continue to live your lives in him, 7rooted and built up in him, strengthened in the faith as you were taught, and overflowing with thankfulness.

This paragraph, along with the closely related 2:8-15, is the heart of Colossians.[3] In these two verses Paul succinctly summarizes the basic response that he wants from his readers. Paul ties these verses to their context by reflecting language and ideas found earlier in the letter.[4] The positive exhortation to *continue to live in Christ*, which is elaborated in a series of four participles (vv. 6-7), is very similar to what Paul has prayed for in 1:10-12.[5] And the warning about avoiding false teachers (v. 8) echoes 2:4-5 and, to a lesser extent, 1:23.

6 If 2:6-15 is the heart of Colossians, this verse (along with vv. 9-10) is the heart of 2:6-15. It serves as the hinge between the first major section of the letter (1:3–2:5) and the second (2:6–4:6). The first clause succinctly restates the key theological argument of the letter to this point: Jesus Christ is Lord, and we have entered into his Lordship. The second clause then summarizes the specific commands and warnings that follow: we are to *continue to live in him*, to work out just what it means in both our thinking and our acting to live under the Lordship of Christ.

Paul's choice of the verb "receive" in the first clause is significant. This verb *(paralambanō)* is usually used by Paul to refer to the "receiving" or "accepting" of tradition about Christ and his significance (1 Cor. 11:23; 15:1, 3; Gal. 1:9, 12; 1 Thess. 4:1; 2 Thess. 3:6; the verb occurs with other senses in Phil. 4:9; Col. 4:17; 1 Thess. 2:13). In keeping with the christological focus of this letter, however, Paul refers here not to the receiving of teaching, or tradition, or the word of God (cf. 1 Thess. 2:13), but of Christ himself (this is the only occurrence of *paralambanō* in Paul with a personal object).[6] To "receive Christ" — in this verse at least — is not only a matter of believing "in" his person; it also involves a commitment to the apostolic teaching about Christ and his significance. This tradition, which the Colossians have heard from the faithful Epaphras

3. E.g., Dibelius-Greeven, 26; O'Brien, 104; Dübbers, *Christologie und Existenz im Kolosserbrief* (Tübingen: Mohr Siebeck, 2005), 180-82.
4. See esp. MacDonald, 88; W. T. Wilson, *The Hope of Glory* (Leiden and New York: Brill, 1997), 241-42.
5. Wolter, 112; Dübbers, *Christologie und Existenz*, 191.
6. Wolter, 117-18.

(1:7-8), stands in contrast to the "human tradition" of the false teachers (v. 8).[7]

This point is underscored in the way Paul describes Christ: *ton Christon Iēsoun ton kyrion* (literally, "the Christ Jesus the Lord"). Paul exhibits considerable variety in the way that he uses these three names, or titles, from the simple "Jesus" or "Christ" or "Lord" to combinations of two or three of them. But never elsewhere does he use exactly the same sequence of names and articles that we find here; indeed, this combination is found nowhere else in the New Testament.[8] Views on just what this unusual construction might indicate vary. Some think "Christ," because of its prominence in Colossians, is the main object of the verb and that "Jesus the Lord" is added to explain further who this Christ is: for example, "you have received Christ [who is both] Jesus and Lord."[9] These two qualifications of "Christ" might, then, be directed to aspects of the false teaching, "Lord" summing up the high Christology of 1:15-20 and "Jesus" emphasizing the real humanity of Christ or the public ministry and teaching of Christ.[10] But the name "Jesus" is too common in such phrases to justify this assumption; nor, again, does Paul anywhere else in Colossians make a point of Jesus' humanity or earthly life. Others suggest that the phrase conceals a double confession: that Jesus is Christ (the Messiah) and Lord; cf. NJB, "you received Jesus as Lord and Christ."[11] It is likely, indeed, that "Christ" is not simply a proper name here — that it carries with it implications, however weak, of Jesus as the promised deliverer/King of Old Testament and Jewish expectation. But it would seem more likely that the article before *kyrios* sets it apart and that it is this title that receives the

---

7. See esp. Bruce, 93. A number of commentators (e.g., Wright, 99; Wolter, 117) think that Paul may allude specifically to a baptismal confession (see v. 12).

8. The three key words are found together 74 times in the NT. They occur in the following combinations, listed by frequency: [article] κύριος ἡμῶν Ἰησοῦς Χριστός ("our Lord Jesus Christ") (35 occurrences); κύριος Ἰησοῦς Χριστός ("Lord Jesus Christ") (16 occurrences); [article] κύριος Ἰησοῦς Χριστός ("the Lord Jesus Christ") (8 occurrences); Χριστὸς Ἰησοῦς [article] κύριος ἡμῶν/ὑμῶν/μου ("Christ Jesus our/your/my Lord") (7 occurrences); Ἰησοῦς Χριστὸς [article] κύριος ἡμῶν ("Jesus Christ our Lord") (5 occurrences); Ἰησοῦς Χριστός κύριος ("Jesus Christ the Lord") (1 occurrence); [article] Χριστὸς Ἰησοὺς [article] κύριος ἡμῶν ("Christ Jesus our Lord") (1 occurrence). This last example, not coincidentally from Ephesians (3:11), is the closest to the formulation here in Colossians.

9. Lightfoot, 176; Harris, 88; Lohse, 93. See RSV; NRSV; ESV; NASB; HCSB; NAB.

10. An emphasis on Jesus' humanity is suggested especially by those who identify the false teachers with (proto-) Gnostics, since the Gnostics famously denied the humanity of Christ (see, e.g., Lightfoot, 176; Abbott, 244). Dunn (140-41), on the other hand, thinks that "Jesus" might simply be added to remind the Colossian Christians, living distant from Palestine, of the public ministry and teaching of Jesus on which their faith ultimately rests.

11. Moule, 90.

emphasis in the verse.[12] Furthermore, coming after a transitive verb such as "receive," the title may function predicatively; hence TNIV's *Christ Jesus as Lord* (see also NLT; NET; REB; TEV).[13] Paul is probably intentionally echoing, then, what was arguably *the* early Christian confession: that "Jesus is Lord" (cf. Rom. 10:9; 1 Cor. 12:3). And "Christ" is added to this formula in two texts that may (despite the different syntax) be cited as close parallels of what Paul probably intends here: "For what we preach is not ourselves, but Jesus Christ as Lord *(Christon Iēsoun kyrion)*" (2 Cor. 4:5); "and every tongue acknowledge that Jesus Christ is Lord *(kyrios Iēsous Christos)*, to the glory of God the Father" (Phil. 2:11). By alluding to this confession here at a key transitional point in the letter, Paul connects a fundamental expression of what it means to be a Christian with the Christology that he has developed in the earlier part of the letter. "Jesus Christ is Lord" is a succinct way of saying that he is "the image of the invisible God," "the firstborn over all creation" (1:15), "the head of the body, the church" (1:18), "the mystery of God" (2:2; cf. 1:27), and the repository of "all wisdom and knowledge" (2:3). It is this central confession, with all its varied and far-reaching implications, to which the Colossians need to return in order to ward off the threat of the false teaching.

Paul has earlier prayed that the Colossians might learn to *live a life pleasing to the Lord* (1:10, where, we suggested, "the Lord" is Christ). Paul makes the same connection here, urging the Colossians, since they have received Christ Jesus *as Lord*, to *continue to live your lives in him.* "Continue to live your lives," as in 1:10, translates the Greek verb *peripateō*, "walk" (and see the notes on 1:10 for the significance of this word). The word "continue" in the TNIV is intended to bring out the significance, in this place, of the present form of the imperative verb (so also NLT; NET). Paul is telling them, in effect, to "remain where you are!"[14] *In him* will have its usual "local" sense: "conduct your lives as incorporated in him,"[15] setting the stage for the important use of this idea in the following passage (vv. 7, 9, 10, 11). The polemical context in which Paul writes (see v. 8) justifies our seeing in this language an exclusive emphasis typical of the letter as a whole: "Let Christ — and no other! for he is Lord — establish your values, guide your thinking, direct your conduct."

7 We have noted earlier the similarity between Paul's prayer in 1:10-12 and his exhortation in vv. 6-7. In both texts, Paul uses four participles to elaborate the nature of the "life" or "walk" that should character-

---

12. See, e.g., O'Brien, 106; Barth/Blanke, 299, 302; Gnilka, 116; Aletti, 161.
13. On this so-called "adverbial accusative," see Wallace, *Greek Grammar*, 198-99 (who classifies Col. 2:6 as an uncertain example).
14. Hay, 85.
15. Moule, 90.

ize believers. Both series of participles employ a horticultural metaphor, and both conclude with a reference to thanksgiving. The parallelism is a striking example of the way Paul will use his opening prayer to anticipate some themes of the letter to follow. It also suggests what for Paul was his central concern for the Colossian Christians. The participles in v. 7 are assigned various syntactical labels by interpreters,[16] but, however we label them, it is clear that they tell us how we can continue to live a life that gives Christ his rightful place as Lord. The first two — *rooted* and *built up* — are closely related: they express a similar idea, they both govern the phrase *in him*, and the former, in its only other New Testament occurrence (Eph. 3:17), is paired with a verb similar to "built up" (Eph. 3:17, "rooted and established [from *themelioō*, "lay a foundation"] in love").[17] To be sure, *rooted* and *built up* connote different metaphorical associations. The former (from the verb *rhizoō*) is obviously taken from the world of horticulture. Its few appearances in biblical Greek (only five in the LXX in addition to the two New Testament occurrences) are all metaphorical in character (as in Philo also). The imagery in the LXX passages (see esp. Isa. 40:24 and Jer. 12:2) reveals that, at least for some *koinē* writers, it was still a "live" metaphor (that is, it would continue to connote horticultural associations to those using the verb).

Built up, equally obviously, is a construction metaphor. As the form of the underlying Greek word suggests, the verb basically has the sense of "build [something] on [something else]" (*ep-* ["upon"] *oikodomeō* ["build"]).[18] But the word sometimes loses the local "upon" idea, simply expressing the process of building, and this would seem to be the case in our verse. As with the verb "root," "build [up]" occurs in biblical Greek only with a metaphorical sense (1 Cor. 3:10, 12, 14; Eph. 2:20; Col. 2:7; Jude 20 [a variant in 1 Pet. 2:5]; it does not occur in the LXX). In Paul's other uses of the verb, the "construction" metaphor remains quite

16. Perhaps they are best categorized as "attendant circumstance" (Harris, 89); but, in any case, dependent on περιπατεῖτε in v. 6, they are "imperatival in character" (Barth/Blanke, 303) (cf. NJB; REB; NLT).

17. The ideas expressed by these two verbs (though not the identical verbs) occur together in a number of other passages, showing that the combination of horticultural and construction images was a natural one; in addition to Eph. 3:17, see 1 Cor. 3:9; 1QS 8:5; 11:8; Philo, *Allegorical Interpretation* 1.48 (see O'Brien, 107). The phrase ἐν αὐτῷ, to be sure, need not depend on both participles, but it would be awkward for the participle ἐρριζωμένοι to stand without any completing idea ("rooted" where?). NJB, REB, and NAB are the only translations that expressly connect both participles to the "in him" phrase, but it is undoubtedly implied in the others as well.

18. Josephus, e.g., speaks of a king who "*built* an idol altar *upon* God's altar" (*Ant.* 12.253); cf. also 1 Cor. 3:10a: "By the grace God has given me, I laid a foundation as a wise builder, and someone else is *building on* it."

strong: Paul and his associates "build" a community "on" foundations laid by others (1 Cor. 3:10, 12, 14); the people of God are "built on the foundation of the apostles and prophets" (Eph. 2:20). But, in common with Jude 20, the metaphor fades a bit here in Colossians 2:7.[19] Together, these participles emphasize that believers can live lives that exemplify the Lordship of Christ only by remaining, like branches, firmly attached to the vine in which God has himself placed them (cf. John 15) and by continuing to allow God to integrate them, like stones, into the new structure that is nothing other than Christ himself (cf. 1 Pet. 2:5-8; "body of Christ" in 1:18, 24; and esp. 2:19). We have deliberately used the language of "remaining" with respect to "rooted" and "continuing" with respect to "built up" to reflect the probable distinction that Paul intends by putting the former into the perfect tense and the latter into the present tense; see NASB: "having been firmly rooted and now being built up in Him."

The third participle may shift metaphors yet again, for *bebaioō* occurs in legal texts to mean "validate" or "guarantee."[20] But the word does not occur often enough in this specific sense to justify our finding a legal metaphor here.[21] It is used generally in the LXX and New Testament, where it means "confirm" (Rom. 15:8; 1 Cor. 1:6; Heb. 2:3), but, especially with a personal object (as here in Colossians), "strengthen" or "establish" (Pss. 40:13; 118:28; 1 Cor. 1:8; 2 Cor. 1:21; Heb. 13:9). "Establish" (as in most English versions) is preferable to TNIV's "strengthen" because it brings out better the basic sense of the word-group: "firm" or "solidly grounded."[22] With this participle, Paul summarizes what he expects to happen as a result of the first two: by sticking to their roots and being built up, the readers will be established in faith.[23] Like the first two participles, this one also is in the passive mood, implying that it is God who does the establishing — as he does the "rooting" and the "building up" — and, like the second, in the present tense, suggesting an ongoing process of "becoming established."

It is uncertain just what Paul means when he qualifies this "establishing" with the word *pistei* ("in faith").[24] The word might refer, as it

19. See the analysis of the verb in BDAG; O. Michel, *TDNT* 5.148.
20. Cf. the use of the cognate words βεβαίωσις and βεβαίως in Lev. 25:23, 30, respectively (H. Schlier, *TDNT* 1.602); MM, 108; Dunn, 142.
21. Wilson, 193.
22. Schlier, *TDNT* 1.601-2.
23. Abbott, 244; O'Brien, 107.
24. In place of the simple dative τῇ πίστει most MSS have a prepositional phrase, ἐν πίστει or ἐν τῇ πίστει. The presence of two other occurrences of ἐν in the verse may have led to its being added here. In any case, there is virtually no difference in meaning.

usually does in Paul, to one's own believing, in which case it might indicate the means by which the establishing — "established by means of faith"[25] — or what the establishing is in reference to — "established with reference to one's own faith," "established in one's own faith" (cf. NASB; NET; TEV).[26] But Paul occasionally uses the word to refer to *the* [Christian] faith, that is, to the content of what one believes rather than to the believing itself.[27] In this case, again, "the faith" might be the means of becoming established (NJB?) but is more likely, with this meaning, to indicate the sphere in which being established takes place: "being established in the faith" (cf. TNIV; RSV; NRSV; ESV; NLT; HCSB; REB; NAB).[28]

With the phrase *as you were taught,* Paul returns to where this sentence began, with the "tradition" that the Christians have received. It is unclear what it is that the Colossians were taught: the faith (cf. NJB, "the faith you have been taught"; also NLT)? That they should be "established in the faith" (so, probably, TNIV; REB)? Or that they should be "rooted and built up in him, established in the faith" (so, apparently, RSV; NRSV; ESV; NASB; HCSB)?[29] The first option, while it makes very good sense, is unlikely on syntactical grounds.[30] Deciding between the other two is almost impossible, especially since, as we have seen, "being established" summarizes the first two. In any case, Paul wants again to remind the Colossians that Epaphras has faithfully conveyed to them the true message of Christ, an emphasis that we have seen at several points in chapter 1 (vv. 5-8 esp.; cf. also v. 23; and cf. Eph. 4:21; 1 Thess. 2:15). The allusion to what the Colossians have already been taught interrupts the flow of participles, causing *overflowing with thankfulness* to stand by itself as al-

25. Lightfoot, 177; Pokorný, 112.

26. The dative might specifically indicate "reference" (e.g, Abbott, 245; Dunn, 142) or "sphere." The same basic meaning results from either. See also Barth/Blanke, 305.

27. As we noted, this meaning is often adopted in 1:23. See also the following (though there is disagreement about almost every occurrence): Rom. 12:6; 1 Cor. 16:13; 2 Cor. 13:5; Gal. 1:23; 6:10; Eph. 4:13; Phil. 1:27; Col. 1:23; 1 Tim. 1:2, 19; 3:9; 4:1, 6; 5:8; 6:10, 21; 2 Tim. 3:8; 4:7; Titus 1:4, 13; 3:15; Phlm. 6. The clearest example is outside of Paul, in Jude 3: "Dear friends, although I was very eager to write to you about the salvation we share, I felt compelled to write and urge you to contend for the faith that the Lord has once for all entrusted to us, his people." The tendency for the word to occur in this sense more often in the Pastoral Epistles has led many to suggest that this meaning reflects a post-Pauline "objectifying" of faith. But there are a number of probable examples of this meaning in the earlier, uncontested letters; the particular situation (as well as perhaps the date) of 1 Timothy and Titus explains the prominence of this meaning there.

28. Harris, 90; R. P. Martin, 78; Lohse, 94; Wilson, 193; Gnilka, 117; Wright, 99.

29. So Harris, 91.

30. It would be unusual for a καθώς clause to modify a preceding substantive. Had this been Paul's intention, we would have expected a relative clause (τῇ πίστει ἣν ἐδιδάχθητε, "the faith that you were taught").

most an afterthought.[31] But we should not thereby underestimate its significance. As we have noticed already, thanksgiving plays a prominent role in Colossians, Paul apparently being convinced that true gratitude for God's grace is an important "offensive" measure against the false teaching (see the notes on 1:12).[32]

B. The Threat to Christocentric Living: Warning about False Teachers (2:8-23)

Paul's strategy for urging the Colossians to resist the false teaching in their midst is to begin with the positive: they need to hold onto the authentic teaching about Christ and his Lordship that they had already received (vv. 6-7). And he continually returns to this positive side of the necessary response in the verses that follow. But vv. 8-23 are dominated by the negative. They are governed by three, roughly parallel, warnings:

> v. 8: "See to it that no one takes you captive through hollow and deceptive philosophy"
> v. 16: "Therefore do not let anyone judge you"
> v. 18: "Do not let anyone who delights in false humility and the worship of angels disqualify you."

The section falls into two basic parts. In vv. 8-15 Paul develops a powerful positive theological argument against the false teaching by rehearsing the completeness of the spiritual victory we share with Christ. In vv. 16-23, he repeats his warning but here backs it up by detailing some of the erroneous beliefs and practices of the false teachers.

1. Spiritual Fullness in Christ (2:8-15)

⁸See to it that no one takes you captive through hollow and deceptive philosophy, which depends on human tradition and the elemental spiritual forces of this world rather than on Christ. ⁹For in Christ all the fullness of

---

31. Some manuscripts, including the majority text (reflected in the KJV and NKJV), read instead of ἐν εὐχαριστίᾳ ("[overflowing or abounding] with thanksgiving") ἐν αὐτῇ ἐν εὐχαριστίᾳ ("[overflowing or abounding] in it [i.e., "faith"] with thanksgiving"). Still others have ἐν αὐτῷ ἐν εὐχαριστίᾳ ("[overflowing or abounding] in it [i.e., perhaps, the "teaching"] with thanksgiving") or simply ἐν αὐτῇ ("[overflowing or abounding] in it [i.e., faith]"). The first variant, which has the strongest support, is probably an assimilation to 4:2, γρηγοροῦντες ἐν αὐτῇ ἐν εὐχαριστίᾳ (Metzger, *Textual Commentary*, 555-56).

32. David Pao, *Thanksgiving* (Downers Grove, Ill.: InterVarsity, 2003), 89-90.

the Deity lives in bodily form, ¹⁰and in Christ you have been brought to fullness. He is the head over every power and authority. ¹¹In him you were also circumcised with a circumcision not performed by human hands. Your sinful nature was put off when you were circumcised by Christ, ¹²having been buried with him in baptism, in which you were also raised with him through your faith in the working of God, who raised him from the dead. ¹³When you were dead in your sins and in the uncircumcision of your sinful nature, God made you alive with Christ. He forgave us all our sins, ¹⁴having canceled the charge of our legal indebtedness, which stood against us and condemned us; he has taken it away, nailing it to the cross. ¹⁵And having disarmed the powers and authorities, he made a public spectacle of them, triumphing over them by the cross.

This key paragraph begins with a warning about the false teachers (v. 8) but is then dominated by a theologically rich explanation of why the Colossians should reject this teaching (vv. 9-15). Again Paul picks up language and ideas found earlier in the letter. The warning about avoiding false teachers (v. 8) echoes 2:4-5 and, to a lesser extent, 1:23. At the same time, the theological teaching of vv. 9-15 picks up the Christology of 1:15-20. Both passages claim that the "fullness [of God] dwells in" Christ (2:9; 1:19); both label Christ the "head" (cf. 2:10 and 1:18); both proclaim his supremacy over the "powers" (cf. 2:10 and 1:16); and both tie his victory over the powers to the cross (compare 2:15 with 1:20). But vv. 9-15 also elaborate the significance for believers of Christ's supremacy and exclusivity. Christ is the one universal Lord, and Christians, by identifying with Christ in faith, experience the benefits of that Lordship. Or, to follow the play on words that Paul uses: Christians experience spiritual "fullness" (v. 10) because they are in Christ, in whom "all the fullness of the Deity lives" (v. 9). All that human beings can know or experience of God is found in Christ, and so Christians, simply by virtue of being *Christians*, have access to all this knowledge and all these experiences. We need look nowhere else. In vv. 11-15, Paul elaborates this "fullness" that Christians experience in Christ. That fullness is ours because we are "in" Christ (v. 11); and we have therefore "with" Christ been buried, raised from the dead, and given new life (vv. 12-13). And that "fullness" includes (though not, of course, being limited to) victory over sin (v. 11), new life (v. 13), full and final forgiveness, and protection from the power of evil angels (vv. 14-15; cf. v. 10b).

   8 Just as vv. 6-7 introduce and sum up the specific exhortations to live out the Lordship of Christ that follow (3:1–4:6), so v. 8 stands in a similar relation to the warnings in the rest of chapter 2 (vv. 16-23). The summarizing character of the verse may be suggested by its lack of any

formal connection to what precedes (e.g., "asyndeton"; there is no conjunction or particle introducing the verse). *See to it* translates a verb *(blepō)* that means "see," "look," and that takes on the sense "look carefully" and therefore "watch out [for]" when followed by a negative, as here *(mē,* captured in the TNIV with *no one)* (see, e.g., Matt. 24:4; Mark 13:5; Luke 21:8; Acts 13:40; 1 Cor. 8:9; 10:12; Gal. 5:15; Heb. 12:25).[1] Paul wants his readers to watch out lest someone *take you captive.* The verb translated in this way by the TNIV (and in most English versions) is a rare one, used only here in biblical Greek and sparsely elsewhere.[2] It vividly expresses the danger that the readers may be "carried off as plunder" by an alien and fundamentally anti-Christian form of teaching. Those responsible for the teaching are not named, but, as Lightfoot points out, Paul uses the indefinite form we find here — *one (tis)* — elsewhere to refer to specific teachers (e.g., Gal. 1:7).[3] Paul has undoubtedly been informed by Epaphras about the threat of false teachers, although he may not know any of them by name. However, the singular form of the word does not imply that he has a specific individual in mind.[4]

Paul now indicates the means *(dia,* "through") by which the false teachers are seeking to carry off the Colossians as captives: *hollow and deceptive philosophy.* The TNIV has here interpreted the Greek syntax, which uses a single article to govern two parallel substantives: "[the] philosophy and vain deceit." Greek writers used a single article with two or more substantives to suggest some kind of association among the words. Sometimes the association is very close, as the substantives basically come to modify each other. The TNIV is probably correct to interpret the construction in this manner (see also NET; REB; NAB).[5] If this view is correct, then it becomes quite clear that Paul has no intention of criticizing "philosophy" as such, but only the kind of philosophy being propagated by the Colossian false teachers. Our use of the word "philosophy" is narrower than was the case in Paul's day, when it could be applied to virtually any system of thought. Josephus (perhaps, to be sure, with one eye on his Roman audience), for instance, describes Judaism as well as the various

---

1. The construction βλέπετε μή . . . is normally followed by a subjunctive, but here by a future indicative. It has been suggested that this construction suggests "the reality of the danger" (Lightfoot, 176; Abbott, 246; Wilson, 193). But it is almost certainly simply a stylistic variant (BDR §369.3).

2. It is very unlikely that Paul has chosen the word as a "contemptuous pun" on the word συναγώγη ("synagogue"), as Wright (100) suggests.

3. Lightfoot, 176.

4. Contra Abbott, 246. Note the parallel constructions in Matt. 24:4/Mark 13:5, where the threat is indefinite.

5. Lightfoot, 178; Harris, 92.

"parties" within Judaism (e.g., Pharisees, Sadducees, etc.) as "philosophies."[6] The word provides no help, then, in identifying the false teaching in Colossae.[7] The positive connotations of the word suggest that it was probably the false teachers themselves who chose to describe their teaching as a "philosophy."[8] Paul does not refute that claim but makes clear just what kind of "philosophy" it is: one that is "vain" (kenēs) and characterized by "deceitfulness" (apatēs).[9] The former, translated hollow in the TNIV, means, when used in a physical sense, "empty" (see 2 Kgs. 4:3) and so, in a metaphorical sense, refers to people or teachings that are "devoid of intellectual, moral, or spiritual value" (e.g., Jas. 2:20; Eph. 5:16).[10] Apatēs, a noun, is translated for English sense as an adjective, deceptive, in the TNIV. Its sense in the New Testament can be gauged from the contexts in which it is used. Wealth (Matt. 13:22/Mark 4:19), desire (Eph. 4:22), and sin (Heb. 3:13) are the kinds of things that "deceive" human beings and so lead them astray (cf. also 2 Thess. 2:10; in 2 Pet. 2:13 the word apparently means "pleasure"). In direct contrast to these descriptions stands the gospel: where the "philosophy" deceives people, the gospel is "true," "reliable" (1:5); where the "philosophy" is "empty," "devoid of spiritual value," the gospel is powerful and transforming (1:6, 23).

Paul continues his strong denunciation of the "philosophy" by further characterizing it with three parallel prepositional phrases, all using the same preposition. The repetition of this preposition, kata, lends both rhythm and emphasis to the characterization: "according to human tradition, according to the elements of the world, and not according to Christ" (TNIV translates kata as depends on in the first phrase and does not repeat it in the latter two). This preposition has a very broad range of meanings and can therefore be precisely defined only by its context. In the first phrase, it probably connotes the source of the "philosophy"; but in the second and third phrases, it may specify the content of the teaching.[11] In contrast to the "tradition" that the Colossians have received (see v. 6), which is from God (cf. 1:25, 27), the false teachers' "philosophy" depends on human tradition. This phrase reminds us especially of Jesus' critique of the Pharisees and teachers of the law for following their own "tradition"

6. Against Apion 1.54, Antiquities 18.11, respectively.
7. Wright, 101, thinks that Paul refers directly to Judaism, labeling it as just another ancient system of thought.
8. R. E. DeMaris, The Colossian Controversy (Sheffield: JSOT Press, 1994), 47-49; Lindemann, 39; O'Brien, 109.
9. In the Greek text, κενῆς modifies ἀπάτης: "vain deceit." But if this whole phrase modifies φιλοσοφίας, it is natural to interpret both of them as modifying φιλοσοφίας.
10. BDAG.
11. Lightfoot, 177-78.

rather than the word of God (Mark 7:1-23 par. Matt. 15:1-20).[12] Wright and Dunn, indeed, suggest that Paul is using the phrase here as Jesus does in the Gospels, to characterize a Jewish teaching.[13] But this is not clear. Even if Paul alludes here to Jesus' teaching — and this is possible — he need not be applying the phrase to the same kind of teaching.[14] What is clear is that the description is pejorative: the "philosophy" is the product of mere human speculation and does not put its adherents in touch with divine truth.

The second *kata* phrase is clearly pejorative as well, but its precise meaning is difficult to determine. Indeed, the meaning of the phrase that Paul uses here, *ta stoicheia tou kosmou* ("the elements of the world"), is one of the more intractable problems in New Testament interpretation. It occurs here and again in v. 20 with reference to the false teaching, and also in Galatians 4:3 and, in a different formulation, Galatians 4:9 (*ta asthenē kai ptōcha stoicheia*, "the weak and miserable elements"). *Stoicheion* is a "formal" word, meaning "fundamental component" or "element," and thus can take on a wide variety of specific senses, depending on the context in which it is used.[15] It can, for instance, refer to the letters of the alphabet, the notes of a musical scale, or the propositions of geometry. But three meanings (or applications) of the word are particularly relevant to the interpretation of the phrase in Colossians.

(1) In Paul's day (and after), the word was most often used to denote the "fundamental components" of the universe, the "elements" from which all matter was composed — usually identified as air, earth, fire, and water.[16] The word is used in this sense in its three LXX occurrences (4 Macc. 12:13; Wis. 7:17; 19:18), in most of its occurrences in Philo, Josephus, and the apostolic fathers, and in two of the six New Testament

12. The connection has good lexical support. The exact phrase τὴν παράδοσιν τῶν ἀνθρώπων occurs only in Col. 2:8 and Mark 7:8 in the NT; and eight of the thirteen occurrences of παράδοσις in the NT come in these narratives.

13. Wright, 101; Dunn, 148.

14. O'Brien, 110. Note Peter's description of the (probably) Gentile background of his audience in 1 Peter as "handed down to you from your ancestors" (πατροπαραδότου; literally, "tradition of the fathers").

15. See esp. Andrew J. Bandstra, *The Law and the Elements of the World: An Exegetical Study in Aspects of Paul's Teaching* (Kampen: Kok, 1964), 31-46. As Walter Wink (referring to Bandstra) summarizes: "It [*stoicheion*] denotes merely an irreducible component; what it is an irreducible component of must be supplied by the context in which it is used" (*Naming the Powers* [Philadelphia: Fortress, 1984], 68).

16. This is also the usual meaning in Philo and Josephus. As an example of this meaning (using the same phrase we find in Colossians), see *Sib. Or.* 2.206: "And then all the elements of the world will be bereft — air, land, sea, light, vault of heaven, days, nights."

occurrences (2 Pet. 3:10, 12). (2) The word was also used in the sense of the "essential principles" of a particular area of study.[17] This meaning is also found in the New Testament, in Hebrews 5:12, where the author refers to "the elementary truths *(ta stoicheia tēs archēs)* of God's word." (3) Finally, *stoicheia* came to be used for spiritual beings. The word is never given this application in any pre-Christian writing; its first extant use in this way comes in the post–New Testament *Testament of Solomon.*[18] But many scholars are convinced that the word was being used this way in Paul's day.[19]

Each of these meanings has been given to the phrase here in Colossians 2 (and in Galatians 4), and each can marshal strong lexical and/or contextual evidence. Before we canvass these options, two methodological issues should be settled. First, the rarity of the expression makes it overwhelmingly likely that the phrase has the same meaning (at least in a general sense) in Galatians as in the Colossians texts. Second, and for the same reason, it is probable that the phrase is Paul's own way of characterizing the teaching in each situation rather than the false teachers' own label.[20] For it would strain credulity to suppose that two different sets of false teachers — advocating doctrines that are at least to some extent different — would have chosen the same rare phrase to describe their views.

The third meaning — the "elements" as spiritual beings — is the most popular option among contemporary scholars, as is evidenced by its adoption in the majority of modern translations (TNIV; RSV; NRSV; ESV; NET; REB; TEV).[21] This interpretation has strong contextual support, since the two passages where the phrase occurs both refer significantly to spiritual beings. Note Galatians 4:8-9: "Formerly, when you did

---

17. See, e.g., Xenophon, *Memorabilia* 2.1.1: ". . . how would you educate them? If you wish, let us consider it, beginning with food, as one of the elementary issues" (my translation).

18. In 8:2 the στοιχεῖα are called "the cosmic rulers of darkness" (cf. also 18:2). The *Testament of Solomon* is difficult to date (1st-3d centuries A.D.), but is certainly post-NT.

19. Although Bruce thinks that Paul himself may have been the first to give the word this application (98-100).

20. See, e.g., E. Percy, *Die Probleme der Kolosser- und Epheserbriefe* (Lund: Gleerup, 1946), 166-67; T. J. Sappington, *Revelation* (Sheffield: JSOT Press, 1991), 169; contra, e.g., Lohse, 99; Wolter, 158.

21. Note, however, that almost every one of these versions has a footnote giving an alternative rendering. For this view of στοιχεῖα, see, e.g., Percy, *Die Probleme der Kolosser- und Epheserbriefe*, 156-67; Harris, 93; O'Brien, 129-32; Lohse, 96-99; Dibelius-Greeven, 27-29; Bruce, 98-100; Hübner, 76-79; A. T. Lincoln, *Paradise Now and Not Yet* (Cambridge and New York: Cambridge University Press, 2004), 114; Wright, 101-2; C. Arnold, *Colossian Syncretism* (Tübingen: Mohr Siebeck, 1995), 159-66.

not know God, you were slaves to *those who by nature are not gods.* But now that you know God — or rather are known by God — how is it that you are turning back to those *weak and miserable forces (stoicheia)?* Do you wish to be enslaved by them all over again?" And in Colossians 2, Paul refers to Christ's supremacy over "every power and authority" in v. 10, to Christ's victory over these same "powers" in v. 15, and to angels in v. 18 (and see, of course, 1:16, 20). Moreover, it is alleged, the reference to "Christ" in the third *kata* phrase of v. 8 suggests that its contrasting phrase would also contain a reference to personal beings. In Galatians, Paul would be saying, the Judaizers, by insisting that their Gentile converts place themselves under the authority of the Mosaic law, would be, in effect, forcing them back into an earlier stage of their religious experience, when the various spirits of this world dominated their existence. In Colossians Paul would be criticizing the false teachers for giving far too much attention to spiritual beings and the "rules" associated with them, elevating them to a position in which they were, in effect, taking away the central place of Christ. The main problem with this view is lexical: as we noted above, there is no evidence that the word *stoicheia* was used to refer to spiritual beings until the third century A.D. Advocates of this view, however, rightly note that the move from *stoicheia* as a reference to physical elements to *stoicheia* as a reference to spiritual beings would have been an easy one in the context of the ancient worldview. Most ancient people did not neatly distinguish the material and the spiritual in the way in which we do today. The heavenly bodies, in particular, were regularly associated with, or even identified with, spiritual beings;[22] hence many commentators speak here in Colossians of "astral spirits."

The second interpretation does not suffer from the same problem as the third that we have just described, since the meaning "elementary principles" is well attested, even if not exactly widespread, in Paul's day. It is also said to fit the contexts of each relevant passage quite well and finds a place in several English versions (KJV; NKJV; NASB; NIV; NJB). In Galatians 4 Paul uses the maturation of a child as a metaphor for the course of salvation history. Israel under the law is like a child who has not yet received his or her inheritance. It would, then, be very natural for Paul to describe the law and its peculiar requirements — circumcision, abstinence from certain foods, the celebration of holy days — as "elementary principles" that have now been put aside in the new era of salvation history. Similarly, whatever else we can learn from Colossians 2 about the

22. Evidence for the association of heavenly bodies with spiritual beings is both early and extensive. On the other hand, and contrary to some exponents of this view, the evidence for the *identification* of the stars with spirits is not widespread.

false teaching, one thing is clear: it also stressed the observance of Jewish holy days (v. 16) and obedience to certain "rules" (vv. 20-23). Again, therefore, characterizing the false teaching as being preoccupied with "elementary principles" to which Christians have "died" in Christ (v. 20) would make good sense.[23] And if advocates of the "astral spirits" view stress that their view provides a natural contrast with Christ in the third *kata* clause, advocates of the "principial" view note the natural parallel that their view would create with the reference to "tradition" in the first *kata* phrase.

In contrast to the "astral spirits" view, which must overcome the lexical evidence, and in comparison with the "principial" view, which can easily fit the lexical evidence, the first view, that *ta stoicheia tou kosmou* refers to the material components of the universe, has lexical evidence solidly in its favor. As we noted above, this was by far the dominant meaning of the word *stoicheia* in Paul's day. Moreover, every instance of the phrase [*ta*] *stoicheia* [*tou*] *kosmou* from Paul's general time period apparently has this meaning.[24] The difficulty this view faces is contextual: how would a reference to material components fit in with the false teaching that Paul describes in Galatians 4 and Colossians 2? Two related answers to this question can be given. First, as we have noted, the false teachers in both Galatians and Colossians are criticized for following rules that focus on material realities: food (in both texts: Gal 2:11-14; Col. 2:21), observance of days (in both texts: Gal. 4:10; Col. 2:16), circumcision (in Galatians: 2:3; 5:2-12; 6:12-15; possibly, by implication, in Colossians: 2:11; 3:11).[25]

Second, and more important, is again the need to take seriously the ancient worldview. The material components of the universe were often associated with spiritual beings or the gods; as Philo puts it,

---

23. Advocates of this view include Lightfoot, 180; Moule, 90-92; Thompson, 53; Sappington, *Revelation*, 164-70; and see, on Galatians, esp. Ernest de W. Burton, *A Critical and Exegetical Commentary on St. Paul's Epistle to the Galatians* (ICC; Edinburgh: T&T Clark, 1921), 510-18.

24. See the summary of a TLG search by Dietrich Rusam, "Neue Belege zu den στοιχεῖα τοῦ κόσμου (Gal 4,3.9; Kol 2,8.20)," *ZNW* 83 (1992), 119-25. He finds nine occurrences, in addition to the eleven that Josef Blinzler had already discovered ("Lexikalisches zu dem Terminus τὰ στοιχεῖα τοῦ κόσμου bei Paulus," in *Studiorum Paulinorum Congressus Internationalis Catholicus* [2 vols.; AnBib 17-18; Rome: Pontifical Biblical Institute, 1963], 2.429-43).

25. Note in this respect the consonance between the assertion in v. 20 that Christians have "died" to the "elements of the world" and the series of words focusing on physical things: "handle," "taste," "touch," "things that are all destined to perish with use," "humility" (= ascetic practices; see v. 18), "harsh treatment of the body," "sensual indulgence" (σάρξ) (vv. 21-23).

"Some nations have made divinities of the four elements, earth and water, and air and fire. Others, of the sun and moon, and of the other planets and fixed stars. Others, again, of the whole world" (*On the Decalogue* 53). This tendency to "spiritualize" or "divinize" the material elements was a strong cultural current that the people of God had to fight against. The Lord, for instance, warns the Israelites: "And when you look up to the sky and see the sun, the moon and the stars — all the heavenly array — do not be enticed into bowing down to them and worshiping things the LORD your God has apportioned to all the nations under heaven" (Deut. 4:19). The characterization of pagan religion as involving worship of physical elements as well as warnings against it are found throughout Jewish and early Christian apologetics. The first-century B.C. Jewish book Wisdom furnishes a typical example: "For all people who were ignorant of God were foolish by nature; and they were unable from the good things that are seen to know the one who exists, nor did they recognize the artisan while paying heed to his works; but they supposed that either fire or wind or swift air, or the circle of the stars, or turbulent water, or the luminaries of heaven were the gods that rule the world"[26] (13:1-2). In light of this background, then, a reference to the material elements of the universe in a religious text such as Colossians 2 would almost certainly include some reference to those deities or spirits who were so closely associated with the elements.[27] The Colossian "philosophy," by its preoccupation with rules about material things, was, in Paul's view, treating them like the pagans did, as if they were fundamental cosmic powers that needed to be pla-

26. See also Philo, *On the Contemplative Life* 3, who mentions people who "honor the elements, earth, water, air, and fire." Among the Christian apologists, see, e.g., *The Kerygma Petrou*; Tertullian, *Idolatry* 4; Aristides (the Apologist) 2-6; Clement of Alexandria, *Exhortation to the Greeks* 5 (commenting on Col 2:8).

27. For this view in general, see esp. Wolter, 122-24; Luz, 220; McDonald, 97-98; Blinzler, "Lexikalisches"; Rusam, "Neue Belege"; DeMaris, *The Colossian Controversy*, 52-55; N. Kehl, *Der Christushymnus im Kolosserbrief* (Stuttgart: Katholisches Bibelwerk, 1967), 138-57; Wink, *Naming the Powers*, 67-77 (though he takes this view only in 2:8; he takes the "principial" view of 2:20). See also I. K. Smith, *Heavenly Perspective* (Edinburgh: T&T Clark, 2006), 87. Eduard Schweizer puts a particular spin on this general interpretation, suggesting that a Pythagorean teaching that emphasized abstinence from various material substances as a means of spiritual purification explains the Colossian false teaching (see his commentary, 128-33, and in more detail, "Die 'Elemente der Welt': Gal. 4:3, 9; Kol. 2:8, 20," in *Beiträge zur Theologie des Neuen Testaments* [Zurich: Zwingli, 1970], 147-63). Bandstra's view, which is often categorized with the "principial" interpretation, may ultimately fit better in this category. For he views the στοιχεῖα as the "elementary forces" of flesh and the law (*The Law and the Elements of the World*, 68-72). See also Dübbers, *Christologie und Existenz*, 206-9. Somewhat similar are the views of Pokorný, 114, and Dunn, 149-50.

cated. They were, in effect, putting them in the place of Christ (thus the contrast between the second and third *kata* phrases) and failing to recognize that believers had "died" to them with Christ (v. 20). The translations of the HCSB — "elemental forces of the world" — and NAB — "elemental powers of the world" — perhaps reflect this interpretation.

We believe that this final view provides the best explanation for the phrase. The rarity of the phrase and Paul's failure to provide any explanation of it suggest that he is using it in the way it was most often used in his day.[28] It makes good sense in both Galatians 4 and Colossians 2. It gives to the word *kosmos* ("world") a meaning — "universe," "all creation" — that it often has in Paul.[29] It avoids the problem of "why this phrase?" associated with both of the other views. In Colossians, especially, it is difficult to understand why Paul would abandon the vocabulary he usually uses to describe spiritual beings (see 1:16, 20; 2:10, 15) and substitute this unusual, and perhaps unprecedented one. And the same objection applies to the "principial" interpretation; note, for instance, that in Hebrews 5:12, where the word does have this meaning, it is not used absolutely but in dependence on *logiōn tou theou*, "words of God," and in association with *tēs archēs*, "the beginning." Moreover, the interpretation we are advocating incorporates some of the strengths of both other views. It retains the sense of a "basic" reality that is central to the "principial" view, and, like the "astral spirits" view, it alludes to the notion of cosmic power. Indeed, the "powers and authorities" to which Paul refers in this context (vv. 10, 15) can be seen as indirectly included in the *stoicheia tou kosmou*.

Whatever precise sense we end up giving to "the elements of the world," it is at any rate clear that the real sting in Paul's characterization

---

28. As J. Louis Martyn notes, the lexical evidence means that we should assume that στοιχεῖα refers to the material elements of the universe unless a convincing contextual case to the contrary can be made (*Galatians: A New Translation with Introduction and Commentary* [AB 33A; New York: Doubleday, 1997], 393-95).

29. See Rom. 1:20; 1 Cor. 3:22 (?); 4:9; 7:31; 8:4; Eph. 1:4; Phil. 2:15. Bandstra (*The Law and the Elements of the World*, 57) argues that the word should be given a pejorative sense (in this sense of "this world") based on normal Pauline usage. But in fact only a minority of Paul's uses of κόσμος have this pejorative sense. In Colossians, apart from the phrase τὰ στοιχεῖα τοῦ κόσμου, Paul uses κόσμος two other times: in 1:6, to refer to the "world" of human beings; and, of particular relevance to our text, since it comes immediately after Paul's claim that believers have died to "the elements of the world," in v. 20: "Why, as if you are living in the world, are you submitting to decrees?" (my translation). "World" here might mean "the fallen world" from which believers have been delivered but could also, and perhaps more naturally, mean "the created world" "in" which believers no longer live, in the sense that they are no longer under its power. See the commentary on v. 20.

of the false teachers comes in the third, negative description: it is not "according to Christ." The false teachers are proclaiming a doctrine and demanding practices that do not *depend . . . on Christ* (TNIV). In this short phrase the dominant theological teaching of the letter is brought to bear on the central purpose of the letter. Christ is the one in whom God exclusively is to be found, the one through whom the world was created and through whom it is redeemed, and the one who has decisively defeated all the hostile powers. Any teaching that in any way detracts from Christ's exclusive role is by definition both wrong and ineffective. The teachers themselves are probably not denying that Christ was central to God's saving purposes. They seem rather to be arguing that certain practices must be added on in order to achieve true spiritual fulfillment. But, for Paul, in this case, addition means subtraction: one cannot "add" to Christ without, in effect, subtracting from his exclusive place in creation and in salvation history.

9 The "for" *(hoti)* at the beginning of this verse ties the argument of vv. 9-15 to v. 8, and especially to the last phrase of v. 8. In effect, these verses elaborate the negative "not according to Christ" by detailing the flip, positive side: in Christ, and Christ alone, is found "the fullness of God" (v. 9); and believers have been made "full" in him (vv. 10-15). As Michael Dübbers, for instance, has noted, v. 9 is an "interpretative paraphrase" of a key line from the christological "hymn" of chapter 1.[30] According to 1:19, "God was pleased to have all his fullness dwell in him [Christ]." The dependence of 2:9 on 1:19 is clear from the tautologous repetition *all the fullness* and from the use of the same verb, *katoikeō*, "dwell" (a parallel that the TNIV unfortunately fails to reflect, translating "dwell" in 1:19 and "live" here). In contrast to 1:19, however, Paul explicitly indicates that the "fullness" has to do with God by adding the qualification "of the Deity." The particular Greek word Paul uses here — *theotēs* — focuses on the divine nature, as opposed to the divine essence (which would be expressed with *theiotēs*).[31] As we noted in the comments on 1:19, this language of "dwelling" probably alludes to Old Testament teaching about the dwelling of God in the Temple (esp. Ps. 68:16).[32] And this background may help explain why Paul qualifies the "dwelling" here with the adverb *sōmatikōs* (TNIV, "in bodily form"). God in his full-

---

30. Dübbers, *Christologie und Existenz*, 213.

31. E.g., Lightfoot, 181. The Greek word Paul uses — θεότης — occurs only here in the NT. The word θειότης, on the other hand, occurs once — in Rom. 1:20. BDAG, e.g., define the former as "the state of being God" and the latter as "the quality or characteristic(s) pertaining to deity" (see also, e.g., Abbott, 248-49; Lohse, 100). Barth/Blanke, 312, question whether the two terms were so distinguished in Paul's day.

32. See 131-33.

ness has not taken up residence in and therefore revealed himself in a building but in a body. Characteristic of the new covenant administration is the replacement of the Temple with Christ as the focus for God's presence and as the nucleus of God's people. We are presuming, with this interpretation, that the adverb *sōmatikōs* means "bodily," "in a human body" (NLT; and so, basically, all the English versions). This adverb does not occur elsewhere in the New Testament (and never in the LXX, Philo, or Josephus), so its meaning must be deduced from the very common cognate noun *sōma* (usually "body"). And this word occurs three times in Colossians 1–2 with the meaning "physical body" (generally in 2:23; with reference to Christ's body in 1:22; 2:11 is debated).[33]

But Paul also uses *sōma* in this context with another meaning, "substance," "reality" (2:17), and *sōmatikōs* could, then, correspondingly, mean "really," "actually."[34] And he uses *sōma* several times in Colossians as a metaphor for the church (1:18, 24; 3:15), so *sōmatikōs* might also include the notion of "expressed in and through the church as Christ's body."[35] However, since the adverb denotes the manner of the dwelling, this last option is unlikely. Either of the other options makes good sense in the context,[36] but the focus is probably on the "bodily" nature of God's manifestation in Christ. The word therefore suggests the idea of incarnation that is so clearly expressed elsewhere in the New Testament (e.g., John 1:14), and, since the verb *katoikei* is in the present tense, also suggests that this indwelling of God in Christ is permanent. Paul's use of the adverb here, in preference, for instance, to "in a body" or "in the flesh," may be intended to show that his disparaging remarks about the material elements of the universe (v. 8) conceal no dualism. Paul is not advocating the view, so common in his day, that true spirituality was to be found by abandoning or by strictly subduing the "body" (see v. 23).[37] Rather, God has chosen precisely a body in which to take residence and through that

33. See also Harris, 99; O'Brien, 112-13; Moule, 92-94.

34. Aletti, 168; Pokorný, 122-23; Dübbers, *Christologie und Existenz*, 215-17; cf. J. Jervell, *Imago Dei* (Göttingen: Vandenhoeck & Ruprecht, 1960), 222-24 (who thinks the term may reflect the εἰκών ["image"] idea). In favor of a meaning other than "bodily," it could be noted that the one clear reference to the body of Christ in Colossians (1:22) as well as the one debated reference (2:11) are qualified with the phrase τῆς σαρκός ("of the flesh").

35. Gnilka, 129; Lohse, 100-101; Masson, 124-25. Geurt Hendrik van Kooten (*Cosmic Christology in Paul and the Pauline School: Colossians and Ephesians in the Context of Graeco-Roman Cosmology* [WUNT 2.171; Tübingen: Mohr Siebeck, 2003], 23-27) suggests that "bodily" here has a cosmological sense, based on the assumption that "body" in the original form of the hymn (1:18) referred to the cosmos.

36. Wright thinks both may be intended (103).

37. Lähnemann, *Der Kolosserbrief*, 118.

body, sacrificed on the cross (1:22; 2:15) and raised from the dead (2:13), to win the ultimate victory over the powers of darkness.

10 The initial sentence explaining why a "philosophy" that is "not according to Christ" is so problematic (v. 8) continues in this verse with a second independent clause — *and in Christ you have been brought to fullness*. The TNIV rightly brings out the play on words that we find in vv. 9-10, although Paul actually uses a verb in this verse rather than the noun of v. 9: "you have been filled" *(este . . . peplērōmenoi)*. The Greek perfect tense of this verbal form is often said to express a "past action with present consequences." In fact, however, the past action element of the perfect often receives little emphasis, so that the perfect tense comes to express simply an existing state of affairs. This would seem to be the case here. The Colossians will have no interest in listening to the false teachers once they realize that they are already "filled."

But filled with what? We must assume that Paul has deliberately chosen to use (unusually for him) the verb absolutely in order to encompass a broad range of ideas and to facilitate the wordplay with v. 9.[38] All the "fullness" of the deity resides in Christ; believers, who are "in Christ,"[39] are "filled" (cf. John 1:16, "Out of his [the Word's] fullness we have all received grace in place of grace already given"; and, illustrating the typical tension of "indicative" and "imperative" in Paul, Eph. 3:19, where the ultimate goal of his prayer is that "you may be filled to the measure of all the fullness of God"). As we noted in our comments on 1:19, Paul may use the language of "fullness" in Colossians because he is directly countering a claim of the false teachers.[40] "We," they perhaps were saying, "offer you the means to attain real spiritual fullness, to move on from Christ to a deeper spiritual experience." Their claim would then fall into line generally with the kinds of claims that false teachers throughout the centuries have made. And against those claims Paul asserts again the exclusivity of Christ. In him, and in him alone, God has decisively and exhaustively revealed himself. All that we can know or experience of God is therefore found in our relationship with him.

---

38. When Paul uses the passive of the verb πληρόω elsewhere, it either has an inanimate subject (e.g., "the entire law is fulfilled" [Gal. 5:14]) or is completed with a word (in the dative or the accusative or with the preposition εἰς) indicating what a person has been filled with (Rom. 1:29; 15:14; 2 Cor. 7:4; Eph. 1:23 [possibly]; 5:18; Phil. 1:11; Col. 1:9; 2 Tim. 1:4). The only exception is Phil. 4:18, where Paul claims that he has been "filled" because of the gift from the Philippians that he has received through Epaphroditus.

39. It is possible to take the verb ἐστε absolutely, with the participle expressing a further circumstance: "And you are in Christ, having been filled" (Lightfoot, 130). But a periphrastic construction is much more likely (e.g., Harris, 100). The ἐν ("in [Christ]") should be given a local rather than an instrumental ("through Christ"; cf. HCSB) meaning.

40. See, here, O'Brien, 113.

The rest of v. 10 confirms that Paul still has the false teachers very much in view. For it is hard, otherwise, to know why he would add the specific claim that Christ is *the head over every power and authority.* "Power" *(archē)* and "authority" *(exousia)* refer to spiritual beings, as they did in 1:16 (cf. also v. 15). Paul continues to apply to his readers the theology of the great Christ hymn of 1:15-20, where it was asserted that Christ is the one through whom "all things were created," "things in heaven and on earth," "whether thrones or powers or rulers or authorities" (v. 16). The authority of Christ over spiritual beings that the language of 1:16-17 (and 20) implies is explicitly claimed here. "Head" *(kephalē)* is a metaphor that undoubtedly includes this notion of "authority over." Yet, as we noted in our comments on 1:18, authority is only one aspect of a broader metaphorical allusion. As the head is the animating and directing force of the body, so Christ is the source of the spiritual beings' existence (1:16) and the one who ultimately determines what they can and cannot do.[41] Christians need not fear these "powers," therefore, because they are firmly under the control of their own "head," the one in whom all the fullness of deity has come to reside.

11 In vv. 9-10, Paul reminds us of an enduring theological reality — "all the fullness of the deity dwells [present tense] in Christ" — and of the state of spiritual affairs that derives from it — "you have come to fullness [perfect tense] in Christ." Now, in vv. 11-15, Paul explains how that state of fullness has come into being (using aorist tenses). The *also* (translating *kai*) at the beginning of v. 11 connects the "in Christ" in v. 10a with the "in him" here. This concept of being in Christ and therefore of experiencing things "with" him is the leitmotif of vv. 11-13: "in him you were circumcised," "buried with him in baptism," "raised with him," "made . . . alive with Christ." The last three, as we will see as we comment on them, all have parallels in Paul's teaching elsewhere. But the idea of Christians being "circumcised" in what Paul calls later in the verse "the circumcision of Christ" (my own rather neutral translation; cf. ESV) has no parallel elsewhere in the New Testament (though Paul expresses a possibly related idea in Phil. 3:3, where he claims that "it is we [Christians] who are the circumcision" [and cf. Rom. 2:28-29]). A number of interpreters think the concept is introduced here as a direct polemic against the false teaching (as, perhaps, in Philippians 3). The false teachers, it is argued, must have been insisting on circumcision, leading Paul to coun-

---

41. Lightfoot, 183. Supremacy is singled out as the main emphasis in the metaphor by Moule, 94; Bruce, 102; and C. E. Arnold, "Jesus Christ: 'Head' of the Church," in *Jesus of Nazareth: Lord and Christ* (Grand Rapids: Eerdmans, 1994), 364. "Derivative source" is singled out by, e.g., Dübbers, *Christologie und Existenz,* 220-21.

ter their demand with the claim that Christians had, in fact, already undergone a "circumcision."[42] And 3:11, with its claim that the "new self" knows no distinction between "circumcised" and "uncircumcised," is thought to confirm this line of thinking. Paul, of course, draws the imagery from the Old Testament and Judaism; and, as in Philippians 3:3, reference to the "circumcision of Christ" indirectly asserts the claim of the Christian movement to be the fulfillment and eschatological expression of the true people of God.[43] But there are two reasons to hesitate before concluding that the false teachers themselves had introduced circumcision into the debate. First, negatively, it is strange, had circumcision been a part of the false teachers' program, that it is never directly countered anywhere in the letter, especially in 2:16-23.[44] Second, positively, a sufficient explanation for Paul's introduction of circumcision here is the apparent focus on conquering or subduing the flesh, or the body, that seems to have been an important component of the false teaching (see esp. 2:23).[45] Against the false teachers' advocacy of rules and ascetic practices as the means of subduing the flesh (2:16, 18, 20-21), Paul asserts that Christians have already experienced "the stripping off of the body of flesh" (my own literal translation) in their union with Christ. No other practice or obedience to a rule is needed.

Physical circumcision was, of course, instituted by God to be a sign of the covenant between him and people of Israel (Gen. 17:1-14). But already in the Old Testament it was also being used as a metaphor, Moses himself calling for the "circumcision of the heart" (Deut. 10:16; 30:6; cf. Jer. 4:4). Paul takes up this concept, claiming that it is the circumcision of the heart, performed by the Spirit — not physical circumcision as such — that marks a person as belonging to the people of God (Rom. 2:28-29). It is this nonphysical circumcision that Paul has in mind here, as the qualification "not performed by human hands" suggests. The TNIV phrase translates rather literally a single Greek word (acheiropoiētos) that occurs twice elsewhere in biblical Greek (Mark 14:58; 2 Cor. 5:1). In each case, its basic negative meaning connotes a strong positive sense: "not made with hands" means, effectively, "made by God," and it is for this reason that TNIV (see also NET; NJB) translates "human hands."[46] The word does not

42. E.g., Lightfoot, 183; Lähnemann, Der Kolosserbrief, 51; George R. Beasley-Murray, "Second Chapter of Colossians," RevExp 70 (1973), 473; Wright, 104; Dunn, 155-56; Masson, 125; Lindemann, 41-42; Dübbers, Christologie und Existenz, 227-28, 232-34.

43. Pokorný, 124.

44. O'Brien, 115.

45. See esp. Lincoln, 623-24.

46. This negative sense is probably also a reflection of the use of the word χειροποίητος in the LXX, where it always refers to idols, the products of "human hands"

necessarily mean that the circumcision is nonphysical (contra NRSV), since the "building from God," "not made by human hands" in 2 Corinthians 5:1 refers to the resurrection body. But when it is taken in conjunction with the biblical tradition about the "circumcision of the heart" to which we have referred, Paul clearly uses "circumcise" as a metaphor for the transition from the old life to the new.

But when, or in what manner, has this transition taken place? The TNIV, in line with some other English versions (NLT, NJB, REB) and many commentators, implies that it is the moment of each person's conversion that is in view, that moment when one is "circumcised by Christ" and the "sinful nature is put off." But both of these translations are quite interpretive. The former translates a phrase in which two key nouns, "circumcision" and "Christ," are connected with a genitive, a construction notorious for its ambiguity. The TNIV has chosen one option, a subjective genitive — "circumcision performed by Christ" — but the genitive could also be objective — "circumcision performed on Christ" — or possessive — "Christ's circumcision," or, effectively, "Christian circumcision."[47] Similarly, the TNIV's "sinful nature is put off" translates a phrase that could be "literally" rendered "the putting off of the body of the flesh." "Sinful nature" in the TNIV is, of course, an attempt to capture in English the negative theological nuance that Paul often gives the word *sarx*. But this word could also have a physical sense here, an option perhaps given greater likelihood by the fact that it here modifies *sōma* ("body") and by the fact that the only other time that Paul (or any biblical writer) uses the phrase "body of flesh" is earlier in this same letter, where it refers to Christ's body given in death for us (Col. 1:22).

Putting these various translation options together yields three basic possible interpretations of the end of v. 11. First, the reference might be to Christian conversion, pictured as a "circumcision" performed on us by Christ, who removes not a piece of physical "flesh," but the enveloping, enervating power of our "fleshly" nature or propensity.[48] Second, in light of v. 12, where baptism is explicitly brought into the picture, Paul could

(Lev. 26:1, 30; Isa. 2:18; 10:11; 16:12; 19:1; 21:9; 31:7; 46:6; Dan. [LXX] 5:4, 23; Dan. [Theod.] Bel 5; Jdt. 8:18; Wis. 14:8). This LXX usage gives particular strength to Stephen's claim (with allusion to Solomon's temple) that "the Most High does not live in houses made by human hands" (Acts 7:48; cf. also Acts 17:24; Heb. 9:11, 24). But especially pertinent to Col. 2:11 is Eph. 2:11, which refers to people "who call themselves 'the circumcision' (which is done in the body by human hands [χειροποιήτου])."

47. C. Beetham ("Echoes of Scripture" [Ph.D. diss., Wheaton College, 2005], 230) claims that, in the ten other places in Jewish Greek contemporary with Paul where περιτομή is followed by a genitive, the genitive is in each case objective.

48. Lightfoot, 183-84; Harris, 102-3; Arnold, *Colossian Syncretism*, 296-97.

be referring to baptism as the Christian equivalent to Old Testament/ Jewish circumcision, the rite through which, or in conjunction with which, our bodies dominated by the flesh are "put off."[49] Third, the reference could be to Christ's own death, "circumcision" being used as a metaphor for violent death, and "body of flesh" (as in 1:22) referring to Christ's own physical body, "stripped off" when he died on the cross. It is in and with Christ's own death, then, that believers were themselves brought from death to life.

This last interpretation has two very strong points in its favor. First, by taking "body of flesh" as a reference to Christ's body, it can give this phrase the same meaning it has earlier in the letter, which is, as we have noted, the only other occurrence of the phrase in biblical Greek. Second, interpreting "circumcision of Christ" as a reference to his death, in which believers participate, fits perfectly into a theological pattern found elsewhere in Paul. The basic gospel message, Paul claims, is that Christ "died for our sins," "that he was buried," and that "he was raised on the third day" (1 Cor. 15:3-4). In Romans 6 Paul teaches that it is through identification with these three key redemptive-historical events that Christians have been set free from sin: they have "died with Christ," they have been "buried with him," and they will be "united with him in a resurrection like his." Moreover, it is in conjunction with baptism that believers are so identified with these events (vv. 3, 4). The parallel with Colossians 2:11-12 is obvious. Here also it is through baptism that believers are "buried with him" and "raised with him." All that is missing from the sequence is "dying with Christ," which, on this interpretation, is found in v. 11.[50]

Attractive though this interpretation is, it is not without its problems. The phrase "body of flesh" is more naturally taken as the body possessed by Christians, the subject of the sentence, than that possessed by Christ, who is mentioned only at the end of the verse. Second, though it is true that "stripping off the body of flesh" is a strange metaphor on any account, taking it as a reference to Christ's death comes dangerously close to a kind of docetic idea in which Christ's body is a negative encumbrance to be disposed of rather than, as in orthodox theology, a neutral, albeit weak, vessel destined for transformation through resurrection.

49. Lohse, 102-3; Abbott, 250; Pokorný, 124-25; MacDonald, 99-100; Gnilka, 131-32.

50. O'Brien, 117-18; Dunn, 157-58 (idem, "The 'Body' in Colossians," in *To Tell the Mystery* [Sheffield: JSOT Press, 1994], 167-70); Moule, 95-96; Barth/Blanke, 364-68; R. C. Tannehill, *Dying and Rising with Christ: A Study in Pauline Theology* (BZNW 32; Berlin: Töpelmann, 1966), 49-50; G. R. Beasley-Murray, *Baptism in the New Testament* (Grand Rapids: Eerdmans, 1962), 152-53; Robert H. Gundry, *Sōma in Biblical Theology with Special Emphasis on Pauline Anthropology* (SNTSMS 29; Cambridge: Cambridge University Press, 1976), 41-42; Wilson, 201-4; E. Martin, 111-12.

Third, interpreting "circumcision" as a metaphor for death does not fit with the actual rite to which it makes allusion as well as a reference to conversion/entrance into the people of God.

We therefore slightly incline to the first view outlined above: "the circumcision of Christ" is a metaphor for the conquering of the power of sin that takes place when a person comes to Christ. "Body of flesh," on this view, will be equivalent to "body of sin" in Romans 6:6.[51] In both verses Paul intends to describe the body not as sinful in itself but as under the domination of sin/the flesh (cf. also "body of death" [Rom. 7:24]; "body of humiliation" [Phil. 3:21]; and note Col. 3:5, where Paul commands us to "put to death" our "earthly members" [TNIV, "whatever belongs to your earthly nature"]). In line with the circumcision metaphor, it is this body of flesh, not simply a piece of flesh (as in physical circumcision), that is "put off" or "stripped off." The Greek noun behind this English expression is very rare, but a verbal cognate occurs in 2:15 and 3:9.[52] The latter verse expresses a concept similar to what we are advocating here, speaking of the "old self" as having been "stripped off." The "circumcision of the heart" that Moses called for and that Paul identified as marking the new covenant people of God has been definitively accomplished in our union with Christ. This is "Christ's circumcision" (possessive genitive),[53] and it fully provides for that subduing of the "flesh" for which the false teachers were advocating elaborate and strenuous rules.

12 At the beginning of v. 11, Paul claims that it is "in Christ" that we are "circumcised" by having our sinful impulse "stripped off." In vv. 12-15 Paul elaborates this "in Christ." Christians have participated "with" Christ in his burial and resurrection (v. 12), bringing us new life in him (v. 13) by virtue of having our sins forgiven (vv. 13b-15). The "with Christ" language that Paul uses here is the tip of an important Pauline theological iceberg.[54] As Romans 5 and 1 Corinthians 15 in particular reveal, Paul views Christ, as he does Adam, as a "corporate" figure. As all people were somehow included "in Adam" when he sinned and brought death into the world, so all people (or all Christians) were "in Christ"

51. The fact that these phrases both occur in contexts in which Paul is discussing the effects of baptism on our new life in Christ is suggestive. Note also that Paul uses the fairly rare expressions "old self" (ὁ παλαιός [ἡμῶν] ἄνθρωπος) in both Rom. 6:6 and in Col. 3:9 and that it is in the latter passage that we find the verbal cognate to the word ἀπέκδυσις ("stripping off") in v. 11.

52. The Greek word is ἀπέκδυσις, a word that does not appear elsewhere before its occurrence here. The cognate verb in 2:15 and 3:9 is ἀπεκδύομαι (for which see the notes on 2:15).

53. For the possessive genitive, see Harris, 102; Abbott, 251; Wright, 105; Masson, 126.

54. See, e.g., Pokorný, 126-28, who points especially to Romans 6.

when he died, was buried, and was raised to new life. By being identified with Christ in these key redemptive events, Christians experience in themselves the "change of eras" that God in Christ has brought to pass. No longer are we dominated by those "powers" of the old era, sin, death, and the flesh; we are now ruled by righteousness, life, grace, and the Spirit (see esp. Rom. 5:12–8:17; 12:1-2; Gal. 1:4; 5:14–6:2).

To be sure, Paul says nothing explicitly about this "change of realms" in Colossians (though cf. 1:13; 3:9-11), but this basic redemptive story undoubtedly lies behind and informs the language of these verses. Similarly, we hear little or nothing about some of the key "powers" that are prominent elsewhere in Paul, for example, grace or the Spirit. The reason, of course, is that Paul is deploying his typical redemptive-historical theology to counter the false teaching in Colossae, false teaching that appeared above all to be insisting on adherence to ascetic-oriented rules as a means of conquering the fleshly impulse, appeasing the hostile powers, and thereby securing final forgiveness for sins. All these, Paul insists, are provided the believer "in Christ." The importance of the theology in this verse is evident from the way in which it serves as the basis for Paul's negative and positive argument with reference to the false teaching in the following sections. In 2:20, Paul appeals to the fact that we have "died with Christ" (an idea implicit in v. 12a) as the basis for resisting the false teaching. And in 3:1, he appeals to our having been raised with Christ as the ground for the transformed attitude and lifestyle of the believer.

Verse 12 is connected to v. 11 by means of a participle, translated fairly literally in the TNIV: *having been buried with him* (cf. also ESV; NASB).[55] The English construction "having been" might suggest that our burial with Christ takes place before our being circumcised (v. 11). But this is probably not the case. Although the participle is aorist, it is almost certainly indicating a contemporaneous action: it is "when we were buried with Christ" that we were circumcised (see NRSV).[56] As he does in Romans 6:4, Paul "locates" our being buried with Christ "in baptism."[57]

55. The HCSB and NET attach the participle to the following verb, "you were raised." This reading of the syntax seems unlikely in light of the relative clause ἐν ᾧ (which neither version explicitly includes), but it does not materially differ from the interpretation that we are advocating.

56. Harris, indeed, suggests that the participle might connote an action subsequent to our being circumcised. This works especially well if we take the circumcision in v. 11 as equivalent to our having "died" with Christ (p. 103).

57. The manuscripts vary between βαπτίσματι and βαπτισμῷ. The former is the usual word in the NT to depict either John's baptism or Christian baptism; the latter denotes Jewish purification rites in two of its other three NT occurrences (Mark 7:4; Heb. 9:10 [v.l. in Mark 7:8]), while the occurrence in Heb. 6:2 may also refer to these rites, but also probably with some reference to Christian baptism. Because βαπτισμός is less usual

The reference is certainly to water baptism (as opposed, e.g., to "baptism in the Spirit"). Why Paul brings in baptism at this point (as in the generally parallel Rom. 6:3-4) and what theology of baptism it implies are quite debated. As we noted in our comments on v. 11, a good number of commentators hold that it is the reference to circumcision in v. 11 that accounts for the presence of baptismal references here. As circumcision was the old covenant rite by which God's people were brought into relationship with him, so baptism now functions similarly in the new covenant. But this is a misreading of our passage.[58] Paul does not compare baptism with (literal) circumcision; he identifies baptism as the "place" where our spiritual circumcision takes place.

Paul's logic runs like this: you have been spiritually "circumcised." This "circumcision" took place when you were buried with Christ and raised with him. And this burial and resurrection with Christ happened when you were baptized. As this paraphrase of Paul's argument also reveals, the popular explanation that Paul uses baptism as a symbol of our death to the old life (when we are plunged beneath the water) and resurrection to new life (when we arise out of the water) is also wide of the mark. Baptism does not symbolize what happened when we were converted; it somehow is integrally involved in that conversion itself. The best way to account for this and at the same time to do justice to Paul's constant emphasis on our faith as the key to our coming to Christ (as he does at the end of this very verse, as if to guard against a possible misunderstanding) is again to recognize a broadly attested New Testament theological concept dubbed by James Dunn "conversion-initiation." The New Testament connects our coming to Christ (being converted and initiated into the new covenant community) to faith, to repentance, to the gift of the Spirit, and to water baptism, in various combinations. Any of these, in a kind of metonymy, could be used to connote the whole experience — implying, of course, in each instance, the presence of all the others. Water baptism, then, as a critical New Testament rite intimately connected to our conversion experience, could be used as shorthand for the whole experience.[59] But it is also striking that it is just in the two most im-

---

as a reference to Christian baptism (contrast, e.g., the roughly parallel Rom. 6:4), it is generally preferred here as the more difficult reading (e.g., Harris, 103-4; Lightfoot, 184; Bruce, 102; Dunn, 145).

58. Everett Ferguson ("Spiritual Circumcision in Early Christianity," *SJT* 41 [1988], 485-97) notes that early patristic writers compared circumcision with the gift of the Spirit, not with baptism.

59. Paul is bringing baptism into the argument, then, because of the theological tradition that we see also in Romans 6. This makes it most unlikely that, as MacDonald argues, "baptism was at the heart of the conflict at Colossae" (107).

portant Pauline passages about our being buried "with Christ" that baptism is brought into the picture in this way (when it is not frequently referred to elsewhere in Paul in this fashion). This may indeed suggest, additionally, that early Christians associated the waters of baptism with Christ's burial.

We have already tipped our hand on one of the most debated syntactical issues in v. 12: the antecedent of the relative pronoun "which" *(hō)* in the second clause of the verse. The form of this pronoun (it could be either masculine or neuter [relevant if the variant *baptismati* is read]) allows us to translate either "in whom [Christ] you were also raised" or "in which [baptism] you were also raised." The context is not decisive. The nearest antecedent is, of course, "baptism," but the concept of being "in Christ" is also a dominant motif in this paragraph (vv. 9, 10, 11, 15 [?]). Nevertheless, we slightly prefer a reference to baptism, because (1) the combination "you were raised with him in him" is a bit awkward; and (2) it provides a somewhat better explanation for the "also" *(kai):* in addition to being buried with him in baptism, you were *also* raised with him in that same baptism.[60]

As we have seen, Colossians 2:12 has many parallels with Romans 6:3-11. Both texts assert that believers have been "buried with Christ in/through baptism." While Colossians does not explicitly assert that believers have "died with Christ," 2:20 — "if therefore you died with Christ" — shows that Paul thinks it is implicit in what he has said here; and this also has clear parallels in Romans (vv. 5, 8; cf. v. 3). And both Romans and Colossians assert that believers participate with Christ in his resurrection. On this last point, however, there is a difference — one that certain scholars have made a great deal of. In Romans, most scholars insist, our resurrection with Christ is future: "if we have been united with him in a death like his, we *will* certainly also be united with him in a resurrection like his" (v. 5); "Now if we died with Christ, we believe that we *will* also live with him" (v. 8). In Colossians, however, sharing the perspective of Ephesians (2:6), our resurrection with Christ is pictured as a completed event: "you *were* also raised with him" (v. 12); "Since, then, you have been raised with Christ" (3:1).

60. A slight majority of commentators favor this construal (see, e.g., Lightfoot, 185; Harris, 104); and see also Beasley-Murray, *Baptism*, 153-54. Favoring "in Christ" is, among others, O'Brien, 118-19. He notes that Eph. 2:6 uses both "with Christ" and "in Christ" and that in Romans 6 baptism is connected to burial but not to resurrection with Christ. In response to the latter, however, Colossians differs from Romans in speaking explicitly of a past identification with Christ's resurrection; and, on the former, Eph. 2:6 is a bit more complex than Col. 2:12b, making the combination of "with Christ" and "in Christ" there less awkward.

This shift from "future" to "realized" eschatology is often held up as one of the main reasons that Paul could not have written Colossians.[61] However, this objection is groundless, for two reasons. First, Romans 6 is not nearly as future-oriented in its portrayal of our resurrection with Christ as is often implied. Paul clearly asserts a present dimension to our new life in Christ in v. 13, calling Christians "those who have been brought from death to life." The reality of a new life with Christ enjoyed in the present is also implied by the logic of v. 4, in which Christ's resurrection is the basis for our living a new life. It is just this logic, in fact, that leads some scholars to suggest that the future tenses in vv. 5 and 8 are "logical futures," asserting, in effect, a present experience of resurrection with Christ.[62] But even if these futures are genuine temporal futures (as I suspect they are), the point is that Romans 6 plainly teaches an "already–not yet" dimension to our participation with Christ in his new resurrection life. Second, then, a focus on the "already" side of our new life with Christ, such as we find in Colossians and Ephesians, is a small step for Paul to take — and a natural step in light of the false teaching that he is opposing. For it is the definitive experience of new life in and with Christ that counteracts the false teachers' insistence that a Christian must go on to add something to his or her experience in order to attain spiritual fullness and find liberation from the "powers."[63]

Having said that our resurrection "with Christ" takes place "in baptism," Paul now adds that it also takes place *through your faith*.[64] This addition reminds us that baptism, while important in its own right as a natural component of "conversion-initiation," has no power apart from faith. The balance of Scripture must be respected at this point: faith is highlighted repeatedly as the critical, necessary, and sufficient (when properly defined) human response to God's converting grace. Paul usually uses the word "faith" absolutely, without an object (as in Col. 1:23 and 2:7).[65] His decision here to specify *the working of God, who raised him*

61. See, e.g., H. E. Lona, *Eschatologie im Kolosser- und Epheserbrief* (Wurzburg: Echter, 1984), esp. 155-62; Wolter, 132-33; Lohse, 103-4.

62. Dübbers, *Christologie und Existenz*, 244-46; N. T. Wright, *The Resurrection of the Son of God* (London: SPCK, 2003), 251-52.

63. See, on the consonance of Colossians' eschatology with Paul's, Lincoln, *Paradise Now and Not Yet*, 131-34; Sappington, *Revelation*, 225-28; Barth/Blanke, 458-61; and, on the application of the "realized eschatology" to the false teaching, Arnold, *Colossian Syncretism*, 300-302.

64. The possessive "your" in the English translations reflects, appropriately, the article before "faith" (τῆς πίστεως).

65. Paul uses the noun πίστις over a hundred times without an object. Some of these, of course, come in constructions where an object would be awkward; but the overall tendency remains quite striking. God is the object of πίστις only once in Paul (1 Thess. 1:8),

from the dead, as the object of our faith requires explanation, especially since this is the only place where Paul specifies "working" *(energeia)* as the object of "faith."[66] One of the reasons for the inclusion of the reference to God's working is that it provides a natural lead-in to the reference to God's raising of Jesus from the dead. And this reference, of course, supports Paul's claim that we have been raised "with Christ." In addition, however, it also signals, as the resurrection often does in Paul, the arrival of a new age (e.g., Rom. 1:4; Gal. 1:1), a new era in which sin and the powers no longer hold sway.[67] However, as Romans 4:24 reveals, Paul could have simply said here that our faith is in "the God who raised Jesus our Lord from the dead." The emphasis on God's "working" probably has the false teaching in mind, Paul reminding us that our being raised with Christ provides all the power we need to conquer the sinful impulse.

13 The new sentence in the TNIV appropriately represents a break in the syntax of the passage.[68] A *kai* ("and," not translated in the TNIV) connects the verse with what comes before, but the subject changes from "you" in vv. 11-12 to "he" in v. 13. Moreover, Paul places the object of the main verb "he made alive" at the beginning of the verse, followed by a long participial clause modifying that object: "you, being dead, . . . he made alive." Indeed, so long is the modifier that Paul repeats the object pronoun immediately after the verb. The ESV captures the flow of the syntax very well, though I have added the word in brackets to reflect the repetition of the object: "And you, who were dead in your trespasses and the uncircumcision of your flesh, God made [you] alive together with him." As in 1:22-23, where Paul uses a similar syntactical structure to accentuate our reconciliation, he highlights the significance of our being made alive with Christ by "fronting" the condition from which that new

---

while Christ is the object fourteen times (I include in my count verses such as Rom. 3:22, 26; Gal. 2:16; 3:23, where the significance of the genitive is debated — they are probably objective in each case). Christ is the object of πίστις in Col. 1:4 and 2:5. The verb πιστεύω, which occurs less often than the cognate noun in Paul, has as its object God (four times), Christ (four times), and the "message" (once).

66. We are assuming that τῆς ἐνεργείας is an objective genitive, along with the English translations and the vast majority of commentaries. The idea that it could be a subjective genitive — "faith produced by the working of God" (Harold H. Buls, "Luther's Translation of Colossians 2:12," CTQ 45 [1981], 13-16; Barth/Blanke, 324) — is not at all likely. While Eph. 1:19 adds κατὰ ἐνεργείαν immediately after τοὺς πιστεύοντας, the former almost certainly modifies τὸ ὑπερβάλλον μέγεθος τῆς δυνάμεως earlier in the verse: "his surpassingly great power for us who believe, the power that is according to his working . . ." (so most English versions).

67. See, e.g., Wright, 108.

68. Some think this break may signal the beginning of a "baptism liturgy" that Paul quotes in vv. 13-15 (K. Wengst, *Christologische Formeln und Lieder des Urchristentums* [Gütersloh: Gütersloher Verlag, 1973], 186-94).

life arose. Paul sums up his teaching in vv. 11-12 about being circumcised "in Christ" and having been buried and resurrected with him with the broader claim about new life.[69]

And as an appropriate foil to this new life, Paul describes our previous state as one of death. This "death," in the sense that Paul uses the word here, refers especially to condemnation, a present state that afflicts all humans in their natural state because of Adam's "original" sin (Rom. 5:12, 18-19). Physical death is included only in the sense that the pain and loss that now accompany death are the outcome of spiritual death. The association of death and sin is, of course, a basic teaching of Scripture, from the creation story onward. So it is natural for Paul to attribute the Colossians' original state of death to "your sins and the uncircumcision of your sinful nature." Most English versions are content to render the preposition that Paul uses here (en) straightforwardly as "in." But, in fact, this may be one of those places where the usual locative or instrumental sense of en is stretched into a causal sense: we are dead "because of our sins" (NLT; NJB; REB).[70] The word for "sins" is paraptōmasin, sometimes translated "trespasses" (e.g., ESV; HCSB) or "transgressions" (e.g., NASB; NET). This word originally had the sense "false step," and Paul uses it in several texts to refer to human sinning.[71] It is doubtful, however, whether the word here has any different sense than the more usual hamartia (Col. 1:14).[72] In the closely parallel Ephesians 2:1, 5, both terms occur: "As for you, you were dead in your transgressions (paraptōmasin) and sins (hamartiais), . . . [God] made us alive with Christ even when we were dead in transgressions (paraptōmasin)."

In distinction from this text in Ephesians, however, Paul in Colossians adds that his readers were at one time dead also because of "the uncircumcision of your sinful nature." "Uncircumcision" translates a word (akrobystia) that means, basically, "foreskin," but that came to be used among Jews, by a natural extension, of people who possessed their foreskins, that is, who were uncircumcised — in a word, "Gentiles."[73] "Sinful nature" is the TNIV rendering of sarx, often translated "flesh." So

69. See Pokorný, 134.
70. Harris, 106; O'Brien, 122; Lightfoot, 186; Lohse, 107.
71. It occurs only in this verse in Colossians; in Paul, see Rom. 4:25; 5:15, 16, 17, 18, 20; 11:11, 12; 2 Cor. 5:19; Gal. 6:1; Eph. 1:7; 2:1, 5; and, in the NT, Matt. 6:14, 15; Mark 11:25.
72. E.g., Lohse, 107; contra M. Wolter, EDNT 3.33.
73. The basic sense of the word is evident in the consistent LXX usage (e.g., Exod. 4:25: "But Zipporah took a flint knife, cut off her son's foreskin (τὴν ἀκροβυστίαν) and touched Moses' feet with it"). The word is mainly Pauline in the NT (nineteen of twenty occurrences).

the whole expression "uncircumcision of your flesh" would naturally suggest that the Colossian Christians were Gentiles. As Paul puts it in another text in Ephesians, Gentiles are "called 'uncircumcised' (*akrobystia*) by those who call themselves 'the circumcision' (which is done in the body by human hands)" (2:11). In light of this Ephesians text in particular, then, some interpreters think that the phrase here in Colossians hints strongly at the mainly Jewish flavor of the false teaching.[74] However, without denying that there is some reference here to the Colossians' ethnic identity (and cf. Col. 3:11), the real point of the phrase lies elsewhere. In v. 11, as we have seen, *sarx* refers to the sinful impulse that dominates the body of the non-Christian, which body is stripped off in the circumcision accomplished by Christ. This makes it likely that *sarx* here also has primarily a metaphorical rather than a physical meaning.[75] And this, in turn, makes it likely that the phrase "uncircumcision of your flesh" as a whole has a primarily metaphorical sense in this context, ruled by the bold language that Paul has used in v. 11. "Uncircumcised flesh" is the condition that "Christ's circumcision" removes, the condition of having "flesh" — the sinful impulse or "sinful nature" — that has not yet been stripped off. Paul thus attributes spiritual "deadness" both to "the actual definite transgressions" and to "the impure carnal disposition which prompts to them."[76]

In the TNIV, the last clause of v. 13 begins a new sentence: *He forgave us all our sins.* This decision makes perfectly good sense in terms of English style (which does not like a long string of subordinate verbs), but the verb *forgave* actually translates a participle that is connected to the verb *God made you alive with Christ.* Most of the versions that translate the verb with a participle suggest that it designates an action that precedes the "making alive" (e.g., "having forgiven" in ESV; contrast NRSV, "when he forgave").[77] This may make good sense here (on logical, not grammatical grounds[78]), with the participle denoting the basis for being "made alive": "God made us alive with Christ because he forgave us all our sins."[79] But Paul may not intend so specific a relationship between the two, perhaps

74. E.g., Dunn, 163.
75. So, e.g., Lohse, 107; Wolter, 134-35.
76. Lightfoot, 186.
77. So also Abbott, 254.
78. Aorist participles (like χαρισάμενος here) can, of course, indicate action antecedent to the verb they modify (though more often doing so when they precede the verb — cf. S. E. Porter, *Verbal Aspect in the Greek of the New Testament* [New York: Lang, 1989], 383-84), but the aorist tense in itself tells us nothing about the temporal relationship (contra, e.g., Eadie, 161).
79. See, e.g., O'Brien, 123.

intending simply to indicate that forgiveness is bound up with our being made alive with Christ. Paul uses the same word for "sins" *(paraptōmata)* that he used earlier in the verse, and he shifts the person of the pronoun from second person to first person — "God made *you* alive with Christ. He forgave *us* all our sins."[80] This shift in pronoun, along with the occurrence of some unusual words in the next two verses, has led a number of commentators to suppose that Paul is quoting a tradition, or at least using traditional language.[81] The latter is possible,[82] but it must also be said that some of the distinctive language is quite Pauline in character,[83] and Paul often shifts the person of his pronouns in mid-sentence.

14 The forgiveness that we enjoy in Christ is total: *"all our sins"* are forgiven (v. 13). The completeness and definitiveness of our forgiveness are the theme of v. 14, which Paul presents via two striking word pictures. Paul's first word picture portrays a document that all human beings have signed, an "IOU," in which we pledge complete allegiance to God. Our sins stand as conclusive evidence that we have failed to give God that allegiance, and so that document is "against us" and "condemns" us. But God has taken that document and wiped it clean; indeed, he has taken it completely out of the picture. He has, in fact, in a second word picture that both highlights the completeness of the removal and the means by which it was accomplished, "nailed it to the cross." The third stanza of Horatio Spafford's hymn "It Is Well with My Soul" beautifully captures the point of the verse:

My sin, oh, the bliss of this glorious thought!
My sin, not in part but the whole,
Is nailed to the cross, and I bear it no more,
Praise the Lord, praise the Lord, O my soul!

The TNIV rightly connects the opening of v. 14 with the last clause of v. 13: "He forgave . . . having cancelled. . . ." As in v. 13, the participle *(exaleipsas)*, again in the aorist tense, could denote action that occurs before and is perhaps the basis for the forgiveness (as the TNIV may sug-

80. To be sure, a few manuscripts have the second-person pronoun (ὑμῖν) here as well, but the reading is clearly a secondary assimilation to the earlier pronoun.

81. See, e.g., Gerhard Schille, *Frühchristliche Hymnen* (2d ed.; Berlin: Evangelische Verlagsanstalt, 1965), 31-37 (who sees all of vv. 9-15 as a baptismal liturgy); Wengst, *Christologische Formeln*, 181-89; G. E. Cannon, *The Use of Traditional Material in Colossians* (Macon, Ga.: Mercer University Press, 1983), 44-47; Lohse, 106.

82. Pokorný, 135-36.

83. E.g., ἀπεκδυσάμενος (only here and in Col. 3:10 in the NT; cf. also ἀπεκδύσις in v. 11); θριαμβεύσας (only elsewhere in the NT in 2 Cor. 2:14); δόγμασιν (cf. Eph. 2:15); αἱρέω ἐκ [τοῦ] μέσου (1 Cor. 5:2).

gest), but it could also be contemporaneous and describe the means by which forgiveness was attained (cf. ESV: "by cancelling . . ."). The verb has the primary meaning "cause to disappear by wiping," seen, for example, in Revelation 7:17 and 21:4, where John predicts that "God will *wipe away* every tear from their eyes." But, by extension, the word could also simply mean "remove," "cause to disappear," as, for instance, in Genesis 7:4, where God promises "to wipe from [LXX, *exaleipsō*] the face of the earth every living creature that I have made." Sins could be the object of this removal (Isa. 43:25; Acts 3:19), and this could fit our context. But the object of the verb here is not sins but a document, so the more pertinent parallels are those in ancient Greek documents where the word is used to denote the "blotting out" of a written record (cf. Rev. 3:5).[84] Hence the English versions variously translate "cancel" (TNIV; ESV; NLT; NASB; REB); "obliterate" (NAB); "erase" (NRSV; HCSB); "destroy" (NET).

What is wiped out is, according to the TNIV, *the charge of our legal indebtedness*. Two Greek words whose meaning is hotly contested are included in this rendering: *cheirographon* and [*tois*] *dogmasin*. The standard meaning of the former word is "certificate of indebtedness," a document recording debts that one is obliged to pay, what we would call an "IOU." The word is not used elsewhere in biblical Greek, but its meaning is well illustrated in *Testament of Job* 11:11, where Job responds to the pleas of debtors by "bringing before them the note and read it granting cancellation as the crowning feature" (cf. also Tob. 5:3; 9:2, 5). Various suggestions for a more specific identification of this "IOU" have been proposed. The most popular view in the early church was that the reference was to a document "signed" by Adam (and/or by all humans) and held over us by Satan. Other interpreters note that the word was occasionally used to refer to the widespread Jewish concept of a manuscript recording human deeds that is brought out as a basis for judgment in the heavenly court.[85] And still others think that the word may refer to the Mosaic law,[86] viewed by Paul as a record of human obligation that has not been met. But, as Hay points out, this last view fits a bit awkwardly with the basic sense of

84. According to MM, the word was used to denote the "washing out" of a piece of papyrus so that it could be used again.

85. See esp. the (Jewish) *Apocalypse of Zephaniah* 3:6-9 and the (Christian) *Apocalypse of Paul* 17. For the general idea, see also Rev. 20:12. See, e.g., Dunn, 164-65; Lincoln, *Paradise Now and Not Yet*, 113-14; idem, 625; Sappington, *Revelation*, 214-17. Bandstra (*Law and the Elements of the World*, 158-63), building on Oliva A. Blanchette ("Does the Cheirographon of Col 2:14 Represent Christ Himself?" *CBQ* 23 [1961], 306-12), takes this idea further, suggesting that Christ himself becomes this "indictment" by taking on himself our sin.

86. Abbott, 255; Wright, 111-12; O'Brien, 125 (Mosaic law for Jews, conscience for Gentiles).

the word, since, of course, an IOU is written not by the one to whom the obligation is due (God, the author of the law), but by the one who is in debt (human beings).[87] And, on the whole, there is insufficient evidence to give to the word any nuance beyond its general well-attested meaning of "IOU." As Moule succinctly puts the idea, "'I owe God obedience to his will. Signed, mankind.'"[88]

The second Greek word behind the TNIV's *charge of our legal indebtedness* is [*tois*] *dogmasin*, "the decrees." This word is used in the LXX and New Testament to refer to decrees issued by kings (e.g., the "decree" of Caesar Augustus that all the world should be taxed; Luke 2:1). Since the word has so general a nuance, many interpreters think that it refers here to the "decrees" that the false teachers were imposing on converts, a view that could receive support from the fact that the verb cognate to *dogma*, *dogmatizō*, is used with such a reference in 2:20.[89] But it is hard to see how these clearly illegitimate decrees could feature in any way in the objective state of indebtedness that required Christ's sacrifice on the cross to erase. Another view, popular especially among the Greek fathers, was that the "decrees" are the "teachings" of the gospel. On this view, the form of the Greek word (a dative case) is tied to the verb "cancel" in an instrumental relationship: "having cancelled the charge of indebtedness by means of the [gospel] teachings."[90] But the plural "decrees" would be an unprecedented (and unusual) way of referring to the gospel.

A more likely interpretation arises from comparison with Ephesians 2:15, the only other place where the word occurs in Paul. Here Paul uses it to describe the commandments of the Mosaic law as consisting in "decrees." Colossians, of course, lacks any reference to the Mosaic law, but it would be typical of Paul's theology of the law to extend the word to include all those "decrees" of God that regulate human conduct, whether found in the law of Moses or more generally in God's revelation to all human beings.[91] Dunn usefully refers to Romans 1:32 in this regard, where Paul sums up his indictment of human beings in general by saying that, "Although they know God's righteous decree that those who do such things deserve death, they not only continue to do these very things but also approve of those who practice them."[92] On this view, the word "de-

87. Hay, 97.

88. Moule, 97.

89. Schweizer, 145-46; Ernst, 204-5; Pokorný, 138-39; Lincoln, *Paradise Now and Not Yet*, 114.

90. See Lightfoot, 188, for the evidence from the Greek fathers.

91. E.g., Lightfoot, 187; Luz, 223.

92. Dunn, 165. It should be noted that the Greek word for "decree" in Rom. 1:32 (δικαίωμα) is not the same as the one in Col. 2:14.

crees" could elucidate the "charge of indebtedness" (cheirographon): "the charge of indebtedness that consists in decrees."[93] But this implies a closer identification between the "charge sheet" and the decrees than we think likely.

A preferable interpretation, then, is to view the "decrees" as explaining the reason why the "IOU" was "against us."[94] All we humans had, as it were, "signed" an IOU promising God perfect obedience, and this document has come to stand against us "because" of God's "decrees" that we have failed to keep. Paul emphasizes the negative verdict of the IOU by stating it twice: it *stood against us* and *condemned us* (more literally, "was opposed to us").[95]

In the Greek text, a *kai* ("and," "now") breaks the flow of Paul's syntax in the middle of v. 14. TNIV represents the break with a semicolon (cf. also RSV; NASB NJB; REB); other versions start a new sentence here (ESV; NLT; NET).[96] The basic flow of vv. 13-14, then, runs as follows: "God has made alive with Christ us who were dead by forgiving our sins, in that he has cancelled the IOU; in fact, God removed this IOU from the situation by nailing it to the cross." Both the syntax and the wording of this last clause lend it emphasis. "Removed from the situation" is my translation of a Greek idiom that has the sense "take out of the midst";[97] in this context, it may highlight the fact that the IOU has no more bearing on our "case." It is by "nailing it to the cross" that the IOU has been decisively removed from having any power over us. The imagery probably has nothing to do with any ancient means of canceling debts[98] but arises from the actual nature of Christ's crucifixion.[99] In causing him to be

93. Harris, 108-9; Wilson, 209; Lincoln, *Paradise Now and Not Yet*, 114. In *NewDocs* 1.110-11, it is noted that the χειρόγραφον was generally a private document; so the "decrees" could be the means by which it is made public. See also J. Luttenberger, "Der gekreuzigte Schuldschein: Ein Aspekt der Deutung des Todes Jesu im Kolosserbrief," *NTS* 51 (2005), 80-95, who cites papyrus texts that speak of δόγματα as the content of the χειρόγραφον.

94. O'Brien, 125; Lohse, 109; Barth/Blanke, 329-30.

95. Harris surmises that the second phrase extends the former by emphasizing the "active hostility" of the IOU (p. 108).

96. This καί makes it unlikely that the participle ἐξαλείψας ("having cancelled") at the beginning of the verse modifies the verb ἦρκεν ("he has taken") (contra HCSB; NAB).

97. The combination of the verb αἴρω and ἐκ [τοῦ] μέσου occurs elsewhere in Paul only in 1 Cor. 5:2, where he demands the removal of a notorious sinner "from the midst" of the Corinthian congregation. The same prepositional phrase, with different verbs, occurs in Matt. 13:49; Acts 17:33; 23:10; 2 Cor. 6:17; 2 Thess. 2:7.

98. Contra Adolf Deissmann, *Light from the Ancient East* (New York: Doran, 1927), 332, who thought that the allusion may have been to the custom of canceling a bond by crossing it out with the Greek letter χ.

99. Cf. John 20:25, which refers to the "marks" on Jesus' hands made by the nails.

nailed to the cross, God (the subject of the verb) has provided for the full cancellation of the debt of obedience that we had incurred. Christ took upon himself the penalty that we were under because of our disobedience, and his death fully satisfied God's necessary demand for due punishment of that disobedience.

15 With this verse, Paul brings to a conclusion his explanation of how we have been brought to "fullness" in Christ (v. 10). In a reflection of a key concern in Colossians, the verse ends as the section began, with a focus on the "powers and authorities."[100] In v. 10, Paul asserted simply that Christ is the "head" of those spiritual powers. Now he shows how that headship has been expressed, as God, through the cross of Christ, has won a victory over the rebellious powers. To some extent, then, vv. 10 and 15 complement one another in the same way as do the earlier verses where the spiritual powers featured, 1:16 and 20.[101] As the former verse establishes Christ's supremacy over the powers by virtue of creation, so the latter expresses the activity by which God through the cross of Christ has "pacified" those powers. In both texts a rebellion against God's rule on the part of at least many of these spiritual beings is assumed.[102]

The TNIV translation of the opening clause of the verse — *And having disarmed the powers and authorities* — is essentially reproduced in almost all the other major English versions. But this unanimity is misleading, for the interpretation of the clause is difficult and disputed. The problem is the verb that Paul uses: *apekdyomai*. This rare verb (it is not attested anywhere before Colossians) means "strip off," "take off [clothes]," and occurs again in 3:9, where it refers to believers' "stripping off" "the old self" (the cognate noun, as we have seen, occurs in 2:11). The form in which the verb occurs here (the middle voice) would normally convey a reflexive idea — "he stripped off from himself the powers and authorities"— and this seems certainly to be the meaning in 3:9 (e.g., believers have stripped off from themselves the old self).[103]

It should be no surprise, therefore, that many interpreters have tried to make sense of what Paul says here by adopting this usual meaning of

100. Arnold, *Colossian Syncretism*, 275.
101. It is unfortunate (and somewhat perplexing) that the TNIV translates ἀρχαί as "powers" here in 2:10 and 15 but as "rulers" in 1:16.
102. We are assuming, with the majority of interpreters, that the "rulers and authorities" in 2:15 are implicitly viewed as hostile to God and humanity, contra W. Carr (*Angels and Principalities* [Cambridge and New York: Cambridge University Press, 2005], 61-63) and R. Yates ("Colossians 2:15: Christ Triumphant," *NTS* 37 [1991], 573-91), who argue that they are good angels who accompany and praise Christ in his triumphal procession.
103. All the biblical Greek occurrences of the simpler form of this verb, ἐκδύω, in the middle voice have this sense of "take one's own clothes off."

the verb. The early fathers were virtually unanimous in adopting this meaning, making Christ the subject of the verb and either (1) making "the powers and authorities" the object — "Christ divested himself of the powers and authorities" — or (2) making an understood "flesh" the object of the verb, with "powers and authorities" being taken as the object of the following verb; hence, "he divested himself of the flesh and made a public spectacle of the powers and authorities." J. A. T. Robinson has adopted the latter view,[104] while Lightfoot, in his classic commentary, adopted the former. Lightfoot's interpretation, the more likely of the two, is rooted in the recognition that Christ, as fully human, was subject to the influence of these malignant spiritual beings. At the cross, however, the victory over these beings was accomplished; in the oft-quoted words of Lightfoot, "The powers of evil, which had clung like a Nessus robe about His humanity, were torn off and cast aside for ever."[105]

Despite the fact that this line of interpretation has a strong lexical and grammatical basis, there are reasons why most English versions and commentators instead think that the verb here has an active sense, "he stripped [clothes] from the powers and authorities," and hence, as an extension of meaning, "he disarmed the powers and authorities."[106] First, the interpretations of the Greek and Latin fathers require that "Christ" be the subject of the verb. But, as universally agreed, the subject of the verb "he made alive with [Christ]" in v. 13 is God, and there has been no indication of a change of subject since then.[107] Second, the concept of Christ being enveloped by "flesh" or by the "powers" depends to some extent on applying the somewhat similar language of v. 11, "stripping off the body of flesh," to Christ. But we have seen that this is unlikely. Third, the lexical and grammatical evidence is not nearly as favorable to the "Christ stripped himself" interpretation as is sometimes suggested.

A key factor that is not always given due recognition is the personal object that follows the verb here.[108] When the related verb *ekdyō* is followed by a personal object in biblical Greek, the idea is always that

104. J. A. T. Robinson, *The Body: A Study in Pauline Theology* [SBT 5; London: SCM, 1952), 41.

105. Lightfoot, 190; cf. also Moule, 101-2. The reference to the robe of Nessus comes from Greek mythology. Nessus was a centaur whose blood-soaked garment, mixed with poison, was wrapped about Heracles, thereby causing his death.

106. Good defenses of this view can be found in, e.g., O'Brien, 127; Lohse, 111-12.

107. Lightfoot thinks that the subject shifts to "Christ" in v. 14b (p. 189).

108. This consideration does not, of course, apply to those, like the Latin fathers and Robinson, who take the participle ἀπεκδυσάμενος absolutely (with τὰς ἀρχὰς καὶ τὰς ἐξουσίας the object of ἐδειγμάτισεν). But an absolute use of the verb is quite unlikely.

"someone stripped clothes off someone else."[109] Matthew 27:28 is a good example: "They [the soldiers] stripped *(ekdysantes)* him and put a scarlet robe on him [Christ]." To be sure, the verbs in all these cases are active. But we have no example of a middle of this verb followed by a personal object, and it is well known that middle forms in biblical Greek are often used equivalently to active forms.[110] There is, then, some objective basis on which to argue that the occurrence of the verb here should be translated slightly differently than the occurrence in 3:9 (where the object is not personal).[111]

These reasons, we think, combine to make the interpretation adopted in most of our English versions the most likely option. To be sure, we have no example of this verb or its simpler form *ekdyō*, meaning "disarm." But in all three places where Paul uses the word-group *apekdy-* in Colossians, the basic sense of "taking off [clothes]" has the extended metaphorical sense of "strip of power." Christians strip off the body of flesh in conversion and are thus freed from its power (2:11). Christians likewise strip off the "old self" and are freed from its controlling influence (3:9). So God in Christ has "stripped" the rulers and authorities of their power.

God's victory over the powers did not remain a private matter: "having disarmed" them, God *make a public spectacle of them*. The verb has the sense "expose publicly" (cf. the only other New Testament occurrence, Matt. 1:19, where Joseph chooses to divorce Mary quietly rather than "expose her to public disgrace").[112] This idea of public display is strongly accentuated with the participle *thriambeusas*, which alludes to the Roman custom of awarding victorious generals a "victory parade." Behind the general as he rode in splendor through the city would follow, in chains, prisoners from the successful campaign just concluded. It is this activity of "leading in triumphal procession" that the verb refers to, as its one other occurrence in the New Testament reveals. In 2 Corinthians 2:14, Paul compares his service to Christ with being "led as captives

---

109. Gen. 37:23; 1 Sam. 31:9; 1 Chr. 10:9; Ezek. 16:39; 23:26; Hos. 2:5 (2:3); 2 Macc. 8:27; Matt. 27:28, 31; Mark 15:20; Luke 10:30.

110. E.g., BDF §316 (1); Turner, *Syntax*, 55; Zerwick, *Biblical Greek* §235 (they all specifically mention Col. 2:15).

111. Contra, e.g., A. T. Lincoln and A. J. M. Wedderburn, *The Theology of the Later Pauline Letters* (Cambridge: Cambridge University Press, 1993), 45, who object to translating such a rare verb in two different ways within the space of a chapter.

112. In the Greek text the verb ἐδειγμάτισεν ("expose publicly") is qualified by a prepositional phrase: ἐν παρρησίᾳ. The phrase is clearly adverbial, but it is difficult to know whether it introduces a slightly different idea — "expose publicly in a bold way" (e.g., Lightfoot, 191; Harris, 111) — or simply reinforces the idea inherent in the verb — "expose publicly in a public way" (e.g., BDAG).

in Christ's triumphal procession." Our English versions, then, in translating "triumphing" or "triumphed" (so, e.g., TNIV; ESV; NASB; HCSB), do not quite capture the nuance of public display contained in this verb. Paul is pulling out all the stops to make as clear as he can that God has removed any claim that the spiritual powers might have over us, and that he has done so clearly and publicly.

But just what does Paul have in mind by this public display of victory over the powers? The answer to this question hinges partly on how we translate the last phrase in v. 15. The antecedent of the pronoun that Paul uses in this phrase — en autō — could be either the "cross" (TNIV; NRSV; NET; NAB)[113] or "Christ" (ESV; NLT; HCSB; NASB).[114] The former is certainly the closest explicit antecedent (end of v. 14), and Paul has explicitly referred to the cross in a passage that has some parallels with this one, 1:20. On the other hand, of course, God's work on our behalf "in" and "with" Christ has been a leitmotif of this whole passage. A decision between the two is very tough, but we are inclined slightly to think that Christ might be the antecedent. If this is so, it means, in turn, that the display of God's triumph over the powers may refer not to the cross (as most assume) but to the resurrection and ascension of Christ.[115] Certainly this latter reference fits well with other New Testament texts. In Ephesians, for instance, Paul asserts that God raised Christ from the dead and seated him in the heavenlies "far above all rule and authority, power and dominion" (1:20-21). In Romans 1:3-4, Paul claims that Christ was "marked out" as "Son-of-God-in-power" through the resurrection. Peter in his Day-of-Pentecost speech similarly argues that it is the resurrection that demonstrates the reality of God's presence in and with Christ (Acts 2:32-36). And, in what many (including myself) think the most likely interpretation of 1 Peter 3:19-22, it is when Christ goes into heaven to the right hand of the Father (v. 22) that Christ "proclaims" his victory over evil spiritual beings (v. 19). This pattern suggests that we might have a temporal progression in v. 15: it was on the cross (v. 14b) that God "disarmed" the rulers and authorities, but it was in Christ's resurrection and ascension that God put on public display the reality of that victory over the powers.[116]

Paul seems to imply in the sequence of vv. 14-15 a relationship between the forgiveness of our sins and the disarming of the powers. In what has been called the "classic" view of the atonement, the connection

113. So, e.g., Lightfoot, 192; Moule, 102.
114. So most commentators; e.g., O'Brien, 128; Dunn, 145; Wright, 114.
115. See also Arnold, *Colossian Syncretism*, 286.
116. The aorist tense of the opening participle, ἀπεκδυσάμενος, is certainly conducive to, though by no means conclusive of, such a temporal pattern.

between these is seen in the power that Satan and his minions hold over human beings because of their sin. God pays the debt that we all owe to Satan because of sin in the provision of Christ. Without adopting the questionable concept that God had to "buy off" Satan in some sense, we may find some basis for this understanding of Christ's death in our passage. We can imagine the false teachers in Colossae, feeding on a widespread ancient fear of various celestial spirits, insisting that believers needed to follow their own rules-oriented procedure for finding freedom from the power of these spirits. In response, Paul insists that God, by sending Christ to the cross as the final and definitive means to take care of the sin problem, has removed any power that these evil spirits might have over us. This victory, celebrated and displayed in the resurrection and ascension of Christ, is what believers need to grasp as their own. Christ's authority over the rulers and authorities (v. 10) has been decisively manifested; and "in him" believers share that authority.

2. The Empty Promise of the False Teaching (2:16-23)

[16]*Therefore do not let anyone judge you by what you eat or drink, or with regard to a religious festival, a New Moon celebration or a Sabbath day.* [17]*These are a shadow of the things that were to come; the reality, however, is found in Christ.* [18]*Do not let anyone who delights in false humility and the worship of angels disqualify you. Such people also go into great detail about what they have seen, and their unspiritual minds puff them up with idle notions.* [19]*They have lost connection with the head, from whom the whole body, supported and held together by its ligaments and sinews, grows as God causes it to grow.*

[20]*Since you died with Christ to the elemental spiritual forces of this world, why, as though you still belonged to the world, do you submit to its rules:* [21]*"Do not handle! Do not taste! Do not touch!"?* [22]*These rules, which have to do with things that are all destined to perish with use, are based on merely human commands and teachings.* [23]*Such regulations indeed have an appearance of wisdom, with their self-imposed worship, their false humility and their harsh treatment of the body, but they lack any value in restraining sensual indulgence.*

In v. 8, Paul brings his central concern in writing to the Colossians to clear expression: "See to it that no one takes you captive through hollow and deceptive philosophy, which depends on human tradition and the elemental spiritual forces of this world rather than on Christ." In vv. 9-15, he elaborates "on Christ," setting forth the alternative to the false teaching: the fullness of spiritual experience to be found "in Christ," in whom all of

God's fullness dwells. Now, in vv. 16-23, he turns to the false teaching itself, developing each of the points he made briefly in v. 8.[117] The central
point of v. 8, an exhortation not to follow the false teaching, is also the
heart of vv. 16-23, expressed twice, in v. 16 — "do not let anyone judge
you" — and v. 18 — "Do not let anyone . . . disqualify you." In v. 8 Paul
justifies his warning in two ways: positively, by characterizing the teaching as human in orientation and based on "the elements of the world"
and, negatively, by asserting that the teaching is not based "on Christ." So
also in vv. 16-23, the false teaching is characterized as being "based on
merely human commands and teachings" (v. 22) and (indirectly) as having to do with "the elements of the world" (v. 20, my trans.), and the
teachers themselves are criticized for not "holding onto the head
[Christ]" (v. 19, my trans.).

The rest of the paragraph is an elaboration of these key points, as
Paul goes into some detail about both the false teachers themselves and
about their teachings. They are worshiping angels and bragging about visions they claim to have received (v. 18). They teach that Christians
should avoid certain kinds of food, observe special days (v. 16; cf. v. 21),
and, in general, apparently, follow an ascetic lifestyle (v. 23). Along the
way Paul again touches briefly on the positive antidote to this false teaching, which is, as we might expect by this time, resolutely christological.
Christ is the "substance" of which the various rules and celebrations
these teachers advocate are the "shadow" (v. 17); he is the "head" of the
body, the source of all true spiritual nourishment for the members of the
body (v. 19); and "with Christ" believers have died to the "elemental spiritual forces" and so need pay no more attention to the demands of these
forces (v. 20). The section divides into two paragraphs, marked formally
by the conditional clause in v. 20 — "since you died with Christ" — and
materially by a renewed focus on the "rules" that seem to have been a
key element in the false teachers' "philosophy."

This paragraph gives us the only really specific explicit information
about the false teaching in Colossae. Unfortunately, while explicit, the information Paul provides is not always clear. Interpreters differ significantly on the interpretation of some of the things that Paul says about the
teachers and thereby reach quite different conclusions about the overall
shape of the teaching (see the Introduction, 46-60). One conclusion that
seems justified is that Paul was particularly concerned about the false

117. Some interpreters, noting the parallelism between "dying with Christ" in v. 20
and being raised with him in 3:1, prefer to think of 2:16–3:4 as an integral section (e.g.,
Dübbers, *Christologie und Existenz*, 262-64). Despite the parallel, however, it is better to
see 3:1 as beginning a fresh section (see the notes on 3:1-11). Others (e.g., Gnilka, 155) put
a major break in the letter between 2:19 and 2:20.

teachers' imposition of certain rules about bodily discipline. He touches on this matter in v. 16 and then, significantly, returns to it and develops it in vv. 20-23. Some commentators think that Paul's failure to address the false teachers directly shows that they were not part of the Christian community.[118] But Paul's claim that the teachers have "lost connection with the head" (v. 19) suggests otherwise.[119]

Particularly significant for our overall perspective on the teaching, and thus on Paul's response to it, is the degree to which the false teaching was Jewish in orientation. The fact that the teachers were advocating the observance of religious festivals, New Moon celebrations, and — especially — the Sabbath day (v. 16) shows that the teaching was to some extent Jewish. Some recent interpreters, moving out from this sure ground, therefore advocate an interpretation of virtually all the other disputed references in Jewish terms. On this view, then, the false teaching was essentially, or even totally, Jewish. The more traditional view, however — which still finds many advocates — is that the false teaching was syncretistic, with Jewish and pagan elements given different proportions in the "mix" by different interpreters. As we will argue with respect to some of the detailed references below, we believe this latter view is closer to the truth (see also the Introduction, 46-60).

16 The *therefore* at the beginning of v. 16 connects the theology about "fullness in Christ" in vv. 10-15 with Paul's exhortation to resist the false teachers in this verse and following. Because it is in Christ that you have spiritual fullness, Paul is saying, do not let anyone impose upon you a program of spiritual development that does not have Christ at its heart. Turning to specifics, Paul begins by warning the Colossians: *Do not let anyone judge you by what you eat or drink, or with regard to a religious festival, a New Moon celebration or a Sabbath day.* Paul's use of the singular *anyone (tis)* might indicate that he has a particular prominent false teacher in view.[120] However the singular is more likely simply generic (see our comments on v. 8). *Judge*, like its Greek equivalent *(krinō)*, can have a neutral — "he judged that it was time to go" — or negative connotation — "she judged him for his false conduct." The word here is clearly negative, paralleled by being "taken captive" in v. 8 and being "disqualified" in v. 18. The latter parallel in particular could suggest that Paul means not just that the false teachers were "criticizing" the Colossian Christians (cf. NJB and REB) but that they were pronouncing God's judgment on them.[121]

118. E.g., Wolter, 140.
119. Luz, 218.
120. E.g., Abbott, 263; O'Brien, 138; Dunn, 171.
121. See Wright, 119, who thinks that the false teachers (from a Jewish viewpoint) were excluding the (Gentile) Colossian Christians from the people of God.

The latter idea might find support from a passage that has many parallels with vv. 16-23, Romans 14:1–15:7. Paul there chastises the "strong in faith" for "judging" their brothers and sisters, noting that it is before God's judgment seat that all must eventually stand (14:10). This passage implies that some Christians were taking upon themselves the role of judge that only God can exercise (see also Jas. 4:11-12). Perhaps the rendering "pass judgment" (RSV; ESV; NAB) best captures the sense.

Paul enumerates two sets of issues on the basis of which the false teachers are "passing judgment": food and drink, and the observance of special religious days. These are also just the matters dividing the "strong" and the "weak" in the Roman community (Rom. 14:2, 5). And in both passages, there is considerable debate about the source of such regulations. While Paul does not directly say so here, his reference to "rules" such as "do not handle" and "do not taste" (vv. 20-21) make it clear that the false teachers were advocating abstinence from some kinds of food and drink. Similarly, it is virtually certain that the teachers were advocating (rather than, e.g., criticizing) observance of special days.[122] Our text gives no information about just what foods or kinds of drink were being prohibited. (In Romans 14–15, the "weak" were avoiding meat [14:2] and perhaps also wine [14:21].) The Old Testament law, of course, prohibits the eating of certain food deemed "unclean," but it does not generally prohibit any kind of drinking.[123] However, both the Old Testament and Judaism reveal that many Jews living in Gentile environments chose to abstain from all meat and wine in order to avoid possible ritual contamination.[124] This is probably the rationale for the prohibitions in Romans 14–15, and, with explicit allusion to Jewish festivals later in this verse, it is natural to think that it is the same here. And the "shadow"/"reality" comparison of v. 17 also points to a probable contrast between Old Testament and New. Nevertheless, what is missing in Colossians, in comparison with Romans, is any direct reference to the Mosaic law or to divisions between Jews and Gentiles. These omissions are especially significant in light of the fact that Paul explicitly mentions just these matters in some

122. Contra, e.g., D. R. de Lacey, "The Sabbath/Sunday Question and the Law in the Pauline Corpus," in *From Sabbath to Lord's Day: A Biblical, Historical and Theological Investigation* (ed. D. A. Carson; Grand Rapids: Zondervan, 1982), 182.

123. The law prohibits drinking only on certain specific occasions: the people are not to drink contaminated water (Lev. 11:34-36); the priests are not to drink wine when entering the tent of meeting (cf. Lev. 10:9); and those who take a Nazirite vow are to drink no wine for the period of their vow (Num. 6:1-3). The Rechabites (Jer. 35:1-19) also abstained from wine.

124. See esp. Dan. 1:8; 10:3; also Tob. 1:10-12; Jdt. 12:2, 19; Add. Esth. 14:17; *Jos. and As.* 7:1; 8:5; Josephus, *The Life* 14; *m. 'Abot* 3:3.

passages in Ephesians that are closely parallel to ones in Colossians (cf. esp. Col. 1:24-29 with Eph. 3:1-13 and 2:14-15 with Eph. 2:11-22). We should therefore at least keep open the possibility that the Colossian false teachers' abstinence from food and drink had its origins elsewhere, since many ancient Greco-Roman philosophical and religious traditions also featured prohibitions of meat and wine.[125]

An Old Testament/Jewish derivation for the false teachers' insistence on keeping certain religious "days" is much more likely.[126] The threefold *religious festival (heortē)*, *New Moon celebration (neomēnia)*, and *Sabbath day (sabbatōn)*[127] is common in the Old Testament (e.g., 1 Chr. 23:31; 2 Chr. 2:3; 31:3; Ezek. 45:17; Hos. 2:13);[128] and "Sabbath," while occasionally observed by Gentiles, is, of course, a distinctly Jewish phenomenon. In the Old Testament, "festivals" include both the annual "pilgrimage" festivals (Passover/Unleavened Bread; Booths, or Tabernacles; and Weeks/Firstfruits) and other special times of community observance.[129] But the New Testament elsewhere uses the word to refer to the annual pilgrimage festivals, so that is probably the referent here also.[130]

Although there is, then, universal agreement that the false teachers' insistence on observance of days was influenced by Judaism, dispute remains over the degree and nature of that influence. Some interpreters think that the false teachers were representing what we might call a "mainstream" Jewish viewpoint.[131] Noting the importance of the observance of special days in the Dead Sea Scrolls, others have thought that a "sectarian" Jewish viewpoint such as found at Qumran might be the background.[132] Most interpreters, however, persist in thinking that the false

125. See esp. Lohse, 115, for examples.

126. *With regard to* in the TNIV translates ἐν μέρει, "in the matter of," "in connection with." Harris theorizes that Paul might have introduced the phrase to avoid a succession of five datives (119). It is perhaps more likely, however, that Paul simply wanted to divide the five issues into two natural groupings.

127. The plural form here (σαββάτων) is regularly used in a singular sense, reflecting the underlying Aramaic, שַׁבְּתָא.

128. As Lightfoot (193-94) notes, the three terms here correspond to the first three (placed in different order) that Paul enumerates in Gal. 4:10: ἡμέρας ("days" = Sabbaths), μῆνας ("months" = New Moon celebrations), καιρούς ("seasons" = "festivals"). The order in Galatians moves from more to less frequent (the last of the list is "years"), while that in Colossians moves from least to most frequent.

129. The LXX uses ἑορτή to translate both חַג, which usually refers to the pilgrimage festivals, and מוֹעֵד, a more general term for any kind of festal gathering.

130. The word ἑορτή occurs elsewhere in the NT only in the Gospel narratives. It is especially prominent in John, since the evangelist organizes his life of Jesus to some extent around trips to Jerusalem to observe the major festivals. See, e.g., Lightfoot, 194.

131. See esp. Dunn, 172-73; Wright, 118-20.

132. E.g., Abbott, 263.

teachers had integrated the observance of Jewish special days into a larger syncretistic system. As Lohse, a good representative of the view, puts it, "The 'philosophy' made use of terms which stemmed from Jewish tradition, but which had been transformed in the crucible of syncretism to be subject to the service of 'the elements of the universe.'"[133] A decision among these options is difficult, although influence from Qumran, since the community observed a solar-based calendar, might be unlikely.[134] The Old Testament–derived language, the "shadow"/"reality" comparison of v. 17, and allusions elsewhere in the passage to Jesus' teaching on ritual cleanness (see v. 22) certainly favor a strong Jewish element in the false teaching. Moreover, Lohse's claim that the false teachers observed these days "in service of 'the elements of the universe'" is an inference, not a sure conclusion (despite the fact that it is repeated in many commentaries). It presumes, perhaps, a definition of these "elements" in terms of "astral spirits" that we have questioned (see v. 8), and it does not necessarily distance the teaching from Judaism, since Paul brings the Jewish law and the "elements" together in Galatians 4 (vv. 3, 9). On the other hand, as we have noted, specific references to the law and Judaism, such as we might have expected had the false teaching been purely (or even mainly) Jewish, are lacking in our text. Furthermore, v. 18 suggests practices that are more likely to stem from broader religious traditions in the region of Colossae. On the whole, then, it seems best to view the practices in v. 16 as basically Jewish in origin and perhaps even orientation while still recognizing that they have been taken up into a larger mix of religious ideas and practices.

One implication of this larger discussion for the application of our passage is the continuing role of Sabbath observance within the Christian church. A casual reading of this verse would suggest that Sabbath observance is treated as entirely optional: one must not judge another Christian over it. But a number of interpreters argue that this kind of reading fails to reckon with the context in which the Sabbath is being observed in our passage. Only Sabbath observance that is connected inappropriately to a wider religious viewpoint is here being condemned.[135] These interpreters are quite right to emphasize the importance of interpreting contextually and historically. And they are also right, we have suggested, to argue that Sabbath was taken up into a larger, syncretistic mix.

133. Lohse, 116; see also, e.g., Lightfoot, 192-93; O'Brien, 139; Gnilka, 146; Lincoln, 631; Wilson, 216-17, 218-19.

134. Bruce, 115.

135. While he is not explicit about the matter, O'Brien's comments tend in this direction (p. 139). See, more explicitly, Samuele Bacchiocchi, *From Sabbath to Sunday: A Historical Investigation of the Rise of Sunday Observance in Early Christianity* (Rome: The Pontifical Gregorian University Press, 1977), 343-64.

But there is still reason to think that Paul calls into question here Sabbath observance per se. The language and logic of v. 17 suggest that the primary problem with Sabbath observance was a failure to reckon with the "fulfillment" of such institutions in the new era of salvation. As Lincoln puts it, "That Paul without any qualification can relegate Sabbaths to shadows certainly indicates that he does not see them as binding and makes it extremely unlikely that he could have seen the Christian first day as a continuation of the Sabbath."[136] In a way similar, then, to Romans 14:5, Colossians 2:16 can validly be used, we think, to conclude that the observance of a Sabbath day is no longer a requirement of God's people in the new realm.[137]

17 Paul does not explicitly connect v. 17 to v. 16 (there is no conjunction in Greek). Thus TNIV, along with most versions, has a new sentence begin in this verse. But the logical relationship between the two verses is clear enough: it is wrong for anyone to pass judgment on someone else over the matters mentioned in v. 16, *because* these matters are only the "shadow" of the reality that Christians now find in Christ.[138] The pronoun *these* (translating the Greek relative pronoun *ha*) refers to the prohibitions of food and drink and the observances of special days in v. 16. In referring to them (collectively) as *a shadow,* Paul taps into a popular Hellenistic image with its roots in Greek philosophical speculation. Plato had famously used the contrast of "shadow" and "substance," or "reality" to compare the material realities to their corresponding "ideals."[139] The distinction was taken up in a variety of ways in Hellenistic thinking. The comparison was usually between "shadow" *(skia)* and "form" or "image" *(eikōn),* but it could also be expressed, as Paul does here, as a contrast between "shadow" and "substance" *(sōma).* A good example of the general contrast, utilizing just these terms, is found in the Jewish philosopher Philo, who spoke of the "letter" of the Old Testament as the "shadow," while his own allegorical interpretations were the "substance," the "higher values . . . [that] really and truly exist" (*On the Confusion of Tongues* 190). In Hellenistic philosophy, the contrast of "shadow"/ "substance" was often, as in the Philo text, a contrast between appearance and reality.

---

136. A. T. Lincoln, "From Sabbath to Lord's Day: A Biblical and Theological Perspective," in *From Sabbath to Lord's Day,* 368.

137. See esp. on this whole matter, *From Sabbath to Lord's Day.*

138. Hence the NLT's "for" at the beginning of v. 17 is quite justified on contextual grounds.

139. The most famous example of the imagery comes in the allegory of the cave in *The Republic* 514A-520A, which Plato uses to contrast true reality (or "the good") with the shadows that most people see.

But Paul, like the author to the Hebrews, who applies the same contrast in a similar way (Heb. 10:1), uses popular language to convey a historically oriented contrast between one era and another. He signals this orientation with the phrase *that were to come*, which refers to those realities that have now come in Christ but were still to come from the perspective of the original institutions.[140] According to the fundamental salvation-historical perspective of the New Testament writers, the Old Testament, and especially the law, belonged to the time of promise, to the time when God was preparing his people and the world for salvation in Christ. With the coming of Christ, the new era of fulfillment has dawned. The old era and the law have now been brought to their "culmination" (Rom. 10:4). Believers who belong to the new era through their incorporation into Christ therefore experience the reality to which the Old Testament and its law pointed. And they are no longer compelled to follow the laws of that earlier era. The Colossian Christians should not let anyone insist on their observing the rules and ceremonies of the earlier era that has now passed. As we noted in our comments on v. 16, then, Paul's use of this particular imagery makes clear that he views the "things" of v. 16 as having positive value. This makes sense if the rules about eating and observance of days are based on the Old Testament law, but it would be most unusual for Paul to accord such a stature to rules derived from pagan religion.

As we noted above, ancient writers typically used the word "form" in contrast to "shadow." Paul, however, chooses to use the word *sōma*. This word can be translated "reality" or "substance," but, of course, more often is translated "body." And since Paul uses this word in Colossians to refer to Christ's own body (1:22) and to the "body" of the church (1:18, 24; 2:19; 3:15), it is often thought that he has chosen to use this particular word to convey a theological point, namely, that the "substance" to which the shadow pointed is the Christian church. "The reality which exists solely with Christ is shared only by those who, as members of the body of Christ, adhere to the head."[141] NJB tries to capture the dual meaning by translating *sōma* twice: "the reality is the body of Christ." Lending some support to this interpretation is the particular phraseology

---

140. *That were to come* translates a Greek phrase, τῶν μελλόντων, that could also be translated "what is to come" (RSV; NRSV; NASB; cf. ESV; NET; NAB; TEV). This translation most naturally suggests that the "things" of which Paul here speaks were still to come from the perspective of Paul and his readers. But the context makes this interpretation unlikely (see, e.g., O'Brien, 140; Gnilka, 47); the translation of TNIV (see also NIV; HCSB; NJB; REB) is to be preferred.

141. Lohse, 117; cf. also Gnilka, 148; Moule, 103; Masson 131; Luz, 224; Wright, 120-21; Dunn, 177; Pokorný, 144-45; MacDonald, 111; Thompson, 65.

that Paul has used. He does not straightforwardly say that "the substance *is* Christ" but that "the substance is *of Christ* or *belongs to Christ*" (see ESV; NASB).[142] Certainly Paul draws attention to the "body" of Christ, the church, in this context (v. 19). On the other hand, as we have seen, *sōma* was sometimes contrasted with "shadow," and we should respect the general linguistic principle that discourages double meanings unless the context makes it pretty clear. The context here is suggestive but not decisive. We conclude, then, that an allusion to the church is possible but not clearly established.[143]

18 This verse furnishes the most important evidence about the false teaching, but it is also arguably the most difficult verse in Colossians to interpret. The beginning and the end of the verse are clear enough. As he did in v. 16, Paul again urges the Colossians not to let *anyone* stand in judgment over them. The translation *disqualify* in the TNIV (and also ESV; NRSV; HCSB; REB; NAB) reflects the use of certain forms of the Greek word used here to refer to the negative verdict of an umpire in an athletic contest.[144] But the evidence for this particular nuance of the word group in Paul's day is not overly strong; the basic verb seemed most often simply to mean "judge" (see Col. 3:15). Therefore it is likely that the stronger form of the verb here means "judge against," for example, "condemn" (NLT; cf. NET).[145]

The bulk of the verse is made up of three descriptions of the false teachers. The last one is clear enough: *their unspiritual minds puff them up with idle notions.* "Puff up" translates a verb that occurs elsewhere in the New Testament only in 1 Corinthians (4:6, 18, 19; 5:2; 8:1; 13:4). Its basic meaning, "blow up, inflate" (as one might blow up a bellows), suits it beautifully to express the idea of arrogance. The arrogance of the false teachers expressed itself in their arrogating to themselves the right to stand in judgment over others. Such arrogance, Paul asserts, has no basis in the facts: it is "without reason" (ESV),[146] and it originates in their *un-*

142. That is, rather than saying τὸ δὲ σῶμα ἐστιν ὁ Χριστός, Paul writes τὸ δὲ σῶμα τοῦ Χριστοῦ. Schweizer conjectures that "Christ" was originally in the nominative (157-58), but there is no evidence for this.

143. Sharing our skepticism about a double reference are O'Brien, 141; and Ernest Best, *One Body in Christ* (London: SPCK, 1955), 121-22.

144. See, e.g., Lightfoot, 195; Harris, 120. The Greek verb in this verse is κατα-βραβεύω, which is found only here in biblical Greek and is very rare elsewhere. The simple form of the verb, βραβεύω, occurs in Col. 3:15 and Wis. 10:12 and fairly often in Philo (13 occurrences) and Josephus (14 occurrences).

145. So, e.g., Abbott, 266; Bruce, 117; O'Brien, 141.

146. Gk. εἰκῇ, which modifies the verb φυσιούμενος that follows. TNIV apparently takes the word as an associative dative, expressing the form in which the false teachers' arrogance expresses itself: "with idle notions."

spiritual minds. "Unspiritual" translates *sarx* (often "flesh"), which Paul uses here in his typical fashion to refer to that which belongs to this world and which therefore often fails to take into consideration the truth of the "spiritual" realm.[147] It is possible that these false teachers — as false teachers often do — were taking on intellectual airs, priding themselves on their superior "minds." Paul's characterization would then be directly polemical: they have minds, alright, but minds that are thoroughly oriented to this world rather than to the next.[148]

Paul says two other things about these people who arrogantly claim to stand in judgment over others: they *delight[s] in false humility and the worship of angels* and they *go into great detail about what they have seen.*[149] The verb translated in TNIV as "delight in" (see also NASB; NET; NAB) can also be translated "insist on" (e.g., ESV; NLT; HCSB). The latter has in its favor a slightly more natural connection with the main verb: "Don't let anyone condemn you by insisting that you. . . ."[150] However, the lexical evidence for the verb (*thelō*, "will," "wish") favors the TNIV rendering.[151] The meaning "delight in" for this verb reflects a Hebrew phrase that has this sense: for example, "the king has delight in you" (1 Sam. 18:22, ESV).[152] Paul does not then say that the false teachers are trying to force the Colossians to adopt the practices he refers to here (although it may be implied). He simply describes what it is that the false teachers themselves are delighting in.

The first of these is *false humility*, the TNIV interpretive rendering of

147. Dunn, however, thinks that σάρξ here, in keeping with the general usage of the word in Colossians, has a more neutral/physical connotation (185).

148. Lightfoot, 198.

149. In the Greek text, Paul qualifies μηδείς, "no one," with three parallel adjectival participles: θέλων ("delighting [in]"), ἐμβατεύων ("going into" or "entering"), and φυσιούμενος ("puffed up"). All three are singular. The TNIV retains the singular of the first in translation. But in order to avoid reading a "masculine" identity into the false teachers that the grammatically masculine forms in the verse do not clearly convey, the TNIV puts the second two descriptions of the false teachers in a separate sentence, and translates the singular verbs as plurals. If, as we have argued, Paul uses "no one" generically, this shift of number does not change the sense of the passage.

150. See, e.g., Harris, 121, who thinks that the participle is modal: the false teacher condemns "by insisting on. . . ."

151. Lightfoot, 195-96; Moule, 104; Dunn, 178; and esp. Percy, *Die Probleme der Kolosser- und Epheserbriefe*, 145-47. Others, not convinced that Paul would use so strong a "Hebraism," try to interpret the phrase with the usual sense of the word, "will," "wish," sometimes connecting the word to what precedes; e.g., the false teachers condemn others "by their own will," "willfully" (Dibelius/Greeven, 34; cf. Abbott, 267).

152. The Greek is θέλων ἐν, which represents the Heb. ‏חָפֵץ בְּ‎. Forms of θέλω or θέλημα plus ἐν translate this Hebrew (or equivalents) in 1 Sam. 18:22; 2 Sam. 15:26; 1 Kgs. 10:9; Pss. 16:3; 18:20; 147[146]:10; Eccl. 5:3; Mal. 1:10.

a word in Greek that means simply "humility." The New Testament generally speaks positively of this virtue (e.g., Col. 3:12), but it is clear in this context that Paul does not think the false teachers' interest in "humility" is a good thing. The TNIV rendering *false humility* suggests that the problem is attitudinal: the false teachers, like Uriah Heep in *David Copperfield*, pretend to a humility that they don't really feel. Another option, however, is that the word connotes ascetic practices, especially fasting (cf. ESV, "asceticism"; HCSB, "ascetic practices"; and NASB, "self-abasement"). Several texts connect "humility" with fasting,[153] and Paul has just referred to the false teachers' concern with what they eat and drink (v. 16). Moreover, Paul may refer to the false teachers' interest in visionary experiences later in the verse *(what they have seen)*, and fasting was often encouraged as a means of preparing for visions.[154] A direct reference to fasting per se is probably too specific, since there is no evidence that the word Paul uses here (or its cognates) could, by itself, refer to fasting. But the context (see v. 23) does suggest that the word refers in general to ascetic practices that the false teachers may have used to prepare themselves for or to stimulate visionary experiences.

The second thing in which the false teachers take delight is *the worship of angels*. This English rendering most naturally suggests that the false teachers were involved in worshiping angels; and this has been the traditional understanding of the phrase.[155] But the phrase could also mean (in Greek, perhaps, more easily than in English) "worship that the angels are offering," and this view of the passage has gained considerable popularity in recent years.[156] According to this interpretation, the false teachers are seeking to join with the angels in the worship of God. Such a

153. See, e.g., Ps. 35:13; Isa. 58:3; Jdt. 4:9; Hermas, *Visions* 3.10.6; *Similitudes* 5.3.7.

154. See, e.g., Dan. 10:1-5. This interpretation was given wide exposure by F. O. Francis as a part of his larger interpretation of the Colossian false teaching (see "Humility and Angelic Worship in Col 2:18," in *Conflict at Colossae* [Missoula: Scholars Press, 1973], 167-71). He has been followed by a significant number of recent interpreters (e.g., O'Brien, 142; Lincoln, *Paradise Now and Not Yet*, 111; Dunn, 178). The reference to "humility" again in v. 23 makes it unlikely that the ascetic practices are being ascribed to the angels (on the assumption that the following phrase refers to worship that angels are engaging in; cf. Sappington, *Revelation*, 159-61).

155. On this view, the genitive τῶν ἀγγέλων after θρησκείᾳ is objective. The NLT, NJB, and REB make this interpretation explicit. This interpretation was assumed without argument in the classic commentaries of Lightfoot and Abbott.

156. This interpretation takes τῶν ἀγγέλων as a subjective genitive. See esp. Francis, "Humility and Angelic Worship"; and also O'Brien, 142-43; Lincoln, *Paradise Now and Not Yet*, 112; Barth/Blanke, 345; Dunn, 180-81; Sappington, *Revelation*, 158-59; Craig A. Evans, "The Colossian Mystics," *Bib* 63 (1982), 197-201; William L. Lane, "Creed and Theology: Reflections on Colossians," *JETS* 21 (1978), 216-18; Smith, *Heavenly Perspective*, 122-27.

participation with angels in the worship of God in heaven features in many Jewish mystical and apocalyptic writings. This interpretation, it is argued, fits well into the context, which seems to focus on visionary experience.

However, the more traditional interpretation should probably be preferred.[157] First, from a purely linguistic point of view, the phrase is more likely to mean "worship offered to angels" than "worship offered by angels."[158] Second, while many Jewish apocalyptic texts refer to angelic worship, and some refer to humans observing or imitating that worship, very few speak of humans joining with angels in such worship.[159] It is questionable, in other words, whether the simple (and very ambiguous) phrase "worship of angels" would have been capable of connoting such a relatively rare concept. Third, as we have noted, a key concern of Colossians has been to accentuate the superiority of Christ over spiritual beings (1:16, 20; 2:10, 15). Such a concern to minimize the significance of the angels would make very good sense if, indeed, the false teachers were worshiping them. Fourth, Clinton Arnold has suggested a plausible background for Paul's accusation that the false teachers were worshiping angels. He notes the importance of invoking angels as a means to ward off evil in the ancient world in general and the geographic region of Colossae in particular.[160] Paul would be characterizing this calling on angels for protection as tantamount to the worship of angels.[161]

Debate about the precise shape of the false teaching continues as we come to the final description of the false teachers in this verse (the second participle in the series): *Such people go into great detail about what they have seen.* The TNIV translation reflects an interpretation adopted by most of

157. See, e.g., Harris, 121; Lohse, 118-19; Gnilka, 149-50; Wolter, 146; R. P. Martin, 93-94.

158. See esp. Arnold, who does not find any clear case of a subjective genitive following θρησκεία (*Colossian Syncretism*, 90-93).

159. A number of the texts often cited for this idea refer to humans using angelic "speech" in praising God (e.g., *T. Job* 48–50) or of humans being in the presence of God with angels (*1 En.* 71:11-12), or of humans praying with angels (*Apoc. Zeph.* 8:2-4) or of humans in congregation with angels (e.g., 1QH 3:20-22 and other DSS references). But the actual concept of humans worshiping God with angels seems to be present only in *Apoc. Ab.* 17 (see v. 3) (1st-2d cent. AD); *3 En.* 1:9-12 (5th-6th cent. A.D.); *Mart. Ascen. Isa.* 8:17; 9:28-33 (2nd cent. A.D. [?]). For these texts, see Francis, "Humility and Angelic Worship," 176; Sappington, *Revelation*, 91-94; cf. also Dunn, 180-81.

160. *Colossian Syncretism*, 61-101.

161. On this view, the "worship of angels" would be Paul's polemical description of what the false teachers were doing (see Arnold, *Colossian Syncretism*, 95; Masson, 133-34; Percy, *Probleme der Kolosser- und Epheserbriefe*, 169; Wright, 121-22; Wolter, 160-61). For the other view, that the phrase reflects the false teachers' own language, see, e.g., O'Brien, 141-42; Lohse, 117-18.

the other English versions. It takes the verb "go into" *(embateuō)* in a metaphorical sense, "go into detail about" (see ESV), and construes *ha heoraken* as a relative clause dependent on it, "which things he/she has seen."[162] This latter phrase is then taken to refer to "things seen" in a vision. On this view, the false teachers are "hung up on" the visions that they have been receiving, relating them endlessly to anyone who would listen and perhaps bragging about them as well (see the end of v. 18).

But there are two important alternatives to this view.[163] The first rests on a technical meaning of the verb "enter" *(embateuō)*. There is evidence that this word was associated with "entry" into the sanctuary where the very popular mystery religions were celebrated. Visions were often associated with the experience of the worshiper in these sanctuaries. So the whole phrase could mean "which things he/she has seen when entering [the sanctuary]": that is, the false teachers have had visions of ascetic practices and angel worship when they participated in the mystery rites.[164] But there are two problems with this view. The first is whether we have enough evidence to think that Paul would be using the verb "enter" in such a specific way.[165] The other problem is whether it makes sense to see ascetic practices and angel worship as the object of vi-

162. In the Greek phrase ἃ ἑόρακεν ἐμβατεύων, then, this view construes the relative pronoun ἃ as the object of ἑόρακεν and assumes that its antecedent is implicit in the verb. The Greek verb ἐμβατεύω is rare, found only here in the NT and only seven times in the LXX, where it means "enter and take possession" (of the land; Josh. 19:49, 51), "enter militarily," e.g., "invade" (1 Macc. 12:25; 13:20; 14:31; 15:40), and "go into" in the sense of our "going into" a matter (2 Macc. 2:30: "To enter into questions and examine them thoroughly from all sides is the task of the professional historian" [NAB]). The last meaning is the one adopted on this view.

163. Indeed, the text is so difficult that as sober an exegete as Lightfoot suggested that it be emended (pp. 196-97; cf. also Percy, *Die Probleme der Kolosser- und Epheserbriefe*, 173-74). Scribes also apparently had difficulty with the text, adding a negative (either μή [many MSS] or οὐ [a few MSS]) before the indicative verb ἑόρακεν: "going into things which he/she had *not* seen." While certainly secondary, these additions do suggest that the early scribes were interpreting ἐμβατεύων in the sense of "investigate."

164. See esp. M. Dibelius, "Isis Initiation," in *Conflict at Colossae*, 61-121 (original date 1917); also Bruce, 120-21; Lohse, 119-20; Gnilka, 151; Pokorný, 146-47. Advocates of this view take the relative pronoun ἃ as referring back to the items earlier in the verse. Arnold's view (*Colossian Syncretism*, 121-24) is difficult to classify. He asserts that ἃ ἑόρακεν must be the object of ἐμβατεύων (with view one), but also thinks that ἐμβατεύων describes entry into the sanctuary (with Dibelius).

165. The idea that the word ἐμβατεύω was a technical term from the mysteries was argued by William Ramsay (*The Teaching of Paul in Terms of the Present Day* [London: Hodder & Stoughton, 1913], 286-305) and Dibelius, "Isis Initiation." The data have been much debated since, but Arnold appears at least to have established the possibility that the term could have had such a technical meaning in Colossians (*Colossian Syncretism*, 107-20).

sions. The second alternative view at least partially answers both of these objections. It takes "enter" to mean "enter into heaven" (in a vision) and "which things he/she has seen" to refer especially to visions of the angels' "humility", and worship.[166] But this view also has its problems. The plural relative pronoun (*ha*; "what") implies that Paul must be referring both to angelic worship and to "[ascetic] humility"; but it is difficult to see how the ascetic practices preceding a vision could be the object of the vision itself. And, second, of course, we have argued against taking "worship of angels" to mean worship conducted by the angels. On the whole, then, and in spite of relatively sparse support from recent commentators,[167] we are inclined to follow the interpretation represented in most of the translations: the false teachers, Paul claims, are recounting in great detail the things they have seen in their visions.

To summarize this difficult verse, then, we find Paul to be asserting four things about the false teachers: (1) they put a great deal of stock in ascetic practices, perhaps to induce visions; (2) they are so concerned with calling on angels as a means of protection from evil forces that they are virtually worshiping them; (3) they focus on visions they have experienced, perhaps citing the content of those visions in their teaching; and (4) they display, perhaps because of their boasting about visions, an arrogance that reveals a worldly orientation. Placing a label on the general viewpoint that encompasses these characteristics is impossible, partly because our information is so tantalizingly unspecific and partly because there were so many possible religious currents and crosscurrents in the Colossian context. Perhaps the best option, however, is the kind of folk religion that Arnold presents in his important monograph: a syncretistic mix that draws from various religious sources in the environment of Colossae (including, certainly, Judaism).

19 As we noted in the introduction to this paragraph, vv. 16-23 elaborate the basic points Paul made about the false teachers in v. 8. Structural similarities between that verse and vv. 18-19 are particularly close. In both texts Paul's main point is a warning not to succumb to the false teachers' program: "See to it that no one takes you captive"; "Do not let anyone . . . disqualify you." In both passages Paul justifies this warning by first describing the false teaching/false teachers: it is "a hollow and deceptive philosophy, which depends on human tradition and the elemental spiritual forces of this world"; they pride themselves on ascetic practices and worship angels. And in both texts Paul clinches his case

166. See, e.g., O'Brien, 144-45; Dunn, 183; Wright, 123; Schweizer, 161; Sappington, *Revelation*, 154-58.
167. Although see Harris, 122; Barth/Blanke, 348.

against the false teachers by accusing them of not depending on Christ, "the head" (cf. v. 10).

In the Greek text, vv. 18-19 comprise one sentence, governed by an imperative with four participles: "Let no one disqualify you . . . delighting in . . . going into great detail . . . puffed up . . . not holding onto" (this structure is preserved in NASB and ESV). For ease of reading in English, TNIV has divided this sentence into three, without, however, changing the sense of the text (most English versions do something like this).[168] *They have lost connection with the head* probably implies, as we noted earlier, that the false teaching has arisen from within the larger Christian community.[169] This conclusion is disputed by some, who note that the verb Paul uses here could be translated "grasp," "seize," and that Paul might therefore be criticizing the false teachers for failing to "come to grips" with Christ (note NJB: "such a person has no connection with the Head").[170] But most commentators, as well as the English versions, rightly decide that the verb in this context must mean "hold onto," "adhere to."[171] The false teachers were apparently professing Christians, who, because of their preoccupation with rules and spiritual beings and visions, had lost contact with the only effective source of spiritual growth. Working from a metaphor that Paul has introduced earlier in Colossians (1:18; 2:10), Paul calls Christ *the head* (capitalized in ESV; NJB because it is taken as a title).

As the rest of this verse indicates, the metaphor of the human body governs Paul's imagery here. As we noted in our comments on 1:18, many ancient writers used the analogy of the physical body, and particularly the head-body relationship, applying it to a wide variety of subjects. Since the head was considered to be the animating and directing part of the body, the analogy would usually connote either authority, or empowerment, or both. Christ's authority is the focus in 2:10, but in 1:18 and here probably both the ideas of authority and of "source of provision" are

168. The TNIV (see also REB) also continues in this verse to render the Greek singular participle (κρατῶν) as a plural ("They have lost connection"). Since the plural functions as well as the singular to convey a generic sense, this introduces no change of meaning.

169. Dunn's suggestion (p. 185) that the reference might be to a Jew who should have recognized that his or her "head" was the Messiah is unlikely in light of the distinctly Christian imagery of "head" and "body" in this verse.

170. See, e.g., Wright, 123.

171. The notion of force ("seize," "take") is usually present when the verb κρατέω connotes a taking hold of something that one does not have (see BDAG). In this sense, the verb in the NT can refer to an arrest (e.g., Matt. 14:3; Acts 24:6) or to "taking" someone by the hand to lift them up (e.g., Matt. 9:25). For the sense of the word in our text, BDAG cite Song 3:4: "I held (ἐκράτησα) and would not let him go." See O'Brien, 146.

in view. Christ is the authority to whom the church should look for its rules and commandments and the one who empowers its members to grow spiritually.[172] For it is Christ, our "head," *from whom*[173] *the whole body, supported and held together by its ligaments and sinews, grows as God causes it to grow.* There has been some discussion about the exact denotation of the Greek words translated in TNIV as "ligaments" and "sinews" (note ESV, "joints and ligaments"). In general, however, it appears that both terms referred to the small "bands" or "fasteners" that connected the parts of the body. "Ligaments," the tissue that connects bones to other bones within the joint, and "sinews," the tissue that connects muscles to bones (also "tendons"), are therefore appropriate English renderings.[174] It makes perfect sense, then, for Paul to say that these parts "support" and "hold together" the body. The latter translation is quite appropriate, the word Paul uses suggesting the idea of something being "joined" or "knit" together.[175] The other word that Paul uses *(epichorēgeō)* means "make provision for," "furnish," and many commentators conclude that it must refer to the nourishment supplied by the ligaments and sinews to the body (see ESV; NRSV; HCSB). Of course, this strains to the breaking point the underlying analogy, since ligaments and sinews do not function this way. But writers frequently use such analogies with considerable freedom, so this is not an insuperable problem. Nevertheless, the idea of "support" in the sense of "provide support for the body" is probably within the semantic range of this verb, and should probably be preferred. Note also the parallel text in Ephesians, where Paul uses the cognate noun: "Instead, speaking the truth in love, we will in all things grow up into him who is the head, that is, Christ. From him the whole body, joined and held together by every supporting *(epichorēgias)* ligament, grows and builds itself up in love, as each part does its work."

However we take Paul's language about the ligaments and the sinews, it is probable that he introduces the imagery here to suggest the same point he explicitly makes in the Ephesians text: the body of Christ grows as its members, or parts, support and learn from each other. And,

---

172. See esp. Arnold, "Jesus Christ: 'Head' of the Church," 360.

173. The Greek behind the pronoun "whom" should be feminine, since its antecedent is clearly "head," a feminine noun (κεφαλή). But it is, in fact, masculine (οὖ), reflecting the person (Christ, Χριστός) to whom "head" refers. See, e.g., Wallace, *Syntax*, 338.

174. See Barth/Blanke, 351-52; BDAG. Lightfoot appeals to the ancient physician Galen's writings in an attempt to distinguish the two in terms, respectively, of "contact" and "attachment" (pp. 198-99), but the distinction is not clear enough or widespread enough to read it into this passage.

175. The word is συμβιβάζω, used also in Col. 2:2 (for which see our notes) and Eph. 4:16 in this sense. Elsewhere in the NT (Acts 9:22; 16:10; 19:33; 1 Cor. 2:16) it means "prove" or "instruct."

of course, Paul's more extensive use of the "body"/"members" metaphor in 1 Corinthians 12 significantly develops this point. At the same time, Paul's main point here is not how the members facilitate growth but how the ultimate source of the body's growth is Christ, its head. It is through him that the body *grows as God causes it to grow.*[176] The "growth" Paul has in view here is probably the growth in maturity of the existing "members" of the body rather than the growth of the body by the addition of new members.[177] For it is the matter of how individual believers find spiritual "fullness" that is the precipitating issue in the letter. Identifying both Christ — "from whom" — and God as the source of the body's growth is typical of the way that Paul associates the work of the Father and the Son in his conception of the Christian life.[178]

20 Verse 20 is not explicitly connected with what precedes by means of a conjunction or syntactical dependence. Paul also shifts from the third-person singular imperative that dominates vv. 16-19 — "let no one judge you" (v. 16); "let no one . . . disqualify you" (v. 18) — to direct address in the second-person plural: "Since you died, . . . why . . . do you submit?" These factors suggest that a minor break in the argument occurs at this point. Indeed, some think the break is a major one. Noting the parallel between v. 20 and 3:1 — "you died with Christ"/"you have been raised with Christ" — they argue that v. 20 marks the beginning of the hortatory section of the letter[179] or that 2:20–3:4 constitutes a distinct section in the letter. However, while the relationship between v. 20 and 3:1 is obvious, the continuing focus on the rules that characterize the "philosophy" of the false teachers in vv. 20-23 suggests that these verses are more closely connected with the portrayal of the false teaching in the preceding verses than with what follows. They function as the hortatory climax of Paul's discussion of the false teaching.

The "if" clause, or protasis, in v. 20 reminds us of a key theological point that Paul has made earlier: believers have "died with Christ." To be sure, Paul has not said this in so many words. But his teaching about believers "being buried with" Christ in baptism implies that we have also

---

176. The Gk. is αὔξει τὴν αὔξησιν τοῦ θεοῦ. The accusative αὔξησιν, cognate to the verb, is an accusative of content, while τοῦ θεοῦ is a subjective genitive (Harris, 124); thus: "grows with a growth that is given by God" (ESV; cf. NASB). The TNIV expresses the same idea in more natural English.

177. O'Brien, 148. Dunn (186) thinks that both numerical growth and growth in maturity may be included.

178. Thus there is no need to categorize τοῦ θεοῦ as a qualitative genitive ("a divine type of growth"; cf. REB: "grows according to God's design") to avoid the dual source identification (contra O'Brien, 148).

179. See esp. Gnilka, 155.

died with him (v. 12).[180] Most English versions introduce the conditional clause with the normal conditional indicator, "if." The TNIV rendering, *since*, reflects the fact that conditional clauses in Greek often assume the reality of the condition.[181] That is clearly the case here, but, from a rhetorical standpoint, it is nevertheless better to retain "if" in translation. Paul is not simply stating the fact that we have died with Christ; he is inviting us to consider whether, indeed, we have died with Christ and thus ponder its implications.[182] As we noted in our comments on vv. 12-13, Paul frequently portrays the believer as one who has participated "with" Christ in the great inaugural events of the new covenant era. This "with" must not be reduced simply to a comparison, as if Paul were saying that we died in the same way that Christ did. With the biblical worldview of "corporate solidarity" as his basis, Paul claims that we really did die with Christ, were buried with him, and were raised with him. Just as all humans were appointed by God to be "with" Adam in his sin, so he has appointed all humans (or all believers) to be "with" Christ in the events that reversed and more than canceled the effects of Adam's sin (see esp. Rom. 5:12-21 and cf. Rom. 6:1-6). We enjoy the benefits that Christ has won in his death because of our union with Christ.

But Paul's concern in this verse is not simply to remind us of our death "with Christ," but to indicate the effects of that experience: we have *died with Christ to the elemental spiritual forces of this world*. Most versions follow the TNIV in rendering "died . . . to," but, in fact, the Greek preposition here would usually be rendered "from" (*apo*). By using this preposition, Paul appears to emphasize not just severance, but "the freedom that follows severance."[183] NLT catches the idea with its paraphrase: "You have died with Christ, and he has set you free from the evil powers of this world." NLT's "evil powers of this world" translates the very controversial phrase *ta stoicheia tou kosmou* that we first encountered in v. 8. We argued there that the phrase refers primarily to the basic "components" of the physical universe and, secondarily, to the spiritual forces often thought to be associated with those physical components. TNIV's *ele-*

180. Many interpreters also think that the metaphor of circumcision in v. 11 might refer to Christ's death, with which we are associated.

181. This is especially the case in the so-called "first class" condition, which, as in v. 20, uses the particle εἰ and the aorist or imperfect form of an indicative verb in the protasis.

182. See on this esp. Wallace, *Greek Grammar*, 692, who aptly comments, "To translate εἰ as *since* is to turn an invitation to dialogue into a lecture."

183. Harris, 127. This is the only place where Paul uses the preposition ἀπό (connoting separation — cf. BDF §211) after the verb ἀποθνῄσκω ("die"). When he uses the verb in this sense, he usually follows it with the dative case (see Rom. 6:2, 10; 14:8; Gal. 2:19).

mental spiritual forces of this world captures this secondary sense at the expense of minimizing the primary focus of the phrase. As we noted in our comments on v. 8, NAB — "elemental powers of the world" — and HCSB — "elemental forces of this world" — offer the translations that match most closely our interpretation of the phrase.

As we have mentioned above, the construction in Greek that Paul uses here emphasizes the reality of being set free from the power of these "elemental forces." Many people in Paul's day lived in fear of these "forces" and sought ways to live in harmony with them. The sense of bondage to these powers appears to have been what made the false teachers' program especially seductive. Paul is therefore at pains to show that Christ's victory over the spiritual beings that are included in the "elemental forces" was complete and final (vv. 14-15) and that people who are in union with Christ share in that victory. In this and the following verses it becomes clear that the main "remedy" for appeasement of the "elemental forces" being suggested by the false teachers was a set of rules focusing on an ascetic lifestyle.

Thus, in the "then" clause (the "apodosis") of his conditional sentence, Paul asks *why, as though you still belonged to the world, do you submit to its rules? As though you belonged to the world* is a good contextual rendering of the Greek here, which would more literally be rendered "as living in the world."[184] Clearly Paul does not mean to imply that believers do not continue to live in "the world," whether we define "world" as the physical universe or as the fallen and sin-prone state of existence.[185] His point, rather, is that believers no longer count the world as their true home or as the place that dictates who they are or how they are to live. By dying with Christ, we have been set free from the elements of this world, and we no longer therefore "belong" to the world over which they rule. How foolish, then, to continue to submit to the rules of this world! "Submit to its rules" (which translates the Greek verb *dogmatizesthe*) has the sense "permit yourselves to be put under," "to be dictated to."[186] Paul uses the present tense of the verb to suggest that the readers of the letter

184. The Greek is ὡς ζῶντες ἐν κόσμῳ. The sense of the verb ζάω here is similar to its sense in 3:7: "You used to walk in these ways, when you *lived* (ἐζῆτε) in them" (my trans.).

185. In favor of the latter ("the old way of life"), see, e.g., O'Brien, 149. We incline to the former rendering, mainly because this is the meaning we believe κόσμος has in the preceding phrase ("the elemental forces of the world"). See esp. Schweizer, 165-66.

186. See BDAG, who take the verb — δογματίζεσθε — as a "permissive passive" (see also, e.g., BDF §314; Wallace, *Greek Grammar*, 441; Lightfoot, 202; O'Brien, 149). Abbott, however, takes it as a middle (p. 272) (by form it could be either middle or passive), but the difference in meaning is slight. The verb is fairly rare in biblical Greek, occurring only here in the NT and seven times in the LXX. It is unusual for the verb in the passive to have a personal subject.

were, in fact, in danger of allowing themselves to be "dictated to" by the false teachers.[187]

21 Paul now provides some examples of the rules that the false teachers were trying to impose on the Colossian Christians. It is most unlikely that he is quoting the rules as the false teachers themselves presented them. Rather, as the somewhat sarcastic tone of the staccato listing of those "rules" suggests, Paul is giving us his own interpretive paraphrase of what those rules amounted to. As Augustine puts it, "Sure he used these words in mockery of those by whom he did not want his followers to be deceived and led astray."[188]

The second of these "rules," *Do not taste!*, reflects the issue of "eating and drinking" that Paul introduced as one of the matters on which the false teachers were passing judgment (v. 16). Paul does not mean, of course, that the false teachers were prohibiting all eating and drinking. Rather, they were apparently arguing that living in harmony with the "elemental forces" required abstinence from certain food and drink, perhaps especially the eating of meat and drinking of alcohol. By framing the prohibition with the word "taste" rather than "eat," Paul can include with one word both eating and drinking. But the word choice might also be ironic: "these false teachers run around trying to keep you from even 'tasting'" anything!"

What Paul means by the other two rules he "quotes" is more difficult to determine. First, the difference between the two is not at all clear. The TNIV rendering, *Do not handle! . . . Do not touch!*, is echoed in most of the English versions and reflects the view of a number of commentators that the former verb is stronger than the second.[189] In fact, however, there is little basis in the Greek for any difference at all between the verbs: both mean simply "touch."[190] The "touching" involved here may relate to the issue clearly stated in the second prohibition: people are not even to "touch" certain kinds of food and drink. But there is little basis for think-

187. Hooker, on the other hand, argues that the verb should here be rendered "why submit?" ("Were There False Teachers in Colossae?" in *Christ and Spirit in the New Testament* [Cambridge: Cambridge University Press, 1973], 317-18; cf. also Dunn, 188).

188. Quoted in *ACCS* 11.43 (from Augustine, *Letter* 149.2.23).

189. See, e.g., Lightfoot, 203; Harris, 129. Lightfoot notes that the former verb, ἅπτομαι (middle of ἅπτω), has the etymological sense "take hold of," and he cites a couple of passages where he thinks it is stronger in meaning than the other verb, θιγγάνω.

190. The former, ἅπτομαι ("handle"), is quite common (thirty-eight NT occurrences), while the latter, θιγγάνω ("touch"), is quite rare (three NT occurrences; one LXX). The two do occur together in Exod. 19:12, where no difference in meaning can be discerned: "Put limits for the people around the mountain and tell them, 'Be careful that you do not approach the mountain or touch (θιγεῖν) the foot of it. Whoever touches (ἀψάμενος) the mountain is to be put to death."

ing that either of the verbs for "touch" would refer to food in particular. Others suggest that one or both of the verbs may refer to sex.[191] Paul certainly uses the former to refer to sexual relations in 1 Corinthians 7:1, where he quotes one of the Corinthians' slogans: "'It is good for a man not to have sexual relations ["touch," *haptesthai*] with a woman." However, the verb nowhere else in the New Testament has this meaning. We know it has this meaning in 1 Corinthians 7:1 only because the verb "touch" is followed by the object "woman." Probably, then, both of the prohibitions of touching are Paul's way of mockingly summarizing the general approach to the physical world that the false teachers were taking. Once again, it is unclear just what general philosophy might have given rise to these specific concerns about the physical world. Verse 22, as we will see, clearly alludes to Jesus' teaching about Jewish ritual purity, so it is likely that Old Testament/Jewish rules about defilement arising from eating certain foods or touching certain objects is part of the background.[192] But Paul's claim that the rules involved here are closely related to "the elemental forces," and that they are "worldly" in orientation (v. 20), also suggests that these Jewish-related or -oriented rules have been taken up into a larger and syncretistic religious philosophy.[193]

22 In vv. 22-23 Paul justifies his rejection of the false teachers' rules by making three points: (1) the rules have to do with matters of this world; (2) the rules reflect human and not divine teaching; and (3) the rules cannot bring spiritual transformation. The first two of these points are made in v. 22. The verse begins in Greek with a relative pronoun (*ha*, "which"), which most versions implicitly take to be a reference to the physical matters to which the rules of v. 21 apply; see, for example, NET: "These are all destined to perish with use." This provides the most straightforward rendering of the Greek of v. 21a, but runs into a problem with v. 23. This verse also begins with a relative pronoun, which most naturally refers to the rules of v. 21. And this suggests that the rules of v. 21 are also the antecedent of the relative pronoun in v. 22. Indeed, the opening parts of vv. 22 and 23 are parallel in the Greek text.[194] Therefore,

191. E.g., MacDonald, 121.
192. See, e.g., Dunn, 191-92. A text that both parallels Col. 2:21 and summarizes a widespread Jewish attitude is *Let. Aris.* 142: "So, to prevent our being perverted by contact with others or by mixing with bad influences, he [God] hedged us in on all sides with strict observances connected with meat and drink and touch and hearing and sight, after the manner of the Law." Note also that one of Paul's only three uses of the verb ἅπτομαι comes in a quotation about ritual purity from Isa. 52:11: "'Come out from them and be separate, says the LORD. Touch (ἅπτεσθε) no unclean thing, and I will receive you.'"
193. See, e.g., Wilson, 227-28.
194. Both begin with a relative pronoun (ἅ/ἅτινα) followed by the verb ἐστιν.

the TNIV is probably to be followed in translating the relative pronoun as *these rules.*

Paul asserts two things about the rules in v. 22: they *have to do with things that are all destined to perish with use;*[195] and they are *based on merely human commands and teachings.*[196] The second phrase (introduced with the Greek preposition *kata*) is probably not directly dependent on the first clause, as the NIV suggests: "These are all destined to perish with use, because they are based on human commands and teachings."[197] Rather, it should be seen as a second negative evaluation of the "rules" of v. 21, roughly parallel to the former. Indeed, this second point would appear to be the most important of the two. The TNIV reflects the relative importance of the two clauses by turning the former into an English relative clause: *these rules, which are all destined to perish with use, are based on merely human commands* (other versions reflect the same idea by putting the first clause in parenthesis [ESV; NASB]).[198] Paul, of course, would not want us to take his criticism of rules having to do with material things in a dualistic way, as if Christians were too spiritual to be bothered with material things. We live in bodies in a material world, and how we relate to the physical world around us has significant bearing on our spirituality. Paul had to make this point to the Corinthians, who had apparently adopted just this kind of dualistic outlook (see esp. 1 Cor. 6:12-20).

Paul's point, as v. 23 will make rather more clearly, is that the false teachers have been making far too big a deal of matters that do not get to the essence of true Christian spirituality: the change of heart and mind that leads to true holiness. Jesus made a very similar point in his rebuke of the Pharisees for their preoccupation with their own rules of ritual un-

195. As we mentioned in the text, the advantage of a rendering such as NET is that it can translate more straightforwardly the whole Greek clause, ἅ ἐστιν πάντα εἰς φθοράν. A rendering such as TNIV must infer that ἅ, "which things," while referring to the rules, also has in view the physical elements to which the rules apply: "These rules are [about matters that] all are destined to perish." It is most unlikely that the "rules" could themselves be what is destined to perish (as the NLT has it). The preposition εἰς in this clause carries the sense of "destined for," while "perish" translates a word, φθορά, that refers to the inevitable dissolution of all created things (see 2 Pet. 2:12; 1 Cor. 15:42, 50; Rom. 8:21).

196. The English versions imitate the TNIV in taking the final genitive τῶν ἀνθρώπων as modifying both τὰ ἐντάλματα ("the commandments") and διδασκαλίας ("teaching"). The grammars point to this phrase as an instance of an article governing nouns of two different genders (BDF §276.1; Turner, *Syntax*, 181; Moule, *Idiom Book*, 110).

197. Contra Barth/Blanke, 357-58.

198. The compound form of the word ἀποχρήσει ("use") (only here in biblical Greek) has led a few commentaries in the past to translate it "abuse" and construe the whole of v. 22a as a continuation of the false teachers' rules: "Do not touch those things that are destined to perish when they are misused." See Lightfoot for comment and rebuttal (204).

cleanness: "Nothing outside you can defile you by going into you. Rather, it is what comes out of you that defiles you" (Mark 7:15). Indeed, it is quite likely that Paul is here referring to this saying of Jesus, since the second part of v. 22 is parallel to another teaching of Jesus from this same context. Paul's criticism of the false teachers' rules for being *based on merely human commands (entalmata . . . tōn anthrōpōn) and teachings (didaskalias)* sounds very much like Jesus' characterization of the Pharisees' traditions: "'They worship me in vain; their teachings *(didaskalias)* are merely human rules *(entalmata anthrōpōn).*' You have let go of the commands of God and are holding on to human traditions" (Mark 7:7-8). To be sure, Mark 7:7 is quot-·ing Isaiah 29:13, so it could be that Jesus and Paul are independently using the same Old Testament text.[199] But it is more likely that Paul, even if he has Isaiah in mind, is also alluding to Jesus' teaching.[200]

23 As we have noted in our comments on v. 22, the relative pronoun that opens v. 23 in Greek *(hatina)* probably refers back to the "rules" of v. 21. TNIV thus translates *Such regulations,* perhaps implying also in this rendering a "qualitative" interpretation of the indefinite relative pronoun — not simply "these regulations" but "regulations such as these."[201] Our interpretation of this verse can proceed no further without making a decision about its structure. The Greek text is very difficult, and every way of putting the verse together suffers from some kind of problem. Some interpreters have gone to the extent of proposing emendations, but these should never be accepted unless the text is really not comprehensible at all — and matters are not quite so desperate here.[202] So the decision is really which of the options has fewest problems. Bypassing for now some of the minor syntactical issues, the root issue is where to find the main clause of the verse and then to determine just what it means. The subject of the sentence as a whole is, as we have seen, the "regulations" being imposed by the false teachers. The main verb is probably simply "are" *(estin).*[203] In

---

199. E.g., Gnilka, 159; Beetham, "Echoes of Scripture," 251-88. Isaiah 29:13 records the Lord's criticism of his people: "These people come near to me with their mouth and honor me with their lips, but their hearts are far from me. Their worship of me is based on merely human rules they have been taught (LXX ἐντάλματα ἀνθρώπων καὶ διδασκαλίας)."

200. Lightfoot, 204; Dunn, 193-94; Pokorný, 154.

201. See, for this qualitative sense of the indefinite relative pronoun, Wallace, *Greek Grammar,* 344-45; cf. Lightfoot, 205. Of course, the definite and indefinite relative pronouns are often indistinguishable in NT Greek (BDF §293).

202. Some of the difficulty arises because Paul is trying to weave into his sentence language or even slogans of the false teachers (Gnilka, 161).

203. The less attractive alternative is to take ἐστιν . . . ἔχοντα as a periphrastic construction, with an understood ἐστιν functioning as the main verb (e.g., BDF §353.4; Harris, 131; Abbott, 275). But the difference in meaning is negligible.

what becomes in effect a subordinate clause Paul then describes the false teaching in terms of its "appearance" or "reputation" ("wisdom," "self-imposed religion," "humility," "harsh treatment of the body"). This clause calls out for a contrasting clause that would then state what these regulations really are from Paul's perspective: for example, "although the regulations have this reputation, they really are. . . ." But, as we have said, identifying this clause and determining what it means are the real difficulties in the verse.[204] Structurally, there are two options.

(1) The main, contrasting clause consists of the last two phrases of the verse. These phrases, together, can be taken in two different ways.

(a) "[The regulations] have no value in restraining the indulgence of the flesh."[205] The TNIV reflects this interpretation: *Such regulations indeed have an appearance of wisdom, with their self-imposed worship, their false humility and their harsh treatment of the body, but they lack any value in restraining sensual indulgence.*

(b) "[The regulations] do not lead, in any honorable way, to the [legitimate] satisfaction of the body." The idea, in this case, is that the false teachers, by imposing their prohibitions, do not allow people to enjoy appropriately the bodies God has given them.[206]

(2) The main, contrasting clause consists of the last phrase of the verse only, the second to the last phrase being part of the subordinate clause. The NET captures the resulting sense very well: "Even though they have the appearance of wisdom with their self-imposed worship and false humility achieved by an unsparing treatment of the body — a wisdom with no true value — they in reality result in fleshly indulgence."

Option 1a is chosen by most modern commentators and English versions; option 1b is found in a number of church fathers; and option 2 is adopted by a few modern interpreters.[207] We judge that there is good reason why most commentators and translations prefer option 1a. While certainly not without its problems, it has fewer, we think, than the others. We will therefore adopt this way of reading the verse in our more detailed comments that follow.

---

204. The subordinate clause is marked with a μέν, but it is the fact that there is no corresponding δέ anywhere in the verse that leaves several options open.

205. See esp. the classic defense of this option in Lightfoot, 206-8; also Moule, 108-10; Wright, 128.

206. On this general approach, the main clause answering to the subordinate clause begins with οὐκ. Structurally, then, the two occurrences of ἐν in the verse would mark the contrasting evaluations of the "wisdom" of the false teaching.

207. E.g., Bruce Hollenbach, "Col. 2:23: Which Things Lead to the Fulfillment of the Flesh," *NTS* 25 (1978-79), 254-61; B. Reicke, "Zum sprachlichen Verständnis von Kol. 2:23," *ST* 6 (1952), 39-53; O'Brien, 154-55.

The verse as a whole both summarizes and concludes Paul's rebuttal of the false teaching. Appropriately, then, the three specific components of the false teaching that Paul enumerates in the initial subordinate clause have all been mentioned previously in the paragraph: *self-imposed worship* is related to "the worship of angels" in v. 18; *false humility* has also been mentioned in v. 18; and *harsh treatment of the body* refers to the ascetic practices of v. 16 — "what you eat or drink" — and the prohibitions of v. 21.[208] These matters, notes Paul, give to the false teaching an *appearance,* or "reputation," *of wisdom (sophia).*[209] We should recall that Paul has labeled the false teaching a "philosophy" *(philo-sophia)* (v. 8), probably borrowing the false teachers' own proud characterization of their system. Now what has been implicit in Paul's argument all along becomes explicit: their claim to offer a wise and comprehensive system of spiritual growth is nothing but a sham. For "*all* the treasures of wisdom and knowledge" are found in Christ (2:3).

The false teachers' system, Paul says, consists, first of all, in *self-imposed worship.* This is the translation of yet another rare word, and it is unclear whether it has the sense (1) "worship freely chosen"; (2) "worship joyfully entered into"; or (3) "would-be worship."[210] The context requires that the word have a basic positive sense (or it would hardly have "an appearance of wisdom"),[211] and, of these options, the first probably makes the best sense.[212] The term may have been chosen by the false teachers to gain accolades for themselves: they have freely chosen a form of worship that involves such "rigor of devotion."[213] As we noted, the *self-imposed*

208. Not included in this summarizing list are the observance of days (v. 16) and visionary experiences (v. 18).

209. As BDAG note, Greek λόγος, the object of ἔχοντα ("having") has the meaning "appearance" here (so most English versions); cf. also "reputation" in HCSB. See also, e.g., Lightfoot, 205; O'Brien, 152.

210. The Greek word is ἐθελοθρησκία, and it occurs for the first time here. According to BDF §118.2, the first part of the word (ἐθελο-, "will") governs the second part (θρησκία, "worship," "religion," "service"). See Reicke, "Kol. 2:23," 45, for the options above.

211. This consideration rules out also the negative translation of REB, "forced piety"; cf. Wolter, 154, "self-made worship" ("selbstgemachte Verehrung").

212. A possible parallel, noted by many, is the word ἐθελοδουλεία, "self-chosen servitude," found in Plato and elsewhere (cf. MM, 181). As Dunn notes, however, it is tempting to see this word as derived from Paul's earlier characterization of the false teachers as θέλων ἐν . . . θρησκείᾳ, since the same two Greek roots occur in both places (195). This would favor the second option, "worship that one delights in."

213. Lohse, 104. This phrase is found in RSV to translate ἐθελοθρησκία, and, while it is not a very good translation of this word (note that both NRSV ["self-imposed piety"] and ESV ["self-made religion"] have changed it), it captures in a single phrase an important aspect of the false teachers' worship program.

worship here is surely related to the "worship of angels" in v. 18 (the same Greek root, *thrēsk-*, occurs in both places). The formulation Paul uses here could certainly cohere with either of the two interpretations of this latter phrase. But it is certainly most natural to assume in this verse that it is the false teachers' own worship that is in view, and this favors a reference in v. 18 also to the false teachers' own worship (of angels).[214]

The second source of the purported wisdom of the false teachers' program is their insistence on *false humility*. As we noted in our comments on v. 18, where the same word *(tapeinophrosynē)* occurs, the TNIV rendering is not quite on target here; the reference is almost certainly to the program of asceticism being propagated by the false teachers (ESV translates "asceticism"; HCSB, "ascetic practices"). On this understanding of the word "humility," *harsh treatment of the body*, the third characterization of the false teachers' program, is closely related to it: the ascetic practices of the false teachers embrace various disciplines, especially fasting and the avoidance of certain food and drink (vv. 16, 21).[215]

As we argue above, the main clause of the verse, which proves that the wisdom of the false teaching is, indeed, an "appearance" only, begins at this point, and makes the single point that the false teaching, in fact, cannot take care of the problem of the "flesh." As TNIV puts it, the regulations of the false teaching *lack any value in restraining sensual indulgence.* The meaning of each of the Greek terms standing behind the four key words in this claim — "value," "restraining," "sensual," and "indulgence" — is debated. We think the TNIV (and most of the English versions, which have something basically comparable) has it basically right in each case.[216]

214. Contra Harris, 131, it is not particularly clear that the "worship" here in v. 23 must be directed to God; on the contrary, if τῶν ἀγγέλων in v. 18 is objective (as we think), then the understood object of "worship" here could well be the angels (Pokorný, 156; Lohse, 104).

215. The connection between "humility" (ταπεινοφροσύνη) and *their harsh treatment of the body* is indicated in most English versions (including the TNIV) with "and." This "and" has an explicit Greek counterpart (καί) in the majority of Greek manuscripts of this verse; and it is adopted by the UBS translation committee (but by a close vote; see Metzger, *Textual Commentary*, 556-57). But many commentators (e.g., Lightfoot, 206; Dunn, 188) feel it is secondary, in which case the phrase *harsh treatment of the body* will directly relate to *false humility*. The idea could be instrumental (see NET: "false humility achieved by an unsparing treatment of the body") but is more likely simply appositional (Dunn, 188; Lincoln, 634).

216. TNIV's "value" translates τιμή, which is a standard translation of the word. Some, however, think that this meaning in this kind of context is unusual (BDAG suggest that it might be a "Latinism"). Perhaps the most problematic, and crucial, translation is the rendering of the Greek preposition πρός as "restraining" (NASB, "against"; ESV, "stopping"; NRSV, "checking"). This preposition would normally indicate the direction

When Paul presented the Christians' "fullness" in Christ as the alternative to the false teaching (vv. 11-15), he highlighted the problem of *sarx* ("flesh"). In Christ believers have "the body of flesh" (TNIV, "sinful nature") stripped off (v. 11), curing the problem of "uncircumcised flesh," or "the uncircumcision of your sinful nature" (TNIV,) that produced death (v. 13). Paul's use of that language may imply that the false teachers were promising, through their attempt to placate hostile spiritual beings and their ascetic devotional practices, to take care of this problem of the "flesh," the bent within fallen humans toward self and the world, the "sinful nature" or "sinful impulse." It is especially attractive to think that the problem of temptation, which can be viewed as a struggle to allow one's mind to control one's body, could be solved if only the body could be subdued through harsh treatment. Indeed, the lure of asceticism as a way of managing the sin problem and finding true spiritual enlightenment is seen in many religions throughout human history. It is a natural impulse. Paul, of course, does not want to suggest that appropriate discipline of the body is of no spiritual importance; we are, he insists, supposed to "honor God with our bodies" (1 Cor. 6:20). But the false teachers were both imposing rules on others that they had no right to impose (vv. 16 and 18) and, more seriously, elevating their rules and practices and giving spiritual beings so much credit that they were, in effect, losing contact with Christ, the only source of spiritual power and growth (v. 19). It is for this reason that the "regulations" of the false teachers could not accomplish the "subduing" of the sinful nature that they were promising.

---

in which something tends, and this is one of the main reasons why a number of interpreters want to connect it directly to "the regulations" at the beginning of the verse: "the regulations," Paul would be suggesting, are bad because they "tend toward (πρός) indulgence of the flesh." But πρός can mean "against" (BDAG cite nine other NT instances, including Col. 3:13: ἐάν τις πρός τινα ἔχῃ μομφήν, "if anyone has a grievance *against* someone"), and the difficulties created by all the other options suggest we should adopt it here. TNIV's "indulgence" is a straightforward rendering of πλησμονή, which normally implies the "satisfaction" that comes from eating one's fill (e.g., Ps. 78:25: "Human beings ate the bread of angels; he sent them all the food they could eat [πλησμονήν]"). "Sensual," finally, is the TNIV rendering of the genitive τῆς σαρκός, "of the flesh." As we noted above, some of the Fathers took this word in a neutral sense, as equivalent basically to "body" — "the regulations . . . did not properly provide for the legitimate satisfaction of the body." However, as we noted above, σάρξ is used in this context in a negative sense, and it fits here (cf. also NRSV, "self-indulgence"). Dunn (197) suggests that the word might connote the idea of Jewish ethnic identification, since Paul elsewhere uses σάρξ in connection with circumcision (see v. 13) and the larger issues of Jewish "badges of identity." But this requires us to import a bit too much into this context.

C. Living a Christocentric Life (3:1–4:1)

Like the "theme verse" displayed on a banner at a conference, Paul's call to keep Christ Jesus as Lord at the center of Christian experience (2:6b) hangs over the body of the letter (2:6–4:6). Because Paul writes in response to the immediate threat of false teachers, he begins by elaborating this basic summons negatively. And so he warns his readers about the false promise of these false teachers in 2:8-23. Now, beginning in 3:1, Paul elaborates this call to remain centered on Christ positively. Taking up the key christological teaching of chapters 1–2, Paul shows how identification with Christ leads to a new way of life. He proceeds in three basic steps. He begins, appropriately, with an overall summons to adopt a mind-set that reflects our new identity in Christ (3:1-4). He then elaborates this new way of thinking in 3:5-17 by means of a contrast between the old way of life that we must "put off" (vv. 5-11) and the new way of life we are to "put on" (vv. 12-17). Paul concludes with a reminder that the new life in Christ does not absolve Christians of their responsibilities to one another within earthbound institutions but provides, in fact, a new impetus and new motivation to live them out appropriately (3:18–4:1).

1. Heavenly Thinking (3:1-4)

1Since, then, you have been raised with Christ, set your hearts on things above, where Christ is seated at the right hand of God. 2Set your minds on things above, not on earthly things. 3For you died, and your life is now hidden with Christ in God. 4When Christ, who is your life, appears, then you also will appear with him in glory.

Two parallel commands constitute the heart of this brief paragraph: "set your hearts on things above" (v. 1)/"set your minds on things above" (v. 2). Paul grounds these commands with reminders of the believer's identification with Christ in both death (v. 3) and resurrection (v. 1). And he concludes with an expression of confidence that this identification will extend to Christ's second coming, when believers will "appear with him in glory" (v. 4). The positive tone of the commands in these verses contrasts with the negative focus in 2:8-23. From what the believer is not supposed to do — allow false teachers to impress their agenda on them (cf. esp. vv. 8, 16, 18) — Paul now turns to what believers are to do — focus on the new, heavenly dimension of reality that has dawned with the coming of Christ. In this sense, 3:1-4 returns to and elaborates the key positive imperatives of 2:6-7. But the addition of the negative "not on earthly things" in v. 2 reveals that Paul has not entirely left the negative behind.

The "things above" that Paul wants his readers to concentrate on stands in contrast to the "earthly things" of the false teaching. And the basis for his commands picks up the theology that Paul has already developed in chapter 2: "since . . . you have been raised with Christ" repeats 2:12 (cf. also "God made you alive with Christ" in 2:13); and "you died" (v. 3) repeats in abbreviated form "you died with Christ" in v. 20 (cf. vv. 11-12).

From a broader perspective, vv. 1-4 bring to a climax and summarize much of the key theology of chapters 1–2 as a whole. As he has been throughout, Christ is the focal point (the title "Christ," the only title Paul uses in these verses, appears four times[1]). But the christological focus of these chapters has always been (despite the impression that vv. 15-20 on their own could convey) on the significance of Christ for the status and experience of believers. And this note dominates vv. 1-4, as Paul focuses on the believer's union with Christ. The *past* experience of dying with him and being raised with him is the basis for our *present* status as people whose heavenly identity is real and secure, yet hidden, an identity that will be gloriously manifested in the *future*.[2] But if the paragraph looks backward, it also looks forward, laying the groundwork for the more detailed elaboration of Christian thinking and its outworking in Christian behavior in 3:5–4:6.[3] Therefore, Colossians 3:1-4 occupies a transitional place in the argument of the letter.[4] It applies the key theological concept of union with Christ, which Paul develops negatively in vv. 16-23 to counter the false teaching, in a positive direction, calling on believers to recognize the basic implications of their status as "dead" to the "elements of the world," "alive" with Christ in heaven, and destined for glory.

1   As we have suggested in the paragraph above, Paul now draws positive conclusions from the same theological premises that he used in 2:8-23 to warn the Colossians about the false teaching. The rules of the false teachers, having to do with the things of this world, cannot subdue the power of the sinful nature (vv. 22-23) and serve, indeed, to sever believers from their "head," the only true source of spiritual strength (v. 19). "Therefore" (TNIV, *then* [Gk. *oun*]) believers need to focus on what is "above," where Christ is himself to be found. Verse 1 is a conditional sentence of a type very common in the New Testament. The theology con-

---

1. See Dunn, 208.

2. Arguing for a major break between 2:23 and 3:1 are, e.g., Wright, 128; Dunn, 199-200; Ernst, 220; J. Lähnemann, *Der Kolosserbrief* (Gütersloh: Mohn, 1971), 60; W. T. Wilson, *The Hope of Glory* (Leiden and New York: Brill, 1997), 229.

3. Thus, e.g., Luz, 225, F. Zeilinger, *Der Erstgeborene der Schöpfung* (Vienna: Herder, 1974), 60-63, and Bruce, 137, argue for a major break between 3:4 and 3:5.

4. See, e.g., MacDonald, 129; A. T. Lincoln, *Paradise Now and Not Yet* (Cambridge and New York: Cambridge University Press, 2004), 110.

tained in the protasis (or "if" clause) provides the basis for the exhortation of the apodosis (the "then" clause). TNIV, along with NJB and NLT, translates the Greek *ei* of this apodosis with "since," reflecting the obvious fact that Paul assumes the protasis to be true. However, as we noted in our comments on 2:20, it is better for rhetorical reasons to translate "if," since this rendering forces the reader or listener to assent to the proposition.

The claim of this "if" clause is significant and controversial: *you have been raised with Christ.* The controversy arises because many interpreters allege that the claim of a past "being raised" with Christ contradicts the theology of the "authentic" Paul, who always taught that the believer would be raised with Christ only in the future. Transferring this resurrection with Christ from the future to the present, it is argued, is the most evident symptom of the "overrealized" eschatology of Colossians (and Ephesians, which shares this perspective). The author of Colossians has turned Paul's temporal orientation into a spatial one, according to which Christians no longer have to wait to be identified with Christ's resurrection in the future, but can even now join Christ "above" in the heavenly realm.[5]

These interpreters are certainly right to point out that the actual language of "being raised with" Christ occurs only in Colossians (here and in 2:12) and Ephesians (2:6). But, as we have argued in our comments on 2:12, the concept of "sharing with Christ in his resurrection power" is certainly present in uncontested Pauline letters such as Romans (6:4, 12) and Philippians (3:10). It is but a small step from this concept to the use of the language of "raised with Christ" to express it. Especially is this the case since v. 4 in this very paragraph continues unambiguously to affirm the temporal category of a future sharing with Christ in glory.[6] In response to the false teachers, with their insistence on ascetic practices and rules as the means of spiritual fulfillment, this letter affirms strongly that spiritual fulfillment is found in Christ and that it is therefore "in Christ" that believers experience this fulfillment themselves (2:9-10). It would be quite natural in this context for Paul to use the category of resurrection to express the participation of the believer with Christ in the present time.[7]

5. Lohse provides a succinct summary of this viewpoint (145-46).
6. See, for these points and others, esp. Lincoln, *Paradise Now and Not Yet*, 122-23; also the Introduction, 68-69; and the monograph by F. J. Steinmetz, *Protologische Heils-Zuversicht* (Frankfurt am Main: Knecht, 1969), who acknowledges the different eschatological emphases of Ephesians and Colossians while showing that they cohere with the eschatology of the "major" Pauline letters.
7. Especially is this true if the false teachers were bragging about their own (mystical) ascents into heaven (see I. K. Smith, *Heavenly Perspective* [Edinburgh: T&T Clark, 2006], 174-81).

And with this point we turn to our second issue, the significance of the language. Without denying the reality of a future resurrection with Christ, Paul, following his typical "already/not yet" paradigm, asserts that those who belong to Christ have already experienced a "spiritual" resurrection with Christ. Because they are "in him" and Christ has himself been raised to sit at the right hand of the Father, so believers can be said to have been "raised with" him.[8]

The TNIV rendering of Paul's imperative, *set your hearts on things above*, attempts to bring out the sense of the Greek *zēteite*, "seek." The meaning of this verb in this context could be illustrated by means of some parallels: "But *seek* first his kingdom and his righteousness" (Matt. 6:33a); "[you] do not *seek* the glory that comes from the only God" (John 5:44b); "To those who by persistence in doing good *seek* glory, honor and immortality, he will give eternal life" (Rom. 2:7). Nevertheless, there is an important difference in nuance between Colossians 3:1 and these parallels. For Paul is not saying so much that believers should seek to *possess* "the things above" as that they are to seek to orient themselves totally to these heavenly realities. We are not to strive for a "heavenly" status, since that has already been freely given us in Christ. Rather, we are to make that heavenly status the guidepost for all our thinking and acting. And, by using the present tense, Paul indicates that believers should be constantly occupied in striving for this orientation. Only here and in v. 2 does Paul use the phrase "the things above" *(ta anō)*, although he uses the adverb *anō* ("upward," "above") in Galatians 4:26 — "the Jerusalem that is above" — and in Philippians 3:14 — "the upward call." "Above," then, is another way of referring to heaven, the abode of God and the sphere to which believers truly belong by virtue of their identification with Christ (see Phil. 3:20). Believers "seek the things above" by deliberately and daily committing ourselves to the values of the heavenly kingdom and living out of those values.

As we noted above, Paul in this paragraph continues implicitly to interact with the false teaching. This teaching apparently offered its adherents access to the heavenly realm (2:18). As Lincoln puts it, then, Paul "by no means completely disparages his readers' concern with the heavenly realm. Instead, he attempts to redirect it. In the process it emerges that two antithetical positions about participation in the heavenly realm are in confrontation. The philosophy's advocates take the earthly situa-

---

8. See also, on this whole issue, N. T. Wright, *The Resurrection of the Son of God* (London: SPCK, 2003), 238-39, who, among other points, notes the similarities between Col. 3:1-4, with its call to "think" a certain way because of the reality of our heavenly identity and future transformation, and the uncontested Pauline text of Phil. 3:19-21.

tion as their starting point, from which by their own efforts and techniques they will move beyond the body, gain visionary experience, and ascend into heavenly spheres. The writer moves in the reverse direction, seeing the starting point and source of the believer's life in the resurrected Christ in heaven, from where it works itself out in earthly life."[9]

By reminding us that the heavenly realm is *where Christ is, seated at the right hand of God*, Paul not only defines that realm but, more importantly, provides motivation for us to seek to orient ourselves to that heavenly realm.[10] Spiritual growth, Paul has made clear, comes only from Christ, so it is naturally incumbent on us to focus on the "place" where he is. Moreover, our identification with Christ in his resurrection means, in effect, that, in some ultimate sense, heaven is where we truly are also. It is only natural that we seek to align our whole being with our true, "heavenly" identity. The attentive reader may notice that our quotation of the last part of v. 1 above differs from the TNIV in one respect: the comma after "is." This reflects the view of most translators and commentators that "is" *(estin)* should be construed as an independent verb rather than as part of a periphrastic construction.[11] This punctuation places the emphasis where it belongs, on the simple fact of where Christ *is* rather than on what he is doing. The language of Christ "sitting at the right hand of God" comes originally from Psalm 110:1, although the idea becomes so common in the New Testament that it is doubtful whether Paul intends a conscious allusion here to that verse.[12] The "right hand" signifies the place of honor and prominence (see, e.g., 1 Kgs. 2:19; Mark 10:37).

2   Revealing just how important this perspective is for believers, Paul repeats the essence of his command in v. 2 (the lack of explicit connection ["asyndeton"] with v. 1 fits well with the repetition). However,

---

9. Lincoln, 638. O'Brien (160) suggests that Paul's choice of ζητεῖτε, "seek," may also be polemical, since the false teachers were apparently "seeking" visionary experiences. But one of his reasons for suggesting a polemical force is the claim that this is the only place where Paul uses the word as a "direct command," in contrast to "indirect commands," a distinction that cannot very well be maintained (cf. esp. 1 Cor. 10:24; 14:12).

10. O'Brien, 161; Harris, 137.

11. ESV; NASB; NET; NJB; NRSV; RSV; HCSB; REB; and see, e.g., Lightfoot, 209; Dunn, 202. Only KJV and NAB follow NIV and TNIV in taking ἐστιν . . . καθήμενος as a periphrastic construction. Only four other texts (three of them synoptic parallels) use the participle of κάθημαι in referring to Ps. 110:1 (Matt. 26:64 par. Mark 14:62 par. Luke 22:69; Eph. 1:20), and none has the verb "to be." Other allusions to Ps. 110:1 preserve the imperative of the original (Matt. 22:44 par. Mark 12:36 par. Luke 20:42; Acts 2:34; Heb. 1:13 — all "quotations"), shift to the indicative (Heb. 1:3; 8:1; 10:12; 12:2), or drop the verb κάθημαι (Acts 2:33; 5:31; Rom. 8:34; 1 Pet. 3:22).

12. On Ps. 110:1 in the NT, see David Hay, *Glory at the Right Hand: Psalm 110:1 in Early Christianity* (SBLMS 18; Nashville: Abingdon, 1973).

the verse also nuances the basic point, in two ways. First, Paul shifts from the rather colorless "seek" to the more specific "think" (*phroneō*). Paul likes this verb: twenty-three of the twenty-six New Testament occurrences are his. It refers not to a purely mental or intellectual process, but to a more fundamental orientation of the will. Thus many versions, like the TNIV, translate "set your minds on" (ESV; NRSV; RSV; HCSB; NASB). The verb suggests the basic inner attitude that lies behind and is part of the "seeking" of v. 1,[13] and, like "seek" in v. 1, it is also in the present tense, suggesting a "habit of the mind" (cf. NET: "Keep thinking about things above"). It may also be a further polemical dig at the false teachers, who are perhaps advocating a spiritual orientation that focused on the emotions at the expense of the mind.[14]

But it is the second nuance added in v. 2 that is the real point of the verse: we are not to have our minds set *on earthly things*. Paul has probably repeated the initial command of v. 1, in a slightly varied form, simply to set up this additional point. Paul is almost certainly suggesting that it is the false teachers who are preoccupied with "earthly things" at the expense of "the things above" — which is quite an ironical twist. For, as 2:18 suggests, the false teachers, because of their preoccupation with their visionary experiences, would have been the ones bragging about their focus on the "things above." In reality, Paul effectively responds, by bragging about those visions and by cutting themselves off from Christ (2:19), the false teachers have their minds set on the things of this world. "Things above," Paul is making clear, are tied to Christ, enthroned above, and must reflect the values of the kingdom that he has inaugurated. Anything else, or less, is no more than "worldly" thinking. Philippians 3:12-21, with its focus on the "heavenward" (Gk. *anō*) direction of his call (v. 14), the criticism that false teachers are "thinking" (*phroneō*; cf. also v. 15) about "earthly things" (v. 19), and the reminder that our "citizenship is in heaven" (v. 20), furnishes a fuller example of the kind of Pauline focus that we find in vv. 1-2:

> Not that I have already obtained all this, or have already arrived at my goal, but I press on to take hold of that for which Christ Jesus took hold of me. Brothers and sisters, I do not consider myself yet to have taken hold of it. But one thing I do: Forgetting what is behind and straining toward what is ahead, I press on toward the goal to win the prize for which God has called me heavenward in Christ Jesus. All of us, then, who are mature should take such a view of things.

13. Harris, 138.
14. E.g., Wright, 131; Lincoln, *Paradise Now and Not Yet*, 125.

And if on some point you think differently, that too God will make clear to you. Only let us live up to what we have already attained.

Join together in following my example, brothers and sisters, and just as you have us as a model, keep your eyes on those who live as we do. For, as I have often told you before and now tell you again even with tears, many live as enemies of the cross of Christ. Their destiny is destruction, their god is their stomach, and their glory is in their shame. Their mind is set on earthly things. But our citizenship is in heaven. And we eagerly await a Savior from there, the Lord Jesus Christ, who, by the power that enables him to bring everything under his control, will transform our lowly bodies so that they will be like his glorious body.

3 Following his typical pattern, Paul now grounds (*for;* Gk. *gar*) the imperatives of vv. 1 and 2 with an appeal to theology: *you died, and your life is now hidden with Christ in God.* His readers have *died* not physically, of course, but spiritually; specifically, this brief assertion is a reminder of what he has said in 2:20: "you died with Christ to the elemental spiritual forces of this world." For the purposes of his polemic with the false teachers, Paul highlights our separation from these powers. But we can infer that Paul would also have in view our deliverance from sin and the bondage of the law, "powers" that he elsewhere claims we have "died to."[15] As we have noted, the believer's union "with" Christ in death (v. 20), burial (v. 12a), and resurrection (v. 12b; cf. 13) provides the Colossians with the spiritual security that they were craving, including especially forgiveness and protection from evil spiritual powers (vv. 13-15). Christ's death, burial, and resurrection are the essential moments of the climactic salvation-historical drama (1 Cor. 15:3-5), and they mark the transition from the old era to the new. By believing in Christ, the Colossians have identified with Christ in these events and so experience all the benefits they confer. Paul bookends his imperatives in vv. 1 and 2 with reminders of this fundamental theology: "since . . . you have been raised with Christ" (v. 1a); "you died [with Christ]" (v. 3a). Setting our hearts and minds on "the things above" and not on "earthly things" is both necessary and possible. It is necessary because our union with Christ means we no longer belong to the realm of this earth but to the heavenly realm; and it is possible because our union with Christ severs us from the tyranny of the powers of this world and provides us with all the power needed to live a new life (cf. 1:10-14).

15. Paul speaks of our "dying" to sin in Rom. 6:2 (with ἀποθνῄσκω) and 6:11 (with νεκρός), and of our "dying" to the law in Rom. 7:5 and Gal. 2:19 (with ἀποθνῄσκω) and in Rom. 7:4 (with θανατόω).

Paul takes the significance of our union with Christ two steps further here, referring both to our present status (v. 3b) and to our future transformation (v. 4). The latter, as we have suggested in our comments on v. 1, probably reflects the same basic idea that Paul refers to with the language of being "raised with Christ" in Romans 6. The former, however, is not mentioned explicitly in other passages where Paul speaks of our union with Christ. We are probably justified, then, in surmising that he brings up this point here because of its particular relevance to the Colossian context. But just what is his point? Nowhere else in the New Testament is there reference to believers being "hidden." Of course, we have met the language of hiddenness earlier in Colossians, and in a context that parallels 3:3-4. For just as the life of the believer is now "hidden" (kekryptai) and will "appear" (phanerōthēsesthe), so the "mystery" had been "hidden" (apokekrymmenon) and has now been "revealed" (ephanerōthē) (1:26).

As we noted in our comments on 1:26, this "hidden"/"revealed" motif is fundamental to the widespread Jewish apocalyptic worldview. According to this perspective, many things relating to God and his purposes exist in the present, but because they are in heaven, they are hidden from human sight. But the apocalyptic seer is given a vision of these things, things that will one day be revealed as they come to pass and are seen by people on earth. So, Paul suggests, at the present time our heavenly identity is real, but it is hidden. We have certainly not been physically transported to heaven; nor do we, who belong to the heavenly realm, look any different from those around us who still belong to this world. Verse 4 affirms that this will one day change. In the meantime, our true status is veiled; and, though we may not look any different than those around us, Paul's point in this context is that we certainly need to behave differently.

But Paul may intend another nuance in asserting that our lives are "hidden" with God. BDAG classify kryptō ("hide") in this verse under the meaning "hide in a safe place." This extension of meaning is quite natural, since hiding is often the way that people find safety and security when enemies are pursuing them (e.g., 1 Sam. 13:6). Several Old Testament texts suggest that "hide" can carry the connotation of safety and security. Psalm 27:5 is especially clear: "For in the day of trouble he will keep me safe in his dwelling; he will hide me in the shelter of his tabernacle and set me high upon a rock" (see also, e.g., Ps. 31:20; Isa. 49:2; Matt. 13:44; 25:18).

The phrase "in God" at the end of the verse may also point in this direction.[16] Therefore, Paul's claim that the lives of believers are now hid-

---

16. The phrase ἐν τῷ θεῷ ("in God") probably modifies κέκρυπται ("hidden"); see Harris, 139. Schweizer cites this phrase as an argument against Pauline authorship; but

den with Christ may be more than simply the "setup" for the emphasis on future revelation in v. 4. It may also remind us that the time between our initial identification with Christ and the revelation of that status on the last day is a time when God is working to keep us secure in that relationship.[17] As Paul has put it earlier: we have a "hope stored up for [us] in heaven" (1:5).

4 Verse 4 lacks a direct connection to v. 3,[18] but the relationship between the two is clear enough. The verb *appear* (the Greek verb is *phaneroō*)[19] is the counterpart to "hidden" in v. 3. At the same time, "your life" in v. 3 is picked up and elaborated in v. 4, as Paul identifies Christ as the one who is *your life*.[20] This identification reflects the relentless christological focus of Colossians (see, e.g., 1:15-20, 27; 2:2, 3, 19; and the Introduction, 61-63). And it reminds us of Paul's autobiographical remark in Galatians 2:20: "I have been crucified with Christ and I no longer live, but Christ lives in me. The life I now live in the body, I live by faith in the Son of God, who loved me and gave himself for me" (cf. also Phil. 1:21). These verses reflect Paul's conviction that the life and destiny of the believer are inextricably bound up with Christ. As Christ died, so believers die with him (Col. 2:20; 3:3). When he died, believers were buried with him (2:12). As he was resurrected, so believers were raised with him (2:13; 3:1). And when he appears in glory at the time of his return, believers will appear with him.

Our identification with Christ, now real but hidden, will one day be manifest. As John puts it, "Dear friends, now we are children of God, and what we will be has not yet been made known *(ephanerōthē)*. But we know that when Christ appears *(phanerōthē)*, we shall be like him, for we shall see him as he is" (1 John 3:2). Because Christ is now "in us," we have "the

his claim that the phrase is not found in Paul is wrong (see Rom. 5:11; and, without the article, Rom. 2:17; 1 Thess. 1:1 [cf. also 2 Thess. 1:1]).

17. See, e.g., C. E. Arnold, *Colossian Syncretism* (Tübingen: Mohr Siebeck, 1995), 307; Harris, 139; O'Brien, 166; Schweizer, 176; E. D. Martin, 136-37.

18. The asyndeton may lend emphasis to the verse (O'Brien, 166).

19. The same verb is used with reference to the Parousia in 1 Pet. 5:4; 1 John 2:28; 3:2. See also 1 Cor. 4:5; 2 Cor. 5:10.

20. Most English translations read "your life," reflecting the text found in some early and diverse manuscripts (ὑμῶν). But NASB, RSV, and REB read "our life," based on the text of a large number of other manuscripts (ἡμῶν). The latter reading is adopted by a majority of the commentators (e.g., Lightfoot, 210; Moule, 112; Lohse, 134; O'Brien, 157; Dunn, 202; Wilson, 240), who think it likely that a scribe replaced an original ἡμῶν with ὑμῶν under the influence of the phrase ἡ ζωὴ ὑμῶν in v. 3. But the external evidence for ὑμῶν is stronger (according to Metzger, the reason that the UBS committee adopted it [*Textual Commentary*, 557]), and it is possible that a scribe sought to "universalize" the text by changing an original ὑμῶν to ἡμῶν (Harris, 140; Pokorný, 162; Barth/Blanke, 398). Little, if any, difference in meaning is involved.

hope of glory" (Col. 1:27), and it is that same union, expressed in the other direction — we "in Christ" — that will bring hope to its certain accomplishment. As the text in 1 John suggests, the believer's appearance "in glory," or "in a state of glory,"[21] will mean a final transformation into the "image" of Christ (see esp. Rom. 8:29) by means of resurrection (1 Cor. 15:43; cf. also Rom. 8:18; Phil. 3:20-21). In Christ God has restored the definitive and perfect "image of God" that was marred in the fall (Col. 1:15), and believers who are joined with him will share that image.[22] All this is typical Pauline teaching, showing that the emphasis on a present "spatial" presence with Christ in heaven (3:1) firmly remains within (though, to be sure, toward one end of) the apostle's customary spectrum of the "already . . . not yet" tension.[23]

2. Putting Off the Practices of the "Old Self" (3:5-11)

> [5]Put to death, therefore, whatever belongs to your earthly nature: sexual immorality, impurity, lust, evil desires and greed, which is idolatry. [6]Because of these, the wrath of God is coming. [7]You used to walk in these ways, in the life you once lived. [8]But now you must also rid yourselves of all such things as these: anger, rage, malice, slander, and filthy language from your lips. [9]Do not lie to each other, since you have taken off your old self with its practices [10]and have put on the new self, which is being renewed in knowledge in the image of its Creator. [11]Here there is no Gentile or Jew, circumcised or uncircumcised, barbarian, Scythian, slave or free, but Christ is all, and is in all.

As the similarity in wording indicates, the initial imperative in this paragraph — "put to death" in v. 1 — bears particular relation to the assertion in v. 3 that "you died." But, conceptually and more generally, this imperative, as well as the others that follow in these verses — "rid yourselves" (v. 8); "do not lie" (v. 9) — and, indeed, in the paragraphs after them, is rooted in the teaching of vv. 1-4 as a whole. And these verses, as we have noted, refer to much of the theology that Paul has taught in chapters 1–2. Verses 5-11 are dominated by the two negative commands that we noted

---

21. The prepositional phrase ἐν δόξῃ could refer to Christ's glory, "in" which the believer shares (e.g., Harris, 141), but more likely it refers to the state of glory in which the believer will one day be manifest.

22. See esp. Dunn, 209, on the "Adam Christology" that might inform this verse; and, more generally, S. Kim, *The Origin of Paul's Gospel* (Grand Rapids: Eerdmans, 1982), 260-67.

23. See esp. O'Brien, 168-69; and also Luz, 226; J. D. G. Dunn, *The Theology of Paul the Apostle* (Grand Rapids: Eerdmans, 1998), 307.

above: "put to death" (v. 5) and "rid yourselves of" (v. 8). Paul draws at-tention to the parallel between these two by elaborating on them in simi-lar ways. In both verses, Paul follows the imperative with an object that denotes a general class of sins, elaborates this class by enumerating five specific vices, and then concludes with a brief characterization of the last vice in the list:[24]

v. 5 put to death   whatever belongs to your earthly nature
                                  sexual immorality
                                  impurity
                                  lust
                                  evil desires
                                  greed
                                        which is idolatry

v. 8 rid yourselves of   all such things as these
                                  anger
                                  rage
                                  malice
                                  slander
                                  filthy language
                                        from your lips

The first exhortation is reinforced by the reminder that God will judge such conduct (v. 6) and that such conduct belongs to the Colossians' for-mer way of life (v. 7). The second list is connected to the first by one of Paul's favorite devices: a "once" (v. 7)/"but now" (v. 8) contrast. He then elaborates this second list of vices with a follow-up imperative, "do not lie" (v. 9a), which in turn is grounded in another reminder of the funda-mental change in status that the readers have undergone. Using imagery widespread in the New Testament, Paul reminds them that they have "taken off" one set of clothes — "the old self with its practices" — and have "put on" a new set of clothes — the "new self" (vv. 9b-10a), whose significance is elaborated in vv. 10b-11.

    The lists of sins that we find in vv. 5 and 8 have parallels in a num-ber of other New Testament texts and are sometimes matched by compa-

---

24. The five-fold structure of the two "vice lists" in vv. 5 and 8 as well as of the "virtue list" in v. 12 is thought by some scholars (e.g., Lohse, 136) to reflect an Iranian reli-gious conception, according to which human beings have five "members" (see v. 5), with deeds relating to each of these members. Dependence on this specific tradition is un-likely, although Paul may be influenced by a broader tendency to use lists of five (Schweizer, 185-87).

rable lists of virtues (see v. 12).[25] Scholars have dubbed these, respectively, "vice lists" and "virtue lists" and have argued that they represent a literary "form" that the New Testament writers have borrowed from their environment.[26] Whether this is the case or not, what is more important for the interpretation of Colossians 3 is the degree to which the vices listed here reflect actual problems in the Colossian community. The list of sins in v. 5 focuses on sexual sins, while the one in v. 8 singles out sins relating to interpersonal relationships. The virtue list of v. 12, along with many of the positive exhortations of vv. 13-17, also focuses on community relations.

Scholars have traditionally thought that the vice and virtue lists in the New Testament reflect traditional ethical teaching that is not especially tailored to its particular context. And there are several indications that this may be the case in Colossians 3: the general nature of the sins enumerated; the many parallels to them in other letters of Paul; the traditional nature of much of the language; and the lack of any good basis to connect the sins specifically with the teaching or behavior of the false teachers or with the Colossian Christian community.[27] This may well be the case with respect to the list of (mainly) sexual sins in v. 5. But the degree to which Paul concentrates on interpersonal relationships in his ethical teaching in vv. 8-17 suggests that the Colossian Christians may have been failing to live out their common life in Christ as they should have

25. The most famous pair of lists is the contrasting "works of the flesh" vs. "fruit of the Spirit" in Gal. 5:19-23. Lists of vices also occur in, e.g., Rom. 1:29-31; 1 Cor. 5:9-11; 6:9-10; Gal. 5:19-21; Eph. 4:31; 5:3-5; 1 Tim. 1:9-10; 6:4-5; 2 Tim. 3:2-4; Titus 1:7; 1 Pet. 4:3; Rev. 21:8; 22:15, with lists of virtues in Eph. 6:14-17; Phil. 4:8; 1 Tim. 3:2-3; 6:11; Titus 1:7-8; Jas. 3:17; 2 Pet. 1:5-8.

26. Lists of vices (often with contrasting virtues) are first found in Aristotle and became especially popular among the Stoics, from whom a number of scholars think Paul has borrowed this "form" (e.g., B. S. Easton, "New Testament Ethical Lists," *JBL* 51 [1932], 1-12). But Jewish writers use similar lists, borrowing perhaps from the widespread Old Testament tradition of the "two ways" tradition (e.g., Psalm 1). It must also be noted that (1) the lists of vices and virtues in the NT take a variety of specific contextually oriented forms; and (2) such lists are to some extent a rather natural way to refer to ethical conduct. For studies of NT vice and virtue lists and their background, see esp. A. Vögtle, *Die Tugend- und Lasterkataloge im Neuen Testament, exegetisch, religions- und formgeschichtlich untersucht* (NTAbh 16; Münster: Aschendorff, 1936); E. Kamlah, *Die Form der katalogischen Paränese im Neuen Testament* (WUNT 7; Tübingen: Mohr Siebeck, 1964); S. Wibbing, *Die Tugend- und Lasterkataloge im Neuen Testament und ihre Traditionsgeschichte unter besonderer Berücksichtigung der Qumran-Texte* (BZNW 25; Berlin: Töpelmann, 1959); M. J. Suggs, "The Christian Two Way Tradition: Its Antiquity, Form, and Function," in *Studies in the New Testament and Other Early Christian Literature: Festschrift for A. P. Wikgren* (ed. D. E. Aune; NovTSup 33; Leiden: Brill, 1972), 60-74.

27. See, e.g., Lohse, 137-38; Bruce, 138.

been. We can imagine, from our own experiences, that Christians in Colossae would react in different ways to the false teaching, and that these varied reactions could easily lead to strained interpersonal relationships. Note, for instance, a similar focus on dissension and critical speech in Galatians 5:19-21, which also addresses a community beset with false teaching.

5 The relationship between the first paragraph (vv. 1-4) and this one (vv. 5-11) is marked with the inferential conjunction *therefore*. In a general way, Paul is probably suggesting that, since we are to have a "heavenly mind-set," we should be eager to get rid of behavior that does not reflect that mind-set. There is also undoubtedly a particular connection with v. 3a: "you died. . . . therefore put to death."[28] Or, to use the language often applied to this general theological concept: "become what you are."[29] We who have died to "the elements of the world" (3:3; 2:20) and to the power of sin (Rom. 6:1-6) because of our union with Christ are to "become" dead to sin in the realities of everyday life. But this "putting to death" of sin is not only demanded by our incorporation into Christ; it is also empowered and effected by it. Union with Christ, because it puts us in a new relationship to sin and brings us into the sphere of the Spirit's power, *will* impact the way we live. Ultimately, then, the imperative "put to death" in this verse must be viewed as a call to respond to, and cooperate with, the transformative power that is already operative within us.

In light of the parallels we have cited — "died to the elements of the world" (2:20); "died to sin" (Rom. 6:2) — the object of the verb *put to death* is somewhat unexpected: *whatever belongs to your earthly nature,* or, more literally, "the members which are on the earth" (cf. KJV; NKJV). "Member" (Gk. *melos*) is ordinarily used to refer to the parts of the human body (see, e.g., Matt. 5:29-30; Jas. 3:5-6; 4:1). Paul applies the word to Christians in his well-known extended metaphor of the church as a "body," believers being the "members" of that body.[30] More pertinent to the usage here, however, are those places in the New Testament where the word refers more generally to the "faculties" of people, faculties that in the old sphere

28. Wright, on the other hand, thinks the connection may be with v. 4 in particular: our new life, though hidden until Christ's return, is nevertheless to be lived out now (133).

29. Or, as Lohse puts it, "Let the old man [cf. v. 10], who has already died in baptism, be dead" (137). Paul uses the verb νεκρόω, which he uses elsewhere only in Rom. 4:19 (and the only other NT occurrence is in Heb. 11:12; it is not used in the LXX).

30. Rom. 12:4, 5; 1 Cor. 12:12-27; Eph. 4:25; 5:30. Masson (142) suggests that τὰ μέλη is used in this sense in this verse, the word being understood as a vocative — "members [of Christ's body], put to death. . . ." However, it is unlikely that it would have this sense apart from explicit comparison of the church with a "body."

of life are used in the service of sin and unrighteousness but that in the new realm are to be given to Christ. See, for example, Romans 6:19b: "Just as you used to offer yourselves (ta melē) as slaves to impurity and to ever-increasing wickedness, so now offer yourselves (ta melē) as slaves to righteousness leading to holiness" (see also Rom. 6:13; 7:5, 23; Jas. 4:1). The language Paul uses here, then, reflects the general biblical view that the human body, while not itself sinful, is particularly susceptible to the influence of sin. Romans 8:13 is a close parallel to our text: "if by the Spirit you put to death (thanatoute) the misdeeds of the body (tas praxeis tou sōmatos), you will live." It is also possible, since language of the "old self" lurks in the contexts of both Romans 6 (v. 6) and Colossians 3 (v. 9), that the word "members" functions as part of this metaphor: as Robert Gundry puts it, "members" would be "a figurative expression for sins which constitute the earthly 'old man.'"[31] Granted this sense of the word in these contexts, the TNIV's decision not to render this word explicitly, either in Romans 6:19 or in Colossians 3:5, seems justified (and most of the other versions do the same: ESV; HCSB; NET; NJB; NLT).

A few commentators suggest that *put to death whatever belongs to your earthly nature* is a self-contained, general command, and that the following list of vices depends on an assumed verb such as "put off" (see v. 8).[32] But this is unnecessary. It is more natural simply to view the list of vices as in apposition to "members on the earth." The first three of the five specific manifestations of the "earthly nature" that Paul enumerates probably have to do especially with sexual sin. This is clear with the first of the terms, "sexual immorality" (porneia), which refers to any kind of sexual sin. The second, "impurity" (akatharsia), refers more generally to any kind of moral corruption, but it is applied quite often to sexual sins.[33] And the third, "lust" (pathos), refers to sexual sin in its two other New Testament occurrences (both Pauline: Rom. 1:26; 1 Thess. 4:5).

The last two sins in the list of five appear at first sight to have a more general meaning. *Evil desires* translates a Greek phrase that is singular in form: *epithymian kakēn*, "evil desire." The word "desire" by itself can have a positive or neutral meaning, but, when it has a negative connota-

31. R. Gundry, *Sōma in Biblical Theology* (Cambridge and New York: Cambridge University Press, 1976), 42; cf. also R. C. Tannehill, *Dying and Rising with Christ* (Berlin: Töpelmann, 1967), 50-51; Harris, 146; O'Brien, 190; Bruce, 140-41. However, there is no need to import the influence of Iranian mythology to explain this language (contra Lohse, 137; Gnilka, 178-80).

32. Lightfoot, 211; Abbott, 280-81; Moule, 116.

33. It is paired with πόρνεια in 2 Cor. 12:21; Gal. 5:19; Eph. 5:3 (where πλεονεξία ["greed"] also occurs); Rev. 17:4. The related form πορνός ("immoral person") occurs with ἀκάθαρτος ("unclean person") in Eph. 5:5.

tion, it can refer to the basic human tendency toward sin. See James 1:14-15: "but each of you is tempted when you are dragged away by your own evil desire (*epithymia*) and enticed. Then, after desire (*epithymia*) has conceived, it gives birth to sin; and sin, when it is full-grown, gives birth to death." The phrase, then, could refer here also to this "evil impulse." But a reference to the basic human tendency toward sin would be odd coming as the fourth in a list of other vices. Moreover, when "desire" refers to this sinful impulse, it occurs on its own, whereas it is here modified by "evil." It is more likely, then, that the phrase refers not to *the* evil desire, but to "evil desire" as a generic category; and we often express this idea in English with the plural (hence the plural form of the phrase in TNIV, NJB, NLT). Moreover, "desire" sometimes refers to sexual desire in particular (see esp. 1 Thess. 4:5), so, considering the context, it might have this connotation here also.[34]

Greed (Gk. *pleonexia*), the last item in the list, likewise usually has the general sense of an "inappropriate desire for more," but this general sense would, of course, include the uncontrolled desire for more and greater sexual experiences.[35] This being the case, and considering the general meaning of the word, Paul might intend to suggest that "greed," or "covetousness" (RSV; ESV), is the source of the other four sins.[36] And Paul's additional description of "greed," *which is idolatry,* might also point in this direction. The idea has its roots in the Old Testament and has parallels in Judaism and in the New Testament. The Old Testament frequently sets wealth in competition with God as a source of security (e.g., Ps. 52:7; Jer. 48:7; Prov. 10:15). Philo claimed that the first commandment prohibits "money-lovers" (*On the Special Laws* 1.23). And the New Testament frequently highlights the love of material possessions as offering a particularly enticing and entrapping alternative to the love of God (e.g., Matt. 6:25-34; 1 Tim. 6:17; Heb. 13:5).[37] Ephesians, as usual, offers the closest parallel: "For of this you can be sure: No immoral, impure or greedy person — such a person is an idolater — has any inheritance in the kingdom of Christ and of God" (5:5). The word used in the Ephesians text (*eidōlolatrēs,* "idolater") occurs along with "immoral person" (*pornos*) and

---

34. Schweizer (143) suggests that "impurity," "lust," and "evil desires" all elaborate the first word in the list, "sexual immorality."

35. The word is used generally of "greed" (often in contexts referring to money or power) in Mark 7:22; Luke 12:15; 2 Cor. 9:5; 1 Thess. 2:5; 2 Pet. 2:3, 14. Its meaning in Rom. 1:29, where it occurs in another vice list, is unclear.

36. Barth/Blanke, 404.

37. See on this topic esp. Brian S. Rosner, "The Concept of Idolatry," *Them* 24.3 (May 1999), 21-30; idem, *Greed as Idolatry: The Origin and Meaning of a Pauline Metaphor* (Grand Rapids: Eerdmans, 2007), passim.

"greedy person" *(pleonektēs)* in 1 Corinthians 5:10, 11 and with "immoral person" in 1 Corinthians 6:9 and Revelation 21:8; 22:15. Clearly, then, we are dealing with a customary cluster of terms and ideas. Jewish writers habitually traced the various sins of the Gentiles back to the root problem of idolatry; and especially was this true of sexual sins. Putting some other "god" in the place of the true God of the Bible leads to the panoply of sexual sins and perversions that characterized the Gentile world.[38] Paul reflects this tradition here: sexual sins arise because people have an uncontrolled desire for more and more "experiences" and "pleasures"; and such a desire is nothing less than a form of idolatry. It is not necessary, then, to suppose that the Colossian Christians were particularly guilty of such sins. Rather, the list reflects the kinds of sins to which Gentiles who came to Christ were generally prone.

6   Vice lists in the New Testament often conclude with a reminder that God will judge the kind of conduct outlined in the list (e.g., Gal. 5:19-21; 1 Cor. 6:10-11; Eph. 5:3-6). They differ in this respect from their counterparts in the larger Greek world, which were concerned simply to foster moral improvement. In the New Testament, in contrast, the vice lists function to depict the lifestyle of people who are in enmity with the holy God of the Bible and who thus suffer eternal condemnation. The "vices" are therefore elevated to a whole new level of seriousness. The warning of judgment in this verse therefore underscores the need to take seriously the exhortation that Christians do away with such conduct. Putting to death sins like those mentioned in v. 5 is vital because God will visit with his wrath those who continue to practice them. And putting to death sins like these is possible (even "natural") because God has given his people, through his Spirit, a new power to conform their conduct to God's holy demands.

God's wrath has been a controversial topic among some modern interpreters, who think that the concept is out of keeping with the biblical portrayal of a loving God. To be sure, if "wrath" is viewed in terms of the capricious and selfish anger of the Greek gods, attributing it to the God of the Bible would be problematic. But the scriptural notion of God's wrath runs in quite a different direction. It is tied directly to the holiness of God and depicts the necessary reaction of a personal God to any violation of his character or will. Particularly noteworthy in our context is the fact that the warning about wrath is directed to "God's holy people in Colossae." God's true people are guaranteed deliverance from wrath

---

38. Perhaps the clearest example is Wisdom 14–15, on which Paul probably depends in Romans 1–2. Idolatry and sexual lust are linked also in *T. Reuben* 4:6; *T. Judah* 23:1. Note also *T. Judah* 19:1, where the love of money is said to lead to idolatry.

(1 Thess. 5:9; Rom. 5:9), but, at the same time, they are repeatedly warned that persistent sinful behavior will bring God's judgment. Relating these two clear biblical principles to one another is an ongoing theological challenge. But, however we finally resolve this matter, it is at least clear that the warnings of verses such as this are designed to encourage God's people to engage seriously and passionately in the process of divesting themselves of the attitudes and lifestyle characteristic of this world.

The verb in this verse is in the present tense (Gk. *erchetai*), and this might signify a reference to a present continuing judgment (perhaps HCSB, "the wrath of God comes"). And Paul can portray God's wrath as operating in the world of our day (Rom. 1:18; 1 Thess. 2:16). However, his typical pattern is to associate God's wrath with the final judgment. See, for instance, 1 Thessalonians 1:10, where Paul, with similar language to what we find here, refers to Jesus as the one "who rescues us from the coming *(erchomenos)* wrath." We probably have a similar use of the present tense here in Colossians. And this, after all, fits the particular meaning of this verb. To say that something "is coming" is not to say that something has arrived, but that it is on the way. So Paul's point here is that the final outpouring of God's wrath is on its way, it is "imminent," in the sense that God has predicted it and it could arrive at any time. The same point is expressed in other terms in 1 Corinthians 6:9 and Ephesians 5:5-6, part of which we quoted above: "For of this you can be sure: No immoral, impure or greedy person — such a person is an idolater — has any inheritance in the kingdom of Christ and of God. Let no one deceive you with empty words, for because of such things God's wrath comes on those who are disobedient" (5:5-6; cf. also Eph. 2:2). We see again the close relationship between Colossians and Ephesians.

And this close relationship is an important factor in evaluating the textual variant that occurs at the end of v. 6: "coming on those who are disobedient" (TNIV footnote). This reading has strong manuscript support[39] and is adopted in most of the English versions (with KJV; NKJV; HCSB; NRSV; NASB; NET; TEV). On the other hand, TNIV, along with RSV, ESV, and NLT, has chosen not to include these words in the text on the basis of a well-established text-critical principle: one should suspect any reading as secondary that has a close parallel in another text. The reason for this principle is the known tendency of scribes to accommodate texts to other familiar texts. Perhaps the most important "inter-

---

39. The Greek is ἐπὶ τοὺς υἱοὺς τῆς ἀπειθείας, and it is included in all the major manuscripts except P⁴⁶ and B (two of the best manuscripts of the Pauline letters). "Sons of disobedience" (a literal rendering of the contested phrase) is a Semitic way of characterizing people; hence: "those who are disobedient" (NRSV) or simply "the disobedient" (HCSB).

nal" argument in favor of the inclusion of the phrase is the transition from v. 6 to v. 7. Verse 7 begins with a Greek phrase that could most naturally be translated "you yourselves also . . ." (*kai* [untranslated in the TNIV] *hymeis*). This "also" seems to imply that Paul has already referred to a group of sinners: "you yourselves *also* [in addition to those I just mentioned] walked in these sins."[40] But only if we include the disputed words would we have such a reference. These two considerations are finally balanced. However, because we do not need to translate "also" in v. 7 (there is another way to explain *kai*; see below), we hesitantly conclude that the phrase has been added to Paul's original texts by scribes influenced by Ephesians 5:5-6.[41]

7 Verse 6 is phrased as a general theological principle: God's wrath is going to be revealed in the last day because of all the sins that humans commit. Verse 7 now applies this principle. Paul reminds the Colossians that they were "once" *(pote)* people who were condemned to suffer this wrath because of their own sinful lifestyle. As a basis for our comments on this verse, we first need to get before us a rather literal rendering of the Greek: "in which you *(kai)* walked, when you were living in these." Two key initial issues require decision: the meaning and translation of *kai*, which we have left untranslated; and the antecedents of the two pronouns "which" (the relative pronoun *hois*) and "these" (the demonstrative pronoun *toutois*). If "coming on those who are disobedient" (v. 6b) is included as part of the original text, then the initial pronoun could refer to "disobedient people": "among which people you once walked."[42] But, quite apart from the textual uncertainty of this phrase, normal Pauline style would suggest, rather, that this pronoun refers to

40. The UBS *Greek New Testament* committee found the decision very difficult but ultimately decided to include the phrase (Metzger, *Textual Commentary,* 556). See esp. Benoit for a comparison with the Ephesians text and the syntactical argument (Pierre Benoit, "Rapports littéraires entre les Épîtres aux Colossiens et aux Éphésiens," in *Neutestamentliche Aufsätze: Festschrift für Prof. Josef Schmid zum 70. Geburtstag* [ed. J. Blinzler, O. Kuss, and F. Mussner; Regensburg: Friedrich Pustet, 1963], 14-17). The relationship between text and syntax is nicely reflected in the RSV and NRSV. The former, which does not include the phrase in v. 6, does not translate the καί in v. 7, whereas the latter, which does include the phrase in v. 6, also translates the καί ("also").

41. The ultimate consideration in deciding among textual variants is which of the variants is best able to explain the existence of the others. The addition of the phrase on the basis of the Ephesians parallel is easy to explain, but its omission is not (interpreters who defend its originality appeal to an "accidental" omission, but what kind of accident?). Most commentators prefer to omit the phrase (see, e.g., Lightfoot, 213; Gnilka, 183; O'Brien, 173), but others argue for its inclusion (Abbott, 281-82; Wright, 135; Lindemann, 55; Dunn, 210).

42. In this case, of course, the relative pronoun οἷς ("which") will be masculine. See Dunn, 217.

"these" in v. 6a, which, in turn, of course, refers to the list of sins in v. 5.[43] And this reading receives some confirmation from a parallel passage in Ephesians 2:1-2: "As for you, you were dead in your transgressions and sins, *in which you used to live* (or "walk," *periepatēsate*) when you followed the ways of this world and of the ruler of the kingdom of the air, the spirit who is now at work in those who are disobedient." The antecedent of the second pronoun in the verse could, then, be the "disobedient people" in v. 6 (assuming that the relevant phrase is original), and this would make good sense of the verse: "You used to walk in these sins when you lived among those disobedient people."

But it is a bit difficult to think that the antecedent of this last pronoun could go back to v. 6. It would be more natural for this pronoun to refer to the immediately preceding pronoun at the beginning of v. 7. If this is right, then the sequence of the two clauses in the verse must rest on a difference in the significance of the verbs "walk" and "live." The internal logic of the verse would then go something like this: "You indulged in these very sins when you were still living in the world where such things are typical."[44] What, then, of the *kai*? As we have noted in our comments on v. 6, the most natural meaning of the word, in conjunction with the emphatic pronoun "you" *(hymeis)*, is "also": "You also [along with these disobedient people just mentioned] walked in these sins."[45] However, Paul can also use *kai* in such a construction in an emphatic sense: "You indeed," "you yourselves."[46] We think this meaning best fits the context here (and also in the following verse, where the same construction occurs). In v. 7 Paul, after inserting the general principle of v. 6, uses an em-

43. When Paul uses the locution περιπατέω plus ἐν, the object of the preposition normally refers to sins or to a way of life (Rom. 6:4; 2 Cor. 4:2; 10:3; Eph. 2:2, 10; 4:17; 5:2; Col. 4:5; 2 Thess. 3:11, however, is an exception; cf. also Col. 2:6). See also, e.g., Lightfoot, 213; O'Brien, 186.

44. For this distinction in the verbs, see Harris, 149; Wright, 136. Lightfoot (213) distinguishes them as, respectively, the "character of their practice" and the "conduct of their life." The shift from the aorist περιεπατήσατε ("you walked") to imperfect ἔζησαν ("you were living") fits with this sequence, the former simply stating the fact of the Colossians' former lifestyle and the latter focusing attention on the duration of that time (see Wallace, *Greek Grammar*, 503, on the persistence of this form with ζάω).

45. On this view, if the reference to the "disobedient" in v. 6 is not original, the comparison will be implicit.

46. The construction in question is the sequence καὶ ὑμεῖς. The καί in this combination can sometimes in Paul have conjunctive force — "and you" (e.g., 1 Thess. 1:6) — but more often is adverbial. In this usage, the word normally reinforces a comparison: "you also" (e.g., Col. 3:13). But there are also instances of an adverbial usage that are not clearly comparative and in which the καί appears simply to reinforce the emphasis perhaps conveyed by the use of the nominative pronoun (see 1 Cor. 16:16; Eph. 5:33; Phil. 4:15; 1 Thess. 2:19). See Lightfoot, 213.

phatic construction to return his attention to the Colossians. "God will visit his wrath on these kinds of sins. And you yourselves were committing just these sins at one time — when you were living in the world where such things are typically done." The verb "live" has the same connotation in the previous chapter, when Paul rebukes the Colossians for submitting to regulations "as if you were still living in the world" (v. 20b; my translation).[47] The TNIV's "in the life you once lived" therefore captures the nuance of the Greek here quite accurately.

8 *But now* contrasts the former way of life of the Colossians with the action that they are now to take as people who have "died" to the powers and regulations of this world. As we noted in our comments on v. 7, Paul uses here again the combination of a nominative personal pronoun — *hymeis*, "you" — with *kai* ("and," "also," "even"). Most interpreters think that the *kai* suggests an implicit comparison: "you also, along with other Christians."[48] But, as in v. 7, we think the combination is emphatic: "you yourselves," "you in particular." In vv. 6-7 Paul underscores how vital it is for Christians to deal with sin in their lives by reminding us (1) that sinful behavior is a hallmark of our past life that we have left behind; and (2) that God's wrath falls on people who engage in such behavior. These verses therefore support the two calls to put away sin that frame them: "put to death . . ." (v. 5); "you must rid yourselves . . ." (v. 8).

As we have noticed, these two exhortations are parallel in formulation: a command to put away sin is followed by a collective expression, which is then enumerated in five specific examples, the last of which is given an additional qualification. However, while structurally parallel, the verses differ in content. In the former (v. 5), Paul calls on the Colossians to "put to death" sins, whereas he here urges them to "rid yourselves" *(apothesthe*, from *apotithēmi)* of them. This latter verb can refer to the taking off of clothes (cf. Acts 7:58), and, since the New Testament frequently uses the imagery of a change of clothes to depict the transition from the old life to the new (including in this context; see vv. 9, 10, 12), a number of interpreters believe that the word may have such a connotation here.[49] But the verb only rarely refers to divesting oneself of

47. The verb ζάω ("live"), of course, often has theological meaning in Paul — "live in relation to God," "live eternally" — but he also uses it fairly often with this more prosaic sense (see Rom. 7:9[?]; 8:12; 14:7; 1 Cor. 7:39; 9:14; 2 Cor. 5:15; 6:9; 13:4; Gal. 2:14; cf. Gal. 2:20; 5:25; Phil. 1:21, 22; Col. 2:20; 2 Tim. 3:12; Titus 2:12).

48. See, e.g., Abbott (282), who suggests that the two ὑμεῖς καί phrases nicely balance one another: "you also, along with other pagans" (v. 7); "you also, along with other believers" (v. 8).

49. E.g., Gnilka, 184; O'Brien, 186. Note that ἀποτίθημι is apparently contrasted with ἐνδύω ("put on [clothes]") in Rom. 13:12 (14) and Eph. 4:22 (24).

clothing in the Bible, and it is doubtful whether any such allusion is intended.[50] It means generally and simply "take away," "put off" (see esp. the roughly parallel uses in Rom. 13:12; Eph. 4:22, 25; Heb. 12:1; Jas. 1:21; 1 Pet. 2:1).[51] In all these passages, including Colossians 3:8, the tense of the verb (aorist) connotes a general exhortation simply to do what is commanded. What we are to do is, literally, "put off all things." This phrase could refer to what precedes, in which case the logic of this verse would be: "put off all these things I have mentioned above, and, in addition. . . ." But it more likely introduces what follows, as the English translations recognize: *rid yourselves of all such things as these. . . .*[52]

Determining the exact referents of the five items that follow depends, first, on deciding just what the concluding prepositional phrase, *from your lips,* modifies. (TNIV's "lips" translates Gk. *stoma,* "mouth," with "lips" used to connote the speaking function of the mouth.)[53] If it modifies the verb, then all the sins listed here will have to be, in some sense, sins of speech: "put away from your mouth all such things as these. . . ." *Anger, rage,* and *malice* will then refer to verbal expressions of these emotions rather than to the emotions themselves.[54] But giving this extended meaning to these words does not have good lexical support. More likely, then, *from your lips* should be attached to the end of the list as a way of reinforcing the last two sins: "put off all these things: anger, rage, malice; and put away from your mouth *slander* and *filthy language.*"[55]

On either reading of the syntax, Paul's concern is especially that Christians would avoid unnecessarily critical and abusive speech. The first three sins in the list refer to those attitudes that give rise to such speech. *Anger (orgē)* and *rage (thymos)* are often used virtually interchangeably in Scripture, and they probably cannot be distinguished here.[56] *Malice*

50. Dunn, 218.

51. The reflexive pronoun found in the TNIV — "rid *yourselves*" — may reflect a decision to interpret the middle voice of ἀπόθεσθε as an "indirect middle," according to which the action has particular reference in some way to the subject. On the other hand, this rendering may simply be a matter of English style, since it is questionable whether the middle form of this verb carries any special force (e.g., it is probably deponent: all occurrences of this verb in the NT are in the middle).

52. Moule, 118.

53. See BDAG for this translation of στόμα.

54. See esp. Moule, 117-18, who claims that the alternative reading of the syntax is unnatural Greek.

55. See, e.g., O'Brien, 187. Most of the versions also imply such a reading of the syntax. Wright (136) believes that the reference is to the sins in both vv. 5 and 8.

56. The rough equivalence of the terms is indicated by the fact that the LXX, on almost 40 occasions, combines the two in a genitive relationship (usually translated "fierce anger"); cf. also the ὁ θυμὸς ὀργῆς in Rev. 16:19; 19:15.

translates a word with a very general meaning *(kakia),* and receives its specific meaning from its context. Both here and in Ephesians 4:31 and 1 Peter 2:1, it occurs in a context where sins of speech are the focus, suggesting the idea of "malice" found in most of the English versions. Paul's purpose is not to single out three specific sins but to use the three words together to connote the attitude of anger and ill will toward others that so often leads to hasty and nasty speech. Jesus reminds us that "the things that come out of the mouth come from the heart" (Matt. 15:18), and it is this principle that undergirds v. 8.[57] "The things that come of the mouth" in this case are *slander* and *filthy language.* The Greek behind the former word is *blasphēmia* ("blasphemy"), which can, of course, refer to defamation of God and what belongs to him (Matt. 12:31; 26:65; Mark 3:28; 14:64; Luke 5:21; John 10:33; Acts 6:11; Rev. 13:1, 5, 6; 17:3). But it also regularly applies to defamatory speech directed to fellow humans (Matt. 12:31; 15:19; Mark 7:22; Eph. 4:31; 1 Tim. 6:4). The Greek word behind *filthy language (aischrologia;* literally, "shameful words") is rare, occurring only here in biblical Greek. It seems to have the general sense of "obscene language," and probably, in combination with *slander,* refers to the use of coarse language when defaming another person.[58] As we noted in our comments at the beginning of this section, Paul's concern with the problem of critical speech (note also "do not lie" in v. 9) suggests that Epaphras had told Paul that the false teachers had stirred up a certain amount of animosity and strife among the Colossian Christians themselves.

9-10 The focus on sins of speech that comes as the climax of v. 8 is reinforced by a new command: *Do not lie to each other.* The lack of explicit connection between this command and the previous verses may indicate that the prohibition of lying is something of a summary,[59] or at least a particularly notable example of the inappropriate speech that Paul wants to banish from the community. Lying is not a sin that features often in the Old Testament law, but a prohibition of lying does occur in Leviticus 19:11, among a series of prohibitions that has influenced the New Testament quite significantly: the command to love the neighbor occurs in Leviticus 19:18.[60] It is also possible that the prohibition of lying reflects the

---

57. Indeed, Pokorný (168) thinks that the phrase ἐκ τοῦ στόματος αὐτοῦ alludes to this saying of Jesus. The suggestion has some merit, since the identical phrase occurs in Matt. 15:11, 18, and Paul has alluded to this same context in 2:22 (see the notes on that verse).

58. See the note in BDAG.

59. See, e.g., Schweizer, 193; Barth/Blanke, 408.

60. Leviticus 19:11 reads: "Do not steal." "Do not lie." "Do not deceive one another" (the LXX for "one another" is πλησίον, "neighbor," which occurs of course also in the love command).

Decalogue commandment, "You shall not give false testimony against your neighbor" (Exod. 20:16; Deut. 5:20).[61] Only in Ephesians does Paul elsewhere explicitly condemn lying in his ethical teaching; see Ephesians 4:25: "Therefore each of you must put off falsehood *(pseudos)* and speak truthfully to your neighbor, for we are all members of one body." (Significantly, this prohibition comes in a context where Paul also refers to the "putting off" of "the old self" and the "putting on" of the "new self" [vv. 22-24; cf. Col. 3:9b-10].) Since Paul identifies the gospel with "truth" (e.g., Col. 1:5; cf. 1:6), it is possible that the "lying" he prohibits is the kind of speaking against the true faith that the false teachers were engaged in.[62]

But the mutuality emphasized by "each other" stands against this interpretation. The prohibition is more likely a general one, singling out lying as a particularly clear form of community sin. The form of the imperative verb (present tense) could have the nuance "*stop* lying to one another" (NAB).[63] But it more likely signifies simply "never lie to each other."[64] As many commentators note, Paul forbids Christians from lying to one another because he is preeminently concerned in this context with the health of the Christian community — not because it is permissible for Christians to lie to non-Christians.

From a strictly grammatical point of view, vv. 9b-11 ground the prohibition "do not lie to one another" in v. 9a. But conceptually these verses provide the basis for all the commands and prohibitions in vv. 5-9a.[65] To be sure, the *since* in the TNIV has nothing explicitly corresponding to it in the Greek text. But the translation is justified, since it is almost certain that the two participles in vv. 9b and 10a — translated *have taken off* and *have put on* — have a causal nuance in this context.[66] Christians are to

61. Gnilka (185; cf. also Dunn, 218-19) buttresses this suggestion by arguing that the context reflects an early Christian ethical tradition built on the Decalogue. He notes that, if "lying" from v. 9 is included, Paul alludes to the seventh and eighth commandments in v. 5 ("You shall not commit adultery"; "you shall not steal") and to the sixth and ninth in vv. 8-9 ("You shall not murder" [= anger; cf. Matt. 5:21-22]; "you shall not give false testimony"). However, while these commandments undoubtedly influenced early Christian moral teaching, direct dependence on the Decalogue here is unlikely.

62. Gnilka, 185; Pokorný, 172. Note the association of lying and false teaching in 2 Thess. 2:9, 11; 1 John 2:21, 27.

63. Bruce, 146; O'Brien, 188; Dunn, 220.

64. Cf. Harris, 150, for these two options. Moule, *Idiom Book*, 21, singles out Col. 3:9 as an instance where it is difficult to account for the tense of the imperative.

65. Aletti, 229.

66. Most English versions therefore translate accordingly (NASB[!]; NET; NKJV; HCSB; NLT; NAB). A few commentators think that these participles — ἀπεκδυσάμενοι ("putting off") and ἐνδυσάμενοι ("putting on") — are imperatival: "put off"; "put on" (Lightfoot, 214-15; Lohse, 141; Pokorný, 168-69). In the parallel Ephesians text the compa-

avoid the vices listed in vv. 5 and 8 as well as the "lying" of v. 9a because they have *taken off the old self* and *have put on the new self* (v. 10a).

The verb behind *have taken off* (*apekdyomai*) is the same verb that Paul used in 2:15 to describe God's "stripping" of the power of the powers and authorities, and, significantly, is cognate to the noun that Paul uses in 2:11 to refer to the "stripping off" (*apekdysei*) of the "sinful nature" that takes place in "Christian circumcision." Paul is here returning to that earlier conception with different imagery. As Christians have "put off" the "sinful nature," so they have also "put off" the "old self." As we noted in our comments on 2:15, the verb Paul uses here in 3:9 is first attested in these texts in Colossians, but it almost certainly has the same basic meaning as the related verb *ekdyomai*, "take off" or "strip off." This latter verb normally refers to a literal "taking off" of clothes (e.g., Matt. 27:28, 31; Mark 15:20; Luke 10:30).

The same is true of the verb used in v. 10a, *endyomai*, "put on," which refers to the donning of clothes fourteen times in the Gospels, Acts, and Revelation. While, then, it was not clear that the verb "rid yourselves" in v. 8 alluded to a change of clothes, the case for such an allusion here is considerably stronger. A change of clothes is a rather natural symbol for a change in life or situation; and a kind of "ritual" changing of clothes therefore featured in a number of ancient religions.[67]

But many interpreters think that Paul may be alluding to a particular "change-of-clothes" scenario: the baptismal ritual. People baptized in the early church symbolized the radical change of life associated with baptism by taking off their normal clothes and then, after their baptism, putting on fresh, often white, clothes. Note, for instance, Galatians 3:27: "for all of you who were baptized into Christ have clothed yourselves (*endyomai* is the verb) with Christ"[68] — a verse particularly relevant because Paul echoes Galatians 3:28 in v. 11 of our passage. And, of course, Paul has already associated in Colossians the believer's transition from the old life to the new with baptism (2:11-13). So it is quite likely that Paul would associate the "taking off" of the old self and the "putting on" of the new with baptism — baptism, however, being understood, in typical

---

rable verbs are infinitives, which perhaps unfold what is meant by the gospel that the readers have heard and been taught (v. 21); cf. TNIV: "You were taught . . . to take off the old self . . . to be renewed . . . to put on the new self" (Eph. 4:21-24; see P. T. O'Brien, *The Letter to the Ephesians* [Grand Rapids: Eerdmans, 1991], 326-27; though see HCSB). But syntax and context in Colossians are quite different; and the translations and most of the commentators are correct to view the participles as genuinely adverbial.

67. Especially relevant for Colossians is the elaborate clothing rituals found in some of the mystery religions (cf. Lohse, 141).

68. E.g., Lohse, 141; Pokorný, 168.

Pauline fashion, as inseparable from faith (see the notes on 2:12).[69] Whether Paul alludes specifically to a physical change of clothes associated with baptism is more doubtful, however. Both the verb "take off" (*apekdyomai*) and "put on" (*endyomai*) are used in the New Testament in a purely metaphorical sense (for the former, see Col. 2:15; for the latter, Rom. 13:12, 14; 1 Cor. 15:53, 54; Gal. 3:27; Eph. 4:24; 6:14; 1 Thess. 5:8); and the earliest evidence for a ritual change of clothes as part of Christian baptism comes from the mid-second century.[70]

Believers are to take off *the old self (ton palaion anthrōpon)* and put on *the new self (ton neon [anthrōpon])*.[71] Paul uses similar language, as we have noted above, in Ephesians 4:22-24, where he summarizes the gospel that the Ephesians were taught as involving a putting off of the old self and a putting on of the new, and in Romans 6:6, where he affirms that "our old self was crucified with him [Christ]." These contrasting expressions, especially in their more traditional translations "old man" and "new man," have figured importantly in various conceptions of the Christian life. The phrases have frequently been interpreted as "natures," and debates have then ensued over whether the Christian possesses a "new nature" that has been added to the "old nature" (as the Ephesians text might suggest) or whether the Christian's "new nature" simply replaces the "old nature" (as Romans, with appeal to the "new creation" language of 2 Cor. 5:17, is thought to imply).

But we suggest that these competing schemes of the Christian life have introduced a key, but unfounded, assumption: that "old self" and "new self" refer to natures, or "parts" of the human being. The text before us in Colossians goes on to claim that "here" (most likely a reference to the "new self") "there is no Gentile or Jew, circumcised or uncircumcised, barbarian, Scythian, slave or free" (v. 11). This language strongly suggests that the "new self" is not a part of an individual or even an individual as a whole, but some kind of corporate entity. This suspicion finds strong confirmation in Ephesians 2:15, where Paul speaks of God's intention to incorporate both Jews and Gentiles in the church: "His purpose was to

69. See, e.g., J. Jervell, *Imago Dei* (Göttingen: Vandenhoeck & Ruprecht, 1960), 233-34.

70. Lincoln, 643. The allusions come in the *Gospel of Philip* 101; Hippolytus, *Apostolic Tradition*.

71. Some (esp. older) interpreters think that νέος ("new") suggests, in contrast with καινός, the nuance of "radically new" (e.g., Abbott, 284; Lightfoot, 215; cf. also Gnilka, 187). But most interpreters rightly regard the two adjectives as having the same meaning in most contexts. Note that νέος in v. 10 is followed by a form of καινός (ἀνακαινούμενον) and that καινός is used in Eph. 4:24 to denote the "new self." See on this esp. O'Brien, 190.

create in himself one new humanity *(kainon anthrōpon)* out of the two, thus making peace" (see also Eph. 4:13). Similarly, we should recall that Romans 6:6 follows closely Paul's discussion of the corporate significance of Adam and Christ in Romans 5:12-21.

These contextual clues suggest strongly that, for Paul, the "old self," or "old man," is first of all Adam and the "new self," or "new man," is Christ. Note, in this regard, that Paul can speak of "putting on Christ" as apparently parallel to "putting on the new self" (Gal. 3:27; Rom. 13:14). It is therefore our "Adamic" identification, with its servitude to sin, that we have "put off" in coming to Christ; and it is our "Christic" identification, with its power over sin, that we have "put on." We have been brought into a new realm of existence, a realm in which the "old self," Adam and all that he represents, no longer dictates our thinking or our behavior. We have, then, made a decisive break with the "old self": we are no longer identified with Adam, and his sin and death no longer rule us (Rom. 6:6; Col. 3:9-10). On the other hand, this real and decisive separation from Adam's "lordship" does not mean that we cannot yet be influenced by Adam's pattern of behavior. For while transferred into Christ's realm, we are still prone to think and live as people who still belong to Adam's realm. Hence, with the celebration of a decisive change, there arises also the constant need for appropriation of that change (Eph. 4:22-24).[72]

The contrast of "old self" and "new self" alludes to one of Paul's most fundamental theological conceptions: the contrast between a realm in opposition to God, rooted in Adam's sin and characterized by sin and death, and the new realm, rooted in Christ's death and resurrection and characterized by righteousness and life. (This same theology lies behind Paul's argument in 2:12-13 [see our comments on those verses].) In our text Paul wants to remind us that we have been transferred into this new realm and that because of this transfer we are both empowered and required to live in a new way. The *practices* characteristic of the "old self" must be "put off" (v. 9b; cf. vv. 5 and 8). And the practices characteristic of the "new self" must be "put on" (see 3:12-17).

The need to work out in daily life the reality of our transfer into the new realm, or "new self," reflects Paul's typical "already–not yet" tension. While "already" detached from the "old self" and attached to the "new self," we yet live in a time when the old has not been finally defeated and destroyed. The old realm continues to exist and to exercise its influence

72. For this general interpretation of "old self" and "new self," see esp. H. N. Ridderbos, *Paul* (Grand Rapids: Eerdmans, 1975), 62-64; Tannehill, *Dying and Rising with Christ*, 24-30; John Murray, *Principles of Conduct* (Grand Rapids: Eerdmans, 1957), 211-19; Darrell L. Bock, " 'The New Man' As Community in Colossians and Ephesians," in *Integrity of Heart, Skillfulness of Hands* (Grand Rapids: Baker, 1994), 158-60.

over us who still live in unredeemed bodies. Paul alludes to this tension when he goes on to say that the new self *is being renewed in knowledge in the image of its Creator.* The present durative force of the verb (a present participle in Greek) makes clear that the "new self," the new reality ruled by Christ, is not in its final state: it is in a state of "becoming." Paul uses this same language to make a similar point in 2 Corinthians 4:16 — "Though outwardly we are wasting away, yet inwardly we are being renewed day by day" — and Romans 12:2 — "Do not conform to the pattern of this world, but be transformed by the renewing of your mind."

Paul qualifies this ongoing renewal with two prepositional phrases: it is taking place *in* or "for" *knowledge;* and it is taking place "according to" (or "in") *the image of its Creator.* In the former phrase, knowledge is probably the goal or object of the renewal (so most translations) rather than its means (NLT). This idea can be expressed in English with the preposition "in," as in most versions (TNIV; RSV; NRSV; ESV; HCSB; NET), but also with "for" (as in NASB; NAB); see NJB: "you have put on a new self which will progress towards true knowledge the more it is renewed." This *knowledge* is, of course, knowledge of God, an understanding of who he is in terms of Christ and what that understanding means for living rightly. It is this knowledge that human beings lost in the fall into sin (Gen. 2:17; 3:5, 7; see Rom. 1:28) and that incorporation into Christ makes possible once again.[73] However, as Paul has made clear earlier in the letter by praying that the Colossians might be filled with this knowledge (1:9, 10), we do not gain this knowledge automatically. It may well be, then, that we should find an implied exhortation in v. 10b: "make sure you are allowing this renewal to take place!"[74]

Image of its Creator, in a context that alludes to Adam (the "old self"), inevitably draws our attention to Genesis 1:26-27: "Then God said, 'Let us make human beings in our image *(eikona),* in our likeness. . . . So God created human beings in his own image *(eikona),* in the image of God he created them." As God created human beings originally to be in his "image," an image defaced in the fall, so God is now working to renew human beings "in accordance with" (Gk. *kata*) his image.[75] Redemption is itself, in a certain basic and fundamental sense, a "new creation" (cf. 2 Cor. 5:17; Gal. 6:15).[76] However, we will also recall that Paul has already

---

73. Dunn, 222.

74. Lohse, 143.

75. It is possible that *Creator* (κτίσαντος) is Christ (so a number of ancient commentators and G. D. Fee, *Pauline Christology* [Peabody, Mass.: Hendrickson, 2007], 303-4), but it is more likely, considering the typical biblical usage of κτίζω and cognates, to refer to God the Father.

76. Wright, 138-39.

claimed in this letter that it is Christ himself who is supremely "the image *(eikōn)* of God" (1:15). It is Christ who supplies the pattern for the renewal of the "new self," as Romans 8:29 makes clear: "For those God foreknew he also predestined to be conformed to the image of his Son, that he might be the firstborn among many brothers and sisters."

11 This "new self," we must recall, is not a "new nature" or even a "new person"; it is a new "humanity." As O'Brien puts it, "The renewal refers not simply to an individual change of character but also to a corporate recreation of humanity in the creator's image."[77] The corporate nature of the "new self" comes very much to the fore in this verse. The *here* (*hopou*; it could also be translated "where") opening the verse refers to the "new self" in v. 10a: "Here, in the new humanity being created by God in Christ and in accordance with Christ, there is neither. . . ."[78] What follow are eight designations intended to accentuate the inclusiveness of the new humanity. Six of the eight form pairs arranged in a contrasting pattern: *Gentile or Jew,*[79] *circumcised or uncircumcised, slave or free.*[80] All three oppositions are very common in Paul: "Gentile and Jew" occurs as a pair of opposites in Romans 1:16; 2:9, 10; 3:9; 10:12; 1 Corinthians 12:13; Galatians 3:28; "slave and free" in 1 Corinthians 12:13; Galatians 3:28; Ephesians 6:8. "Circumcision and uncircumcision" are never paired in quite the same fashion in Paul, although Galatians 5:6 and 6:15 come close. But they are frequently contrasted (Rom. 4:9-11; 1 Cor. 7:18-19).

The "odd men out" in this list are the two designations *barbarian*

---

77. O'Brien, 191.

78. The ἔνι has been explained as the original (strengthened) form of the preposition ἐν ("in"), with the verb (ἐστιν) being understood (Abbott, 285; Harris, 154). But others take it to be a shortened form of ἔνεστιν, from ἔνειμι, "be, exist" (BDF §98). The form occurs also in Jas. 1:17; Gal. 3:28 (three times). The meaning of the verse is the same in either case.

79. The Greek behind TNIV's "Gentile" is Ἕλλην, "Greek" (see most of the English translations); but Paul uses this word virtually as the singular form of ἔθνη, "Gentiles" (Paul never uses the singular ἔθνος to refer to an individual human being). It is truer to Paul's intention, therefore, to translate this word "Gentile" rather than "Greek" (which could be restricted to a person from Greece; cf. also NLT). See also Rom. 1:16; 2:9, 10; 10:12; 1 Cor. 12:13; Gal. 3:28; and the plural in Rom. 3:9. "Greek"/"Greeks" is retained in the TNIV of 1 Cor. 1:22, 24; 10:32 because of the focus in those contexts on Greek ethnicity per se.

80. The designations in the first and second pair are separated with a καί ("and," rendered "or" in TNIV because it is governed by a negative), while the final four terms are not (cf. ESV; although a few manuscripts do supply a καί between δοῦλος and ἐλεύθερος). On semantic grounds, the final two words can be seen to constitute a contrasting pair; but the shift in form may suggest that the fifth and sixth words — "barbarian, Scythian" — do not; especially since contrasting pairs in the parallel texts (Gal. 3:28; 1 Cor. 12:13) always have a conjunction.

and *Scythian*. Paul uses the former elsewhere, but never elsewhere contrasted with *Scythian*, which occurs only here in the New Testament. Granted the context, it is of course natural to think that Paul intends these two words also to be in opposition to one another. But it is difficult to find a clear opposition between them. "Barbarian" is an onomatopoeic word (one that sounds like what it means), used by Greeks to mock the way non-Greeks spoke ("bar bar bar"). It accordingly is used of any non-Greek, often with an implied nuance of cultural inferiority (it occurs in the NT in Acts 28:2, 4; Rom. 1:14; 1 Cor. 14:11). *Scythian* refers to a person who lives in Scythia, a region just north of the Black Sea.[81] The evidence we have from ancient sources suggests that the Scythian was generally thought to be the "epitome of unrefinement and savagery" (cf. the NLT translation "uncivilized").[82] If this is so, *barbarian* and *Scythian* would not be in opposition to each other; *Scythian* would be simply an extreme example of a *barbarian*. To be sure, attempts to rescue an opposition between these two words have been made by giving *Scythian* a different sense, but they have not been successful.[83] Probably, then, Paul intends both *barbarian* and *Scythian* as further examples of the general category *uncircumcised*, though perhaps with special emphasis on their social identity: "barbarians," that is, "non-Greeks," as opposed to "Greeks" (the first word in the list).

The three contrasting pairs occur in two texts that closely resemble Colossians 3:11:

Galatians 3:27-28: for all of you who were baptized into Christ have clothed yourselves with Christ. There is neither Jew nor Gentile, neither slave nor free, neither male nor female, for you are all one in Christ Jesus.

81. On the Scythians in general, see Karen S. Rubinson, *ABD* 5.1056-57.
82. BDAG; O. Michel, *TDNT* 7.447-50. See Josephus, *Contra Apion* 2.269: "Scythians, who delight in murdering people and are little better than wild beasts." See also Philo, *On the Embassy of Gaius* 1.10; 2 Macc. 4:47; 3 Macc. 7:5.
83. Douglas Campbell, e.g., has argued that the "Scythian" might refer to a slave, since slaves were often purchased from the region of the Black Sea. "Barbarian," then, could refer to the slave owner (Douglas A. Campbell, "Unravelling Colossians 3.11b," *NTS* 42 [1996], 120-32). But Campbell's evidence is not compelling. Eckhard Schnabel also thinks that "Scythian" might refer to a slave and that Paul might therefore be contrasting free non-Greeks ("barbarians") with slaves ("barbarian and Scythian" would then repeat, in reverse order, the contrast "slave and free," just as "circumcised and uncircumcised" repeat, also in reverse order, the first contrast, "Gentile and Jew"). (*Early Christian Mission*, vol. 2: *Paul and the Early Church* [Downers Grove, Ill.: InterVarsity, 2004], 2.1245). The problem with Schnabel's otherwise very attractive interpretation is that it presumes an emphasis on "free" in the word "barbarian" that is unlikely.

> 1 Corinthians 12:13: For we were all baptized by one Spirit so as to form one body — whether Jews or Gentiles, slave or free — and we were all given the one Spirit to drink.

All three texts refer or allude to water baptism;[84] all three make a principial statement about the inclusiveness of the new people of God; and all three use two or more pairs of opposites to illustrate this inclusiveness. We have good grounds for thinking, then, that Paul "quotes" in Colossians 3:11 an established tradition.[85] Those who belong to Christ constitute a "new humanity," within which the distinctions of this world, while not obliterated, are relativized. As the "household" code in 3:18–4:1 makes clear, the Christian community is comprised of people who maintain their gender, familial, and social identities. Jews are still Jews in Christ; Gentiles are still Gentiles in Christ; slaves are still slaves in Christ. But these earthly identities are no longer what is most important: solidarity in Christ is now the ruling paradigm for the new community.[86]

As Paul typically does when he cites tradition, he modifies it to suit the particular point he is making. What do his modifications here tell us about his intention? Paul omits the pair "male or female" that is found in the Galatians text, and interpreters have speculated about what this might mean.[87] But speculate is all that we can do; we just do not know enough to suggest even a plausible explanation. Moreover, the absence of this pairing in the 1 Corinthians text might suggest that it was not a standard part of the tradition. The two additions Paul makes to the tradition may be more significant. First, his addition of the circumcised/uncircumcised pair emphasizes the polarity already present in the Jew/Gentile pairing. This addition has led a number of recent commentators to stress the Jewish character of the false teaching at Colossae.[88] Second, Paul elaborates the category "uncircumcised" by mentioning both barbarians and Scythians. Perhaps this indicates a concern, in opposition to a

---

84. We argued above that Col. 3:9-11 probably has water baptism in view. The meaning of ἐν ἑνὶ πνεύματι . . . ἐβαπτίσθημεν in 1 Cor. 12:13 is debated. But we think a reference to water baptism, empowered by the Spirit, is more likely than a reference to a baptism "in the Spirit."

85. For an exploration of this tradition and its origin, see Michel Bouttier, "Complexio Oppositorum: sur les formules de I Cor 12:13; Gal 3:26-8; Col 3:10, 11," *NTS* 23 (1976), 1-19.

86. See esp. D. G. Horrell, *Solidarity and Difference* (London and New York: T&T Clark, 2005), 124-29.

87. E.g., Pokorný, 170, speculates that there may have been a tendency toward an androgynous view among the false teachers, while MacDonald, 146, thinks the pairing was omitted because of tendencies toward asceticism.

88. See esp. Dunn, 223-24.

tendency among the false teachers to exclusivity, to stress that the new humanity is inclusive of every nation and every social class.[89]

Paul concludes by showing that the polarities of worldly existence are overcome in Christ — the one who is *all, and is in all*. To claim that Christ is "all" is briefly to reiterate the high Christology that Paul has set forth in 1:15-20: Christ is the center point of both creation and redemption, the one in whom and through whom all things now "hold together." The second "all" *(pasin)* could also assert Christ's penetration of "all things" *(pasin* as neuter). But in this context it more likely asserts that Christ brings unity because he is the one who indwells "all people" *(pasin* as masculine) who make up the new humanity.[90] This last phrase may echo the tradition Paul is citing: the end of Galatians 3:28 claims that "you are all one in Christ Jesus."[91]

3. Putting On the Practices of the "New Self" (3:12-17)

[12]*Therefore, as God's chosen people, holy and dearly loved, clothe yourselves with compassion, kindness, humility, gentleness and patience.* [13]*Bear with each other and forgive one another if any of you has a grievance against someone. Forgive as the Lord forgave you.* [14]*And over all these virtues put on love, which binds them all together in perfect unity.*

[15]*Let the peace of Christ rule in your hearts, since as members of one body you were called to peace. And be thankful.* [16]*Let the message of Christ dwell among you richly as you teach and admonish one another with all wisdom through psalms, hymns and songs from the Spirit, singing to God with gratitude in your hearts.* [17]*And whatever you do, whether in word or deed, do it all in the name of the Lord Jesus, giving thanks to God the Father through him.*

In Colossians 3:1-4, Paul has called on us to take a "heavenly" perspective on all of life, a perspective that emerges naturally from our new identity as those who have died with Christ and been raised with him. The specifics of this heavenly perspective are spelled out in a mainly negative fashion in vv. 5-11, where Paul focuses on those vices that we are to "put to death" (v. 5) and "rid [our]selves of" (v. 9). But at the end of this paragraph, Paul comes back to the positive side of our new identity: we are people who belong to the "new self, "being renewed in knowledge in the image of its Creator." In vv. 12-17, Paul enumerates positively some of the

89. Luz, 230.
90. Harris, 154; Wright, 140.
91. Dunn, 227.

attitudes and behavior that should typify the "new self." And in keeping with the collective significance of the new self, the focus in these verses is on those virtues that foster community identity and cohesion. Nor is this a new emphasis. As we have noted, the previous paragraph also focuses on those vices that would tend to bring dissension into the Christian community: "anger, rage, malice, slander, and filthy language" (v. 8); lying to one another (v. 9). The "new self" brings together people from different ethnic, religious, and social backgrounds, and believers should put aside the prejudices that might arise from those backgrounds in order to facilitate the unity of the body. This "new self," as we noted, alludes fundamentally to Christ himself. Through faith, we are joined to Christ; we become his "body." The basic theological truth that undergirds Paul's commands in vv. 12-17 involves just this point: we are "members of one body" (v. 15).[92]

While the paragraph unfolds without major breaks, four basic parts can be identified. Three of the four explicitly maintain the strongly christological focus of this letter. Paul begins by reminding us of our privileged position as God's "chosen people, holy and dearly loved," and urges us to "clothe ourselves" with five virtues that will enable us to live together harmoniously in one body (these five virtues may, indeed, be deliberately contrasted with the five vices in v. 8 that hinder such unity). The call to "bear with each other" and "forgive one another" in v. 13 shows how these virtues are fleshed out. And the grounding for all of this is Christ's own ("the Lord"; see our comments on v. 14) forgiveness of us. The call to love in v. 14 is the second basic part of the paragraph. Paul pictures love as the garment, or "coat," that goes on over all the other virtues and enables them all to work together. The third section of the paragraph (vv. 15-16) is marked by a shift in syntax. The second-person plural imperatives of vv. 12-14 — "clothe yourselves," "bear," "forgive," "put on" — give way to third-person passive imperatives: "Let the peace of Christ rule," "Let the message of Christ dwell." These two parallel exhortations again focus on Christ. The passage concludes with a general exhortation (returning to the second plural imperative active form) to do all we do "in the name of the Lord Jesus" (v. 17). These three phrases — "the peace of Christ," "the message of Christ," and "the name of the Lord Jesus" — reinforce and apply the Christocentric message of Colossians.[93] The passage ends with another reference to "thanksgiving" (see also v. 15), a recurring motif in Colossians. The attitudes and behavior that Paul calls on the community to display in this paragraph are quite general and do not

92. See Jervell, *Imago Dei*, 252-54.
93. E.g., E. D. Martin, 175.

seem to be closely related to the false teaching with which the letter is so preoccupied in chapters 1–2. But this should not surprise us. Though the writing of Colossians is clearly stimulated by the false teaching, we would expect Paul to take the opportunity to encourage the Christians in Colossae to develop those distinctly Christian characteristics that should mark them as the new covenant people of God.

12 *Therefore* connects the paragraph that begins here with what Paul has just said about the "new self." This "new self," the Christian community formed by and in Christ, transcends the boundaries of religious background, ethnicity, and social status — and any other "boundary" drawn from this world that we might like to draw. Whatever our worldly background or status, we all now have our fundamental identity determined by Christ and the people of Christ to whom we belong. But this new identity, while given in Christ, also must be achieved in practice. The barriers erected by our identity in this world must be overcome in reality as we live out the new relationship in the body of Christ. At the same time, Paul implies that this "new self" is rooted in history. The Christians in Colossae, Gentiles though they are, have the privilege of belonging to the historical people of God. The "new self" is the "new Israel."[94]

This identification is clearly indicated in the description of the Colossians as *God's chosen people, holy and dearly loved.* All three are standard ways of describing Israel in the Old Testament and the church as the people of God in the New Testament. As is suggested in the TNIV translation, the governing concept is "chosen people," with "holy" and "dearly loved" expressing aspects of that key idea.[95] *Chosen people* (in Greek simply "God's chosen") reflects standard Old Testament teaching that the existence and status of Israel depend on God's decision to choose them and to form them as his people — which he does through the events of the exodus, the giving of the law, and the entrance into the promised land.[96] In distinction from the Old Testament where God selects his people mainly from one nation, Israel, God now forms his new covenant people by choosing (or "electing") individuals from among both Jews and Gentiles (see esp. Rom. 9:24-25; also Rom. 8:30; Eph. 1:4; and cf. v. 15 in our passage).

94. Wright, 141; Dunn, 228. Dunn sees this as further evidence for the essentially Jewish nature of the false teaching.

95. See, e.g., Lightfoot, 220-21; Harris, 161; O'Brien, 198.

96. The concept is, of course, very widespread; but the actual language that Paul uses here — ἐκλεκτοί, "chosen ones" — appears only in 1 Chr. 16:13; Pss. 105:6, 43; 106:5; Wis 4:15; Isa. 43:20; 45:4; 65:9. In the NT, see Rom. 8:33; 2 Tim. 2:10; Titus 1:1; 1 Pet. 1:1; 2:9; Rev. 17:14.

It is because of this gracious act of God that Israel is *holy*. This language is a very common designation of God's people Israel and is taken up in the New Testament as one of the most common ways to describe the church as well (e.g., Col. 1:2). The word "holy," of course, suggests the notion of being "set apart for God," and it not surprisingly therefore often occurs with the idea of election. Note, for instance, Deuteronomy 14:2: "you are a people holy to the LORD your God. Out of all the peoples on the face of the earth, the LORD has chosen you to be his treasured possession." *Dearly loved* in the TNIV represents a passive participle that could be translated simply "loved" (e.g., HCSB) or "beloved" (ESV) — the implied subject is clearly God. God's love for his people is often featured in the Old Testament, sometimes as a response to the people's obedience (e.g., Deut. 5:10) but often also as the fundamental basis for God's election of the people (e.g., Deut. 4:37; 10:15; Ps. 78:68; Isa. 41:8). Paul also brings together God's love and his election of his people (1 Thess. 1:4; 2 Thess. 2:13; cf. also Jude 1). In this verse, then, as *holy* designates the result of God's election, so *dearly loved* may suggest its basis. Nowhere else in Scripture do we find together in a description of God's people the three Greek words used here *(eklektos, hagios, agapaō)*. But we do find a similar constellation of ideas. See, in the Old Testament, Deuteronomy 7:6-7: "For you are a people *holy* to the LORD your God. The LORD your God has *chosen* you out of all the peoples on the face of the earth to be his people, his treasured possession. The LORD did not *set his affection* on you and choose you because you were more numerous than other peoples, for you were the fewest of all peoples."[97] In the New Testament, Paul's address to the Roman Christians touches on these same three conceptions: "to all in Rome who are *loved by God* and *called* to be his *holy* people." See also 1 Peter 2:9-10: "But you are a chosen people, a royal priesthood, a holy nation, God's special possession, that you may declare the praises of him who called you out of darkness into his wonderful light. Once you were not a people, but now you are the people of God; once you had not received mercy, but now you have received mercy."

Paul uses the clothing imagery that he has employed earlier to urge the community of God's people in Christ to cultivate virtues that will foster that community in practice. *Clothe yourselves* translates the same verb that Paul has used in v. 10 ("put on"; cf. "taken off" in v. 9). Paul names five specific virtues, almost surely intentionally paralleling the five vices of v. 5 and v. 9. A significant aspect of these virtues is that they are often attributed to, or associated with, Christ. It is as if Paul is saying, in the

---

97. The LXX uses ἅγιος ("holy"), as does Col. 3:12, but for both "chose" and "set his affection" it employs προαιρέω ("choose"); the Hebrew in v. 7a is חָשַׁק, "love," "desire").

words of Romans 13:14, that we are to "put on Christ." And, of course, this christological focus neatly elaborates the key idea in vv. 10-11. Having put on "the new self," identified with Christ himself, it is necessary at the same time to put on those virtues that characterize Christ.[98]

Compassion translates a phrase that can be rendered literally "bowels of mercy" (KJV). "Bowels" (Gk. *splanchna*), as the English makes clear, has an originally physiological sense, referring to the inner parts of a person. See Acts 1:18, where Judas's death is recounted: "his body burst open and all his intestines *(splanchna)* spilled out." But the parts of the human body were often in the ancient world (and in ours) associated with psychological aspects of the person. "Bowels" was very often associated with the seat of the emotions and especially love. The word is used this way regularly throughout the New Testament (Luke 1:78; 2 Cor. 6:12; 7:15; Phil. 1:8; 2:1; Phlm. 7, 12, 20; 1 John 3:17). In our text, then, "bowels of mercy" means "love characterized by mercy," "heartfelt compassion" (NAB; HCSB), or "tenderhearted mercy" (NLT).[99]

Kindness, the second virtue in the list, sometimes denotes God's own "goodness," especially as it is expressed in his gracious acts (e.g., Pss. 31:19; 67:11; 119:68; Rom. 2:4; 11:22; Eph. 2:7; Titus 3:4). Here, of course, the reference is to the human attribute of kindness (see also Rom. 3:12; 2 Cor. 6:6; Gal. 5:22).

Humility is a typically Christian virtue, which was often viewed negatively in the ancient world, where it was understood in terms of servility or cowardice. The call to humility in the New Testament is based on the supreme act of "humbling," Christ's taking on human form and going to death on the cross on our behalf (Phil. 2:3, 8). The Philippians text also provides a nice commentary on "humility," as involving valuing "others above yourselves" and "not looking to your own interests but . . . to the interests of others" (vv. 3b, 4; note also the reference to "heartfelt compassion" [*splanchna*] and "compassion" [*oiktirmoi*] in v. 1). Paul wants the Christian community to display this true humility toward one another, in contrast to the "humility" of the false teachers, which apparently consisted mainly of ascetic practices (see 2:18, 23, where the same Greek word as appears here [*tapeinophrosynē*] is used).

A fourth community-fostering virtue is *gentleness (praütēta),* which the standard Greek lexicon for the New Testament nicely (if somewhat expansively) defines as "the quality of not being overly impressed by a

98. See, e.g., Bruce, 152.
99. The genitive οἰκτιρμοῦ is probably qualitative: "love characterized by mercy" (e.g., Harris, 161). This is the only place in the NT where the word occurs in the singular (the plural form elsewhere probably reflects the underlying Heb. רַחֲמִים [BDF §142], O'Brien, 198]). The singular is probably used because it depends on a lead noun.

sense of one's self-importance."[100] The model is again Jesus, who claimed to be "gentle *(praüs)* and humble *(tapeinos)* in heart" (Matt. 11:29; cf. 21:5; 2 Cor. 10:1). The New Testament letters frequently call on Christians to follow Christ's example in this self-giving (Gal. 5:23; 6:1; Eph. 4:2; 2 Tim. 2:25; Titus 3:2; Jas. 1:21; 3:13; 1 Pet. 3:16).

The final virtue in the list, "patience" *(makrothymia),* is once more an attitude that both God the Father and Christ display toward sinful creatures (Rom. 2:4; 9:22; 1 Tim. 1:16; 1 Pet. 3:20; 2 Pet. 3:15) and that we, as his people, should display toward one another (2 Cor. 6:6; Gal. 5:22; Eph. 4:2; Col. 1:11; 2 Tim. 3:10; 4:2; Heb. 6:12; Jas. 5:10). If "kindness," Wright suggests, refers to our basic approach to people, so "patience" refers to the kind of reaction we should display toward them.[101] As the biblical references in the previous sentences reveal, the attributes in this list appear together elsewhere in the New Testament in a rich variety of combinations. This suggests that Paul is using the list of virtues in v. 12 to draw a general picture of what a member of Christ's new covenant community should look like.

13 Paul now indicates what this fundamental attitude should look like in action: *Bear with each other and forgive one another.* The participles of the Greek text are accurately rendered as imperative verbs in the TNIV (see also NIV; NRSV; NJB; NLT),[102] but they make clear that there is a close relationship between the actions commanded in v. 13 and the attitudes in v. 12. Paul may view these actions as the product of patience (the last virtue in the list in v. 12) specifically,[103] but he more likely intends to present these actions as the natural outgrowth of the general attitude conveyed by all five virtues together. The two commands in the verse are, of course, related, but there is also a progression. The verb "bear with" *(anechomai),* as the translation suggests, indicates a somewhat grudging willingness to "put up with" difficult circumstances (e.g., persecutions — 2 Cor. 4:12; 2 Thess. 1:4) or people (Jesus asks, referring to an "unbelieving and perverse generation," "how long shall I put up with you?" [Matt.

---

100. BDAG.

101. Wright, 142.

102. A few commentators (e.g., Lohse, 147) identify the participles as imperatival. But Wallace is probably right to caution us about taking participles with such independent force unless they clearly cannot be dependent (*Grammar*, 652). Here, then, the participles are more likely to express "attendant circumstance" (Harris, 162 — as one possibility). However, since such participles often take their mood from the verb they "modify" (in this case the imperative ἐνδύσασθε ["clothe yourselves"] in v. 12), the result is the same. (Harris is right to criticize the identification of the participles as modal [e.g., Lindemann, 61 — "by bearing with and forgiving"] since this would reverse the logical connection of the verses.)

103. O'Brien, 201-2.

17:17; par. Mark 9:19; Luke 9:41]).[104] In the New Testament, it is only in the closely parallel Ephesians 4:2 that "bearing with each other" is presented, as here, so positively: "Be completely humble and gentle; be patient, bearing with one another in love." Therefore, while not requiring the greatest display of Christian kindness and patience, "bearing with one another" is nevertheless a first and necessary step in establishing community. The demand acknowledges that every Christian fellowship is made up of all kinds of people and that we will accordingly sometimes find ourselves in close fellowship with people who are very different than we are. For the sake of maintaining community, we will sometimes have to "put up with" people with whom we would not normally choose to associate.

But, of course, more than this is ultimately called for. Not only must we "bear with each other"; we must also *forgive one another*.[105] "Forgive" translates a Greek verb (*charizomai*) that conveys the idea that forgiving others is an act of grace, freely offered, often not "deserved."[106] Paul frankly recognizes that in the Christian community there will be times when a person will have a *grievance*, a "cause for complaint," against someone else within the fellowship.[107] In such cases, believers are to imitate their Lord, who has "graciously forgiven" them. The normal New Testament pattern is to feature God as the one who forgives, "in" or "because of" Christ; see Colossians 2:13, where the same verb is used, and the Ephesians parallel, in 4:32: "Be kind and compassionate to one another, forgiving each other, just as in Christ God forgave you." This being

104. See also Acts 18:14; 1 Cor. 4:12; 2 Cor. 11:1, 4, 19, 20; 2 Thess. 1:4; 2 Tim. 4:3; Heb. 13:22. Barth/Blanke, 422, find a more positive connotation of the verb based on its use in the LXX of Isa. 46:4. But, considering the rather free nature of the LXX translation of Isaiah, this occurrence provides a slim basis for such a meaning.

105. The TNIV shift from "each other" to "one another" mirrors a shift of Greek pronouns, from the reciprocal ἀλλήλων to the reflexive ἑαυτοῖς. The two often convey different ideas, the former referring to relations within a group of people ("one another") and the latter to action that "reflects" back on the subject. Philippians 2:3, where Paul calls on the believers to "treat one another (ἀλλήλους) as more important than yourself (ἑαυτῶν)" (NET), illustrates the distinction. Older scholars (e.g., Lightfoot, 221) often sought to distinguish the two here in Colossians, but it is generally recognized now that they simply reflect a general tendency to use them interchangeably with a reciprocal sense (BDF §287; Turner, *Syntax*, 43-44).

106. The verb here, χαρίζομαι, is, in fact, something of a distinctly Pauline word, since only he among NT authors uses it to refer to the forgiveness of others (see also 2 Cor. 2:7, 10 [3 times]; 12:13; Eph. 4:32; Col. 2:13; the verb occurs in Luke 7:42, 43 in reference to "canceling" or "forgiving" a debt). The verb more often used in the NT generally for "forgive" (ἀφίημι) occurs in Paul with this sense only once, and then in an OT quotation (Rom. 4:7).

107. "Grievance" translates μομφή, which occurs only here in biblical Greek.

the case, the "Lord" here in Colossians could refer to God the Father.[108] But, apart from Old Testament quotations, Paul apparently invariably uses *kyrios*, "Lord," to refer to Christ (see, e.g., the distinction in 1 Cor. 8:6), and this pretty well settles the matter here. Identifying Christ as the one who forgives fits with the resolutely christological focus of this paragraph ("peace of Christ" [v. 15]; "message of Christ" [v. 16]; "in the name of the Lord Jesus" [v. 17]) and of the letter as a whole.[109] And the notion is hardly a significant departure from Paul's standard way of speaking (as some suggest who find here further evidence of the un-Pauline character of Colossians). Paul's references to divine forgiveness are few (Rom. 4:7; Eph. 1:7; 4:32; Col. 2:13; 3:13), so one can hardly speak of a pattern. And it is a small step from asserting that God forgives "in Christ" (Eph. 4:32; cf. Eph. 1:7; Col. 1:14) to saying that Christ himself forgives. The formal structure of this last sentence in the verse suggests a comparative idea: we should forgive "in the same way as" the Lord forgives.[110] But the construction might also include a causal nuance: we are to forgive *because* the Lord has forgiven us. Christ establishes not only the pattern but the possibility of forgiveness.[111] The general sense is similar to Jesus' teaching about forgiveness in Matthew 18:23-35.

14 The connection between this verse and the preceding context is left quite ambiguous in the Greek text, which, literally translated, reads "and upon all these love." The verb to be supplied, as the versions and commentators agree, is "clothe yourselves" *(endysasthe)* from v. 12. But it is less clear how the preposition I have translated "upon" *(epi)* functions. It might simply suggest that believers need to adopt the virtue of love "in addition to" the other virtues mentioned in this context (NET; NASB).[112] But the clothing imagery that is picked up from v. 12 suggests rather that love is being pictured as a garment that is to be put on "on top of" the other items of dress that Paul has enumerated in v. 12. In this case, the implication would be that love is not just another virtue to be added but the supreme virtue. Some of the translations suggest this idea by rendering

---

108. One manuscript, in fact, has "God" as the subject, another has "God in Christ," while a larger number have "Christ." But "Lord" is almost certainly original, since (1) it is strongly supported in the manuscripts (P[46], A, B, etc.); and (2) it offers a good explanation for the origin of the other variants. See Metzger, *Textual Commentary*, 557-58.

109. E.g., Aletti, 238.

110. The *as* in the TNIV represents two Greek conjunctions that are related to each other: "καθώς ["just as"] the Lord has forgiven οὕτως ["in this way"] you also [should forgive]."

111. See the same construction in 1 Thess. 2:4: it is *because* Paul and his companions have been entrusted with the gospel that they speak. On the causal use of καθώς, see BDAG.

112. BDAG; Zerwick, *Biblical Greek* §128; Harris, 163.

"above all" (KJV; RSV; NRSV; ESV; HCSB; NASB), while TNIV, by translating *over all these,* explicitly preserves the clothing imagery (see also
NAB and even more clearly NJB: "over all these clothes").[113] While clear
syntactical parallels for this second sense are lacking,[114] we still prefer
this interpretation on contextual grounds: it fits with the clothing imagery of v. 12 and sets the stage for the unifying effect of love that the second part of this verse highlights.

In this second part of the verse Paul asserts that love *binds them all
together in perfect unity.* The TNIV reflects a particular interpretation of a
rather dense Greek construction, but one that we think brings out the
sense quite accurately. A rather literal translation would run "which is
the bond of perfection" (cf. NKJV).[115] The phrase has two ambiguities:
what does the "bond" bind together, and in what sense does "perfection"
qualify that bond? "Bond" translates a word that means, essentially, "that
which binds together" *(syndesmos).*[116] In the New Testament, it is used to
refer to fetters that bind (Acts 8:23) and to the connecting parts of the human body (the "sinews"; Col. 2:19). We can assume, then, that the word
here pictures love as a binding or unifying force. This sense is clear in the
somewhat parallel Ephesians 4:3, where Paul pictures the Spirit as the
"binding force" that fosters unity within the body of Christ. In that text it
is Christians whom the Spirit binds together, and a number of interpreters fill out Colossians 3:14 in the same way: love "binds us all together in
perfect harmony" (NLT).[117] But, as we suggested above, the interpretation followed by the TNIV, which implicitly identifies the virtues
("them," referring to the "virtues" in v. 14a) as what is bound together by
love, is to be preferred. Possible parallels to this general conception are
found in the Greco-Roman world; and it is a bit more natural to supply
the object of the binding from v. 14a, which refers to the virtues ("them"
in v. 14b in the TNIV refers to "all these virtues" in v. 14a).[118] Moreover,
while the New Testament elsewhere does not clearly view love as having
a unifying force among the virtues, love is frequently highlighted as that

113. See, e.g., Moule, 123; O'Brien, 203.

114. There are no examples, within biblical Greek at least, of the verb ἐνδύω followed by ἐπί in the sense of "put on top of."

115. The phrase is connected to the earlier part of the verse with the phrase ὅ ἐστιν.
"Love" (feminine ἀγάπη) is the antecedent of ὅ, even though the latter is neuter. The
phrase ὅ ἐστιν is a kind of set phrase that does not change depending on the gender or
number of the antecedent (e.g., Robertson, *Grammar,* 713-14).

116. BDAG.

117. E.g., Lohse, 148-49; O'Brien, 203-4; Barth/Blanke, 424.

118. See, e.g., Lightfoot, 222; Harris, 164; Moule, 123; Wright, 142-43. The Pythago-
reans highlighted φιλία ("friendship") as the force that binds the virtues together (references in Lohse, 148-49).

virtue without which others cease to have the value they are meant to have (see esp. the well-known 1 Cor. 13:1-3). "Compassion," "kindness," "humility," "gentleness," and "patience" attain their full power only when they are unified by and empowered by love. The qualifier "of perfection," could, on this reading, describe the quality of the bond: "a bond characterized by perfection," for example, "a perfect bond" (NET; HCSB; NASB). But it is probably better, since Paul presents "perfection" earlier in Colossians as the goal of his ministry (1:28), to think that perfection is the goal of the binding force of love.[119] While in the earlier text, however, it was "each person" whom Paul sought to bring to perfection, here, in the context, it is the "new self," the community, that will be brought to perfection when love binds the virtues together.

15 Paul's concern for the unity of the body becomes explicit in this verse. It begins with a *kai* — "and" (untranslated in the TNIV; see, e.g., ESV) — which suggests that this next command continues the theme that Paul has been developing since v. 12.[120] "And [in addition to putting on these virtues, forgiving each other, and making love supreme] *let the peace of Christ rule in your hearts.*"[121] Paul highlights "peace" as one of the key blessings of Christian experience. This is clear from his customary letter opening, in which he prays that his readers might experience "grace" and "peace" (e.g., Col. 1:2). Moreover, the transition from "love" (v. 14) to "peace" is a natural one, as the somewhat parallel text in Ephesians 4:2-3 suggests: "Be completely humble and gentle; be patient, bearing with one another in love. Make every effort to keep the unity of the Spirit through the bond (*syndesmos*; cf. v. 14) of peace." The "peace" that God brings to us in Christ is sometimes the objective state of "peace with God," or reconciliation (Rom. 5:1; cf. vv. 10-11). Paul has used the cognate verb in this

---

119. The genitive τῆς τελειότητος, on this view, would be objective. See, e.g., Turner, *Syntax*, 212; Harris, 164-65; Lohse, 148; Pokorný, 172; Wolter, 187. The TNIV of Col. 1:28 has as the goal of Paul's ministry a person "fully mature." But the Greek word there is τέλειος, which is cognate to the Greek word used here. A connection between 3:14 and 1:28 is rendered more likely by the fact that v. 16 in our paragraph picks up the "admonishing" and "teaching" language of 1:28.

120. The καί might also serve to set out the parallel vv. 15 and 16 as a subunit within the paragraph (note the καί introducing v. 17 in this regard).

121. The "peace of Christ" is a phrase that occurs only here in Paul, and some interpreters are quick to suggest that this provides further evidence of a non-Pauline author. But (1) Paul uses the comparable phrase "peace of God" only once (Phil. 4:7), so we can hardly speak of a standard Pauline "formula"; (2) Paul uses the phrase "the Lord of peace," almost certainly referring to Christ, in 2 Thess. 3:16; and (3) Paul identifies Christ so closely with God in the securing of peace that a shift from one to the other is quite natural. See esp. Eph. 2:14, where Christ is identified as "our peace" (of course, this text is also often attributed to a post-Pauline author); and the confusing mixture of pronouns in Col. 1:19-20 (on which see our comments).

sense in Colossians 1:20, where he claims that God has "reconciled" all things to himself "by making peace through [Christ's] blood." As we noted in our comments on that verse, the peace established through Christ is *shalōm*, the eschatological state of cosmic restoration that the Old Testament prophets anticipated.

In our verse, however, Paul seems to have a specific facet of this universal peace in view. For, first, he calls on the Colossians to let the peace of Christ "rule." "Rule" translates a Greek verb that refers to the activity of the "umpire," who renders verdicts in contested situations. The verb thus naturally takes on the connotation of "control"; the standard Greek lexicon paraphrases, let the peace of Christ "be the decisive factor."[122] In general, then, Paul wants the Colossians to make "peace" the arbiter, the factor that should be given preference over competing concerns and interests.[123] And in the context it is in their relationships with each other that the "peace of Christ" should play this role. Without sacrificing principle, believers should relate to one another in a way that facilitates and demonstrates the peace that Christ has secured for them (cf. Rom. 14:19).

A second indicator that Paul is not thinking here of our "peace with Christ" in an objective sense is the addition of the phrase *in your hearts*. To be sure, this phrase could indicate that the peace here is the "inner peace" of a contented and satisfied heart. But Paul is not saying that the peace is in our hearts; he is saying that the peace should rule "in the heart." Note particularly in this regard the use of this same phrase at the end of v. 16: "singing . . . in your hearts." Here Paul is clearly not saying that the singing is to be an activity that takes place within each person. Rather, his point is that the singing should be "heartfelt," sincere, proceeding from the inner being of each singer. In this verse, then, similarly, Paul is saying that the peace that characterizes the "new self" should be a ruling principle or virtue in our innermost being and that it should affect all our relationships — and, in this context, our relationships with one another. "The peace of Christ," then, is "the peace that he both embodies and brings."[124] It was Jesus himself who said, "Peace I leave with you; my peace I give you" (John 14:27; cf. 16:33).

---

122. BDAG. The verb occurs only here in the NT and only in Wis. 10:12 in the LXX. A verb cognate to this one does, however, occur in Col. 2:18: καταβραβεύω, "decide against," "disqualify."

123. Schweizer, 209; cf. also Lightfoot, 223; Wright, 143. O'Brien (204), however, doubts if any nuance of "arbitrate" is to be found in the verb (see also Barth/Blanke, 425). The basic sense of this exhortation would be found also in Rom. 5:1 if the variant subjunctive verb (ἔχωμεν) were to be read — "let us enjoy peace with God."

124. The genitive τοῦ Χριστοῦ is, then, difficult to classify, but it probably is at least partly subjective (cf. NLT; Harris, 165).

The interrelational focus of the imperative in v. 15a is confirmed by the second part of the verse, which provides the reason why the peace of Christ should rule: *since as members of one body you were called to peace.* To be sure, the *since* of the TNIV is somewhat interpretive, since the Greek conjunction here is simply *kai,* "also" (HCSB) or "indeed" (ESV; NASB). But the logical relationship between the clauses is clearly causal, so the "since" (cf. "for" in NET and NLT; "because" in NJB) captures the sequence of thought. *You were called* picks up the language of election that Paul used in v. 12 — "God's chosen people." Paul frequently uses the verb "call" *(kaleō)* to denote God's gracious and powerful summons to human beings, by which they are transferred from the realm of sin and death into the realm of righteousness and life.[125] And Paul will sometimes, as here, specify particular virtues or blessings "to" which or "into" which believers have been called. Particularly illuminating for this text are 1 Corinthians 7:15, where Paul (referring to husband and wife) says that "God has called us in *(en)* peace"; Galatians 5:13, "you were called to *(epi)* freedom"; Ephesians 4:4, "you were called in *(en)* one hope"; 1 Thessalonians 4:7, "God did not call us to *(epi)* uncleanness but for *(en)* holiness"; 2 Timothy 1:9, "God has saved us and called us to [dative case] a holy life."[126] In all these texts the point is that God has chosen his people not simply to be his people but to live a certain kind of life. That life is bound up with the calling and cannot be separated from it.

As these texts also indicate, Paul uses a variety of Greek constructions to denote this purpose in God's calling. In v. 15b he uses the preposition *eis* but then adds a second prepositional phrase, introduced with *en:* "in one body." As in some of the parallel texts, this *en* phrase could indicate the purpose of God's calling: "you have been called to be one body." But it is awkward to make both this and "peace" the objects of the calling. Therefore, we should take "in one body" to indicate the mode of our calling.[127] The gospel is inescapably individual in its focus: each of us, on our own, is "called" by God and responds in faith on our own. Yet, at the same time, the gospel is inescapably corporate: we are called along with other people, with whom we make up "one body." The TNIV captures the sense well: *as members of one body.* Paul does not define this "one body," and a few interpreters have thought that the phrase may simply be a way of saying that we have been called "together," "as one unit." But the explicit references to the church as the "body of

---

125. Rom. 8:30; 9:24; 1 Cor. 1:9; 7:15, 17, 18, 20, 21, 22, 24; Gal. 1:6; 5:8, 13; Eph. 4:1, 4; 1 Thess. 2:12; 4:7; 5:24; 2 Thess. 2:14; 1 Tim. 6:12; 2 Tim. 1:9.

126. These translations are my own.

127. O'Brien, 205.

Christ" earlier in the letter (1:18, 24; cf. 2:19) make it far more likely that Paul has in view that specific "body." As Christ's own body, the "new self," we belong inextricably to one another, and the pursuit of peace as a reigning principle follows naturally from that corporate reality. It is difficult to decide whether Paul thinks of the "one body" as the local church or as the universal church. The latter would fit with Paul's use of the metaphor elsewhere in Colossians (1:18, 24; 2:19) and with the "one body" parallels in Ephesians (2:16; 4:4).[128] But the context, with its focus on forgiveness of one another (v. 14) and mutual edification through singing (v. 16), suggests that the local church may be in view.[129] But our decision between these options makes little difference. Clearly, for Paul, what is true for the universal church is true as well for the specific, localized expressions of the church. We do not need to make a choice here. The oneness of the universal church comes to expression in local communities of believers.

The brief exhortation *be thankful* at the end of v. 15 is, on the one hand, unexpected but, on the other, not unexpected at all.[130] It is unexpected in that it seems to break the flow of a passage focused on the relations of believers to one another. But "thanksgiving" has also been given an unexpected prominence earlier in the letter (1:12; 2:7; and see v. 16 [probably], v. 17, and 4:2). Believers who are full of gratitude to God for his gracious calling (v. 15a) will find it easier to extend to fellow believers the grace of love and forgiveness and to put aside petty issues that might inhibit the expression of peace in the community.

16 No conjunction or particle links v. 16 to v. 15, perhaps as a way of enhancing the obvious parallelism between the two: "let the peace of Christ rule in *(en)* your hearts" parallels *let the message of Christ dwell among (en) you* (the Greek word order is even the same). TNIV's "message" translates *logos*, which, of course, can also be translated "word." References to the "word of God" are extremely common in the New Testament, but "word of Christ" is rare (only here and in Heb. 6:1; "word of the Lord [referring to Christ]" occurs in 1 Thess. 1:8; 4:15; 2 Thess. 3:1; 1 Tim. 6:3 [plural]).[131] Probably Paul means not "the word, or message,

---

128. Harris, 166.
129. Dunn, 235.
130. The Greek takes the form of the imperative of γίνομαι ("be," "become") plus the adjective εὐχάριστοι ("thankful"). No particular connotation should be attributed to Paul's use of γίνομαι, since the imperative form of εἰμί is rare in the NT (the second plural imperative of εἰμί occurs nowhere in biblical Greek).
131. There are, of course, many places in the Gospels that refer to a particular "word" or saying that Jesus uttered (e.g., John 18:32; 1 Thess. 4:15 may fit in this category also).

that Christ proclaimed" but "the message that proclaims Christ," "the message about the Messiah" (HCSB; NLT; cf. "the word of the gospel" in Col. 1:5).[132] Paul uses the phrase to summarize the authentic teaching about Christ and his significance, an immediately relevant example of which we have in the first two chapters of Colossians.[133] The HCSB, by translating *Christos* as "Messiah," usefully reminds us that this name often continues in Paul to have titular significance, pointing to Jesus as the eschatological anointed King of Old Testament and Jewish expectation.[134] TNIV's *among you* translates a phrase that could also be translated "in [each of] you." (The "in you" found in many versions would most naturally suggest this concept.) Some interpreters argue for this individualized application based on the parallelism with v. 15 ("in your hearts").[135] But the rest of this verse, with its focus on the worship of the collective body, suggests rather that Paul is urging the community as a whole to put the message about Christ at the center of its corporate experience.[136] Specifically, Paul urges them to *let* it *dwell richly* among them. The message about Christ should take up permanent residence among the Colossians (NJB: "find a home with you"); it should be constantly at the center of the community's activities and worship.[137] "Richly" suggests that this constant reference to the word of Christ should not be superficial or passing but that it should be a deep and penetrating contemplation that enables the message to have transforming power in the life of the community.[138]

The rest of v. 16 is governed by three participles (in the Greek text), the first two of which are clearly coordinate: "teaching and admonishing"; "singing." But their relationship to one another and, especially, the relationship of the various modifying phrases to them, are debated. These re-

132. That is, the genitive τοῦ Χριστοῦ is probably objective rather than subjective. See Harris, 166; O'Brien, 206; contra, e.g., Lightfoot, 224; Bruce, 157; Moule, 125.

133. Wright, 144.

134. See D. J. Moo, "The Christology of the Early Pauline Letters," in *Contours of Christology in the New Testament* (ed. Richard N. Longenecker; Grand Rapids: Eerdmans, 2005), 186-87.

135. E.g., Lightfoot, 224.

136. See, e.g., Bruce, 157; Masson, 147.

137. The verb is ἐνοικέω, "dwell in." Paul's other uses of the verb support the concept of a permanent "residence": of the Holy Spirit in believers (Rom. 8:11; 2 Tim. 1:14), of God among his people (2 Cor. 6:16, quoting Lev. 26:12; Jer. 32:38; Ezek. 37:27), or of "faith" in Timothy's grandmother Lois and mother Eunice (2 Tim. 1:5). The verb occurs only in Paul's letters in the NT, as does the basic verb οἰκέω, which has a similar meaning to the compound verb.

138. See the other occurrences of "richly" (πλουσίως) in the NT: 1 Tim. 6:17; Titus 3:6; 2 Pet. 1:11.

lationships should be clarified before we look at the details. The three main options are reflected, respectively, in the TNIV, ESV, and HCSB:[139]

TNIV:

"as you teach and admonish one another with all wisdom through psalms, hymns and songs from the Spirit, singing to God with gratitude in your hearts"

ESV:

"teaching and admonishing one another in all wisdom, singing psalms and hymns and spiritual songs, with thankfulness in our hearts to God."

HCSB:

"teaching and admonishing one another in all wisdom; and singing psalms, hymns, and spiritual songs, with gratitude in your hearts to God."

These three translations differ in the way they make two key decisions. The first is whether "psalms, hymns, and songs from the Spirit" modifies the previous participles, "teaching and admonishing" (TNIV; cf. also KJV; NKJV; NASB) or the following participle, "singing" (ESV; HCSB; cf. also NRSV; NAB; NJB; NLT). Commentators are pretty evenly divided, and a decision between these two options is indeed difficult.[140] But the former option (followed in the TNIV) is perhaps the better. As O'Brien points out, it has three things in its favor: (1) it provides a better balance between the two clauses; (2) it deals seriously with the lack of an "and" *(kai)* before "singing"; and (3) it matches the structure of the parallel in Ephesians 5:19: "speaking to one another with psalms, hymns and songs from the Spirit. Sing and make music from your heart to the Lord."

---

139. We pass over in the text a third issue. The Greek phrase translated by "in all wisdom" (ἐν πάσῃ σοφίᾳ) comes between "Let the message of Christ dwell among you richly" and "teaching and admonishing." It could, therefore, modify the preceding imperative, as the NKJV (following, of course, KJV) has it: "Let the word of Christ dwell in you richly in all wisdom, teaching. . . ." But this option receives little support in the literature (though see Lightfoot, 224), and the parallel in Col. 1:28 strongly suggests that the usual view, attaching the phrase to what follows, is preferable.

140. For the connection with "teaching and admonishing" (διδάσκοντες καὶ νουθετοῦντες), see, e.g., O'Brien, 208; Pokorný, 174; G. D. Fee, *God's Empowering Spirit* (Peabody, Mass.: Hendrickson, 1994), 652-53. For the connection with "singing" (ᾄδοντες), see, e.g., Harris, 167; Bruce, 158; Dunn, 211; Martin Hengel, "Hymnus und Christologie," in *Wort in der Zeit: Neutestamentliche Studien. Festgabe für Karl Heinrich Rengstorf zum 75. Geburtstag* (ed. Wilfrid Haubeck and Michael Bachmann; Leiden: Brill, 1980), 2-3.

The second difference reflected in the three translations above is whether to take the phrase governed by "singing" with the immediately preceding participles — in which case "singing" modifies in some way "teaching and admonishing" (TNIV; ESV) — or to take them back to the main verb of the verse — in which case "teaching and admonishing" and "singing" are parallel ways in which the "message of Christ" dwells richly in the community. This latter option appears to be implied by the HCSB decision to add an "and" before "singing" (cf. also NIV). But it is just the fact that there is no *kai* corresponding to the HCSB "and" in the Greek text that makes this option less attractive than the alternative. We conclude, then, that the TNIV has the basic structure of the verse right: Paul wants the community to teach and admonish each other by means of various kinds of songs, and he wants them to do this singing to God with hearts full of gratitude.

If this is the basic structure of the verse, then it falls into three parts, each of which is slightly subordinate to the part before it:

"Let the message of Christ dwell among you richly
   as you teach and admonish one another . . .
      singing to God with gratitude in your hearts."

The question then arises as to just how each clause modifies the one before it. As we noted, the Greek equivalents to "teach" and "admonish" are in the form of participles. It would make some sense to identify them as instrumental, in which case the "teaching and admonishing" would be the means by which the word would dwell richly in the community.[141] But this may inappropriately restrict the ways in which the message of Christ is to take root in the community. Another option is to see the particles as imperatival. However, while they undoubtedly take on a commanding aspect by virtue of their connection with the imperative "let . . . dwell," they are probably not independent imperatival participles.[142] The best option, then, is to see them as loosely connected to the preceding imperative, indicating two of the modes in which the word of Christ establishes its central place in the community. The "as you teach and admonish" construction in the TNIV brings this out quite well, as does the "teaching and admonishing" construction chosen in many other translations. The relationship between the second and third parts of the verse is much easier to determine. The participle "singing" in the last part picks up the reference to the various types of songs in the second and adds in-

141. Harris, 168.
142. See, again, Wallace, *Greek Grammar,* 652, on the need to restrict the category of "imperatival" participle (technically conceived) to truly independent participles.

formation about how that singing is to take place: "to God"[143] and "with gratitude in your hearts."[144]

The pair "teach" *(didaskō)* and "admonish" *(noutheteō)* is found earlier in Colossians, in Paul's description of his ministry (1:28). As we noted in our comments there, "teaching" refers to the positive presentation of Christian truth, while "admonishing" refers to the more negative warning about the danger of straying from the truth. The similarity to this earlier text continues in the insistence that these activities take place "in all wisdom" *(en pasē sophia):* that is, that those doing the teaching and admonishing do them in appropriate ways, governed by insight into the situation and the people being addressed. And, of course, in contrast to the previous text, this text gives to each member of the congregation the responsibility to teach and admonish other members.[145] Our text, as we have argued, without limiting the means to these activities, identifies "psalms, hymns and songs from the Spirit" as the way in which believers teach and admonish each other. Whether we can distinguish the meanings of these three terms is questionable. The same three words are found in Ephesians 5:19. "Psalm" refers generally in Greek to a song that is sung to the "plucking" (Gk. *psallō)* of the strings of an instrument (esp. a harp).[146] In the New Testament, following the LXX, the word is usually applied to the Old Testament Psalms (Luke 20:42; 24:44; Acts 1:20; 13:33). In 1 Corinthians 14:26, however, it appears to be used generally of a Christian "song" or "hymn." "Hymn" *(hymnos)* occurs only here and in the parallel Ephesians 5:19 in the New Testament. In the LXX, it is translates a variety of Hebrew words referring to religious songs and especially to songs of praise to God. This general sense of a song in praise of a god imitates the usage of the word in general Greek. "Song," finally, is a

143. "To God" (τῷ θεῷ), which comes last in the verse in Greek, could modify "in gratitude" (ἐν [τῇ] χάριτι) (cf. ESV; HCSB; NET) but is more likely to modify "singing," as the TNIV indicates.

144. It should be noted that "gratitude," the rendering found in most of the English versions, translates the Greek word χάρις, which, of course, is often translated "grace" in the NT. Particularly, then, if the textual variant that has an article before the word is followed (τῇ, found in some very good MSS), it is possible to take this phrase as a reference to "the grace of God" (so, e.g., Lohse, 152; Gnilka, 201), perhaps as modifying the songs previously mentioned: "songs that are in the grace of God" (Lightfoot, 225-26). But, whether the article is read or not, it is preferable to take the word here in its well-known sense of "gratitude," "thanks" (BDAG; Abbott, 291; Moule, 126; O'Brien, 210; comparable occurrences are in 1 Cor. 10:30; Col. 4:6 [?]). "In your hearts" could modify "singing" but is more likely to modify "with gratitude" (Wright, 144-45); hence "with gratitude in your hearts," found in most of the English translations.

145. The Greek behind "one another" is again the reflexive ἑαυτούς, used here in a reciprocal sense (see on v. 13).

146. LSJ.

very general term, used in secular Greek and the LXX of all kinds of songs.[147] It occurs very often in the LXX titles of psalms. If we follow the TNIV in attaching *pneumatikais* to this last word in the series only, then it possibly refers to a spontaneous, musical praise of God or Christ prompted by the Spirit. In this case, it is attractive to identify "psalms" as songs based on Scripture, "hymns" as songs about Christ, and "songs" as spontaneous compositions "prompted by the Spirit."[148] Whether these distinctions are maintained or not, it is perhaps probable that *pneumatikos* does qualify only the last of the three terms, since only the last term was general enough to require a qualification that would limit its meaning to religious songs.[149] And the translation "from the Spirit" is also appropriate, since it preserves the distinctive role of the Spirit that is basic to Paul's thinking; "spiritual," especially in modern English, is too vague to capture this sense.[150]

This verse is one of the very few that provide us with any window at all into the worship of the earliest Christians. It is, of course, too brief, and its specific contours too uncertain, to give us much specific information. But it does make three points that are worth emphasizing. First, the "message about Christ," or, more broadly, we could say, "the word of God," was central to the experience of worship. Second, various forms of music were integral to the experience. And, third, teaching and admonishing, while undoubtedly often the responsibility of particular gifted individuals within the congregation (such as Paul [Col. 1:28] or Epaphras [Col. 2:7]) or elders (1 Tim. 3:2; 5:17; see also, e.g., 1 Cor. 12:28; 2 Tim. 2:2), were also engaged in by every member of the congregation.

17 Paul concludes this paragraph of exhortations focused on community life with a general command: *And whatever you do, whether in word or deed, do it all in the name of the Lord Jesus, giving thanks to God the Father through him.* He thereby brings to a conclusion the central exhortatory section of the letter. That this is a concluding summary is suggested not only by its broad concern but also by specific similarities to the opening statement of this section, in 2:6-7. As in this text, where the touchstone of Christian conduct is *the Lord Jesus,* so there also: "As you received Christ Jesus the Lord, continue to live your lives in him" ("Jesus" has not oc-

---

147. Philo, in *On the Embassy to Gaius* 1.44, e.g., uses ᾠδή ("song") with "dancing" and "acting" as activities that are unlikely to influence the "ruler of all the earth and sea."

148. Harris, 169; cf. Lightfoot, 225 and Dunn, 238 (on the first two).

149. Contra, e.g., Lohse, 151; Wolter, 190; O'Brien, 210, who think all three terms are modified by πνευματικαῖς. (The dative plural feminine form agrees technically only with ᾠδαῖς; but it could still modify all three.)

150. O'Brien, 210; Bruce, 159; Gnilka, 200; Dunn, 239.

curred since that text).[151] Christology, in a manner wholly in keeping with the overall message of Colossians, bookends the Colossians' required response as they face the threat of the false teaching.

The combination "word" *(logos)* and "deed" *(ergon)* is a common way of referring to the totality of one's interaction with the world (Luke 24:19; Acts 7:22; Rom. 15:18; 2 Thess. 2:17; cf. 1 Cor. 10:31): everything, including what we say and what we do, should be governed by the consideration of what it means to live in the realm of the risen Christ.[152] Perhaps we can discern something of a progression from v. 16. Just as the worship gathering should be focused on the "message of Christ" (v. 16), so all of life must be seen as an experience of worship (cf. Rom. 12:1-2). The phrase "name of the LORD" is ubiquitous in the Old Testament, where the "LORD" is, of course, Yahweh. It is, then, another (less direct) sign of the high Christology of this letter (and of the New Testament in general) that the "LORD" is now identified with Jesus Christ.[153] The phrase "in the name of the Lord" takes on a wide variety of nuances, but often the focus is on the nature or character of the Lord. To do all things "in the name of the Lord Jesus," then, does not mean simply to utter Jesus' name but to act always in concert with the nature and character of our Lord.[154] When believers are baptized "in the name of Jesus" they come under his authority and are called to conform to his character; they are, indeed, baptized "into union with" Christ (Gal. 3:27; Rom. 6:3). Since we have put on that Lord, becoming as a community the "new self" who is none other than Jesus, the totality of our existence must now be lived out with him constantly in mind.

The concluding participial clause again highlights thanksgiving as an important component of Christian obedience and, at the same time, an important source of that obedience (see also 1:11; 2:7; 3:15, 16; 4:2). Thankfulness for what God has accomplished for us in Christ is an obvious and powerful stimulus to live under his Lordship. But more than attitude is called for here. Gratitude in the heart (v. 16) must come to expression in actual, verbal giving of thanks to the Father "through" Christ. Some inter-

---

151. Dunn, 241; Wright, 145; J. Callow, *A Semantic and Structural Analysis of Colossians* (Dallas: SIL International, 2002), 130.

152. "Whatever you do, whether in word or deed" is an absolute nominative clause, standing first in the verse for emphasis. The clause anticipates "all" in the main clause of the verse. The Greek text has no explicit verb in this clause, but, as often in Greek, the verb ποιεῖτε, "do" (reflecting ποιῆτε in the first clause), should be supplied.

153. "In the name of the Lord" (בְּשֵׁם יהוה) is a constant refrain in the OT, while it has no clear precedents in the larger Greco-Roman world (Dunn, 240).

154. Barth/Blanke suggest that the phrase here may have the connotation of actions that "proclaim the name of this Lord, or, in other words, that Jesus is the Lord" (430).

preters think that Christ is the basis for the giving of thanks.[155] But Paul's choice of construction should be honored: the giving of thanks is not "because of" Christ (*dia* with accusative) but "through" Christ (*dia* with genitive).[156] In keeping with the way in which Colossians persistently presents Christ as the mediator of all that God is to the world and to the believer, so Christ mediates our thanksgiving to the Father.[157] One might think specifically of Christ, as our High Priest, "transmitting" our thanksgiving to God. But, since this idea is not prominent in Paul, it is probably better to think generally of Christ as the one (in possible contrast to the angels of the false teachers) who has opened the way for us to approach God.[158]

4. The Lordship of Christ in Earthly Relationships (3:18–4:1)

[18]Wives, submit yourselves to your husbands, as is fitting in the Lord.
[19]Husbands, love your wives and do not be harsh with them.
[20]Children, obey your parents in everything, for this pleases the Lord.
[21]Fathers, do not embitter your children, or they will become discouraged.
[22]Slaves, obey your earthly masters in everything; and do it, not only when their eye is on you and to curry their favor, but with sincerity of heart and reverence for the Lord. [23]Whatever you do, work at it with all your heart, as working for the Lord, not for human masters, [24]since you know that you will receive an inheritance from the Lord as a reward. It is the Lord Christ you are serving. [25]Those who do wrong will be repaid for their wrongs, and there is no favoritism.
[4:1]Masters, provide your slaves with what is right and fair, because you know that you also have a Master in heaven.

In vv. 12-17, Paul elaborates some of the ways in which the Christian community is to live out its identity as the "new self," the new humanity that God is creating in and according to Christ (vv. 10-11). The essence of this new humanity is mutuality. In the "new self," there is no longer "Gentile or Jew, circumcised or uncircumcised, barbarian, Scythian, slave or free" (v. 11). Christians are therefore to view themselves as members of "one body" (v. 16), within which an attitude of consideration and love for

---

155. Lohse, 153.
156. O'Brien, 212.
157. "God the Father" occurs a bit less frequently in the NT than "God and Father," and this is probably why some manuscripts have τῷ θεῷ καὶ πατρί instead of the better-attested τῷ θεῷ πατρί. See Metzger, *Textual Commentary*, 558.
158. E.g., Calvin, 354; O'Brien, 212-13; Dunn, 241.

"one another" should prevail. In 3:18–4:1, on the other hand, Paul turns his attention from the spiritual family to the physical family. He addresses the household members in terms of their particular roles within that entity: wives are to submit to their husbands, and husbands are to love their wives (3:18-19); children are to obey their parents, and fathers are not to embitter their children (3:20-21); slaves are to obey their masters, and masters are to treat their slaves equitably and fairly (3:22–4:1). The inclusion of slaves in this series of household regulations might appear odd to us, but not so to the original readers. Slaves often composed an integral component of the ancient household, serving the family in a wide variety of capacities.

This section of Colossians has, as usual, its closest parallel in Ephesians. Ephesians 5:22–6:9 addresses these very same household roles, in the same order, and calling for basically the same behavior as does the Colossians text. But we also find at least partial parallels to Colossians 3:18–4:1 in other passages in the New Testament. Paul asks Titus to require wives to "submit" to their husbands (2:5) and slaves to "submit" to their masters (2:9). First Peter 2:18–3:7 also exhorts slaves to "submit" to their masters (2:18), wives to "submit" to their husbands (3:1), and husbands to "live considerately" with their wives (3:7). To be sure, there are significant differences among these passages. But they are similar in addressing various household members and in assuming some kind of hierarchical pattern within the household relationships. These parallels raise the possibility that we are faced in these passages with a popular early Christian "form" of teaching that focused on household affairs. Lending support to this suggestion is the relatively loose connection between this paragraph and its surrounding context as well as the rapid-fire command style of the passage. And this possibility is turned into a strong probability when we recognize that the same pattern is attested in various other ancient writings. Luther dubbed this form of teaching the *Haustafeln*, "household table," and considerable attention has been devoted to it and its implications for New Testament teaching. Three issues require brief mention.

First, scholars have long debated the particular source from which the New Testament writers have derived this form. It is not necessary here to rehearse the various suggestions, since, as Dunn notes, recent scholarship has quite rightly settled on the general Greco-Roman ethical topic of "household management" *(oikonomia)* as the source of these passages.[159] A good example, and one of the earliest, comes from Aristotle,

---

159. Dunn, 243. For elaboration, see esp. David L. Balch, "Household Codes," in *Greco-Roman Literature and the New Testament: Selected Forms and Genres* (ed. David Aune; Atlanta: Scholars Press, 1988), 25-35 (who also provides a useful overview of theories and

who divides the essential relations of the household into three — master and slave, husband and wife, and father and children — and stresses the natural superiority of the master over the slave and the male (as husband or father) over wife and children.[160] The *Haustafeln* appears in various Greco-Roman writers and was taken up by Philo and Josephus in the Jewish world. This form of teaching, then, was "in the air," and it is not surprising that New Testament writers utilize it to instruct early Christians in their household responsibilities.[161]

A second issue pertaining to these codes is of greater significance for our interpretation of Colossians 3:18–4:1 and related passages. In keeping with their antecedents in the wider culture, the New Testament household tables, as we have noted above, require certain household members (wives, children, slaves) to "submit to" or "obey" others. These exhortations reflect the Roman household pattern, according to which the husband/father/slave owner, the *paterfamilias*, exercised *patria potestas*, "paternal power," over the household. But this hierarchical pattern stands in some apparent tension with the New Testament teaching about the "equality" of all people in Christ. In Christ, as Paul puts it in the famous Galatians 3:28, "there is neither Jew nor Gentile, neither slave nor free, neither male nor female, for you are all one in Christ Jesus." Paul has said much the same thing in this context (v. 11), and vv. 12-17 reinforce this point with exhortations that call on Christians to flesh out the mutuality of their "one body" existence.

The modern drive toward "liberation" has quite naturally focused attention on such passages. But, at the same time, this concern has brought such "conservative" passages as the household codes under severe scrutiny. These passages are said to represent a capitulation to the prevailing cultural norm, a reinforcement of a patriarchal status quo that cannot be reconciled with the more fundamental "liberating" New Testament message. A draconian solution to this problem is to dismiss all the codes as late insertions into their respective books[162] — a suggestion that has rightly received little support. More commonly, these passages are marginalized. Because they occur in books that are widely thought to be pseudepigraphical

scholars); and also, e.g., Barth/Blanke, 462-74 and Lincoln, 652-54. Popular specific proposals are that the codes reflect Stoic teaching (e.g., Lohse, 154-57) or Hellenistic Judaism (James E. Crouch, *The Origin and Intention of the Colossian Haustafeln* [FRLANT 109; Göttingen: Vandenhoeck & Ruprecht, 1972]).

160. *Politics* 1.2.1-23; 1.5.1-12.

161. See esp. Balch, "Household Codes."

162. Winsome Munro, *Authority in Paul and Peter: The Identification of a Pastoral Stratum in the Pauline Corpus and 1 Peter* (SNTSMS 45; Cambridge: Cambridge University Press, 1983).

(Ephesians, Colossians, Titus, 1 Peter), the codes are often viewed as something of a departure from the "authentic" New Testament view (e.g., Galatians). However, a strong case for apostolic authorship of all these contested books can be made, and, in our opinion, convincingly. And it should be noted that the "liberating" principle of Galatians 3:28 is repeated in Colossians 3 (v. 11): the two perspectives lie here side-by-side. We must therefore accord full canonical weight to these passages as we seek to construct a full-bodied Christian ethic on these matters.

Other interpreters, including many evangelicals, give full weight to these passages but argue that the exhortations to submission are deliberate accommodations to the prevailing culture. People in the Greco-Roman world were suspicious of new religious movements, particularly ones that proclaimed revolutionary ideas such as the equality of all people. Paul and other New Testament writers urge Christians to respect the hierarchical structure of the Greco-Roman household as a means of defending the new faith from charges that it was intent on overthrowing existing social structures.[163] This concern to allay suspicion about the gospel was indeed one motivation for some of these passages (see Titus 2:10; 1 Pet. 3:1).

But there is reason to be cautious about concluding thereby that the ethics taught in these passages are simply an accommodation to the culture. For one thing, all the passages are suffused with appeals to distinctly Christian principles. For another, it is perhaps unlikely that the New Testament authors would be so concerned to commend the church that they would teach less than a genuine New Testament ethic. Moreover, we should, perhaps, exercise a "hermeneutic of suspicion" on our own interpretive tendencies: it would be all too easy to impose on the New Testament our own modern preoccupation with and certain definition of "liberation" that does not reflect the balance of New Testament teaching on these issues. We suggest, then, that the instructions within the household code, while obviously directed toward and thereby reflecting the culture of that time (e.g., by addressing slavery), are not simply reflections of that culture. They must be "heard" as an authentic New Testament voice, integrated with, and not simply overridden by, the very important insistence on "equality" in Christ.

One approach to the integration of these two "tendencies" is to view the household codes, along with some other similar texts, as a response to an unbalanced appropriation of the "all one in Christ" principle. While the

163. See esp. David L. Balch on 1 Peter (*Let Wives Be Submissive: The Domestic Code in I Peter* [SBLMS 26; Chico, Calif.: Scholars Press, 1981], 23-80) and, on the Pastoral Epistles, David C. Verner, *The Household of God: The Social World of the Pastoral Epistles* (SBLDS 71; Chico, Calif.: Scholars Press, 1983); see also Wall, 158, on Col. 3:18–4:1.

principle is exceedingly important, setting forth a fundamental dimension of the "new creation," it was clearly never intended to eradicate all distinctions between men and women, husbands and wives, children and parents. Yet some Christians in the early church apparently interpreted the principle in just this way, suggesting, it seems, that marriage, for instance, was an institution of this world best avoided by "liberated," Spirit-filled Christians or that, if one were married, at least sex should be avoided (1 Cor. 7; 1 Tim. 4:3). One can understand how such excesses could arise from the call to Christians to set their hearts and minds on "things above" (Col. 3:1-2). And it is quite possible that the false teachers, with their ascetic tendencies, were themselves downplaying the role of something so mundane as the household.[164] The household codes may be responses to such excesses, reminding Christians that certain institutions continued to exist in the new age and that believers needed to relate appropriately to one another within these institutions.[165] The new family of God gave believers their fundamental identity, but the spiritual family did not eliminate the continuing significance of the physical family and the relations appropriate to its smooth functioning. Colossians 3:18–4:1, like the other household codes, is best seen as giving guidance for the way Christians are to bring all of life under the Lordship of Christ.

Nevertheless, this way of viewing the passages faces a difficult question: how does slavery fit into the picture? Do the household codes support, by implication, the continuing existence of the institution of slavery as part of the "right order" of society? The codes have often been read as if such were the case, with interpreters then drawing two opposite conclusions: (1) the New Testament does not, in fact, oppose all forms of slavery;[166] or (2) the household codes must be relativized in some way, since biblical principles clearly outlaw all forms of slavery.[167] We certainly agree that slavery is ultimately incompatible with consistent biblical teaching, and it is to the church's great discredit that it took so long to recognize that fact. But must we then "relativize" the teaching in these passages? We answer "no" — but with a caveat. We answer negatively simply because the logic set out above makes a crucial, but, in our view, wrong assumption: that these passages endorse slavery. They do not.[168]

---

164. E.g., Hay, 147.

165. Crouch, *Origin and Intention*, 120-45; Pokorný, 178; Dunn, 245-46.

166. E.g., Murray, *Principles of Conduct*, 91-106.

167. E.g., Kevin Giles, "The Biblical Argument for Slavery: Can the Bible Mislead? A Case Study in Hermeneutics," *EvQ* 66 (1994), 3-17.

168. Contra, e.g., Giles, "Biblical Argument," 3, 11. The claim that 1 Tim. 6:1-3 endorses the institution is simply not true; as in the other relevant NT texts, Paul's concern is with individual slaves and masters who are caught up in the existing status quo.

They simply address an institution that happened to be a significant element of ancient society. For various reasons, some theological and some practical, the New Testament writers do not attack the institution of slavery as such. (See the Introduction to Philemon, 369-78, for more on this point.) The household codes are practical and specific: they require believers who occupy these roles to relate to each other in certain ways. Whether those roles should continue or are endorsed by the author or by God is simply not in view. Other biblical texts make clear enough that marriage (wives and husbands) and the family (children and fathers) are to endure as long as this world lasts. There is nothing even approaching any such endorsement of slavery, however.

But we do need to add a caveat. While the silence of the New Testament on the *institution* of slavery is not unexpected, it is somewhat perplexing that the New Testament never calls on Christian slave owners to release their slaves from their bondage. Again, there are reasons for this silence (see once more the Introduction to Philemon, 369-78). But we might also tentatively suggest that the New Testament writers themselves had not yet worked out the full implications of their own theology on this matter.[169]

And there is a further point to be made about this whole argument that must not be overlooked: the degree to which the household codes are "countercultural." As we noted above, they consistently reflect a distinctly Christian ethos, including the new equality among persons that is intrinsic to the gospel.[170] The explicit and repeated basis for the behavior Paul calls for in 3:18–4:1 is the Lordship of Christ. This theme is mentioned seven times in these nine verses.[171] Moreover, while other ancient household codes did occasionally address the "subordinate" members within the household (wives, children, slaves),[172] they were especially concerned to maintain "order" and focused on the head of the household.

169. See on this point esp. William J. Webb (*Slaves, Women, and Homosexuals: Exploring the Hermeneutics of Cultural Analysis* [Downers Grove, Ill.: InterVarsity, 2001]; see also Richard N. Longenecker, *New Testament Social Ethics for Today* [Grand Rapids: Eerdmans, 1984], esp. 26-28; 51-54). Webb provides some helpful perspective on this whole issue, even if his overall proposal is not without some problems. We discuss this matter, and Webb's book, more fully in the Introduction to Philemon, 377-78.

170. O'Brien, 216; Wright, 146-47.

171. Wolfgang Schrage, *Ethik des Neuen Testaments* (Grundrisse zum Neuen Testament 4; Göttingen: Vandenhoeck & Ruprecht, 1982), 239-40; David B. Capes, *Old Testament Yahweh Texts in Paul's Christology* (WUNT 2.47; Tübingen: Mohr Siebeck, 1992), 73.

172. Balch, e.g., notes that Dionysius of Halicarnassus addresses wives before their husbands in his version of a "household code" (*Roman Antiquities* 2.25.4–26.4) (*Let Wives Be Submissive*, 55).

Colossians 3:18–4:1, with the other New Testament codes, is remarkable for the identical tone Paul uses in addressing each group.[173]

A third issue may be addressed more briefly. While we think the academic consensus that Colossians 3:18–4:1 and similar passages reflects a common form of teaching is correct, it is also the case that each specific code takes a particular form appropriate to its context. A comparison with the Ephesians passage, for instance, reveals that the Colossians code gives proportionately greater space to slavery than to the family (five verses out of nineteen are devoted to slavery in Ephesians; five out of nine in Colossians). There may be explanations for this difference in the circumstances that we do not know about. Or the Colossian Christian community may have had a relatively large number of slaves.[174] But if we view Colossians as a letter of Paul himself, then a simpler historical explanation lies near at hand: this letter is being sent along with Onesimus, a slave who is returning to be reconciled (Paul strongly hopes) with his master, Philemon.[175] Some verbal parallels between vv. 22-25 and Philemon support this connection.[176] And, considering the whole code generally, it is also important to note how well it fits within a letter that focuses on the universal significance of Jesus Christ. Christ governs the entire universe, including the mundane affairs of the household. As John Barclay puts it, the household code "is thus entirely consistent with the universalizing thrust of the letter as a whole, in which the tendrils of the Christ-event spread out, as it were, to cover the whole surface of life."[177]

18 The household code opens rather abruptly, with no indication of the relationship between this passage and what has come before. Some interpreters therefore think that the code is a bit of an "add-on," with the general exhortation of v. 17 marking the end of the exhortation section proper.[178] But, as we have suggested above, it is better to view the injunc-

173. John M. G. Barclay, "Ordinary but Different: Colossians and Hidden Moral Identity," *ABR* 49 (2001), 41; Schweizer, 221. A concern for subordinate and more "helpless" members of the household also typifies some of the Jewish codes.

174. O'Brien, 226; Pokorný, 182.

175. See, e.g., Abbott, 294; Lightfoot, 222; Garland, 242; Fee, *Pauline Christology*, 329-30.

176. Compare esp. v. 25 — "those who do wrong (ἀδικῶν) will be repaid for their wrongs (ἠδίκησεν)" with Phlm. 18: "if he has done you any wrong (ἠδίκησεν) or owes you anything, charge it to me."

177. Barclay, "Ordinary but Different," 44.

178. E.g., Pokorný, 175, who suggests that the "thanksgiving" in v. 17 functions with the thanksgiving in 1:3 as an *inclusio* around the body of the letter. R. P. Martin, noting the context in which other household codes appear, thinks that Paul might be heading off any possible disorder in worship (see v. 16) (*Colossians: The Church's Lord and the*

tions of the household code as integral to Paul's ethical exhortation. They make clear that the creation of a new humanity in Christ does not mean an erasure of existing social relationships but their transformation as they are lived out under the Lordship of Christ. Paul begins by exhorting the wives,[179] *submit yourselves to your husbands*.[180] The TNIV's "submit yourselves" (so also KJV) differs from most English versions, which render "submit" (ESV; NET; NLT) or "be subject" (NRSV; NASB; NJB) or "be submissive" (HCSB).[181] The verb being translated is *hypotassō*, which etymologically could be rendered "order" *(tassō)* "under" *(hypo)*. The verb is not common in pre–New Testament Greek but does occur thirty times in the LXX, where it occasionally refers to humans "submitting" to God (2 Macc. 9:12) but more often refers to submission in the secular sphere, particularly to the military and the state. The verb occurs thirty-eight times in the New Testament, twenty-three of them in Paul. It can denote a forcible "subjecting," as when evil spiritual beings are "subjected" to the authority of God or Christ (Luke 10:17, 20; 1 Pet. 3:22) or when God "subjects" all things to Christ (1 Cor. 15:27; cf. Heb. 2:5, 8 [both quoting Ps. 8:7]; Eph. 1:22; Phil. 3:21) or when God, because of humanity's fall into sin, puts creation in "subjection" (Rom. 8:20).

But particularly characteristic of New Testament usage are exhortations to voluntarily "put oneself under" the authority or direction of someone or something else: all believers to God (Heb. 12:9; Jas. 4:7) or to his law (Rom. 8:7); the church to Christ (Eph. 5:24); Jews to God's righteousness (Rom 10:3); humans to governing authorities (Rom. 13:1, 5; Titus 3:1; 1 Pet. 2:13); Christians to their leaders (1 Cor. 16:16); slaves to masters (Titus 2:9; 1 Pet. 2:18); young men to older men (1 Pet. 5:5); children to their parents (Luke 2:51); wives to their husbands (Eph. 5:22; Col. 3:18; Titus 2:5; 1 Pet.

Christian's Liberty: An Expository Commentary with a Present-Day Application [Grand Rapids: Zondervan, 1972], 129-30).

179. The Greek is αἱ γυναῖκες, which can function as either nominative or vocative. In this context, it is obviously vocative (an address). The article is typical in this case (Robertson, *Grammar*, 757; Harris, 178), perhaps a reflection of Semitic syntax (Moule, *Idiom Book*, 117; Lightfoot, 226). The word γυνή means both "woman" and "wife," and in some contexts it is difficult to be sure which is intended (e.g., 1 Tim. 2:12). The context here, however, makes it clear that the reference is to wives.

180. The "your" in English translations has no equivalent pronoun in Greek, but it is widely agreed that the article with ἀνδράσιν has this purpose. The KJV's "your own" reflects a secondary variant reading found in some MSS, ἰδίοις.

181. It is unclear whether these translational differences reflect different decisions about the form of ὑποτάσσεσθε or are simply stylistic decisions. The form of the verb can be either middle or passive. Most scholars assume that the form here is middle, perhaps a "direct" middle (noted in Robertson, *Grammar*, 807, as possible): "submit yourselves." But the passive — literally, simply "be subject" — could have much the same sense.

3:1, 5). Ephesians 5:21 — "Submit to one another out of reverence for Christ" — is debated. Some commentators contend that the word retains the notion of "under authority." In this case, the "one another" is not fully reciprocal (as if every Christian must submit to every other Christian), but restricted to the particular relationships that Paul goes on to enumerate (wives submit to husbands, children to parents, slaves to masters). But it might better be taken as an exhortation for all believers to "put themselves under" other believers in the sense spelled out in Philippians 2:3b-4: "Rather, in humility value others above yourselves, not looking to your own interests but each of you to the interests of the others."[182]

Ephesians 5:21 is sometimes then used to restrict the meaning of *hypotassō* in the immediately following v. 22 and in the parallel Colossians 3:18 to something like "respect," a respect that should, according to Ephesians 5:21, be mutual — in the marriage relationship as elsewhere. For instance, *The Message* translates Colossians 3:18 "understand and support your husbands." But as the data above reveal, this illegitimately weakens the meaning of the verb. To be sure, as the husband loves his wife, he will often, in effect, "put himself under" her, deferring to her interests and needs (Phil. 2:3-4). But this "submission" of the husband to the wife is of a different character than the submission required of the wife to the husband. In this latter sense, the wife "puts herself under" her husband in recognizing and living out an "order" established by God himself within the marriage relationship (and by extension, in the family of God, the church). As Paul puts it in 1 Corinthians 11:3, "the head of a wife is her husband" (ESV) — the husband, as the "prominent" and "directing" member of the relationship, is to take the lead in the marriage relationship.[183]

This submission of the wife can, of course, take the form of "obedience." But three caveats at this point must be introduced in order to strike the right balance in Paul's teaching. First, it is probably significant that the household code here in Colossians urges wives to "submit" to their husbands but children and slaves to "obey" their fathers and masters, respectively (3:20, 22). This pattern is typical, though not universal, in the New Testament,[184] and suggests that the New Testament writers put the

---

182. G. Delling paraphrases ὑποτάσσω in NT exhortation as "to lose or surrender one's own rights or will" (*TDNT* 8.40).

183. The meaning of "head" (κεφαλή) in this passage is, of course, greatly disputed. For a survey and balanced conclusion, see Anthony C. Thiselton, *The First Epistle to the Corinthians: A Commentary on the Greek Text* (NIGTC; Grand Rapids: Eerdmans, 2000), 812-23; see also our comments on 1:18.

184. Slaves are urged to "submit" to their masters in Titus 2:9 and 1 Pet. 2:18; and 1 Pet. 3:6 cites Sarah's "obedience" to Abraham as an illustration of wives' "submission" to husbands.

relationship of wife to husband in a different (and less "authoritarian") category than these others. "Obedience" naturally fits a situation in which orders are being issued and in which the party obeying has little choice in the matter. Submission, on the other hand, suggests a voluntary willingness to recognize and put oneself under the leadership of another.[185] To "submit" is to recognize a relationship of order established by God. But submission to any human is always conditioned by the ultimate submission that each believer owes to God: in any hierarchy we can imagine, God stands at the "top of the chart." This means, then, that a wife will sometimes have to disobey a husband (even a Christian one) if that husband commands her to do something contrary to God's will. Even as she disobeys, however, she can continue to "submit," in a sense, by recognizing that her husband remains her head — just not her ultimate head.

Second, the submission of the wife to the husband is inevitably and necessarily conditioned significantly by the demand that husbands love their wives, and, in so loving them, will often "submit" to their needs, desires, and wishes (Eph. 5:21). The mutuality implied by the one-flesh union of husband and wife and the husband's love of the wife must be given full weight, even as the need for wives to recognize the headship of their husbands is upheld.

Third, we might cautiously suggest that, without eviscerating the word of its meaning, "submission" may take different forms in different cultures. Paul's was a patriarchal culture, in which a man, husband of a wife, father of children, master of slaves, "ruled" the household. The New Testament certainly does not abolish a certain kind of "patriarchy" — although it must be said that the etymological sense of "rule" in the word is not the best way to express the New Testament concept of the headship of the husband. Nevertheless, we may tentatively suggest that the New Testament teaching about the "oneness" of all in Christ, coupled with the demand that husbands love their wives (as Christ did the church; Eph. 5:23-24), sets a trajectory that leads to a more equal sharing of all dimensions of the marriage relationship.

Some interpreters have suggested that the concluding part of v. 18 might specifically qualify the nature or degree of submission that the wife is required to render to the husband.[186] They would presumably endorse the translation in *The Message:* "wives, understand and support your hus-

185. The middle form may connote this; cf. G. Delling, TDNT 8.42; Schweizer, 221; O'Brien, 224.
186. See, e.g., Schweizer, 165; Dunn, 248. BDAG give some countenance to this meaning by paraphrasing "(in such a way) as is fitting."

bands by submitting to them *in ways that* honor the Master" (my emphasis). However, as much as it may be true in general (as we have pointed out above) that the wife's submission to her husband is always conditioned by the "higher" submission she owes to her Lord, this is not the point that Paul makes here. As the majority of English translations suggest, this last clause does not limit the submission of the wife but explains why it is necessary.[187] She must submit not because it was necessary for the order of society (as the secular household codes usually emphasized) or (only) because it was appropriate to that time and place but because it is the kind of behavior that is "fitting"[188] to those who "live in the sphere of the Lord." As we noted above, it is this theme of what is required of those who belong to the Lord that undergirds the household behavior Paul requires in this passage. And it is this same theme that suggests that these admonitions are of permament validity for the people of God.

19 As is fitting for such a list of "rules" for the household, Paul turns quickly and somewhat abruptly from wives to husbands.[189] Requiring wives to submit to husbands, as we have noted, matches widespread Greek and Jewish teaching about marriage. Requiring husbands to love their wives does not. The concern in the secular codes was usually effective household management — especially since the household was typically viewed as a key building block of society and of the state. Accordingly, the focus of the codes was on the *paterfamilias* — the "head of the household" — and what he should do to maintain order and decorum in his household. Referring to a husband's love for his wife would not fit this purpose — and, indeed, no other code we have discovered from the ancient world requires husbands to love their wives.[190] More-

187. See, e.g., O'Brien, 222-23. The conjunction ὡς ("as"), which occurs here, can, in fact, indicate cause (BDAG).

188. "Fitting" translates ἀνῆκεν, an imperfect form of the verb ἀνήκω. The imperfect does not refer here to a past action ("as was fitting") but to the present (Turner, *Syntax*, 90), with perhaps the connotation that the behavior has been and continues to be "fitting" (Harris, 179). The verb is rare in the NT (only elsewhere in Eph. 5:4 and Phlm. 8) and has, as O'Brien (222) puts it, a "Stoic ring" (because it was so widely used by the Stoics in their moral teaching). But the presence of this word is in itself insufficient basis to hold that Paul has derived the household code from Stoicism.

189. There is no conjunction or particle to connect the verses, an omission somewhat rare in Greek. Husbands are addressed in the same way (nominative form, vocative in meaning) as the wives are in v. 18. The word that Paul uses — ἄνδρες, a form of ἀνήρ — refers to a male, either "man" generally or "husband" specifically (and it can occasionally, contra some scholars, also refer to human beings without reference to gender). The context here shows that the reference is to husbands.

190. When ancient authors spoke of love between marriage partners, their focus was often on sexual love, and a few Jewish texts extend the general call to love the neighbor (Lev. 19:18) to the love of the husband for his wife (Str-B 3.610).

over, the word for "love" here is *agapaō*, the distinctly (though certainly not uniquely) Christian word for the kind of sacrificial, self-giving love whose model is Christ himself (the connection brought out in the Ephesians parallel, 5:25). Perhaps significantly, the only other occurrence of the verb "love" in Colossians refers to God's love for us, his people (3:12). As the people loved by God, Paul urges us to "put on love" (3:14). Now Paul applies this requirement to husbands specifically. But why are only husbands urged to love their wives? The pattern of requiring submission of the wife and love of the husband is consistent in the New Testament (see also Eph. 5:22-25; in 1 Pet. 3:1-7, wives are urged to "submit" and husbands to live considerately with their wives and respect them). Perhaps this pattern reflects the particular susceptibilities of each partner in the relationship: wives may be tempted to chafe under the "headship" of their husbands; and husbands are prone to abuse their leadership role. Whatever the explanation, the command that husbands love their wives introduces a somewhat revolutionary note of reciprocity that is a hallmark of this household code.

If, positively, husbands are to love their wives, negatively, they are commanded not to *be harsh with them*. *Be harsh* translates a verb whose basic sense is "make bitter." The verb occurs elsewhere in the New Testament only with a physical sense: water (Rev. 8:11) or the stomach (Rev. 10:9, 10) is turned "bitter" or "sour." The corresponding noun is used four times, in each case condemning an attitude of bitterness (Acts 8:23; Rom. 3:14; Eph. 4:31; Heb. 12:15), while the adjective occurs twice, once with reference to "bitter" (as opposed to sweet or fresh) water (Jas. 3:11) and once modifying "envy" (Jas. 3:14). Words from the Greek root of the word used here occur in other ancient Greek writings to refer to rulership that is domineering and harsh. Paul is probably reflecting this tradition, urging husbands not to act with a heart of bitterness toward their wives.[191] Verse 19 may thus be seen as Paul's attempt to explain or even "soften" the rights of the husband implied in the requirement that wives

191. Wolter, 199; W. Michaelis, *TDNT* 6.125. Ancient texts illustrating this sense include Josephus, *Against Apion* 1.210; 2.277 ("cruel [πικρόν] master" in both cases). Perhaps the closest parallel is Plutarch's admonition to male readers: "[do not] rage bitterly against women" (πρὸς γυναῖκα διαπικραίνονται) (*Moralia* 6.457A); here we find the compound form of the same verb that Paul uses (πικραίνω) followed by the same preposition that Paul uses (πρός). On the basis of the passive form of the verb in Colossians, Dunn suggests that the attitude must be that of the husband: he therefore proposes that Paul is saying that the unreasoning expectations of the husband can lead to bitterness (249). But the passive verb (which is intransitive here [BDAG]) refers to the husband's attitude in the usual interpretation also. In this context, that attitude is expressed toward (πρός) the wife. Note, e.g., Jer. 37:15 (44:15, LXX), which also uses the passive form of the verb: "They were angry with (ἐπικράνθησαν . . . ἐπί) Jeremiah."

submit to them. The leadership that husbands rightly exhibit in marriage is not to be carried out harshly or selfishly, but lovingly. To love one's wife therefore will often mean to put her interests ahead of the husband's — thus approaching (though not quite the same as) the "mutual submission" required by Ephesians 5:21.[192]

20 Paul turns abruptly — again, with no intervening conjunction — to address the *children*. The reciprocity that characterizes the Colossian code surfaces here again; in contrast to most ancient moral treatises, the children are "addressed as responsible persons within the congregation."[193] Putting the matter in these terms raises the question of just what kind of children Paul might have in view. The Greek word used here *(teknon)*, much like our English "children," can refer to almost any age group. The ancient "household" would often have included adult, and even married, children, so it is possible that Paul's exhortation applies to all children, of any age.[194] On the other hand, the comparable text in Ephesians, after urging children to obey their parents, requires that fathers "bring them up in the training and instruction of the Lord" (6:4). This language suggests that the concern is with young children.[195] Of course, despite the close relationship of Ephesians and Colossians, we have to be careful not to read what is said in Ephesians into the Colossians text. Perhaps the best option steers between that of limiting the reference to very young children and expanding it to include all children. Paul's concern is with the household, and we might therefore infer that he includes any children who are part of that household and therefore technically under the "authority" of the *paterfamilias*.

As we noted in our comments on v. 18, "submission" and "obedience" are distinct but overlapping concepts. Submission is the broader concept, implying a general "order" in a particular relationship that renders it appropriate for one party to defer to another. Obedience is the specific form that submission will often take. For instance, 1 Peter 3:22 claims that Christ, by virtue of his resurrection and ascension, has "angels, authorities and powers in submission to him." It is on the basis of this (forceful) "subduing" of the powers that Jesus (proleptically, in anticipation of his victory) can command evil spirits and they "obey" him (Mark 1:27). But obedience implies a relationship in which one party issues "orders" to another, a circumstance generally incompatible with a husband's

---

192. Barth/Blanke, 438.
193. O'Brien, 224.
194. E.g., Barth/Blanke, 439.
195. O'Brien, 224; Wall, 159.

sacrificial love for his wife but fitting for the relationship of children (especially younger children) with their parents.[196]

Paul emphasizes the absolute and sweeping character of this relationship by adding that children must obey their parents *in everything*. This universal and apparently unqualified requirement of obedience naturally raises questions about its implementation in our culture. We do not (especially in the west) have households of the sort that Paul had in view in this passage. This does not mean, of course, that his exhortation can simply be dismissed. But it does mean that wisdom, rooted in broad biblical principles, will be required to apply the requirement of "obedience in all things" to children in our culture. As long as children are living under the protection of their parents, we would suggest, they are expected to obey their parents. (Although even here, of course, exceptions, in the case, for instance, of abusive parents, must be recognized.) But when children are no longer under the protection and care of their parents, we would suggest that, while deference and "honor" are still appropriate, obedience is no longer necessarily to be expected.

In addition to the reciprocal nature of the relationships in this passage, the thoroughly "Christianized" nature of the household requirements stands out as especially characteristic of this household code. So we are not surprised to find Paul again referring to the Lord (Jesus Christ) as the touchstone for the obedience of children. In the Ephesians parallel, Paul requires children to obey their parents because it is "right" *(dikaion)* and then quotes the fifth commandment of the Decalogue as justification (6:1-2). As he does throughout the admonitions to husbands and wives, children and parents, here in Colossians Paul abbreviates, claiming simply that children should obey their parents, *for this pleases the Lord*. The "Lord" is again the Lord Jesus Christ (see v. 17). And the wording of the Greek suggests that Paul is not so much saying that "this is pleasing to the Lord" but that it is pleasing "in the Lord," that is, the obedience of children is appropriate behavior within the community that acknowledges Christ as their Lord (see NRSV; NET; HCSB).[197] Paul may

196. Some interpreters (e.g., Schweizer, 223) claim the call to obey human authorities in Ephesians (6:1, 5) and Colossians (3:20, 22) is another mark of their post-Pauline origin, since the "authentic Paul" uses obedience language only with reference to the divine commandments or apostolic teaching (Rom. 1:5; 5:19; 6:16, 17; 10:16; 15:18; 16:19, 26; 2 Cor. 7:15; 10:5, 6; Phil. 2:12; 2 Thess. 1:8; 3:14; in Rom. 6:12, 16, Paul speaks of obedience to sin or its desires, and it is not clear whether Phlm. 21 refers to obedience to Paul's personal request or to God's will [see the commentary on that verse]). This claim has little merit, since Paul requires obedience only of children and slaves, with reference to whom the language is common and appropriate. The lack of such references in the other letters is simply because Paul does not there treat these topics.

197. Paul uses the preposition ἐν ("in") before κυρίῳ ("Lord"), the only place in the

305

emphasize this point in opposition to some "enthusiastic" Christians who might have dismissed such mundane and hierarchical ideas as a wife's submission to her husband or a child's obedience of parents as inappropriate for the new humanity being created in and by Christ. On the contrary, Paul may be responding, these family obligations continue to be required in the new community.

21 The focus on reciprocity (especially in contrast with other ancient household codes) that we have seen as Paul deals with marriage carries over into the parental sphere. As children are to obey their parents, so *fathers* are not to *embitter* their children. The Greek word for *fathers (pateres)* can sometimes refer to both parents, as in Hebrews 11:23: "By faith Moses' parents *(pateres)* hid him for three months after he was born, because they saw he was no ordinary child, and they were not afraid of the king's edict." The standard Greek lexicon of the New Testament suggests that this is what the word means here in Colossians and in the Ephesians parallel (6:4); see NJB.[198] However, the primary referent is probably the father, since this fits the culture of that time, in which the man was the head of the household and would have had primary responsibility for issuing orders to children. The Romans called this power *patria potestas*, "the power of the father," and it was a basic assumption about the way the household in the Hellenistic world should function. And Paul's shift from the word *goneis* — which can only mean "parents" — in v. 20 to *pateres* here is probably significant. Nevertheless, it is possible that, while primarily addressing the father, Paul would have had both parents in view.[199] And certainly a reference to mothers as well as fathers is justified from the standpoint of cultural translation. Fathers are addressed in Colossians because they were the ones who had ultimate authority over children in the ancient household. But since in the modern family mothers often appropriately take equal responsibility for raising children (and, indeed, in many families are the only parental authority), it is entirely valid to apply this verse to both fathers and mothers.

Fathers (or parents in general) are, Paul says, not to *embitter* their children. This admonition is roughly parallel to what Paul has said to husbands in v. 19. As wives submit to their husbands, their husbands are not to "be harsh" with them; so here, as children obey their fathers, their

---

NT where εὐάρεστος is followed by this preposition (it is followed elsewhere by the dative [Rom. 12:1; 14:18; 2 Cor. 5:9; Eph. 5:10; Phil. 4:18], ἐνώπιον ["before"] [Heb. 13:21], or absolutely [Rom. 12:2; Titus 2:9]). For this interpretation, see, e.g., Turner, *Syntax*, 263; O'Brien, 225; MacDonald, 154-55. A conditional reading of the clause — "provided that the children's obedience is ἐν κυρίῳ, on a truly Christian level of motive" (Moule, 130) — is unlikely.

198. BDAG.

199. E.g., Schweizer, 223; O'Brien, 225.

fathers are not to "embitter" them.[200] Missing, of course, from v. 21 is the command to love that we find in v. 19. Why Paul does not urge fathers to love their children is the kind of question that is impossible to answer. But, in comparison with the typical approach to these matters in the ancient world, another issue is even more glaring by its absence: the call to fathers to "rule" or "govern" their children. To be sure, this function is assumed in the call to children to obey their parents (v. 20). But it is still striking that, as in Paul's address of the husband, he omits any reference to their actual exercise of "authority" with respect to their children.

Despite the formal similarity to v. 19, Paul uses a different word here to describe what the father is to avoid in his handling of his children. The word here (the verb *erethizō*) means, in the lengthy paraphrase of BDAG, "to cause someone to react in a way that suggests acceptance of a challenge." This meaning is illustrated in the only other New Testament occurrence of the verb, where Paul says that the enthusiasm of the Corinthians to give to the Collection has "stirred to action" most of the Macedonians (2 Cor. 9:2). Most occurrences of the verb, however, as here in Colossians 3:21, refer to a negative reaction, as when, for instance, a "sly tongue" is said to "provoke" a "horrified look" (Prov. 25:23). The text most relevant to Colossians 3:21, however — and one that Paul may well have had in mind — is Deuteronomy 21:20, where parents are charged with bringing a disobedient son before the elders and proclaiming, "This son of ours is stubborn and rebellious (LXX, *erethizei*). He will not obey us. He is a profligate and a drunkard." Paul, in effect, is exhorting fathers to raise their children in such a way that they do their utmost to avoid provoking this kind of rebellious attitude in them.

This point is accentuated by the final "negative purpose" clause: do not "embitter" (or "exasperate" [NASB; HCSB] or "provoke" [ESV; NET] or "aggravate" [NLT]) your children, *or they will become discouraged* (or "with the purpose that they not become discouraged"). The Greek word for "become discouraged" *(athymeō)* occurs only here in the New Testament and is rare in the LXX (nine occurrences), but its meaning in this kind of context is clear enough: Paul does not want to see the children of Christian families disciplined to such an extent that they "lose heart" (NASB; NJB; NRSV) and simply give up trying to please their parents.[201]

---

200. A number of manuscripts read, instead of ἐρεθίζετε, παροργίζετε ("provoke to anger"). This reading is secondary, an assimilation to Eph. 6:4.

201. Dunn (252) suggests that Paul might have a particular circumstance related to the false teachers in view: that younger people in the Christian community were vulnerable to becoming disenchanted because of their parents' adherence to a strange sect, neither Jewish nor pagan. But the parallel exhortation to fathers in Eph. 6:4 suggests that this was a typical feature of early Christian household teaching.

22 The third household relationship Paul addresses is that of slave and master. As we noted in the introduction to this paragraph, the ancient household was often far larger than our typical modern "nuclear" family, including not just parents and their young children, but older children (and sometimes their spouses) as well as domestic slaves. The context makes clear that it is this kind of slave that Paul has specifically in view here. At the same time, the popular homiletical decision to apply Paul's exhortations in vv. 22-25 to workers in general is probably justified. To be sure, historical and cultural accuracy requires that we carefully distinguish "slaves" and "employees." It is true that ancient slavery differed in some important ways from the slavery practiced, for instance, in nineteenth-century America (see the Introduction to Philemon, 369-78). But it is also true that ancient and modern slavery, in its various forms, has in common the basic fact that one human owns and has virtually ultimate control over another. Some forms of employment in the ancient world and in history might come close to this situation (e.g., the "indentured servant"), but most employees do not work in this kind of legally binding framework. We must, then, take into account this basic difference before we apply what Paul says here about slaves to workers in general. Having said that, however, it is also true that Paul's advice to slaves here enunciates some basic principles about how Christians should "serve" someone else that are broadly applicable.

At first sight, Paul's command that slaves obey their masters seems simply to endorse the status quo. But we need to see that what he writes here also subtly undermines it. First, it is significant that Paul chooses to address slaves at all, implying not only that they are assembled with the other Christians of the Colossian church to hear the letter being read but that they are responsible people who need to choose a certain kind of behavior. Second, Paul clearly relativizes the status of the slave's master by repeatedly reminding both slave (vv. 22, 23, 24) and master (4:1) of the ultimate "master" to whom both are responsible: the Lord Jesus Christ. Third, Paul never hints that he endorses the institution of slavery. He tells slaves and masters how they are to conduct themselves within the institution, but it is a bad misreading of Paul to read into his teaching approval of the institution itself. (For more on slavery in the ancient world and Paul's response to it, see the Introduction to Philemon, 369-78.)

Paul's admonition to slaves begins by following the pattern that we have seen in the household code so far. He introduces this next class of persons abruptly, omitting any formal connecting word. He addresses them, using the same Greek form — the articular nominative plural — that he uses throughout. Since they are the "subordinate" group, he urges them to *obey*, just as he commands the children to "obey" (v. 20) and wives to "submit" (v. 18). As wives are to submit to their husbands and children obey their parents, so slaves are to obey their *earthly masters*. And, as with the children, he urges the slaves to obey *in everything (kata panta)*.

In other ways, however, Paul significantly departs from the pattern we see in these other two relationships. First, rather than simply naming the slaves' *masters*, he characterizes them: *earthly masters*. TNIV's *earthly* translates a phrase using that notoriously slippery Greek word *sarx: kata sarka*, which could be rendered simply "according to the flesh" (KJV). It is perhaps significant, however, that here even the NASB ("on earth") and ESV ("earthly") abandon any attempt to retain the English "flesh" for *sarx*. As we have noted (see the comments on 1:22), Paul uses this Greek word to connote the human realm, sometimes rather neutrally (Christ came in a "body made up of flesh" [1:22]) and other times negatively (the false teachers have minds "dominated by the flesh" [2:18]). Here the word is being used in its neutral sense: the slaves' masters belong to the human realm. But, as is often the case even when Paul uses *sarx* "neutrally," there is an implicit contrast intended: the slave has a master on earth, but he or she also has a "master" in heaven. In English, we miss some of what Paul intends here because we cannot easily reproduce his play on the Greek word *kyrios*, which is translated in this context both "master" (v. 22a; 4:1a, b) and "Lord" (vv. 22b, 23, 24). Only in 4:1 does the TNIV (along with most other English translations) preserve this word-play in English. But a similar, though more subtle, play on the word occurs in this verse also: slaves are to obey their earthly masters, but they are to "fear" their (ultimate, heavenly) Master.

Paul also departs from the pattern he has established thus far by adding a series of more specific admonitions to the slaves, focusing on the manner of their service (vv. 22-23), the reward they can expect from faithful service (v. 24), and the penalty they will incur if they do not serve faithfully (v. 25). As we suggested above, it is probably the delicate situation of Onesimus, who is accompanying the letter carrier (4:8-9), that explains this material. In the rest of v. 22, then, Paul elaborates on the way in which slaves are to obey their masters. He makes two basic points: their obedience is to be sincere and their obedience is to be conditioned by their fear of the Lord. He conveys the focus on sincerity with two contrasting adjectival phrases: slaves are to *do it* [e.g., obey their masters] *not only when their eye is on you and to curry their favor, but with sincerity of heart.* The TNIV's *eye on you* translates a single Greek compound word that is made up of the words for "eye" *(ophthalmos)* and "service" *(doulia)*. It occurs only here and in the parallel text in Ephesians (6:6) in biblical Greek. It has the sense "service that has to do with the eye," and connotes the attitude of the servant who works hard only when the master's eye is on him or her. The appropriateness of renderings such as that found in the TNIV is manifest when one tries to make sense of the literal "eye-service" (ESV, which goes back, via the RSV, to KJV); note the similar attempts to capture the sense in English in, for example, NRSV — "while being watched" — and NJB — "when you are under their eye." The temporal translations of these versions, along with the addition of words such as "only," are legitimate ways of capturing the sense of the Greek in English.

And Paul makes the point even more clear by adding a further description: *to curry their favor*. The Greek behind this clause is an adverbial clause made up of "as" *(hōs)* and another compound word, composed of the word for "person" *(anthrōpos)* plus the word for "pleasing" *(areskos)*: hence, literally, "as people-pleasers" (ESV) (this word, like the former one, occurs only here and in the Ephesians parallel text [6:6] in the New Testament).[202] The TNIV again accurately captures the sense of the phrase. The two compound words reinforce each other, conveying the sense of an obedience that is superficial and hypocritical, concerned with appearances rather than reality.

By way of contrast, Paul urges Christian slaves to obey their masters *with sincerity of heart*. "Sincerity" *(haplotēs)* has the sense of "singleness." Its meaning is illustrated by the use of a cognate word in Matthew 6:22, brought out very well in the traditional rendering of the KJV: "The light of the body is the eye: if therefore thine eye be single, thy whole body shall be full of light." The "single" eye has a concentrated focus that leads a person consistently in the same direction.[203] So, here, "singleness of heart" (the KJV rendering) refers to a focused and unvarying concentration of the will that produces consistent conduct. The sense is accurately captured in the English translations "sincerity of heart" (TNIV; ESV; NASB; cf. NET, "a sincere heart"; NLT, "sincerely") and "wholeheartedly" (NRSV; NJB; HCSB).

But the conduct of *Christian* slaves is, as we would expect, most fundamentally to be oriented toward their heavenly "master," the Lord Jesus. The TNIV, along with most of the English versions, understands this

202. The negative sense of the compound word might be influenced by the fact that the simple ἄρεσκος often has a negative nuance: "obsequious" (LSJ).

203. The Greek word is ἁπλοῦς, used only here and in the parallel Luke 11:34 in the NT. A related word is the adverb ἁπλῶς, used with similar meaning in Jas. 1:5. The word that is found here in Colossians — the noun ἁπλότης — is used in the Ephesians parallel (6:5) and in several other passages in Paul (Rom. 12:8; 2 Cor. 1:12; 8:2; 9:11, 13; 11:3). Many interpreters think that the word means "generously" in some of these texts (and this is reflected in many English translations). But it is probable that the word has the basic sense of "singleness," "sincerity," in each of these texts (see BDAG).

last participial clause to indicate the manner in which slaves are to obey: *fearing the Lord*. However, the clause could also be causal, giving the reason why slaves should obey with sincerity of heart rather than superficially or hypocritically (cf. NLT: "because of your reverent fear of the Lord").[204] The "fear of the Lord" is, of course, a prominent theme in the Old Testament, combining a sense of appropriate awe in the presence of God with submission to his will. But the theme is by no means absent from the New Testament (e.g., 2 Cor. 7:1; 1 Pet. 2:17; Rev. 11:18; 14:7; 15:4; 19:5), where, in a move typical of the "christological monotheism" of the early church, the Lord is sometimes defined as Christ (Acts 9:31; 2 Cor. 5:11; Eph. 5:21). This is certainly the case here, as the high Christology of the letter to the Colossians as a whole is again brought to bear on the ordinary situation of the Christian household.[205]

23 This focus on the Lord Christ as the ultimate motivation of the slave's labor receives strong emphasis in vv. 23-24. The principle of doing everything with respect to Christ that Paul set forth for Christians in general in v. 17 is now applied specifically to Christian slaves. They are to work at whatever they do *with all your heart*. In v. 22 "heart" translates *kardia*, whereas here it translates *psychē*, the word often translated "soul." The two words are essentially interchangeable in a context such as this. Both of them indicate the true and authentic inner person: something done "from the soul" is something "done from the vital heart of the person, with all the individual's life force behind it."[206] Our phrase "from the heart" captures the idea very well (see also NAB; and NJB, "put your heart into it"). "Work at it with enthusiasm" (NET; see also HCSB) strikes the wrong note, however, suggesting that Paul was concerned with the degree of effort rather than the motivation for the effort. The *as (hōs)* that connects the first part of the verse to the second indicates the reality of the situation: slaves should do their work "with the constant realization" that they are working for the Lord Christ and not just for human master.[207] The Greek puts the contrast simply: "the Lord" versus "humans"

---

204. Harris, 183.

205. O'Brien, 227; Dunn, 255. The "majority text," along with a few other manuscripts, reads θεόν (reflected in the KJV and NKJV).

206. Dunn, 255. Cf. Mark 12:30: "Love the Lord your God with all your heart (ἐξ ὅλης τῆς καρδίας) and with all your soul (ἐξ ὅλης τῆς ψυχῆς) and with all your mind and with all your strength." Dunn suggests that Colossians might echo this text.

207. BDF §425.3; Harris, 184. Τῷ κυρίῳ and ἀνθρώποις are datives of advantage (see, again, BDF §188; Harris, 184): "for the benefit of the Lord"/"for the benefit of humans." There is no verb in this clause in the Greek text, but the verb from the first part of the verse — ἐργάζεσθε, "work" — is to be read (as a participle, ἐργαζόμενοι, "working") in the second part of the verse (e.g., BDF §425.4).

(e.g., NET: "as to the Lord and not for people"); the TNIV has added the specific referent from the context — *human masters.*

24 This verse grounds the two main admonitions of v. 23: slaves should work "from the heart" and they should do their work with reference to Christ the Lord *because* they will receive an inheritance as a reward from that same Lord. The TNIV makes explicit the causal function of the verse, translating the Greek participle (*eidotes,* "knowing") *since you know* (see also NET and NRSV). The TNIV does not, however, make clear that *the Lord* is placed first in the Greek word order, almost certainly for emphasis and in continuation of the last part of v. 23: "you are working for the Lord and not for human masters, since you know that *it is from the Lord himself* that you will receive the inheritance as a reward." (Many other versions reproduce this emphasis in English [NASB; ESV; KJV; NKJV; ESV; RSV].) The translation *an inheritance . . . as a reward* is almost certainly the right way to understand a phrase that would be literally translated from the Greek "the reward of the inheritance" (*tēn antapodosin tēs klēronomias*). In this kind of construction the two nouns refer to the same thing but in different ways.[208] The "inheritance" that they will receive will have the nature of a reward, a fair recompense for their faithful service.[209] We have met the language of "inheritance" earlier in Colossians (1:12), where we noted its rich Old Testament associations.[210] "Inheritance" language is used especially often in the Old Testament to denote the promised land, but the land becomes a tangible symbol of all that God promises to do for his people. In the New Testament, therefore, the "inheritance" is "the kingdom of God" (1 Cor. 6:9, 10; 15:50; Gal. 5:21) or "salvation" (Heb. 1:14), an inheritance now "kept in heaven for you" (1 Pet. 1:4) and to be given to God's people in the last day. Adding poignancy to this language is the fact that most slaves in the Roman Empire would have had little hope of any earthly inheritance. The situation is, of

208. The genitive of apposition (see Robertson, *Grammar*, 498).

209. The Greek word ἀνταπόδοσις conveys this notion of "exchange" — "a giving in place of." This word usually occurs with a negative sense, referring to condemnation in the judgment as a "retribution" for evil behavior. See, e.g., Ps. 94:2 — "Rise up, Judge of the earth; pay back to the proud what they deserve" (and also Judg. 16:18; Pss. 68:23; 90:8; Isa. 34:8; 59:18; 61:21; 63:4; 66:6; Jer. 28:56 [LXX 51:56]; Hos. 9:7). Only three LXX texts use the word, as in Col. 3:24, in a positive sense: Pss. 18:12; 102:2; 130:2. Although the noun occurs only here in the NT (it occurs as a variant in Rom. 2:5), a similar noun (ἀνταπόδομα) occurs twice, once with a neutral sense (Luke 14:12) and once with a negative sense (Rom. 11:9), while the cognate verb (ἀνταποδίδωμι) occurs six times, three times with a neutral sense (Luke 14:14; Rom. 11:35; 1 Thess. 3:9) and three times with a negative sense (Rom. 12:19; 2 Thess. 1:6; Heb. 10:30).

210. To be sure, the Greek word in 1:12 is κλῆρος ("portion" [of an inheritance]), whereas here it is κληρονομία. But the sense is very similar.

course, quite specific, but Galatians 4:30, where Paul claims that the "slave woman" will not receive the "inheritance" (Gen. 21:20), might at least be illustrative. Slaves who come to Christ may not have an inheritance in this world to look forward to. But they can look forward to a far more important inheritance — one that "can never perish, spoil or fade" (1 Pet. 1:4), and one that they will share on precisely equal terms with all other Christians, including their masters.

The TNIV, with most of the English versions, takes the last clause of v. 24 as a statement: *It is the Lord Christ you are serving.* Read this way, this clause both reminds the slaves of the point that Paul made briefly in v. 23 — "as working for the Lord" — and explains why they can anticipate a spiritual inheritance. However, the verb that Paul uses here *(douleuete)* can also be read as an imperative, and, somewhat surprisingly, the commentators are generally out of step with the translations, favoring the imperative rendering by a large margin.[211] We think they are right. An assertion about whom the Christian slaves ultimately serve could certainly make sense. But the imperative better explains the way this clause sits in its context. On the one hand, Paul does not use any conjunction or particle to tie this clause to what comes before it. This is exactly how Paul has introduced the other imperatives in this paragraph (vv. 18, 19, 20, 21, 22; 4:1), and, if he had intended this clause to support v. 23a, we might have expected a conjunction such as "for" *(gar).* On the other hand, this is just the conjunction that we find at the beginning of v. 25, suggesting that this verse explains or supports v. 24. It is very natural (though certainly not necessary) to view v. 25 as the reason why Paul urges slaves to "serve the Lord Christ" (NET; see also NAB).[212] This command is in some ways the center of 3:18–4:1, enunciating the fundamental reality underlining the entire household code and bringing together the titles "Lord" and "Christ" as a way of tying this section firmly to the overall Christocentric message of Colossians. It should be noted at this point that the usual translation "serve" for this verb misses the connotation of bond service that the Greek verb suggests: *douleō* and its cognate, *doulos,* are the standard ways of referring to slavery in ancient Greek and in the New Testament.[213] It is tempting, therefore, to

211. E.g., Abbott, 295; Moule, 131; Harris, 185-86; O'Brien, 229; Wright, 150; Lohse, 161; Lincoln, 658; Garland, 250. Commentators who support the indicative reading are, e.g., Lightfoot, 229; Lindemann, 67.

212. The sequence "Lord Christ" (κυρίος Χριστός) is found only once elsewhere in Paul (Rom. 16:18) and is probably emphatic, suggesting an implicit contrast with another "lord": "it is the Lord Christ whom you are to serve (and not merely your human lord)" (Barth/Blanke, 448).

213. It is instructive to note that the TNIV translates δουλεύω with "serve" when the verb is used to denote "service" of God or Christ, whereas it tends to use "slavery"

translate, with the NAB, "Be slaves of the Lord Christ." Unfortunately, this rendering, particularly against the backdrop of nineteenth-century American slavery, might be too strong. In any case, in this context Paul is obviously reminding the slaves that their true and ultimate "master" is Christ, not the earthly master to whom they are enslaved. They need to serve the Lord Christ not only in order to receive their inheritance but also to avoid punishment for doing wrong (v. 25).

25 This reading of the sequence between vv. 24 and 25 takes a position on another debated point: the intended addressee of v. 25. The verse uses a play on words to warn that people who "do wrong" *(adikōn) will be repaid for their* "wrongs" *(ēdikēsen,* which is from the same root as the verb "do wrong"). But who are these people? Is Paul still referring to the slaves, warning them of the consequences if they fail to continue to serve their earthly masters as they live out their "slavery" to Christ?[214] Or does he anticipate 4:1, warning masters that they will be punished if they do not treat their slaves properly?[215] Or is the verse a janus, looking in two directions at once: back to the slaves and forward to the masters?[216] A decision is not easy, but as we have already suggested, we think a reference to slaves is a bit more likely. The most important consideration, of course, is that Paul does not explicitly turn to address "masters" until the next verse. It would be unprecedented in New Testament household codes for an author to refer to household members before they had been addressed. A warning to slaves in this verse would also make good sense of the probable background.

As we have noticed, slaves are given proportionally more attention in this household code than in the very similar Ephesians code. We have suggested that the most natural explanation for this attention is that the situation of Onesimus, whom Paul is sending back to his master Philemon, is uppermost in Paul's mind. As the letter to Philemon reveals, this situation is a tricky one. Paul does not deny Philemon's "rights" over his slave under the law, and he is very careful to give Philemon room to make his own decisions. But he also clearly wants Philemon not only not to punish his runaway slave but to accept him back as a brother in Christ. Paul goes so far as to promise to repay Philemon for any "wrong"

---

language in contexts where the "master" is something negative, such as sin. On the significance of "slavery"/"service" language in Paul, see esp. M. J. Harris, *Slave of God* (Downers Grove, Ill.: InterVarsity, 2001); and see his specific translation proposals on 183-91.

214. E.g., O'Brien, 230-31; Lohse, 161; Masson, 150; MacDonald, 158; Garland, 250.
215. E.g., Abbott, 295; R. P. Martin, 123.
216. Lightfoot, 229; Schweizer, 226-27; Gnilka, 224. Gnilka suggests that v. 24a — "serve the Lord Christ" — also refers to both slaves and masters (222-23).

Onesimus has done (Phlm. 18). In this verse in Philemon Paul uses the same verb *(adikeō)* that he uses twice here in Colossians 3:25. It seems quite likely, then, that Paul has the possible ramifications of Philemon's forgiveness and acceptance of Onesimus in view here. He does not want other slaves in Colossae to think that they can "do wrong" with impunity, avoiding any penalty for their actions because they are now in Christ.[217]

As we have noted above, it is a misreading of what Paul is teaching in passages such as this to conclude that he endorses slavery as an institution. But it is equally clear that he is in these passages seriously concerned that slaves do not view service to their new master, Christ, as reason to treat lightly the obligations they bear to their human masters. Thus he warns them of the judgment that they will incur if they do wrong. This judgment could consist of the punishment that a master would inflict on a disobedient slave. But the connection with v. 24b suggests that Paul is rather thinking of eschatological judgment.[218]

The last clause of v. 25 is the strongest reason to adopt the opposite view that we have defended in the last paragraph. For the principle that *there is no favoritism* makes especially good sense as a warning to masters, who would naturally be prone to presume that their high social position in this world would put them in a different category from that of their slaves. Moreover, the same principle functions in the parallel Ephesians 6:9 as a warning to masters. Nevertheless, it can also stand as a reminder to the slaves that God will not overlook the wrongs they do, as if their servile status might exempt them from accountability. It is just possible, in addition, that this last clause of v. 25 is a reminder to both slaves and masters that they will have to stand before an impartial and discerning judge to answer for their conduct. The judge before whom they will stand is the Lord. NLT makes this explicit, "For God has no favorites." However, we should probably supply "the Lord" (as a reference to Christ) rather than God.[219] Paul has consistently appealed to the Lord Christ in this context, and in the parallel Ephesians text Paul says, "you know that

217. See J. Knox, *Philemon among the Letters of Paul* (London: Collins, 1960), 32-33; Garland, 250.

218. The verb κομίσεται ("will be repaid") is therefore probably a true future (Harris, 187). The somewhat parallel verse in Eph. 6:8 uses the same verb to promise a reward for both slave and master: "you know that the Lord will reward (κομίσεται) each one of you for whatever good you do, whether you are slave or free" (6:8). As we suggest above, the Onesimus situation explains the focus on slaves and the presence of a warning instead of a promise in Colossians. Paul's only other use of the verb κομίζω also comes in a verse about eschatological judgment: "For we must all appear before the judgment seat of Christ, that everyone might receive (κομίσηται) what is due them for the things done while in the body, whether good or bad" (2 Cor. 5:10). See also Heb. 10:36; 1 Pet. 1:9; 5:4.

219. E.g., Harris, 187.

315

he who is both their Master and yours is in heaven, and there is no favoritism with him." The word *favoritism* translates a Greek word that means, literally, "receiving the face"; the Greek word is a (literal) translation of a Hebrew idiom.[220] It means treating people on the basis of (mere) appearance and is thus accurately translated "favoritism" or "partiality" (NRSV; ESV; NASB; NAB). As the quotation above suggests, the word occurs elsewhere in Ephesians 6:9 and also in Romans 2:11 and James 2:1 (the cognate verb occurs in Jas. 2:9 and the cognate adjective in Acts 10:34).

4:1 Paul turns, finally, to the sixth member of the household: masters of slaves.[221] In reality, of course, the husband (3:19), father (3:21), and master are three related roles carried out by the *paterfamilias*, the "head of the household." In this case, as in the previous two exhortations to the "head of the household," Paul's admonition is remarkable, in comparison with secular parallels, for its concern with the kindness and "other-regard" with which the duties of household management are to be carried out. Specifically, Paul calls on the masters to *provide your slaves with what is right and fair*. The TNIV (along with HCSB; KJV; NKJV; NJB) is a bit awkward here, suggesting that Paul is urging masters to give their slaves something (what?) that has the qualities of "rightness" and "fairness." But the Greek can be straightforwardly translated "provide justice and fairness to your slaves."[222] The idea seems best conveyed in English with adverbs, and this is the choice most of the translations make; see, for example, ESV: "treat your slaves justly and fairly." "Justly" translates a Greek adjective used as a noun, *dikaios*, "just," "right." It occurs often in the Greek Bible to refer to conduct that meets the standards set by God (often in the covenant). "Fairly" translates a word that means "equality" (*isotētēs*; see its two other New Testament occurrences [2 Cor. 8:13, 14]). Some interpreters have therefore suggested that Paul may be, in effect, requesting masters to treat their slaves as "equals" with the revolutionary social consequences that would follow.[223] But the word had also devel-

220. The NT word προσωπολημψία is a compound noun derived from the LXX expression πρόσωπον λαμβάνειν (taken over in Luke 20:21), which in turn is used to render the Hebrew phrase "receive the face" (see, e.g., Lev. 19:15; Ps. 81:2; Mal. 1:8, 9; 2:9; see also 1 Esd. 4:39; Sir. 4:22, 27; 35:13; 42:1).

221. Paul addresses the masters in the same way that he has addressed the five other household relationships in this context: with an articular nominative — οἱ κύριοι — and without any connecting conjunction or particle.

222. Paul uses the middle form of the verb παρέχω, which BDAG translate "grant something to someone," and two nouns as objects of the verb. Some interpreters think that the choice of the middle form (as opposed to the active) might have significance here (e.g., Lightfoot, 230; Harris, 187), but BDR (§316.3) argue that the active and middle forms of this verb do not differ in meaning.

223. Meyer, 405.

oped the sense of "fairness," and this is the way it is normally used when it occurs in conjunction with "right" *(dikaios)* language.[224] Moreover, this word was used in secular Greek to refer to the appropriate treatment of slaves, in the sense of giving them what was "due" them.[225] The two words occur together in popular moral philosophy, sometimes as virtual synonyms, at other times with "fairness" viewed as an extension or dimension of "what is just." In this context, Paul might intend the second to reinforce and explicate the former: treat your slaves in the right way, that is, treat them with scrupulous fairness.[226] The New Testament is not alone in urging fair treatment of slaves (the Roman Seneca has much to say on the matter), but it is comparatively unusual.

Masters are to treat their slaves fairly *because you know that you also have a Master in heaven.* The TNIV, along with most of the English translations, preserves Paul's play on words by translating the Greek *kyrios* — which is normally translated "Lord" when the reference is to Christ — as "Master." Slave owners might pride themselves on their position in society and in the household, and they would naturally be very tempted to abuse that position at times. But Christian slave owners need to remember that they are answerable to a higher master, the Lord Jesus. They are, in fact, "slaves" themselves; as Paul puts it in 1 Corinthians 7:22, "For those who were slaves when called to faith in the Lord are the Lord's freed people; similarly, those who were free when called are Christ's slaves." The "Master" in heaven (cf. 3:1) will show no "favoritism" (3:25) when he judges, meting out to slaves and their owners with scrupulous impartiality just what their conduct merits on the day of judgment. The reciprocity that is a hallmark of this Colossians household code emerges here again in emphatic form. Slaves and masters ultimately serve the same Lord, and that fundamental spiritual reality not only relativizes their earthly relationship but even sets the stage for its abolishment.

D. Exhortation to Prayer and Christian Witness (4:2-6)

2Devote yourselves to prayer, being watchful and thankful. 3And pray for us, too, that God may open a door for our message, so that we may proclaim the mystery of Christ, for which I am in chains. 4Pray that I may proclaim it clearly, as I should. 5Be wise in the way you act toward outsiders;

224. BDAG.
225. BDAG.
226. O'Brien, 232.

make the most of every opportunity. ⁶Let your conversation be always full of grace, seasoned with salt, so that you may know how to answer everyone.

With this paragraph, Paul concludes his series of general exhortations about the way the Lordship of Christ is to be lived out in daily life (3:5–4:6). It also brings to a close the letter body. This central section of Colossians is driven by imperatives that spell out how the believers in Colossae are to manifest the Lordship of Christ, the Head of creation and the church (2:6-7). In the earlier part of this letter body (2:8-23), the focus is on the need to assert Christ's exclusive role in salvation and Christian living with respect to the rival claims being put forward by the false teachers. In the second part of this letter body, however, explicit concern with the false teachers fades and is replaced with exhortations relating to the Christian life in general (3:1–4:1). Almost all of this material has been inward-looking, focusing on relationships within the Christian community.

Colossians 4:2-6, however, looks outward, with a focus on Paul's evangelistic work and the community's relationships with non-Christians. The paragraph has some connection with 3:17, focusing on the "words" that the community should use to glorify the Lord and picking up the theme of "thanksgiving" (v. 2; see also, perhaps, "grace" in v. 6 and our notes).[1] (But these connections do not justify the conclusion that the intervening material, the household code in 3:18–4:1, is an "interruption.")[2] There are other connections with earlier parts of the letter: Paul's request for prayer for his ministry (vv. 3-4), for instance, echoes, in content and wording, 1:24–2:5.[3] The movement of the paragraph is easy to follow: a general encouragement to pray (v. 2) → a request to pray for Paul's evangelistic ministry (vv. 3-4) → exhortations regarding the Colossians' evangelistic ministry (vv. 5-6). The Greek text closely matches this structure. Imperative verbs occur in vv. 2 and 5, dividing the paragraph into two basic parts.[4] Verses 3-4 are attached to v. 2 with a participle that carries on the exhortation to prayer in v. 2. Verse 6 is not formally attached to v. 5, though it (implicitly) carries over the imperative force of v. 5.

Formal parallels to this section in the other Pauline letters are not easy to identify. Paul elsewhere includes requests that his readers pray (Eph. 6:18; Phil. 4:6; 1 Thess. 5:17) and particularly for the ministry of himself and his associates (Rom. 15:30-32; Eph. 6:19-20; 2 Thess. 3:1-2) in

1. E.g., O'Brien, 235; Wilson, 289.
2. As Lohse, 164, does.
3. Wright, 151.
4. See, e.g., Gnilka, 227; Pokorný, 185.

his letter closings. As is usually the case, Ephesians furnishes the closest parallel to Colossians 4:2-4, in both structure and language:

> And pray in the Spirit on all occasions with all kinds of prayers and requests. With this in mind, be alert and always keep on praying for all the Lord's people. Pray also for me, that whenever I speak, words may be given me so that I will fearlessly make known the mystery of the gospel, for which I am an ambassador in chains. Pray that I may declare it fearlessly, as I should. (Eph. 6:18-20)

These parallels might suggest that Colossians 4:2-6 functions as the opening of the letter closing rather than the conclusion of the letter body.[5] Of course, the issue — particularly when we put it this way! — is somewhat pedantic. While study of ancient letters enables us to identify a standard structure of "letter opening" — "letter body" — "letter closing," the transition from one of these to the other will not always be clearly marked or easy to identify. Colossians 4:2-6 might, therefore, be transitional, belonging neither to the letter body nor to the letter closing per se. Nevertheless, we think the general tendency to include 4:2-6 with what precedes is probably correct.[6] One factor leading us to tilt in this direction is Paul's advice to the community about its relationship to "outsiders" in vv. 5-6. These verses have no formal parallel in the Pauline letter closings, but a rather close parallel is found in the body of Ephesians (5:16). Verses 5-6 also raise another issue: why does Paul spend more time here in Colossians on this matter than he does in Ephesians? We can only speculate, but it might be that Paul does not want his warnings about avoiding false teachers to lead the Colossian Christians to distance themselves from non-Christians generally. They must resist the false teachers, but they must also continue to reach out to their fellow citizens.

2   Verse 2, and thus the paragraph vv. 2-6 as a whole, is not explicitly connected to its preceding context (it lacks the linking particle or conjunction that is so typical of Greek style). Nevertheless, the exhortation to pray clearly marks a shift of focus away from the household code of 3:18–4:1. Paul highlights the need not only to pray, but to make prayer a standard feature of the Christian life: *Devote yourselves to prayer*. The point, then, is not that believers should pray with intensity when they pray but that they should pray habitually and with perseverance. We "should always pray and not give up" (Luke 18:1); "pray continually" (1 Thess. 5:17) (cf. NAB,

5. E.g., P. Lamarche, "Structure de L'épître aux Colossiens," *Bib* 56 (1975), 461-63; Luz, 239.
6. See, e.g., Lincoln, 664, who takes 4:2-6 to be the conclusion of the main section of the letter body, with vv. 7-9 as the conclusion of the letter body.

"persevere in prayer"; ESV, "continue steadfastly in prayer"). Other New Testament texts that call for persistent prayer, in fact, use the same verb that Paul has used here (*proskartereō; see* Acts 2:42; 6:4; Rom. 12:12). "Prayer" (*proseuchē*) is a general word, encompassing every kind of praying (Mark 11:17; Acts 1:14; 2:42; 16:13). But it often implicitly refers more specifically to petitionary prayer, that is, to requests made to God in prayer (Matt. 21:22; Acts 12:5; Rom. 1:10; 15:30; Phil. 4:6; Col. 4:12; Phlm. 22; Jas. 5:17). It might have this sense here, since Paul moves so easily from a general exhortation to pray (v. 2) to a specific request to pray for him (v. 3).[7]

Paul elaborates his call to constancy in prayer by indicating the manner in which we are to pray: *being watchful and thankful.*[8] The word translated *being watchful* (the participle *grēgorountes*) has the basic sense of being "awake" and alert. In 1 Thessalonians 5:10, for example, the same verb, translated in TNIV "we are awake," is contrasted with being "asleep." This 1 Thessalonians text also illustrates another facet of this verb in the New Testament: it often calls for Christians to be alert or watchful in light of the imminent return of Christ (twelve of the twenty-two New Testament occurrences are in such a context: Matt. 24:42, 43; 25:13; Mark 13:34, 35, 37; Luke 12:37; 1 Thess. 5:6, 10; Rev. 3:2, 3; 16:15). What the "watching" believers are to do in these texts is not watch for Christ's return, but watch their own life in light of the return of Christ. Believers need constantly to be "awake" to the nature of the times they live in — the "last days" of eschatological "fulfillment without consummation" — and to orient their lives accordingly.[9] The verb here could well connote this idea: the devotion to prayer that Paul calls for should be characterized by a strong sense of expectation about Christ's near return that governs and motivates prayer.[10] To be sure, the one time the verb occurs elsewhere in the New Testament with a call to pray it has no evident eschatological connotation (Matt. 26:41), and it is used elsewhere generally of the need to be "watchful." See, for instance, 1 Peter 5:8: "Be alert and of sober mind (*grēgorēsate*). Your enemy the devil prowls around like a roaring lion looking for someone to devour." Note also the Ephesians parallel: "And pray in the Spirit on all occasions with all kinds of prayers and requests. With this in mind, be alert (*agrypnountes*) and always keep on praying for all the Lord's people" (6:18). Yet even in these contexts, the

---

7. O'Brien, 237.

8. Some interpreters take the participle as imperatival (Harris, 192; Lohse, 164; cf. KJV; HCSB). However, while the participle may have some imperatival flavor because it modifies an imperative, it is best seen as subordinate in sense.

9. See esp. E. Lövestam, *Spiritual Wakefulness in the New Testament* (Lund: Gleerup, 1963).

10. O'Brien, 237-38; Dunn, 262.

sense of alertness to the nature of the "times" in which believers live is present. We are probably justified therefore in concluding that, in light of Colossians 3:1-4, "watchfulness" here alludes to the salvation-historical situation of believers, "raised with Christ" already, yet awaiting the day when we will "appear with him in glory." Here is yet another (to be sure, somewhat veiled) allusion to the typical Pauline sense of eschatological imminence that many interpreters allege is absent from Colossians.[11]

A second attitude that should mark believers' prayer life is, not surprisingly, thankfulness.[12] We say "not surprisingly" because, as we have noted in several other places, thanksgiving is a motif that is woven throughout the argument of Colossians (1:12; 2:7; 3:15, 17). A true appreciation of the believer's status, "dead" to the world and its powers, "alive" to God in Christ with all one's sins forgiven, and destined for glory, will inevitably produce thanksgiving. And such an attitude of thanks will serve as a powerful deterrent to the inroads of the false teachers as well as a stimulus to pray.

3 From prayer in general Paul moves to prayer for himself and others engaged in ministry. Almost all the versions translate v. 3 as a command: *And pray for us, too* (exceptions are KJV, NKJV, NASB).[13] This translation is undoubtedly warranted, since the participle Paul uses — *proseuchomenoi* — takes on imperatival force from the fact that it modifies the imperative "be devoted to prayer" in v. 2.[14] As the Colossians pray, Paul asks them to pray specifically for *us*. Since Paul can sometimes refer to himself alone with such a plural pronoun, he may mean here, in effect, "pray for me." But the three occasions when he requests prayer for "us" occur in letters that include one of Paul's associates in the letter opening: 1 Thessalonians 5:25 and 2 Thessalonians 3:1 (Silas and Timothy), and here in Colossians 4:3 (Timothy) (and contrast Rom. 15:30, where, in a letter without a co-sender, Paul asks prayer for "me"). Probably, then, Paul is requesting prayer for himself and Timothy, and perhaps also the other

---

11. Schweizer's claim that the verse betrays a move away from imminence to an expectation of an extended time before Christ's return (231-32) has no basis.

12. In the Greek text this idea is indicated in a prepositional phrase — ἐν εὐχαριστίᾳ — attached to γρηγοροῦντες ("being watchful"); see ESV: "being watchful in it with thanksgiving." TNIV's *being watchful and thankful* expresses the idea clearly enough; see also NLT: "devote yourselves to prayer with an alert and thankful heart."

13. The Gk. ἅμα καί ("at the same time also") with the participle is a construction comparatively rare in the NT but widespread in classical Greek. It serves to reinforce the temporal relation between the participle and its governing verb (Robertson, *Grammar*, 1139-40).

14. This is not to say that the participle is "imperatival," which is a designation best confined to those situations (rare in the NT) where a participle is used on its own to issue a command. See on this Wallace, *Greek Syntax*, 652.

coworkers he mentions in the following context (esp. Epaphras; cf. 1:7 as well as 4:12, 13).[15] Nevertheless, the return to the first-person singular in the following verse — "that I might proclaim it clearly, as I should" — shows that he is thinking especially of his own ministry.

The content of Paul's request is that God might open *a door for our message*.[16] An "open door" is a natural metaphor for the idea of ready access to an opportunity and is therefore widely used in the ancient world.[17] It occurs in the New Testament to refer to an opportunity for evangelistic ministry (Acts 14:27; 1 Cor. 16:9; 2 Cor. 2:12; cf. Rev. 3:8, 20). These parallel texts, along with the context here, make it probable that Paul is asking prayer for his (and others') evangelistic ministry in particular. Strikingly, however, Paul does not pray that he or some other minister might have an open door to walk through, but that there might be an open door for *our message*. As O'Brien puts it, "the emphasis falls on the dynamic, almost personal, character of the 'word'"[18] (*logos*, translated "message" in TNIV, NET, HCSB, NJB, etc.). It is the word that must be given entrance because it is the word that has the power to transform human beings. This emphasis echoes the beginning of the letter, where Paul gives the word a similar active role, as the word "grows and bears fruit" among the Colossians (1:6) and in all the world. In requesting prayer for the opening of a door for the word, Paul implies that it is God who prepares the way for the message of the gospel. He provides opportunities; he softens the hearts of listeners by his grace. The fact that Paul makes this request while imprisoned not only tells us something about the nature of that confinement — perhaps a "house arrest" — but also about Paul's passion for the gospel.

The TNIV is probably correct to take the next clause (governed by an infinitive in Greek) as indicating result. Paul wants a door for the word to be opened so that *we may proclaim the mystery of Christ*.[19] "Pro-

---

15. O'Brien, 238; Harris, 193; Dunn, 263.

16. The "that" here in the TNIV and in most other versions translates Gk. ἵνα, which usually indicates the content rather than the purpose of praying (Harris, 193).

17. See J. Jeremias, *TDNT* 3.174. Somewhat different in nuance are Ps. 78:23, where God "opens the doors of heaven" to pour manna on his people; Isa. 45:1, which speaks of God "opening doors" (gates of cities?) for the conquests of Cyrus; Rev. 4:1, which refers to the opening of a door in heaven through which John can enter to see his visions; and Rev. 3:20, which urges the community to open its "door" for the Lord to enter (probably).

18. O'Brien, 239. He cites 2 Thess. 3:1.

19. Robertson, *Grammar*, 1090. Harris (194) holds that the infinitive indicates purpose; and here, as so often in Scripture, the distinction between purpose and result is a fine one. Translating the Greek infinitive straightforwardly as an English infinitive produces a puzzling collocation: "that God may open to us a door for the word, to declare the mystery of Christ" (ESV; cf. also HCSB; NAB, etc.). With no explicit subject, "declare" would seem to depend on "word."

claim" translates a verb with a broad meaning (*laleō*, "speak," "say"). It is applied to virtually every form of verbal communication. The context here certainly justifies the sense "proclaim" (also NET) or "declare" (ESV) or "announce" (NJB).[20] In identifying the content of what he proclaims as "the mystery of Christ," Paul harks back to the description of his ministry in 1:24–2:5. In this earlier text he also identified the content of his proclamation as "the mystery," "kept hidden for ages and generations" but now "disclosed to the Lord's people" (1:26). As we noted in our comments on those verses, "mystery" is a term derived from Scripture (esp. the book of Daniel) and is used by Paul to denote various aspects of the gospel message that God had not clearly revealed to his people in the past but that were now revealed in Christ. Because of Paul's particular role in salvation history, he often focuses on one element of this mystery: the inclusion of Gentiles as full members of the new covenant people of God (an idea touched on in 1:27).[21] But the focus in Colossians, in a manner wholly distinctive to this letter, is christological. The mystery, Paul said earlier, is "Christ in you, the hope of glory" (1:27) or, simply, "Christ" (2:2). These texts suggest that we should understand "the mystery of Christ" not as "the mystery that Christ proclaims" (taking *Christou* as a subjective genitive) or even "the mystery about Christ" (objective genitive; see NLT) but "the mystery which is Christ" (an epexegetic genitive).[22] God is therefore here once again defined in christological terms: God opens the door for the mystery of Christ to be proclaimed.[23]

The verse closes with a brief reminder of Paul's circumstances: *for which I am in chains.*[24] The TNIV is quite compact; "for the sake of which I am in chains" (NJB) might convey the idea more clearly. The TNIV also preserves the concrete imagery — "in chains" — while other versions "translate" more abstractly: "in prison" (e.g., ESV; HCSB; NAB; NRSV).

---

20. It is sometimes suggested that the verb λαλέω has the nuance of informal speech, but, as Louw-Nida note after suggesting the possibility, "this cannot be clearly and consistently shown from NT contexts." Paul uses λαλέω far less frequently than he does λέγω, and a distinction between the two is very difficult to maintain. Paul uses λαλέω often in contexts where somewhat formal gospel proclamation is intended (e.g., 1 Cor. 2:6, 7, 13; Eph. 6:20; Phil. 1:14; 1 Thess. 2:2, 4, 26; Titus 2:1, 15). And in Rom. 3:19 he uses both λαλέω and λέγω to refer to what the OT "says" with no difference in meaning. In Colossians, λαλέω occurs only in this verse and the next, while λέγω is found in 2:4; 4:11, 17.

21. Dunn, 263 (who sees this as further evidence of the Jewish nature of the false teaching).

22. E.g., Harris, 194.

23. See Gnilka, 227.

24. This translation is found, essentially, in all the English translations and is supported by almost all the commentators.

Either translation gets the point across. (The Greek actually uses a verb here: for which "I am bound" [*dedemai*].) This is the first time in the letter that Paul has mentioned his status as prisoner. We lean toward the view that this verse refers to Paul's imprisonment in Rome described at the end of the book of Acts. That account makes clear that Paul was held in loose custody, living in his own rented rooms while probably chained to his guard.[25] It is because of "the mystery," Paul says, that he is in chains ("mystery" must be the antecedent of the relative pronoun "which" because its Greek equivalent, *ho*, is neuter). Paul, of course, was not officially arrested because he was proclaiming the mystery. But he ended up in Roman custody because he was seeking to advance the cause of the gospel, offering a sacrifice in the Temple to signal his continuing loyalty to the Jewish people (Acts 21:26-36). Note especially how Tertullus, the spokesperson for the Jewish elders, puts the matter: "We have found this man to be a troublemaker, stirring up riots among the Jews all over the world. He is a ringleader of the Nazarene sect and even tried to desecrate the temple; so we seized him" (Acts 24:5-7). It was Paul's bold proclamation of Christ that stimulated such strong reactions, leading even to "riots," among the Jews. But what is of greater relevance for this text is why Paul chose to bring up the matter of his imprisonment at this point in the letter. Probably he does so to illustrate the power of God in opening doors for the gospel even when humans conspire to close them. See especially 2 Timothy 2:9, where he says about the gospel: "for which I am suffering even to the point of being chained like a criminal. But God's word is not chained."

4 In the Greek text, this verse consists of a purpose clause, and it can be connected to the previous context in three ways.

(1) It could depend on the last clause of v. 3:
"Because of the mystery I am in chains, with the purpose that I might proclaim it clearly"[26]

(2) It could depend on "pray" at the beginning of v. 3:

25. See esp. Brian Rapske, *The Book of Acts and Paul in Roman Custody*, vol. 3 of The Book of Acts in Its First Century Setting (Grand Rapids: Eerdmans, 1994), 177-81.

26. Barth/Blanke, 454. Further supporting this construal of the syntax is the suggestion that, in v. 3b, we should read the Greek letters that are normally divided into two words — δι' ὅ, "because of which" — as one word — διό, "therefore." (Most early manuscripts did not include accents, breathing marks, or even spaces between words.) If we read this word, then this clause would be translated, "Wherefore it is to this end that I have been imprisoned," namely, in order to "make manifest the gospel . . ." (v. 4) (see Markus Bockmuehl, "A Note on the Text of Colossians 4:3," *JTS* 39 [1988], 489-94). But the usual way of reading the text is to be preferred (see esp. Aletti, 259-60).

Pray
(a) "that God might open a door" [and]
(b) "that I might proclaim the mystery clearly"[27]
(3) It could depend on the clause "that God might open a door":
Pray that God might open a door
(a) "so that we may proclaim the mystery" [and]
(b) "so that I may proclaim it clearly"[28]

Probably the third option makes best sense of the flow of thought. Paul's general reference to the proclamation of the mystery (note the "we") is filled out more specifically with concern that he might himself, in his imprisonment (v. 3b), continue boldly and clearly to proclaim the gospel. Paul refers to a similar concern in other letters written from prison (Phil. 1:12-18; Eph. 6:19-20; 2 Tim. 4:17). At first sight, it might seem that the TNIV, by introducing the imperative "pray" at the beginning of v. 4 and making the verse a new sentence, is supporting the second syntactical option (see also NET; NJB; NLT). But this is not necessarily the case. Trying to attach v. 4 to the already complex sentence in v. 3 makes for some awkward, "run-on" English (see NASB; NRSV; ESV and HCSB try to ease the problem by introducing a dash at the beginning of v. 4). Starting a new sentence simply makes for better English while still leaving the syntactical options open.

We may, then, reconstruct the sequence of thought in vv. 3-4 as follows: Paul requests prayer that God might provide an "open door" for himself and his co-workers to proclaim the gospel (v. 3a). He then notes, almost as a parenthesis, that it is for the sake of this gospel that he is in prison (v. 3b). And this reference to his own circumstances leads him to return to the purpose for which God opens the door, but now in terms of his own ministry specifically: that Paul might, despite his difficult circumstances, proclaim it clearly. In v. 3a, "proclaim," as we noted above, translates a rather general and colorless Greek verb (*laleō*, "speak"). Here, however, it translates the more pointed verb "manifest," "make clear" (*phaneroō*; cf. ESV; HCSB). Paul has used this verb earlier in Colossians to refer to Christ's final "appearance" in glory (3:4) and, of greater relevance to this verse, in 1:26 with reference to "the mystery," which, he says, "has been kept hidden for ages and generations, but is now disclosed (*ephanerōthē*) to the Lord's people." Indeed, as we noted in our comments on 1:26, Paul regularly uses this verb to refer to the revelation, or manifes-

27. See Harris, 195. This option has in its favor making the two ἵνα clauses parallel to each other.
28. O'Brien, 240.

tation, of eschatological events, whether ones connected with Christ's first coming (e.g., Rom. 3:21; 16:26; 1 Tim. 3:16; 2 Tim. 1:10) or his second (1 Cor. 4:5; 2 Cor. 5:10). Paul can also use the verb, as he does here, for his own proclamation of God's revelation (2 Cor. 2:4; 3:3; 11:16). In doing so, he implies that his own preaching stands in continuity with God's own revelation: what God has revealed in history, Paul now reveals in his own preaching.[29] This verse therefore points to the significant salvation-historical role that Paul claims for himself more explicitly elsewhere (e.g., Rom. 11:13-15; Eph. 3:1-10; Col. 1:24-28).

The last clause of the verse reinforces this point by reminding us of Paul's sense of calling. Paul was conscious of being specially chosen by God for the ministry of gospel proclamation (esp. among Gentiles) (Gal. 1:11-16), a calling that "compelled" him to preach Christ wherever he could: "For when I preach the gospel, I cannot boast, since I am compelled to preach. Woe to me if I do not preach the gospel!" (1 Cor. 9:16; cf. Rom. 1:14; 15:20). Paul refers to this same sense of divine compulsion in the last part of v. 4, which could be translated, "as it is necessary for me to speak." The verb "it is necessary" *(dei)* often has this sense of divine determination in the New Testament, though not as often in Paul as in other parts of the New Testament. It is not entirely clear, however, whether Paul is saying here simply that he must proclaim the mystery or that he must proclaim it in a "clear" manner (as the TNIV could imply; see esp. NLT: "Pray that I will proclaim this message as clearly as I should").[30] Since the Greek verb refers to the fact of "manifestation" rather than the manner of manifestation, we think the former is more likely.

5 This verse is not formally connected to what comes before it, but the logical connection is clear enough. Having asked the Colossians to pray for the evangelistic efforts of himself and his co-workers (vv. 3-4), Paul naturally thinks of the Colossians' own involvement in evangelism (vv. 5-6). Outsiders, then, refers to people outside the Christian community (NLT: "those who are not believers"). Some commentators think that the false teachers may be particularly in view, in which case the verse would focus more narrowly on how the Colossian Christians should respond to this teaching. But a general reference to non-Christians is more likely, since this is how Paul uses the Greek phrase translated "outsiders" elsewhere (*hoi exō*, "those outside"; see 1 Cor. 5:12, 13; 1 Thess. 4:12; and cf. Mark 4:11).[31]

---

29. O'Brien, 240; Schweizer, 233.

30. O'Brien, 240.

31. Gnilka (230-31) thinks that there the reference is generally to "outsiders," but with particular reference to the false teachers.

With respect to these "outsiders," Paul says, the Colossian Christians are to be wise in the way they act. Paul again employs the widespread biblical idiom of "walking": "walk in wisdom" is a more literal rendering of the Greek (cf. HCSB). Here, as elsewhere (see our notes on 1:10 and 2:6), English translators choose a variety of ways to convey this idiom: "Conduct yourselves wisely" (RSV; NRSV; ESV; NAB); "act wisely" (NJB; cf. TEV); "Live wisely" (NLT). All these translations get the point across clearly enough: believers should govern their conduct with unbelievers on the basis of biblical wisdom. Just what this conduct will look like specifically is left unsaid. "Wisdom," of course, is a very broad concept, occupying in biblical thought a crucial intermediate stage between thought and action. As believers immerse themselves in the life of Christ, having put on the "new man" (3:10-11), their minds are renewed by God's Spirit (Rom. 12:2; Eph. 4:23). Wisdom will enable us to determine just how, in given situations, our new way of thinking, our new set of biblical values, should be put into effect. At the beginning of the letter, Paul reported that he was continually praying to God "to fill you with the knowledge of his will through all the wisdom and understanding that the Spirit gives, so that you may live a life worthy of the Lord and please him in every way." Colossians 4:6 picks up this basic concern, applying it now specifically to those outside the community.[32] Paul's concern at this point makes very good sense in a letter that focuses so much on the need for Christians to distance themselves from certain kinds of "outsiders" (the false teachers). While resisting the wrong kind of outside influence, the Colossian Christians nevertheless need to stay engaged with their fellow citizens and seek to win them to Christ.

In the Greek text, v. 5b is a participial clause that is tied to the command to "be wise toward outsiders" in v. 5a: cf. ESV, "making the best use of the time." The translation of this verb as an imperative in TNIV — *make the most of every opportunity* (cf. also NLT) — is simply a choice related to English style. The participle, while syntactically tied to the verb *be wise*, is only very generally tied to that verb conceptually, and an independent verb in English is a good way to translate it.[33] More difficult is the meaning of the verb. This verb *(exagorazō)* is a compound verb made up of the preposition "out of" *(ek)* and the simple verb "buy" *(agorazō)*. Putting these together would yield the meaning "buy out of," and this, in fact, is basically what the word means in two of its four New Testament occur-

---

32. Dunn, 265, notes that 4:6 therefore forms an *inclusio* with 1:9-10.

33. The participle ἐξαγοραζόμενοι is, in other words, a participle of "attendant circumstances" (see Wallace, *Syntax*, 640). O'Brien (241), on the other hand, thinks the participle is instrumental: "Be wise . . . by thoroughly using the time."

rences: Galatians 3:13 — "Christ redeemed us from the curse of the law" — and Galatians 4:(4)-5 — "God sent his Son . . . to redeem those under the law." In both of these verses, the verb has the sense of "buy out of slavery": on the cross, God in Christ has "paid the price" to buy sinners out of their captivity to sin. A few interpreters think the verb might have this meaning in the two other places it occurs in the New Testament, here in Colossians 4:6 and in the generally parallel Ephesians 5:16. As God in Christ has bought humans out from their slavery to sin, so Christians need to "buy" time "out of" its captivity to sin and Satan (see KJV, "redeeming the time").[34]

The idea that time might itself be evil or be under the sway of evil could be inferred from the Ephesians text, where Paul follows up his exhortation to "redeem the time" with the reminder that "the days are evil." But no such indication is found in Colossians, and it is generally very difficult to think of an inanimate concept such as "time" being redeemed. Most interpreters therefore have rejected this interpretation in favor of other options. Methodologically, of course, the most obvious place to look for help would be the LXX. And, in fact, we find, in the only occurrence of this verb in the LXX, in Daniel 2:8, a rather close parallel to Colossians 4:6 and Ephesians 5:16. In the Daniel text King Nebuchadnezzar accuses his astrologers of trying to "buy time" before his threatened punishment (for their failure to interpret his dream) falls on them. Not only does Daniel have the same verb as we find in the New Testament texts, but it also has the same object, "time." But the verb in this text appears to have the sense simply of "buy," and the whole phrase means to "stall for time" — a meaning that surely does not fit either Colossians 4:6 or Ephesians 5:16. The Daniel text does, however, illustrate the fact that the preposition added to the front of the verb might have an intensive meaning: "buy thoroughly," or, more idiomatically, "buy up."[35] Most interpreters feel that this is the best option for the verb in Colossians and Ephesians.[36] Paul would be encouraging us to "buy up" all the time that is available to us — or, as the TNIV puts it, "make the most of every opportunity."

The word for "time" here, *kairos*, can sometimes have the sense of a particular time, or opportune moment (as opposed to *chronos*, which usually refers to time in a general way). It is not clear whether the word has

34. See J. Armitage Robinson, *St. Paul's Epistle to the Ephesians* (London: James Clarke, n.d.), 202.

35. See F. Büchsel, *TDNT* 1.128.

36. E.g., Lightfoot, 232; O'Brien, 242; Moule, 133-34; Wright, 153. The verb is in the middle voice, probably an "indirect" middle, connoting that Christians "buy back" time "for themselves" (e.g., Wallace, *Grammar*, 421; Harris, 196).

that particular nuance here or not, but it does not make much difference to the meaning. More significant is the wider salvation-historical significance of the concept "time" here. Paul views the time in which believers find themselves as caught in the tension of the "already . . . not yet." Believers live after the initial coming of Messiah and the inauguration of the redemptive kingdom. But they also live in expectation of a second coming of Messiah to complete the work of redemption. Paul has alluded to this tension in 3:1-4, and his call for believers to "watch" in v. 2, as we have seen, may also allude to this eschatological sense of time. Therefore the need to "buy time" is especially imperative because of Paul's sense of the "shortness of the time" (1 Cor. 7:29).[37] He does not mean by this that the Lord will return within a specified short period of time, but that the return of the Lord is always impending, rendering it entirely uncertain how much time we will yet be given. An important aspect of wise living is to use the (short) time God has given us to best effect. In Colossians, because of the focus on "outsiders," this will refer specifically to making the most of the "open doors" (cf. v. 3) that God gives us to evangelize.[38]

6 The end of this verse — *so that you may know how to answer everyone* — shows that Paul continues to elaborate the basic command at the beginning of v. 5. Acting wisely toward outsiders includes "making the most of every opportunity" (v. 5b) and speaking to them in the right manner (v. 6).[39] But what kind of "speaking" does Paul refer to here? The answer to this question is not obvious, because he uses the general word *logos*, which can refer to anything from casual conversation to proclamation of the gospel. Complicating matters is the equally ambiguous reference to *charis*, which can refer to divine "grace" or simply to human "graciousness." Thus, at one end of the spectrum of possibilities, we can view v. 6a as exhorting Christians to make sure that their gospel "message" — their "witnessing," we may call it — is empowered by and mixed with divine grace. Translations that may suggest this interpretation are, for instance, NASB: "Let your speech always be with grace." At the other end of the spectrum, Paul may be making a point about ordinary "conversation," exhorting Christians to speak "graciously." See, for

37. See Dunn, 265-66. Lohse, 168, denies that any sense of imminence is conveyed by this phrase, contrasting the perspective of Colossians on eschatology with Paul's own perspective. However, while an allusion to imminence is certainly not clear, Lohse denies the possibility too strongly, thereby driving an unwarranted wedge between Colossians and Paul.

38. MacDonald, 173.

39. The opening words of v. 6, in context, must clearly be an exhortation, even though no verb is explicit. We are to assume the verb ἔστω (third singular present imperative active of εἰμί).

example, NJB: "Always talk pleasantly."[40] A consideration of the context might initially favor the former view, since Paul has used *logos* in v. 3 to refer to the gospel message (a door for "our message"). And, of course, *charis* usually refers to divine "grace" in Paul (and in three of its four other occurrences in Colossians: 1:2, 6; 4:18).

Nevertheless, good reasons to favor the second view can also be cited. Especially important are extra-biblical parallels where we find the same cluster of words that Paul uses here (*logos, charis, halas* ["salt"]) to refer to human speech in general.[41] And Paul can certainly use *logos* with this more general sense; see, for example, Colossians 3:17: "whatever you do, whether in word *(logos)* or deed." The main problem with this second view, however, is the fact that Paul never uses *charis* in the sense of graciousness (though Luke does; see the reference to Christ's "gracious words" [*tois logois tēs charitos*] in Luke 4:22). It is possible, then, that *logos* might refer to ordinary human speech while *charis* retains its distinctive Christian meaning.[42] This is the interpretation apparently reflected in the TNIV: *Let your conversation be always full of grace*[43] (and perhaps also in KJV; NASB). A decision among these options is not easy to make. Perhaps in this case, however, we should view the significant clustering of words (the "syntagmatic" consideration) as the most important and conclude tentatively that Paul is exhorting Christians to exhibit in all their speech (whether casual conversation or overt gospel witness) a gracious and attractive tone.

The next phrase, which further describes the kind of speech Paul wants the Colossian Christians to exhibit, is also difficult. The translation is straightforward, and most of the English versions agree on something like the TNIV's *seasoned with salt*. Paul is using a metaphor; but what does the metaphor connote? The word "salt" is used in two other contexts in the New Testament, both of them metaphorical and both of them uncertain in meaning: Matthew 5:13: "You are the salt of the earth. But if the salt loses its saltiness, how can it be made salty again? It is no longer good for anything, except to be thrown out and trampled underfoot"; Mark

40. The Greek prepositional phrase ἐν χάριτι can have an adverbial force; hence "graciously."

41. This consideration leads the majority of commentators to favor a reference here to "gracious" speech (e.g., Lightfoot, 232; Abbott, 298; O'Brien, 242; Lohse, 168; Wolter, 312).

42. Gnilka, 231; Barth/Blanke, 456-57. Pokorný (188) thinks that χάρις refers to both divine grace and human graciousness.

43. To be sure, the English word "grace" is itself somewhat ambiguous, since we can use it to refer to a human quality; e.g., "he exhibited grace in responding to his accusers." Nevertheless, the phrase "in grace" within the "language game" of scriptural teaching would naturally suggest a reference to divine grace.

9:50 (parallel in Luke 14:34): "Salt is good, but if it loses its saltiness, how can you make it salty again? Have salt in yourselves, and be at peace with each other."[44] Most interpreters, citing parallels in Greco-Roman literature, think that the reference in Colossians 4:6 is to speech that is "winsome or witty."[45] Others, however, note that there is some basis in rabbinic literature to associate salt with wisdom.[46] And a call for Christians to exhibit wisdom in their speech would cohere with v. 5a and also fit in very well with the end of v. 6. For the goal, or result, of the speech that Paul is calling for is that believers would be prepared to "answer" unbelievers, and it is a bit easier to see how "wise speech" could do this than "winsome" or "witty" speech.

Again, however, we think that the parallels between the word cluster found here in Paul (especially since this is the only place he uses the word "salt") and in Greco-Roman literature should be the decisive criterion. We take it, then, that Paul is calling on Christians to speak with their unbelieving neighbors and friends with gracious, warm, and winsome words — all with the purpose of being able to "answer" unbelievers.[47] By putting it this way, Paul assumes that unbelievers will be raising questions about the faith of the Colossian Christians, questions that may be neutral or even, perhaps, hostile. An appropriate Christian response will, of course, communicate the content of the gospel, but it will also be done in a manner that will make the gospel attractive. Peter makes a similar point: "Always be prepared to give an answer to everyone who asks you to give the reason for the hope that you have. But do this with gentleness and respect" (1 Pet. 3:15b). As Dunn puts it, Paul envisages a church "expected to hold its own in the social setting of marketplace, baths, and meal table and to win attention by the attractiveness of its life and speech."[48]

44. This latter text (and its Lukan parallel) is also the only other passage in biblical Greek where the verb ἀρτύω, "season," occurs. The form in Col. 4:6 is a perfect participle (ἠρτυμένος), the perfect tense being used because Paul refers simply to the "state" or character of the speech.

45. BDAG; see also, e.g., Lightfoot, 232; Moule, 135; Lohse, 168; Wright, 153. Texts regularly cited are Plutarch, *Moralia* 514EF, which, however, may not be relevant since it does not compare conversation to salt but refers to "the salt of conversation" (see Moule, 135); *Moralia* 684E-685C, where Plutarch explains that salt is highly esteemed as the "crowning season," and for imparting flavor to food, for preserving bodies, and as an aphrodisiac (!); and Diogenes Laertius 4.67, where the third-century B.C. Timon is quoted as saying of the school of philosophers known as the "Academics," that their speech was "unseasoned by salt" (i.e., not to the point?).

46. See W. Nauck, "Salt as a Metaphor in Instruction for Discipleship," *ST* 6 (1952), 165-78; R. P. Martin, 128; Bruce, 175; O'Brien, 243.

47. The end of v. 6 is an infinitive clause in Greek (εἰδέναι, "to know") that is probably telic in significance (Harris, 197).

48. Dunn, 267.

III. THE LETTER CLOSING: GREETINGS, PLANS, AND INSTRUCTIONS (4:7-18)

7Tychicus will tell you all the news about me. He is a dear brother, a faithful minister and fellow servant in the Lord. 8I am sending him to you for the express purpose that you may know about our circumstances and that he may encourage your hearts. 9He is coming with Onesimus, our faithful and dear brother, who is one of you. They will tell you everything that is happening here.

10 My fellow prisoner Aristarchus sends you his greetings, as does Mark, the cousin of Barnabas. (You have received instructions about him; if he comes to you, welcome him.) 11Jesus, who is called Justus, also sends greetings. These are the only Jews among my co-workers for the kingdom of God, and they have proved a comfort to me. 12Epaphras, who is one of you and a servant of Christ Jesus, sends greetings. He is always wrestling in prayer for you, that you may stand firm in all the will of God, mature and fully assured. 13I vouch for him that he is working hard for you and for those at Laodicea and Hierapolis. 14Our dear friend Luke, the doctor, and Demas send greetings. 15Give my greetings to the brothers and sisters at Laodicea, and to Nympha and the church in her house.

16After this letter has been read to you, see that it is also read in the church of the Laodiceans and that you in turn read the letter from Laodicea.

17Tell Archippus: "See to it that you complete the work you have received in the Lord."

18I, Paul, write this greeting in my own hand. Remember my chains. Grace be with you.

The TNIV divides the "letter closing" of Colossians into five parts: a reference to the men carrying the letter to the Colossians (vv. 7-9); a series of greetings (vv. 10-15); a request for an exchange of letters between Colossae and the neighboring town of Laodicea (v. 16); an exhortation to Archippus, probably related to his ministry (v. 17); and a final "signature," with a brief prayer request and grace wish (v. 18).[1] One might arrange the material slightly differently, for instance grouping together the material in vv. 15-17 or 16-17 or even 10-17.[2] But it makes little difference to the meaning of this section, which, as is typical of Paul's letter closings,

---

1. See also Dunn, 267.
2. The NA[27] Greek text follows the first (see also O'Brien, 246; Lohse, 170; Gnilka, 233 [who puts v. 18 with vv. 15-17]); Wolter (214) advocates the second; while Moule (138) and Dunn (267) assume the third.

moves rapidly from one topic to another. These letter closings tend to follow a general pattern, with many of the same elements recurring in each one. But there is also considerable variation, so one should avoid speaking of any kind of "set" series of topics or of drawing too many implications from what is included or left out in any given closing.

Nevertheless, we might note that the request to share letters between two cities is unique in Paul's letter closings, probably reflecting the unusual geographic proximity of two important early centers of Christianity. On the other hand, it is somewhat surprising that Paul makes no reference to his own travel plans in this section, since, according to Philemon 22, he apparently contemplates a visit to the city. Paul's "indirect" relationship to the Colossians (he had never met them [2:1]) might account for the lack of such a detail.[3] But some interpreters see this omission as one indication of the post-Pauline character of Colossians.[4] They argue that a Pauline disciple, writing shortly after the apostle's death, would naturally not include such a reference. But how, then, does one account for the other personal details in this passage? And how does one explain the "apostolic signature" in v. 18? Defenders of the pseudepigraphic nature of the letter argue that these details were included in order to reinforce the authority of Paul's co-workers in his absence. The "Pauline community" had lost its founder and leader and required new authorization to carry on its teaching.[5] At the same time, of course, these details would lend an air of authenticity and authority to the letter itself.[6]

One can readily understand how these details could, indeed, serve such a purpose. What is much harder to understand is how the inclusion of such fictional details would actually have functioned. On the one hand, the readers may have been fooled by these details into thinking that Paul really was writing the letter. In this case, however we might try to gloss over the issue, it is hard to see how Colossians could be viewed as anything but a deceptive fraud. On the other hand, the readers may have recognized a sort of literary technique here, seeing exactly what the post-Pauline author was attempting to do. But in this case, it is hard to see how the letter could achieve its alleged purpose, since, in effect, members of the Pauline school would be accrediting themselves. Moreover, we could assume that the first readers would have read these details as a transparent literary device only if we had convincing evidence that the

---

3. E. Percy, *Die Probleme der Kolosser- und Epheserbriefe* (Lund: Gleerup, 1946), 474.
4. E.g., Gnilka, 233; MacDonald, 186.
5. For a brief and lucid defense of this reading of these verses, see esp. MacDonald, 185-88; see also W. Marxsen, *Introduction to the New Testament* (Philadelphia: Fortress, 1968), 177-86.
6. See Lohse, 175-77.

personalia in ancient letters had such a function. Such evidence is, how-ever, lacking. These personal details therefore leave us with only two rea-sonable conclusions: (1) Paul has written the letter; or (2) the letter is a fraud and unworthy of serious consideration. As we have argued in the Introduction (28-41), we think that the case against Pauline authorship has been overstated and that there are sound reasons to endorse the deci-sion of the early church to accept this letter as authentically Pauline.

7 As he often does at the end of his letters, Paul in vv. 7-9 singles out for special mention some people who are with him and who are being sent to the letter's destination to tell the Christians there more about his circumstances. The closest parallel is in Ephesians (6:21-22), where Paul also mentions Tychicus and describes him and his mission in similar lan-guage: "Tychicus, the dear brother and faithful servant in the Lord, will tell you everything, so that you also may know how I am and what I am doing. I am sending him to you for this very purpose, that you may know how we are, and that he may encourage you." (Compare also 1 Cor. 16:10; Titus 3:12.) Almost certainly these people were the ones charged with car-rying the letter Paul has written to its destination. As one would expect in a time before mail service, a letter-writer would have had to depend on a courier to deliver his or her letter. But Paul's couriers were more than passive letter-carriers. As fellow ministers of the gospel, they were in a position not only to deliver the letter but also to elaborate on it and fill in blanks.[7]

Tychicus was apparently the person chiefly responsible for deliver-ing the letter. Since he plays the same role in Ephesians (6:21) and is ac-companied by Onesimus (v. 9), and since Ephesus and Colossae are no more than 120 miles apart, we can reasonably surmise that he is carrying the letters to the Ephesians, to the Colossians, and to Philemon at the same time. Tychicus makes his first appearance in the New Testament as a Christian from the Province of Asia who accompanied Paul on his trip to Jerusalem to deliver the "collection" (Acts 20:4). In addition to Ephe-sians 6:21 and Colossians 4:7, he is also mentioned in Titus 3:12 (Paul is sending him from his place of writing [Nicopolis?] to Titus on Crete) and 2 Timothy 4:12 (Paul has sent him to Ephesus). Clearly, then, he was a trusted — and much-traveled! — associate of Paul's, perhaps a convert from Paul's three-year ministry in Ephesus.[8] When he arrives in Colossae, he will tell the Christians there *all the news about me*. "All the

---

7. E.g., *NewDocs* 7.56.

8. Dunn (271-72) suggests that he may have been a late convert, since he appears only in the later part of Paul's ministry (from approximately A.D. 57 and later). Paul's ministry in Ephesus (the chief city of the Province of Asia) lasted from around 53 to 56.

news" translates the Greek phrase *ta kat' eme panta*, "all the things concerning me" (the same phrase, without the *panta* ["all"], occurs with a similar sense in Eph. 6:21 and Phil. 1:12).

Paul is obviously concerned to establish the "bona fides" of Tychicus so that the Colossians will give him a respectful hearing when he arrives. Nowhere else in his letters does Paul describe a co-worker with the same threefold description that we find here — *a dear brother, a faithful minister and fellow servant in the Lord* — though Paul's commendation of Epaphroditus in Philippians 2:25 is similar: "brother, co-worker and fellow soldier." The language Paul applies here to Tychicus is very similar to the way he has earlier described Epaphras: "our dear (*agapētos*) fellow servant (*syndoulos*), who is a faithful minister (*pistos . . . diakonos*) of Christ on our behalf" (1:7). The language of "dear brother" is very common in Paul, and may, in this context, mean not simply that Tychicus was a fellow Christian but that he was a fellow worker with Paul.[9] Despite their close association, Paul probably thinks of the "faithfulness" that Tychicus displays in his ministry as directed not to himself but to the churches in general.[10] Why Paul would choose to use "fellow servant" here instead of the more common "fellow worker" (*synergos*; cf. 4:3, 11; also Rom. 16:3, 9, 21; 1 Cor. 3:9; 2 Cor. 1:24; 8:23; Phil. 4:3; 1 Thess. 3:2; Phlm. 1, 24) is difficult to say. "In the Lord," which should probably be connected to both "faithful minister" and "fellow servant,"[11] might, because of the context, mean "in the Lord's work" (NLT), but it is more likely to have its more basic sense as a reference to the sphere in which Tychicus carries out his ministerial duties.

8 The commentators almost universally view the aorist verb *epempsa* as a so-called "epistolary aorist," according to which the "sending" is viewed from the perspective of the readers of the letter as already accomplished.[12] In English, then, the verb is better rendered "I am sending" (TNIV; NAB; NJB; NKJV) than "I have sent" (RSV; NRSV; ESV; HCSB; NET; NLT), since the latter could imply that Paul had sent Tychicus to them before writing the letter. Paul repeats, perhaps for emphasis, what he has said about Tychicus's mission in v. 7: he is sending him *for the express purpose* of informing the Colossians about his *circumstances*.[13] As we

9. E.g., O'Brien, 247.
10. See our notes on 1:7; and also Bruce, 176; contra Lightfoot, 234.
11. Lighfoot, 234. It is also possible, because the three nouns are associated through a common governing article — ὁ . . . ἀδελφὸς . . . διάκονος . . . σύνδουλος — that ἐν κυρίῳ goes with all three (mentioned as a possibility by Harris, 201).
12. See, e.g., BDF §334; Moule, *Idiom Book*, 12; Turner, *Syntax*, 73.
13. NKJV's "that he may know your circumstances" (cf. KJV) reflects a variant reading in the Greek text that is unlikely to be original. In place of γνῶτε τὰ περὶ ἡμῶν —

noted in the introduction to this section, the people who carried Paul's letters to their destinations were usually trusted co-workers who would be able to elaborate the content of the letter as well as to inform the readers in more detail about Paul's situation. This latter information would be especially important when Paul is in prison, since they would naturally be especially anxious to learn about his condition and prospects. However, while Paul explicitly mentions only Tychicus's conveying of personal information, he likely is thinking also of his role as letter-reader and interpreter in the final purpose clause: *that he may encourage your hearts*.[14] Paul has used a similar expression in 2:2 to describe the purpose of his apostolic prayer ministry (see also Eph. 6:22; 2 Thess. 2:17).[15]

9 Accompanying Tychicus on his mission to Colossae is Onesimus. He is, of course, the slave about whom the letter to Philemon is written. From that letter, we can conclude that Onesimus encountered Paul in his place of imprisonment, that he was converted through Paul's ministry (v. 10), and that Paul became deeply attached to him (vv. 12, 15). Many of the details "behind the scenes" are very unclear — how did Onesimus and Paul meet? what was Onesimus's role in Paul's ministry? — and we will investigate these matters in our comments on Philemon.

Here Paul contents himself with a brief and fairly colorless description. Onesimus is a *faithful and dear brother*, a description that has close parallels in the description of Tychicus (v. 7) and Epaphras (1:7). In contrast to these other two men, however, Onesimus is not described as a "fellow servant" or "minister." The former term would certainly be inappropriate, since it could also be translated "fellow slave" (*doulos* is the root). And, as the letter to Philemon makes clear, it is exactly Onesimus's status as a slave that is at issue. While we should be careful not to read too much into Paul's silence on the matter, it is perhaps also the case that Onesimus was not part of Paul's "ministry team."[16] Nevertheless, Paul clearly treats Onesimus as on the same level as his trusted associates Epaphras and Tychicus — a quite astonishing thing to do in light of Onesimus's status as a slave. Here we find a practical example of the principle that in the new creation there is "no . . . slave or free" (3:11). Paul also notes that Onesimus is *one of you*, this wording suggesting not

---

"that *you* might know *our* circumstances" — a significant number of manuscripts read γνῷ τὰ περὶ ὑμῶν — "that *he* might know *your* circumstances." As Metzger points out, the latter reading is almost certainly an attempt to make sense out of some other minor (mis-)readings of the text (*Textual Commentary*, 559).

14. O'Brien, 248.

15. See Wolter, 214, who views this as yet another indication of the intention of the pseudepigraphical author to authorize the next generation in the "Pauline school."

16. Dunn, 273.

that he is a Christian, as they are, but that he is from the city of Colossae.[17] As Harris notes, Paul thereby "highlights the radical nature of the conversion of one of their own."[18] He will join Tychicus in informing the Colossians of *everything that is happening here.*

10 Verses 10-15 are held together by the theme of "greeting." Paul passes on greetings to the Colossians from three Jewish co-workers — Aristarchus, Mark, and Justus (vv. 10-11) — and from three Gentile coworkers — Epaphras, Luke, and Demas (vv. 12-14). He then asks that his own greetings be conveyed to the Christians at Laodicea and to Nympha and the church that meets in her house (v. 15). Greetings of the sort that we have in these verses are found in seven of the other twelve Pauline letter closings. Only in Romans (16:3-16), however, does Paul convey greetings from more individuals (twenty-six) than he does here in Colossians (he conveys greetings from four individuals in 2 Timothy [4:21] and five in Philemon [23-24]). And, as we might expect from the close relationship of the letters, five of the six men mentioned here in Colossians are also mentioned in Philemon (only Justus is missing from Philemon).[19] On the other hand, missing here in Colossians is the general greeting from "all the brothers and sisters here" (1 Cor. 16:20; cf. 2 Cor. 13:13; Phil. 4:21-22; 2 Tim. 4:21; Titus 3:15) that we find in other letters. Paul may drop this general greeting in Colossians because his imprisonment kept him from significant contact with a community of believers. On the other hand, the specific mention of six individuals by name is probably not the mark of a post-Pauline author trying to gain credibility for Paul's co-workers but Paul's own concern to make contact with a community that he has neither founded nor visited (the number of people who send greetings in Romans 16 may reflect the same concern).

Paul first extends greetings from *Aristarchus.* Paul uses the simple indicative form of the verb "greet" here and in vv. 12 and 14: "Aristarchus greets you" (KJV; NKJV; RSV; NRSV; ESV; HCSB), put into a slightly more "formal" style in TNIV and most English versions: *Aristarchus sends you his greetings.* Aristarchus, like Tychicus (see v. 7), figures in the later stages of Paul's ministry, being mentioned first as a "traveling companion" of Paul's from Macedonia during the apostle's Ephesian ministry (Acts 19:29; c. A.D. 52-55). According to Acts 20:4, he hails from Thessalonica. He accompanied Paul on at least the early stage of his voyage to Rome (Acts 27:2) and may have gone all the way to Rome with Paul. This

17. The Greek is ἐξ ὑμῶν; cf. BDAG, "who is a fellow-countryman of yours."
18. Harris, 202.
19. A few interpreters have read Phlm. 23 in such a way that Justus would be included, but this reading is improbable (see our notes on the verse).

might be particularly likely if, as we think, Paul is writing this letter from Rome shortly after his arrival there. Paul does not characterize Aristarchus as a "dear brother" or "minister" or "fellow worker," but as a "fellow prisoner" (synaichmalōtos). Interpreters are divided over whether this word should be understood literally — Aristarchus is "here in prison with me" (NJB)[20] — or metaphorically — Aristarchus, like Paul, has been taken captive by the Lord to serve him.[21] The word that Paul uses occurs only twice elsewhere in the New Testament: in Philemon 23, which simply duplicates the reference to Aristarchus, and in Romans 16:7, where it refers to two other co-workers of Paul, Andronicus and Junia. Some proponents of the metaphorical interpretation claim that the word we find here would be inappropriate if taken literally, since it strictly connotes a military prisoner.[22] Had Paul intended a reference to literal imprisonment, he would have used syndesmios, which is built on his usual word for "prisoner" (desmios; see Eph. 3:1; 4:1; 2 Tim. 1:8; Phlm. 1, 9).[23] But Paul seems to use the simple verb cognate to the word Paul uses here (aichmalōtizō) in a metaphorical sense, as, for instance, in 2 Timothy 3:6, where Paul speaks of women being "taken captive" by false teachers (see also Rom. 7:23; 2 Cor. 10:5; the simple noun aichmalōtos occurs in Luke 4:18). Moreover, had a metaphorical meaning been intended, we would have expected Paul to say "fellow prisoners of Christ," or something of the sort. The literal interpretation is, then, to be preferred. We do not know how Aristarchus ended up in prison with Paul, but we can speculate that he volunteered to share the apostle's imprisonment in order to be of help to him.[24]

Mark, the cousin[25] *of Barnabas,* is the same Mark who had a checkered career in Paul's early missionary labors. Mark, whose other name was John, was the son of a woman in whose house the early Jerusalem Christian community met (Acts 12:12). After Barnabas and Saul had de-

---

20. E.g., O'Brien, 249-50; Abbott, 300; Dunn, 275-76; Lohse, 172; Barth/Blanke, 479; MacDonald, 180; Hübner, 119.

21. Lightfoot, 236; Moule, 136-37; Masson, 185; Harris, 206; idem, *Slave of Christ* (Downers Grove, Ill.: InterVarsity, 2001), 117; Gnilka, 237; George E. Ladd, "Paul's Friends in Colossians 4:7-16," *RevExp* 70 (1973), 509.

22. E.g., Harris, 206.

23. G. Kittel, *TDNT* 1.196-97.

24. Dunn, 275-76; Barth/Blanke, 479. William Ramsay thought that Aristarchus might have been a slave who accompanied Paul on his trip to Rome (*St. Paul: Traveller and Roman Citizen* [repr.; Grand Rapids: Baker, 1962], 316), while Rapske argues that he, along with Luke, voluntarily accompanied Paul as a "friend" (*The Book of Acts and Paul in Roman Custody* [Grand Rapids: Eerdmans, 1994], 372-78).

25. The Gk. ἀνεψιός means "cousin," not "nephew" (as in KJV, "sister's son") (see BDAG).

livered the money collected by the church in Antioch to the Christians in Jerusalem (Acts 11:27-30), they took "John, called Mark," with them back to Antioch. He then accompanied Paul and Barnabas on the first missionary journey, only to abandon the trip in Pamphylia (Acts 15:38). It was for this reason that Paul refused to take Mark with him on the second missionary journey, creating a rift between himself and Barnabas (Acts 15:37-39). This split must have taken place around A.D. 49, and we hear nothing more about Mark until twelve years or so later. Paul's simple conveyance of greetings here and in Philemon 24, along with his commendation of Mark in 2 Timothy 4:11, reveals that they must have become reconciled at some point. Mark apparently had a significant ministry in Rome, since Peter, writing from there, also mentions him (1 Pet. 5:13). And it was probably from Rome that Mark wrote the gospel bearing his name.

Since "Jesus, who is called Justus" in v. 11 carries on the series of nouns governed by "sends you his greetings" in v. 10,[26] Paul's remark about the *instructions* the Colossians received concerning Mark is best taken as parenthetical (so most English versions; NRSV and NLT are exceptions). *Instructions*, the English word used in most of the translations, captures accurately the sense of the Greek *entolas* here. This word would usually be translated "commandments," but there is good reason to think that it has a weaker sense here.[27] Paul touches on a matter that both he and the Colossians know something about, and so he is quite elliptical. Our ability to reconstruct just what is going on is very limited; about all we can do is guess. Lightfoot, for instance, suggests that Paul is reinforcing instructions about Mark that he had given the community on some earlier occasion.[28] Had Paul issued these instructions, however, we might have expected him to be more direct about it: for example, "I have given you instructions about him."[29] Perhaps, then, the instructions came from Peter and/or Barnabas, who had already requested that the Colossians "reinstate" Mark. Paul would then simply be adding his own *imprimatur*.[30] The way Paul mentions Barnabas (as Mark's cousin) certainly sug-

26. Ἰησοῦς is then the third noun (after Μάρκος and Ἀρίσταρχος) that depends on the singular verb ἀσπάζεται. This construction is not unusual, the verb agreeing with the first noun in the series with the others as sort of "add-ons": "Aristarchus greets you — as does Mark and also, by the way, Jesus" (see Harris, 206).

27. Paul normally uses ἐντολή to refer to divine commandments (Rom 7:8, 10, 11, 12, 13; 13:9; 1 Cor. 7:19; 14:37; Eph. 2:15; 6:2); the only exceptions are 1 Tim. 6:14, where the word may refer to the commission of Timothy, and Titus 1:14, which refers to "human commands" (perhaps in implicit contrast to divine commands).

28. Lightfoot, 238; Bruce, 180.

29. Lohse, 172.

30. O'Brien, 250-51.

339

gests that he was already known to the Colossians, and it may be that he had taken up some of Paul's responsibilities in Asia in the Apostle's absence (the New Testament is silent about the ministry of Barnabas after his split with Paul[31]). Further indication that Mark was not "under Paul's command" is the uncertain way in which Paul talks about his coming to the Colossians.[32]

11 Paul conveys greetings from a third individual, *Jesus, who is called Justus.* "Jesus" was a popular name among first-century Jews, fading in popularity only in the second century because of growing Jewish/Christian tensions.[33] In the multilingual environment of the first century, Jews often took a second Greek or Roman name, often one that sounded like their "original" Hebrew name (hence, e.g., Saul/Paul). In the Greek text, this name stands on its own, the verb having to be supplied from the beginning of v. 10; see ESV: "Aristarchus greets you . . . and Mark . . . and Jesus." The TNIV (also NET; NJB; NLT; NRSV) eases the "run-on" syntax by repeating the verb from v. 10. "Justus" is a surname that is borne by three different men in the New Testament: one of the candidates to take the place of Judas among the Twelve, "Joseph called Barsabbas (also known as Justus)" (Acts 1:23); a Gentile "God-fearer" in Corinth, "Titius Justus" (Acts 18:7); and the "Jesus Justus" in this text. We know nothing else about this man, though the name "Justus," as Lightfoot notes, was common among Judeans and Gentile proselytes.[34]

In the second part of v. 11, Paul further describes the three men whose greetings he has conveyed in vv. 10-11a. But just what Paul is saying about them is difficult to establish. The uncertainty arises from some awkwardness in the Greek syntax, which allows for at least three different interpretations:

(1) "Jesus, who is called Justus, also sends greetings. These are the only Jews among my co-workers for the kingdom of God, and they have proved a comfort to me." (TNIV; see also RSV; NRSV; ESV; NASB; NLT; NKJV)

(2) ". . . and so does Jesus who is called Justus. These alone of the circumcision are my co-workers for the kingdom of God, and they have been a comfort to me." (HCSB; see also NET; NJB)

---

31. Assuming an early date for Galatians.

32. It is possible, however, that the construction ἐάν plus aorist subjunctive (ἔλθῃ) has more the sense of "when he comes" than "if he comes" (see Harris, 207; and see Wallace, *Greek Grammar*, 470-71, for the broad range of meaning encompassed by the "third-class" conditional form).

33. See, e.g., W. Foerster, *TDNT* 3.284-93.

34. Lightfoot, 238.

(3) "and Jesus, who is called Justus, who are of the circumcision; these alone are my co-workers for the kingdom of God, and they have been a comfort to me." (NAB; see also KJV)[35]

The first option has Paul contrasting Aristarchus, Mark, and Jesus Justus with his other co-workers: these three were Jewish; the ones mentioned in the following verses were not. According to the second option, on the other hand, Paul is contrasting these three men with other Jews in his vicinity: only these three, of the Jews or Jewish-Christians around him, are working for the kingdom of God. On the third view, the Jewish identity of the three men is incidental, and Paul's main point is to single them out as the only co-workers among his current Christian associates. This last view, while it represents a legitimate interpretation of the Greek, is difficult contextually: Paul certainly seems to present Epaphras, Luke, and Demas (vv. 12-14) as three other co-workers who are with him (and he does so explicitly in Phlm. 24). A decision between the other two is harder to make. The first option is preferred by most of the English translations and also by most commentators.[36] But the second option is probably the most natural way to read the Greek syntax.[37] And it also provides a better explanation of why Paul has included this reference. It is hard to see how distinguishing between Paul's Jewish and Gentile co-workers would add to his argument.[38] But a reference to the comparatively few Jewish-Christians who are participating with Paul in gospel ministry would serve to remind his readers of the tensions that Paul's Gentile-oriented ministry had created. If, as we think, Colossians is written from

35. The difficulty in the Greek has to do with the relationship between two clauses that follow the reference to Jesus Justus: the substantival participial clause οἱ ὄντες ἐκ περιτομῆς — "the ones from the circumcision" — and the predicative assertion οὗτοι μόνοι συνεργοὶ εἰς τὴν βασιλείαν τοῦ θεοῦ — "these are the only co-workers for the kingdom of God." The first two options tie the clauses together, but they differ on how they are related. The former takes the initial participial clause as modifying συνεργοί: — "these are the only *co-workers* who are from the circumcision" — while the second attaches it to οὗτοι: "*these* only from among the circumcision are co-workers." The third option, on the other hand, separates the clauses, viewing the participial clause as a loosely attached modifier of the three names with οὗτοι starting a new clause.

36. See esp. Harris, 208, for analysis and in support of this conclusion.

37. As Abbott (301) points out, the use of a "nominative absolute" to introduce a subject that is then taken up in the following clause is standard Greek. Here, then, we would read the flow of the Greek in this manner: "these men are of the circumcision; and they are the only ones of the circumcision who are my fellow workers for the kingdom."

38. Although Dunn (278-79) suggests that Paul could be seeking to highlight the cooperation of Jews in his mission in order to counter a Jewish form of false teaching (see also Wall, 172). But the "only" seems to put the accent not on the positive ("look how many Jews are cooperating") but the negative ("look at how few Jews are cooperating").

Paul's Roman imprisonment, then Philippians (which we also think was probably written at that time) would provide something of a parallel:

> And because of my chains, most of the brothers and sisters have become confident in the Lord and dare all the more to proclaim the gospel without fear. It is true that some preach Christ out of envy and rivalry, but others out of goodwill. The latter do so out of love, knowing that I am put here for the defense of the gospel. The former preach Christ out of selfish ambition, not sincerely, supposing that they can stir up trouble for me while I am in chains. But what does it matter? The important thing is that in every way, whether from false motives or true, Christ is preached. And because of this I rejoice. Yes, and I will continue to rejoice. . . . (Phil. 1:14-18)

Some also cite as a parallel Romans 9:1-5, where Paul expresses his deep sadness at the spiritual state of so many of his fellow Jews.[39] But this text is probably not a true parallel, since the context ("co-workers for God's kingdom") pretty clearly suggests that Paul is thinking in this context of Jewish-Christians rather than simply of Jews.

But this raises a further interpretational issue. As a comparison of the translations above reveals, where the TNIV has "Jews," other versions have a reference to those "of the circumcision." The latter is the straightforward rendering of the Greek (*ek peritomēs*), and there is some debate about the precise meaning of the phrase. Circumcision, of course, is a basic badge of Jewishness, so the phrase could simply be identifying the three men as Jewish (so TNIV; NET; NLT).[40] The same phrase is used with this meaning in Acts 10:45; 11:2; Romans 4:12. However, in Galatians 2:12 and Titus 1:10, Paul uses the phrase in a narrower sense, to identify people who are propagating circumcision, "the circumcision group" (the TNIV translation in both texts). Some therefore think that Paul might be characterizing these three men as Jewish-Christians who were more conservative than Paul on issues of the law and who worked with the apostle in evangelism.[41] But there are insufficient grounds in this context to limit the reference in this way. Paul is probably simply identifying them as Jewish — not in the sense of their religion, of course, but in terms of their national identity.

39. E.g., Gnilka, 239.
40. So, e.g., Lightfoot, 238.
41. E. Earle Ellis, "The Circumcision Party and the Early Christian Mission," in *Prophecy and Hermeneutics: New Testament Essays* (WUNT 2.18; Tübingen: Mohr Siebeck, 1978), 116-28. Ellis bases this identification partly on a historical reconstruction of the "Hebraist" vs. "Hellenist" distinction in Acts 6.

Paul commends these Jewish-Christian ministers for their labor with him *for the kingdom of God*. Paul might be thinking of the future consummation of the kingdom: these men are working to "bring about" *(eis)* the kingdom of God. However, as we have noted in our comments on 1:13, Paul refers to the present, "inaugurated" kingdom more often than is sometimes recognized; and this is probably the meaning here.[42] Luke describes Paul's own mission during this same time period (A.D. 60-61, imprisoned in Rome) in similar terms: "He [Paul] proclaimed the kingdom of God and taught about the Lord Jesus Christ — with all boldness and without hindrance!" (Acts 28:31). But not only have Aristarchus, Mark, and Jesus Justus contributed to the work of the kingdom generally; in addition, *they have proved a comfort to me*.[43] We do not know just how they comforted Paul, whether through their hard work for the kingdom or (as is more likely) in their personal ministry to Paul in his imprisonment.

12 A minor break occurs between vv. 11 and 12, which have no explicit connection. This break is marked also by the similarity in language between the opening of this verse and the beginning of v. 10: the Greek verb for "greet" *(aspazetai)* followed by its object, "you" *(hymas)*, and then its subject, "Epaphras" ("Aristarchus" in v. 10). Epaphras, of course, has already been mentioned in the letter (1:7-8). It was he, perhaps a convert of Paul's from his Ephesian ministry, who first brought the gospel to Colossae. As this verse makes clear, Epaphras is part of the Colossian community *(one of you)*. In 1:7, Paul described Epaphras as his "dear fellow servant *(syndoulos)*" and a "faithful minister *(diakonos)* of Christ." Here he abbreviates, calling him simply *a servant of Christ Jesus*. The Greek word translated "servant" is *doulos*, which, as we have noted (see our comments on 1:7), can also be translated "slave" (e.g., HCSB; NAB; NET). This word, of course, applies to slaves in legal status (e.g., 3:11, 22; 4:1), but it can also be applied to people who have been enlisted in the service of the Lord. Significantly, however, the only individuals he names as "servants" in this sense are himself (Rom. 1:1; 2 Cor. 4:5;[44] Gal. 1:10; Titus 1:1) and Timothy (Phil. 1:1; 2 Tim. 2:24). Naming Epaphras a "servant of Christ Jesus," then, emphasizes his status and significance for the community. And the further description of Epaphras confirms this emphasis: like Paul, he is "always . . . in prayer" for the Colossians (cf. 1:3); like

---

42. Bruce, 180-81; O'Brien, 252; Gnilka, 239.

43. "They" translates the Greek indefinite relative pronoun οἵτινες, which often in these contexts has a qualitative force: "who are of the sort that. . . ." "Comfort" translates παρηγορία ("a source of encouragement, comfort"), a word that occurs only here in the NT (and in 4 Macc. 5:12; 6:1 in the LXX).

44. The plural form in 2 Cor. 4:5 could refer to Paul along with other apostles but is probably restricted to Paul himself.

Paul, he "wrestles" or "contends" for them (cf. 1:29); like Paul, he seeks their "maturity" (cf. 1:28); and, like Paul, he wants them to be confirmed in "all the will of God" (cf. 1:9).[45] Advocates of the pseudepigraphical nature of Colossians see in this association of Epaphras with Paul an indication of a post-Pauline author trying to buttress the authority of a new generation of leaders. But the commendation makes perfect sense as a comment from Paul himself, who wants to assert Epaphras's authority vis-à-vis the false teachers.[46]

But it is not only, or primarily, Epaphras's authority that Paul has in view; it is his deep concern for the Colossian Christians. Epaphras, says Paul, is *always wrestling in prayer for you, that you might stand firm in all the will of God, mature and fully assured.* "Wrestling in prayer" uses the same Greek verb *(agōnizomai)* that Paul used absolutely of his own "contending" for the Colossians in 1:29.[47] The translation "wrestling" preserves the athletic connotations that the verb often has (see also "battling" in NJB; "contending" in HCSB). In any case, it refers to strenuous and consistent intervention with the Lord on behalf of the Colossians — prayer needed especially in light of the danger posed by the false teachers.

The content of Epaphras's prayer[48] is that they might *stand firm.* This TNIV phrase translates the verb *histēmi,* "stand," which occurs elsewhere in Paul with the sense of firm adherence to, and in, the Christian faith (Rom. 11:20; 14:4; 1 Cor. 7:37; 10:12; 15:1; 2 Cor. 1:24; Eph. 6:11, 13, 14). Some suggest that the passive form of the verb here might have the sense "that you might be made to stand [by God],"[49] but this is unlikely. The passive form of this verb has an intransitive sense, and the addition "and the Lord is able to make them stand" to "they will stand" in Romans 14:4 suggests that the verb means simply "stand."[50]

According to the TNIV, this firm standing for which Epaphras prays has a particular sphere: *in all the will of God.*[51] But the connection of this phrase to the verb is an interpretive decision. Others think that the verb stands on its own and that "in all the will of God" *(en panti thelēmati tou theou)* modifies the words "mature and fully assured"[52] or just the final

---

45. Gnilka, 240.

46. Barth/Blanke, 483. Some speculate that Epaphras may have fallen out of favor with the Colossian Christians (Wall, 173-74).

47. Dunn, 280; O'Brien, 252-53.

48. The Greek particle ἵνα probably introduces the content of the prayer rather than stating its purpose.

49. O'Brien, 253; Dunn, 280.

50. E.g., Zerwick, *Biblical Greek,* §231; Turner, *Syntax,* 57; Harris, 209. Some manuscripts here, in fact, read the active form, στῆτε.

51. Harris, 209; Moule, 138.

52. Moule, 138.

verb, "fully assured."[53] Most of the English versions suggest this latter interpretation by following the Greek word order; cf., for example, ESV: "that you may stand mature and fully assured in all the will of God." Any of these connections makes good sense, and, indeed, they do not differ materially from each other in any significant way. In any case, the point is that Epaphras is earnestly asking the Lord to confirm the Colossians in a mature spiritual stance that would honor all that the Lord has taught them.

There is also some question about the meaning of the verb translated "fully assured" in the TNIV (and similarly in most versions). This verb (*plērophoreō*) can also mean "fulfill" (Luke 1:1; 2 Tim. 4:5, 17), and some interpreters prefer this meaning because the language of "fullness" is clearly significant in the letter. Against the probable claims of the false teachers, Paul argues that true "fullness" is found not in the false teaching but in Christ, and in Christ alone (see 1:18; 2:9); and it is in him that believers are themselves brought to "fullness" (2:10).[54] But the verb in this last verse is a different one (*plēroō*) than the one that Paul uses here, and it is a bit difficult to understand why he would have shifted verbs had he meant basically the same thing. Moreover, as we have seen, Paul appears deliberately to echo here in his description of Epaphras his earlier description of his concern for the Colossians (1:28–2:2); and in 2:2, he expresses his desire that the Colossians have "complete understanding, in order that they might know the mystery of God, namely Christ." "Fully assured" sums up this purpose fairly well.[55] We therefore slightly prefer the usual rendering, "fully assured."

13 Paul's commendation of Epaphras continues in this verse. It is connected to v. 12 by a *gar* ("for") in the Greek text (see, e.g., ESV), but the connection is a loose one, the *gar* functioning not to ground or explain something in v. 12 but simply to add a further thought.[56] "For" in English can sometimes function in this way, so it is certainly not misleading to include it (as most of the English versions do). But English can also indicate such a connection of thought simply by virtue of the juxtaposition of the sentences, so omitting a connecting word works just as well (TNIV; NJB; NLT). *I vouch for him* (TNIV) is a bit interpretive, the Greek expressing the more neutral "I bear witness about him" or "I af-

---

53. Lightfoot, 240; O'Brien, 254.

54. See, e.g., Lohse, 173; O'Brien, 254. A few manuscripts have a form of πληρόω here; hence the KJV/NKJV translation "complete."

55. Gnilka, 240.

56. BDAG explain this usage of γάρ: "Akin to explanatory function is the use of γάρ as a narrative marker to express continuation or connection." They go on to cite ancient grammarians, who noted that γάρ in this sense is basically equivalent to δέ.

firm concerning him."[57] Still, the TNIV translation is not misleading since Paul's "testimony" about Epaphras is clearly positive.

Specifically, Paul brings to the attention of the Colossians the "hard work" of Epaphras. The word for "work" here (which many of the English versions, including TNIV, translate with a verb for stylistic reasons) is not the usual *ergon* but the more rare *ponos*. This word occurs only three other times in the New Testament, all in the book of Revelation, where it means "pain" (Rev. 16:10, 11; 21:14). But the word can also refer to "work," as it does in a number of passages in the LXX (e.g., Exod. 2:11; Deut. 28:33; Ps. 78:46). The question is why Paul would use this unusual word in place of the normal *ergon*. The standard New Testament Greek lexicon suggests an answer by offering the definition, "work that involves much exertion or trouble."[58] While we must be wary of reading one discrete meaning of the word — "pain" — into another — "work" — the passages where the word occurs with this sense seem generally to bear out this connotation.[59] Paul has therefore chosen a word that highlights the difficulty and degree of exertion involved in the "work" that Epaphras is doing for the Colossians. We can only speculate about why Epaphras was having so hard a time. But it is surely natural to think that the onset of the false teaching was the cause. Ministers who are faced with threats to the spiritual well-being of their charges have to devote great energy to the defense of the gospel, and such work brings great stress, out of concern for the spiritual health of the community and because of attacks from opponents. Epaphras surely needed support from Paul in the midst of such a difficult and taxing ministry.

And Epaphras has not only the Colossians to worry about; his hard work also is directed toward the neighboring Christian communities in Laodicea and Hierapolis. We have here yet another echo of Paul's description of his own ministry, for he claims that he was "contending for you and for those at Laodicea, and for all who have not met me personally" (2:1). As we noted in our comments on this verse, Laodicea was an important city about twelve miles west of Colossae. Hierapolis, which is not mentioned in 2:1, was located about fifteen miles northwest of Colossae, thus forming something of a triangle with Colossae and

57. The Greek is μαρτυρῶ αὐτῷ. The closest parallels to this construction are in Rom. 10:2 and Gal. 4:15. The TNIV has apparently taken αὐτῷ as a "dative of advantage" and given the verb a corresponding positive translation.

58. BDAG.

59. At least this is true in the LXX. In Philo, however, who uses the word almost 140 times, this nuance is not as clear. The translations "zeal" (NKJV) or "concern" (NASB) do not represent the Greek word very well. Still less is it justified to think that this "work" involved prayer only (as NLT has it: "he prays hard for you").

Laodicea.[60] All three cities were located on important Roman roads and were therefore significant centers of commerce and industry. Epaphras was probably the founder of churches in all three cities, and this verse makes clear that he continued to exercise pastoral oversight of them.

14 Paul ends the section in which he conveys greetings from ministry associates with references to Luke and Demas. Luke is mentioned by name in the New Testament only here, in the parallel greeting in Philemon (v. 24), and in 2 Timothy 4:11 — "Only Luke is with me." All three letters were written while Paul was imprisoned in Rome, although two different imprisonments are probably involved: Colossians and Philemon from the imprisonment mentioned in Acts 28 (A.D. 60-62) and 2 Timothy from a later incarceration that climaxed in Paul's execution (perhaps around A.D. 64). But the relative paucity of explicit references to Luke by no means represents his true significance for the New Testament. The most likely conclusion to be drawn from the "we" passages in the book of Acts (passages in which the author appears to include himself in the narrative) is that Luke is the person writing on these occasions. This would naturally mean that he is the author of both Acts and the Gospel that bears his name — almost one-fourth of the New Testament.[61] Based on the passages in which Luke refers to himself in Acts, we can conclude that he was a regular companion of Paul, participating with him in ministry in Madeconia (Acts 16:8-17), on his trip back to Palestine after the third missionary journey (Acts 20:5-15; 21:1-18), and on the "shipwreck" voyage to Rome (Acts 27:1–28:16). So it would be natural to think that Luke stayed on with Paul in Rome during his imprisonment there. Very little about Luke can be gleaned from the New Testament itself, and it is, in fact, from this text in Colossians that we learn two things about Luke that we would otherwise not know: that he was a Gentile and that he was a doctor. The former conclusion, to be sure, depends on two other conclusions: that "the circumcision" in v. 11 refers to Jews in general, and that Luke is a co-worker. Some doubt one or both of these points and thus conclude that we have no sure knowledge of Luke's ethnic origins.[62] We have argued the former in our interpretation of v. 11. And the latter is a natural inference from the sequence in the text and from Luke's participation with Paul in ministry in the book of Acts. The common description of Luke as "the beloved physician" (KJV and many versions in this tradition) comes from this text. Why Paul mentions here that Luke is a doctor

60. On Hierapolis, see F. F. Bruce, *ABD* 3.195-96.
61. See D. A. Carson and D. J. Moo, *Introduction to the New Testament* (2nd ed.; Grand Rapids: Zondervan, 2005), 203-6, 290-96, for further details.
62. E.g., O'Brien, 256.

is uncertain. Nothing in the New Testament suggests that he accompanied Paul as his personal physician; perhaps it was a way of distinguishing this Luke from some other man with this name (see, e.g., "Lucius" in Rom. 16:21).

Demas is referred to elsewhere in the New Testament in Philemon 24 and in 2 Timothy 4:10. In the latter text, he is mentioned along with two other co-workers who also appear here in Colossians:

> Do your best to come to me quickly, for Demas, because he loved this world, has deserted me and has gone to Thessalonica. Crescens has gone to Galatia, and Titus to Dalmatia. Only Luke is with me. Get Mark and bring him with you, because he is helpful to me in my ministry. I sent Tychicus to Ephesus. (2 Tim. 4:9-12)

As we noted above, 2 Timothy was written from a Roman imprisonment just three or four years after Colossians. Mark, who was with Paul in Rome for at least part of his first imprisonment, has left, and Tychicus has been sent (or is being sent — the aorist here might be epistolary) on another mission to the Province of Asia. It is possible that Paul's brief reference to Demas here in Colossians might hint at the problem that erupted a few years later.[63] But this might be reading more into the silence of Paul than is warranted.

15 Verse 15 is transitional. Because it continues to convey greetings, it looks back to vv. 10-14. But because the greetings are now Paul's own, it also looks ahead to vv. 16-17, where Paul issues various instructions to the church. Paul has already hinted at the close relationships between the Christians in Colossae and in Laodicea (2:1; 4:13), so it is no surprise that he asks the Colossians to convey his greetings to the believers in the neighboring city.[64] And yet, in another sense it is a surprise, since v. 16 apparently refers to a letter that Paul has sent the Laodiceans. Why ask the Colossians to convey greetings to the Laodiceans when he can do so directly in his letter to them? Lightfoot, noting that Paul does not refer to the "church" in Laodicea but only to the *brothers and sisters at Laodicea*,[65] suggests that the greetings might be directed to a Colossian

---

63. Lightfoot, 242; Dunn, 283.

64. The Greek does not explicitly indicate that Paul is asking the Colossians to convey his greetings to the Laodiceans: Paul simply uses the imperative ἀσπάσασθε. Some versions, therefore, leave open the possibility that Paul is asking the Colossians to greet the Laodiceans (KJV; NKJV; NASB), a possibility that Dunn (284) appears to endorse. But Paul regularly uses this form of the verb to indicate his desire that his own greetings be conveyed to others (e.g., Rom. 16:3-15).

65. TNIV's "brothers and sisters" translates ἀδελφούς, which in this context refers to men and women equally. See the note on 1:2.

family that had resettled in Laodicea.[66] But a reference to Christians in Laodicea generally is more likely. It might be, then, that Paul wants to encourage fellowship between believers in Colossae and Laodicea by asking the former to greet the latter on his behalf. Another question this verse raises is why Paul does not ask for his greetings to be conveyed to Christians in Hierapolis (cf. 4:13). Some, indeed, think that Paul does greet Christians in Hierapolis, arguing that the church in Nympha's house (v. 15b) is located in Hierapolis.[67] This is unlikely. Probably, then, the reason why Paul fails to ask that his greetings be conveyed to Hierapolis is the same as his failure to mention the church in 2:1: that the false teaching had not spread to Hierapolis and so Paul did not need to establish his apostolic authority there.

In the second part of v. 15, Paul requests that his greetings be extended to an individual and the church in that person's house. The gender of this person is not entirely clear, the confusion arising from two sources: (1) the Greek form, depending on how it is accented, could be the name of either a man, "Nymphas," or a woman, "Nympha";[68] (2) the manuscripts differ in the possessive pronoun modifying "church," some having *autou* ("his"), others *autēs* ("her"), and still others *autōn* ("their"). The last option, though defended by Lightfoot,[69] can probably be eliminated. It depends on reading "brothers and sisters and Nympha(s)" together, which is unlikely. The other two variants undoubtedly arose because of uncertainty about the gender of the name Nympha(s). None of the variants commands a very clear preference in terms of external evidence. But the feminine name, with corresponding pronoun, should probably be preferred, since it would be more natural for early scribes to think of a man as the one in whose house a church met rather than a woman. The scribes would therefore have been more likely to change an original feminine pronoun into a masculine one. The feminine "Nympha," then, is the option preferred by most of the modern translations and commentaries.[70] Nympha, then, was perhaps a wealthy widow who used her home and resources to support the church. Because of the sequence in this verse, we should probably conclude that she lived in

66. Lightfoot, 243.
67. Gnilka, 244.
68. Accented as Νύμφαν, the name is feminine, from Νύμφα; accented Νυμφᾶς, it is masculine, from Νυμφᾶς. Most Greek manuscripts lacked accents.
69. Lightfoot, 243.
70. See, e.g., Harris, 211-12; O'Brien, 245-46; Bruce, 183; Dunn, 274. See also Metzger, *Textual Commentary*, 560. Favoring the masculine name are, e.g., Abbott, 303-4; Masson, 156. The KJV and NKJV translate with the masculine form because they are dependent on the "majority text," which reads the masculine here.

Laodicea and that there was, then, more than one "house church" in Laodicea. Why Paul singles out Nympha and the church that met in her house for special mention is impossible to know.

16 In the Greek text, a *kai* ("and"; cf., e.g., ESV) connects this verse with v. 15, as Paul continues to make his own requests of the believers in Colossae. In a culture in which copies of texts were not easily come by and in which not all people were literate, the public reading of a letter sent to a community such as the church at Colossae would be the normal procedure. Paul's opening words assume this practice: *After this letter has been read to you.* The "after" in TNIV (see also NET; NJB; NLT) translates a Greek word that means "when" or "whenever" (*hotan*), but Paul's sentence clearly indicates a sequence: the Colossians are to read the letter and then have it read in Laodicea. The TNIV translation "read *to* you" is a bit more interpretive. The Greek preposition (*para* with the dative) means "among" in this context,[71] and most versions translate accordingly. But the problem with this translation is that it can imply that the letter was passed around among the Colossians, being read by each of them in turn. In reality, however, the standard practice in the ancient world was for someone to read the letter to the assembled group. See, most clearly in the New Testament, 1 Thessalonians 5:27: "I charge you before the Lord to have this letter read to all the brothers and sisters." (We have suggested above that Tychicus, a trusted Pauline co-worker, was probably entrusted with this task.) The TNIV's "to" better conveys this cultural context.

Paul goes on, however, to request an exchange of letters between Colossae and Laodicea — a practice otherwise unknown from the New Testament. First, once they have heard Paul's letter read, the Colossians are to *see that it is also read in the church of the Laodiceans.* Whether this meant that they were to bring the original letter and have it read in the neighboring church or whether a copy was to be made and read there is not clear. In any case, it implies that this particular letter, at least, was not narrowly occasional, as if it had relevance only to the Christians in Colossae. As Dunn notes, this practice of reading a letter written to one community in another suggests that from the beginning Paul viewed some of his letters as having more than local relevance.[72]

At the same time as the Colossians are sharing "their" letter with the Laodiceans, the Laodiceans are to do likewise; Paul wants the Colossians *in turn [to] read the letter from Laodicea.*[73] In this context, the

71. See H. Riesenfeld, *TDNT* 5.732.
72. Dunn, 286.
73. The Greek word order is unusual, the reference to the letter from Laodicea — τὴν ἐκ Λαοδικείας ("the [letter] from Laodicea") — preceding the ἵνα plus ἀναγνῶτε on

phrase "from Laodicea" will almost certainly not mean a letter written *by* the Laodiceans but a letter addressed to the Laodiceans, which is now in their possession and hence is "from" them in the sense that it will be sent from them to Colossae.[74] A lot of scholarly ingenuity has been expended trying to identify this letter. John Knox, as part of his wide-ranging theory about Philemon, suggested that the letter "from the Laodiceans" is, in fact, the letter to Philemon.[75] But this identification would be possible only if Knox's ingenious but implausible general hypothesis were to be accepted (see the Introduction to Philemon, 374, for further detail). Others have suggested that the letter was written by Epaphras,[76] but the parallelism — "you *in turn (kai)* read the letter from Laodicea" — suggests that Paul is the author of both letters. The most plausible suggestion is that the letter is Ephesians.[77] It is quite possible that Ephesians was a circular letter, and Paul may assume that the Laodiceans will have a copy of it that they are to share with the Colossians. But if, as we think, Ephesians and Colossians were written at the same time and dispatched with the same person, this scenario is highly unlikely. Surely Paul simply would have included Colossae in the churches to whom "Ephesians" was to be circulated. It is unlikely, then, that the "letter to the Laodiceans" can be identified with any extant Pauline letter; it has been lost to us.[78]

17 A third request of Paul's (again connected to the context with a *kai*, "and") is that Archippus *complete the work you have received in the*

---

which it depends grammatically. Turner (*Syntax*, 95) takes the ἵνα as imperatival: "and as for the letter from Laodicea — see that it is read." But the ἵνα is more likely to be final, dependent on ποιήσατε earlier in the verse (Harris, 213).

74. Robertson, *Grammar*, 600; BDF §437. A few early church fathers did, however, take "from Laodicea" to mean a letter written by them (according to O'Brien [257], Chrysostom, Theodore of Mopsuestia, Theodoret).

75. John Knox, *Philemon among the Letters of Paul* (London: Collins, 1960), 38-40.

76. Charles P. Anderson, "Who Wrote the Epistle from Laodicea?" *JBL* 85 (1966), 436-40.

77. The suggestion was first made in the early church by Marcion; and see, e.g., Lightfoot, 244; Abbott, 305-6; Wright, 160-61(?). For criticism of the proposal, see Percy, *Die Probleme der Kolosser- und Epheserbriefe*, 453-55.

78. So most commentators; see, e.g., O'Brien, 258. This letter would not be the only Pauline letter to have suffered such a fate; we have also lost the "previous letter" Paul wrote to the Corinthians (see 1 Cor. 5:9). Early writers exploited this reference for their own ends, writing forgeries to fill the gap otherwise left in the Pauline correspondence. Marcionites forged a "Letter to the Laodiceans" that is not extant but is referred to in the Muratorian Canon. And an apocryphal letter of the same name, perhaps originating in the fifth century, has come down to us (cf. Edgar Hennecke and Wilhelm Schneemelcher, *New Testament Apocrypha* [rev. ed.; Westminster: John Knox, 1992], 2.42-45).

Lord.[79] Almost as much scholarly ingenuity has been devoted to this verse as to the "Letter to the Laodiceans," and with equally inconclusive results. Archippus is mentioned again as one of the recipients of Philemon (v. 2). In fact, Knox theorizes that he is the main recipient of the letter and the real owner of Onesimus. The "work" that Archippus is to "complete," then, is the acceptance of Onesimus as a brother in the Lord.[80] But Archippus is almost certainly not the main addressee of Philemon and not, then, the owner of Onesimus (see our notes on Phlm. 2). Not much further help comes from the specifics of Paul's request. The word for "work" is *diakonia*, which can refer to a "service" of almost any kind. In Paul, however, the word usually refers either to service of the risen Lord and his people — that is, "ministry" (so most English versions) — or, more specifically, to the special "ministry" of financial relief that Paul sponsored during this third missionary journey (e.g., Rom. 15:31; 2 Cor. 8:4; 9:1, 12, 13). Since Paul in Philemon 2 identifies Archippus as a "fellow soldier," we can assume that he was engaged with Paul in some kind of ministry. It is unlikely that *diakonia* has an "official" sense, referring to Archippus as a "deacon."[81] From the fact that Paul does not address Archippus directly, Lightfoot infers that he was not resident in Colossae but was pastoring the neighboring church at Laodicea.[82] This is possible, but Paul could also be bringing public pressure to bear on Archippus. All that we can conclude is that Archippus had been given a particular task related to his ministry, but what that task was — preaching?[83] teaching young converts?[84] — we simply cannot know.

18 Paul concludes his letter to the Colossians with (1) an apostolic "signature"; (2) a final prayer request; and (3) a grace wish. All three are

---

79. The sequence of the Greek, with βλέπε ("see!") at the beginning of the sentence and ἵνα αὐτὴν πληροῖς at the end, is maintained in NASB: "Take heed to the ministry which you have received in the Lord, that you may fulfill it." See, on the syntax, Harris, 214-15.

80. Knox, *Philemon*, 49-51; see also Lamar Cope, "On Rethinking the Philemon-Colossians Connection," *BR* 30 (1985), 45-50. Jerome Murphy-O'Connor argues that Epaphras had arrived and conveyed the distressing information that Archippus, who had been an effective minister (Phlm. 2), had deserted the ministry; and so Paul had to ask the Christians in Colossae to "tell" him to get back to his work (*Paul: A Critical Life* [New York: Oxford University Press, 1997], 236-37). But this reconstruction requires an implausibly long interval between the writing of Phlm. 2 and Phlm. 23 (which assumes that Epaphras is with Paul).

81. Contra, e.g., Udo Schnelle, *Apostle Paul: His Life and Theology* (Grand Rapids: Baker, 2005), 378.

82. Lightfoot, 244.

83. O'Brien, 259.

84. Wright, 161.

found in the closing sections of Paul's letters. Letters in the ancient world were often dictated to a trained scribe who could form letters that were small (to conserve valuable papyrus) and neat. The practice of adding a brief note in the author's own hand to authenticate the letter is known from the Greco-Roman world generally and is done by Paul also in 1 Corinthians (16:21), Galatians (6:11), and 2 Thessalonians (3:17) (Philemon also has a signature [v. 19], but it functions slightly differently.) In the latter text, Paul even claims that it is "the distinguishing mark in all my letters," so perhaps he typically took stylus in hand even when he did not explicitly indicate it.[85]

Paul's very brief prayer request — *remember my chains* — is quite poignant. Some think that Paul's point is to "hold up his manacled wrists to impress the readers with his authority as a suffering apostle."[86] But it is more likely that Paul wants his readers to "bring to remembrance" his "chains" as a stimulus to pray for him. The verb "remember" has this sense elsewhere in Paul (1 Thess. 1:3) and in Hebrews (13:7; in 13:3, though with a different Greek verb), and Paul frequently uses the noun "remembrance" *(mneia)* to refer to prayer (Rom. 1:9; Eph. 1:16; Phil. 1:3; 1 Thess. 1:2; 2 Tim. 1:3; Phlm. 4).[87]

Paul includes a "grace wish" to his readers in the closing of all his letters (Rom. 16:20b; 1 Cor. 16:23; 2 Cor. 13:14; Gal. 6:18; Eph. 6:24; Phil. 4:23; 1 Thess. 5:28; 2 Thess. 3:18; 1 Tim. 6:21b; 2 Tim. 4:22b; Titus 3:15b; Phlm. 25), and, in every letter except Romans and 1 Corinthians, it comes last. Paul normally asks the "Lord Jesus" or the "Lord Jesus Christ" to dispense this grace. Here in Colossians, along with Ephesians, 1 and 2 Timothy, and Titus, however, there is no reference to Christ. This grace wish takes the place normally occupied in secular letters by a "farewell." "Grace" *(charis)* is, of course, a rich and foundational theological concept, one that Paul can use to express the essence of the Christian faith (1:6; Rom. 5:2). Paul has begun his letter by asking for "grace" to be upon the Colossians (1:2), and it is fitting that he concludes with a similar wish. Their need to continue and grow in their faith in the face of false teaching will be undergirded and stimulated by the continuing work of God's grace in their midst.

---

85. Jeffrey A. D. Weima (*Neglected Endings: The Significance of the Pauline Letter Closings* [JSNTSup 101; Sheffield: Sheffield Academic Press, 1994], 119) notes that a number of ancient letters feature a shift of handwriting at the end, with no explicit indication of change of writer.

86. R. P. Martin, 132; cf. also Lohse, 177; Moule, 139.

87. See O'Brien, 260.

The Letter
to
PHILEMON

Select Bibliography on Philemon

Commentaries on Philemon

The commentaries listed here are referred to in the commentary with the last name of the commentary author only.

Arzt-Grabner, Peter. *Philemon*. Göttingen: Vandenhoeck & Ruprecht, 2003.
Barth, Markus, and Helmut Blanke. *The Letter to Philemon: A New Translation with Notes and Commentary*. Eerdmans Critical Commentary. Grand Rapids: Eerdmans, 2000.
Binder, Hermann, and Joachim Rohde. *Der Brief des Paulus an Philemon*. THKNT 11.2. Berlin: Evangelische Verlagsanstalt, 1990.
Bruce, F. F. *The Epistles to the Colossians, to Philemon, and to the Ephesians*. NICNT. Grand Rapids: Eerdmans, 1984.
Collange, Jean-François. *L'Épître de Saint Paul à Philémon*. CNT. Geneva: Labor et Fides, 1987.
Dibelius, Martin. *An die Kolosser, Epheser, an Philemon*. 3d ed. rev. H. Greeven. HNT 12. Tübingen: Mohr Siebeck, 1953.
Dunn, James D. G. *The Epistles to the Colossians and to Philemon*. NIGTC. Grand Rapids: Eerdmans, 1996.
Ernst, J. *Die Briefe an die Philipper, an Philemon, an die Kolosser, an die Epheser*. RNT. Regensburg: Pustet, 1974.
Fitzmyer, Joseph. *The Letter to Philemon: A New Translation with Introduction and Commentary*. AB 34C. New York: Doubleday, 2000.
Friedrich, Gerhard. "Der Brief an Philemon." In *Die Briefe an die Galater, Epheser, Philipper, Kolosser, Thessalonicher und Philemon* by Joachim Becker, Hans Conzelmann, and Gerhard Friedrich. NTD 8. Göttingen: Vandenhoeck & Ruprecht, 1981.

SELECT BIBLIOGRAPHY ON PHILEMON

Furter, Daniel. *Les Épîtres de Paul aux Colossiens et à Philémon.* Commentaire
Évangélique de la Bible 8. Vaux-sur-Seine: Faculté libre de théologie
évangélique, 1988.

Garland, David E. *Colossians and Philemon.* NIVAC. Grand Rapids: Zondervan, 1998.

Gnilka, Joachim. *Der Philemonbrief.* HTKNT 10.4. Freiburg: Herder, 1982.

Gorday, Peter, ed. *Colossians, 1-2 Thessalonians, 1-2 Timothy, Titus, Philemon.*
ACCS. Downers Grove, Ill.: InterVarsity, 2000.

Harris, Murray J. *Colossians and Philemon.* Exegetical Guide to the Greek New
Testament. Grand Rapids: Eerdmans, 1991.

Houlden, J. L. *Paul's Letters from Prison.* Harmondsworth: Penguin, 1970.

Huby, Joseph. *Les Épîtres de la captivité: Colossiens, Philémon, Ephésiens, Philippiens.* Verbum Salutis. Paris: Beauchesne, 1947.

Lightfoot, J. B. *Saint Paul's Epistles to the Colossians and to Philemon.* London:
Macmillan, 1897 (repr., Grand Rapids: Zondervan, 1971).

Lohmeyer, Ernst. *Die Briefe an die Philipper, an die Kolosser und an Philemon.*
KEK 9. Göttingen: Vandenhoeck & Ruprecht, 1964.

Lohse, Eduard. *Colossians and Philemon.* Hermeneia. Philadelphia: Fortress,
1971.

Lucas, R. C. *The Message of Colossians and Philemon: Fullness and Freedom.* The
Bible Speaks Today. Downers Grove, Ill.: Inter-Varsity, 1980.

Martin, Ernest D. *Colossians, Philemon.* Believers Church Bible Commentary.
Scottdale, Pa.: Herald Press, 1993.

Martin, Ralph P. *Colossians and Philemon.* NCBC. Grand Rapids: Eerdmans,
1973.

—. *Ephesians, Colossians, and Philemon.* IBC. Atlanta: John Knox, 1991.

Melick, Richard R., Jr. *Philippians, Colossians, Philemon.* NAC 32. Nashville:
Broadman, 1991, 2000.

Meyer, H. A. W. *Kritisch-exegetisches Handbuch über die Briefe an die Philipper,
Kolosser und an Philemon.* KEK 9. Göttingen: Vandenhoeck & Ruprecht,
1859.

Moule, C. F. D. *The Epistles of Paul the Apostle to the Colossians and to Philemon.*
CGTC. Cambridge: Cambridge University Press, 1968.

O'Brien, Peter T. *Colossians, Philemon.* WBC 44. Waco, Tex.: Word, 1982.

Reinmuth, Eckart. *Der Brief des Paulus an Philemon.* THKNT 11.2. Leipzig:
Evangelische Verlagsanstalt, 2006.

Stuhlmacher, Peter. *Der Brief an Philemon.* 4th ed. EKKNT 18. Neukirchen-
Vluyn: Neukirchener and Düsseldorf: Benziger, 2004.

Suhl, Alfred. *Der Philemonbrief.* ZBK 13. Zürich: Theologischer Verlag, 1981.

Thompson, Marianne Meye. *Colossians and Philemon.* The Two Horizons New
Testament Commentary. Grand Rapids: Eerdmans, 2005.

Vincent, Marvin R. *A Critical and Exegetical Commentary on the Epistles to the Philippians and to Philemon.* ICC. Edinburgh: T&T Clark, 1897.

Wall, Robert W. *Colossians and Philemon.* IVPNTC. Downers Grove, Ill.: InterVarsity, 1993.

Wilson, R. McL. *A Critical and Exegetical Commentary on Colossians and Philemon.* ICC. Edinburgh: T&T Clark, 2005.

Wolter, Michael. *Der Brief an die Kolosser. Der Brief an Philemon.* ÖTK 12. Gütersloh: Gerd Mohn, 1993.

Wright, N. T. *The Epistles of Paul to the Colossians and to Philemon.* TNTC. Leicester: Inter-Varsity, 1986.

Other Works on Philemon

Arzt-Grabner, P. "Onesimus Erro: Zur Vorgeschichte des Philemonbriefes." *ZNW* 95 (2004), 131-43.

Banker, J. *A Semantic and Structural Analysis of Philemon.* Dallas: Summer Institute of Linguistics, 1990.

Barclay, J. M. G. "Paul, Philemon and the Dilemma of Christian Slave-Ownership." *NTS* 37 (1991), 161-86.

Barnes, A. *Notes Explanatory and Practical on the Epistles of Paul to the Ephesians, Philippians, and Colossians.* New York: Harper, 1845.

Birdsall, J. N. "Πρεσβύτης in Philemon 9: A Study in Conjectural Emendation." *NTS* 39 (1993), 625-30.

Bratcher, R. G., and E. A. Nida. *A Translator's Handbook on Paul's Letters to the Colossians and to Philemon.* Stuttgart: United Bible Societies, 1977.

Burtchaell, J. T. *Philemon's Problem: A Theology of Grace.* Grand Rapids: Eerdmans, 1998.

————. "Paul's Epistle to Philemon: Toward an Alternative *Argumentum.*" *HTR* 86 (1993), 357-76.

Church, F. F. "Rhetorical Structure and Design in Paul's Letter to Philemon." *HTR* 71 (1978), 17-33.

Cope, L. "On Rethinking the Philemon-Colossians Connection." *BR* 30 (1985), 45-50.

Daube, D. "Onesimus." *HTR* 79 (1986), 40-43.

Derrett, J. D. M. "The Functions of the Epistle to Philemon." *ZNW* 79 (1988), 63-91.

Frilingos, C. "'For My Child, Onesimus': Paul and Domestic Power in Philemon." *JBL* 119 (2000), 91-104.

Glaze, R. E., Jr. "Onesimus: Runaway or Emissary?" *TTE* 54 (1996), 3-11.

Goodenough, E. R. "Paul and Onesimus." *HTR* 22 (1929), 181-83.

Harrill, J. A. "Using the Roman Jurists to Interpret Philemon: A Response to Peter Lampe." *ZNW* 90 (1999), 135-38.

Heil, J. P. "The Chiastic Structure and Meaning of Paul's Letter to Philemon." *Bib* 82 (2001), 178-206.

Knox, J. *Philemon among the Letters of Paul.* London: Collins, 1960.

Lampe, P. "Keine 'Sklavenflucht' des Onesimus." *ZNW* 76 (1985), 135-37.

Marshall, I. H. "The Theology of Philemon." Pages 175-91 in *The Theology of the Shorter Pauline Letters.* Edited by K. P. Donfried and I. H. Marshall. Cambridge: Cambridge University Press, 1993.

Mullins, T. Y. "The Thanksgivings of Philemon and Colossians." *NTS* 30 (1984), 288-93.

Nordling, J. G. "Onesimus *Fugitivus:* A Defense of the Runaway Slave Hypothesis in Philemon." *JSNT* 41 (1991), 97-119.

Petersen, N. R. *Rediscovering Paul: Philemon and the Sociology of Paul's Narrative World.* Philadelphia: Fortress, 1985.

Rapske, B. M. "The Prisoner Paul in the Eyes of Onesimus." *NTS* 37 (1991), 187-203.

Sanders, L. L. "Equality and a Request for the Manumission of Onesimus." *ResQ* 46 (2004), 109-14.

Schenk, W. "Der Brief des Paulus an Philemon in der neueren Forschung (1945-1987)." *ANRW* (1987), 3439-95.

Snyman, A. H. "A Semantic Discourse Analysis of the Letter to Philemon." Pages 83-99 in *Text and Interpretation: New Approaches in the Criticism of the New Testament.* Edited by P. J. Hartin and J. H. Petzer. Leiden and New York: E. J. Brill, 1991.

Still, T. D. "Philemon among the Letters of Paul: Theological and Canonical Considerations." *ResQ* 47 (2005), 133-42.

Vos, C. S. de. "Once a Slave, Always a Slave? Slavery, Manumission and Relational Patterns in Paul's Letter to Philemon." *JSNT* 82 (2001), 89-105.

Winter, S. C. "Paul's Letter to Philemon." *NTS* 33 (1987), 1-15.

Introduction to Philemon

Most Christians have never studied Philemon; many have never heard it taught or preached. It is short — in the New Testament only 2 and 3 John are shorter; it is private — addressed to a fellow worker, but in his private capacity; and it is obscure — scholars are not quite sure just what it is about. No wonder it suffers from neglect. Yet God has providentially seen to it that this short, private, and obscure letter is included in the canon of authoritative Christian Scripture. Why? What is its purpose? What was Paul asking from Philemon? And what is the significance of the letter for Christian belief and practice? These are the questions that will guide our discussion in the commentary that follows. Before turning to the details of the letter, however, we need an overview.

I. A BASIC PROFILE: AUTHOR, RECIPIENT, NATURE, AND PLACE OF WRITING

The letter claims to be written by Paul (vv. 1, 19), and, in contrast to Colossians, there has been no serious challenge to this claim.[1] Christian tradition (reflected in the title) has singled out Philemon, mentioned in v. 1, as the recipient. Most scholars agree, although it should be noted that, in fact, vv. 1-2 appear to list four recipients: "[to] Philemon . . . and to Apphia . . . and to Archippus . . . and to the church that meets in your house" (my own trans.; TNIV reflects an interpretive decision). A few

---

1. The famous nineteenth-century NT critic F. C. Baur and a few other scholars have questioned Paul's authorship.

scholars have argued that it is more natural to single out the last-named individual, Archippus, as the primary addressee and that it was in his house, not Philemon's, that the church Paul mentions was probably meeting.[2] However, the pattern of ancient letters was to list the primary addressee first, and this points to Philemon.[3] The TNIV punctuation captures the resulting sense well: "To Philemon our dear friend and fellow worker — also to Apphia our sister and Archippus our fellow soldier — and to the church that meets in your home."

But why must we identify a "primary addressee"? Why don't we simply identify all three individuals and the church as the recipients of the letter? The first reason for focusing on an individual is the ancient epistolary convention mentioned above. The fact that Paul mentions Philemon's name first is very significant. But more significant is the fact that all the second-person pronouns and verbal forms in vv. 4-22a and vv. 23-24 are singular. This is not always clear in English translations, since modern English suffers from the handicap of not being able to distinguish second-person singular and plural forms. The body of the letter, then, focuses consistently on a single individual. Moreover, although Philemon is a "fellow worker" of Paul's (v. 1), the letter deals not with ministry issues but with personal matters. For these reasons, it is probably justified to think of Philemon as basically a "private" letter.[4]

At the same time, we should not overlook the fact that Paul chooses to include two other individuals and the whole church that meets in Philemon's house in his address. And this is not just a literary convention, as the switch to second-person plural forms in vv. 22b ("your prayers") and v. 25 ("your spirit") reveals. This does not turn the letter into a "public" letter, or an official "apostolic" document.[5] Yet it does suggest that our notion of Philemon as a "private individual" or of his handling of the Onesimus situation as a "private matter" needs rethinking. We may be injecting into the first-century Christian community a contrast of "private" versus "public" that was simply not present there. Indeed, we will suggest that one of the enduring and extremely relevant teachings of Philemon is the degree to which Christians are bound to one another in all their activities through their common faith. Paul's inclusion of the whole church in the address of the letter is not simply, then, a way of putting greater pressure on Philemon ("you had better do as I say or all

2. J. Knox, *Philemon among the Letters of Paul* (London: Collins, 1960), 51-59; see also L. Cope, "On Rethinking the Philemon-Colossians Connection," *BR* 30 (1985), 45-50.

3. Arzt-Grabner, 112-14.

4. This is the traditional interpretation; see, e.g., Lightfoot, 303; O'Brien, 267-68.

5. Contra, e.g., W. H. Ollrog, *Paulus und seiner Mitarbeiter* (Neukirchen-Vluyn: Neukirchener, 1979), 104; Lohse, 187; Fitzmyer, 35.

the church will know you have scorned me"). It is the reflection of a social and theological reality of the early Christian community.

Philemon is usually thought to be a resident of Colossae. Although he is not mentioned anywhere else in the New Testament, his slave, Onesimus, is said to be "one of you" in the letter to the Colossians (4:9). Paul, then, has written a general letter to the church at Colossae along with this "private" note to Philemon at the same time, sending both of them with Tychicus, who is accompanied by Onesimus (Col. 4:7-9). Where was Paul when he wrote these letters? We have considered this question in the Introduction to Colossians, where we noted that, on the evidence of Philemon alone, an Ephesian provenance (and thus a date in the middle 50s) would make good sense.[6] Two features of the letter, in particular, could be cited in favor of Ephesus. (1) Paul's request that a guest room be prepared for him (v. 22) shows that he is planning a trip to Colossae. And not only is it more likely that Paul would be planning to visit Colossae while in Ephesus (120 miles away) than from Rome (almost a thousand miles away), but a visit to Colossae from Rome would appear to contradict Paul's own expressed travel plans. In Romans 15, Paul indicates that he planned to go to minister in Spain after visiting Rome; a projected trip back to the eastern Mediterranean would contradict this plan. (2) It is also more likely that Onesimus, whatever his precise status and motivation, would have chosen to travel to the nearby metropolitan center of Ephesus than to the far-distant Rome. But neither point is decisive. As we suggest in the Introduction to Colossians (44-45), the travel plans Paul put forward in Romans in A.D. 57 may very well have changed after four years or so. And, if we accept the Pastoral Epistles as genuinely Pauline, they pretty clearly indicate that Paul, in fact, did end up traveling back to the Eastern Mediterranean after his release from Roman imprisonment. As to the second point, it is perhaps a bit more likely, if Onesimus had sought out Paul to mediate between himself and Philemon, that Paul would have been in Ephesus rather than in Rome. But if he were a runaway slave, it is very hard to tell which destination would have been the more likely.[7] What finally tips the scales

---

6. As we noted in the Introduction to Colossians (42-43), a few scholars also suggest Caesarea as the place of writing (e.g., B. Reicke, *Rexamining Paul's Letters* [Harrisburg, Pa.: Trinity Press International, 2001], 73-74). Wolfgang Schenk (who thinks Colossians is pseudepigraphical) somewhat strangely suggests Pergamum as the place of writing ("Der Brief des Paulus an Philemon in der neueren Forschung [1945-87]," *ANRW* 2.25.4, 3482-83).

7. S. W. Llewelyn (*NewDocs* 8.45) notes that the evidence we have about runaway slaves reveals that they sometimes remained in their own countries but at other times fled to distant cities. (This assumes, of course, that Onesimus was a runaway; see below, 364-69.)

for us in favor of Rome, however, is the evidence of Colossians and Ephesians (see the Introduction to Colossians, 41-46). We incline, then, toward the majority view that Philemon, along with Colossians and Ephesians, was written early in Paul's "first" Roman imprisonment (Acts 28:11-31). The date of the letter, then, would be A.D. 60-61.

II. THE SITUATION BEHIND THE LETTER

"Mirror reading" is what we call the process of scrutinizing New Testament letters to see what they might "reflect" about the situation and/or arguments that the letter addresses. Nowhere is this task more difficult than in Philemon. One factor that makes it difficult is shared with all the New Testament letters: the writer obviously feels no need to refer explicitly to many of the background issues that both writer and addressee already know about. But a second factor is what makes mirror reading in Philemon especially challenging: Paul's delicacy in approaching Philemon about Onesimus. However we finally reconstruct the situation, it is clearly one that requires considerable diplomacy on Paul's part. He refrains from issuing orders to Philemon, wanting him to act on his own out of love rather than compulsion (vv. 8-9, 14). As a result, Paul often writes indirectly and allusively, contenting himself with dropping hints about what he wants Philemon to do. The allusiveness of the letter gives considerable scope to scholarly ingenuity, as interpreters try to piece together the situation Paul is writing about and identify just what it is that Paul wants Philemon to do. Moreover, the ramifications of these decisions for our understanding of the New Testament perspective on slavery inject a considerable degree of passion into the scholarly argument. Before we assess the different proposals, it will be helpful to have the evidence from the letter before us. We will survey the relevant evidence in textual order, noting significant alternative interpretations as we go.

1. Paul is a "prisoner" (vv. 1, 9, 13). This does not necessarily mean that he was "in prison," since, for instance, if he is writing during his first Roman imprisonment, he was living in his own rented quarters, probably chained to a guard.

2. Paul is "appealing" to Philemon about Onesimus (v. 10). This might mean that his appeal "concerns" Onesimus or that his appeal is "for" Onesimus, in the sense that Paul is requesting Philemon to send Onesimus to him.

3. Onesimus has become a Christian through Paul's ministry while Paul was a prisoner (v. 10).

4. Onesimus is very dear to Paul and has been useful to him (vv. 10, 11, 12, 13, 16). It is not clear whether this "usefulness" consisted in caring for Paul's personal needs or in working with Paul in ministry (or both).

5. Paul is either "sending Onesimus back" to Philemon or he is "referring the case of Onesimus" to Philemon (v. 12). The Greek verb Paul uses here — *anapempō* — could mean either, and its interpretation is a key tipping point in deciding among the various alternatives.

6. Paul would like to keep Onesimus with him if he could (v. 13).

7. Onesimus has been "separated from" Philemon (v. 15).

8. Paul suggests that the purpose of this separation may have been that Philemon could have Onesimus back "forever" (v. 15). It is not clear whether this means "enjoy Onesimus's physical presence for a very long time" or "enjoy eternal spiritual fellowship with Onesimus."

9. Paul suggests, further, that Philemon might have Onesimus back "no longer as a slave but better than a slave" (v. 16). There is some disagreement over whether this means "you will no longer treat Onesimus 'like a slave' (as if he were a slave)" or "you will no longer view him only as a slave (which he is) but also as a fellow Christian."

10. Onesimus, Paul hopes, will now be "dear" to Philemon, both "in the flesh and in the Lord" (v. 16; my translation). Does this mean that Philemon is to treat Onesimus well both as his slave (their "fleshly" relationship) and as a fellow Christian? Or does it suggest more, that Philemon is to translate Onesimus's new status as a "dear brother" into the "fleshly" realm by giving him his freedom?

11. The one explicit request that Paul makes with respect to Onesimus is that Philemon should "welcome" him (v. 17). Again, however, it is somewhat unclear whether this implies a welcome "in person" or a more general welcome into the fellowship of Christ.

12. Paul suggests that Onesimus may have wronged Philemon in some way (v. 18). What this "debt" may have been — had Onesimus stolen money? had he "robbed" Philemon of his required labor? — is not clear; nor is it clear how likely it is that Onesimus has committed a wrong.

13. Philemon has become a Christian through Paul, whether directly or indirectly (as a result of the ministry of Epaphras) (v. 19b).

14. Paul asks generally for "benefit" from Philemon (v. 20).

15. Paul is confident that Philemon will do "even more than I ask" (v. 21). Does this mean that Paul hopes Philemon will do what he has asked very well, or very thoroughly (a "qualitative" interpretation), or that he hopes Philemon will do something beyond what he has explicitly requested (a "quantitative" interpretation)? And, if the latter, what is the "even more"? Might it refer to setting Onesimus free?

Not all the options we have noted above are equally probable. Some of them, in fact, in our opinion, are very improbable. But we wanted to begin by setting out the data as neutrally as possible so that it would be clear why there is such a variety of reconstructions. We turn now to these options.

1. Philemon and Onesimus are physical brothers who have quarreled. Paul is seeking to reconcile them and is sending Onesimus to Philemon for ministry. On this view, the language of "brother" is, at least in some places, literal, whereas the language about "slavery" is not. Onesimus is not a slave at all, and Christian tradition has been wrong to read the letter as if it were about slavery.[8] This view is the most improbable of all the options. The letter clearly uses the language of "brother" in a consistently metaphorical way, while it equally clearly uses the language of "slave" (v. 16) in a literal way (see the notes on v. 16 in particular).

2. Philemon, and his house church, have sent Onesimus, his slave, to Paul as his emissary. Paul writes to request that Onesimus stay with Paul as a freeman.[9] This interpretation is slightly more probable than the first, but still suffers from some insuperable problems. First, had Philemon, or the church, sent Onesimus as their emissary, it is hard to understand why Paul says that "he was separated from you" (v. 15). This passive form strongly suggests that Onesimus left Philemon without the latter's consent. Second, it requires that we interpret the verb *anapempō* in v. 10 as "refer to a higher authority" rather than "send back." Yet this is unlikely, on both lexical and contextual grounds. Third, it must treat the reference to Onesimus being sent back with Tychicus to Colossae in Colossians 4:9 as an unhistorical detail supplied by a later pseudepigraphical author — a view we think is quite unlikely. And, fourth, it has difficulty explaining why Philemon would have sent a "useless" non-Christian to take his place in serving Paul (cf. vv. 10, 13).[10]

3. Onesimus is a runaway slave, a "fugitive." He fled from Colossae and met Paul in his place of detention. Paul converted him, and he is now sending him back to his master, Philemon, for the latter to make a final decision about Onesimus. This is the traditional understanding of the cir-

---

8. Allen Dwight Callahan, "Paul's Epistle to Philemon: Toward an Alternative *Argumentum*," HTR 86 (1993), 357-76; idem, *Embassy of Onesimus: The Letter of Paul to Philemon* (The New Testament in Context; Valley Forge, Pa.: Trinity Press International, 1997).

9. See esp. Sara C. Winter, "Paul's Letter to Philemon," NTS 33 (1987), 1-15. See also, sometimes in modified form, Schenk, "Der Brief des Paulus an Philemon," 3466-75; R. E. Glaze Jr., "Onesimus: Runaway or Emissary?" TTE 54 (1996), 3-11.

10. John M. Barclay, "Paul, Philemon and the Dilemma of Christian Slave-Ownership," NTS 37 (1991), 164.

cumstances of the letter, part of Christian tradition since at least Chrysostom and often assumed without much argument until somewhat recently.[11] And there is good reason for it to have been accepted for so long, for it is able to explain tolerably well the data that we have listed above. It also fits the historical circumstances, since we know that slaves seeking their freedom by running away from their masters were common in the world of Paul's day. But there are also three problems with this reconstruction. First, if Onesimus was indeed a runaway slave, then he had legally "wronged" Philemon. Yet Paul mentions Onesimus's wronging of Philemon only as a possibility (v. 18). Second, and related to this first point, we would have expected a runaway slave returning to his master for reconciliation to express remorse. Yet Paul never mentions Onesimus's repentance or remorse in the letter. In other words, taking these first two points together, we would have expected, if Onesimus were a runaway, for Paul at some point to say, as it were, "Onesimus has wronged you, and he is sorry for it." But the third, and most serious, objection to the "runaway slave" view is the difficulty of imagining how Paul and Onesimus ever would have come into contact with one another. If Onesimus had been arrested for the serious crime of being a *fugitivus*, a runaway slave, it is most unlikely that he would have been confined in the same place as Paul — especially, as we have argued, if Paul at the time was living in his own hired quarters in Rome.[12] Nor, of course, is it likely that a runaway slave would deliberately seek out a friend of his master. So we are left with coincidence: Onesimus just happened to run into Paul, a friend of his master, 120 or (more likely) almost a thousand miles from home. Coincidences happen, of course, but this is a coincidence worthy of a Dickens novel and, many would argue, just as believable.

4. These weaknesses in the traditional reading of the situation behind Philemon have fed the growing popularity of an alternative. According to this hypothesis, Onesimus fled from Philemon not as a "runaway" seeking to gain freedom but in order to enlist Paul's services as mediator in a dispute between himself and his master Philemon.[13] An-

11. Lightfoot, 310-16; Garland, 294-300; John G. Nordling, "Onesimus *Fugitivus*: A Defense of the Runaway Slave Hypothesis in Philemon," *JSNT* 41 (1991), 97-119; Llewelyn in *NewDocs* 8.40-42.
12. See Fitzmyer, 13: Onesimus would have been placed in what the Romans call the *ergastulum*, while Paul was in *custodia libera*.
13. See esp. Peter Lampe, "Keine 'Sklavenflucht' des Onesimus," ZNW 76 (1985), 135-37; and Brian M. Rapske, "The Prisoner Paul in the Eyes of Onesimus," NTS 37 (1991), 187-303; also, e.g., J. M. G. Barclay, *Colossians and Philemon* (New Testament Guides; Sheffield: Sheffield Academic Press, 1997), 98-102; Wolter, 227-35; Fitzmyer, 17-23; Peter Arzt-Grabner, "Onesimus Erro: Zur Vorgeschichte des Philemonbriefes," ZNW

cient sources refer to this kind of a situation, the slave in such circumstances not being regarded legally as a "fugitive" as long as he had no intention of seeking his freedom and as long as he went directly to the mediator. On this scenario, the problem of coincidence is removed: Onesimus deliberately sought out Paul. We can assume that, as a member of Philemon's household, he had come to realize how highly Philemon regarded Paul. It is even possible that Onesimus, accompanying his master on a business trip to nearby Ephesus, had met the apostle. This explanation of the circumstances also explains the data of the letter quite well. But it also suffers from some problems. First, if Paul is indeed in Rome (as we think), it might be considered unlikely that Onesimus, presumably subject to arrest the whole time, would choose a mediator so far away. The second problem is the lack of any clear reference in the letter either to wrongs on Philemon's part or remorse on Onesimus's. If Paul is mediating between the two, then either Philemon has wronged Onesimus or Onesimus has wronged Philemon. If the former is true, it is somewhat disingenuous of Paul to praise Philemon as strongly as he does. In the latter case, which, in light of v. 18, is the more likely, it is hard to explain why Paul does not convey any remorse from Onesimus. The letter from Pliny to Sabiniasus, often cited as a parallel to this particular scenario in Philemon, is full of strong expressions of just such remorse.[14] Of course, as is often the case in such situations, there may be fault on both sides, and Paul may for strategic reasons be reluctant to suggest blame. But it is still strange that he says nothing about any remorse from Onesimus.[15]

We think it impossible to decide with any degree of certainty between these last two scenarios. But we lean slightly toward the runaway slave hypothesis because it better explains two points in the letter. First, the attention that Paul draws to his decision to send Onesimus back (v. 12) (in contrast to his preference to keep Onesimus with him [v. 13]) suggests

---

95 (2004), 131-43; idem, 102-8; I. Howard Marshall, "The Theology of Philemon," in *The Theology of the Shorter Pauline Letters* (with Karl P. Donfried; Cambridge: Cambridge University Press, 1993), 177-78 (hesitantly); J. Murphy-O'Connor, *Paul: A Critical Life* (New York: Oxford University Press, 1997), 176-78. A variation of this view is that Paul's residence might have been considered a "sanctuary" where a fugitive such as Onesimus could take refuge (Erwin R. Goodenough, "Paul and Onesimus," *HTR* 22 [1929], 181-83; Bruce, 196-97). But it is most unlikely that Paul's residence, wherever it was, would have qualified as a sanctuary (Rapske, "The Prisoner Paul," 192-95).

14. Pliny ("the Younger") was a Roman administrator in the second century A.D. The text and translation of his letter (*Epistle* 9.21) can be found in Lohse, 196-97.

15. Llewelyn, *NewDocs* 8.41-42. We should also note that Lampe's appeal to Roman jurists to establish the "mediator" scenario has been questioned (J. Albert Harrill, "Using the Roman Jurists to Interpret Philemon: A Response to Peter Lampe," *ZNW* [1999], 135-38), although it is not clear that these objections are fatal to the view.

that the sending back itself was an important, and difficult, step. This would not be the case if Paul were mediating a dispute and Onesimus had all along intended to go back. But if Onesimus were a runaway, sending him back — whether it was legally required or not[16] — would be a significant matter for both Paul (who benefited from Onesimus's presence) and Onesimus (who had attained some measure of freedom). A second feature of the letter that slightly favors the runaway slave scenario is the emphasis that Paul places on the changed spiritual condition of Onesimus. Philemon can "have Onesimus back forever — no longer as a slave, but better than a slave, as a dear brother" (vv. 15b-16a). This emphasis suggests that the key issue is not a past quarrel between the two but an entirely new situation that has arisen because of Onesimus's conversion. How, then, can we explain the "coincidence" of Onesimus meeting Paul? Perhaps the best solution is to assume that Onesimus had begun to have doubts about his decision to run away from his master. Having heard of Paul or met him on some occasion, he seeks out Paul to enlist his help in intervening with Philemon.[17] While, then, we slightly prefer the "traditional" runaway slave explanation of the circumstances of the letter, we cannot be sure about it. Accordingly, we will not assume it in the course of the commentary below.

III. THE PURPOSE AND SIGNIFICANCE OF THE LETTER

The delicacy with which Paul writes to Philemon not only makes it difficult to be sure about the circumstances behind it; it also makes it hard to be sure just what Paul's purpose in writing really is. As Barclay notes, "the letter is skilfully designed to constrain Philemon to accept Paul's request, and yet, at the same time, it is extremely unclear what precisely Paul is requesting!"[18] Yet this claim must be modified to a certain extent. Verse 17 is very clear about what Paul wants Philemon to do: "welcome him [Onesimus] as you would welcome me." The beginning of this verse — "if you consider me a partner" — sums up some key ideas from the first part of the letter. And this request also features the first imperative verb in the letter. It is therefore a key moment in the letter. Paul's desire

16. It is not clear in the circumstances whether Paul would have been legally required to send Onesimus back to Philemon (Llewelyn, *NewDocs* 8.42).
17. See, e.g., Moule, 20.
18. Barclay, "Paul, Philemon and the Dilemma of Christian Slave-Ownership," 170-71.

that Philemon receive his slave Onesimus back as a brother in Christ must, then, be central in any estimation of the purpose of the letter. The debate about the purpose of the letter focuses on what the further implications of this basic request might be. Verse 21, where Paul expresses his confidence that Philemon will do "even more" than he asks, certainly suggests that Paul hopes for more than he has explicitly set out in v. 17. What is this "even more"? Based on hints in the letter, there are two main possibilities.

First, Paul might be requesting that Philemon make Onesimus available for ministry, whether in Colossae or, more likely, alongside Paul.[19] This possibility is based on Paul's praise of Onesimus as one who had become "useful" in "serving" Paul (v. 13). The Greek verb behind "serve" is *diakoneō*, and words from this root regularly refer to Christian ministry in the New Testament. Paul makes clear that he would have liked to keep Onesimus with him, so it makes some sense to identify the "even more" that Paul hopes Philemon will do as the return of Onesimus to him for further ministry. However, as we point out in the commentary, the verb *diakoneō* itself is not often used for Christian ministry, and it is especially unlikely to refer to ministry when the one to whom ministry is directed is, as here, a person (Paul) rather than the Lord. While the "help" (see the TNIV translation) that Onesimus was to Paul may certainly have included Christian ministry, even this, then, is not clear. Moreover, it is unlikely that Paul wants Philemon to send Onesimus back to him since he himself plans to visit Colossae soon (v. 22). We are not convinced, then, that Paul is asking Philemon to release Onesimus for Christian ministry.[20]

A second possibility is that the "even more" that Paul wants Philemon to do might be the immediate manumission of Onesimus.[21] To deal adequately with this possibility requires that we step back a bit and set this matter in the larger context of the vexing issue of slavery in the New Testament and the New Testament world. Many interpreters are convinced that the letter to Philemon, while perhaps setting forth some principles that would tend to undermine the institution of slavery, implies nothing directly about the manumission of Onesimus. They argue

19. O'Brien, 267; Knox, *Philemon*, 18-27; Ollrog, *Paulus und seiner Mitarbeiter*, 103-4. Marshall puts it quite strongly (referring to v. 21): "If this is not a request for Onesimus to join Paul's circle, I don't know what is" ("Theology," 188). Some who hold this view combine it with the next, arguing that Onesimus could not have served in ministry with Paul unless he were set free (e.g., Garland, 304-5).

20. See also, e.g., Wright, 166-68.

21. We use the word "immediate" because, as S. Scott Bartchy has pointed out, most slaves, at least in urban areas, would have expected that they would be set free at some point (*ABD* 6.70).

that the issue of Onesimus's legal freedom would simply not have entered into Paul's thinking. By demanding that the letter say something on this legal point, we make the mistake of reading our modern categories of thinking into the first-century church. There is much to be said for this perspective, and it is certainly right in some respects. The issue of slavery would have looked quite different to a first-century Christian than it does to many of us in modern liberal democracies — and in four respects.

First, slavery was an integral part of the social and economic world of the first century. Estimates vary widely, but one scholar reckons that one-third of the people in cities such as Colossae would have been slaves.[22] Slaves served in all kinds of capacities, from the grim and frightful mine workers (the "salt mines") whose life expectancy was very short, to trusted and respected household slaves who helped run businesses and raise children. Slavery was so much a part of the world of that day that, as an institution, it would almost have escaped the notice of early Christians — much as, for instance, the underlying economic systems in which we live simply don't make the moral "radar screen" of many Christians.

Second, "freedom," or "liberation," was not in the first-century world the obvious good that it is for us in the modern world. Many of us, whose knowledge of slavery is determined by the institution as it existed in the antebellum United States South, think of slavery in terms of the forced subjugation of a certain race of people. However, while many people in the ancient world became slaves by force (through war, for instance), many others voluntarily sold themselves into slavery. Nor was slavery in the Greco-Roman world racially based: slaves came from all races and ethnic groups. And because they were spread over so many occupations and social classes, ancient slaves had little sense of solidarity. The result, as Bartchy has put it, is that "any such call as 'slaves of the world, unite!' would have fallen on completely deaf ears."[23] Moreover, legal freedom was by no means always a positive move for a slave. The treatment slaves received from their owners naturally varied greatly, but all owners had reason to treat their slaves tolerably well since they were an important economic investment for them. Once set free, however, former slaves ("freedmen") were on their own and often found it very difficult to make a living. Legal freedom would not, then, have been the obvious good in the first century that we would consider it to be today.[24] Nor

22. William L. Westermann, *The Slave Systems of Greek and Roman Antiquity* (Philadelphia: The American Philosophical Society, 1955), 127, referring to cities in Asia Minor during the Empire.

23. Bartchy, *ABD* 6.66.

24. See Dunn, 337; Reinmuth, 48; Bartchy, *ABD* 6.71. Barclay has also raised a number of practical problems involved in any decision on Philemon's part to manumit

would Onesimus's manumission necessarily have changed his relationship to Philemon all that much; many freed slaves were still obliged to work for their former masters in virtually the same conditions as when they were slaves.[25]

Third, the New Testament Christians were a tiny religious group living within an all-powerful, authoritarian empire. They lacked the power to influence government policy. More important, they lacked the categories (simply assumed by those of us who live in liberal democracies) within which they could conceive of what we would call "social action."

Finally, fourth — and most important, perhaps — the early Christians did not understand their calling in these terms. They rejoiced in their identity as the people of the new realm inaugurated by God through Christ. But they also knew quite well that the "old realm" continued to exist and that it would exist until Christ returned in glory. Granted this realism about the continuing existence of the "world that is," with its many social injustices, the New Testament Christians focused on the creation of an alternative society, a realm in which, whatever the realities around them, kingdom values would be lived out. Slavery, for instance, was not going to be abolished anytime soon; it was a reality that the early Christians lived with. Their focus, then, was on encouraging Christians to realize, in their relationships with each other, that their "new realm" of existence was what ultimately mattered and that this existence must dictate the way they would relate to one another.[26] The realities of one's social or cultural identity could not usually be changed. What mattered was that these "earthly" realities were seen to be trivial in comparison with eternal spiritual realities (see esp. 1 Cor. 7:17-24). The letter to Philemon certainly shares this overall perspective. Paul seeks to reconfigure the relationship between Philemon and Onesimus in terms of their shared faith and the "fellowship" that faith creates (v. 6). Whether this new relationship would transform Onesimus's existing "worldly" relationship to Philemon was not the most important thing. As Thompson puts it, "If a Christian owned a slave, the highest duty to which that master could be called was not to set the other free but to love the slave with the self-

---

Onesimus ("Paul, Philemon and the Dilemma of Christian Slave-Ownership," 176-77). But Barclay may overestimate these difficulties (see Craig S. de Vos, "Once a Slave, Always a Slave? Slavery, Manumission and Relational Patterns in Paul's Letter to Philemon," *JSNT* 82 [2001], 89-105).

25. S. Scott Bartchy, *MALLON CHRESAI: First-Century Slavery and the Interpretation of 1 Cor. 7:21* (SBLDS 11; Missoula, Mont.: SBL, 1985), 72-82; de Vos, "Once a Slave, Always a Slave?" 100-102.

26. See, e.g., Wright, who argues that "a lost protest [against slavery], at that moment in social history, would have functioned simply on the level of the old age" (169).

giving love of Christ."[27] Certainly this is the perspective found in the New Testament "household codes," which do not call on Christian masters to liberate their slaves but to treat them fairly and justly (Eph. 6:9; Col. 4:1; 1 Tim. 6:2).

These are all valid and important points, and scholars who doubt that Philemon has anything to say about the manumission of Onesimus justly bring them up. And yet. . . . We still wonder whether a continuation of the existing master-slave relationship is compatible with Paul's request that Philemon treat Onesimus as a "dear *brother.*" As Barclay has noted, Paul's basic appeal with respect to Onesimus is encapsulated here, and its implications must be explored. As he puts it, "Paul has presented Onesimus as having undergone such a major change in identity that we are bound to ask what happens next."[28] It is particularly significant that Paul asks Philemon to treat Onesimus as a dear brother not only "in the Lord" but also "in the flesh" (my translation). This last phrase is, in a sense, superfluous. For Paul would not entertain the idea that there is any sphere of existence for the believer that lies outside the all-encompassing "in the Lord." The idea of two equal and competing spheres of existence — what believers are "in the Lord" and what they are "in the flesh" — is foreign to the New Testament understanding of the Lordship of Christ. The believer's existence "in the Lord" affects all his or her relationships, whether "sacred" or secular.[29] And the fact that Paul nowhere else contrasts "flesh" with the Lord points to the unusual nature of the contrast here.

By adding "in the flesh," therefore, Paul brings forcefully to Philemon's attention the implications of Onesimus's new status for their existing worldly relationship. As has often been pointed out, to *own* someone one calls a "dear brother" seems inherently problematic. There is something finally inconsistent about this dual relationship. We think that Paul here may be hinting at this fact to Philemon.[30] And certainly such a hope would dovetail naturally with what is the one explicit request that Paul does make in the letter: to "welcome him [Onesimus] as you would welcome me" (v. 17). If Paul is hinting at a request that Onesimus be freed, the preservation of this letter makes it likely that Paul's request was granted. What ultimately became of Onesimus we cannot know for sure. Some scholars think that Onesimus was not only freed but became the Bishop of Ephesus, since an early Christian source mentions an "Onesimus" in that

27. Thompson, 266. See also James Tunstead Burtchaell, *Philemon's Problem: A Theology of Grace* (Grand Rapids: Eerdmans, 1998), 20-34.
28. Barclay, *Colossians and Philemon*, 111.
29. This point is rightly emphasized by Reinmuth, 47-48.
30. See, further, the notes and bibliography on v. 15.

role early in the second century.[31] But the name was common enough that this identification is by no means clear.[32] Still other scholars, more speculatively, have thought that Onesimus might have written the letter to the Ephesians and/or been responsible for an early collection of the letters of Paul.[33] But these speculations are even more unlikely.[34]

Whether the letter to Philemon *implicitly requests that Onesimus be set free or not*, it inevitably raises larger questions about the New Testament view of slavery and its significance for Christian theology and practice. As Stuhlmacher has noted, the history of interpretation of this matter reveals tendencies toward opposite extremes.[35] On the one hand, beginning with Chrysostom in the early church, continuing with Luther at the time of the Reformation, and seen in its most extreme form among defenders of slavery in nineteenth-century United States, there is an "antienthusiastic," or "conservative," tendency to stress the degree to which Paul in the letter upholds the status quo.[36] He does not ask Philemon to manumit Onesimus; he praises him, even though he owns slaves, for his "love and faith" (v. 5); he follows the dictates of the law and sends the runaway slave back to his master. And, of course, it is argued that what

---

31. Ignatius is the early first-century Christian leader who refers to an Onesimus as Bishop of Ephesus, in his *Letter to the Ephesians*. Those who hold that this Onesimus is the one who features in Philemon include Knox, *Philemon*, 79-80; Bruce, 202; Moule, 21; Stuhlmacher, 19.

32. See, e.g., *NewDocs* 4.179-81; R. P. Martin, 168.

33. This case is argued in an intriguing and wide-ranging monograph by John Knox *(Philemon)*. Knox (as we noted above) argues that the letter of Philemon was, in fact, written to Archippus, a part-time Christian worker in Colossae. Archippus was the owner of Onesimus, and Paul is writing to him to request that Onesimus be released for Christian ministry. Philemon's name appears in v. 1 because he is the overseer of the churches of the Lycus valley, and Paul sends the letter through him to enlist his support. But Philemon lives in Laodicea, so the "letter to the Laodiceans" of Col. 4:16 is, in fact, this letter to Archippus via Philemon. Knox further suggests that, as Bishop of Ephesus, Onesimus initiated the collection of Paul's letters and insured that this letter of great personal significance would be included. At this point, Knox's theory has some parallel with Goodspeed's theory that Onesimus was the writer of Ephesians, as a kind of "cover letter" for the Pauline corpus (Edgar J. Goodspeed, *The Meaning of Ephesians* [Chicago: University of Chicago Press, 1933]).

34. Knox's theory, impressive for providing answers to so many difficult issues, has fatal exegetical weaknesses. See, e.g., the succinct critique of Moule, 16-18.

35. Stuhlmacher, 58-69.

36. Many conservative theologians in early nineteenth-century America defended slavery on the basis of sustained biblical and theological arguments. For an overview of these defenses, see, e.g., Larry E. Tise, *Proslavery: A History of the Defense of Slavery in America 1701-1840* (Athens, Ga.: University of Georgia Press, 1987); Elizabeth Fox-Genovese and Eugene D. Genovese, "The Divine Sanction of Social Order: Religious Foundations of the Southern Slaveholders' World View," *JAAR* 55 (1987), 211-33.

we find in Philemon in this regard simply echoes the general New Testament approach to slavery, where the institution is never questioned, slaves are required to obey their masters "in the Lord," and masters are never challenged to free their slaves. A relatively recent defender of this general line of interpretation — albeit in a mild form — is evangelical theologian John Murray, who argues that the Bible does not condemn slavery per se but only certain forms of slavery or the abuse of slaves.[37]

At the other end of the spectrum are interpreters who espouse liberation as a dominating value and seek to find in Philemon a basis for their program (or at least to deprive Philemon of any "anti-liberation" implications). Most evangelical interpreters have steered a middle course, acknowledging, for the reasons we have given above, that Philemon makes no frontal attack on the institution of slavery or even, perhaps, implies that Philemon should set Onesimus free, but insist nevertheless that, in Lightfoot's classic way of putting it, "a principle is boldly enunciated, which must in the end prove fatal to slavery."[38] We would like to think this is the case; but we are not sure. For the "principle" to which scholars appeal is the fact that Philemon and Onesimus are "brothers" — it is finally inconsistent for "brothers" to own one another. But unless we read into this language the rather unlikely idea of "the brotherhood of mankind," the letter suggests the inappropriateness of one *Christian* owning another. It is not clear that the principle can validly be extended to slavery in general.[39] Using the New Testament to think theologically about the *institution* of slavery therefore requires a broader theological and hermeneutical approach; and the task of crafting such an approach is beyond our scope here.[40]

37. John Murray, *Principles of Conduct* (Grand Rapids: Eerdmans, 1957), 91-106.

38. Lightfoot, 325. This sentiment has been echoed again and again; see, e.g., Bruce, 197-98 (Philemon creates "an atmosphere where it [slavery] could only wilt and die"); Moule, 11 (Paul "applies an explosive charge to the whole institution"); M. J. Harris, *Slave of Christ* (Downers Grove, Ill.: InverVarsity, 2001), 59. There is debate over the degree of influence that Christianity had on the amelioration of slavery in the later Roman Empire (e.g., Westermann, *Slave Systems*, 159-62). And it is also pointedly asked why, if the principle were so clear, it took so long for slavery to be eradicated (and against the arguments of some of the most biblically oriented Christians of the time) (see Wayne Meeks, "The 'Haustafeln' and American Slavery: A Hermeneutical Challenge," in *Theology and Ethics in Paul and His Interpreters* [ed. E. H. Lovering and J. L. Sumney; Nashville: Abingdon, 1996], 249-50).

39. Although note Marshall's suggestion: ". . . once it has been realized that Christian masters must treat their Christian slaves as brothers and sisters in the flesh and in Christ, is it not inevitable that they should treat their other slaves as brothers and sisters in the flesh — with all that implies?" ("Theology," 190).

40. David Horrell has recently analyzed Paul's ethics with particular interest in the move from community ethics to broader societal ethics (*Solidarity and Difference* [London and New York: T&T Clark, 2005]).

In saying what we have above, we do not want to minimize the implications of what Philemon says about masters and slaves being "brothers" in Christ for the Christian community. Calling another person "brother" or "sister" is, indeed, ultimately inconsistent with the ownership of that brother or sister. But, if this is true, it raises rather insistently another question: why did Paul, and other New Testament Christians, not appear to recognize this and require Christian slave owners to release their slaves? Granted the personal focus of the New Testament, it is this question — not the question of why the New Testament does not advocate the overthrow of the institution of slavery — that is the really difficult one.[41] The New Testament certainly does not endorse the institution of slavery; nor does it encourage Christians to buy or own slaves.[42] It presumes that some Christians do own slaves, and encourages them to bring to bear on that relationship their Christian principles and values.

The problem, then, is the silence of the New Testament about Christian slave owning. If slave owning is a moral evil, why doesn't Paul condemn it as such?[43] We suggest two possible responses to the problem. First, as we noted above, freedom for the first-century slave was by no means an unqualified good thing. Again, we insist, we run the danger when discussing this issue of elevating "freedom" to a level of moral supremacy that was not recognized in first-century society — or in the Bible for that matter — and which reflects our own modern prejudice. A Christian slave owner who immediately released all his or her slaves might be condemning many of them to poverty and starvation. Perhaps the contemporary problem of polygamy among new converts is something of a parallel. Should a man who has converted to Christianity and come to recognize monogamy as a biblical principle immediately send all but one

41. Barclay, "Paul, Philemon and the Dilemma of Christian Slave-Ownership," 183. It must also be said, however, that the silence of the New Testament on the institution of slavery has sometimes been defended on less than convincing bases. For instance, it is often suggested that the NT writers did not condemn the institution because it would have brought chaos to society (e.g., Lightfoot, 323: "Slavery was woven into the fabric of society; and to prohibit slavery was to tear society to shreds"). However, (1) the tiny Christian movement could, of course, have had no such effect on society in general; (2) the Christians could, as, e.g., the Essenes apparently did, prohibit slavery among themselves; and (3) is it such a bad thing to "tear to shreds" a society shot through with evil?

42. See, e.g., Harris, *Slave of Christ*, 62-68; contra, e.g., K. Giles, "The Biblical Argument for Slavery," *EvQ* 66 (1994), 3, 11 (who uses what he claims is the Bible's endorsement of slavery to argue that the Bible is not finally authoritative in matters of social relations).

43. See esp. on this issue, Barclay, "Paul, Philemon and the Dilemma of Christian Slave-Ownership," 161-86; idem, *Colossians and Philemon*, 161-83. Barclay opts finally to express disappointment with Paul's failure to press this matter. Murray, on the other hand, who raises the same question, thinks that it implies that Paul does not, in fact, condemn slavery per se (*Principles of Conduct*, 94).

wife away — even if, in doing so, he condemns those women to a life as outcasts and economic hardship? While going some way toward answering the problem, this factor still does not go all the way; for we still might have expected Paul to have encouraged Christians to release their slaves in a timely and compassionate way.

We might, then, very tentatively suggest that Paul, and the other New Testament writers, did not always recognize all the implications of the theological principles that they themselves enunciated. We believe that God preserved them from contradicting those principles. But we are not sure that he always enabled them to see the full range of application of those principles. From our vantage point, Paul's principle of "neither slave nor free in Christ" (Gal. 3:28; Col. 3:11) jars with his failure to ask Christian slave owners to release their slaves (see Col. 4:1). And we rightly draw from Paul's principle the conclusion — that Christians must not own slaves — that he did not explicitly draw in his own day.[44]

---

44. See Marshall, "Theology," 190. This way of viewing ethical issues in the New Testament has some affinities with W. J. Webb's advocacy of a "redemptive-movement" hermeneutic in analyzing the NT teaching on a variety of issues (*Slaves, Women, and Homosexuals* [Downers Grove, Ill.: InterVarsity, 2001]). The proposal has received strong criticism from Wayne Grudem ("Should We Move beyond the New Testament to a Better Ethic?" *JETS* 47 [2004], 299-346). There are, indeed, some problems with Webb's proposal and especially the particular ways that he works it out. We think that Webb tends too easily to assume what an "ideal ethic" might be, sometimes appearing to adapt the ethic of modern liberal democracies without sufficient critique. We also believe that he fails adequately to recognize the degree to which the NT itself might qualify how far the "redemptive movement" should go and what its limitations might be (particularly in his application of his method to the issue of the roles of women). Nevertheless, we also think that Webb's proposal has some merit as a way to explain the silence of the NT on issues such as slave ownership. As we suggest above, scholars tend to explain this silence in three basic ways. (1) The NT is silent on the matter because it does not, in fact, condemn at least some forms of slavery; nor should we (Murray). (2) The NT is silent on the matter because it does not condemn slavery; but, of course, we must. This shows that the NT is not adequate for providing ethical direction today (e.g., Barclay; Giles, "The Biblical Argument for Slavery"). (3) The NT is silent on the matter because, although it sets forth principles that are incompatible with slavery, (a) slavery was part of the fabric of first-century society; and (b) the NT was not fundamentally interested in "earthly" liberation (most evangelical scholars). We feel that the third explanation correctly stresses the incompatibility between biblical theology and slavery, but we question whether it adequately explains the silence of the NT. With respect to point (a), as we have suggested above in the text, while it provides a generally convincing explanation of why the NT does not condemn the *institution* of slavery, it does not explain why it does not require Christian slave owners to free their slaves. Point (b), on the other hand, while preserving a measure of truth (again, see the text above), tends uncomfortably toward a dualistic, "two kingdom" ethic according to which the NT speaks to the spiritual side of life but not to the physical and earthly side of life. We hold that Webb and others are correct to point out the inadequacy of the usual responses to this problem. And as Webb rightly

As important as it is, however, slavery is not what Philemon is ultimately "about." It is important not to allow this pressing modern problem to derail us from recognizing and applying the key theological teaching of the letter. As we have seen above, Paul's one clear request with respect to Onesimus is that Philemon accept him as a Christian brother, with all that this acceptance would entail (v. 17). Paul builds his case for this acceptance on the new relationship of Philemon and Onesimus in the Lord. And he urges Philemon to do what he asks on the basis of his close relationship to Philemon in the Lord. The letter to Philemon, as Petersen has especially emphasized, reconfigures the existing social relationships among these three men.[45] By his conversion, Onesimus is Paul's "son" in the faith (v. 10), and he is therefore a "brother" of Philemon, whom Paul has also brought to faith. This nexus of relationships requires each of the key players in this drama to do something that would not have been the "natural" thing for them to do: Paul has to send back to Philemon "his very heart" (v. 12); Onesimus, who has gained some measure of freedom, has to go back to his master; and Philemon has to accept back this slave as if he were Paul himself!

As Wright has particularly emphasized, then, the central theme of Philemon is *koinōnia*, "fellowship."[46] This word is featured in v. 6, as Paul is laying the foundation for his appeal, and he picks it up, in another form (*koinōnos*), as he transitions to his central appeal (v. 17; "partner" in TNIV). As we argue in the commentary, the phrase in v. 6 where this word appears has the sense of "the fellowship that is the product of our mutual faith in Christ." Believing in Christ joins us to other believers in an intimate family unit. Within that new relationship, which takes pride of place in all our relationships and dictates how those other relationships are to be lived out, we bear responsibilities for one another. It is those responsibilities that Paul spells out in this letter. This short private letter stands, then, as an important reminder of the communitarian aspect of Christianity that many of us, in our individualist cultures, are so prone to forget. In Christ we belong to one another; we enjoy each other's company and support; and we are obliged to support, to the point of sacrificing our own time, interests, and money, our brothers and sisters.

---

points out, his proposal is not an entirely new one (William J. Webb, "A Redemptive-Movement Hermeneutic: Encouraging Dialogue among Four Evangelical Views," *JETS* 48 [2005], 334-35; note, e.g., R. N. Longenecker, *New Testament Social Ethics for Today* [Grand Rapids: Eerdmans, 1984], and the reference to Marshall above).

45. Norman R. Petersen, *Rediscovering Paul: Philemon and the Sociology of Paul's Narrative World* (Philadelphia: Fortress, 1985); see also Wolter, 256-57.

46. Wright, 170, 183-87.

Commentary on Philemon

I. THE LETTER OPENING (vv. 1-3)

> ¹*Paul, a prisoner of Christ Jesus, and Timothy our brother,*
> *To Philemon our dear friend and fellow worker* — ²*also to Apphia our sister and Archippus our fellow soldier* — *and to the church that meets in your home:*
> ³*Grace and peace to you from God our Father and the Lord Jesus Christ.*

The openings of ancient letters fall into a rather natural pattern: identification of writer, identification of sender, a greeting. The letter of James to believers in Antioch, Syria, and Cilicia, conveying the decision of the Jerusalem Council, is the purest New Testament example of this form: "The apostles and elders, your brothers, To the Gentile believers in Antioch, Syria and Cilicia: Greetings" (Acts 15:23b). Paul also follows this form in his letters, although he usually elaborates each part, sometimes briefly, sometimes at considerable length. Philemon 1-3 is easily identified as the letter opening and exhibits a modest expansion of the three typical features.

1 Paul (the Greco-Roman equivalent of Saul [see the notes on Col. 1:1]) usually identifies himself as an "apostle" in his letter openings. The exceptions are Philippians, 1 and 2 Thessalonians, and Philemon. In the former three epistles, Paul may drop the "apostle" title because he associates one or more of his co-workers with him in the writing of the letter. In Philemon, on the other hand, the absence is probably to be explained by the more personal nature of the letter. In place of "apostle" we find *prisoner*. Philemon is, therefore, one of five letters that Paul wrote while in custody. On the basis of content, destination, and references to co-workers, it

379

is closely associated with Ephesians and Colossians. While certainty is impossible, we tentatively conclude that all three were written while Paul was in custody in Rome around A.D. 60-61 (Acts 28:28-30) (see the Introduction to Colossians, 41-46). However, while all three of these letters, along with Philippians and 2 Timothy, were written while Paul was in prison, it is only in Philemon that he begins by calling himself a "prisoner." Some commentators think that this designation functions in a way similar to his usual claim to be an apostle. By identifying himself as a *prisoner of Christ Jesus*, Paul may be asserting his authority, the authority of one who has been sent to jail for his commitment to carry out his apostolic calling.[1] But it is likely that Paul has a different purpose. He identifies himself as a *prisoner* not only because he is writing a private letter but also because he has decided to pursue a particular argumentative strategy. Paul's appeal to Philemon is laced with allusions to the various relationships in which the key figures of the letter find themselves.[2] Paul's imprisonment is a subtle reminder of his own sacrifices for the sake of the gospel and should lead Philemon to look on his request with sympathy.[3] "Paul empties himself of his rights to compel Philemon also to waive his rights" (Luther).[4] With his reference to being a prisoner, Paul also aligns himself with the weak and powerless Onesimus.[5] At the same time, the title *prisoner of Christ Jesus* also serves another key implicit theme of the letter: the reconfiguration of relationships in terms of the gospel. Paul may appear to be a "prisoner of Caesar," but he is, in a deeper sense, a "prisoner of Christ Jesus."[6] This does not mean that "prisoner" has a spiritual sense here, as if Paul is claiming to have been captured by Christ for gospel ministry.[7] But it does suggest that Paul's imprisonment is not finally a matter of human decision; he is in prison because of, and at the direction of, Christ.[8]

Joining Paul as one of the senders of the letter is Timothy. Colos-

---

1. Lohse, 189; Wilson, 332.

2. See esp. N. R. Petersen, *Rediscovering Paul* (Philadelphia: Fortress, 1985); Chris Frilingos, "'For My Child, Onesimus': Paul and Domestic Power in Philemon," *JBL* 119 (2000), 91-104.

3. See, e.g., Lightfoot, 333; O'Brien, 272; Dunn, 311.

4. Quoted in Garland, 316.

5. Thompson, 206.

6. Reinmuth, 22-23.

7. Contra Erwin R. Goodenough, "Paul and Onesimus," *HTR* 22 (1929), 182-83. Barth/Blanke, 245-47, think that "prisoner" has both physical and spiritual connotations.

8. Χριστοῦ Ἰησοῦ after δέσμιος is one of those hard-to-classify genitives that probably indicates a general relationship between "prisoner" and "Christ Jesus" that should not be confined to one particular nuance. Paul is in prison because he has been preaching Christ; he is in prison for the sake of Christ; he is a prisoner who belongs to Christ. See Harris, 244.

sians opens in the same way, and we argued in our comments on Colossians 1:1 that the reference to Timothy does not mean that he was a co-author. It is more a courteous acknowledgment that Timothy is with Paul as he writes, included perhaps because Timothy is known to Philemon (Timothy was with Paul during at least part of his three-year ministry in nearby Ephesus [Acts 19:22]).[9] Philemon, even more than Colossians, bears the unmistakable imprint of Paul's own personality. The letter is addressed to Philemon, whom Paul calls *our dear friend and fellow worker*. "Dear friend" translates the word *agapētos*, "beloved," which could function in this context as an adjective; see ESV, "beloved fellow worker" (see also NJB; RSV; NLT).[10] But it is probably better to keep the two separate: Philemon is both a close and well-loved friend of Paul's and one of his fellow laborers in the cause of the gospel. Paul can use "fellow worker" to denote Christians in general (2 Cor. 1:24) but generally applies this designation only to people who have worked closely with him in significant ministry (Rom. 16:3, 9, 21; 1 Cor. 3:9; 2 Cor. 8:23; Phil. 2:25; 4:3; Col. 4:11; 1 Thess. 3:2; Phlm. 24). Colossians 2:1, along with Paul's claim that he has only "heard" about Philemon's love and faith (v. 5), might suggest that they had never met. But "fellow worker" suggests a close personal relationship, and v. 19 probably implies that Paul was instrumental in Philemon's conversion. We might, then, surmise that Philemon was converted during a visit to Ephesus and that he and Paul worked together in ministry there for a time before Philemon returned to the Lycus valley. Paul talks about "hearing" of Philemon's love and faith because it has been so long since they have been together.

2   The title of this letter in our Bibles (which is not original) and our own comments on the letter thus far in the commentary single out Philemon as the addressee of the letter. But, as this verse makes clear, Paul appears to address the letter not only to Philemon but also to *Apphia our sister and Archippus our fellow soldier*, and *to the church that meets in your home*. Indeed, some interpreters argue that the primary addressee is found in this verse. John Knox, in his famous alternative interpretation of this letter and its significance, argued that Archippus is the person to whom Paul addresses himself: he is the owner of Onesimus, and the church meets in his house.[11] This latter point, Knox argues, is clear from the order of the

---

9. O'Brien, 272; Reinmuth, 23. The English versions suggest this interpretation by rendering the Gk. ὁ ἀδελφός as "our brother." This is a valid interpretation of the Greek article, but it does distance Timothy from any role in writing the letter.

10. This translation takes the Gk. τῷ ἀγαπητῷ καὶ συνεργῷ ἡμῶν as a hendiadys (see Harris, 245).

11. J. Knox, *Philemon among the Letters of Paul* (London: Collins, 1960), 51-59; see also L. Cope, "On Rethinking the Philemon-Colossians Connection," *BR* 30 (1995), 45-50.

Greek text: Archippus is the nearest antecedent to the pronoun "your" (*sou*) that modifies "church." Philemon is mentioned first simply because Paul knows him and wants to enlist his help in mediating between himself and Archippus. But these arguments are not convincing. In Greco-Roman letters it is virtually always the first-named individual who is the main recipient of the letter. Most interpreters agree, then, that Philemon is the basic addressee. He was the owner of Onesimus and the church mentioned in this verse met in his house. Most of the English translations leave this matter open or even imply that Archippus is the owner of the house (by virtue of being the closest antecedent). But the TNIV reflects the usual interpretation by placing *also to Apphia our sister and Archippus our fellow soldier* between dashes and thereby making clear that Philemon is the antecedent of the *your* at the end of v. 2.

If Philemon is the person whom Paul truly addresses in the letter, why, then, does he include these other names in this prominent place in the letter opening — something that Paul does in none of his other letters?[12] Other Greco-Roman letters that mention several names at the opening are addressed to a single individual, so Paul is not doing something unprecedented.[13] And the bulk of the letter reveals that Paul has a single person in view, since the Greek behind the pronoun "you" throughout vv. 4-22 is singular in form. Why, then, does Paul mention Apphia, Archippus, and Philemon's house church? He may include them simply as a courtesy, especially if Apphia and Archippus belong to Philemon's household. Although Paul refers to *Apphia* simply as *our sister* (i.e., a fellow Christian),[14] it is possible that she was Philemon's wife.[15] She may have been active in ministry with her husband Philemon, and we find other examples of such husband-and-wife ministry teams in the New Testament (Aquila and Priscilla being the most prominent [Acts 18:2, 18-19; Rom. 16:3-4]; see also, probably, "Andronicus and Junia" [Rom. 16:7]). However, it is also possible that, if Apphia were Philemon's wife, she is mentioned simply because the issue addressed in the letter is a "household" matter that affects her as well as her husband.[16] On this

---

12. The only possible parallel is Phil. 1:1, where Paul addresses "all God's holy people in Christ Jesus at Philippi, together with the overseers and deacons." But in this case the overseers and deacons are significant people included in the overall address.

13. See Arzt-Grabner, 112-14.

14. Paul uses "sister" (ἀδελφή) when he refers to a single female believer (Rom. 16:1, 15), to a group of female believers (1 Tim. 5:2), or to a representative female believer (1 Cor. 7:15; 9:5).

15. So most commentators; see, e.g., Lightfoot, 306; Vincent, 176; Lohse, 190; O'Brien, 273; Gnilka, 16; Stuhlmacher, 30.

16. E.g., Dunn, 312.

reading, then, Archippus might be included simply because he was Philemon's son.[17] However, by calling Archippus a *fellow soldier,* Paul suggests that he was a significant supporter of Paul and his ministry (the only other person whom Paul calls a "fellow soldier" is Epaphroditus, the emissary to Paul from the Philippian church [Phil. 2:25]). Paul's demand in Colossians 4:17 that Archippus "complete the work you have received in the Lord" also shows that he was engaged in ministry of some kind. It may be, then, that both Apphia and Archippus are included in Paul's address not because they were related to Philemon but because they were both prominent figures in the Colossian church.[18] We finally do not have enough data to make a decision one way or the other. But, with considerable hesitation, we think it more likely that Apphia was Philemon's wife and Archippus his son. There is nothing, of course, to prevent Archippus from being both a ministry associate of Paul's and the son of Philemon; and the unusual inclusion of these names makes best sense if they are tied to the letter's distinctive nature and purpose.

Whether Apphia and Archippus are members of Philemon's household or simply fellow believers, they are of course included in the last, general addressee: *the church that meets in your home.*[19] The inclusion of Philemon's house church in the address is significant. The mention of Apphia and Archippus may have been little more than a courteous gesture, but the mention of the entire church cannot function in quite this way. Moreover, Paul gives indications in the letter that he has a larger audience in view. For while the bulk of the letter is addressed to an individual, with second-person singular forms, Paul also uses second-person *plural* forms: in v. 3 — "grace and peace to *you*"; in v. 22 — "I hope to be restored to *you* in answer to *your* prayers"; and in v. 25 — "The grace of the Lord Jesus Christ be with *your* spirit." These references seem to imply that the whole community would have been present as the letter was publicly read.[20] By making the issue of Onesimus a public one, Paul increases the pressure on Philemon to respond as he wishes. But we should not view the public nature of the letter as simply a lawyer's tactic to win

17. Lightfoot, 309; Bruce, 206; Binder, 30.
18. Barth/Blanke, 256; Reinmuth, 24-25. To claim that Apphia was an independent leader in the church may, however, be going too far (contra Allen Dwight Callahan, *Embassy of Onesimus: The Letter of Paul to Philemon* [The New Testament in Context; Valley Forge, Pa.: Trinity Press International, 1997], 25). Houlden's evaluation of the thesis that Archippus was Philemon's son — "an instance of legend active when history fails" (p. 228) — is witty but too severe.
19. The construction τῇ κατ' οἶκόν σου ἐκκλησίᾳ — "the 'in-your-house' church" — refers to a congregation of Christians meeting in a particular home (see Rom. 16:5; 1 Cor. 16:19; Col. 4:15; and Fitzmyer, 89).
20. Dunn, 313; Garland, 317-18.

383

his case; it rather reflects the corporate nature of early Christianity, in which no matter was "private" but inevitably affected, and was affected by, one's brothers and sisters in the new family of God.[21]

3   The letter opening ends with the theologically significant salutation that Paul usually uses in place of the common Greco-Roman "greetings." *Grace* and *peace* both touch on a central gospel truth. While grace was of course hardly absent from God's dealings with his old covenant people, it especially marks the extraordinary free and unmerited gift of his Son that stands at the center of the gospel (e.g., John 1:16; Rom. 3:24; 4:4-5; 5:2; 2 Cor. 8:9; Gal. 5:4; Eph. 1:6-7). "Peace," on the other hand, has deeper Old Testament roots, used by the prophets as a way of summarizing the universal "well-being" *(shalōm)* that God would establish in the last days (see esp. Isa. 52:7; 55:12; 66:12; Jer. 30:10; 33:6; 46:27; Ezek. 34:25; 37:26; Hag. 2:9; Zech. 9:10). This "peace" has been established by God through the word of his Son (cf. Eph. 2:14-17; Col. 1:20), and so it is appropriate that Paul traces the source of both this peace and grace to *God our Father* and *the Lord Jesus Christ.* This, too, is the common pattern of Paul's salutations, and it implies that Paul puts Christ on the same level with God the Father.[22]

II. THANKSGIVING: THE "FELLOWSHIP OF FAITH" (vv. 4-7)

> [4]*I always thank my God as I remember you in my prayers,* [5]*because I hear about your love for all his people and your faith in the Lord Jesus.* [6]*I pray that your partnership with us in the faith may be effective in deepening your understanding of every good thing we share for the sake of Christ.* [7]*Your love has given me great joy and encouragement, because you, brother, have refreshed the hearts of the Lord's people.*

A thanksgiving that acts as a bridge between the letter opening and the body of the letter is customary in the letters of Paul (it is omitted only in Galatians and Titus).[1] The thanksgiving section in Philemon, as we might expect in so relatively short a letter, is brief (the shortest in Paul's letters)

---

21. Thompson, 210.

22. Harris, 246; Dunn, 314.

1. This thanksgiving section is usually thought to have formal parallels with the "health" wish in Greco-Roman letters. Arzt-Grabner, however, doubts whether the parallels are close enough to justify a formal comparison (135-36; cf. also "The Epistolary Introductory Thanksgiving in the Papyri and in Paul," *NovT* 36 [1994], 29-46).

and focuses on Philemon personally. But it still has the features common to Paul's thanksgivings. Simplified, four discrete elements can be discerned. Paul (1) expresses thanks for Philemon (v. 4a); (2) reports that he constantly prays for him (v. 4b); (3) explains why he gives thanks for Philemon, mentioning his love and faith (v. 5); and (4) tells Philemon what he is praying for him (v. 6). These verses find their closest parallels in Colossians 1:3-4 and 1 Thessalonians 1:2-3. Verse 7 is not formally part of the thanksgiving. It is transitional, elaborating the thanksgiving and preparing the way for Paul's appeal to Philemon in v. 8.[2] But it is best included with vv. 4-6,[3] since its focus on Philemon's love elaborates v. 5. Thus vv. 5-7 fall into a chiastic arrangement: love — faith (v. 5) — faith (v. 6) — love (v. 7).[4] Verse 7 also functions with these other verses to introduce some of the key ideas that Paul will come back to in the body of the letter: "love" (*agapē*) (see v. 9); "partnership" (or "fellowship"; *koinōnia*) (see v. 17), "good thing" (*agathos*) (see v. 14, "favor" [*agathos*]); "refresh" (*anapauō*) (see v. 20); "heart(s)" (*splanchna*) (see vv. 12, 20). In no other letter does Paul "rehearse" so many of the key points of the letter in the thanksgiving section.[5] While working in fellowship with Paul, Philemon has already come to understand "every good thing," and he has refreshed the hearts of God's people out of his deep love. So Paul will ask Philemon to reveal the depths of his love and fellowship with Paul by refreshing his heart with a "favor," or good deed.

4 The fact that Paul expresses his thanksgiving with the first-person singular — *I always thank my God* — strongly suggests that Timothy is introduced in v. 1 not as co-author but as a co-worker only loosely connected with the writing of this letter. This contrasts with Colossians, where Timothy is also mentioned in the salutation and where the thanksgiving is expressed in the first-person plural. Presumably the more personal focus of Philemon explains the difference. Paul also expresses thanks to *my God* in Romans 1:8, 1 Corinthians 1:4, and Philippians 1:3. The expression is not intended to be exclusive — "my God" as opposed to yours — but, following the pattern of the Psalms, expresses a sense of deep personal relationship.[6] As is the case in several of Paul's thanks-

---

2. Lohse, 192; O'Brien, 276.

3. So most commentators and English versions. See, however, Arzt-Grabner, 58-59, who argues that it belongs with vv. 8ff.

4. Dunn, 315.

5. Wolter, 255; see the full chart of parallels in W. Schenk, "Der Brief des Paulus an Philemon," *ANRW*, 3452; also F. Forrester Church, "Rhetorical Structure and Design in Paul's Letter to Philemon," *HTR* 71 (1978), 23.

6. "My God" occurs over sixty times in the Psalms; see, e.g., 17:30; 18:6; 25:1; 103:33; 145:2.

givings (see our notes on Col. 1:3), there is uncertainty about which word the adverb *always* modifies. Does it modify "give thanks" — "I always thank my God" (TNIV and most versions)? Or does it modify "remember in prayer" — "making mention of you always in my prayers" (NKJV)? The former is a bit more likely because it fits the Pauline thanksgiving pattern.[7] But the two verbs are so closely related that it does not make much difference, the second verb — *I remember you*[8] — in any case limiting the meaning of *always:* it is when Paul prays that he "always" thanks God for Philemon.[9] Still, Paul's claim about the frequency with which he mentions Philemon in prayer is impressive, especially when we remember that Paul says much the same thing about many other individuals and churches. If Paul is not exaggerating in these verses (and we have no reason to think he is), they reveal a man who spent quite considerable time in prayer for Christians all over the Mediterranean world — an implicit testimony to Paul's view of the significance of prayer.

Paul often uses the language of "remembering" for prayer (Rom. 1:9; Eph. 1:16; Phil. 1:3; Col. 4:18; 1 Thess. 1:2, 3; 2 Tim. 1:3). "Remembering" is a significant activity in Scripture, involving not just the recall of facts but a pondering on or presenting to someone those facts with a view toward changing one's attitude. When Moses calls on the people of Israel to "remember" the day on which the Lord brought his people out of Egypt (Exod. 13:3), he is asking the people to bring the events and the significance of those events to mind in a way that stimulates their greater devotion to the Lord. "Remembering" people in prayer, then, involves not only the mental activity of considering them and their needs but also calling on God to consider them and act for their benefit.[10]

5 Verse 5 is subordinated to v. 4 by means of a participle in Greek, a participle that is universally taken to have causal significance (hence all

7. The adverb πάντοτε must modify the verb εὐχαριστέω in 1 Cor. 1:4, 1 Thess. 1:2, and 2 Thess. 1:3. On the other hand, albeit in a different construction, it modifies the expression of prayer in Rom. 1:10 (see v. 8) and Phil. 1:4. Most commentators also take πάντοτε with εὐχαριστῶ (see, e.g., Lightfoot, 234; Vincent, 177), but a few think it modifies μνείαν . . . ποιούμενος ("making remembrance") (Wolter, 251-52; Stuhlmacher, 32). See also our note on Col. 1:3.

8. The Greek uses the construction μνείαν ποιούμενος, "making remembrance." The verb ποιέω, which has an incredibly wide range of meaning, is often used in these kinds of constructions and often in the middle voice, as here (BDF §310[1]). The construction is therefore accurately rendered "when I pray for you" (NLT; see Burton, *Moods and Tenses*, §203) or, in an attempt to preserve the possible significance of the "memory" idea (see above), "when I remember you in my prayers" (or similar; so most versions).

9. Vincent, 178; Harris, 249.

10. Barth/Blanke, 270.

the modern translations render "because I hear"). It is also generally agreed that the causal clause depends on "I always thank my God" in v. 4. Only in Colossians and Philemon does Paul use the verb "hear" to explain why he gives thanks for his addressees. We might expect this language in Colossians, since Paul does not personally know them (see 2:1). But, as we have noted, it is likely that Paul is personally acquainted with Philemon. Nevertheless, these contacts are some years in the past by the time Paul writes this letter — at least three years if Paul is writing from Rome. Paul's choice of the present tense of the verb, then, is probably significant (contrast Col. 1:4): he is continuing to hear positive reports about Philemon's relationship to Christ and commitment to other believers. Paul may have received this information from Onesimus himself, or perhaps from Epaphras (see Col. 1:7-8).[11]

What Paul is hearing about Philemon is that he has *love* and *faith*.[12] And this love and faith are directed toward *the Lord Jesus* and *all his people*. The Greek word order allows two different arrangements of these words. One possibility is that Philemon's love and faith are both directed to both the Lord and his people. This is the option reflected in most of the English versions; see, for example, HCSB: "I hear of your love and faith toward the Lord Jesus and for all the saints" (see also, basically, KJV; NAB; NJB). Other versions are similar but, by inserting a definite article before "faith," may imply (whether intentionally or not) that it is Philemon's faith (only) that is directed to the Lord and to his people: "I hear of your love and of the faith that you have toward the Lord Jesus and all the saints" (ESV; see also RSV; NASB). No commentator, however, argues for this reading of the verse, so perhaps these versions really intend both love and faith to be directed toward the Lord and to the "saints." The other possibility is that Philemon's love is directed to the Lord's people and his faith to the Lord Jesus only; see, for example, TNIV: "I hear about your love for all his people and your faith in the Lord Jesus" (see also NIV; NRSV; NET; NLT; TEV).[13]

11. For the former, see Fitzmyer, 93 (cautiously); for the latter, Barth/Blanke, 271.

12. Both nouns are in the accusative case (τὴν ἀγάπην, τὴν πίστιν). In classical Greek, the verb ἀκούω with the accusative case would normally indicate "hearing with understanding," while ἀκούω with the genitive case would denote simple physical hearing. This distinction may continue to be observed in some NT texts (it is often cited as the difference between Acts 9:7 and 22:9), but is not strictly followed in general. It is certainly difficult here to see any emphasis on "hearing with understanding" (Wallace, *Greek Grammar*, 133).

13. If we translate in this way, the relative pronoun that serves as the object of "you have" (ἔχεις) — ἥν — might be singular because it goes with τὴν πίστιν alone (Harris, 250) or, more likely, because it has as its antecedent both τὴν ἀγάπην and τὴν πίστιν, but individually: "which (faith) you have in the Lord Jesus and which (love) you have for the Lord's

In favor of the first option is the fact that it duplicates in English the word order of the Greek text. Paul would, in effect, be saying two things about Philemon: he loves both the Lord and his people; and he displays "faith" toward both the Lord and his people.[14] The first assertion fits well into Paul's usual teaching, since he speaks of Christians as loving the Lord (though not often: Rom. 8:28; 1 Cor. 2:9; 8:3; Eph. 6:24) and, of course (very often), as loving fellow Christians. But the second assertion is more difficult. Since "having faith for all the saints" does not make much sense, the noun *pistis* must mean, in relationship to the saints, at least, "faithfulness." And this word does (though not very often) have this meaning in Paul.[15] But nowhere else does Paul speak of Christians having *pistis* in or toward one another (the same is true of the cognate verb, *pisteuō*). And, though Paul does refer to Christians "loving" God (with the verb *agapaō*), he rarely, if ever, refers to them having *agapē* ("love," the noun) for God or Christ.[16]

On the other hand, arguing in favor of the second option are passages very similar to this one, where Paul refers distinctly to believers' faith in the Lord and love for other Christians. See, for example, Colossians 1:4: "we have heard of your faith in Christ Jesus and of the love you have for all his people" (see also Eph. 1:15). On this view, Paul has arranged the words of the Greek text chiastically:

A *tēn agapēn*, "love"
  B *tēn pistin*, "faith"
  B′ *pros ton kyrion Iēsoun*, "toward the Lord Jesus"
A′ *eis pantas tous hagious*, "toward all the Lord's people"

---

people." This singular relative pronoun may be one of the reasons that RSV, ESV, and NAB translate as they do (see above).

14. See, e.g., Bruce, 208; Gnilka, 36; Dunn, 317; Barth/Blanke, 293-94; Arzt-Grabner, 178. Vincent (178) thinks that faith goes with the Lord alone while love goes with both the Lord and the "saints."

15. Paul clearly uses πίστις to mean "faithfulness" only in Rom. 3:3, and perhaps in Gal. 5:22 (see TNIV) and 1 Tim. 2:7. And, though the matter is disputed, the word may have this meaning also in a number of other passages, including some where the reference is to the "πίστις of Christ." The Heb. אֱמוּנָה, which lies behind πίστις in several key Pauline texts (e.g., Hab. 2:4, quoted in 1 Cor. 1:17 and Gal. 3:11), certainly often means "faithfulness," sometimes in combination with "faith."

16. Several passages where Paul uses a genitive after ἀγάπη are in dispute: e.g., does 2 Cor. 5:14 refer to "our love for Christ" (objective genitive) or "Christ's love for us" (subjective genitive); see also Rom. 5:5. The similar constructions in 1 Tim. 1:14 and 2 Tim. 1:13 — μετὰ πίστεως καὶ ἀγάπης τῆς ἐν Χριστοῦ Ἰησοῦ/ἐν πίστει καὶ ἀγάπῃ τῇ ἐν Χριστῷ Ἰησοῦ — could refer to "faith and love *in* [directed to] Christ Jesus"; but they might also mean "faith and love that we have in our union with Christ Jesus."

We think this interpretation is the more likely.[17] As we have seen, it matches the usual way Paul speaks of faith and love, and there are parallels in Paul to the way he expresses the matter here.[18]

Two other points about the verse deserve comment. First, TNIV's *his people* translates the Greek *hagious*, normally rendered in English as "saints." However, as we noted in our comments on Colossians 1:2, this familiar translation may obscure Paul's real intent. In modern English, "saints" is widely used to designate especially good or holy people, whereas Paul uses the word, against its Old Testament background, to refer simply to the people of God. Second, the unusual word order that Paul follows in this verse is probably due to his concern to highlight the love of Philemon. When Paul refers both to faith and love, he almost always puts the former first. The reversal of that order here not only explains the unusual chiastic order for which we have argued but also reflects the purpose of the letter.[19] Paul never again refers to Philemon's faith (although, of course, he takes it for granted), but he appeals twice more to Philemon's "love" as a way of motivating him to extend grace to Onesimus (vv. 7, 9).

6 This verse is universally recognized as the most difficult in Philemon. A glance at several English translations will reveal several key differences in interpretation. And these differences begin right with the opening words, reflecting different decisions about how the verse is to be related to its context. The conjunction that links the verse to the previous verses *(hopōs)* could indicate purpose or result. If we give the word this meaning, then v. 6 will indicate the purpose or result of Philemon's faith and love (v. 5; see KJV, NKJV).[20] But this connection does not make very good sense. Most of the versions, therefore, introduce the verb "pray" as a way of suggesting that v. 6 indicates the purpose or content of Paul's prayer in v. 4b (so, e.g., TNIV). The conjunction used here can certainly have this meaning, and this reading makes much better sense of the flow of thought.[21]

17. See also, e.g., BDF §477(1); Lightfoot, 334; Lohse, 193; Harris, 250; O'Brien, 278-79; Collange, 48-49; Fitzmyer, 96; Suhl, 27; Wolter, 253.
18. Paul uses the preposition πρός to express faith (πίστις) "toward" God in 1 Thess. 1:8; and he uses the preposition εἰς to speak of believers' love (ἀγαπή) in several texts (e.g., in Eph. 1:15, cited above). The small number of occurrences certainly does not constitute a pattern of usage in Paul; but perhaps rather than seeing the shift from πρός to εἰς as a pure stylistic variation (so Turner, *Syntax*, 256; Lohse, 193; O'Brien, 279; Dunn, 317-18), these examples may suggest a tendency that Paul follows here (Lightfoot, 325; Vincent, 179).
19. Bieder, 19.
20. Wolter, 253-54; Arzt-Grabner, 182.
21. ὅπως functions, just as ἵνα does, to indicate the purpose or content of a prayer (see esp. Acts 8:15; Jas. 5:16; BDAG; BDF §369[4]). Most commentators support this option; see, e.g., Lightfoot, 335; Moule, 142; O'Brien, 279; Fitzmyer, 96; also David L. Allen,

The diversity of translations reveals the difficulty of the next phrase. The two key words in the phrase, *koinōnia* (usually translated "fellowship") and *pistis* ("faith"), have a variety of meanings, and they can then be related to each other in different ways. Paul is the only New Testament writer who uses *koinōnia* in a theologically significant way.[22] It has at its root an active sense, referring to one's "participating in" or "sharing in" the realities of new covenant blessings or the "sharing with" other believers in those realities. Thus believers can be said to "share in" God's Son, Jesus Christ our Lord (1 Cor. 1:9), or in "his sufferings" (Phil. 3:10), or, through the eucharist, in the blood and body of Christ (1 Cor. 10:16). The opposite expression of this concept is Paul's concern that believers have no partnership with wickedness, which he illustrates by asking, "What fellowship can light have with darkness?" (2 Cor. 6:14). Paul can also refer to the Philippians' "partnership" with him in the gospel (Phil. 1:5). And this active sharing with other believers can take concrete form, in giving money to believers in need (Rom. 15:26; 2 Cor. 8:4; 9:13).[23] On two other occasions, Paul uses this word with reference to the Spirit, where it is not clear whether Paul refers to "our fellowship with the Spirit" or "our fellowship with others through the Spirit" (2 Cor. 13:14; Phil. 2:1). The second word in this construction, *pistis,* also normally has an active sense in Paul, referring to "the act of believing." But it can also sometimes have a passive sense, denoting "that which one believes," for example, the "Christian faith."[24] Once one decides on what each of these words means in this context, one must then also decide how they are related to each other (they are joined by the notoriously ambiguous genitive construction in Greek). Taking these variables into account and considering the context, four different interpretations appear to be reasonable options.

1. Paul could be praying that Philemon's participation with Paul, and/or other Christians, in the Christian faith, or in Christian ministry, or in the act of believing, might become effective. The difference between these options is in the meaning to be given to *pistis,* which can denote either "the faith that one believes," for example, "the Christian faith," or "the

---

"The Discourse Structure of Philemon: A Study in Textlinguistics," in *Scribes and Scripture: New Testament Essays in Honor of J. Harold Greenlee* (ed. David Alan Black; Winona Lake, Ind.: Eisenbrauns, 1992), 85.

22. It occurs only three times in the LXX and in Acts 2:42; Heb. 13:16; 1 John 1:3 (twice), 6, 7 outside Paul in biblical Greek.

23. Four of five occurrences of the cognate verb κοινωνέω in Paul have this active sense of "sharing [material things]" with others (Rom. 12:13; 15:27; Gal. 6:6; Phil. 4:15; cf. also 1 Tim. 5:22). The adjective κοινωνός refers, like the verb, to one who actively "participates in" something else (1 Cor. 10:18, 20; 2 Cor. 1:7; 8:23; Phlm. 17).

24. See our notes on Col. 2:7.

faith that one exercises." The TNIV appears to reflect the former interpretation — *I pray that your partnership with us in the faith may be effective* — and the NET the second: "I pray that the faith you share with us may deepen..." (perhaps also HCSB).[25] These two renderings agree on two crucial points: *koinōnia* expresses an active idea, referring to a participation or sharing in something; and the "faith" is the "object," the thing in which one participates. The difference, as we have noted, is in the particular sense of *pistis*. The NET rendering suggests that Paul is referring to the "act of believing" that Philemon shares with others: they are all, in effect, believers. The TNIV, on the other hand, suggests a reference to the Christian faith in general. But, it might also suggest, by using the word "partnership," that Paul is referring to Philemon's intimate participation with *Paul* (or perhaps Paul and Timothy). This specific interpretation finds some support in Paul's use of the cognate word *koinōnos* in v. 17 to denote his "partnership" with Philemon. If this more specific interpretation is what Paul intended, then he would already be hinting here at the request that he will be making later in the letter: Philemon's "partnership with Paul" will find concrete expression in his acceding to Paul's request about Onesimus.

2. Paul could be praying that Philemon's "sharing" of the Christian faith, or his personal believing, might be effective. See ESV: "I pray that the sharing of your faith may become effective ..." (so also RSV; NRSV; NIV). This option is very similar to the first, and it may be that the translations intend basically the same thing. But the choice of the English word "sharing" would tend to imply, for Christian readers at least, a reference to Philemon's evangelism. That this may be intended by these versions finds some confirmation in their relationship (direct or indirect) to the KJV, which translates here "communication of thy faith." Few interpreters support this reading,[26] mainly, no doubt, because it finds little support in Paul's use of the word *koinōnia*.

3. Paul could be praying that Philemon's fellowship with other believers, based on faith, might be effective. *Koinōnia*, as in the first two options, has the active sense of "participating in," but, in distinction from the first two views, "faith" is not the object of fellowship but the basis for it.[27]

25. This is the most popular option among the interpreters. Supporting the first reading are, e.g., Stuhlmacher, 33-34; Wolter, 254; Reinmuth, 30; Garland, 320; Thompson, 215; supporting the second are, e.g., Vincent, 180; Dunn, 318.
26. Although see Vincent, 179 and (perhaps) Fitzmyer, 97.
27. Wright, 175-76; Arzt-Grabner, 182; George Panikulam, *Koinōnia in the New Testament: A Dynamic Expression of Christian Life* (AnBib 85; Rome: Pontifical Biblical Institute, 1979), 88-89; I. H. Marshall, "The Theology of Philemon," in *The Theology of the Shorter Pauline Letters* (Cambridge: Cambridge University Press, 1993), 183. Wallace, *Greek Grammar*, 116, treats the genitive τῆς πίστεως as subjective.

The faith that Christians share produces a fellowship, or participation with one another, that Paul is praying might become effective in Philemon's case.

4. Paul could be praying that Philemon's "act of fellowship," or generosity, which stems from his believing, might be effective.[28] So, apparently, NLT: "I am praying that you will put into action the generosity that comes from your faith." As in view 3, "faith" is the basis for *koinōnia*, but, differing from all three views above, *koinōnia* is taken to refer specifically to a particular manifestation of fellowship, almsgiving — a sharing with or generosity toward others.

We begin our evaluation of these options with the last one. As we noted above, Paul uses *koinōnia* to refer to the "collection" for the believers in Jerusalem. However, even in these instances, the word refers not to the collection per se, but to the collection as an "act of fellowship." Dunn is, then, probably correct to argue that *koinōnia* always has an active sense in Paul,[29] and this consideration probably eliminates this fourth option. We have already suggested the second option is unlikely, so we are left with a choice between the first and the third. Here a decision is more difficult. But perhaps the third option better accounts for the prominence of the word *koinōnia* in this verse, especially in light of the overall argument of the letter. Paul could have prayed simply that Philemon's "faith" might become more effective. But, instead, he puts *koinōnia* in the key position. The word captures a central concern of the letter: to highlight the reality of the close and intimate "fellowship" that Christians enjoy with one another as a fundamental basis for the way we perceive ourselves and for the way that we are to respond to specific situations.[30] "Fellowship based on faith, or produced by faith," rather than "fellowship in faith" better captures this significance. This being the case, we think Wright's paraphrase of the phrase comes close to capturing its sense: "the mutual participation proper to your faith."[31] When people believe in Christ, they become identified with one another in an intimate association and incur both the benefits and responsibilities of that communion. Philemon is fundamentally all about those responsibilities, as Paul, Onesimus, and Philemon, bound together in faith, are forced by circumstances to think through the radical implications of their *koinōnia*.

28. Lightfoot, 335; Bruce, 208-9; Harris, 251; O'Brien, 280.
29. Dunn, 318.
30. See, esp. Wright, 175-76; J. Hainz, *EDNT* 3.304, who claims that κοινωνία is the "key to the total understanding of the letter"; and that "the letter is a concrete demonstration of what Paul understands by κοινωνία."
31. Wright, 176; and see esp. his *Climax of the Covenant* (Minneapolis: Fortress, 1992), 51-52.

Paul assumes, then, that Philemon exists in fellowship with other believers. His prayer is that that fellowship might *be effective in deepening your understanding of every good thing we share for the sake of Christ.* The TNIV reflects several key decisions about ambiguous Greek constructions and words. The first words are clear enough: "effective" is a good translation (adopted in most of the versions) for a Greek word that connotes activity and energy *(energēs).*[32] Paul undoubtedly thinks of Philemon's fellowship being activated in particular with reference to the matter of Onesimus that Paul writes about. But he does not say this, preferring to lay the groundwork for his request in more general terms. Here he speaks rather of a *deepening* of Philemon's *understanding.* These words in the TNIV translate a prepositional phrase, *en epignōsei,* "in knowledge." "Deepening" is an attempt to capture the relationship between "effective" and "knowledge" that is communicated by *en.* The sense seems to be that the effectiveness for which Paul prays "consists in" knowledge.[33] And, since Paul uses a compound rather than simple form of the Greek word for "knowledge," many interpreters argue that a "full" or "complete" knowledge is intended.[34] Hence the idea of "deepening understanding" (see also NET). But this compound word *(epignōsis)* probably refers, at least here, not to a "deeper" knowledge but to a practical, experiential knowledge: "to know is both to possess and to perform."[35] Paul wants Philemon to "understand and put into practice" *every good thing.* The expression is deliberately vague, referring broadly to all the "good" that Christians are called to do (see, e.g., Rom. 15:2; Gal. 6:10; 1 Thess. 5:15).[36] Again Paul deftly introduces a concept that will appear later and more

32. The word is rare in biblical Greek, occurring elsewhere only in 1 Cor. 16:9, where Paul uses it to describe a "door" for "effective work"; and in Heb. 4:12, in the famous reference to the word of God as "living" and "active."

33. Harris, 251. This is preferable to taking the ἐν as instrumental — "become effective through knowing" (HCSB) — or temporal — "become effective when you perceive" (NRSV).

34. See esp. Lightfoot, 336; O'Brien, 281. This meaning is not dependent on the fact that Paul uses the compound form ἐπίγνωσις. Modern lexicographers rightly warn against the tendency to assume that a compound form of a word in NT Greek must have a different and more "intense" meaning than the simple form of the word: as the language developed, prepositions added to the front of words that originally expressed emphasis tended to lose that emphasis. But there is good basis in Paul's use of ἐπίγνωσις (and γνῶσις) to conclude that he often uses the word with the sense of "experiential knowledge." See esp. Rom. 3:20, "knowledge of sin"; Eph. 1:17, "in knowing him [Christ]"; "knowledge of his will" (Col. 1:9); "knowledge of the truth" (1 Tim. 2:4; 2 Tim. 2:25; 3:7; Titus 1:1) (my translations). See also Rom. 1:28; 10:2; Eph. 4:13; Phil. 1:9; Col. 2:2; 3:10.

35. Lightfoot, 336.

36. O'Brien (280-81), on the other hand, suggests that it refers to all the blessings that Philemon should experience.

specifically in the letter: if Philemon does learn to do "every good thing" *(pantos agathou)*, he will be glad to comply with Paul's request that he do a specific "good thing" *(agathon)* (v. 14; "favor" in the TNIV). Paul qualifies "every good thing" with a prepositional phrase that might mean either "in us" (RSV; ESV; HCSB; NAB) or "among us" *(en hēmin)*.[37] The focus on fellowship in the verse makes the latter more likely, in which case it probably has the sense of "every good thing that we have" (NLT) or "share" (TNIV; cf. also RSV; NRSV).[38] The "us" may be confined to Paul and Philemon (see v. 17),[39] but probably it has reference to Christians generally.[40]

This difficult verse ends with yet one last ambiguity: Paul's prayer that Philemon learn to recognize and do "every good thing" is, finally, *eis Christon* ("unto Christ"). Paul's choice of preposition means that he probably does not mean simply "in Christ" (as NET and NLT translate),[41] though the phrase might have the sense of "incorporation into Christ."[42] Since Paul has referred already to faith and love in this context, some interpreters think it only natural that he might allude to hope, taking the phrase to mean "[as we look] toward Christ [at his return]."[43] Still others think the phrase means "for the glory of Christ" (HCSB).[44] But perhaps the general sense of direction or goal is the simplest and best option: "for the sake of Christ" (TNIV; ESV; NASB; cf. NRSV; NJB).[45]

We summarize our exegetical decisions in this verse in a paraphrase: "Philemon, I am praying that the mutual participation that arises from your faith in Christ might become effective in leading you to understand and put into practice all the good that God wills for us and that is found in our community; and do all this for the sake of Christ."

37. The pronoun ἡμῖν ("us") is replaced with ὑμῖν in a number of manuscripts, including the majority text (hence "in you" in KJV and NKJV). External support for ὑμῖν is strong (it is assumed also in NASB and NET), but most commentators think that it probably arose as an assimilation to the other second-person pronouns in the context (Metzger, *Textual Commentary*, 588).

38. Wolter, 254-55.

39. Wolter, 254.

40. Fitzmyer, 98.

41. Paul generally distinguishes between ἐν, which has a locative sense ("in"), and εἰς, which has a "directional" sense ("to," "toward," "for").

42. Bruce, 209; O'Brien, 281; Harris, 252-53.

43. Collange, 51; Suhl, 28; Stuhlmacher, 33. Note, e.g., Phil. 1:6, where Paul expresses his confidence that "he who began a good work in you will carry it on to completion until the day of Christ Jesus (ἄχρι ἡμέρας Χριστοῦ Ἰησοῦ)."

44. Vincent, 181; Lohse, 194-95.

45. Lightfoot, 336; Thompson, 215. Somewhat related is Moule's suggestion: "bringing us closer to Christ" (see NAB). Wright suggests that "Christ" (= "Messiah") might have a corporate sense, so the idea would be that we grow together "into the fullness of Christian fellowship" (*Climax of the Covenant*, 53-55).

7   As we have noted above, the formal thanksgiving section ends with v. 6. To it Paul now adds a personal note about his own experience of and appreciation of Philemon's love, connected to the previous context with a *gar* ("for" [e.g., ESV], untranslated in TNIV). The theme of love ties this verse back to v. 5, completing a chiasm: Philemon's love and faith (v. 5) — Philemon's faith (v. 6) — Philemon's love (v. 7). At the same time, the verse functions as a personal reflection on all of vv. 4-6.[46] But v. 7 also looks ahead: with its focus on Philemon's love and his refreshing of the "hearts" *(splanchna)* of believers, it lays further groundwork for the appeal that follows ("love" in v. 7; "heart" [*splanchna*] in vv. 12, 20).[47]

Paul has had *great joy and encouragement* because of Philemon's love.[48] The meaning of "joy" is clear enough, but the word translated "encouragement" in TNIV *(paraklēsis)* could also mean "comfort" (RSV; ESV; NASB; NLT).[49] In fact, the semantic range of the word encompasses both of these closely related ideas, tilting in some cases toward "comfort" (e.g., 2 Cor. 1:3, 4, 5, 6, 7) and in other texts toward "encouragement" (2 Thess. 2:16). Here perhaps the sense is closer to "encouragement," since "comfort" fits better a circumstance of difficulty or hurt — not in view here. The love that has brought encouragement and joy to Paul may have been expressed in Philemon's ministry,[50] although we cannot be certain about this.[51]

The TNIV, along with most of the English versions, by translating "because" (= *hoti*), suggests that the second part of the verse expresses the reason why Paul finds encouragement and joy on the basis of Philemon's love: *because you, brother, have refreshed the hearts of the Lord's people* (see also

46. Wolter, 255; similar is Wright, 178. Lightfoot (336), on the other hand, feels that the verse provides further motivation for Paul's thanksgiving in v. 4.

47. For the transitional character of the verse, see esp. Lohse, 192; O'Brien, 281. Paul's strong commendation of Philemon functions, to some extent, as a *captatio benevolentiae*, a rhetorical device used to flatter someone in the interests of gaining their adherence to a teaching or course of action (Ernst, 132; Wolter, 255).

48. In the Greek, Paul is the subject of this clause, with "joy" and "encouragement" as its objects. For reasons of English style, TNIV switches the subject and the object. The verb is ἔσχον, an aorist, which Fitzmyer, 99, takes as an epistolary aorist: "I have. . . ." The English translations are correct to assume that πολλήν ("great," "much") modifies both χαράν ("joy") and παράκλησιν ("encouragement") (Harris, 253).

49. The word is cognate to the word παράκλητος that occurs in the Farewell Discourse of John's Gospel, referring to the Holy Spirit (John 14:16, 26; 15:26; 16:7; cf. 1 John 2:1). A similar debate about the meaning of this word (complicated by background issues) rages over that word as well.

50. Dunn, 320-21.

51. In 2 Cor. 7:13, Paul uses three of the words that occur together here to refer to his own "encouragement" (παράκλησις) and to Titus's "joy" (χαρά) because his spirit was "refreshed" (ἀναπαύω) by the Corinthians.

NASB; RSV; NRSV; ESV). But this clause could also indicate the way in which Philemon's love has been manifested, an interpretation captured well in the NJB: "I have received much joy and encouragement by your love; you have set the hearts of God's holy people at rest."[52] As we have noted earlier, the Greek word translated "hearts" is an important one in Philemon. Three of Paul's eight references to the word occur in this short letter: Onesimus, says Paul, is his very "heart" (v. 12) and, as Philemon refreshes the hearts of God's people generally (v. 7), so Paul asks that he might refresh his own heart also (v. 20). The Greek word behind "heart" is *splanchna*, which has the physiological meaning "inward parts," "entrails" (hence KJV's "bowels") (see Acts 1:18), but which is generally used in the New Testament (as well as in Greek generally) in an extended sense to connote the "seat of the emotions." It can also refer to the expression of deep love or sympathy that comes from the inner being (see Col. 3:12), but in Philemon it has the former sense, "the total personality at the deepest level."[53] Paul uses this word to stress that Philemon's love had "refreshed" the people of God at the deepest and most significant level of their being. Some interpreters think that Paul may be referring to one particular act of kindness on Philemon's part.[54] But this is not clear, and it is perhaps more likely that he reflects on the lasting effects of Philemon's ministry over a period of time.[55] "Refresh" translates a word that Paul uses elsewhere in a very similar sense, to refer to the heartening and encouraging effect that effective ministry has on people (1 Cor. 16:18; 2 Cor. 7:13).[56] Many ministries can appear to be successful but have, in fact, only a superficial and therefore very temporary impact on believers. Philemon's influence was not like that. The TNIV, for reasons of English style, puts the address "brother" at the beginning of the second clause in the verse. In fact, however, Paul puts this word at the end of the verse, perhaps for emphasis. While he uses the plural *adelphoi* ("brothers and sisters") very frequently to address believers, he uses the singular form to address believers only here and in v. 20 — yet another indication of the way in which this transitional verse paves the way for the appeal to follow.

---

52. O'Brien, 282.

53. H. Köster, *TDNT* 7.555; cf. also BDAG.

54. E.g., Lohse, 195, who thinks that the perfect form of the verb ἀναπέπαυται points in this direction.

55. Contra Lohse (see the previous note), the perfect may simply draw attention to the continuing effects of Philemon's ministry.

56. The verb is ἀναπαύω, which also means "rest on" (1 Pet. 4:14) or "rest (from physical labor)," "be drowsy" (Matt. 26:45; Mark 6:31; 14:41; Luke 12:19; Rev. 6:11; 14:13). The word has a similar meaning in Jesus' famous saying: "Come to me, all you who are weary and burdened, and I will give you rest (ἀναπαύσω)."

III. THE LETTER BODY: PAUL'S APPEAL
CONCERNING ONESIMUS (vv. 8-20)

[8]Therefore, although in Christ I could be bold and order you to do what you ought to do, [9]yet I prefer to appeal to you on the basis of love. It is as none other than Paul — an old man and now also a prisoner of Christ Jesus — [10]that I appeal to you for my son Onesimus, who became my son while I was in chains. [11]Formerly he was useless to you, but now he has become useful both to you and to me.

[12]I am sending him — who is my very heart — back to you. [13]I would have liked to keep him with me so that he could take your place in helping me while I am in chains for the gospel. [14]But I did not want to do anything without your consent, so that any favor you do would not seem forced but would be voluntary. [15]Perhaps the reason he was separated from you for a little while was that you might have him back forever — [16]no longer as a slave, but better than a slave, as a dear brother. He is very dear to me but even dearer to you, both as a fellow man and as a brother in the Lord.

[17]So if you consider me a partner, welcome him as you would welcome me. [18]If he has done you any wrong or owes you anything, charge it to me. [19]I, Paul, am writing this with my own hand. I will pay it back — not to mention that you owe me your very self. [20]I do wish, brother, that I may have some benefit from you in the Lord; refresh my heart in Christ.

Most interpreters agree that the body of the letter to Philemon begins at v. 8.[1] The "therefore" *(dio)* signals a transition from the opening elements of salutation, address, greeting, and thanksgiving to the central concern of the letter. Where the transition from the body of the letter to its closing occurs is more difficult to decide. The TNIV suggests that this break comes at the end of v. 22, by inserting a major break between vv. 22 and 23 (see also ESV; HCSB; NLT).[2] Others think that that the body of the letter ends with Paul's expression of confidence in Philemon in v. 21 (see NJB; NRSV).[3] Still others think that Paul's direct appeal to "welcome"

1. White, however, thinks a break occurs between vv. 6 and 7 and concludes that vv. 7-22 make up the "body" of the letter (John L. White, "The Structural Analysis of Philemon: A Point of Departure in the Formal Analysis of the Pauline Letter" [*SBLSP*; Missoula, Mont.: Society of Biblical Literature, 1971], 26; see also Binder/Rohde, 51-52). John Banker (*A Semantic and Structural Analysis of Philemon* [Dallas: Summer Institute of Linguistics, 1990], 14) takes vv. 4-22 to be the letter body.

2. See Wright, 178-79; I. H. Marshall, "The Theology of Philemon," in *The Theology of the Shorter Pauline Letters* (Cambridge: Cambridge University Press, 1993), 180; C.-H. Kim, *Form and Function of the Greek Letter of Recommendation* (SBLDS 4; Missoula, Mont.: Scholars Press, 1972), 124.

3. Wolter, 256-57.

Onesimus in v. 17 marks the end of the body.[4] But the majority of commentators place a major break between vv. 20 and 21, and this seems to be the best option.[5] Verse 21, which in the Greek is not formally connected to v. 20 and repeats the verb "write" from v. 19, seems to be a bit of a new beginning. Moreover, this verse picks up two key terms from the end of the letter opening: "brother" and "refresh the heart" (see v. 7). These verses, then, provide something of a frame around the body of the letter.

The heart of the letter body is Paul's "appeal" for Onesimus (v. 10). Paul, however, does not spell out the specifics of his appeal explicitly until v. 17, where he asks Philemon to "welcome" Onesimus. Paul delays this specific request until then because he is pursuing a rhetorical strategy of persuasion. Paul wants to persuade Philemon to act on his own, without compulsion (v. 14), on the basis of love rather than because Paul commands it (vv. 8-9). Paul's means of persuasion focus on three relationships:

(1) Paul's relationship to Onesimus. Onesimus has become a Christian through Paul's ministry (v. 10) and is proving "useful" (v. 11) to Paul in his imprisonment (v. 13). But, more than that, he is Paul's "dear brother" (v. 16), his "son" (v. 10), his "very heart" (v. 12).

(2) Paul's relationship to Philemon. Philemon has also become a Christian through Paul (v. 19) and is a "partner" with him in ministry (17; see also vv. 2 and 6). Significantly, Paul does not appeal to his status as an "apostle" in talking about his relationship to Philemon. Rather, he refers to himself in a remarkable series of personal references designed to win Philemon's sympathy: "an old man" (v. 10), a "prisoner" (v. 9), "in chains" (vv. 10, 13), a "partner" (v. 17), and a "brother" (v. 20).

(3) Philemon's relationship to Onesimus. For whatever reason, Onesimus had been "useless" to Philemon in the past (v. 11); in fact, in some manner, it would appear, he had defrauded Philemon (v. 18). Now, however, he is "useful" to Philemon as well as to Paul (v. 11). Most importantly, as one who, like Philemon, has been "fathered" by Paul, he is now Philemon's "brother in the Lord" and therefore very dear to him (v. 16).

These relationships, of course, flow from the fundamental fact that each of these men has a relationship with Jesus Christ, and this relationship brings them into intimate fellowship as members of a spiritual family

---

4. Lightfoot, 337; Arzt-Grabner, 190-91. J. A. D. Weima (*Neglected Endings* [Sheffield: JSOT Press, 1994], 230-32), on the other hand, thinks that the body ends with v. 18, while Church, analyzing the letter in terms of Greco-Roman "deliberative rhetoric," views vv. 8-16 as the "proof" (F. F. Church, "Rhetorical Structure and Design in Paul's Letter to Philemon," *HTR* 71 [1978], 21-23; see also D. A. Allen, "The Discourse Structure of Philemon," in *Scribes and Scripture* [Winona Lake: Eisenbrauns, 1992], 87; Bartchy, *ABD* 5.305).

5. E.g., O'Brien, 284; Dunn, 324, 343; Stuhlmacher, 36; Wilson, 362.

(see v. 6). It is this fellowship built on faith that provides the fundamental theological grounding for Paul's appeal to Philemon. This fellowship brings great blessing; it also imposes obligations. Paul has an obligation to treat his brother and fellow worker Philemon with love and respect. Onesimus has an obligation to defer to his master Philemon. And, though Paul is cautious about spelling it out, the central thrust of this letter is that Philemon also has an obligation: to recognize that his Christian family constitutes a far more fundamental consideration than the worldly relationships of household or society and that he must govern his attitude and actions toward Onesimus on the basis of this spiritual relationship.

Paul interweaves references to these three relationships throughout the body of the letter, and attempts to discern a sequence or structure based on one or another of these relationships are not convincing.[6] Paul is attempting to persuade Philemon to take a certain course of action.[7] And because this course of action might not be easy for Philemon to take and because it might even be objected that Paul has no right to ask it of Philemon, Paul proceeds cautiously and indirectly. He does not come right out and make clear what he wants Philemon to do. He builds up to his request, waiting to make it explicit until v. 17. (And even then, as we will see, it might be that he has left unstated his ultimate request.) With these rhetorical considerations in view, then, we may tentatively suggest a division of the body of the letter into three basic parts: vv. 8-14, vv. 15-16, and vv. 17-20.

The first section, vv. 8-14, is marked by an *inclusio*. In both vv. 8-9 and v. 14 Paul refers to the basis on which he wants Philemon to act: not because Paul commands it (v. 8), so that Philemon feels "forced" (v. 14), but out of love (v. 9), as a voluntary act (v. 14). In both parts of this *inclusio* Paul also makes clear that Philemon is, in fact, going to be presented with a course of action that he must choose: there is something he "ought to do" (v. 8), a "favor," or "good thing" (v. 14), that Paul is going to request. That this favor has something to do with Onesimus Paul also makes clear (v. 10). In vv. 10b-13, then, Paul does three things that contribute to his appeal. First, he explains the circumstances that have led to the appeal: Onesimus has come into contact with Paul (implied); Onesimus has been converted through Paul (v. 10); Paul is sending Onesimus back to Philemon (v. 12). Second, he puts pressure on Philemon by reminding him of his difficult circumstances (an "old man" [v. 9], a prisoner [vv. 9, 10, 13]). Third, he puts further pressure on Philemon by making it clear

---

6. Contra, e.g., Wolter, 257; Wright, 178-19; Collange, 24.

7. The letter may, then, be broadly considered a species of what ancient authors labeled "deliberative" rhetoric (see, e.g., Church, "Rhetorical Structure").

that he, Paul, is having to do something difficult himself: send back to Philemon one who is his "very heart" (v. 12) and who promises to be very helpful to Paul (v. 13).

In vv. 15-16, Paul takes his argument to the next level. He suggests that the circumstances he has just narrated might have a divine purpose: to bring Onesimus and Philemon together forever as brothers in Christ.

Finally, then, in vv. 17-20, Paul tells Philemon explicitly what he wants him to do: "welcome" Onesimus (v. 17). He concludes the body by adding powerful personal reasons for Philemon to respond as he asks (vv. 18-20).[8]

This basic outline reflects the structural clues found in the Greek text, which we might (overly literally) set out as follows:

> "Therefore" (dio; cf. vv. 4-7), I "appeal" (parakalō) to you on the basis of love (vv. 8-9)
> > "I appeal" (parakalō) to you for Onesimus (v. 10a)
> > "whom" (hon) I gave birth to (v. 10b)
> > > that is, the one who was formerly useless but is now useful (v. 11)
> > "whom" (hon) I am sending back to you (v. 12)
> > "whom" (hon) I wish I could keep with me (v. 13)
> Now (de) I want you to respond voluntarily (v. 14)

> For (gar) the purpose behind Onesimus's story is that you might be together forever, as brothers (vv. 15-16)

> Therefore (oun) welcome him (v. 17)
> > And (de) I will repay any debts he owes (v. 18)
> > I guarantee what I say with my own signature (v. 19)
> > Truly (nai), brother, "refresh my heart" (cf. v. 7) (v. 20)

8 Paul marks the transition from the letter's thanksgiving (vv. 4-7) to its body (vv. 8-20) with a "therefore" (dio). This word might function to indicate the general relationship of these two sections of the letter. Paul would, in effect, be saying: Philemon, because you are a dear friend and fellow worker (v. 1), and because you have shown in your ministry the quality of your faith and love (vv. 4-5, 7), and because you understand the fellowship with me and others created by your faith (v. 6), "therefore" I

---

8. Our proposal bears some resemblance to the chiastic structure discerned by John Paul Heil, "The Chiastic Structure and Meaning of Paul's Letter to Philemon," Bib 82 (2001), 178-206.

appeal to you for Onesimus (v. 10). On this view, "therefore" in v. 8 would go with "appeal" in v. 10, with vv. 8b-9 being something of a parenthesis.[9] But the syntactical structure of vv. 8-9 suggests rather that the "therefore" functions more specifically, connecting the focus on Philemon's love in vv. 4-7 (and esp. v. 7) with Paul's decision to base his appeal to Philemon on that love (vv. 8-9). Paul's concern about the manner of his appeal surfaces again in this paragraph (v. 14), showing that it is more than an incidental point for him. He emphasizes the point here by way of a contrast: *although in Christ I could be bold and order you to do what you ought to do, yet I prefer to appeal to you on the basis of love.*[10] The contrast is between Paul's apostolic authority and what we might call the "moral" authority arising from the *koinōnia* that exists between Paul and Philemon (v. 6). Our relationships to one another in Christ create expectations and impose obligations that cannot be ignored and that often go far beyond what any "law" might impose. Love is foundational to Christian ethics (e.g., Rom. 13:8-10; Gal. 5:13-15) and makes Christian ethics something that is open-ended, incalculable (as Jesus' Parable of the Good Samaritan illustrates).

In v. 8, then, Paul reminds Philemon of the authority that he could have used in addressing him but that he has chosen to set aside. The adjective "bold" in the TNIV translates a Greek noun, *parrēsia*.[11] This word is formed from Greek words that mean "full speech," and it was used by the Greeks to refer to the rights of people in a democracy openly to express their opinion. This meaning of the word — "openness" — carries over into the New Testament, as, for instance, Jesus' words in John 18:20a illustrate: "I have spoken openly (with *parrēsia*) to the world."[12] But the idea of "openness" in speech easily morphs into the idea of having the

9. Wolter, 258-59. Some basis for this reading of vv. 8-9 might be found in the absolute use of παρακαλῶ in v. 9. When Paul uses this verb in the active mood to mean "exhort," he usually follows it with an object indicating who is being exhorted. This might suggest that Paul intended to complete the verb in v. 9 with σε, "you," but interjected a parenthetical comment instead, requiring him to repeat the verb with its object in v. 10. The force of this argument is blunted, however, by the fact that Paul does use παρακαλέω in the active mood to mean "exhort" without an object (Rom. 12:8[?]; 1 Cor. 4:13; 2 Cor. 5:20; 1 Tim. 2:1; 2 Tim. 4:2).

10. The "although" clause (v. 8) translates a Greek participial clause — ἔχων . . . — the participle being universally recognized (on the basis of the logic of the sentence) as having concessive force (hence the "although" in all the English translations).

11. This change from Greek noun to English adjective arises from the decision to reflect in English the concessive force of the participle ἔχων. "Although I have boldness" is possible in English (e.g., HCSB; NET, etc.), but it is not as natural as "although I could be bold."

12. The word has this meaning eight other times in John's Gospel (7:4, 13, 26; 10:24; 11:14, 54; 16:25, 29) and once in Mark (8:32). See also Col. 2:15, where Paul speaks of the "public" manifestation of God's victory in Christ over the powers and authorities.

"confidence" or "boldness" to speak out. Luke accordingly refers to the early Christians having the *parrēsia* to proclaim the word of God (Acts 2:29; 4:13, 29, 31; 28:31). Here in Philemon 8, some interpreters think that the word has more the former sense, referring to Paul's sense of "openness" because of his fellowship with Philemon.[13] However, while no neat line between the meanings "boldness" and "openness" can be drawn, Paul's use of the word tends toward the former idea. It is because he has a hope grounded in the glory of new covenant ministry that he has the right and courage to be "very bold" (2 Cor. 3:12; see also Eph. 6:19; Phil. 1:20). We therefore believe that the word here hints at the "boldness" or "confidence" that Paul possesses because of his apostolic status.[14] It is "in Christ," that is, in light of who he is in his union with Christ, that he possesses the boldness that would enable him to *order* or "command" Philemon. Paul nowhere else uses the Greek word for "command" that we have here (*epitassō*), but he does use other Greek words to refer to his apostolic "commanding" authority (e.g., *parangellō* in 2 Thess. 3:4, 6, 10, 12; cf. 1 Tim. 4:11; 5:7). Paul could, then, use his apostolic rights to command Philemon to "do what he ought to do." The language Paul uses here is, as the English translations make clear, quite general and undefined[15] — reflecting Paul's hesitancy throughout the body of the letter to spell out what he wants of Philemon. But it does make clear that there is some action that is the "proper" or "fitting" thing for Philemon to do in this situation. Philemon's status as a Christian and "brother" of Paul means that he has an obligation to act in a certain way.[16]

9 But this obligation is not something that Paul will impose on Philemon as a command; rather, he appeals to Philemon *on the basis of love*. *Appeal* is a good rendering here for the verb *parakaleō*. This verb often has the stronger sense "exhort" (on the basis of apostolic authority) in Paul, but the context of Philemon suggests the milder translation, adopted in most of the English versions.[17] The delicacy of the situation explains the way in which Paul broaches the matter of this "appeal." Before he even indicates what, in general, the appeal is about (v. 10) — far less indicating just what it is that he wants of Philemon — Paul indicates that what he is going to ask will only be given on the basis of love. This

---

13. See esp. O'Brien, 287-88; Dunn, 325; Gnilka, 41.

14. So most commentators; see, e.g., Lohse, 198; Ernst, 133; Stuhlmacher, 36-37.

15. The Greek is τὸ ἀνῆκον, "what is fitting, proper." The verb ἀνήκω is rare in the NT, used only by Paul here and in Eph. 5:4 and Col. 3:18.

16. Wright, 180. O'Brien (288) is correct to emphasize that the obligation is not a "legal" one (contra H. Schlier, *TDNT* 1.360: "almost legally obligatory"), but one that arises from the context of his Christian commitment (see also Fitzmyer, 104).

17. BDAG suggest the translations "request," "implore," "entreat."

"love," in context, of course, might well refer to Philemon's own proven love for God's people (v. 7; cf. NJB, "your love").[18] Yet the omission of any personal pronoun in the Greek text might suggest that Paul refers more broadly to Christian love in general (cf. NLT, "our love").[19] Paul's reason for making love rather than a command the basis for Philemon's action is, as v. 14 makes clear, that he wants Philemon to act of his own free will. But it must also be said that the nature of Paul's appeal hardly lets Philemon "off the hook." Indeed, by appealing to Philemon on the basis of love, Paul raises the stakes and puts even greater pressure on Philemon. Obeying a command may be onerous, but it is rather straight-forward and can be accomplished grudgingly. But Paul puts the ball into Philemon's court: he is, in effect, testing the depths of Philemon's love and the extent of his understanding of Christian fellowship. He must not only do what Paul wants him to do; he must do it for the right reasons. And the pressure on Philemon is all the greater when we remember that this appeal is being heard by his entire house church (see v. 2).

Paul continues with this subtle but unmistakable pressure in the second part of v. 9 by reminding Philemon of who he is: *It is as none other than Paul — an old man and now also a prisoner of Christ Jesus.* The way in which this reference to himself fits into its context is not clear. There are three main options, represented clearly in, respectively, TNIV, ESV, and NJB:

(1) TNIV: "I prefer to appeal to you on the basis of love. It is as none other than Paul — an old man and now also a prisoner of Christ Jesus — that I appeal to you for my son Onesimus" (see also HCSB). This way of punctuating the verses (the original MSS, of course, have little or no punctuation) reflects the decision to make "Paul" the subject of the following "I appeal" (in v. 10) and to treat the references to Paul being an "old man" and "prisoner" as parenthetical.

(2) ESV: "for love's sake I prefer to appeal to you — I, Paul, an old man and now a prisoner also for Christ Jesus — I appeal to you for my child, Onesimus" (see also RSV; NASB; NET). On this reading of the syntax, the entire clause containing both the name Paul and the characterizations of him is a parenthesis that interrupts the flow of thought. Paul begins to speak of his "appeal" only to pause to remind Philemon of the one making the appeal before resuming the syntax with the repetition of "I appeal."

18. Harris, 259; O'Brien, 289.

19. Lightfoot, 336; Lohse, 198. The article with ἀγάπη could, of course, indicate anaphora/possession — the love of Philemon that I have already mentioned — but it could also serve to "tighten up" the sense of love by focusing on Christian love in particular (see Wallace, *Greek Grammar*, 226-27 for this general idea).

(3) NJB: "I am rather appealing to your love, being what I am, Paul, an old man, and now also a prisoner of Christ Jesus. I am appealing to you for a child of mine" (see also KJV; NKJV; NAB; NLT). This reading of the verses is similar to the second, with the difference that the reference to Paul is attached syntactically to the first "I appeal" verb in v. 9.[20]

The Greek syntax makes it likely that the clause depends on the first "I appeal" (as in view 3). But the repetition of "I appeal" also suggests that Paul views the clause as an interruption in the syntax.[21] The second punctuation best captures this sequence.

Paul's intention in this parenthesis is clear enough. The Greek construction he uses to introduce the clause highlights his intention to remind Philemon of just who he is: *It is as none other than Paul* (TNIV); "since I am such a person as Paul" (NASB).[22] The name "Paul" itself would have considerable force for Philemon, since Paul was instrumental in his conversion (v. 19) and is his "partner" (v. 17), "brother" (vv. 7-20), and "fellow worker" (v. 2). But Paul adds to the emotional impact of his self-reference by reminding Philemon that he is also an *old man* and a *prisoner*. It is, however, possible that Paul calls himself here not an "old man" but an "ambassador." This possibility, although reflected only in the RSV among the English translations, is, in fact, widely supported in the literature.[23] The possibility of translating "ambassador" here is argued by some on the grounds of a textual emendation. The Greek text in all extant manuscripts of Philemon has *presbytēs*, "old man." But the word for "ambassador" differs from this word only in one vowel — *presbeutēs* — and so it is thought that the former has inadvertently been substituted for the latter. Such an emendation, however, is unlikely;[24] and most interpreters who defend "ambassabor" here do so on strictly lexical grounds, arguing

---

20. This is the punctuation adopted in NA[27]; and see Lightfoot, 338; Harris, 260; O'Brien, 289. Wright (181) suggests that the clause functions to elaborate "love," the emphasis being on the final words, "Christ Jesus," which he thinks allude to Christ's self-sacrificial giving. But the latter notion reads a lot into "Christ Jesus."

21. The verb in the clause is the participle ὤν, which is most naturally taken as adverbial and dependent on the preceding παρακαλῶ ("I appeal").

22. The Greek is τοιοῦτος ὢν ὡς Παῦλος, literally translated as "being such a one as Paul." But the ὡς following τοιοῦτος has the sense of "in my character as" (BDAG; they translate the phrase "since I am the sort of person").

23. Lightfoot, 339; Moule, 144; Bruce, 212; O'Brien, 290; Harris, 259-60; Wright, 180; Stuhlmacher, 37-38; Suhl, 31; Barth/Blanke, 321-23; N. R. Petersen, *Rediscovering Paul* (Philadelphia: Fortress, 1985), 125-28.

24. See esp. J. N. Birdsall, "Πρεσβύτης in Philemon 9: A Study in Conjectural Emendation," *NTS* 39 (1993), 627-28.

that the word *presbytēs* can have this meaning. And they think that this is the likely meaning here, for two reasons. First, it fits with the parallel in Ephesians 6:19a-20: "Pray also for me, that whenever I speak, words may be given me so that I will fearlessly make known the mystery of the gospel, for which I am an ambassador in chains." And, second, it suits the context, since the "now" and the parallel in v. 11 — "formerly useless . . . but now . . . useful" suggests that Paul intends to contrast *presbytēs* and "prisoner." An "ambassador" but "now" a prisoner creates such a contrast; an "old man" and "now" a prisoner does not.[25]

We do not, however, find the case for "ambassador" to be convincing. First, the evidence for thinking that the word can mean "ambassador" is, at best, very slim.[26] We would need very strong contextual reasons, indeed, to entertain this meaning here. But these reasons are not forthcoming. The parallel with v. 11 is not necessarily apropos, since the construction is different, and there is no reason why Paul should intend the same kind of contrast.[27] Positively, a reference to Paul's old age fits the rhetoric of Philemon better than "ambassador" would. For, as we have seen, Paul appeals to Philemon not on the basis of his authority (cf. v. 8; and the omission of "apostle" in v. 1), but on the basis of their personal relationship.[28] Paul may therefore calculate that he would gain Philemon's sympathy by reminding him that he was an old man. Another possibility has been suggested by Hock. He notes that old age in Greco-Roman society often was associated with helplessness and the consequent need for family members to provide for their elders. Paul has

25. See esp. Petersen, *Rediscovering Paul*, 125-28. It is also argued that the participle ὤν, like ἔχων in v. 8, must be concessive; and, again, it is only the meaning "ambassador" that makes sense in a concessive relationship (U. Wickert, "Der Philemonbrief — Privatbrief oder apostolisches Schreiben?" *ZNW* 52 [1961], 233-35).

26. The standard Greek lexicon, BDAG, does not list this meaning for πρεσβύτης, and, of the texts usually cited to confirm this meaning (2 Chr. 32:31 [in B]; 1 Macc. 14:22 [in ℵ]; 15:17 [in ℵ]; 2 Macc. 11:34), three are uncertain because the case rests on the substitution of this word in some MSS (where the question of whether the intended meaning is the same arises). On the other hand, the word is used over forty-five times in the LXX and in its two other NT occurrences (Luke 1:18; Titus 2:2) with the meaning "old man." Lightfoot and others have also cited places where the words πρεσβύτης and πρεσβυτής are substituted for one another in manuscripts. But the confusion of these two is, in fact, fairly rare (Ronald F. Hock, "A Support for His Old Age: Paul's Plea on Behalf of Onesimus," in *The Social World of the First Christians: Essays in Honor of Wayne A. Meeks* [ed. L. Michael White and O. Larry Yarbrough; Minneapolis: Fortress, 1995], 73).

27. In v. 11, a clear contrast is established by the collocation of ποτέ — "formerly" — and νυνί — "now." Verse 9 lacks the ποτέ, and νυνί on its own, while retaining its normal temporal sense, could have an ascensive force. See TNIV: "an old man and now also a prisoner."

28. Lohse, 199; Fitzmyer, 106.

found in Onesimus a "son" to help him in his defenseless condition (v. 10), and so it would be natural for him to appeal to his age as a reason why he does not want to send Onesimus back to Philemon (v. 13).[29] "Old man," then, on both lexical and contextual grounds, is a better translation than "ambassador."[30] The word is appropriately applied to Paul at this point in his life, since it often indicated an age of between 50 and 56.[31]

Paul reinforces this personal appeal to Philemon by reminding him that he is doubly helpless: not only an old man, but an imprisoned old man.[32] Three times in this context Paul mentions his status as a prisoner (also vv. 10, 13), not only, perhaps, to stress his helpless condition but also, perhaps, as an ironical contrast to the freedom that he wishes for Onesimus.[33]

10 As we have seen, Paul approaches the actual content of his appeal to Philemon cautiously, first indicating the manner of that appeal — on the basis of love rather than command (vv. 8-9a) — and then reminding Philemon of the circumstances in which he makes the appeal (v. 9b). Only now does he indicate just what the appeal is about. "I appeal" (*parakalō*) repeats the verb that Paul has already used in v. 9a, the repetition being required after the parenthesis about Paul's circumstances in v. 9b. The TNIV translates, *I appeal to you for my son Onesimus;* and most other versions are similar. But this translation masks three issues in the Greek text that deserve comment. First, in saying that he is appealing "for" Onesimus, Paul does not mean that he is directly asking for Onesimus to be restored to him (a meaning that the English "appeal for" could convey). To be sure, a few interpreters have thought that this is exactly what Paul intends here,[34] but the Greek simply cannot bear this meaning.[35] The "for" indicates, in a general manner, the content or focus

29. Hock, "A Support for His Old Age," 77-79.

30. The tendency among recent interpreters is to adopt the meaning "old men" (see, e.g., Dunn, 322; Reinmuth, 36-37; Wilson, 348; Gnilka, 43; Wolter, 261; Fitzmyer, 105). There is no need to think that Paul is saying the same thing here that he is in the very different context of Eph. 6:20.

31. See Philo, *On the Creation of the World* 105; BDAG.

32. "Prisoner" (δέσμιος) is almost certainly literal (though M. J. Harris, *Slave of Christ* [Downers Grove, Ill.; InterVarsity, 2001], 118, suggests that it might here be both literal and figurative; cf. also Vincent, who paraphrases δέσμιος Χριστοῦ Ἰησοῦ "one whom Christ brought into captivity").

33. Ernst, 133.

34. J. Knox, *Philemon among the Letters of Paul* (London: Collins, 1960), 19-20; S. C. Winter, "Paul's Letter to Philemon," *NTS* 33 (1987), 6; W. Schenk, "Der Brief des Paulus an Philemon," *ANRW* (1987), 3466; Bruce, 212-13.

35. The combination παρακαλέω plus περί never, apparently, introduces the actual appeal but refers to the issue or person "concerning which" the appeal is being made (see

of Paul's appeal (see NET: "I am appealing to you concerning my child") or, perhaps, the one on whose behalf the request is being made (NAB: "I urge you on behalf of my child Onesimus").[36] Second, TNIV's *son* translates a word that generically means "child" (*teknon;* cf. most other versions). Paul prefers to use this word to depict his relationship to beloved associates, so it is no surprise that he uses it here of Onesimus.[37] Third, the TNIV translation "my son Onesimus" also conceals the fact that the name Onesimus is withheld until the very end of the verse.[38] A few English versions retain this sequence; see, for example, HCSB: "I appeal to you for my child, whom I fathered while in chains — Onesimus" (see also NET; NJB). Paul is not, of course, concealing anything from Philemon or the others who are listening to the letter; Onesimus is there among them as the letter is being read! But it is nevertheless rhetorically effective for Paul to characterize Onesimus first as his "son," and then describe the manner in which he became his son before actually naming him.[39]

The name Onesimus, which means "useful" (see v. 11), was a common one, especially often given to slaves in the hope that they would live up to their name.[40] The TNIV's *became my son* translates a Greek verb (*gennaō*) that means "give birth to" (when the focus is on the mother's role) or, more generally, "beget" or "become the parent of" (when the focus is on the father's role; cf. HCSB: "whom I fathered").[41] The imagery of giving birth was used in a variety of ancient traditions to connote conversion to a new way of life. The rabbis described a convert to Judaism as a "child just born."[42] Paul frequently speaks of converts as his "children" (1 Cor. 4:14, 17; Gal. 4:19) and describes his role in people's conversion

---

esp. Arzt-Grabner, 101-2; and almost all the commentators [e.g., O'Brien, 290; Dunn, 328; Fitzmyer, 106]). Paul does not elsewhere use this combination; but he consistently states the content of his "exhortations" or "appeals" with an infinitive or ἵνα plus subjunctive.

36. For this latter sense, see esp. Harris, 261, who notes the overlap between περί ("concerning") and ὑπέρ ("on behalf of").

37. For instance, Paul calls Timothy his τέκνον six times (1 Cor. 4:17; Phil. 2:22; 1 Tim. 1:2, 18; 2 Tim. 1:2; 2:1) but never his υἱός.

38. The name, or at least person, of Onesimus is already in Paul's mind, however, as is seen in his use of a masculine relative pronoun (ὅν) after the neuter word τέκνον ("child"). This "construction according to the sense," according to which the relative pronoun refers to natural rather than grammatical gender, is common (Wallace, *Greek Grammar*, 337; see also BDF §294).

39. Harris, 261.

40. *New Docs* 4.179-81.

41. In the former sense, see, e.g., Luke 1:57: "When it was time for Elizabeth to have her baby, she gave birth to (ἐγέννησεν) a son"; in the latter, Acts 7:29: "When Moses heard this, he fled to Midian, where he settled as a foreigner and had (ἐγέννησεν) two sons."

42. *b. Yebamot* 22a. See David Daube, "Onesimus," *HTR* 79 (1986), 40-41.

with birth imagery (1 Thess. 2:7; cf. Gal. 4:19, where the imagery is applied to Christian maturation). And, again in imitation of Jewish tradition, he refers to younger men who are working with him in ministry as his "sons" (e.g., Phil. 2:22; 1 Tim. 1:2; 2 Tim. 1:2; Titus 1:4). The context here, with its explicit mention of Paul's role in "fathering" Onesimus, makes clear that it is Onesimus as convert rather than as younger fellow worker that is uppermost in Paul's mind.

We can only speculate about the circumstances that would have brought Onesimus into contact with Paul, who was at this point *in chains*. As we have argued, Philemon was probably written while Paul was in custody in Rome, living in his own quarters and able to receive visitors. Whether Onesimus as a runaway slave ran into Paul by "accident" or whether he sought him out to act as intercessor with Philemon is impossible to say. In either case, as Paul hints at rather clearly in v. 15, Onesimus's encounter with Paul was providential. Calling Onesimus Paul's son obviously touches on the close relationship between the two and provides emotional grounds for Paul's appeal to Philemon. But the emphasis here falls on Onesimus's new status as one who, by God's grace and through the ministry of Paul, belongs to the "new creation" (2 Cor. 5:17; Gal. 6:15).[43] Paul is saying to Philemon, in effect, that his appeal is not for the Onesimus whom Philemon has known in the past but for a new Onesimus, one who has been "born again" (see John 3:3, 5, 7; cf. 1 John 2:29; 3:9; 4:7; 5:1, 4, 18).

11 Most English translations (like the TNIV) punctuate v. 11 as a new sentence, but in the Greek this description of the change in Onesimus's character is syntactically dependent on the name Onesimus at the end of v. 10: "Onesimus, the one who . . ." (see NAB; NASB; NET). This description is a bit of an add-on (it is treated as a parenthesis in RSV; ESV). But the point is one that Paul obviously feels is important: Onesimus's new birth has transformed his character. Paul indicates this transformation with a wordplay that was rather common in the ancient world: Onesimus is no longer *achrēstos* but is now *euchrēstos*. Fortunately, the wordplay is easy to preserve in English: "useless"/"useful" (most versions); "unprofitable"/"profitable" (KJV; NKJV). Almost all the commentaries refer to Lightfoot's marshalling of evidence to suggest that slaves from Phrygia (where Colossae was located) had a bad reputation.[44] The conclusion may be justified, although it would be easy to overinterpret casual references of this sort. In any case, Onesimus himself had not, apparently, been a very valuable slave. Now, however, he is use-

43. Wolter, 262; Stuhlmacher, 38.
44. Lightfoot, 310.

ful *both to you and to me*. The order of the pronouns suggests that Paul
wants to foreground the worth of the "new" Onesimus for Philemon
himself. Whether Onesimus is already proving his worth by serving Paul
in the place of Philemon (see v. 13) or whether Paul anticipates the value
of Onesimus's work once he returns to Philemon is difficult to say.[45] But
"both to you and to me" might suggest the former.[46]

A more important question is whether Paul intends a second wordplay in his *achrēstos/euchrēstos* contrast. For, as a glance at the transliteration of these Greek words reveals, the basic word used to form them —
chrēstos — is quite similar to the word for "Christ": *Christos*. A famous reference in the Roman historian Suetonius suggests that these words could,
indeed, be confused: he refers to unrest in Rome that occurred at the insti-
gation of "Chrestos" — which most scholars think is a reference to dis-
putes among the Jews in Rome over the claims of Jesus to be the
"Christ."[47] It is possible, then, that Paul intends not only to claim that
Philemon has moved from being "useless" to being "useful" but that he
has also moved from being "without Christ" (*a-Christos*) to being a "good
Christian" (*eu-Christos*).[48] Advocates of this interpretation cite two contextual factors in its support. First, a reference to Onesimus's Christian
status would explain how Paul can claim that he is now "useful" to both
Paul and Philemon. And, second, Paul frequently uses the "once . . . but
now" contrast found in this verse to refer to the transformation in life and
circumstances brought about by the power of the gospel (Rom. 11:30; Gal.
1:23; Eph. 2:13; 5:8; Col. 1:21-22; 3:7-8).[49] But this latter point is adequately
explained by the fact that it is Onesimus's conversion to Christian faith
that has turned him from being "useless" into being "useful." And, as we
have noted above, Onesimus's usefulness to both Paul and Philemon can
be adequately explained without explicit reference to his Christian status.
Since, then, all the contextual data are fully accounted for on the single

45. See, e.g., Thompson, 218, for the former; and Dunn, 329, for the latter.
46. The "both" in this translation (TNIV) apparently assumes the text (found in a
few MSS) that includes a καί before both σοί and ἐμοί (hence "both you and me"). But the
majority of manuscripts omit the former καί, in which case we might translate simply "to
you and to me" (e.g., RSV; ESV; NET; NKJV; see Barth/Blanke, 343-44).
47. Suetonius, *Life of Claudius* 25.2; for analysis of this reference, see esp. E. M.
Smallwood, *The Jews under Roman Rule* (SJLA 20; Leiden: Brill, 1976), 210-16.
48. A hint of this wordplay is found in the middle of the second century, in Justin,
Apology 1.4.1, who speaks of "Christians" as people who are accused of hating what is
"useful" (χρηστόν). Advocates of this wordplay here include, e.g., Lohse, 200; Wright,
182; Stuhlmacher, 39; Suhl, 32; Garland, 330; Wolter, 263-64; Thompson, 218.
49. All these texts use the same words found here to create the contrast: ποτέ and
either νῦν or νυνὶ δέ. A similar contrast is found in other texts with slightly different wording (e.g., Rom. 3:21; 6:22; 7:6).

interpretation of the *achrēstos/euchrēstos* contrast, we conclude that the case for a second contrast falls short.[50]

12 This verse, like v. 11, is attached grammatically in the Greek to the name Onesimus at the end of v. 10. The decision of most translators to begin a new sentence here simply reflects the difference between Greek (which often features very long sentences with many subordinate clauses) and modern English (which does not tolerate long, complex sentences). This verse continues the implicit narrative that stands behind Paul's request of Philemon. Much of this story is assumed or only hinted at in the letter, mainly because Philemon was already aware of some of it. Thus Paul mentions as a recognized fact his status as a "prisoner" (vv. 9, 10) because Philemon, perhaps through Epaphras, must already have known that Paul was in custody. He similarly alludes to Onesimus's departure from Philemon (v. 15a) only generally, since, of course, Philemon is well aware of these circumstances also. Implicit in the narrative is the fact that Onesimus somehow met up with Paul. But Paul is explicit about the next two stages in the narrative because they are each important for his appeal: Onesimus has been converted to Christ through Paul (v. 10), and Paul is sending Onesimus back to Philemon (v. 12). The former circumstance is, of course, foundational to Paul's appeal, since it is Onesimus's new status that explains why Philemon must respond to him as Paul wants him to do. But the latter act, though of course quite obvious to Philemon by the time he hears the letter read, is important also.[51] For implicit in Paul's way of putting the matter is his authority over Onesimus. He does not say that "Onesimus has repented of any wrongs he has committed (see v. 18) and has decided to return."[52] This is exactly what Paul would have been expected to say if he wanted to create in Philemon a sympathetic attitude toward Onesimus. Instead, however, Paul takes the initiative: "I am sending him back." This is not to say that Onesimus was not willing, or even anxious, to return. The point is that Paul chooses

---

50. Another problem for this second interpretation is that the most natural word to describe a "non-Christian" would, on the analogy of χριστιανός in Acts 11:26, be ἀχριστιανός (Reinmuth, 42-43). In the parallel cited from Justin (see above), e.g., he uses χριστιανός before playing on this word with the word χρηστός. See also Lightfoot, 340; Fitzmyer, 109.

51. A few scholars have suggested that Paul here expresses his intention but that he did not, in fact, send Onesimus back with this letter, hoping instead that Philemon would allow Onesimus to stay with Paul (esp. Knox, *Philemon*, 25). But this interpretation is not the natural way to understand this verse, far less v. 17. And it can be sustained only if Colossians is regarded as a later pseudepigraph (see Col. 4:9).

52. As Barclay notes, this failure to mention any remorse on the part of Onesimus is striking (J. M. G. Barclay, *Colossians and Philemon* [Sheffield: Sheffield Academic Press, 1997], 103-11).

rather to highlight his decision on this matter. As vv. 12b-13 make clear, the focus is then on the sacrifice that Paul is making. It is this "fellowship of love" between himself and Philemon that Paul wants to make the basis of Philemon's response.

The English versions are agreed in rendering the opening verb in v. 12 as "send back," and most put the verb into the present tense. This is quite appropriate, even though the Greek verb is in the aorist, since the aorist is certainly "epistolary" (the Greeks would often present an action contemporary with the writing of a letter in the aorist because it would be "past" by the time the letter was read). This verb (*anapempō*) can mean "send up to a higher authority" (Luke 23:7, 15; Acts 25:21), and a few interpreters think that Paul might use the verb in this sense. Some of these, as part of an overall "revisionist" reading of the letter, hold that the reference in that case is to Paul's dispatch of Onesimus as an emissary on his behalf.[53] Others think that Paul simply hints at the fact that he is "referring" this matter of Onesimus to Philemon for his decision.[54] But both these interpretations are probably reading too much into the verb. It can simply mean "send back" (as in Luke 23:11), and this meaning makes perfect sense here without adding any further nuances from another meaning of the word.[55] As we have seen, scholars are uncertain about Onesimus's exact situation (see the Introduction, 364-69), and there is some question as to what (if any) Roman laws might have applied to these circumstances. The Old Testament also gave directions for this general situation: "If a slave has taken refuge with you, do not hand them over to their master. Let them live among you wherever they like and in whatever town they choose. Do not oppress them" (Deut. 23:15-16). Bruce has suggested that this law might have led Paul to keep Onesimus with him as long as he did.[56] However, this law in Deuteronomy was apparently intended to apply only to foreign slaves,[57] and so it is questionable whether Paul would have thought it relevant. In any case, Paul's decision to send Onesimus back to Philemon is based on neither Jewish nor Roman law, but on the higher law of love. The fellowship he enjoys with Philemon demands that Philemon be allowed to have final say in the matter of his slave Onesimus.

---

53. A. D. Callahan, *Embassy of Onesimus* (Valley Forge, Pa.: Trinity Press International, 1997), 38-41; Winter, "Paul's Letter to Philemon," 7; Schenk, "Philemon," 3448-49.

54. Moule, 145; Harris, 262; Gnilka, 46.

55. So most interpreters; see esp. Fitzmyer, 109-10.

56. F. F. Bruce, *Paul, Apostle of the Heart Set Free* (Grand Rapids: Eerdmans, 1977), 399-400. On the other hand, Wright (182) and O'Brien (293) doubt that the Deuteronomy text has any relevance.

57. Peter C. Craigie, *The Book of Deuteronomy* (NICOT; Grand Rapids: Eerdmans, 1976), 300; Harris, *Slave of Christ*, 57.

As we have suggested, in vv. 12b-13 Paul accentuates how difficult it is for him to send Onesimus away. The punctuation of the TNIV very nicely captures the emphasis of the Greek text, which highlights Paul's characterization of Onesimus as his "very heart": *I am sending him — who is my very heart — back to you.*[58] "Very heart" is also a good rendering of the Greek word Paul uses, which we have met earlier in Philemon: *splanchna* (see v. 7). Onesimus is not only Paul's "son in the Lord"; he has also quite quickly become a very dear friend and intimate companion.

13 This verse is grammatically tied to the preceding verses, continuing the series of clauses dependent on the name Onesimus in v. 10b: "the one who is now useful" (v. 11), "whom I am sending back" (v. 12), "whom I would have liked to keep with me" (to use some awkward English that represents the Greek constructions). But v. 13 also functions with v. 14 to form a contrast: "I would have liked to keep him with me . . . but I did not want to do anything without your consent."[59] Paul's assertion that he is sending Onesimus back to Philemon is the climax of the brief narrative in vv. 8-12, explaining why he is appealing to Philemon about him. Verses 13-14 explain why Paul is sending him back (v. 14) and why he finds it so hard to do so (v. 13). They are therefore somewhat parenthetical, with v. 15 moving back to the circumstances and purpose of Paul's sending Onesimus back to Philemon.[60]

The contrast between vv. 13 and 14 is established by the pairing "I would have liked"/"but I did not want." This contrast is more marked in the Greek text, involving two simple verbal forms: *eboulomēn/(ouden) ēthelēsa*. In order to keep these verbs from creating a nonsensical contradiction (e.g., "I determined to keep Onesimus with me"/"I determined to do nothing without your consent"), many commentators interpret the former verb as indicating a hypothetical desire.[61] This view is reflected in the TNIV

---

58. Paul accomplishes this in the Greek text by introducing the personal pronoun αὐτόν after his initial statement: "I am sending him back to you — him, that is, my very heart." It is possible that this αὐτόν simply reflects a Semitic style, but it is more likely to be emphatic (see, e.g., O'Brien, 292; Harris, 262). The awkwardness of the Greek that arises from the use of this emphatic pronoun has led to scribal attempts to make "better sense" of the sentence: either by adding the verb "receive" (προσλαβοῦ) (either at the end of the sentence, after αὐτόν, or before αὐτόν); or by introducing "you" as the subject (either in place of or in addition to σοι). This latter text stands behind the KJV and NKJV — "You therefore receive him" — but is clearly secondary. See Metzger, *Textual Commentary*, 589.

59. Many interpreters therefore put a minor break between vv. 12 and 13 (e.g., Stuhlmacher, 36; Reinmuth, 31-32; Barth/Blanke, 119-21; O'Brien, 285).

60. Wolter, 265.

61. Turner, *Syntax*, 65, 91; Wallace, *Greek Grammar*, 551-52; Moule, 146; Harris, 263; Fitzmyer, 111.

— *I would have liked* — and several other English versions (RSV; ESV; KJV; NKJV; NAB). Other interpreters suggest that the tension between the two can be relieved if we press the difference in the tenses between the verbs. The former, being imperfect, might mean "I was wishing for a time," while the latter, an aorist, could mean, in effect, "but then I decided."[62] But there is some question whether we can draw this kind of distinction between the tenses.[63] More important, it is questionable whether we should try in this manner to reduce the tension between the two verbs. Indeed, Paul's whole point here is that he was in conflict, torn between two desires: the desire to keep Onesimus with him and the desire to let Philemon decide the matter. Even as he determined on the latter course of action, he was still "wishing" (*eboulēmen*) that he could keep Philemon with him.[64] This conflict is best captured in English with the kind of straightforward rendering we find in, for example, the HCSB: "I wanted to keep him with me . . . but I didn't want to do anything without your consent."

The verb that Paul uses to indicate that he wanted to *keep* Onesimus with him can mean "hold back," and some think it has this sense here: Onesimus wanted to go back to Philemon, but Paul detained him.[65] But this nuance is by no means clear; the verb can simply mean "hold on to," "keep," "retain."[66] Paul's desire to keep Onesimus "with" him[67] is under-

---

62. Lightfoot, 341 ("the will stepped in and put an end to the inclinations of the mind"); O'Brien, 293; Dunn, 332.

63. Paul uses the verb βούλομαι in the imperfect tense on only one other occasion, where it does not stress duration of time: "Because I was confident of this, I wanted (ἐβουλόμην) to visit you first so that you might benefit twice" (2 Cor. 1:15). The meaning of the verb, of course, lends itself to durative tenses. S. E. Porter (*Verbal Aspect in the Greek of the New Testament* [New York: Lang, 1989], 210) suggests that the imperfect here might not refer to past time at all, but present time. But it is more likely that both ἐβουλόμην and ἠθέλησα refer to the past time of Paul's decision.

64. Vincent, 186. The former verb, from βούλομαι, will then have more the sense of "wish" or desire," while the latter, from θέλω, will connote "decide," "determine." βούλομαι appears to have this sense of "wish" in the majority of Pauline occurrences; see 2 Cor. 1:15, 17; 1 Tim. 2:8; 5:14; 6:9; Titus 3:8. In 1 Cor. 12:11, on the other hand, it has the stronger sense of "determine."

65. See BDAG; Dunn, 330.

66. The verb κατέχω, when used in this sense of "hold on to," can connote the idea of "keep from leaving," as in Luke 4:42: "At daybreak, Jesus went out to a solitary place. The people were looking for him and when they came to where he was, they tried to keep him (κατεῖχον) from leaving them." But the verb normally does not convey this nuance (see Luke 8:15; 14:9; 1 Cor. 7:30; 11:2; 15:2; 2 Cor. 6:10; 1 Thess. 5:21; Heb. 3:6, 14; 10:23). The verb can also mean "restrain" or "hinder" (clearly in Rom. 1:18; 7:6; possibly in the much debated 2 Thess. 2:6, 7); see also the nautical application in Acts 27:40.

67. The Greek is πρὸς ἐμαυτόν, with πρός here (even with the accusative) meaning simply "with" (Wallace notes that this illustrates the general principle that stative verbs can override the usual "transitive" force of prepositions [*Greek Grammar*, 359]).

standable in light of the close and intimate relationship they had developed (v. 12b). But there was another, more important, reason why Paul wanted to keep him with him: *so that he could take your place in helping me while I am in chains for the gospel.* The TNIV translation *helped* suggests that Onesimus was aiding Paul in his personal, day-to-day needs as a prisoner and that Paul wished that Onesimus could continue in this role. But the verb translated by "helped" is *diakoneō*, a verb that Paul sometimes uses to refer to gospel ministry (e.g., 2 Cor. 3:3). Since Paul refers to the gospel in this clause, then, he might intend to portray Onesimus as "serving" in the ministry of the gospel.[68] A number of interpreters further suggest that Paul here hints at what he really wants Philemon to do: allow Onesimus to return and minister with Paul.[69] This view, however, does not fit well with Paul's apparent intention to visit Colossae soon (v. 22): why send Onesimus back to him when he plans to be in Colossae soon? But there is also a more immediate potential problem with this view: the combination "helping [or serving] me" strongly suggests that the interpretation suggested in the TNIV is correct, and that Onesimus's services to Paul were more personal in nature.[70] "Serve" originally referred to waiting on tables at a meal (Acts 6:2), and the word here probably has this more mundane sense (see also, perhaps, 2 Tim. 1:18).

By helping Paul in this way, Onesimus is serving "in the place" of Philemon (TNIV; KJV; HCSB; NET; NJB; NRSV)[71] or "on behalf of" (NKJV; RSV; ESV; NLT; NASB; NAB) Philemon.[72] These two translations reflect different interpretations of the Greek preposition that Paul uses here *(hyper).* The latter might be slightly preferred in light of the general parallel between Onesimus's service to Paul and that of Epaphroditus. The latter was sent by the Philippians to care for Paul in his needs while in prison (Phil. 2:25), and Paul says of him, "He risked his life to make up for the help you yourselves could not give me" (2:30). Geographical distance has prevented Philemon from helping Paul, but, in God's providence, his slave has done what he could not do. Further evidence that this help consisted of personal aid and support rather than "gospel min-

68. O'Brien, 294; W. Bieder, *Der Kolosserbrief* (Zurich: Zwingli, 1943), 36-37; Wolter, 265-66; Binder/Rohde, 57; W. H. Ollrog, *Paulus und seiner Mitarbeiter* (Neukirchen-Vluyn: Neukirchener, 1979), 102-3; Callahan, *Embassy of Onesimus*, 38-39.

69. E.g., W. H. Ollrog, *Paulus und seiner Mitarbeiter*, 103-6.

70. E.g., Bruce, 215; Dunn, 331; Stuhlmacher, 40. Wilson (352-53) suggests that both kinds of service might be in view.

71. Wallace, *Greek Grammar*, 387; Zerwick, *Biblical Greek* §91; Harris, 264; Stuhlmacher, 40; Barth/Blanke, 376-77.

72. Vincent, 186; Dunn, 331. Some who take this view of the genitive think that it implies, further, that Philemon had sent Onesimus to Paul as his emissary (e.g., Callahan, *Embassy of Onesimus*, 38-41; Winter, "Paul's Letter to Philemon," 9).

istry" per se comes in the final words of the verse. Had Paul intended to portray Onesimus as involved in preaching or something similar, we would have expected Paul to say that he was helping him "in the gospel." But by saying, rather, that Onesimus was helping Paul while he was *in chains for the gospel*,[73] he draws attention to his personal circumstances. This is the third time in five verses that Paul has alluded to his imprisonment (see vv. 9, 10). His general purpose in doing so is not simply to evoke sympathy from Philemon, but to remind him that commitment to the gospel will often bring suffering or difficulty. If Paul is willing to suffer chains for the sake of the gospel, Philemon should be willing to respond to his erring slave Onesimus with love.

14 In the nearer context, this verse stands in adversative relationship with v. 13 (hence the *but* [= *de*] in most versions; "however" in NET; NJB). Paul contrasts what he was wishing — to keep Onesimus with him — with what he determined to do — do nothing without Philemon's consent. And he could receive Philemon's consent only by sending Onesimus back to him (v. 12) — not only so that the matter could be thoroughly discussed but, more importantly, so that the personal reconciliation for which Paul hoped might take place. In the larger context, this verse functions with vv. 8-9 to mark off (with an *inclusio*) a stage in Paul's argument. Verse 14 shares with vv. 8-9 a focus on the manner of Paul's appeal to Philemon. In both texts Paul renounces an authoritarian approach — "order you"; "forced" — so that Philemon's response to Paul can be *voluntary*, based on love and not compulsion. This is why Paul is sending Onesimus back to Philemon (v. 12): because he does not want *to do anything without your consent. Consent* is the translation found in most of the versions, and it is accurate enough. But the word that Paul uses implies not just agreement to a course of action, but agreement that arises from a considered opinion about the matter.[74] Only if Philemon has sincerely in

---

73. "For the gospel" translates a genitive, τοῦ εὐαγγελίου, that is hard to classify. The English "for the gospel," adopted in almost all the versions, suggests the idea that Paul is in prison "because of" the gospel, as in the parallel "he was in jail for murder." This would assume that the genitive is a genitive of source or, perhaps, subjective — "in my imprisonment which has resulted from the preaching of the gospel" (Vincent, 187; cf. NJB: "the chains that the gospel has brought me"). This interpretation makes good sense, although others believe that the genitive indicates a broader and less specific idea (O'Brien, 294).

74. The word involved is γνώμη. It has the basic sense "that which is known," and is used in the NT in the extended senses of "purpose" (Acts 20:3; 1 Cor. 1:10; Rev. 17:13, 17) and "judgment" (1 Cor. 7:25, 40; 2 Cor. 8:10). The translation "consent" accurately conveys the result (for the meaning "consent," see esp. R. Bultmann, *TDNT* 1.717, who cites parallel uses in 2 Macc. 4:39 and Josephus, *Antiquities* 20.202) but does not clearly convey the process that leads to that result.

his own mind decided on the appropriateness of what Paul is recommending will his act be truly voluntary and loving. Once again, it is possible that Paul wanted to leave the matter in Philemon's hands out of a concern to "submit to the governing authorities" (Rom. 13:1) — Philemon had the legal right to make decisions regarding his slave. But Paul actually says nothing about legal obligations. What he does say suggests rather that his concern is with the demands of Christian fellowship. What is vital in this matter, Paul suggests, are not the demands of society but the demands of the "new society," the community of faith.

The second half of v. 14 is a purpose clause that explains, as we have seen, why Paul wants to secure Philemon's consent to any course of action. If Paul had acted on his own and then later sought Philemon's agreement, it would have appeared "as if" Philemon were being forced to go along with a *fait accompli*. The Greek here suggests this concern with appearances, a nuance captured in the TNIV — *so that any favor you do would not seem forced* — and also KJV ("as it were"), NASB ("in effect").[75] It would be important for the Christian community to see that Philemon's decision was genuinely his own. But it would also have been important for Philemon's fellow slaveholders to see that his decision was not forced on him by some "foreign" religious authority.[76] (We can too easily ignore the actual social context in which these matters were being played out.) The central contrast in this purpose clause is expressed in Greek in two contrasting prepositional phrases: "according to necessity" *(kata anankēn)* versus "according to free will" *(kata hekousion)*. These two words are not contrasted anywhere else in biblical Greek,[77] but cognates of each are contrasted in 1 Peter 5:2, which illustrates their meanings: "Be shepherds of God's flock that is under your care, watching over them — not because you must *(anankastōs)*, but because you are willing *(hekousiōs)*." Paul's advice to the Corinthians is an especially pertinent example of the word "necessity": "Each of you should give what you have decided in your heart to give, not reluctantly or under compulsion *(ex anankēs)*, for God loves a cheerful giver" (2 Cor. 9:7).

We have noted throughout our discussion the "gradualism" that Paul uses in presenting his appeal to Philemon. He declines to state his appeal at the outset, nevertheless making it clear that there is something

---

75. This nuance is suggested by Paul's inclusion of the particle ὡς before κατὰ ἀνάγκην ("according to necessity"). See O'Brien, 294.

76. Dunn, 332.

77. The word ἀνάγκη, which occurs frequently in the LXX and the NT, can mean "necessity," "compulsion" (Rom. 13:5; Heb. 9:13), or, very often, the "pressure" of affliction or distress (e.g., Ps. 106:6, 13, 19, 28; 2 Cor. 12:10; 1 Thess. 3:7). Ἑκούσιος occurs only here in the NT but is widely used in the LXX to refer to "freewill offerings."

that Philemon "ought to do" (v. 8) with respect to Onesiumus (v. 10). He refers indirectly again in this verse to the appeal that he is leading up to. Paul's reason for not wanting to do anything without Philemon's consent is so that *any favor* that Philemon does will be of his own free will. We quote here the TNIV translation *(any favor you do)*, but this translation could be misleading, in two ways. First, "favor" makes it appear as if what Philemon is being asked to do is for Paul's personal benefit. Of course, Paul has invested himself in the matter, making it clear that he is indeed looking for personal "benefit" from Philemon (see v. 20). But the Greek here simply means "your good," or "your good act" *(to agathon sou)*. Paul usually uses "good" to refer to that which comes from God or is pleasing to him (see, e.g., Rom. 12:9; Gal. 6:10; 1 Thess. 5:15; and the note on v. 6). Paul is probably, therefore, suggesting that what he wants Philemon to do is not so much because it would please him but because it would please God.

The second problem with the TNIV translation of this phrase is the "any," which could suggest that Paul is thinking generally of "good things" that Philemon might do.[78] But the form that Paul uses here suggests that he is thinking of a particular "good deed": what he hopes Philemon will do in response to his appeal about Onesimus (see "your good deed" in HCSB; NET; NKJV; NRSV; also NAB; NJB).[79] Of course, Paul's rhetorical strategy of indirectness means that we have no certain way of knowing what this particular "good deed" might be. It almost certainly refers to Philemon's welcome of Onesimus as a brother in Christ (including therefore full forgiveness for any of Onesimus's wrongs) (v. 17). Others suggest that returning Onesimus to Paul may be included (see v. 13), and this could make sense in terms of the logic of the verse. For the "good thing" that Onesimus could do voluntarily is apparently something that Paul could have prevented if he had done what he wanted.

---

78. See, e.g., Collange, 62. Other interpreters discern a more specific focus in the word: Gnilka (49) points to the philosophical tradition that identifies the "good" as that which is freely chosen; and Dunn (333) sees an allusion to the need for powerful Christians to renounce their rights over the less powerful. The TNIV rendering, to be sure, could be an attempt to capture Paul's rhetorical strategy: "I want any favor that you might happen to choose to do [and of course I have one particularly in view] to be completely voluntary."

79. The Greek phrase is τὸ ἀγαθόν σου. The article with this neuter substantive could be generic, conveying the sense of "that which is good" (as in Rom. 2:10; 12:9, 21; 16:19; Gal 6:10; Eph. 4:28; 1 Thess. 5:15; cf. Rom. 5:7, "the good person"). But this neuter singular form is also used "in an individual sense of a particular definite thing or act" (BDF §263, who refer to this verse), and this makes good sense when the context has suggested such a particularization (cf. also Rom. 7:13 [twice]; 14:16). See also O'Brien, 295. The abstract "goodness" (RSV; ESV; NASB) is possible, but contextually hardly apropos.

And, of course, Paul has already indicated his desire to keep Onesimus with him. More intriguing is the possibility that Onesimus's manumission is included in this "good deed." Whether this further act is included depends on how we interpret v. 21, and especially on how we view the social and legal implications of Philemon's treating Onesimus as a spiritual brother (v. 16). But, to anticipate, we think that manumission is probably implied in these texts and that the setting free of Onesimus is probably included in the "good deed" Paul hopes for from Philemon.[80]

15 The function of vv. 15-16 (which clearly go closely together) in the unfolding argument of the letter is not clear. Although it is not explicitly translated in the TNIV, v. 15 is connected to the previous context with a *gar*, "for" (see, e.g., ESV). This conjunction can sometimes indicate that the material being introduced functions as an explanation or elaboration of the preceding material generally. If this is the case here, then Paul's suggestion about the divine intention behind Onesimus's separation from Philemon (vv. 15-16) might be a kind of "commentary" on the events he has narrated in vv. 8-14. If this is Paul's intention, the omission of "for" in English (which tends to suggest a relationship with the immediately preceding context) is justified (see also RSV; NRSV; NJB; NLT; NAB). Another possibility is that these verses provide a further reason for Paul's decision to send Onesimus back (v. 12): he did not want to get in the way of the possible intention of God, to bring Philemon and Onesimus together.[81] But perhaps the best option is to connect vv. 15-16 with "your good deed" (TNIV, "any favor you do") in v. 14. On the one hand, they hint at the content of this "good deed" by specifying its outcome: Philemon will have Onesimus back forever as a "dear brother." And, on the other hand, they explain why what Paul is asking Philemon to do is, indeed, a *good* deed, "for" it is quite possible that God himself is working in the circumstances to bring out just this outcome.

This last point — that the circumstances in Onesimus's history are providential — is suggested by the combination of the form of the verb that Paul uses in v. 15a and the purpose clause in v. 15b: *the reason he was separated from you . . . that* ("in order that": *hina*).[82] The passive verb "was

---

80. Garland (332) believes that there may be some lexical basis for this conclusion, noting that Philo uses the word ἀγαθόν in commenting on the laws in Deuteronomy about slaves (*On the Special Laws* 2.84). But the word ἀγαθός is perhaps too common to suggest this connection (Philo uses the word over 1,400 times; and it occurs over 750 times in biblical Greek).

81. Lightfoot, 342; O'Brien, 295; A. H. Snyman, "A Semantic Discourse Analysis of the Letter to Philemon," in *Text and Interpretation: New Approaches in the Criticism of the New Testament* (ed. P. J. Hartin and J. H. Petzer; NTTS 15; Leiden: Brill, 1991), 95.

82. The TNIV's "the reason . . . that" translates Gk. διὰ τοῦτο . . . ἵνα. This is a clear instance of a "prospective" τοῦτο, with the ἵνα clause specifying that content of the τοῦτο:

separated" *(echōristhē)* is widely and, in our view, correctly viewed as a "divine passive": a passive verb in which God is the implied agent.[83] And it is the fact that this verb governs a purpose clause that makes this interpretation especially probable. The action of "separation" has the purpose of restoring Onesimus to Philemon forever; and only by seeing God behind this separation does this purpose statement make sense. God caused Onesimus to be separated from Philemon with the purpose that he might bring them back together for good. Interpreters also commonly, and rightly, allude at this point to the Joseph story in Genesis as a comparable example of God at work in a series of apparently random (and even evil) events. Joseph's brothers sinned in selling him into slavery, but "God intended it for good" (Gen. 50:20; cf. 45:4-8).

As we have seen, Paul's appeal to Philemon presumes a narrative of events to which he alludes at various points in his argument. Onesimus has met Paul in his imprisonment (assumed); Onesimus has been converted through Paul (v. 10); Onesimus has been useful to Paul (vv. 11, 13). However, the initial and precipitating event in this story has not been mentioned: Onesimus has left his master Philemon. Now Paul alludes to this event. However, instead of narrating this event he provides an interpretation of it — much to the frustration of interpreters of Philemon, for whom the exact circumstances of Onesimus's departure from Philemon are critical to understanding the significance of the letter. Did Onesimus flee from Philemon with a view to gaining his freedom? Did he leave only briefly to seek reconciliation with his master through Paul? Or did Philemon send Onesimus as his emissary to Paul? This last option, at least, can pretty safely be eliminated, partly on the evidence of this verse. Paul would hardly have described Philemon's sending of Onesimus in the language "separated from you for a little while." On the other hand, this language gives no basis for choosing between the other two options (see, further, the Introduction, 364-69). And, of course, there was no need for Paul to describe the event, since Philemon was very well acquainted with the circumstances. Indeed, Paul's reticence serves his rhetorical strategy. However it took place, the parting between Philemon and Onesimus was hardly cordial; and it would not serve Paul's purposes to remind Philemon of the painful episode.

What suits his argument far better, of course, is to suggest that, however difficult the situation, and however much Onesimus might have been

---

Onesimus was separated "because of this," e.g., "because it was necessary to accomplish this," namely, "that. . . ."

83. E.g., Lohse, 202; O'Brien, 295; Gnilka, 40. Arzt-Grabner, on the other hand, cites examples of the passive of this verb to argue that it means "separate oneself" (103-5; cf. also P. Arzt-Grabner, "Onesimus Erro," *ZNW* 95 [2004], 136-39).

at fault, God had a beneficial intention in view. To be sure, Paul advances this possibility with the caution incumbent on any human trying to discern the intention of God behind the events of history: *perhaps (tacha)*. Describing Onesimus's separation from Philemon as *for a little while*[84] also serves Paul's rhetoric: In the big view of things, they have not been apart for long — especially when the separation may lead to Philemon having him back *forever*. The form of the verb that Paul uses for Philemon's having him back (the active voice of *apechō*) frequently occurs as a technical term in the world of commerce: "provide a receipt for a sum paid in full." See, for example, Matthew 6:2, 5, 16: "They have received their reward in full *(apechousin)*" (in Paul; Phil. 4:18). Some interpreters think that Paul is using the term here with this commercial sense and that he is alluding to his hope that Philemon would set Onesimus free. Paul would, in effect, be suggesting that the temporary separation between Philemon and Onesimus happened "in order that you might freely relinquish your claim on him forever."[85] However, Paul uses this verb here in an unusual construction, suggesting that he is not using the verb in its usual technical sense.[86] Probably, then, as most of the commentators think, it means here simply "receive back."[87]

This leaves to be decided the significance of *forever* in this context. The English "forever" can sometimes be an overtranslation of the word *aiōnion*, which, in a temporal sense, can mean simply "for a long time." In question here is whether Paul uses the word in an "earthly" or in a spiritual sense. Is he saying that Philemon will have Onesimus back "permanently" (HCSB), "for good" (NIV) — in the sense that Onesimus will return as a willing, "useful" slave for as long as Philemon wants?[88] Or is Paul saying that Philemon will have Onesimus back "eternally" (so most versions) — in the sense that they now share a faith that gives them, together, eternal life?[89] This latter view is, we think, by far the more preferable. It is not Onesimus's usefulness *as a slave* that Paul stresses in his reci-

---

84. The Greek is πρὸς ὥραν, "for an hour," ὥρα referring, as it often does, to a short period of time (BDAG; cf. 2 Cor. 7:8; Gal. 2:5).

85. Knox, *Philemon*, 22-24.

86. Of the six times that this verb has this general sense in the NT, only this occurrence has a personal object (αὐτόν). See also Matt. 6:2, 5, 16; Mark 14:41; Phil. 4:18.

87. E.g., O'Brien, 296. Wolter (270) suggests that Paul might use a verb with commercial associations because the ancients viewed slaves as property.

88. E.g., Moule, 146; Wolter, 269; Harris, 266; Stuhlmacher, 41-42; Wilson, 355. Some of these interpreters think that the provisions for marking the possession of slaves in Deut. 15:17 may lie behind Paul's language: "then take an awl and push it through his ear lobe into the door, and he will become your servant for life (εἰς τὸν αἰῶνα)."

89. A slight majority of the commentators favor this view; see, e.g., Lightfoot, 342; O'Brien, 296; Collange, 62-63; Gnilka, 50; Reinmuth, 46; Garland, 333-34.

tation of events in vv. 8-14, but Onesimus's new status as a Christian. And this is just the point reinforced by v. 16: Philemon will have Onesimus back "as a brother." Moreover, it would be a bit odd for Paul to suggest that God's purpose in the separation of Philemon and Onesimus was that so the former could have permanent possession of his slave. But it makes good sense to see Paul attributing to God the circumstances that have led to Onesimus's conversion and to the prospect of his "eternal" fellowship with Philemon.

16 This verse begins clearly enough, as Paul, continuing the purpose clause in v. 15b, speaks about the way in which Philemon should "receive back" Onesimus: *no longer as a slave but, better than a slave, as a dear brother*. But so fraught with significance is this hope (perhaps the climax of the letter)[90] that Paul adds a series of further qualifications, and we end up with an awkward "run-on" clause (masked in the TNIV in an effort to put Paul's Greek into readable English). The phrase *no longer as a slave* could appear to settle the matter of what Paul is expecting Philemon to do: clearly he expects Philemon to set Onesimus free. The Greek word behind "no longer" could suggest that Paul is focusing on the objective status of Onesimus,[91] and the "as" language could also fit this interpretation.[92] On

90. Ernst, 135; Barth/Blanke, 410.

91. Since this opening phrase in v. 16 depends on the subjunctive verb ἀπέχῃς ("have back") at the end of v. 15, "no longer" should be expressed with μηκέτι. Paul's use of οὐκέτι suggests that he is speaking of "facts" rather than hopes here (Lightfoot, 343; Barth/Blanke, 416).

92. Many interpreters insist that Paul's use of the particle ὡς indicates that the condition cannot be "factual." The particle, O'Brien insists (quoting von Soden), "expresses the subjective evaluation of the relationship, without calling its objective form into question" (O'Brien, 297; cf. also Lightfoot, 343; Harris, 267; Dunn, 334-35). They then argue that, if Paul had wanted simply to state that Onesimus was no longer a slave, he would simply have omitted the ὡς. But this is not at all clear. First, it is not clear that the verb ἀπέχω could take a double accusative, as this would require: e.g., "have him (αὐτόν) back (no longer) a slave (δοῦλον)." More important, the particle ὡς here does not depend on a verb of "subjective evaluation," as if Paul said "you should treat him as" or even "receive him as" (v. 17). The verb is the impersonal "you will have him back (as)"; and, at the risk of using English to interpret Greek, an "as" in this kind of sentence can certainly express the true facts of the situation. E.g., after a prisoner is released from confinement, "You will have him back as a free man." 2 Thessalonians 3:15 illustrates very well both uses of ὡς: "Yet do not regard them as (ὡς) enemies, but warn them as (ὡς) fellow believers." The former is clearly subjective: "do not treat them as if they were ememies"; but the second is objective: "warn them as the fellow believers they truly are." The question, then, is how closely we tie this opening phrase of v. 16 to the verb in v. 15. If the tie is close, then an objective interpretation makes the best grammatical sense. But if (as the shift to οὐκέτι might suggest), Paul is implicitly shifting his focus — e.g., "you will have him back forever; receive him back as . . ." — then the subjective interpretation is to preferred.

A. D. Callahan has argued that the particle implies much more than this, suggest-the other hand, Paul goes on to say that Philemon is to treat Onesimus as *more than a slave,* which certainly seems to suggest that Onesimus will remain a slave, at least for the time being.[93] While, therefore, the issue is by no means as clear as some interpreters make it, it is likely that this opening phrase means "no longer as primarily a slave in your view of him." Paul is saying, in effect, "Your relationship with Onesimus will no longer be dictated by your legal relationship (master-slave) but by your spiritual relationship (brothers)."[94] The NLT captures the sense very well: "He is no longer like a slave to you." At this point, then, Paul's concern is with how the returning slave Onesimus should be viewed by his master Philemon.

Philemon will have Onesimus back not merely as a "brother" but as a "dear brother" *(adelphon agapēton).* Paul tellingly refers to Onesimus here with the same language he has used in addressing Philemon himself: a "brother" *(adelphe;* vv. 7, 20) and "dear friend" *(agapētō).* As "children" of Paul via conversion, both Philemon and Onesimus are "dear brothers" in the same spiritual family. This new family relationship, rather than the existing household relationship, is to determine Philemon's view (and treatment) of Onesimus. It is at this point that Paul's syntax becomes rather convoluted. The ESV renders the Greek here pretty straightforwardly: ". . . as a beloved brother — especially to me, but how much more to you, both in the flesh and in the Lord." As the dash suggests, Paul breaks off his sentence to elaborate the significance of Onesimus' new status as a "dear brother" — clearly a fundamental point in the letter. What is confusing in this way of rendering the Greek is the implication that Onesimus is a "dear brother" to Philemon both "in the flesh" and "in the Lord." The former phrase uses "flesh" in a typically Pauline way to refer to "that aspect of human life that is bound by earthly-oriented interests" (cf. NJB, "on the natural plane").[95]

---

ing that ὡς introduces an "unreal" condition: "no longer as if he were a slave" ("Paul's Epistle to Philemon," *HTR* 86 [1993], 362; cf. also Callahan, *Embassy of Onesimus,* 10). But, as Fitzmyer makes clear, ὡς simply does not have this sense in the NT (114; see also Barth/Blanke, 419).

93. The preposition is ὑπέρ, which is followed by the accusative case (δοῦλον). Paul uses this combination only eleven times; two have a local meaning — "above" (Eph. 1:22; Phil. 2:9) — while the other nine all have a comparative meaning — "more than," "beyond" (1 Cor. 4:6a; 10:13; 2 Cor. 1:8b; 12:6, 13; Gal. 1:14; Eph. 3:20; Phlm. 21 [cf. also 2 Cor. 11:23]). See BDAG; BDF §230. It is very unlikely, then, that the construction can indicate that Philemon was to view Onesimus as a brother "instead of" a slave (contra Reinmuth, 46; and J. M. Barclay, "Paul, Philemon and the Dilemma of Christian Slave-Ownership," *NTS* 39 [1991], 173 [who leaves the question open]).

94. See esp. Petersen, *Rediscovering Paul,* 95-97.

95. Fitzmyer, 116. On the complexity of Paul's use of σάρξ, see the comments on Col. 1:22.

But in what sense is Onesimus to be considered a "brother" of Philemon in an earthly sense? A few interpreters have suggested that Paul means, simply, that Philemon and Onesimus were biological "brothers" and that what has happened to Onesimus will enhance that relationship.[96] But this would assume a series of inferences about the letter's background that are, to say the least, improbable. Another possibility, then, is that this additional material describes not "brother" but "dearer."[97] The TNIV captures this idea by putting the additional material in a new sentence and carrying over the word "dear": *He is very dear to me but even dearer to you, both as a fellow man and as a brother in the Lord* (see also NAB; NJB). Yet the word "brother" is probably too significant for it not to be carried over into all the elements of what follows.[98] Probably, then, Paul's point is that Onesimus's new status as "beloved brother" has implications for Philemon's relationship to Onesimus at the purely earthly level as well as at the spiritual level. Paul's role in converting Onesimus and their time together in the difficult circumstances of Paul's imprisonment have made Onesimus an "especially" dear brother to him.[99] Yet the long relationship between Philemon and Onesimus and the prospect of that relationship now being brought to an entirely new level through his conversion will mean that Onesimus will be even more a "dear brother" to Philemon — and this relationship will include their earthly relationship ("in the flesh").

But what will this mean, specifically, for their earthly relationship? In what sense does Paul hope that the relationship between Philemon and Onesimus will be transformed? Does he hope that Philemon might give Onesimus his freedom? This is one of the knottiest problems that the letter to Philemon presents to us, and its implications for the wider and controversial matter of the New Testament view of slavery mean that a great deal of attention is given to it. The question is a difficult one be-

---

96. Callahan, *Embassy of Onesimus*, 49-54. C. S. de Vos ("Once a Slave, Always a Slave?" *JSNT* 82 [2001], 102), on the other hand, thinks that "in the flesh" refers to the household and "in the Lord" to the house church.

97. Fitzmyer, 115; Barth/Blanke, 447.

98. It is sometimes argued that Paul's use of the dative pronouns ἐμοί and σοί show that the word carried over into the last part of the verse is ἀγαπητόν: "beloved to me/to you"; if ἀδελφόν, on the other hand, were assumed, the pronouns would be in the genitive: "a brother of me/of you" (e.g., Barth/Blanke, 447). But this is not conclusive, since the pronouns do not depend directly on either "beloved" or "brother."

99. Since μᾶλλον ("more") is used just after it, μάλιστα almost certainly has an elative meaning ("especially"; so most of the versions). The datives ἐμοί and σοί could be instrumental — "held dear especially by me . . . even more so by you" (Barth/Blanke, 447) — but are probably "ethical datives" — "dear from my perspective/from your perspective" (see Wallace, *Greek Grammar*, 146-47 for the category).

cause, of course, Paul is far from explicit about what he is asking. Partly because he wants Philemon to act on his own initiative, Paul asks nothing more definite than that Philemon welcome Onesimus as he would welcome the apostle himself (v. 17). Furthermore, as we have pointed out in the Introduction (374-78), the New Testament generally refrains, because of both practical issues (the impossibility of fighting institutional evil in an authoritarian regime) and theological principle (the focus on establishing an alternative society in the church), from engaging social and institutional evil. In light of this perspective, then, many interpreters think that Paul implies nothing in this verse about a change in Onesimus's legal status. Paul is suggesting that Philemon should treat his returned slave as a brother, not punishing him and being a kind and attentive master to him.[100]

"Both in the flesh and in the Lord" suggests that Paul may indeed hint at a change in Onesimus's worldly status as well as in his spiritual status. To be sure, Philemon could certainly treat Onesimus as a "dear brother" while continuing to be his master. This is assumed in the "household codes," which do not call on Christian masters to liberate their slaves but to treat them well (Eph. 6:9; Col. 4:1; cf. 1 Tim. 6:2). And we find many examples of strong mutual affection between master and slave in the ancient world. Moreover, granting a slave his or her freedom was not always an unqualified good thing, for the freed slaves, cut off from the "household" of which they had been a part, often had a difficult time finding a way to make a living. Nevertheless, while we grant all this, we still wonder whether a continuation of the existing master-slave relationship is compatible with Philemon's treating Onesimus as a "dear brother" "in the flesh."[101] The contrast that Paul presents here, between Philemon's relationship to Onesimus "in the Lord" and "in the flesh" is striking. Nowhere else does Paul contrast "the Lord" and the "flesh." Moreover, "in the Lord" covers all possible elements of the Christian's existence. Paul must, then, intend some particular emphasis by adding "in the flesh" here. In suggesting, then, that Philemon's embrace of Onesimus as his dear brother must have implications for their earthly relationship, Paul may be hinting at a request for Onesimus' manumis-

---

100. E.g., Lohse, 203; Wright, 185-86; Harris, 268; O'Brien, 297-98; and (at excruciating length) Barth/Blanke, 410-55.

101. Lohse, arguing that Onesimus's status "in the flesh" is surpassed by his status "in the Lord," claims that "in the last analysis it is of no significance to the Christian whether he is slave or free" (203). As Barclay suggests, we may discern in this comment the influence of the dualistic Lutheran "two kingdoms" tradition (*Colossians and Philemon*, 120-21). We would agree and argue that Lohse's "of no significance" should be replaced with "not of ultimate significance" to reflect more accurately the NT perspective.

sion.[102] Treating Onesimus as "more than a slave" will perhaps mean, in the end, not treating him as a slave at all. Of course, Paul is not yet technically asking Philemon to do anything. The sentence we are dealing with is about what Paul suspects might be God's purpose in the circumstances of Onesimus's situation (v. 15). But by suggesting that this might indeed be God's purpose, Paul is, of course, putting considerable pressure on Philemon.[103] To refuse to act toward Onesimus, Paul suggests, would be — "perhaps" — to fly in the face of God's own purposes.

17 Paul finally comes out in the open and makes a direct request of Philemon: *welcome him as you would welcome me.* Paul told us that he had an appeal to make regarding Onesimus (v. 10), and we have suggested that he hints at the ultimate content of that appeal in v. 16. Here, however, he states the content of his immediate appeal.[104] This request is built on the argument of the letter to this point, as the *so (oun)* that introduces it indicates.[105] This conjunction also marks the transition to the third part of the body of the letter (vv. 17-20). Here Paul pulls together the threads of his argument, an argument that focuses on relationships. Onesimus, through his conversion, stands in a new relationship to Philemon, as Paul has just made clear (v. 16). Philemon also has an intimate relationship with Paul: they are "beloved friends," "fellow workers" (v. 1), "brothers" (cf. v. 7), joined in a close bond of fellowship through their faith. In the exhortation in v. 17, which is the dominant point in this paragraph, Paul now, in effect, asks Philemon to actualize that fellowship and give practical recognition to his new relationship to Onesimus. He then turns to practicalities, guaranteeing (with his own "signature") to pay any debts that Onesimus has incurred (vv. 18-19). His general plea that Philemon "refresh" his "heart" (v. 20) then underscores his request in v. 17.[106] Particularly prominent in these verses is the relationship between Paul and Philemon: the text is filled with pronouns referring to Paul and Philemon.[107]

Paul prefaces his appeal to Philemon with a reminder of their "partnership." "Partner" is the word most English versions use to render the

102. See esp. Wall, 211-13; Bruce, 217; Wolter, 270-72; Reinmuth, 48; Fitzmyer, 114-15 (cautiously); Barclay, "Paul, Philemon and the Dilemma of Christian Slave-Ownership," 173; Lucas (187) and Stuhlmacher (43-45) are unsure.

103. Fitzmyer, 102.

104. As, therefore, v. 16 is the theological high point of the letter, this verse is its rhetorical climax (Wolter, 269; Arzt-Grabner, 58).

105. Others (e.g., Vincent, 189; Lohse, 203; Harris, 271; O'Brien, 298) suggest that oὖν is used to resume the main track of Paul's argument after the excursus of vv. 14-15 (or vv. 11-15).

106. Verses 17 and 20 form, then, something of an *inclusio* (Collange, 66).

107. Harris, 271.

Greek *koinōnos* here, but it is questionable whether it strikes quite the right note. For one thing, "partner" tends to suggest a business relationship. To be sure, Winter has argued that the word has virtually this sense here, referring to a formal "partnership" that Philemon and Paul have joined and in which Onesimus is being invited to share.[108] But nothing in the letter or its probable background suggests so specific a nuance. Others think that Paul has chosen to use a commercial term as a way of denoting his participation with Philemon in the common work of ministry; he is "Philemon's partner in the business of the gospel" (v. 1; and see 2 Cor. 8:23, which refers to Titus as a *koinōnos* and "fellow worker" with Paul).[109] However, while the word *koinōnos* can have this commercial sense (see Luke 5:10), it also has a much wider application: to "friends" (Sir. 6:10; 41:19), a marriage "partner" (Mal. 2:14), and, of particular relevance, those who "participate" in a religious experience (1 Cor. 10:18, 20; 2 Cor. 1:7; 1 Pet. 5:1; 2 Pet. 1:4) or are "participants" with others in such an experience (Heb. 10:33). The use of the cognate noun *koinōnia* in v. 6 points strongly toward this sense of the word here. In setting the stage for his appeal, Paul refers to "the fellowship based in faith" that he and Philemon share. This verse should be seen as a reference back to that fundamental sharing of the reality of the new covenant experience that Paul and Philemon have in common.[110] "Comrade" (if we can rid ourselves of its Communist associations!) would not be a bad translation;[111] but it might be better to paraphrase: "if you have any fellowship with me in our common faith."

The "if" language in this clause does not call into question the reality of this fellowship, but puts the onus on Philemon to acknowledge it.[112] And if he acknowledges it, suggests Paul, Philemon will do what Paul asks and *welcome* Onesimus. The sense of the verb *welcome* (the Greek verb is *proslambanō*) can be gauged from the only other place where Paul uses it: to encourage the squabbling factions in the Roman community to "receive" each other, that is, fully to accept one another as fellow members of Christ's body (Rom. 15:7; see also 14:1, 3). This suggests that the word here is commanding Philemon not only to "welcome" Onesimus back into his

108. Winter, "Paul's Letter to Philemon," 11-12.

109. Dunn, 337; see also Barth/Blanke, 474-75; Fitzmyer, 116.

110. Lohse, 203-4; Wright, 187; O'Brien, 298-99; Wolter, 273. As O'Brien notes, Paul has used a number of words with commercial connotations in this context. But this does not mean that the words have a commercial meaning: they are metaphors, taken from the business world, to denote the spiritual realities of the new covenant church.

111. As Fitzmyer (116) suggests.

112. While, then, Paul clearly assumes that the condition is true, we should not translate "since" (contra, e.g., Barth/Blanke, 473), because this would remove the rhetorical force of the condition. See Wallace, *Greek Grammar*, 694, on this so-called "first-class" type of apodosis (εἰ + indicative [in this case the present tense ἔχεις]).

household,[113] but, far more importantly, to welcome him into "the household of faith" (cf. Gal 6:10).[114] A number of interpreters, especially those who hold that *koinōnos* means "partner in ministry," think that Paul may also be hinting at a request that Philemon accept Onesimus as a fellow worker (and send him back to Paul? — see vv. 13, 14).[115] Again, however, we question whether this additional nuance is justified. The focus throughout this verse, in our opinion, is on the need to receive Onesimus as a Christian, with all the revolutionary implications of that action. These implications are underscored by the final words in the verse: welcome him *as you would welcome me.* As Stuhlmacher emphasizes, what Paul says here is startling: Philemon is to give to his slave Onesimus the same welcome he would extend to the apostle Paul.[116] Here is one practical consequence of Paul's great theological principle, that "There is neither Jew nor Gentile, neither slave nor free, neither male nor female, for you are all one in Christ Jesus" (Gal. 3:28; cf. Col. 3:11).

18 Having stated his request, Paul now turns to practicalities: *If he has done you any wrong or owes you anything, charge it to me.* Paul wants nothing to stand in the way of Philemon's welcome of Onesimus. And so he offers to pay any debts that Onesimus might owe to Philemon. This offer is the other side of the "exchange" that Paul mentioned in v. 13: as Onesimus has discharged Philemon's debt to Paul by serving the apostle, so Paul now offers to discharge Onesimus's debt to Philemon and thus return the favor.[117] But what is the nature of Onesimus's debt to Philemon? Or how has he "wronged" him? These questions can be answered only in the context of our general understanding of the situation that has brought Onesimus and Paul together. On the supposition that Onesimus is a "fugitive" slave, the "wrong" and the "debt" may both refer to Onesimus's having robbed his master as he fled.[118] Runaway slaves, not unnaturally, would often finance their flight by such robbery. Or the "wrong" Onesimus did may have been simply his running away and his "debt" what he owed to his master in compensation for the time of his service that had been lost.[119] If, on the other hand, Onesimus has traveled to Paul to mediate a dispute with his master, then the "wrong"

113. See Harris, 272.
114. Reinmuth, 49; Fitzmyer, 116.
115. O'Brien, 299. προσλαμβάνω, it is noted, was sometimes used with κοινωνός to mean "take on as a partner" (LSJ; cf. Knox, *Philemon*, 24; Bruce, 219).
116. Stuhlmacher, 49.
117. Wall, 213-14.
118. Lightfoot, 343; Wright, 187; Stuhlmacher, 49; Nordling, "Onesimus *Fugitivus,*" 110.
119. R. P. Martin, 167; Lohse, 204.

could refer to the dispute between Onesimus and Philemon that has led him to seek refuge with Paul, and the "debt" may refer to something arising out of this dispute or, again, to the loss of Onesimus's services.

But, to back up to a prior issue, it is not even clear that Onesimus has done anything wrong. The particular way that Paul frames the condition (the so-called "first class" condition) simply assumes the reality of the situation for the sake of argument. It begs the question whether Onesimus had really wronged Philemon. Dunn puts it well: ". . . it neatly serves the purpose of taking for granted Philemon's view that Onesimus was guilty of serious misdemeanor, without wholly conceding that Philemon's judgment was entirely correct."[120] We can assume, of course, that Onesimus has told his side of the story to Paul. But Paul wants to gain a hearing from Philemon, and so he presumes nothing about who was right and who was wrong. He simply indicates what he proposes to do if, in fact, Onesimus has wronged Philemon and owes him something: *charge it to me*, Paul says. *Charge*, as is appropriate to this context, is a commercial term. It means "charge to the account of someone" (see most English versions).[121] Paul's offer to compensate Philemon for his loss raises probably unanswerable questions about Paul's own financial situation. Some, indeed, think that, especially in light of v. 19b, Paul's offer is ironic: he did not have the money to reimburse Philemon, and Philemon knew it.[122] But the solemn attestation in v. 19a is incompatible with an ironic offer.[123] Further speculation is only that. Did he have his own private funds that he could draw upon? Did he have financial backers, or "patrons," willing to help?[124] We simply cannot know.

19 Paul's emphasis on his personal investment in the "Onesimus affair" reaches its climax here: *I, Paul, am writing this with my own hand. I will pay it back.* This affirmation could mark the beginning of the letter closing, since it usually occurs in this section in Paul's other letters.[125] But Paul's "signature" functions differently here than in other letters, and it is

120. Dunn, 338.
121. BDAG; MM, 204; H. Preisker, *TDNT* 2.516-17. The verb is ἐλλογέω, and thus the form that we would expect here (for the second singular present imperative) is ἐλλόγει (and some scribes helpfully supplied it; it is read in the majority text and a few other MSS). The use of ἐλλόγα arises from a common confusion between verbs ending in -εω and -αω (BDF §90). The verb occurs only here and in Rom. 5:13 in biblical Greek. Paul's decision to use the present rather than the aorist imperative is hard to explain, but, as Moule notes, the distinction between the tenses in imperatives is not always clear (*Idiom Book*, 135).
122. Wall, 215-16; see also Lohse, 204.
123. Fitzmyer, 117-18.
124. Dunn, 339.
125. Weima, *Neglected Endings*, 230-32.

better to keep v. 19 with v. 18. English translations cannot quite convey the emphasis on Paul's own involvement that we find in the Greek text: both "I"s are expressed in Greek with a pronoun (not strictly required), and the "my" may also be emphatic.[126] What we have here, as Harris puts it, is Paul's "promissory note."[127]

But there is some uncertainty about just what part of the letter Paul has in view when he says, *I am writing.* The TNIV, along with most other English versions (RSV; ESV; NRSV; HCSB; NASB; NJB; NLT), translates with a present tense, suggesting that Paul refers to the "promise" that he is now writing (and perhaps more). And this is a valid interpretation of the verbal form that Paul uses here.[128] But the verb could also be translated "I wrote" or "I have written" (KJV; NET), in which case the reference might be to the previous part of the letter (including, perhaps, the present verse).[129] The issue is complicated by the broader issue of the mechanics of the production of the letter. Has Paul written the letter in its entirety?[130] Or did he dictate most of it to a scribe and then "take up the pen" here to add his signature as a guarantee?[131] We simply cannot know. However, in the other letters where Paul adds such a "signature," it seems likely that an amanuensis has been responsible for the actual mechanical writing of most of the letter, and this may be the case here also.[132] Elsewhere Paul appends his signature to guarantee that the letter is, in fact, from him. Here, however, he uses it to underscore his commitment to repay Philemon anything that Onesimus might owe. And this is also why the signature comes here at the end of the body of the letter rather than at the beginning of the letter closing.[133] In any case, Paul is

---

126. The Greek behind "my" is ἐμῇ, the possessive adjective, which is sometimes more emphatic than the genitive form of the personal pronoun (μου); see Robertson, *Grammar*, 684-85. The point cannot be pressed, however, because there is some evidence that the two forms were being used as virtually equivalent (BDF §285[1]).

127. Harris, 273.

128. The verb ἔγραψα is in the aorist tense, but it may be an "epistolary" aorist (the aorist tense having a "past" reference from the perspective of the readers of the letter). See, e.g., O'Brien, 300.

129. Robertson, 845-46; Wallace, *Greek Grammar*, 563, notes the ambiguity of the aorist form here.

130. Lightfoot, 344; Stuhlmacher, 50; Wright, 188.

131. Bruce, 222; Dunn, 339-40; Weima, *Neglected Endings*, 232.

132. See Galatians (6:11); 1 Corinthians (16:21); Colossians (4:18); 2 Thessalonians (3:17). In the latter three texts, Paul makes clear that his own writing is restricted to the "greeting." In 2 Thess. 3:17, Paul claims that a greeting "in his own hand" is "the distinguishing mark in all my letters"; it might be, then, that, even when Paul does not draw attention to it, a change of handwriting at the end would indicate Paul's "signature." See Weima, *Neglected Endings*, 119; and the notes on Col. 4:18.

133. Dunn, 339-40.

writing this verse in his own hand in order to underscore his promise in
v. 18. As he repeats it here: *I will pay it back*. "Pay it back," like "charge it"
in v. 18, is a technical term drawn from the realm of commerce. Paul is
promising to "pay any damages."[134]

As the dash in the TNIV indicates, the second part of v. 19 is only
loosely connected with the first part of the verse. Various specific explanations of what is an awkward Greek construction are possible.[135] But, in
general, the convoluted syntax probably represents Paul's desire to "have
his cake and eat it too." He is reluctant to bring up as a means of persuading Philemon the ultimate debt that Philemon owes to Paul. But he is going to do it anyway, as a means of persuading Philemon to do what Paul
is asking. As Vincent paraphrases the logic, "The writer delicately protests against saying something which he nevertheless does say."[136] The
NLT captures the nuance well: "And I won't mention that you owe me
your very soul!" What Paul "won't mention" is exactly what he goes on
to mention. Most of us will be familiar with exactly this rhetorical maneu-
ver. As a means of persuading one's child to do a household chore, one
might say, for instance, "Of course, I am not going to mention that I am
paying your room and board."

Paul continues to use commercial imagery in this reminder to
Philemon: *you owe me your very self*. *Owe* translates a different Greek word
(*prosopheilō*) than the one that Paul used in v. 18. The word here has the
sense of "owe besides," which makes sense in this context: quite apart
from all other considerations, Philemon owes Paul his very self.[137] What
Paul means by saying that Philemon owes him his "very self" (*seauton*) is

---

134. BDAG. The verb is ἀποτίνω. It occurs only here in the NT but thirty times in
the LXX, tellingly almost always in legal texts. See, e.g., Exod. 22:1: "Whoever steals an
ox or a sheep and slaughters it or sells it must pay back (ἀποτείσει) five head of cattle for
the ox and four sheep for the sheep." The verb also occurs frequently in papyri roughly
contemporary to Paul with this sense.

135. The second part of the verse is introduced with a ἵνα that does not make sense
if given its usual telic force and connected with either of the verbs in v. 19a: "I am writing
. . . in order that I might not say"; "I will pay it back . . . in order that I might not say."
Probably, then, there is an ellipsis of the main verb on which the ἵνα depends: "I put it this
way in order that I might not have to say to you . . ." (Moule, *Idiom Book*, 145; Harris, 274;
Dunn, 323). The construction may be stereotypical, since we find a similar construction
in 2 Cor. 9:4, which, like Phlm. 19, uses the verb λέγω. Other options are to take the ἵνα as
imperatival — "Let me not mention that . . ." (Turner, *Syntax*, 95) — or to view the clause
as dependent on v. 18 and repunctuate — "charge this to me . . . , not to say: to you, because . . ." (BDF §495[1]; O'Brien, 301; see NASB).

136. Vincent, 190.

137. Harris, 274; BDAG (who note, however, that it is often difficult to find any
"special force" in the preposition that is prefixed to the verbal form here; see also MM,
553). The verb προσοφείλω is a biblical hapax; the simple ὀφείλω is used in v. 18.

that Philemon is in debt to Paul for his eternal life. Paul was used by God in Philemon's conversion. Paul may have been involved indirectly, Philemon having been converted through the ministry of one of Paul's fellow workers (Epaphras).[138] But it is more likely that Paul's involvement was direct, Paul having brought Philemon to faith during a visit of the latter to Ephesus while Paul was resident there.[139] In light of this infinite debt that Philemon owes Paul, he should have no hesitation in accepting Paul's offer to cover Onesimus's debts. The principle is one that Paul states elsewhere. Commenting on the generous giving of Gentile believers to Jewish believers in Jerusalem, he says: "They were pleased to do it, and indeed they owe (opheiletai) it to them. For if the Gentiles have shared in the Jews' spiritual blessings, they owe (opheilousin) it to the Jews to share with them their material blessings" (Rom. 15:27). Perhaps, indeed, this reminder is a subtle suggestion that it would be a bit crass on Philemon's part even to accept Paul's offer. His gratitude to Paul for his spiritual wealth should more than cancel any "debt" that Onesimus, Paul's "child," has incurred. As Barclay puts it, "Philemon is turned from creditor to debtor in the space of two verses, and loaded with a debt so large ('your very self') that he is under limitless obligation to Paul."[140]

20 As we have argued (see the introductory notes on this section), this verse concludes the body of the letter. And it makes a very appropriate conclusion to Paul's appeal, echoing with three key words the conclusion to the opening of the letter (v. 7): "brother" as a vocative address (adelphe), "refresh" (anapauō), and "heart/s" (splanchna). As Philemon has "refreshed the hearts of the Lord's people" in general, so Paul now asks that he might "refresh" his heart. The verb opens with a particle of affirmation, translated "yes" in most of the English versions. This translation works well, since our English "yes" matches the two key meanings of the Greek word (nai): an affirmative answer to a question; or an affirmative repetition of a previous idea. See, for example, Luke 12:5: "But I will show you whom you should fear: Fear him who, after your body has been killed, has authority to throw you into hell. Yes, I tell you, fear him." The TNIV (following NIV) reflects the word with the emphatic "I do wish." Paul, then, adds no new request here; he is simply strengthening, with a final personal appeal, the request he has made in v. 17. This request is that Philemon welcome Onesimus as himself. The tone of this final appeal is evident from the fact that Onesimus is not mentioned again: the focus is entirely on the relationship between Philemon and Paul and

138. Dunn, 340-41; Murphy-O'Connor, Paul, 235-36.
139. So most commentators; see, e.g., O'Brien, 301.
140. Barclay, Colossians and Philemon, 104.

431

what the "obligations" of the former are within that relationship. This emphasis on personal involvement is highlighted again with Paul's use of the (unnecessary) personal pronoun *egō* ("I"). I, the one who is your brother, the one whom you owe your very self, *I* am asking to *have some benefit from you.*[141] The word translated *"benefit"* (the verb *onaimēn*) is somewhat similar to the name "Onesimus" *(Onēsimos)*, and a number of interpreters suggest therefore that Paul might intend another play on words (as in v. 11): "You, Philemon, will truly be 'Onesimus' ("useful") to me."[142] It is argued, to the contrary, that the verb is not all that unusual.[143] But, in fact, the verb is found only here in the New Testament and only once in the LXX, so it is unusual enough. Paul may well intend the pun.

In the last words of the verse (and the body of the letter) Paul becomes a bit more direct, shifting from the language of "wish" or "polite request" to command: *refresh my heart in Christ.* "Heart," as we noted above, translates the Greek word *splanchna* that plays an important role in the rhetoric of the letter. Philemon, who refreshes the "hearts" of God's people (v. 7), is to refresh Paul's "heart" (v. 20) by giving a full Christian welcome to Onesimus, Paul's very "heart" (v. 12). Easily overlooked in the dual appeal Paul makes in this verse are the phrases "in the Lord" and "in Christ."[144] Their casual (and probably unstudied) interchange touches again on a key underlying element in Paul's Christology: his identification of Jesus, the Messiah (the "Christ"), with the "Lord" (with all the significant OT connotations of that title). But more important here is the rhetorical point that they make: Philemon is to respond to Paul because he, Paul, and Onesimus are all "in the Lord/Christ."[145] The fellowship that is created among those who have faith in Christ (v. 6) brings with it obligations to one another.

---

141. The TNIV's "may have some benefit" translates ὀναίμην, which is one of the few uses of the optative mood in the NT (apart from certain stereotyped expressions; e.g., μή γένοιτο, "may it never be"). The optative indicates a wish; hence the EVV's "I want some benefit" (BDF §394).

142. E.g., Lightfoot, 343; Dunn, 341; Wright, 189; Barth/Blanke, 486; Weima, *Neglected Endings*, 233.

143. O'Brien, 302; Fitzmyer, 119; BDF §488(1). They point out that the verb is used in a number of pre-NT texts and also several times in Ignatius (see BDAG).

144. A number of MSS (including the majority text; hence the translation in KJV and NKJV) have κυρίῳ in place of Χριστῷ; but the latter has better support.

145. It is unlikely that these phrases have any more specific function, i.e., as indicating the "Christian manner" in which Philemon is to bring benefit to Paul (R. P. Martin, 167) or as indicating that Onesimus will be freed for service "in the Lord" (Knox, *Philemon*, 25).

IV. THE LETTER CLOSING (vv. 21-25)

21Confident of your obedience, I write to you, knowing that you will do even more than I ask.
22And one thing more: Prepare a guest room for me, because I hope to be restored to you in answer to your prayers.

23Epaphras, my fellow prisoner in Christ Jesus, sends you greetings.
24And so do Mark, Aristarchus, Demas and Luke, my fellow workers.
25The grace of the Lord Jesus Christ be with your spirit.

As we noted above (see the introduction to vv. 8-20), the line between the body of Philemon and its closing is hard to draw.[1] Paul uses several standard features in his letter closings, but he also varies them considerably, making it inappropriate to speak of a hard-and-fast "form."[2] The TNIV suggests, by its spacing, that the closing begins with the greetings in v. 23.[3] Others, however, think that the travel plans of v. 22 introduce the closing,[4] while still others insist that the apostolic "autograph" of v. 19 must be part of the closing, as it is in other letters of Paul.[5] However, as we have noted in our comments on v. 19, Paul "takes up the pen" not to authenticate the letter (as is the case in the parallel texts) but to guarantee his promise to Philemon. It therefore does not function at the level of the letter and need not be included in the letter closing. On the whole, while recognizing that any line must be drawn in soft lead rather than in ink, we think the line between body and closing is best placed between vv. 20 and 21.[6] Four arguments in favor of this division are: (1) the lack of an explicit connecting conjunction or particle in v. 21; (2) the fact that v. 20 makes an appropriate conclusion to the body of the letter (see above); (3) the transitional flavor of the opening of v. 21 ("having become confident"); and (4) the close connection between vv. 21 and 22.

1. J. A. D. Weima (*Neglected Endings* [Sheffield: JSOT Press, 1994], 230) claims that Philemon "is perhaps the most difficult of Paul's letters for determining with certainty the extent of the closing section."
2. See esp. Weima, *Neglected Endings*, 152-55.
3. E.g., Gnilka, 91-95; Wright, 191-92.
4. E.g., Wolter, 279-80.
5. See esp. Weima, *Neglected Endings*, 231. He begins the closing with v. 19, while still others begin it with v. 17 (F. F. Church, "Rhetorical Structure," *HTR* 71 [1978], 17-33) or v. 18 (C.-H. Kim, *Form and Function of the Greek Letter of Recommendation* [Missoula, Mont.: Scholars Press, 1972], 124).
6. See also, e.g., Dunn, 343; Stuhlmacher, 51; Lohse, 206; A. H. Snyman, "A Semantic Discourse Analysis of the Letter to Philemon," in *Text and Interpretation* (Leiden: Brill, 1999).

The letter closing, then, includes four elements: an expression of confidence in Philemon (v. 21); a notice that Paul plans to visit soon (v. 22); greetings from fellow workers (vv. 23-24); and a grace benediction (v. 25). The closing reinforces the rhetorical purpose of the letter, not only in the expression of confidence in v. 21 but also in the subtle pressure put on Philemon by the prospect of Paul's visit (v. 22) and the inclusion of greetings from a number of key fellow workers (vv. 23-24).[7]

21 The lack of any connecting conjunction or particle at the beginning of this verse suggests that Paul has paused for breath, as it were, after v. 20 and that v. 21 marks a new beginning. This impression is reinforced by the construction with which the verse begins, which takes the form of a perfect participle *(pepoithōs)*. Especially with this verb *(peithō,* "persuade"), the perfect tense stresses the current state of Paul's attitude toward Philemon: "having confidence" (KJV), "since I am confident" (HCSB), or simply "confident" (TNIV; RSV; NRSV; ESV).[8] But Paul's confidence is not simply in Philemon but in his *obedience.* This word *(hypakoē)* strikes an odd note in a letter in which Paul has expressly declined to appeal to his apostolic authority (v. 8; cf. also v. 14). A number of interpreters therefore want to soften its meaning, suggesting that it means something like "compliance."[9] But it is doubtful whether the word can be softened quite that far. Others suggest that Paul now makes explicit what, in fact, has been implicit in the letter at a number of points: that, while he wants Philemon to respond voluntarily, there is nevertheless a sense in which Philemon is also under obligation to meet Paul's wishes.[10] There is certainly something to this: as we have seen, by speaking of a "good thing" (v. 6) and something that Philemon "ought to do" (v. 8), Paul makes clear that Philemon's response is not a matter of a neutral decision but of doing what is "right."

But perhaps it is better to think of this obedience as directed not to Paul personally but to what we might call the "gospel imperative." Paul does not use the word "obedience" often, but when he does he often speaks about the general demand that accompanies the gospel: what

---

7. Weima, *Neglected Endings,* 235-36.

8. Generations of Greek students have learned that the perfect tense connotes a "past action with present consequences," and, while true enough, the "past action" focus is often, in fact, very much in the background. The tense therefore often has a simply "stative" connotation. Wallace (*Greek Grammar,* 574-76) sees this as one connotation of the perfect, the intensive, or the resultative perfect, and this is what he classifies πεποιθώς here, while at the same time (580) calling it a "perfect with present force." The stative idea is especially prominent in a verb such as πείθω. Most of Paul's uses of the verb are in the perfect, and all express this idea: see Rom. 2:19; 8:38; 14:14; 15:14; 2 Cor. 2:3; 10:7; Gal. 5:10; Phil. 1:6, 14, 25; 2:24; 2 Thess. 3:4; 2 Tim. 1:5, 12.

9. E.g., Harris, 277-78; Fitzmyer, 121-22.

10. Lohse, 206; Dunn, 344.

Paul calls "the obedience of faith" (Rom. 1:5; 16:26; cf. also 15:18). By this phrase Paul indicates that faith (in Christ) is always accompanied by the call to obedience: that, to put it another way, accepting Christ as Savior is to accept him as Lord. This same general flavor of the word emerges in other texts. In 2 Corinthians 7:15, Paul refers to the Corinthians' repentance and willingness to stand again under the apostolic gospel as their "obedience."; and in 2 Corinthians 10:5, he speaks about the need to "take captive every thought to make it obedient to Christ."[11] While it might be a bit of stretch to think that we can import all this significance into the word here, we believe that Paul's general usage does suggest that he might refer to his idea of general gospel "obedience."[12] The fellowship created by faith (v. 6) carries with it obligations. To believe in Christ is to come under his "law," the law of love. Philemon, Paul suggests, is faced with a situation which, however much he should act voluntarily and on the basis of love, really has only one course of action open to him. And, of course, this obligation is one that Paul has himself suggested to Philemon. In this sense, Philemon's obedience is to some extent related to Paul as well (as the second part of this verse suggests).

Most of the English versions, along with TNIV, translate the next verb in the present tense: *I write to you*. They again reflect the consensus of scholars that the aorist form of the Greek verb *(egrapsa)* looks at the action from the point of view of the readers (i.e., an "epistolary" aorist).[13] Not only is Paul confident about Philemon's "obedience"; he also knows that *you will do even more than I ask*.[14] With this tantalizingly unspecific reference, we again face the vexing question of what it is, ultimately, that Paul hopes Philemon will do with Onesimus. It is possible that this *even more* has a qualitative sense: "I know that you will do what I have asked expeditiously and joyfully." But there does not seem to be much basis to take the word that Paul uses here *(hyper)* in that way. Probably, then, Paul expresses his hope that Philemon will do something beyond what he has already explicitly asked, namely, "welcome" Onesimus as a Christian brother. Many interpreters think, based on v. 13, that Paul is hoping that

11. Paul uses the word elsewhere in Rom. 5:19; 6:16 (twice); 16:19; 2 Cor. 10:6.

12. See also O'Brien, 305; Collange, 73; Gnilka, 87-88; Dunn, 344; Wright, 189; Reinmuth, 52; Garland, 339.

13. As the question mark in the listing in BDF (§334) indicates, however — "[referring to epistolary aorists] Phlm 12, 19 (also 21?)" — there is a bit more uncertainty about this verb. It could look back at the letter, as the NET suggests: "Since I was confident that you would obey, I wrote to you. . . ."

14. The Greek for "more than I ask" is ὑπὲρ ἃ λέγω. The relative pronoun ἃ depends on an assumed demonstrative pronoun, ταῦτα; i.e., "more of those things which I am asking" (see Harris, 278). A number of MSS substitute the singular ὅ for the plural ἃ.

Philemon will "assign" Onesimus to Paul for gospel ministry.[15] This is certainly possible, although, as we have noted, it is unlikely that Paul hopes for Onesimus to return to him: v. 22 makes clear that Paul's plan is to come to Philemon (in Colossae).[16] Other interpreters, without necessarily denying that release for gospel ministry is involved, think that Paul hints here at this hope that Philemon would grant Onesimus his legal freedom.[17] We believe that v. 16 has already hinted at just such a hope and that it is probable, therefore, that Paul does so here again.

As we noted in our comments on v. 16, however, this matter of manumission must be seen in its proper proportion. We can easily make it more important than it was for Paul, Philemon, and Onesimus. For, first, it is likely that Onesimus, like most slaves in the ancient world, could have looked forward to being manumitted at some point; it is therefore possible that what Paul is really asking is that Philemon not use Onesimus's absence as a reason to delay his manumission or, alternatively, that Philemon should free Onesimus immediately.[18] And, second, freed slaves, because of harsh economic realities, were still bound to their masters in all sorts of informal ways. A master could "free" his slave and still treat him almost as badly as before. Paul's concern is fundamentally that, whatever Onesimus's status, Philemon treat him truly as a brother in Christ, perhaps making it possible for him to serve with Paul in ministry.[19] Still, while perhaps not the focus of Paul's concern, the emancipation of Onesimus, we feel, is an action indivisible from what Paul hopes Philemon will do.

22 Paul uses a temporal expression to connect v. 22 to v. 21 (*hama de*, "now, at the same time"). This temporal connection is obscured in the TNIV — *and one thing more* — but is represented in most of the other English versions; see, for example, ESV, "at the same time."[20] The phrase functions much like our equivalent expression to indicate that Paul is adding another request to the one he has just made; and perhaps "one more thing" or the equivalent (cf. NRSV; NLT; NJB; "meanwhile" in NKJV; HCSB) is not a bad way to express the idea. However, there is also a possible connection in Paul's thinking between v. 21 and v. 22. For

15. E.g., O'Brien, 305-6; Lohse, 206; Barth/Blanke, 492.
16. See Wolter, 278-79.
17. E.g., Harris, 278-79; Wright, 189; Stuhlmacher, 53-54; Garland, 334; N. R. Petersen, *Rediscovering Paul* (Philadelphia: Fortress, 1985), 97-98.
18. S. Scott Bartchy, *ABD* 6.71.
19. Thompson, 226.
20. The Greek is ἅμα δέ. As BDAG shows, ἅμα (when used as an adverb) is usually a "marker of simultaneous occurrence" (see Acts 24:26; 27:40; Col. 4:3; 1 Tim. 5:13) but can also be a "marker of association" (see Rom. 3:12).

Paul's request that Philemon prepare a *guest room*[21] implies, of course, that Paul will be visiting Colossae — and perhaps sooner rather than later.[22] It is likely that this is more than a casual request related to Paul's needs, since Paul says nothing about it in Colossians. Rather, it functions as a subtle encouragement to Philemon to respond as Paul hopes he will: Paul will be coming soon to see personally just what has happened with Onesimus.[23]

Paul's coming to visit Philemon and the rest of the Colossians is, however, contingent. He writes, of course, from prison, and so he can only "hope" to be able to visit soon. "Hope" in Paul often has the character of a strong expectation, based on the promises of God. But, as Dunn points out, Paul's use of the verb "hope" in his narration of travel plans has more of an uncertain character.[24] His request that Philemon prepare a room suggests that a release from prison is a strong possibility, but nothing in Paul's language suggests that it is a certainty. Therefore, if Paul is to come to Colossae, it will be through the prayers of the Colossian Christians: the pronouns at the end of the verse — *to you in answer to your prayers* — are plural. These are the first plural pronouns since the opening conventional grace wish in v. 3. The letter is focused on Philemon and Paul's request of him, but we again see that he assumes that it will be read within the context of the community as a whole. TNIV's *restored to you* translates a word that can have two different connotations in this context. The verb is *charizomai,* and Paul uses it to mean "to give graciously" (Rom. 8:32; 1 Cor. 2:12; Gal. 3:18; Phil. 1:29; 2:9) or "to show oneself gra-

21. "Guest room" is undoubtedly the appropriate translation of ξενία in this context (the word means generally "hospitality," but evidence for the specific sense "guest room" is clear; see BDAG). The anarthrous state of the word has suggested to some that Philemon must have been very wealthy, with more than one guest room at his disposal (e.g., Dunn, 346); but this is by no means a necessary interpretation of the anarthrous ξενίαν.

22. Why Paul uses an imperative verb in the present tense (ἑτοίμαζε, "prepare") is not clear, but some think that it might have the nuance "keep ready" (Harris, 279 — as possible). On the other hand, this might be a case in which any difference between aorist and present tense in the imperative is difficult to determine (Moule calls this "an apparently inappropriate present" to make this point [*Idiom Book*, 135]). The focus on Paul's coming visit to Colossae in this verse fits the general contours of what Robert Funk has called the "apostolic parousia." He points to the presence of these kinds of promises to visit in a number of Paul's letter closings. See Robert W. Funk, "The Apostolic *Parousia:* Form and Significance," in *Christian History and Interpretation: Studies Presented to John Knox* (ed. W. R. Farmer, C. F. D. Moule, and R. R. Niebuhr; Cambridge: Cambridge University Press, 1967), 249-69; and also John L. White, *Light from Ancient Letters* (Philadelphia: Fortress, 1986), 219.

23. E.g., Wall, 217-18.

24. Dunn, 346.

cious," to "forgive" (2 Cor. 2:7, 10 [three times]; 12:13; Eph. 4:32 [twice]; Col. 2:13; 3:13 [twice]). The root *charis* ("grace") can easily be recognized. Paul may, then, intend to say that he is hoping that, by God's grace and through their prayers, he may be "given" to them, in the sense that he will be able to visit them. But the word can also have a kind of technical meaning: "to escape death or imprisonment."[25] This meaning is unattested in the New Testament (though see Acts 27:24), but it fits the present context well. If this is so, then TNIV's *be restored*, in the sense "be restored to freedom [so that I can eventually visit you]," is pretty accurate (see also HCSB; NRSV; NJB).

Paul's hope to visit Colossae may have implications for the place from which he writes. In the Introduction to Colossians (41-46), we have tentatively defended the view that Paul writes both Colossians and Philemon from Rome in A.D. 60-61. But many think that this request to prepare a room in Colossae creates a problem for this view, in two ways. First, Paul's planned itinerary for this phase of his missionary career is, according to Romans 15:14-33, to move on to Spain after traveling to Rome. If, then, Paul writes from Rome, why does he speak about returning east when his plan was to move on to the west? As we argued in the Introduction (44-45), one's evaluation of this problem will depend greatly on one's view of the authenticity of the thirteen letters attributed to Paul in the New Testament. If, as we argue, Paul did indeed write all of them, then the Pastoral Epistles must be taken into full account in reconstructing the Pauline chronology. And the most natural reconstruction of the circumstances behind these letters is that Paul, after being released from his "first" Roman imprisonment in A.D. 60-62, returned to ministry in the east. A projected visit to Colossae would perfectly match these circumstances.[26]

The second problem this request raises with a Roman provenance is, of course, geographical. Would it not be more likely that Paul would be planning a visit if he were in Ephesus than if he were in Rome? Perhaps.[27] But the likelihood of a visit would seem to depend more on the needs of ministry and Paul's overall travel plans than on geographical proximity. Certainly, granted the extensive traveling Paul did throughout his ministry, a projected trip from Rome to Colossae would be no big deal. Paul might have been planning a return to Asia Minor after his release from Rome for any number of reasons.[28]

---

25. BDAG.

26. Philippians, if it were written from this same Roman imprisonment, would corroborate these plans (see Phil. 1:25-26; 2:24). But the provenance of Philippians is uncertain enough that it cannot be used positively to make this case.

27. Wright, 190-91.

28. Bruce, 222-23.

23 Passing along greetings from fellow Christians is a normal feature of Paul's letter closings; they are found in seven of the other twelve letters (Rom. 16:3-16; 1 Cor. 16:19-20; 2 Cor. 13:12; Phil. 4:21-22; Col. 4:10-15; 2 Tim. 4:19-21; Titus 3:15). In vv. 23-24, Paul extends greetings from one "fellow prisoner" and four "fellow workers." These greetings are all directed to Philemon himself: the "you" in *sends you greetings* is singular. Probably, then, in addition to the courtesy involved, these greetings also are intended to bring some further pressure on Philemon. Five of his own "fellow workers" (see v. 1) are with Paul, probably aware of what he is writing.

The closest parallel between vv. 23-24 is, as one might expect, with Colossians 4:10-15. But the differences are also instructive:

Colossians 4:10-15	*Philemon 23-24*
Aristarchus, "my fellow prisoner"	Epaphras, "my fellow prisoner"
Mark	Mark
Jesus, who is called Justus	
Epaphras	Aristarchus
Luke	Demas
Demas	Luke
(the latter five are all apparently "fellow workers")	(all four "fellow workers")

Of course, there is no reason to expect exact agreement between the lists; Paul has not memorized a list of associates. Nevertheless, granted the supposition that the two letters were written at about the same time, two differences stand out and require comment. First is the shift in the designation "fellow prisoner" from Aristarchus to Epaphras. This switch would be easy to explain if, as some argue, the language is metaphorical: both Aristarchus and Epaphras have been, like Paul, "captured" by Christ to serve him with the gospel.[29] A metaphorical reference is suggested, it is argued, by the fact that Paul uses a word here that means, literally, "fellow prisoner of war" (*synaichmalōtos*). This word is technically inapplicable to prisoners because of the gospel and different from the one that Paul has used for his own imprisonment (v. 9). The title would then be a kind of honorific that Paul could apply for emphasis on whomever he wanted (the word is used by Paul also in Rom. 16:7 and Col. 4:10).

But it is very unlikely that the word has a metaphorical meaning.[30] As we noted in our comments on Colossians 4:10, the verb from which

29. E.g., Harris, 280; Fitzmyer, 124.
30. See, e.g., O'Brien, 307; Dunn, 348.

the noun here is taken is used by Paul more broadly than in the technical sense of "imprisoned (in war)." And had Paul intended a metaphorical meaning, as in Colossians 4:10, we would have expected him to say "fellow prisoners *of* Christ Jesus." If, then, the word is used to refer to a literal imprisonment shared with Paul, we have two options to explain why the word is applied to Aristarchus in Colossians and to Epaphras here. First, an interval may have come between the writing of Colossians and of Philemon, during which Aristarchus has ceased to be a prisoner and Epaphras has become one.[31] This switch is not unlikely if, as many suppose, these fellow workers of Paul decided voluntarily to share his imprisonment in order to help him. Second, it is also possible that calling someone a "fellow prisoner" does not mean that they are a prisoner at the time of writing but that they had, at some time, shared prison with Paul.[32]

The second difference in the list of associates worth commenting on is the absence of "Jesus, the one called Justus" from the Philemon list. Or is he missing? With the addition of one letter in the Greek text at the end of v. 23 and repunctuation, the name "Jesus" would appear: "Epaphras, my fellow prisoner in Christ, sends you greetings; as does Jesus. . . ."[33] As ingenious as the proposal is, however, it must be dismissed for lack of textual evidence.[34] We can only guess that Jesus left Paul between the writing of Colossians and Philemon.

The Epaphras given the place of honor in this list is the person who first preached the gospel in Colossae (Col. 1:7-8).[35] He was probably converted by Paul during his ministry in Ephesus and then returned as an evangelist to his hometown. Now, during his absence from the city, he is continuing to pray for his fellow Christians there (Col. 4:12).

24 Paul characterizes the other four men who extend their greetings to Philemon through Paul as "fellow workers" — both with Paul and

---

31. Dunn, 347-48.

32. Bruce, 224.

33. In order to read the verse this way, a *sigma* would have to be added to the end of Ἰησοῦ, converting it from a dative ("in Christ Jesus") to a nominative. The proposal was first made by Ernst Amling, "Eine Konjecktur im Philemonbrief," *ZNW* 10 (1909), 261-62 and is adopted by W. H. Ollrog, *Paulus und seiner Mitarbeiter* (Neukirchen-Vluyn: Neukirchener, 1979), 49 and Lohse, 207, who points out that Paul does not elsewhere in Philemon use the expression "in Christ Jesus."

34. In addition, it is unlikely that Paul would refer to any individual simply as "Jesus" without further designation (Dunn, 343).

35. Since the name Ἐπαφρᾶς is a shortened form of Ἐπαφρόδιτος, a few interpreters think that this Epaphras might be the same as the envoy from Philippi to Paul (Phil. 2:25-29; 4:18). But this is unlikely, since Epaphras appears to be from Colossae and Epaphroditus from Philippi.

with Philemon (v. 1).[36] Mark, who is identified as a "cousin of Barnabas" in Colossians 4:10, is almost certainly "John Mark," the son of a woman in whose house the Christians in Jerusalem met for a time (Acts 12:12) and who accompanied Paul and Barnabas on part of the first missionary journey. His failure to complete the journey with them, however, led Paul to distrust him and refuse to take him along on a second journey (Acts 15:38). This text, along with Colossians 4:10, shows that Paul was eventually reconciled with Mark. Aristarchus is, as we have noted, called Paul's "fellow prisoner" in Colossians 4:10. He was active in the second phase of Paul's missionary work, being mentioned during the apostle's Ephesian ministry (Acts 19:29) and as a traveling companion with Paul on his voyage to Rome (Acts 27:2). Demas is known otherwise only from the parallel text in Colossians 4:14 and from 2 Timothy 4:9-12, where his desertion of Paul and the cause of Christ is sadly mentioned. Luke, designated a "doctor" in Colossians 4:14, is the companion of Paul who is almost certainly to be identified as the author of the Third Gospel and the book of Acts. Based on the passages in which Luke refers to himself in Acts, we may conclude that he was a regular companion of Paul, participating with him in ministry in Madeconia (Acts 16:8-17), on his trip back to Palestine after the third missionary journey (Acts 20:5-15; 21:1-18), and on the "shipwreck" voyage to Rome (Acts 27:1–28:16). So it would be natural to believe that Luke stayed on with Paul in Rome during his imprisonment there.

25 A "grace benediction" is found in all Paul's letter closings (Rom. 16:20b; 1 Cor. 16:23; 2 Cor. 13:14; Gal. 6:18; Eph. 6:24; Phil. 4:23; Col. 4:18; 1 Thess. 5:28; 2 Thess. 3:18; 1 Tim. 6:21b; 2 Tim. 4:22b; Titus 3:15b), and it comes as the last word in every letter except Romans and 1 Corinthians. The exact form of the grace wish here is found also in Philippians 4:23.[37] The word "grace" (charis) appears only here and in the grace wish of v. 3 in Philemon, so it creates something of an inclusio around the letter.[38] Continuing the somewhat baffling interchange that we have seen

36. The names in v. 24 pick up the verb ἀσπάζεται in v. 23. The verb is singular because its subject is "Epaphras"; each of the names in v. 24 then goes back and picks up the verb. Most translations represent this by using the transitional phrase and so do or something similar (there is no explicit Greek behind these words). The plural form ἀσπάζονται found in the majority text (see the syntax in KJV) is an obvious attempt to "correct" the syntax.

37. The majority text, along with a few other MSS, adds a ἡμῶν after κυρίου and ἀμήν at the end of the verse; see NKJV: "The grace of our Lord Jesus Christ be with your spirit. Amen." Both are almost certainly secondary, the principle "the shortest reading should be preferred" coming into play here.

38. See Stuhlmacher, 56, who notes some other parallels between vv. 1-3 and vv. 21-25.

throughout vv. 21-25, Paul extends this grace to Philemon's whole house church: the "your" in *your spirit* is plural. A few interpreters have taken *pneuma* as a reference to the Holy Spirit, perhaps as indwelling the community as a whole.[39] But the word almost certainly refers here to the human spirit, as the interchange between this wording and the simple "you" in parallel texts suggests ("your spirit" is found in Gal. 6:18; Phil. 4:23; 2 Tim. 4:22; simply "you" in the other letters).[40] The singular "your spirit" is then distributive: the spirit that each of you has.[41] Since this grace wish is so much a staple of Paul's letter closings, it might be that he adds it here without giving it much thought. But we might wonder whether Paul could ever write about grace without thinking about its significance. And here he might especially be aware of how much the whole community would need a strong measure of grace in order to respond well to the Onesimus affair.

---

39. E.g., Reinmuth, 55-56; Wall, 218 (with the human spirit).

40. Even G. D. Fee, who generally tries to find reference to the Holy Spirit in Paul's πνεῦμα references wherever he can, believes that the reference here is to the human spirit (*God's Empowering Presence* [Peabody, Mass.: Hendrickson, 1994], 635-36); see also Lohse, 208; Dunn, 349; Fitzmyer, 125.

41. Harris, 281.

Index of Authors

INDEX OF AUTHORS

Bock, D. L., 268
Bockmuehl, M. N. A., 155, 324
Bornkamm, G., 34
Bouttier, M., 77, 272
Bradley, J., 57
Brown, R. E., 29, 37, 37, 39, 41, 155
Bruce, F. F., 29, 42, 54, 74, 82, 84, 88, 91,
    98, 102, 115, 124, 127, 128, 133, 136,
    140, 141, 141, 164, 178, 188, 196, 202,
    221, 224, 228, 244, 254, 256, 265, 277,
    286, 287, 290, 331, 335, 339, 343, 347,
    349, 404, 406, 411, 414, 425, 429, 438,
    440
Büchsel, F., 328
Bujard, W., 31
Buls, H. H., 205
Bultmann, R., 415
Burger, C., 108, 114
Burney, C. F., 113
Burtchaell, J. T., 373
Burton, E. D., 190

Callahan, A. D., 366, 383, 411, 414, 421,
    422, 423
Callow, J., 82, 291
Calvin, J., 292
Campbell, D. A., 271
Cannon, G. E., 33, 99, 208
Capes, D. B., 297
Carr, W., 64, 122, 212
Carson, D. A., 38, 347
Cervin, R., 128
Chadwick, H., 174
Church, F. F., 385, 398, 399, 433
Cleveland, R. E., 50
Clines, D. J. A., 66
Collange, J. F., 43, 389, 394, 399, 417,
    420, 425, 435
Collins, R. F., 29, 30
Cope, L., 352, 381
Coutts, J., 36
Craigie, P. C., 411
Crouch, J. E., 294, 296

Daube, D., 407
Davies, W. D., 113, 101
Davis, P. R., 66
Deissmann, A., 211
Delling, G., 300, 301

DeMaris, R. E., 50, 54, 56, 57, 73, 186,
    191
Dibelius, M., 53, 228
Dibelius, M./Greeven, H., 115, 132,
    156, 166, 177, 188, 225
Donelson, L. R., 38, 39
Dübbers, M., 82, 63, 102, 116, 118, 126,
    128, 136, 177, 191, 193, 194, 196, 197,
    204, 217
Duncan, G. S., 42
Dunn, J. D. G., 29, 37, 29, 41, 47, 48, 55,
    56, 57, 58, 73, 75, 76, 78, 83, 86, 94,
    95, 98, 102, 106, 112, 113, 115, 119,
    121, 122, 124, 125, 126, 127, 129, 132,
    133, 138, 139, 139, 141, 142, 146, 148,
    154, 158, 160, 162, 164, 167, 171, 172,
    174, 175, 175, 178, 181, 182, 187, 191,
    197, 199, 202, 202, 207, 209, 210, 215,
    218, 220, 223, 225, 226, 227, 229, 230,
    232, 235, 236, 238, 240, 241, 242, 244,
    247, 251, 252, 260, 263, 265, 269, 272,
    273, 275, 285, 287, 290, 291, 292, 293,
    296, 301, 303, 307, 311, 320, 322, 323,
    327, 329, 331, 332, 334, 336, 338, 341,
    344, 348, 349, 350, 371, 380, 382, 383,
    384, 385, 388, 391, 392, 392, 395, 398,
    402, 406, 407, 409, 413, 413, 414, 416,
    417, 421, 426, 428, 429, 430, 431, 432,
    433, 434, 435, 437, 439, 440, 442
Dupont, J., 171

Eadie, J., 130, 157, 207
Easton, B. S., 254
Ellingworth, P., 115
Ellis, E. E., 38, 74, 77, 82, 91, 342
Ernst, P., 29, 88, 99, 119, 115, 121, 126,
    210, 244, 402, 406, 421
Evans, C. A., 54, 226
Evanson, E., 30

Fee, G. D., 79, 92, 103, 106, 113, 114,
    131, 134, 141, 173, 269, 287, 442
Ferguson, E., 202
Fitzmyer, J., 43, 362, 367, 367, 383, 387,
    389, 391, 394, 395, 402, 405, 406, 407,
    410, 411, 412, 422, 423, 425, 426, 427,
    428, 432, 434, 439, 442
Foerster, W., 340
Fowl, S. E., 110, 121, 128
Fox, M., 64

Index of Subjects

Index of Scripture References

26:41	320	1:18	405	1:14	194
26:45	396	1:51	98	1:16	195, 384
26:64	247	1:57	407	1:18	118
27:28	214, 266	1:78	277	3:3	408
27:31	214, 266	2:1	210	3:5	408
27:52-53	129	2:51	299	3:7	408
		4:18	338	5:44	246
Mark		4:22	330	7:4	401
1:27	304	4:42	413	7:13	401
1:39	146	5:5	162	7:26	401
3:28	264	5:10	426	10:24	401
4:11	326	5:21	264	10:33	264
4:19	186	7:42	279	11:14	401
4:20	88	7:43	279	11:54	401
4:28	88	8:15	88, 413	14:16	395
5:20	146	9:26	102	14:26	395
6:31	396	9:41	279	14:27	283
7	50	10:17	299	15:26	395
7:1-23	187	10:20	299	16:7	395
7:4	201	10:21	156	16:25	401
7:7	238	10:30	214, 266	16:29	401
7:7-8	238	11:34	310	16:33	283
7:8	187, 201	12:5	431	18:20	401
7:15	238	12:11	122	18:32	285
7:22	257, 264	12:15	257	18:36	162
8:32	401	12:19	396	20	181
8:38	102	12:32	131	20:25	211
9:19	279	12:37	320		
9:50	331	13:24	162	**Acts**	
10:37	247	14:9	413	1:14	320
10:45	106	14:12	312	1:18	277, 396
11:17	320	14:14	312	1:20	289
11:24	93	14:34	331	1:23	340
11:25	206	16:2-4	153, 154	2:5	146, 147
12:16	117	18:1	319	2:29	402
12:30	311	19:20	85	2:32-36	215
12:36	247	20:21	316	2:33	247
13:5	185	20:42	247, 289	2:34	247
13:34	320	21:8	185	2:36	130
13:35	320	22:69	247	2:42	320, 390
13:37	320	23:7	411	3:19	209
14:9	146	23:11	411	4:12	146
14:41	396, 420	23:15	411	4:13	402
14:58	197	24:19	291	4:29	402
14:62	247	24:44	289	4:31	402
14:64	264			5:31	247
15:20	214, 266	**John**		6	342
		1:1	118	6:2	414
Luke		1:1-18	118	6:4	320
1:1	345	1:3	120, 121	6:11	264

INDEX OF SCRIPTURE REFERENCES

INDEX OF SCRIPTURE REFERENCES

|---|---|---|---|---|---|
3:14	166, 176, 274, 280, 281, 285, 303	4	164		321, 322, 337, 343, 345, 440
3:15	62, 63, 127, 176, 194, 223, 224, 274, 275, 280, 282, 284, 285, 286, 291, 321	4:1	62, 85, 86, 176, 308, 309, 313, 316, 343, 373, 377, 424	4:12-13	27, 32, 90
		4:2	100, 176, 285, 291, 318, 319, 320, 321, 329	4:12-14	337, 341
				4:13	77, 321, 322, 345, 348, 349
3:15-16	274	4:2-3	282	4:13-16	164
3:16	36, 47, 62, 68, 79, 97, 100, 160, 161, 176, 243, 280, 282, 283, 285, 286, 291, 292, 298	4:2-4	319	4:14	337, 347, 441
		4:2-6	176, 317, 318, 319	4:15	66, 77, 127, 337, 348, 349, 350, 383
		4:3	41, 62, 76, 100, 155, 157, 176, 320, 321, 324, 325, 329, 330, 335, 436	4:15-17	332
				4:16	26, 28, 66, 77, 127, 332, 348, 350, 374
3:16-23	244				
3:17	62, 100, 176, 274, 280, 282, 285, 290, 298, 305, 311, 318, 321, 330	4:3-4	28, 68, 76, 318, 325, 326	4:16-17	332, 348
				4:17	28, 62, 121, 177, 323, 332, 383
		4:4	285, 324, 325, 326	4:18	28, 31, 36, 41, 76, 79, 330, 332, 333, 352, 386, 429, 441
3:18	62, 121, 176, 243, 298, 299, 300, 301, 304, 308, 313, 402	4:5	95, 100, 161, 176, 261, 318, 326, 327, 329, 331		
				1 Thessalonians	
3:18-19	293	4:5-6	318, 319, 326	1:1	76, 79, 82, 83, 251
3:18–4:1	71, 176, 243, 272, 292, 293, 294, 295, 296, 297, 298, 313, 318, 319	4:6	36, 79, 176, 289, 318, 327, 328, 329, 331	1:2	83, 353, 386
				1:2-3	385
		4:7	62, 90, 91, 121, 176, 334, 336, 337	1:3	353, 386
				1:4	276
3:19	176, 302, 303, 306, 307, 313, 316	4:7-8	27, 42, 44	1:5	167
		4:7-9	319, 332, 334, 363	1:6	261, 417
3:20	62, 121, 176, 244, 300, 304, 305, 306, 307, 308, 313			1:8	84, 204, 285, 389
		4:7-14	43	1:10	259
		4:7-15	28, 76	2:2	323
3:20-21	293	4:7-18	332	2:4	96, 280, 323
3:21	176, 200, 306, 307, 313, 316	4:8	165, 335	2:5	257
		4:8-9	309	2:7	408
3:22	142, 176, 300, 305, 308, 309, 311, 313, 343	4:9	42, 334, 336, 363, 366, 410	2:12	96, 105, 284
				2:13	177
		4:10	337, 339, 340, 343, 439, 440, 441	2:15	182
3:22-23	309			2:16	259
3:22-24	62			2:19	261
3:22-25	298, 308	4:10-11	337, 340	2:26	323
3:22–4:1	293	4:10-14	42, 348	3:1	82
3:23	176, 308, 309, 311, 312, 313	4:10-15	332, 337, 439	3:2	76, 335, 381
		4:10-17	332	3:7	416
3:23-24	311	4:11	62, 105, 323, 335, 339, 340, 343, 347, 381	3:9	312
3:24	308, 309, 312, 313, 314, 315			3:11	83
				3:13	102, 143
3:25	298, 309, 313, 314, 315, 317	4:12	62, 90, 162, 320,	4:1	88, 96, 177
				4:5	256, 257

464

INDEX OF SCRIPTURE REFERENCES

Index of Extrabiblical Literature

JEWISH LITERATURE